# GANDHI

# GANDHI

---

*A Life*

## YOGESH CHADHA

John Wiley & Sons, Inc.
New York • Chichester • Weinheim • Brisbane • Singapore • Toronto

This publication is designed to provide accurate and authoritative information in regard to
the subject matter covered. It is sold with the understanding that the publisher is not engaged
in rendering professional services. If professional advice or other expert assistance is
required, the services of a competent professional person should be sought.

*Library of Congress Cataloging-in-Publication Data:*

Chadha, Yogesh.
    Gandhi : a life / Yogesh Chadha.
        p.    cm.
    Includes bibliographical references and index.
    ISBN 0-471-24378-7 (cloth : alk. paper)
    1. Gandhi, Mahatma, 1869–1948—Political and social views.
    2. Statesman—India—Biography.  3. India—Politics and
    government—1919–1947-   I. Title.
    DS481.G73C43   1998
    954.03'5'092—dc21
    [B]                                                      97-37406

Printed in the United States of America

10 9 8 7 6 5 4 3 2 1

# CONTENTS

# Biographer's Note

In discussing Gandhi, too much emphasis is often placed on his being instrumental in freeing India from British rule. Is this perception valid?

When Gandhi appeared on the Indian political scene, the movements for political reform and freedom had already been progressing for some three decades. Even without him, the constitutional approach followed by the Indian National Congress would have continued, with tangible results. Notwithstanding Gandhi's success in taking the Congress from the classes to the masses, and his dominant political leadership, he cannot be acclaimed as the author of India's freedom – though the extraordinary manner in which it was achieved can be pointedly ascribed to him. Gandhi was essentially a humanist, more interested in individuals than institutions. However, the politician in him cannot be underestimated. The combination of Gandhi the politician and Gandhi the humanist was remarkable indeed. But to call him a saint – which is implicit in his title of Mahatma – does not reflect his true personality. While his goodness was of an unusual variety, there was no mystery about his faults.

His genuine religious convictions and spirituality were an integral part of his personality. These attributes would, in time to come, totally eclipse the prevalent notion that Gandhi wrought the miracle of India's freedom. Trite phrases like 'Hindu saint' and 'Father of the Nation' do not describe his true place in the history of human civilization.

Gandhi showed the world that the love of one's people need not be inconsistent with the love of humanity. He strove to free the downtrodden from the shackles of injustice, slavery and deprivation. But he was also obsessed with the future of the human race. 'There is no hope for the aching world except through the narrow and straight path of non-violence,' he wrote. 'Millions like me may fail to prove the truth in their own lives; that would be their failure, never of the eternal law.'

Indeed, when the names of the giants of Indian independence movement are embedded in the fossils of history, Gandhi's name shall shine for his message of truth and nonviolence.

Now a word about the making of this book. The publication of Gandhi's

*Collected Works* by the Publication Division of the Government of India (90 volumes) has opened up the floodgates of information about Gandhi's philosophy and life. This monumental work entailed collecting his speeches and writings – and, where necessary, translating them from his native Gujarati, as well as Hindi, into English – and arranging them in chronological order. This has turned out to be a boon for the present-day Gandhi researcher. However, the sheer wordage that Gandhi has left behind may prove to be a drawback, for there is a danger of one not being able to see the forest for the trees. In addition, there are the endless books and articles that have been written about him. It would appear that nearly everyone who ever spoke to Gandhi and could put pen to paper, felt an overwhelming urge to write something about him.

While dealing with the subject of this book, I have sought to draw a rounded portrait of Mohandas Karamchand Gandhi, and in doing so I have aimed more at clarity than detail.

A biography is part of history. Half-truths and untruths mixed with truth can play havoc with history. The warning of Thucydides remains valid for all historians, famous or not so famous, that history is written 'not as an essay to win the applause of the moment, but as a possession for all time'.

Utmost care has, therefore, been taken to ensure the accuracy of the material incorporated in this book. Some choice pieces of information have been left out for want of authenticity, but even without them there is enough spice and drama in Gandhi's story.

There are, of course, excellent works on Gandhi, by both Indian and Western writers, that can be quite illuminating. The voluminous biographies by Gandhi's chief secretary, Pyarelal, and D.G. Tendulkar, though hagiographical, provide useful source material. But one must heed the Mahatma's own opinion about the disciple-biographer, afflicted with devotional infirmities :

> A disciple cannot write a critical biography. It would be presumptuous for a disciple to do so. The true disciple merges himself in the *Guru* and so can never be a critic of the *Guru*. *Bhakti* (devotion) has no eye for shortcomings.

For better or for worse, I did not have so much as a nodding acquaintance with Gandhi. But I saw the assassinated Mahatma and also witnessed the momentous occasion, on 31 January 1948, when his mortal remains were consigned to flames.

It is imperative that Gandhi is reclaimed as a human being out of the many myths surrounding him. He had his failings and favourites, but to suppress these weaknesses would be to undermine his strengths. It is important to refrain from being oracular and to let Gandhi speak, in the best biographical tradition. To some extent, the writer's opinion is inevitable; but it is desirable that the biographer stands aside and lets the participants play their part. This approach is apparent throughout this work.

# ONE

# The Mahatma: Background and Boyhood

When Mahatma Gandhi was in London in 1931 to plead for India's independence, a small girl started to ask him for his autograph. Then she drew back shyly before this strange little *dhoti*-clad man with a roughly mended coarse shawl over his shoulders, wearing cheap wire-framed spectacles. She looked up at her mother and asked: 'Mummy, is he really great?'

Gandhi's greatness – nay, uniqueness – lies in his role as an innovator in politics. Far from being a mere political theoretician or analyst, he loved humanity with surpassing compassion and, to use his own phrase, 'approached the poor with the mind of the poor'. In fact, he endeavoured to found a new human order. He was the first in human history to extend the principle of nonviolence from the individual to the social and the political plane. He was always optimistic, for he could see with 'the eye of faith'. This expression reminds one of the lines of George Santayana, the American philosopher of Spanish descent:

> Columbus found a world, and had no chart,
> Save one that faith deciphered in the skies;
> To trust the soul's invincible surmise
> Was all his science and his only art.

Paying tribute to Gandhi on the occasion of his seventy-fifth birthday, Professor Einstein wrote: 'Generations to come, it may be, will scarce believe that such a one as this ever in flesh and blood walked upon this earth.'

Mohandas Karamchand Gandhi was born on 2 October 1869 at Porbandar, the capital of a small princely state of that name on the peninsula of Kathiawar that juts into the Arabian Sea. In the 1872 census, Porbandar state (area: 642 sq. miles) had a population of 72,000, and the town of Porbandar a population of 15,000.

The Gandhis belonged to the Modh Bania subdivision of the Vaisya caste, representing the trader class in the traditional Hindu caste system, and were, it seems, originally grocers. But for a considerable period of time the family had been of some consequence in Kathiawar. Gandhi's grand-father, and his father and uncle were each in turn *dewan*, or prime minister, to the ruler of Porbandar; and his father was later prime minister of two other similar tiny states. None of these states was subject to direct British rule, and consequently old Indian customs and traditions were much more in evidence there than in most parts of British India.

Direct British sovereignty was established in India after the Mutiny of 1857. There were two Indias: British India was ruled by the Viceroy from Delhi and with British governors in all its provinces; the other India con-sisted of over 550 princely states which were mere royal instruments with-out possession of any political power. This tactic of divide and rule enabled the British to have tight control over the Indian subcontinent. Professor Rushbrook Williams, in an article in the London *Evening Standard* of 28 May 1930, puts its significance quite succinctly:

> The situations of these feudatory states, checkerboarding all India as they do, are a great safeguard. It is like establishing a vast network of friendly fortresses in debatable territory. It would be difficult for a general rebellion against the British to sweep India because of this network of powerful, loyal, native states.

The princely states covered a third of the subcontinent, and contained a quarter of India's total population. They varied greatly in size and wealth. Some princes were debauched grandees who spent a good deal of their time in the playgrounds of Europe's rich, while there were rajahs who lived on less than £80 a year. There were a few rulers who allocated funds from the state's exchequer for the improvement of the lot of their subjects, but the majority of them considered the maintenance of their living style to be the sole purpose of their rule.

The British deprived the princes of armed force, but allowed them ample liberty within their own domains under the eye of a British resident or agent, whose prime function was to ensure that they behaved themselves inasmuch as they did not endanger British security. The princes were inde-pendent of Delhi and of any laws passed by the Government of India – they owed their allegiance to the British Crown, whose foreign policy they agreed to accept and follow. The British retained the right to intervene in the affairs of the princely states, but they scarcely had the occasion to do so. These princely puppets rarely gave a resident or agent any anxious moments.

Uttamchand Gandhi, Mohandas's grandfather, worked his way up to become the *dewan* of Porbandar. But political intrigues in the princely states were the order of the day. Their rulers behaved like petty autocrats toward their subjects, while displaying utter sycophancy before the British. Once, Uttamchand Gandhi fell out with the queen regent, Rupali Ba, by taking an opposite stand in a domestic dispute involving her maids. Things came to such a pass that Rupali Ba had Uttamchand's house – the house his father, Harijivan, had bought – surrounded by palace guards, who fired at it from a cannon. Uttamchand was forced out of prime ministership of Porbandar into exile in the nearby state of Junagarh. When he went to pay his respects to the nawab, he saluted the prince with his left hand. Asked for an explanation, he said: 'The right hand is already pledged to Porbandar.' Mohandas was proud of such loyalty. 'My grandfather', he wrote, 'must have been a man of principle.'

In 1841 Rupali Ba died and her eighteen-year-old son, Vikmatji, succeeded to the throne of Porbandar. He invited Uttamchand to return and take over as *dewan*. Uttamchand returned to Porbandar, but recommended the fifth, and most gifted, of his sons, Karamchand (Gandhi's father), for the post. In 1847, at the age of twenty-five, Karamchand became *dewan* of Porbandar, an office he held for twenty-eight years.

Karamchand first married when he was fourteen, and for the second time when he was twenty-five. He had a daughter from each marriage, but both wives died without bearing any sons and nothing is known about either of the daughters. The third marriage proved childless and it is believed that this wife was stricken with an incurable ailment which had incapacitated her for life. Karamchand obtained his third wife's permission – a matter of courtesy – to marry again when he was still married to her.

The small, stocky, broad-shouldered, forty-ish Karamchand married Putlibai, just in her teens. She bore him four children. The first child was Raliatbehn, a daughter, who was born in 1862 and died nearly a hundred years later. Laxmidas, the eldest son, was born the following year. Karsandas, the second son, in 1866 and Mohandas Karamchand, the last child, in 1869.

Karamchand, Putlibai and their children lived in the old family house, which had over the years been expanded to a three-storey structure. It is not known when the house was built, but the deed of sale and transfer shows that it was bought in 1777 by Harjivan Gandhi, the great-grand-father of the Mahatma. It was wedged between two temples and looked more like a small fortress than an ordinary dwelling-house. The interior contained a honeycomb of cramped, dark, dingy rooms built around a small courtyard. Only rooms built on the top storey permitted sunlight to penetrate them and were quite airy. Karamchand and his family occupied two ground-floor rooms opening on to a veranda, and the rest of the house was given over to Karamchand's four brothers and their wives and children. Of his father, Gandhi wrote in his autobiography:

> My father was a lover of his clan, truthful, brave and generous, but short-tempered. To a certain extent he might have been even given to carnal pleasures, for he married for the fourth time when he was over forty. But he was incorruptible and had earned a name for strict impartiality in his family as well as outside. His loyalty to the state was well-known . . . My father never had any ambition to accumulate riches and left us very little property . . . He had no education, save that of experience. At best he might be said to have read up to the fifth standard. Of history and geography he was innocent, but his rich experience of practical affairs of the state stood him in good stead in the solution of the most intricate questions and in managing hundreds of men.

Karamchand's long tenure as prime minister of Porbandar was followed by similar positions, though of shorter duration, in the princely states of Rajkot and Wankaner. Once, the British political agent spoke insultingly about the native ruler of Rajkot, Thakore Saheb. Karamchand vehemently defended his chief. The agent strongly objected to the prime minister's attitude and asked him to apologize. Karamchand stoutly refused. The agent ordered him to be detained under a tree till he apologized. Some hours later, seeing that Karamchand was adamant, the agent ordered him to be released.

Karamchand was a moderately religious man, his obeisance confined to frequent visits to temples and listening to religious discourses. However, in his last days, at the instance of a Brahmin friend, he would recite aloud some verses from the *Bhagavad Gita* every day at the time of worship.

But religion was the very breath of Putlibai. She was unlettered but knowledgeable, deeply religious and addicted to prayer and fasting. For her, every day was a holy day. Although she attended to her duties as wife and mother with single-minded zeal, her heart and mind were elsewhere. It was as if she lived mainly to prepare for the journey to the other world. She was a natural ascetic who loved discipline almost for its own sake. In the annual *Chaturmas* (literally: a period of four months), a kind of Lent lasting through the rainy season, she lived on a single meal a day. Not content with that, one year she observed, in addition, a complete fast on alternate days. The following *Chaturmas* she vowed to abstain from food until the sun came out, even though she had grown thin and haggard. Her children, observing her condition, often watched for some rift in the clouds, and when the sun showed through they at once raised a cry for their mother. But Putlibai's vow demanded that she should see the sun herself, and more often than not, as she rushed outdoors, the fugitive sun was hidden again, thus depriving her of her meal. 'That does not matter,' she would cheer-fully reassure her children. 'God does not want me to eat today.' The wife of the prime minister would return to her household duties with a smile. 'The outstanding impression my mother has left on my memory', Gandhi wrote, 'is that of saintliness.'

Gandhi inherited his father's stubbornness, incorruptibility and prac-tical sense and his mother's life of religion, devotion and asceticism. His life was influenced by both Vaishnavism and Jainism, the two religious cults which regard all forms of life as God's creation and hence sacred. He grew up in the midst of a population which would not kill even wild animals that daily destroyed their crops. Saints and sages of all sects visited his house. 'Jain monks', Gandhi wrote, 'would also pay frequent visits to my father and would even go out of their way to accept food from us – non-Jains. They would have talks with my father on subjects religious and mundane.' Karamchand had, besides, Muslim and Parsi friends who would talk to him about their own faiths, and he would listen to them with respect. As his father's nurse, the schoolboy Mohandas had ample opportunities to hear these discussions and have 'glimpses' of religion. 'These many things com-bined to inculcate in me a toleration for all faiths.'

This was also the time when a great devotee of Lord Rama, Ladha Maharaj, recited before Karamchand couplets and quatrains from the *Ramayana*, an ancient Hindu epic centring round the life of Rama, the apostle of *dharma* (duty). Ladha Maharaj would not only sing the couplets and quatrains, but also explain them with such devotion that the thirteen-year-old Mohandas was enraptured. 'That laid the foundation of my deep devotion to the *Ramayana*,' Gandhi wrote. 'Today I regard the *Ramayana* of Tulsidas as the greatest book in all devotional literature.' Nevertheless, he gave credit to his old nurse, Rambha, for making him aware of the sig-nificance of *Ramanama* (the repetition of God's name), which she had sug-gested as a means of dispelling his fears of ghosts and spirits. The repetition of *Ramanama* at a tender age was his introduction to self-realization. 'I think it is due to the seed sown by that good woman Rambha that today *Ramanama* is an infallible remedy for me.'

Humility, tenderness and affection for all living things were the watch-words of the Vaishnavas, or followers of Vishnu, one of the three supreme gods of the Hindu pantheon. The medieval Gujarati saint-poet, Narasaya, had glorified Vishnu and the Vaishnavas in a song which Gandhi heard in his childhood and repeated throughout his life. This song was destined to 'paint so fully the whole cast of Gandhi's mind and the deepest longings of his spirit'. It reads:

He is the true Vaishnava who knows and feels another's woes as his own. Ever ready to serve, he never boasts.

He bows to everyone and despises no one, keeping his thought, word and deed pure. Blessed is the mother of such a one.

He looks upon all with an equal eye. He has rid himself of lust, and reveres every woman as his mother. His tongue would fail him if he attempted to utter an untruth. He covets not another's wealth.

The bonds of earthly attachment hold him not. His mind is deeply rooted in renunciation. Every moment he is intent on reciting the name of God. All the holy places are ever present in his body.

He has conquered greed, hypocrisy, passion and anger.

Young Mohandas's exposure to these teachings does not mean that he had developed a deep faith in religion or in *ahimsa* (nonviolence) at an early age. 'But one thing took deep root in me – the conviction that morality is the basis of things, and that truth is the substance of all morality.' He learned then the guiding principle: 'Return good for evil.' And he began to make everything he did an experiment with truth.

Moniya, as the family affectionately called Mohandas, had an enchanting childhood. He received the special treatment often accorded a youngest child, and he inevitably became the spoiled darling of the family. One of the family members in charge of him was his sister Raliat. Years later she vividly remembered his early childhood days:

Moniya could be said to have grown up on my lap. I used to carry him in my arms when I went out for a walk or for recreation. Mother used to be worried lest I should drop him or lose sight of him. Moniya was restless as mercury, could not sit still even for a little while. He must be either playing or roaming about. I used to take him out with me to show him the familiar sights in the street – cows, buffaloes and horses, cats and dogs. He was full of curiosity. At the first opportunity, he would go up to the animals and try to make friends with them. One of his favourite pastimes was twisting dogs' ears.

The mercurial little Moniya gave his family many an anxious moment. Once, during a carnival of dancing and singing, he slipped out of the house and followed a group of young girls dressed up in ceremonial costumes, with flowers in their hair, to a secluded temple on the outskirts of the town, where he spent the day with them. A frantic search was made for him, without success. At dusk one of the girls brought him home. He could not eat and compained of a burning throat. It was discovered that he had eaten nothing all day except some flowers that fell from the girls' hair. A *vaidya* was summoned. He administered an antidote and also applied a throat paint, and soon young Moniya was relieved of the pain. But he could no more be trusted to be left unaccompanied at any time, and a nurse was engaged to look after him. This was Rambha, whom the Mahatma immortalized in his autobiography.

The nurse had difficulty in coping with her young charge. One afternoon he eluded her vigilance and stole into a temple with some of his cousins while the priest was taking a siesta. The boys wanted real gods and goddesses to play with, as a change from the mud versions they usually had. They stealthily removed some bronze statues from the sanctuary, and were about to run off with the booty when a couple of statues banged together, causing a sudden loud clanging noise around the priest, who gave chase. The boys dropped the statues and managed to get home without being caught.

By this time Karamchand was no longer the *dewan* of Porbandar and had taken up a similar new position of chief *karbhari* (adviser) in the principality of Rajkot, 120 miles to the north-east of Porbandar, so could not be called upon to give his verdict on the temple episode. The priest, who had recognized the boys as all belonging to the large Gandhi clan, reported the matter to one of Karamchand's brothers, a strict disciplinarian. The boys were rounded up and cross-examined. All except one denied that they had had anything to do with the deed. The exception was Mohandas, then about six years old, who not only fearlessly confessed his hand in it but also pointed out the cousin who had put them up to it. Mohandas was, of course, one of the jubilant plotters and thoroughly enjoyed committing the mischief.

Mohandas started school in Porbandar, where he probably attended the local *Dhoolishala*, or Dust School, where the schoolteacher taught the children how to write letters of the Gujarati alphabet in the dust on the floor. He had no difficulty in composing, along with other children, Gujarati rhymed couplets ridiculing the lame teacher, but encountered some problem in mastering the multiplication table. 'My intellect must have been sluggish, and my memory raw,' the adult Mahatma charges the child of six.

He was about five when his father was appointed *dewan* to the Rana of Rajkot, but the *dewan*'s family stayed behind in Porbandar for about two years before moving to Rajkot. In Rajkot Mohandas and his brothers attended first a local primary school and then Alfred High School. He was again a 'mediocre student', but punctual and complained if breakfast was late 'because it will prevent me from going on with my studies'. He was shy, self-conscious about his frail constitution, and avoided all company. 'My books and lessons were my sole companions.' At the end of the school day he ran back home because he could not bear to talk to anybody. 'I was even afraid lest anyone should poke fun at me.' At school he was required to do gymnastics and play cricket, but he had no aptitude for either. He preferred long solitary walks or playing a simple Indian street game called *gilli danda*, which consists of striking a short, sharpened wooden peg with a stick.

Alfred High School, Rajkot, the secondary school in the area, prepared students for college. English was taught in the very first year at this school, and in the upper high school all subjects (arithmetic, geometry, algebra, chemistry, astronomy, history, geography, etc.) were taught in English. 'The tyranny of English', as Gandhi puts it, was great and this difficulty was increased by reason of the fact that 'the teacher's own English was by no means without blemish'.

During Mohandas's first year at the Alfred High School, when he was about eleven, a British educational inspector named Mr Giles attended an examination and set the pupils five words as a spelling exercise. No one made a mistake except Mohandas, who misspelled 'kettle'. The regular teacher noticed the mistake and motioned him to copy from the slate of the boy sitting next to him. Mohandas would not do it. The teacher later chided him for this 'stupidity' which spoiled the record of the class, but Mohandas felt sure he had done the right thing. Years later he wrote in his autobiography: 'I had thought the teacher was there to supervise against copying . . . Yet the incident did not in the least diminish my respect for my teacher. I was by nature blind to the faults of elders.'

Soon Mohandas, in the company of a cousin, began to smoke, eagerly collecting the cigarette butts of an uncle. They also tried smoking cheap cigarettes they bought with coppers stolen from the servants. Sometimes both were penniless, so they made cigarettes from the porous stalks of a wild plant,but found it hard to keep them lighted. As the days passed, and more and more money was stolen, both boys were gripped by a sense of guilt. They found it unbearable that they should be unable to do anything without the permission of the elders. They despaired of ever becoming grown-ups, and decided that death was preferable to remaining children. To honour their suicide pact, they first went into the jungle in search of poisonous *dhatura* (thorn-apple) seeds and thence proceeded, appropriately, to the nearby temple of God to lay down their lives. Mohandas and his cousin made their obeisances and sought out a lonely corner for the final act, but their courage failed them. The 'suicide' bid thus brought their habit of smoking, and of stealing coppers for the purpose, to an abrupt end. 'I realized it was not as easy to commit suicide as to contemplate it,' Gandhi wrote. 'And since then, whenever I have heard of someone threatening to commit suicide, it has had little or no effect on me.'

8

At this stage, the schoolboy Mohandas had a distaste for reading beyond his school books. Doing the daily homework was an important part of his schedule, 'because I disliked being taken to task by my teacher as much as I disliked deceiving him'. But he noticed a book bought by his father *Shravana Pitribhagti Nataka*, a play about the undying devotion of a poor young boy, named Shravana, toward his old and blind parents, and read it with intense interest. Of all the holy pictures publicly displayed by itinerant showmen, it was the one of 'Shravana carrying, by means of slings fitted for his shoulders, his blind parents on a pilgrimage' which left 'an indelible impression' on his mind. The showmen performed the play with slides in a stereopticon, synchronizing it with the playing of musical instruments. Mohandas was overpowered by the agonized lament of the blind parents over the death of dutiful Shravana who, while bringing water for his thirsty parents from a stream, was hit by an arrow inadvertently shot at him by King Dasharath. The parents refused the water offered by the king and dehydrated their bodies to death. 'The melting tune moved me deeply,' he wrote, 'and I played it on a concertina which my father had purchased for me.'

At about that time, Mohandas had obtained his father's permission to see a play performed by a certain dramatic company. This play, *Harishchandra*, essentially centres round a king of immense goodness and unflinching devotion to truth. As the story goes, the gods decide to test him. They send a Brahmin to him, who at first asks for alms. Then he asks for more and more and the king, true to his *dharma*, does not hesitate to give. He ends up depriving himself of all he has, including his kingdom, and becomes a slave. His wife leaves him, taking their son, who soon dies. Harishchandra is posted at the local cremation grounds, where his wife comes with the body of their son for cremation. Harishchandra, true to his new *dharma*, insists on the customary fee, which his wife cannot pay. 'But he is your son,' she pleads. Finally the gods intervene and restore to Harishchandra his kingship and his family.

Gandhi reports in his autobiography:

I could never be tired of seeing *Harishchandra*. But how often should I be permitted to go? It haunted me, and I must have acted Harishchandra to myself times without number. 'Why should not all be truthful like Harishchandra?' was the question I asked myself day and night. To follow truth and to go through all the ordeals Harishchandra went through was the one ideal it inspired in me. I literally believed in the story of Harishchandra. The thought of it all often made me weep. My commonsense tells me today that Harishchandra could not have been a historical character. Still both

Harishchandra and Shravana are living realities for me, and I am sure I should be moved as before if I were to read those plays again today.

Mohandas was now beginning to think about morality and codes of conduct, including the accepted codes of the Hindu caste system. Hindu society had been divided into four castes by Manu, the ancient Hindu sage, philosopher and strategist. These were, in order of hierarchy: Brahmins, Kshatriyas, Vaisyas and Shudras. Although the caste system was based on the birth of a person into a particular section, each section was attributed specific avocations. While Brahmins engaged themselves in learning holy scriptures and dissemination of knowledge, the Kshatriyas wore the mantle of protectors of society and they included kings and warriors. The Vaisyas represented the business class, and the Banias among them (to which Gandhi belonged) were predominantly engaged in trading. The Shudras, the lowest in the social hierarchy, did menial jobs and were particularly forbidden from learning scriptures and transgressing in any way into the domains of the other sections. On the lowest rung were the 'Untouchables' who were casteless.

A scavenger named Uka, who belonged to this lowest group, was employed in the Gandhi house to clean out the latrines. If anyone of a superior caste accidentally touched a scavenger, then it became incumbent upon him to 'purify' himself by performing his ablutions. Young Mohandas told his mother that he did not consider Uka inferior to anyone else, and added that untouchability was not sanctioned by religion; even Rama was taken across the Ganges by an 'Untouchable'. His mother reminded him that it was not necessary for him to perform ablutions after touching a scavenger; the shortest cut to purification was to cancel the contact by touching any passing Muslim who would, no doubt, be free of the taboos of the Hindu religion.

Presently his attention was drawn to more compelling matters. When Mohandas was about thirteen, he married a girl who had been chosen for him. His bride, Kasturbai Makanji, was the daughter of Gokuldas Makanji, a merchant dealing in cloth, grain and cotton, who lived only a few doors away from the Gandhi house at Porbandar. She was almost the same age as Mohandas.

A wedding is a costly feature of Hindu life. The chief item of expenditure is the dowry, which is paid by the parents of the bride, but a certain amount of the expense must be met by the parents of the bridegroom. The prime minister of Rajkot, true to his Bania trait of a shrewd business mind, was not a man to incur debts or to waste money on three wedding feasts when one was sufficient. He therefore arranged that the wedding of

Mohandas should synchronize with those of his elder brother, Karsandas, and a cousin.

The wedding, which took place at Porbandar, was celebrated with great pomp. While the preparations were taking place, Karamchand, on the ruler's advice, remained at Rajkot, attending to matters of state. On the eve of the marriage, instead of making a leisurely journey to Porbandar by bullock cart, he travelled on a stagecoach especially ordered by the ruler. The coach speeded up when it was nearing Porbandar, resulting in an accident. The *dewan* was thrown clear as the coach overturned, but sustained serious injuries in his fall. However, there could be no postponement of the triple wedding, and he attended it wrapped in bandages.

Young Mohandas's notion of marriage was nothing more than 'the prospect of good clothes to wear, drum-beating, marriage processions, rich dinners, and a strange girl to play with . . . I forgot my grief over my father's injuries in the childish amusement of the wedding.'

At the culmination of the festivities, Mohandas rode to Kasturbai's house on horseback in a marriage procession. There he and Kasturbai sat on a dais and prayed. The priests intoned hymns, and the very young couple rose and took the traditional seven steps around a sacred fire, reciting the Hindu marriage vows pledging devotion to each other through all the ensuing years:

'Take one step, that we may have strength of will,' said Mohandas.

'In every worthy wish of yours, I shall be your helpmate,' responded Kasturbai.

'Take the second step, that we may be filled with vigour.'

'In every worthy wish of yours, I shall be your helpmate.'

'Take the third step, that we may live in ever-increasing prosperity.'

'Your joys and sorrows I will share.'

'Take the fourth step, that we may be ever full of joy.'

'I will ever live devoted to you, speaking words of love and praying for your happiness.'

'Take the fifth step, that we may serve the people.'

'I will follow close behind you always and help you to keep your vow of serving the people.'

'Take the sixth step, that we may follow our religious vows in life.'

'I will follow you in observing our religious vows and duties.'

'Take the seventh step, that we may ever live as friends.'

'It is the fruit of my good deeds that I have you as my husband. You are my best friend, my highest *guru* and my sovereign lord.'

Mohandas and Kasturbai then offered one another *kansar*, sweetened wheat-cakes, symbolizing their joy. It was the year 1882.

'And oh! that first night,' Gandhi wrote forty years later, 'two innocent children all unwittingly hurled together into the ocean of life. My brother's wife had thoroughly coached me about my behaviour on the first night. I do not know who had coached my wife.' Both were too nervous to face each other and the 'coaching could not carry me far'. 'But no coaching is really necessary in such matters,' he adds rather ambiguously. 'The impressions of the former birth are potent enough to make all coaching superfluous.'

They gradually began to know each other, but the thirteen-year-old Mohandas took no time 'in assuming the authority of a husband'. This authority appears to have been stretched rather far, as he began to consider it his right to exact faithfulness from his wife, even though he had no reason to suspect her loyalty. His self-inflicted jealousy ensured that he kept a strict vigilance over her movements. She could not go to the temple or visit friends without his permission. 'But Kasturbai was not the girl to brook any such thing,' Gandhi reports. 'She made it a point to go out whenever and wherever she liked.' The little husband got 'more and more cross and refusal to speak to one another thus became the order of the day with us, married children'. Nevertheless he loved her. His 'passion was entirely on one woman', and he wanted it reciprocated. But Kasturbai was just a child. Sitting in his school classroom, he would daydream about her, and 'the thought of nightfall and our subsequent meeting was ever haunting me. Separation was unbearable. I used to keep her awake till late in the night with my idle talk.'

Kasturbai remained virtually illiterate all her life. Her husband was anxious to teach her, but when he 'awoke from the sleep of lust' there was no spare time, for he had already launched forth into public life. Kasturbai was not impatient about her lack of education, and later efforts to instruct her through private tutors also proved futile. 'I am sure,' Gandhi wrote, 'had my love for her been absolutely untainted with lust, she would be a learned lady today, for I could then have conquered her dislike for studies.'

In later years Gandhi would castigate the 'cruel custom of child marriage', saying that it was the prime cause of India's weakness and degeneracy, filling children's minds with lustful thoughts and sapping their strength, retarding their progress in their schoolwork and permitting them to live a debilitating life of senses. 'It is my painful duty to have to record here my marriage at the age of thirteen,' he wrote in his autobiography. 'As I see the youngsters of the same age under my care, I think of my own marriage. I am inclined to pity myself and to congratulate them on having escaped my lot. I can see no moral argument in support of such a preposterously early marriage.'

In 1882, the year of his marriage, his schoolwork suffered. He failed to appear at the annual examination, but on his promise to make up for the loss he was allowed to enter a higher grade. He did exceptionally well the following year. In contrast, Karsandas, his elder brother, could not cope with the temporary uprooting. He bade farewell to school.

Mohandas had had certain fears and hang-ups since childhood and they still remained. He had always been afraid of darkness, and even after his marriage he could not sleep without a lamp burning at his bedside. To sleep in a room alone was an act of bravery for him. 'I was a coward,' he wrote. 'Darkness was a terror to me. It was almost impossible for me to sleep in the dark, as I would imagine ghosts coming from one direction, thieves from another, and serpents from a third . . . How could I disclose my fears to my wife, no child, but already at the threshold of youth, sleeping by my side? I knew that she had more courage than I, and I felt ashamed of myself.'

He envied the bigger, stronger boys, particularly a Muslim named Sheikh Mehtab, who had originally been a friend of Karsandas. The bold, atheletic Mehtab led the timid Mohandas to believe that meat-eaters were always braver and stronger than others, and he ascribed his strength and fearlessness to meat-eating. He would tell Mohandas that he could hold in his hands live serpents, could defy thieves and did not believe in ghosts. And all this was, of course, the result of eating meat. Boys at school used to recite a doggerel of the Gujarati poet Narmadashankar:

> Behold the mighty Englishman,
> He rules the Indian small,
> Because being a meat-eater
> He is five cubits tall.

It began to dawn on Mohandas that he would grow taller, stronger and more daring if he ate meat. 'If the whole country took to meat-eating, the English could be overcome.'

The experiment had to be conducted in secret lest his parents, strictly vegetarians by religious conviction, should be 'shocked to death'. The opposition to and abhorrence of meat-eating among Jains and Vaishnavas was total. Mohandas, in the company of his brother Karsandas and friend Mehtab, went in search of a lonely spot by the river and there he undertook the experiment, the feast consisting of goat meat and baker's bread. He relished neither. He found the goat meat 'as thick as leather' and had to leave off eating. He spent a nightmarish night. 'Every time I dropped off to sleep it would seem as though a live goat were bleating inside me, and I would jump up full of remorse.'

Sheikh Mehtab was not one to give up easily, and for about a year, at regular intervals, Mohandas joined his friend in surreptitious meat-feasts in the Rajkot State House. He increased neither in strength nor in beauty; however, he came to the conclusion that though there was a duty to eat meat and take up 'food reforms' in the country, deceiving and lying to one's parents was worse than not eating meat. He would not eat meat during the lifetime of his parents and when they were no more and 'I have found my freedom, I will eat meat openly, but until such time I will abstain from it'.

Mohandas appears to have had an aversion to telling lies. Yet to have told the truth was quite impossible. It would have been 'far easier for George Washington to confess to the destruction of an entire forest of cherry-trees than for Mohandas to confess to a Vaishnava family that he had tasted meat'. Sheikh Mehtab had a knack of arranging things, and on one occasion he succeeded in leading Mohandas to a brothel. Payment had been made in advance. Mohandas sat near the woman on the bed, tongue-tied and scared out of his wits. The woman had no time for him and promptly showed him the door, hurling some choice abuse at the future Mahatma. 'I then felt as though my manhood had been injured and wished to sink into the ground of shame,' Gandhi reports. 'But I have ever since given thanks to God for having saved me.'

Karsandas continued to partake of meat at Mehtab's feasts and, as a result, ran up a twenty-five-rupee debt. Sheikh Mehtab and Karsandas persuaded Mohandas to carve out a small piece of Karsandas's thick, solid gold armlet and sell it. Mohandas accomplished the task with ease, but soon pangs of guilt hit him. He made up his mind to confess to his father, yet would not dare do it, not because he was afraid of his father giving him a thrashing – he had never done so – but because he was 'afraid of the pain that I should cause him'. However, there could not be a cleansing without a confession. Finally he wrote out his confession and, trembling, handed it to his father. In it he asked for punishment, and knowing his father well he pleaded that Karamchand would not take the guilt upon himself. He also pledged himself never to steal in future.

The *dewan* had not fully recovered from the accident, and in addition he was suffering from a fistula. He sat up in his sickbed to read the note. Suddenly his cheeks were wet and tears were falling on the page. For a few moments he closed his eyes in thought, and then tore up the note. Mohandas also cried. 'I could see my father's agony,' he wrote. 'If I were a painter I could draw the picture of the whole scene today. It is still so vivid in my mind . . . This was, for me, an object lesson in *ahimsa*. Then I could read in it nothing more than a father's love, but today I know that it was pure *ahimsa* . . . I know that my confession made my father feel absolutely safe about me, and increased his affection for me beyond measure.'

The spell of Mehtab even made inroads into Mohandas's home life. His wife, his mother and even his brother Karsandas advised him that the Muslim wastrel was not a good influence on him. But Mohandas was determined to reform him. At one time Mehtab, whose veracity he could never doubt, managed to kindle Mohandas's suspicion about his wife's fidelity. 'I broke her bangles, refused to have anything to do with her and sent her away to her parents for a whole year,' Gandhi wrote fifty years after the event. 'But Kasturbai showed courage. In the end, after four or more years, my suspicion was dispelled.' His friendship with Mehtab appears quite strange. Years later, Mehtab ended up in South Africa as a member of the Gandhi household. At some point he was found in the house in the company of a prostitute and was finally abandoned.

Meanwhile Karamchand's illness was causing anxiety. Hindu *vaidyas*, Muslim *hakims* and even the local quacks were descending on the house to offer their services. There was also a lengthy discussion with an English surgeon in Bombay about an operation on the fistula, but the *dewan*'s personal physician later disapproved of it, saying it could not possibly succeed because of the patient's advanced age.

Mohandas, for his part, spared no effort in his role of nurse. In the evening he compounded the drugs for his ailing father, dressed the wound, massaged his legs, and when Karamchand was feeling somewhat better would go out for a long walk. This was the time when his mind was also occupied with the approaching birth of his first child, for the sixteen-year-old would soon become a father.

Karamchand was getting weaker and weaker and despaired of living any longer. The end came in November 1885. Mohandas was seized with the guilt which over the years never quite left him. He had spent the evening massaging his father's legs, and late at night one of his uncles offered to take over. Mohandas was glad to be relieved of his duty, and returned to his own room. He describes the situation in what, perhaps, is the most celebrated passage in his autobiography:

The dreadful night came . . . It was between 10:30 and 11:00 p.m . . . my wife . . . was fast asleep . . . But how could she sleep when I was there? I woke her up. In five or six minutes, however, the servant knocked at the door. 'Get up,' he said, 'father is very ill' . . . I guessed what 'very ill' meant at that moment . . .

I felt deeply ashamed and miserable. I ran to my father's room. I saw that if animal passion had not blinded me, I should have been spared the torture of separation from my father during his last moments. I should have been massaging him, and he would have died in my arms. But . . . it was my uncle who had the privilege.

This shame of carnal desire . . . at the critical hour of my father's death . . . is a blot I have never been able to efface or forget . . . the poor mite that was born to my wife scarcely breathed for more than three or four days . . .

# TWO

# *Growing Pains*

With Karamchand's death, the family began to experience financial difficulties. He had been receiving a small pension from the ruler of Rajkot, but this ceased with his death. By nature he was no hoarder of wealth, spending all he earned on the education and marriages of his children or on charity. The eldest of the three sons was now the head of the household. Mohandas therefore had to appeal to Laxmidas whenever he needed money. During these years, in fact, they were on close and friendly terms. But later the two brothers were to have a strong difference of opinion over money matters.

Late in 1887, when Mohandas was eighteen, he went to Ahmedabad, the capital of the province to sit for his matriculation at Bombay University. He barely succeeded in passing the examination. His total of 247 marks out of an aggregate of 625 (39 per cent) was by no means a creditable performance (pass marks for individual subjects being 33 per cent). But he managed to enter the small, inexpensive Samaldas College at Bhavnagar, in the princely state of Bhavnagar. For the first time he was living away from home without his wife. He did badly in his studies and felt homesick. He began having headaches and frequent nosebleeds and went back to Rajkot. While he was at college his wife had given birth to a son, who was named Harilal. Mohandas never returned to Samaldas College.

He confided his problems to Laxmidas, and the two brothers went to see an old family adviser, a Brahmin named Mavji Dave. Mohandas told Dave frankly about his total lack of interest in studies, adding that he was not hopeful of succeeding even in the first-year college examination. The priest was critical of the current plans for his education. 'Times have changed,' he told Laxmidas. 'And none of you can expect to succeed to your father's position as *dewan* without proper education.' He advised that since Mohandas was still pursuing his studies, the family should look to him to keep the *dewan*ship. If he spent four or five years getting his BA degree, it would at best qualify him for a sixty-rupee post, not a *dewan*ship. He counselled Mohandas to go to England and become a barrister-at-law – a title reserved for those who studied law in England. The priest's son, Kevalram, a lawyer, had informed him that it was far easier and took much less time to become a barrister-at-law than to qualify as a lawyer in India. The total expense would be about five thousand rupees, and on completion of his studies in England he would get the *dewan*ship for the asking. 'Try to get some scholarship,' he added. 'Apply to Junagarh and Porbandar states. See my son, Kevalram, and if you fail in getting pecuniary help and if you have no money, sell your furniture. You must go to England.'

Mohandas was also interested in medicine, but his suggestion that he go to England to study medicine instead of law was promptly dismissed by Laxmidas: 'Father never liked it. He had you in mind when he said that we Vaishnavas should have nothing to do with dissection of dead bodies. Father intended you for the bar.' Mavji did not take the same dismal view of the medical profession, but stressed that a doctor would have scant chance of becoming a *dewan*. He cautioned them to keep the matter a secret, because there would be objections to the plan on religious grounds. But Laxmidas had no talent for keeping secrets, and before long many of the Gandhi cousins had heard about it. One of them even promised to advance the five thousand rupees, but nothing came of it.

Mohandas was delighted at the prospect of going to England, but a meeting with the priest's son had a sobering effect. 'You will have to spend there at least ten thousand rupees,' he was told. 'You will have to set aside your religious prejudices, if any. You will have to eat meat. You must drink. You cannot live without that. The more you spend, the cleverer you will be. It is a very important thing. I speak to you frankly. Don't be offended, but look here, you are still very young. There are many temptations in London. You are apt to be entrapped by them.'

Young Mohandas's morale suddenly registered a new low. The journey to London had not only become prohibitively expensive, but would also demand that he should drink alcohol, eat meat and submit to the temptations of life in a great metropolis. Timidly, Mohandas asked Kevalram Dave to use his influence to get him a scholarship. The interview came to an abrupt end when the request was refused.

Mohandas was determined to eliminate the several obstacles confronting him. There were religious taboos against anyone of his caste travelling overseas; other members of the family must be in agreement on the subject; there was also his wife to be considered; and then, of course, there was the question of raising the money.

The thought of going to England, however, had emboldened Mohandas to make the four-day journey by bullock cart and camel to Porbandar to obtain, in accordance with his mother's wishes, the consent of his uncle, now head of the Gandhi clan. The uncle pondered over the matter. He was not sure if it was possible to stay in England without prejudice to one's religion. He had met many Indian barristers who were thoroughly Anglicized. 'They know no scruples regarding food,' he said. 'Cigars are never out of their mouths. They dress as shamelessly as Englishmen. All this would not be in keeping with our family tradition.' He was about to go on a pilgrimage, and how could he 'at the threshold of death', give Mohandas permission to cross the seas? This stern sermon was followed by a few reassuring words. 'But I will not stand in your way,' he said. 'It is your mother's permission which really matters. If she permits you, then god-speed. You will go with my blessings.'

In an effort to obtain some financial assistance for his law studies in London, Mohandas made an appointment with Mr Lely, the British agent in Porbandar, who managed the state during the minority of the young prince. Mr Lely rebuffed him without even letting him present his case. 'Pass your BA first and then see me,' he told the nervous and disappointed Mohandas. 'I had made elaborate preparations to meet him,' wrote Gandhi. 'I had carefully learnt up a few sentences, and had bowed low and saluted him with both hands. But all to no purpose!'

Colonel Watson, the British agent at Rajkot, was also approached. He gave Mohandas a 'trivial' note of introduction to someone in England, which, he said, was 'worth a hundred thousand rupees'. The ruler of Rajkot indicated some hope of assistance, but gave him just a signed photograph of himself. Mohandas returned to Bhavnagar and sold off his furniture, thus providing himself with a paltry sum toward his expenses.

Although Kevalram's estimate of living expense amounted to ten thousand rupees, Mohandas was convinced he could manage it more cheaply. However, several weeks of manoeuvres had failed and no money was forthcoming from uncles and cousins who had earlier shown interest in his education plans and promised financial assistance. Laxmidas promised to find the required money somehow. Mavji Dave's estimate of the expense of sending Mohandas to London proved grossly inaccurate. Instead of five thousand rupees, the total expense was in the vicinity of thirteen thousand rupees. If they had known this at the beginning, his chances of going to England would have been remote.

Mohandas's mother had her reservations about his going overseas. She had begun making patient enquiries and was informed that young Indians in London sometimes associated with strange women, consumed liquor and ate meat. 'How about all this?' she asked him. Mohandas reassured her: 'I shall not lie to you. I swear that I shall not touch any of those things.' He reminded her that old Mavji Dave would never have suggested the journey to London if there was any danger of his succumbing to these sins. Another family adviser, a Jain monk named Becharji Swami, was able to allay her anxieties. 'I shall get the boy solemnly to take the three vows and then he can be allowed to go.' So Mohandas solemnly vowed not to touch wine, women or meat. She trusted her son to keep these vows, and gave her blessing to his departure.

On 4 July 1888, his fellow students at the Alfred High School in Rajkot gave him a farewell party. Mohandas rose to make his maiden speech. 'I had written a few words of thanks,' he reports. 'But I could scarcely stammer them out. I remember how my head reeled and my whole frame shook as I stood up to read them.' The substance of his speech was published in the *Kathiawar Times*, a local newspaper: 'I hope that some of you will follow in my footsteps and after your return from England you will work wholeheartedly for big reforms in India.'

This was by no means a political speech. When Gandhi spoke at the school farewell meeting, he had social reforms in mind, though he had no clear concept in this regard. In his brief speech he was only stating the conventional things that were expected of a youth having the rare opportunity of going to England to become a lawyer.

The farewell party was rather premature, for a period of about one month elapsed before he was able to leave Rajkot. 'Sleeping, waking, drinking, eating, walking, running, reading, I was dreaming and thinking of England and what I would do on that momentous day.' At last, on 10 August, the day of departure to Bombay dawned. Gandhi describes the scene of his leaving home:

> My mother was hiding her tearful eyes with her hands, but the sobbing was clearly heard. There were some fifty friends present, and if I wept they would consider me too weak . . . I did not cry even though my heart was breaking . . . then came the leave-taking with my wife . . . I had to see her in a separate room. She of course, had begun sobbing long before. I went to her and stood like a dumb statue for a moment. I kissed her, and she said, 'Don't go.' What followed I need not describe.

Mohandas, accompanied by Laxmidas, Sheikh Mehtab and two others, left for Bombay. Some friends got into the carriage en route, travelled with him a few stations, and then returned. A ship was scheduled to leave on 21 August, and he planned to spend a few days in Bombay, buying proper clothes for the journey, but there were to be more difficulties in store for him.

In Bombay he was told that the Indian Ocean was rough, and since it was his first voyage he should postpone his departure till November when the sea would be calmer. It was also reported that a steamer had just sunk in a gale. Laxmidas was frightened, and he refused to allow Mohandas to sail till the roughness of the Indian Ocean had subsided. He returned to Rajkot, leaving Mohandas in the care of brother-in-law Khushalbhai Makanji, who had been entrusted with the money, and also left word with some friends to afford him whatever help he might need. But there were also enemies around.

Word had passed from one Modh Bania to another that a member of their caste, with plans to go to England, was on the verge of polluting the sanctity of the caste. Nothing was done until Mohandas had actually left Rajkot, but soon after he reached Bombay, he savoured the first taste of Bania orthodoxy. On one occasion, not far from the Town Hall, he was accosted and hooted by a group of caste fellows, while Laxmidas looked helplessly on. Mohandas was determined to tackle this new hurdle that now threatened his departure. He was pestered by many deputations from his caste people; however, they failed to make an impression on him. The boy's full-grown obstinacy came to his rescue, but not before he was virtually dragged out of the house to present himself at a court of elders. The meeting of the caste was well attended as the elders had announced that absentees should be liable to a fine of five annas.

'In the opinion of the caste, your proposal to go to England is not proper,' said the Sheth – the headman of the community – who was a distant relative of Mohandas and had been on very good terms with Karamchand Gandhi. 'We are positively informed that you will have to eat flesh and drink wine in England; moreover, you have to cross the waters; and all this you must know is against our caste rules. Therefore we command you to reconsider your decision, or else the heaviest punishment shall be meted out to you.'

'I thank you for your warnings,' Mohandas said calmly. 'I am sorry I cannot alter my decision. What I have heard about England is quite different from what you say; one need not take meat or wine there. Concerning crossing the waters, if our brothers can go as far as Aden, why could I not go to England? I am deeply convinced that malice is at the root of all these objections.'

'Very well, then,' replied the headman in anger. 'You are not the son of your father.' Then, turning to the audience, he proclaimed: 'This boy shall be treated as an outcast from today. Whoever helps him or goes to see him off at the dock shall be punishable with a fine of one rupee four annas.'

The incident made Mohandas more anxious to sail, lest they should succeed in pressurizing his brother. As he was worrying over his predicament, he heard from friends that a middle-aged Junagarh lawyer, Tryambakrai

Mazumdar, had reserved a passage on the SS *Clyde*, and they suggested that he should take the same ship and even share a cabin with the lawyer. Mohandas approached his brother-in-law for the money, but Khushalbhai referred to the order of the headman and said he could not afford to lose caste. Mohandas then sought the help of a friend of the family to advance him money to cover travelling expenses and sundries. The friend obliged, and it was arranged that he could recover the amount from the brother-in-law. Mohandas finally sailed from Bombay on 4 September 1888.

Tryambakrai Mazumdar was a kindly man. He advised the shy, provincial Mohandas to come out of his self-imposed loneliness and mix with other passengers aboard. But Mohandas hid himself in the cabin, speaking to no one except his new-found friend, living for two days on the sweets and fruits he had brought with him. On board he wore a black suit. He was innocent of the use of knives and forks, and could not pluck up enough courage to enquire what dishes on the menu were free of meat. Finally Mr Mazumdar arranged for Indian vegetarian food to be served, and Mohandas would dine in the company of his lawyer friend and a first-class passenger named Abdul Majid. He was, however, not too pleased with the food and found it somewhat unappetizing.

Mohandas was unaccustomed to conversing in English. Except for him and Mr Mazumdar, all the passengers in the second-class saloon were English. Some of them would come up to speak to him, but he could hardly make out what they were saying. Even when he did understand them, he could not reply. 'I had to frame every sentence in my mind, before I could bring it out.' He took refuge from the loneliness of the cabin by watching the sea from the deck. One night the scene around him completely baffled him, and he recorded this in his journal:

> One dark night when the sky was clear the stars were reflected in the water. The scene around us was very beautiful at that time. I could not at first imagine what that was. They appeared like so many diamonds. But I know that a diamond could not float. Then I thought they must be some insects which can only be seen at night. Amidst these reflections I looked up in the sky and at once found that it was nothing but stars reflected in waters. I laughed at my folly.

When the ship anchored at Aden, he saw young boys rowing out to dive into the clear blue water for the pennies the Europeans flung into the sea. He envied their strength and skill at diving, till a boatman informed him that the boys sometimes lost their limbs to the hungry sharks. He enjoyed driving around Aden with Mr Mazumdar in a carriage which cost him one rupee, and he regretfully noted this expense in his journal.

He was fascinated by the journey through the Suez Canal. The sheer heat would drive him out of the cabin to the deck where it would be somewhat more bearable. He marvelled at the construction of the canal. 'I cannot think of the genius of the man who invented it,' he wrote in his journal. 'I don't know how he would have done it. It is quite right to say that he has competed with nature.' At Port Said, the terminus of the the canal, he was surprised to learn that what he thought was a theatre was merely a coffeehouse, where 'a bottle of lemonade would cost you twelve pence – the one which will cost less than a penny in Bombay'. Listening to music in the coffee-house was advertised as being free; however, later a woman came around and he was obliged to give her sixpence. 'Port Said,' he noted, 'is nothing but a seat of luxury', and he found the men and women in the town 'very cunning'.

By this time he was beginning to come out of his aloofness and even talked to some of the English passengers. On the eve of his departure from India, well-meaning but none-too-knowledgeable friends had told him that he could not do without meat and wine in the cold English climate. One went so far as to advise him to take with him 'eight bottles of whiskey', for after Aden he would need them. An English passenger on the *Clyde*, a certain Mr Jeffreys, had taken very kindly to him. 'The weather has not been severe,' he said to Mohandas, 'but in the Bay of Biscay you will have to choose between death and meat and wine.' He too warned him that he could not possibly survive without meat in the cold climate of England.

When the ship anchored at Brindisi, it was still warm. Mohandas went ashore and was promptly importuned by an enterprising pimp who attempted to lead him to a prostitute. The young traveller was on his guard – he certainly wanted to have nothing to do with the proposal. In his journal Mohandas gives an account of his meeting with the pimp in an oddly exhortative manner. He has pondered over the matter with great care, and offers remedies for avoiding such encounters in future.

When you land at Brindisi, a man would come and ask you, in case you are a black man: 'Sir, there is a beautiful girl of 14, follow me, Sir, and I will take you there, the charge is not high, Sir.' You are at once puzzled. But be calm and answer boldly that you don't want her and tell the man to go away and thereby you will be safe. If you are in any difficulty at once refer to a policeman just near you, or at once enter a large building which you will surely see. But before you enter it, read the name on the building and make sure that it is open to all. This you will be able to make out at once. Tell the porter that you are in a difficulty, and he will at once show you what you should do. If you are bold enough, ask the porter to take you to the Chief Officer and you will refer the matter to him. By a large building I meant that it must be belonging to Thos. Cook or Henry

King or some other such agents. They will take care of you. Don't be miserly at this time. Pay the porter something.

Meanwhile, friendly Englishmen kept goading him to partake of meat and wine. He took their advice seriously and kept a close watch on the weather, but concluded that he would rather die than break the oath he had given to his mother and to the Jain priest.

The weather was still agreeable when the ship reached Malta. Here he was short-changed, this time by the boatman who took him ashore. He carefully noted down the number of the boat, but the rogue could not be brought to book. Mohandas was impressed with the Cathedral of St John, and went down into the crypt to see 'some skeletons of eminent persons'. He also saw some tapestries of Peter Paul Rubens depicting the life of Christ, the first works of European art he had ever looked upon. He went to see the collection in the Armoury Hall and was particularly impressed with the carriage of Napoleon Bonaparte. It was expensive wandering through the city, but what Mohandas really enjoyed was a quiet pool where red and gold fish were swimming.

The next stop-over was Gibraltar. He could not see much of it, and this disappointed him. The ship was now cruising along on the last leg of the voyage.

Mohandas's long-awaited first sight of England was rather a symbolic one. He could see nothing of the land at Plymouth, for it was shrouded in fog and darkness. The passengers were disembarked at the new docks at Tilbury, twenty miles down the Thames from London. At four o'clock in the afternoon of 29 September 1888, he arrived on the boat-train at Victoria Station. He stepped out of the train attired in the white flannel suit which he had bought in Bombay for summer wear. 'I had thought that white clothes would suit me better when I stepped ashore.' But he soon discovered that he was the only one wearing such clothes. It was a bitterly cold day.

# THREE

# Law Student in London

Mohandas had left his baggage in the charge of an agent of Grindlay and Co., since many fellow-passengers had entrusted their baggage to such forwarding agents and 'I must follow suit'. The next day being a Sunday, he could not hope to get his baggage until the following day. His white flannels were still inviting unwelcome glares as he, along with his two Indian companions, arrived at the Victoria Hotel, which stood on Northumberland Avenue, not far from Piccadilly Circus, and was considered one of the finest in the town. Mr Majid, the first-class passenger from the *Clyde*, entered the hotel with the air of a maharajah and did not consider it proper to enquire about the tariff. The cost of the second-floor room which they took was six shillings a day, and he had spoken for all of them.

Mohandas was dazzled by the splendour of the hotel. Never in his life had he seen so ornate and so brightly lit a place as this. He felt somewhat intimidated by the spectacle, and was still more puzzled when a young porter pushed a button 'which I thought was the lock of the door' to summon an elevator. 'The doors were opened and I thought that was a room in which we were to sit for some time. But to my great surprise we were brought to the second floor.' Of the splendour of the place he observed: 'When I first saw my room in the Victoria Hotel, I thought I could pass a lifetime in that room.'

He had with him a letter of introduction to Dr P. J. Mehta, a friend of the Gandhi family. A telegraphic message soon brought the doctor to the hotel. Mohandas was intrigued to see his silken top hat and out of curiosity passed his hands over it to feel the glossy fur. Unfortunately, he rubbed it the wrong way, and the polished doctor took this opportunity to give him some essential lessons in deportment and behaviour. 'Do not touch other people's things,' he said. 'Do not ask questions as we usually do in India on first acquaintance. Do not talk loudly.' There were several of these instructions, and Mohandas was quick to grasp them. Dr Mehta also urged him to move to a more affordable place, and promised to come back in a day or so when he could be more specific about a suitable residence for the young student.

Two days later Dr Mehta returned to the Victoria Hotel. But soon after his luggage had arrived that morning, Mohandas, along with Mr Mazumdar, had moved to a cheap lodging house, forgetting to inform the doctor about the move. Dr Mehta was able to learn the new address from the hotel manager. He inspected the dingy room and its appointments and shook his head in disapproval. 'This place won't do,' he said. 'We come to England not so much for the purpose of studies as for gaining experience of English life and customs.'

Dr Mehta had plans for Mohandas to live with a family, but prior to that he was to serve a period of apprenticeship with a young friend of his, a law student named Dalpatram Shukla, in his lodgings at Richmond. Shukla treated the lonesome Mohandas very kindly. He provided a basic initiation in English ways and manners and made him accustomed to speak English at all times. But introduction to a completely different type of food posed a serious problem. Boiled vegetables without salt and condiments were unpalatable, and the landlady was at a loss to know what to prepare for him. She wondered how long he would be able to survive on a diet of oatmeal porridge for breakfast, and jam, bread and spinach for lunch and dinner.

Mohandas was a good eater and had a 'capacious stomach', but would not ask for more than two or three slices of bread, as he did not deem it correct to do so. For some reason there was no milk available either for lunch or dinner, and this added to his dietary predicament. He shed copious tears at night, and would dream of the country he had left behind him. His companion tried to argue him out of his vow against meat, pointing out that it was no vow at all when at the time he knew nothing of the conditions of life in England. 'What is the value of a vow made before an illiterate mother?' asked Shukla. 'It would not be regarded as a vow in law. It is pure superstition to stick to such a promise.'

One day, in an effort to wean him from his vow, Shukla began to read aloud Bentham's *Theory of Utility*. 'These abstruse things are beyond me,' Mohandas said. 'I admit it is necessary to eat meat, but I cannot break my vow.' As Shukla sought to throw more light on Bentham's work, Mohandas got exasperated. 'A vow is a vow. It cannot be broken.'

He wrote to his brother Laxmidas informing him that despite the cold weather he felt no need to take meat or liquor. 'This fills my heart with joy and thankfulness.'

After about a month of tutelage, Mohandas was considered to be fit to survive by himself, and accommodation was found in the home of an English widow who had for some years lived in India. Her family included her two daughters. The house was at 20 Baron's Court Road, West Kensington. The landlady was aware of Mohandas's vow and was genuinely sympathetic and understanding, but Mohandas found the food quite bland, and was too shy to ask for more than they put in front of him. Sometimes the two girls would offer him an extra slice of bread, while his eyes were set on the whole loaf. He stayed with this family for eight or nine months, paying thirty shillings a week, 'not because the cost of board and lodging was so much or even half so much, but because of the privilege of being allowed their company'. He would also periodically eat out just to show them that he was 'not stingy'. He commended the experience in his unpublished 'Guide to London' in a qualified manner. 'It is generally thought desirable to live in families in order to learn the English manners and customs,' he noted. 'This may be good for a few months, but to pass three years in a family is not only unnecessary but often tiresome. And it would be impossible to lead a regular student's life in a family. This is the experience of many.'

As a law student, he was rather an isolated person. There was no campus life and he had only a few classes or lectures to attend. Once he was admitted to the Inner Temple, one of the four Inns of Court, there were only three conditions to be fulfilled before he was formally called to the Bar: he must keep twelve terms, pass his examinations, and attain the age of twenty-one. 'Keeping term' meant attendance at at least six dinners out of the twenty-four offered at the Inner Temple each term. He ate poorly at these sumptuous meals until he discovered that it was possible to be served with a vegetarian meal. He was a popular guest at the dinners because two bottles of wine were allowed to each group of four, and he did not drink. The examinations were scarcely more difficult than eating the meals, but he took his studies seriously.

The first few months were mainly devoted to exploration and learning to cope with the English way of living. His main problem was still his lack of facility in English. On Dalpatram Shukla's advice he cultivated the regular reading of newspapers, something that must have been quite an experience for him. 'In India I had never read a newspaper.' He would spend about an hour a day glancing over the *Daily News*, the *Daily Telegraph*, and the *Pall Mall Gazette*, and this left him with plenty of time for his jaunts. His landlady had told him about the presence of vegetarian restaurants in the city. He would walk several miles each day and have his fill of bread in cheap restaurants, but would never be satisfied. During his wanderings he ran into a vegetarian restaurant in Farringdon Street, not far from the Inner Temple, which not only served a vegetarian diet but propagated it through literature. He bought H.S. Salt's *A Plea for Vegetarianism* for a shilling, then walked into the dining room and for the first time since he came to England had a hearty meal. 'God had come to my aid,' Gandhi wrote in his autobiography, and added:

I read Salt's book from cover to cover and was very much impressed by it. From the date of reading this book, I may claim to have become a vegetarian by choice. I blessed the day on which I had taken the vow before my mother. I had all along abstained from meat in the interests of truth and the vow I had taken, but had wished at the same time that every Indian should be a meat-eater and had looked forward to being one myself freely and openly some day, and to enlisting others in the cause. The choice was now made in favour of vegetarianism, the spread of which henceforward became my mission.

His faith in vegetarianism was now on a more definite plane, and Salt's book 'whetted my appetite for dietetic studies'. During the following weeks he read most of the available vegetarian literature, including Howard Williams's *The Ethics of Diet* and Dr Anna Kingsford's *The Perfect Way in Diet*. 'The result of reading all this literature was that dietetic experiments came to take an important place in my life,' wrote Gandhi. 'Health was the principal consideration of these experiments to begin with, but later on religion became the supreme motive.'

His growing interest in vegetarianism began to worry his friends. They were afraid that this fad might prove injurious to his health. Dalpatram Shukla, his Richmond friend, was concerned lest he should fritter his life away in experiments, forgetting his own work, and become a crank. Shukla planned a little stratagem which, he thought, might reform Mohandas. He invited him to a dinner to be followed by a visit to the theatre. Dinner was at the luxurious Holborn Restaurant. Perhaps he thought that there at least Mohandas would, if only for decency's sake, accept unquestioningly whatever was brought to the table. The waiter served soup. Mohandas turned to enquire if it was a vegetarian soup. His friend noticed the movement. 'You are too clumsy for decent society,' he exclaimed. 'If you cannot behave yourself you had better go. Feed in some other restaurant and wait for me outside.' Mohandas was delighted: there was a vegetarian restaurant close by where he could have a hearty meal, though disappointment awaited him as it was closed.

Mohandas found living in London very expensive and reckoned that apart from the £650 already provided for, he would require an additional £350 to see him through the entire three-year period. He wrote to Mr Lely, the English administrator in Porbandar, and to Colonel Watson, the political agent at Rajkot, a close friend of his father, requesting financial assistance. Both letters remained unanswered.

There were very few Indian students in England at the time, and although many of them were married, it was a practice with them to affect bachelor status. The institution of child-marriage was virtually nonexistent in England, and in order to save embarrassment, they would rather not admit that they were married. In addition, such an admission would certainly prove a hurdle to going out or flirting with the young girls of the family in which they lived. 'The flirting was more or less innocent. Parents even encouraged it.' Young Gandhi's shyness seems to have been more pronounced in the presence of young women, but he did not hesitate to go about as a bachelor. 'I too caught the contagion,' he wrote. 'But I was none the happier for being a dissembler. Only my reserve and my reticence saved me from going into deeper waters.'

On one occasion he went to Ventnor, on the Isle of Wight, and stayed there with a family. The daughter of the landlady, as was customary in such families, took the guests out for a walk. Gandhi, who as a child was a picture of agility, and as a man could outwalk anyone, describes his outing with the young woman. It was his first encounter with an unchaperoned woman:

> My landlady's daughter took me one day to the lovely hills around Ventnor. I was no slow walker, but my companion walked even faster, dragging me after her and chattering away all the while. I responded to her chatter sometimes with a whispered 'yes' or 'no', or at the most 'yes, how beautiful!' She was flying like a bird, whilst I was wondering when I should get back home. We thus reached the top of a hill. How to get down again was the question. In spite of her high-heeled boots, this sprightly young lady of twenty-five darted down the hill like an arrow. I was shamefacedly struggling to get down. She stood at the foot smiling and cheering me and offering to come and drag me. How could I be so chicken-hearted? With the greatest difficulty and crawling at intervals, I somehow managed to scramble to the bottom. She loudly laughed 'bravo' and shamed me all the more, as well she might.

None of these ladies was aware that he had a wife back in India, and he made the fact known only when an old woman, who had helped him read the menu in a Brighton hotel, appeared to be playing the role of matchmaker. The kind lady invited him to dine with her every Sunday when he returned to London, an invitation which he gladly accepted. On occasions, in order to help him to conquer his bashfulness, she would introduce him to unmarried girls, and would draw him into conversation with them. His shyness and weakness in spoken English would invariably lead to confusion, his words misunderstood and his very silences regarded as breathless adoration. Particularly marked out for these conversations was a girl who stayed with the old lady, and the latter would ensure that the youngsters were left entirely alone together. In the course of time Mohandas began to feel a little more confident and looked forward to Sundays for the interesting conversation with his young friend, but he was in a quandary when he realized what the old lady had in mind. He composed a letter, asking for her forgiveness, for he was married while yet a boy, and was the father of a son. 'I am glad God has now given me the courage to speak out the truth,' he wrote. 'I can assure you I have taken no improper liberties with the young lady you were good enough to introduce to me.' It was a long and laborious letter, written with the utmost honesty and humility. The old lady sent a kind reply, assuring him that 'the untruth you say you have been guilty of is pardonable and it is well that you have acquainted us with the real state of things'. He was welcomed to dinner as usual. 'We shall look forward to hearing all about your child-marriage,' she wrote in a light vein, 'and to the pleasure of laughing at your expense.' But Mohandas was inclined to treat the whole episode in all seriousness, and thus purged himself of 'the canker of untruth'.

Although Gandhi was now a vegetarian by conviction, he had realized that in England vegetarianism, besides being an inconvenience, was a social handicap; and he was determined to make up for this and other social deficiencies by cultivating some accomplishments which would fit him for polite society. For this purpose he undertook the task of becoming an 'English gentleman'. The transformation was so sudden that Indian students in London wondered whether he had inherited a fortune. He discarded the garments he had brought from India and purchased a set of clothes at the Army and Navy Stores. He also went in for a black silk hat costing nineteen shillings. As soon as he was attired in his new suit and his black silk hat, he walked to Bond Street, where the then extravagant sum of ten pounds could buy him an evening suit tailored to order. He dispatched an urgent message to his noble-hearted brother to send him a double watch chain of gold. He was quick to observe the fundamental immorality of a ready-made tie. Having bought the right sort of tie, he sat down before a mirror and proceeded to work out the puzzle. For ten minutes every day he mirrored to himself his daily knotty exercise with the tie and the parting of the hair – little conscious of the parting of the ways. Dr Sachchidananda Sinha, an Indian who was then a student in London, recollected meeting Gandhi in February 1890 in Piccadilly Circus:

> Gandhi was wearing at the time a high silk top hat 'burnished bright', a stiff and starched collar (known as a Gladstonian), a rather flashy tie displaying all the colours of the rainbow, under which there was a fine striped silk shirt. He wore as his outer clothes a morning coat, a double-breasted waistcoat, and dark

striped trousers to match, and not only patent-leather shoes but spats over them. He also carried leather gloves and a silver-mounted stick, but wore no spectacles. His clothes were regarded as the very acme of fashion for young men about town at that time, and were largely in vogue among the Indian youth prosecuting their studies in law at one of the four institutions called the Inns of Court. The Inner Temple, the one in which Gandhi enrolled, was considered by Indians the most aristocratic.

It did not suffice merely to be well dressed. He therefore directed his attention to other qualities that went to the making of an English gentleman. He decided it was necessary for him to take lessons in dancing, French and elocution, and paid three pounds in advance for a set of dancing lessons. The music, however, bewildered him. He could not follow the piano and thus it was impossible to keep time. He thought he should learn to play the violin in order to cultivate an ear for Western music, and spent several more pounds on a violin and fees to a violin teacher. He sought out a teacher to teach him French, and another to teach him elocution, to whom he paid a preliminary fee of a guinea. The elocution teacher recommended the *Standard Elocutionist* of Alexander Melville Bell, the father of Alexander Graham Bell, the inventor of the telephone. Young Gandhi promptly bought the book and began with a speech of Pitt's. 'But Mr Bell rang the bell of alarm in my ear and I awoke.' He was not planning to spend a lifetime in England. What then was the use of learning elocution? And how could dancing make a gentleman of him? He was a student and he ought to go on with his studies. He wrote to the dancing instructor and the teacher of elocution to explain why he would trouble neither of them again. He went personally to the violin teacher with a request to dispose of the violin for any price it might fetch. She was quite understanding, and even encouraged him in his resolve to make a complete change.

Gandhi's infatuation with English finery lasted a few months, but his fastidiousness in dress persisted for years. During the brief spell of 'aping the English gentleman' he kept account of every farthing he spent, and his expenses were carefully allocated. Every little item, including money spent on postage stamps and pennies paid for newspapers, was accounted for and the balance struck before going to bed. With the realization that he was gaining nothing by his expensive mode of life, he began to examine his living habits closely, and came to the conclusion that the thirty shillings he paid each week for room and board at 20 Baron's Court Road was excessive and very largely wasted. The rules were strict in that he had to be punctual at meals. It was customary that occasionally he should take the members of the family out to dinner; he would sometime dine out alone; there were also afternoon teas to be paid for. In all he was spending a tidy sum on extra meals not included in the boarding-house budget. By simplifying systematically, he was able to cut his expenses drastically. He rented a suite of rooms and eventually settled for a single-roomed 'bedsitter'. He studied books on simple living and found that by installing a stove in his room and giving himself oatmeal porridge and cocoa for breakfast and bread and cocoa for dinner, and taking lunch at a cheap restaurant, he could live on one shilling and threepence a day. He economized further by walking where previously he had always taken the train or bus. 'It was mainly this habit of long walks that kept me practically free from illness throughout my stay in England and gave me a fairly strong body.' His total expenses were now only seventeen shillings a week. This change in living did not make his life a dreary affair, but in fact 'harmonized my inward and outward life'. It was, no doubt, in keeping with the means of his family. 'My life was certainly more truthful and my soul knew no bounds of joy.'

He began to ask himself how he could best employ his time. The Bar examinations, he was aware, were not difficult and would not require much study. He thought, therefore, that besides these he should pass some literary examinations which would help to improve his English. Oxford and Cambridge courses he found would be time-consuming and prohibitively expensive. A friend suggested that he should study for the London Matriculation. This would involve hard work, but there would be almost no extra expense. He was somewhat deterred to note that a modern language and Latin were compulsory subjects. The modern language presented no serious problem, as he had already taken up a course in French, but the prospect of learning Latin discouraged him. However, his friend managed to convince him that Latin would be useful to a lawyer, and would give him a better command of English, and so he joined a private matriculation class and settled down to the life of a serious student. In January 1890, after five months of sheer hard work, he took the examination, but was declared unsuccessful, having failed in Latin. Six months later he took the examination again and passed with good marks.

Despite concentration on his studies, he was able to continue to pursue his interest in vegetarianism. At one time he lived on bread and fruit alone, and for a short period on a diet of cheese, milk and eggs. He held that eggs could not be considered meat, as no injury was done to living creatures by consuming them, but he knew that this was a new interpretation, for his mother's definition of meat included eggs. 'As soon as I saw the true import of the vow I gave up eggs and the experiment alike.'

Two attractions of the restaurant in Farringdon Street which Gandhi frequented were the afternoon teas and the celebrities. People would go miles for the privilege of meeting and sitting beside a celebrity over a cup of tea, and hearing him orate. H.S. Salt, the author of *A Plea for Vegetarianism*, used to arrange such tea parties. Stephen Winsten, in his *Salt and His Circle*, observes:

> And in the very early days, an Indian in silk hat and black coat walked in . . . sat among very affable and talkative people and asked where he could get dancing lessons . . . Salt was kindness and understanding itself. 'My name is Gandhi,' he told them, 'you have, of course, never heard of it.' Salt made a note of a possible new member. Years went by and the name was forgotten.

Decades later, however, Gandhi recalled before a gathering of vegetarians in London what he had observed in those days. 'They had a habit of talking of nothing but food and nothing but disease.' This was the 'worst way of going about the business'. Most of them had taken to vegetarianism purely for health reasons, for they were suffering from some ailment or other. They thought that by becoming vegetarians they could 'eat as much lentils, haricot beans and cheese as they liked', and this notion did not help them at all. In order to be healthy, one had to 'eat sparingly and now and then fast. No man or woman really ate . . . just the quantity which the body requires and no more.'

It was at the Farringdon Street restaurant that he learned about the existence of the Vegetarian Society of Manchester and about its journal, the *Vegetarian Messenger* which he would sometimes read. About this time he also came to know of the journal of the London Vegetarian Society, *The Vegetarian*, of which Dr Josiah Oldfield was the editor. In due course Gandhi would meet Dr Oldfield at an International Vegetarian Conference. Dr Oldfield noted in the new recruit to the London Vegetarian Society a rare will-power and devotion to the cause, and soon he had him elected to its executive committee. Gandhi would attend the committee meetings but rarely spoke, not because he was not tempted to express his views on matters – it was just that he could not pick up enough courage to say a few words, and on occasions 'when I mustered up courage to speak, a fresh subject would be started. This went on for a long time.'

His life in London was sober, disciplined and lonely. He went for long walks, which helped him maintain good health and he rarely fell sick. One such occasion was during the autumn when he was preoccupied with preparing for his Bar examination in December. Oldfield reports that a doctor prescribed beef tea and meat as a cure for his bronchitis. 'Come along, my laddie, and be sensible, and drink down this strengthening food,' he urged, holding a cup of steaming beef tea before him. 'You must either take beef tea or die,' the good doctor cautioned him earnestly. Gandhi refused, saying that if it was God's will he would die, but he would not break his vow.

His stay in London was mostly in the area that extends from Kensington to Holborn, and he rarely travelled outside its confines. Once he crossed the Channel to visit Paris to see the Great Exhibition. He found a vegetarian restaurant, rented a room for a week, and did most of his sightseeing on foot with the aid of a map. One of the chief attractions of the Exhibition was the Eiffel Tower. He was impressed by the tower and in his exuberance climbed it more than once, and even 'threw away' seven precious shillings on lunch in a restaurant there 'for the satisfaction of being able to say that I had my lunch at a great height'.

Gandhi seems to have developed an early interest in eccentrics of all kinds – Indian as well as English. At a meeting of the National Indian Association he was introduced to a visiting young Gujarati writer named Narayan Hemchandra, a small, bearded, round-faced pockmarked man, who dressed as he pleased and displayed a total indifference to social custom. He wore 'a clumsy pair of trousers, a wrinkled, dirty, brown coat, no necktie or collar, and a tasselled woollen cap'. He was innocent of English grammar, for which he had a lordly contempt, treated 'horse' as a verb and 'run' as a noun, but had a ferocious intellectual appetite, and intended to learn English, French and German since it was his ardent desire to translate the treasures of these languages into his native Gujarati. He knew or thought he knew Gujarati, Marathi, Bengali and Hindi. He had translated the works of Debendranath Tagore, the father of Rabindranath, from Bengali into Gujarati and had no patience to stop at just that. He was convinced that the knowledge of grammar was of no consequence. What he wanted was copious vocabulary, and he arrived at Gandhi's place with an exercise book. Gandhi had read some of his works and was pleased to make acquaintance with him. 'Narayan Hemchandra's simplicity was all his own,' he wrote, 'and his frankness was on a par with it. Of pride he had not the slightest trace, excepting, of course, a rather undue regard for his own capacity as a writer.'

They met regularly, and would often cook and eat meals together. Gandhi would teach him English and talk to him about Disraeli and Cardinal Manning. The Cardinal's name then was a household one, since it was due to his efforts, along with those of John Burns, that the strike by the London dockworkers had come to an early conclusion. Narayan Hemchandra had to see the Cardinal to congratulate him for his humanitarian work, for hadn't Disraeli paid him a glowing tribute? Since Hemchandra's knowledge of English was rudimentary, Gandhi would act as an interpreter for the famous writer. The Cardinal saw a large number of people almost every day of his life. He would not hesitate to grant an interview to two unknown Indians, and in due course a card fixing the meeting arrived.

Young Gandhi's attire was, no doubt, faultless and his awkward hair brushed with special care. Needless to say, Narayan Hemchandra saw no compelling reason to make the slightest alteration to his appearance. 'Great men never look at a person's exterior,' he proclaimed. So Gandhi in a silk hat and Narayan Hemchandra in a tasselled woollen cap walked together to Cardinal Manning's house for an audience. Hemchandra made a brief speech in Gujarati, in which he solemnly declared that the Cardinal was a sage. Gandhi translated the speech for the benefit of the Cardinal. The Cardinal was glad that they had come; he hoped that their stay in London would agree with them; he gave them God's blessings and promptly dismissed them.

Many of the eccentrics with whom Gandhi came into closest contact were either theosophists or devout Christians, who urged their own faith on him. Towards the end of 1889, while he was studying for his matriculation, he met two theosophist brothers who took a keen interest in Hindu religion. They were reading the *Bhagavad Gita* in Sir Edwin Arnold's translation – *The Song Celestial* – and invited him to read the original. Gandhi found it somewhat embarrassing to confess that he had never read it either in English, Sanskrit or his mother tongue, Gujarati, though he had heard bits of it read aloud to his father. He gladly joined them in reading it in Sanskrit, along with Arnold's English translation. His knowledge of Sanskrit was inadequate; still he hoped to be able to understand the original to the extent of telling where the translation failed to bring out the meaning. Arnold's book struck him as one of immense worth and a passage in the second chapter, with its warning of the danger of desire and passion, left a deep impression on his mind:

If one
Ponders on objects of the sense, there springs
Attraction; from attraction grows desire,
Desire flames to fierce passion, passion breeds
Recklessness; then the memory – all betrayed –
Lets noble purposes go, and saps the mind,
Till purpose, mind, and man are all undone.

The *Bhagavad Gita* (Song of the Blessed), a profound religious poem of the Hindu scriptures, forms part of the great ancient Sanskrit epic the

*Mahabharata*. It consists of 700 verses, divided into 18 chapters, and is in the form of a dialogue between Arjuna, warrior prince, the third of the Pandava brothers, and his friend and charioteer, Krishna, who is also an earthly incarnation of the god Vishnu. The Pandavas are at war with their kinsmen, the Kauravas, who have deprived them of their ancestral kingdom.

The dialogue takes place as the two armies stand opposing each other on the fields of Kurukshetra. As Arjuna surveys them he becomes despondent to think of the impending fight with kinsmen, friends and revered teachers among the opposing forces, which would lead to immense loss of life. But Lord Krishna recalls Arjuna to his sense of duty insisting that as a member of the Kshatriya warrior caste, he must not avoid a battle of righteousness. Krishna's teaching leads Arjuna to abandon doubt; he is heartened, and prepares to enter the battle, which his side is destined to win.

Since the *Gita* is a predominantly theistic work, it often describes the ultimate reality as a personal god, identified with Krishna. Orthodox Hindus regard the *Gita* as the historic account of a battle in which a warrior king seeks to avoid bloodshed but is soon reminded by God of his caste obligation to fight a just war, however violent it might be.

Gandhi, who read the *Bhagavad Gita* with devotion, had come to the conclusion that it was 'not a historical work', but was in fact an allegory. He felt that the battlefield described in the poem 'is the human soul wherein Arjuna, representing higher impulses, struggles against evil. Krishna is the Dweller within, ever whispering to a pure heart.' Gandhi asserted that 'under the guise of physical warfare, the *Gita* described the duel that perpetually went on in the hearts of mankind . . . Physical warfare was brought in merely to make the description of the internal duel more alluring.'

The *Bhagavad Gita* goes far beyond the ethical question with which it starts to consider broadly the nature of the soul, the Absolute God, and the means by which man can know Him. It teaches that when a man breathes his last, only the body dies. The highest part of man, the soul, is essentially birthless and deathless spirit. The *Gita* teaches renunciation of desire and non-attachment to the things of this world, but not withdrawal into a life of inactive contemplation. A man should strive to do his duty in the service of his fellow men; such duty must be performed in a detached spirit, the doer surrendering the results to God. Only through renunciation, non-attachment and acts of service without regard to their fruits can one attain deliverance from the bondage of life and death, and realize identity with the supreme reality, thus attaining spiritual bliss.

Gandhi would read several English translations of the *Bhagavad Gita*, but he regarded Arnold's as the best. 'He has been faithful to the text, and yet it does not read like a translation.' Though he read the *Gita* with the theosophist brothers, it was only after many years that he actually studied it, and then it became a book of daily reading. At their request, he also read Arnold's *The Light of Asia* and found it most absorbing. The brothers took him on one occasion to a meeting at the Blavatsky Lodge and introduced him to Madam Blavatsky and Mrs Annie Besant. A Russian by birth, Helena Petrovna Blavatsky lived for many years in North America and India. In 1875, at the age of forty-four, she founded in New York the Theosophical Society. Gandhi was invited to join the society, but he politely declined. 'With my meagre knowledge of my own religion, I do not want to belong to any religious body.' The scholarly Mrs Besant had earlier been propagating atheism – she was much influenced by Charles Bradlaugh, the exponent of atheism. From being a free-thinker and an atheist, she had recently turned to theism, and since she was already well known for her work as a journalist, Fabian socialist, labour organizer, and fighter for birth control, her conversion was highly publicized. Gandhi attended a meeting where she arose to answer a charge of inconsistency, and the concluding words of her speech never faded from his memory. 'She said as she wound up her great speech,' he recalled, 'that she would be quite satisfied to have the epitaph written on her tomb that she had lived for truth and she died for truth.'

The theosophist brothers urged Gandhi to read Madam Blavatsky's *Key to Theosophy*. 'This book stimulated in me the desire to read books on Hinduism,' he wrote, 'and disabused me of the notion fostered by the missionaries that Hinduism was rife with superstitions.' It appears that Gandhi's mind at this stage was seeking corroboration of Hinduism from various Western thinkers. His reaction to theosophy itself was one of critical interest and he drew from it only a portion of its message – he particularly disapproved of the society's faith in the occult powers. 'Though the Society's rule respecting brotherhood appealed to me, I had no sympathy for its search for occult powers.'

Dr Josiah Oldfield, the editor of *The Vegetarian*, whom Gandhi met in the latter half of 1890 at a vegetarian conference, introduced him to the Bible, emphasizing that neither drinking nor meat-eating were enjoined in holy scriptures. Young Gandhi read Genesis, but found the other books of the Old Testament quite uninspiring and he developed a particular aversion for Numbers. While the reading of the Old Testament 'sent me to sleep', the New Testament appealed to him immensely, particularly the Sermon on the Mount. 'But I say unto you, that ye resist not evil: but whosoever shall smite thee on the right cheek, turn to him the other also. And if any man will sue thee at the law, and take away thy coat let him have thy cloak also' delighted him beyond measure. In the Sermon on the

Mount, the *Bhagavad Gita* and *The Light of Asia* he found the common theme of renunciation. This reading stimulated his appetite for studying the lives of religious teachers. He read Carlyle's *Heroes and Hero Worship* and was pleased with the author's depiction of Mohammed as a spiritual hero, his greatness and his austere living.

Charles Bradlaugh, the uncompromising atheist, died on 30 January 1891. He was a champion of women's suffrage, birth control and trade unionism. Most Indians living in London, including Gandhi, were among a large crowd which attended his funeral. It was not because they subscribed to his atheism, but because they admired his fearlessness. Bradlaugh had been elected to the House of Commons but was refused a seat on the grounds that an atheist could not take an oath of allegiance on a Bible. The rules committee of the House of Commons later reluctantly permitted him to take his seat. He was a champion of the rights of the Indian people, and because of this he was contemptuously described in England by Conservatives as the 'Member for India'. He was highly intelligent and was a spellbinding orator. He was admired by even those who did not quite agree with his views.

On his way back from the funeral, as he was awaiting the train to London, Gandhi heard a staunch atheist heckle a clergyman.

'Well, sir, you believe in the existence of God?' said the atheist.

'I do,' the clergyman replied in a low voice.

'You also agree that the circumference of the earth is about 25,000 miles, don't you?' said the atheist with a self-assured smile.

'Indeed.'

'Pray tell me then the size of God and where he may be?'

'Well, if we but knew, He resides in the hearts of us both.'

'Now, now, don't take me to be a child,' said the atheist triumphantly. The clergyman assumed a humble silence.

Gandhi considered the heckler's attitude as something bordering on vulgarity, and 'this talk still further increased my prejudice against atheism'.

Years later, Gandhi, who talked and worked in the name of God, said that although Bradlaugh delighted to call himself an atheist, he would call him a God-fearing man.

Two and a half years after his admission, Gandhi sat for his Bar Final examination and came out successful. But he could not be called to the Bar, for he had not yet completed his twelve terms. This necessitated his staying in England for some five more months, which would be the happiest time of his life since he arrived.

He was now a regular visitor to church, sampling the various preachers of the time. He was also attending meetings of the Theosophical Society, becoming an associate member in March 1891. But vegetarianism was his foremost interest. So intense was his enthusiasm for propagating the doctrine that he founded his own Vegetarian Club in Bayswater, with Dr Oldfield as the president, Sir Edwin Arnold as vice-president, and himself as the secretary. Dr Oldfield as editor of *The Vegetarian* wrote most of the articles in the journal, with vigour and authority, and Gandhi was so devoted to him that for a while they took rooms together in St Stephen's Square in Bayswater, and spent all their spare time together, carrying the message of peace and vegetarianism from house to house, lecturing at clubs and addressing public meetings, wherever they could get a hearing. 'Those were happy days,' recalled Dr Oldfield many years later, 'of consciousness that we were helping to make the world better.'

The Vegetarian Movement was something more than its name implied. It was a kind of amalgam of the ideas expressed in the transcendentalism of Emerson, Thoreau and Walt Whitman. The vegetarianism that Gandhi discovered in England was rooted in the current humanitarian and socialist ideas which were being disseminated by various groups, some of which had sprung up at the time. All the groups had close links with the Vegetarian Society.

The Vegetarian Club which Gandhi had founded ceased to exist when he moved to another area. Soon he was climbing high in vegetarian circles. He read voraciously and began to write. Between February and June 1891, he penned a series of ten articles. The first six, on 'Indian Vegetarians', were followed by three articles on 'Some Indian Festivals', and were all published in *The Vegetarian*. These articles include a vehement criticism of the importation of alcohol, 'that hated enemy of mankind', into India by the British, and an interesting aside on Indian weakness and its cure. 'Hindus as a rule are notoriously weak,' he wrote, but hesitated to add that this was not because of the absence of meat in their diet. The main cause was 'the wretched custom of child-marriage and its attendant evils'. It was imperative that this moral slackness was eliminated so that the resultant inner regeneration would lead to new strength. This theme would return as the foundation stone of his philosophy.

His last article, entitled 'The Foods of India' and published in the Vegetarian *Messenger*, was in fact the text of his speech delivered on 2 May at Bloomsbury Hall. *The Vegetarian*, which sometimes printed his speeches, announced in its issue of 6 May 1891 that Mr M.K. Gandhi, a Brahmin (*sic*) from the Bombay Presidency, delivered a speech on 'The Foods of India' at Bloomsbury Hall, Hart Street, Bloomsbury, and was 'rather nervous at the beginning'. Gandhi would certainly have found it an understatement. Nevertheless it was an excellent speech, and he delivered it again at a conference held later in the month at Portsmouth. Delegates from all over England arrived in Portsmouth, and Gandhi was one of the official delegates of the London Vegetarian Society. Very characteristic of the Mahatma-to-be is the closing remark in his speech that a time will come 'when the great difference now existing between the food habits of meat-eating in England and [generally] grain-eating in India will disappear, and with it some other differences which, in some quarters, mar the unity of sympathy that ought to exist between the two countries', and finally that 'unity of custom' will lead to 'unity of hearts'.

But a severe ordeal awaited Gandhi in Portsmouth. He was staying in lodgings with an Indian friend, and one evening after returning from the conference he sat down to play a rubber of bridge. The landlady joined in, and soon Gandhi's companion found in her a compatible partner for exchanging salacious jokes. Gandhi was not inclinced to lag behind and he too was caught up in a happy tide of indecency, the landlady making advances and the Indian egging him on, but 'just when I was about to go beyond the limit . . . God . . . uttered the blessed warning: "Whence this devil in you, my boy? Be off, quick."' Remembering the vow he had taken before his mother, he rose from the table and rushed back to his room, 'quaking, trembling, and with beating heart, like a quarry escaped from its pursuer'. He spent a sleepless night, deeply distressed that he had let himself succumb to lustful desires. No woman except his wife had ever moved him this way. He wondered whether he should leave the town forthwith, or if he should stay till the end of the conference. 'I decided to act thenceforth with great caution.'

The following day he had every reason to be satisfied with himself. His paper had been admired by vegetarians much senior to him. A sumptuous six-course vegetarian banquet and a public meeting were to follow the next day's programme. But all this was eclipsed by the shattering experience of the previous night. As soon as the afternoon session was over, he quickly left Portsmouth for Ventnor. 'I did not then know the essence of religion or of God,' he wrote years later, 'and how He works in us. I understood only vaguely that God had saved me on that occasion. On all occasions of trial He has saved me. I know that the phrase "God saved me" has a deeper meaning for me today, and still I feel that I have not yet grasped its entire meaning.'

Gandhi's stay in London was now coming to an end, for he had duly eaten his dinners, passed his examination and been called to the Bar; and it was time to return to India and start work. His family were eager to welcome him home. They expected great things of him as a barrister-at-law.

Before leaving London the young barrister gave a party for his friends at the fashionable Holborn Restaurant on Kingsway, which went vegetarian for the occasion, at least in one of its rooms. When he got up to say a few words of thanks he intended to overcome his nervousness by referring to a well-known story in which the politician, Addison, on giving his maiden speech in the House of Commons, began with the words 'I conceive', and not knowing what else to say repeated the words thrice, whereupon a helpful colleague arose to exclaim: 'The gentleman has conceived thrice but has brought forth nothing.' Gandhi, however, could not muster enough courage to repeat this joke. He spoke briefly, somewhat hesitantly, and abruptly sat down. A few days later *The Vegetarian* described the dinner at some length, and was quite charitable in reporting his speech:

> Mr Gandhi, in a very graceful though somewhat nervous speech, welcomed all present, spoke of the pleasure it gave him to see the habit of abstinence from flesh progressing in England, related the manner in which his connection with the London Vegetarian Society arose, and in so doing took occasion to speak in a touching way of what he owed to Mr Oldfield . . .'

About this time, in an interview with *The Vegetarian*, he spoke of the vow he had taken – the vow not to touch wine, women or meat:

> . . . In conclusion, I am bound to say that, during my nearly three years' stay in England, I have left many things undone, and have done many things which perhaps I might have left undone, yet I carry one great consolation with me that I shall go back without having touched meat or wine, and that I know from personal experience that there are so many vegetarians in England.

Shortly before Gandhi left London he was asked the reason which had first persuaded him to think of coming over to England and adopting the legal profession. Gandhi replied: 'In a word, ambition . . . If I go to England not only shall I become a barrister (of whom I used to think a great deal) but I shall be able to see England, the land of philosophers and poets, the very centre of civilization.' Some months later he would write in *The Vegetarian*:

> So much attached I was to London and its environments; for who would not be? London with its teaching institutions, public galleries, museums, theatres, vast commerce, public parks and restaurants, is a fit place for a student and a traveller, a trader and a 'faddist' – as a vegetarian would be called by his opponents. Thus it was not without deep regret that I left dear London.

On 12 June 1891 he sailed for India on the P&O steamship *Oceana*. He was delighted to be aboard, for the *Oceana* was a massive luxury ship in which the second-class saloon was nearly as comfortable as the first-class. He met a fellow vegetarian, and they were both content to make do with boiled potatoes, cabbage and butter, but a sympathetic steward gave them vegetable curry, brown bread, rice and stewed and fresh fruit from the first-class saloon. They enjoyed the vegetarian meals until they disembarked at Aden, where they were transferred to another ship.

Gandhi was somewhat puzzled to observe passengers devouring large quantities of food. Throughout his stay in England he was not exactly accustomed to observing Englishmen at their meals. He mailed two articles entitled 'On Way Home to India' to *The Vegetarian*, touching on the subject in the first:

> The breakfast menu generally contained oatmeal porridge, some fish, chop, curry, jam, bread and butter, tea or coffee, etc., everything *ad libitum*. I have often seen passengers take porridge, fish and curry, bread and butter, and wash down with two or three cups of tea. Hardly had we time to digest the breakfast, when bang – it was the dinner bell at 1:30 p.m. The dinner was as good as breakfast: plenty of mutton and vegetables, rice and curry, pastry, and what not . . . The dinner fare was so easily digestible that we wanted a 'refreshing' cup of tea and biscuits at 4 p.m. Well, but the evening breezes seemed so soon to take away all the effect of 'that little' cup of tea that we were served a 'high tea' at 6:30 p.m.: bread and butter, jam or marmalade, or both, salad, chops, tea, coffee, etc. The sea air seemed to be so very salubrious that the passengers could not retire to bed before taking a few, a very few – only eight or ten, fifteen at the most – biscuits, a little cheese and some wine or beer . . .

The passengers whiled away their spare time chatting, playing cards or resting. A few participated in sports like tug-of-war and running races for which prizes were awarded. There were also concerts and speeches. Gandhi, disappointed as he was at their eating routine, thought it was about time that he imparted the rudiments of vegetarianism to them. He requested the secretary of the committee of the ship to give him a quarter of an hour for a short speech on vegetarianism. Anticipating a hostile audience, the secretary advised him to be humorous. 'I might be nervous, but humorous I could not be,' he replied. He diligently prepared his speech, but 'to my great mortification,' the meeting didn't come off and the speech was never delivered.

On the homeward voyage, the ship did not anchor at Gibraltar, and Gandhi's trips ashore at Malta, Brindisi and Port Said held little interest for him as he had already seen those places, though in Malta he made it a point to visit the red and gold fish again. The landing at Brindisi was rather uneventful this time, but the 'rogues and rascals' were still making their presence felt at Port Said.

Gandhi had enjoyed the *Oceana*, but the transfer at Aden of India-bound passengers to the *Assam* was like 'leaving London for a miserable village'. The approaching storm made the voyage on the much smaller ship all the more rough. In his second article 'On Way Home to India', he reported to the readers of *The Vegetarian*:

> The second night brought the real storm. Many were sick. If I ventured out on the deck I was splashed with water. There goes a crash; something is broken. In the cabin you cannot sleep quietly. The door is banging. Your bags begin to dance. You roll in your bed. You sometimes feel as if the ship is sinking. At the dinner table you are no more comfortable. The steamer rolls on your side. Your forks and spoons are in your lap, even the cruet stand and the soup plate; your napkin is dyed yellow and so on . . .

The sea had been rough all the way from Aden, and the storm was still raging when the *Assam* docked at Bombay. A sombre-looking Laxmidas was waiting for him, and the two brothers went to the residence of Dr P.J.Mehta who had received Gandhi in London. Dr Mehta again offered to afford all help and invited them to stay with him. Gandhi was very anxious to go to Rajkot to see his mother, but a shock was in store for him when Laxmidas told him that their mother had died while he was still in England. The family wanted to spare him the blow while he was in a foreign land. 'My grief was even greater than over my father's death,' he wrote. 'But I remember that I did not give myself up to any wild expression of grief. I could even check the tears, and took to life just as though nothing had happened.'

Much later in life, when Mahadev Desai, his personal secretary and chronicler asked whether austerity and not saintliness was the appropriate word to describe his mother, Gandhi replied: 'No, I have used the word saintliness deliberately,' and added:

> Austerity implies external renunciation, endurance and sometimes even hypocrisy. But saintliness is an inner quality of the soul. My mother's austerity was only an echo of her inner life. If you notice any purity in me, I have inherited it from my mother, and not from my father. Mother died at the early age of forty. I have been a witness of her behaviour in the flower of youth, but never did I see in her any frivolity, any recourse to beauty aids or interest in the pleasures of life. The only impression she ever left on my mind is that of saintliness.

# FOUR

# *Briefless Barrister*

When Gandhi landed in Bombay a section of his caste was still hostile about the issue of his going overseas. Keeping this in mind, Laxmidas took him to Nasik before they went back to Rajkot, and Gandhi had a ritual bath in the sacred river Godavari. On their return to Rajkot, Laxmidas, in an effort to further diminish the hostility, hosted a ceremonial dinner, inviting some people of his caste. Gandhi had no inclination to go through all these rituals, but he was too devoted to his brother to question, and so 'I mechanically acted as he wished, taking his will to be law.' He did not agitate for his admission to the Modh Bania subcaste which had refused it, nor did he attempt to divide the caste on his account.

Despite his long absence, his relations with his wife did not register a change. He still found himself as jealous as ever. 'I continued my squeamishness and suspiciousness in respect of every little thing, and thus all my cherished desires remained unfulfilled.' He wanted her to learn to read and write and was anxious to assist her in her studies, 'but my lust came in the way and she had to suffer for my own shortcomings'. He decided instead to take in hand the education of his son, Harilal, who was now barely four, and since he had ample time at his disposal he was soon educating all the other Gandhi children too. But he also had the time to quarrel with his wife.

Laxmidas, himself a lawyer, had ensured that some kind of English atmosphere would await Mohandas on his return home. He had built high hopes on his young brother's career as a barrister and, in anticipation of Mohandas's successful practice, persuaded himself to increase his household expenses. After all, a barrister's fees were several times more than those paid to an indigenously qualified lawyer. The house underwent some renovation and new furniture was installed. Crockery and other such things were now in general use. Gandhi introduced oatmeal porridge and cocoa in addition to tea and coffee. European dress too was added and the expenses, which had hitherto been nonexistent, 'had succeeded in tying a white elephant at our door'.

Gandhi's studies of English and Roman law had given him no knowledge of Indian law and no practical experience of the conduct of cases in court.

Aware of his deficiencies, he was content to remain for a while a briefless barrister. Friends advised him to go to Bombay for some time in order to gain experience of the High Court, to study Indian law and to try to get what briefs he could.

The study of Indian law was a tedious business, and the timid barrister was further discouraged by stories of barristers 'vegetating' for many years. 'You should count yourself lucky if you can paddle your own cause in three years' time,' a young law student informed him. He further acquainted Gandhi with the performance of some of the giants of the Bombay Bar such as Sir Pherozeshah Mehta and Badrudin Tyabji. 'The stories of stalwarts such as these would unnerve me.'

His first court case in India was hardly something he was looking forward to. Representing a certain Mamibai in the Small Causes Court, he had anticipated no problem in handling the somewhat easy case. But as he began to cross-examine the plaintiff's witness, nervousness gripped him. 'My head was reeling and I felt as though the whole court was doing likewise,' Gandhi wrote. 'I could think of no question to ask. The judge must have laughed, and the lawyers no doubt enjoyed the spectacle.' He sat down abruptly, returned his thirty-rupee fee to his client, and left the court. He was utterly discouraged. What did he have in common with Sir Pherozeshah Mehta, who roared like a lion and knew the laws of evidence by heart, or Badrudin Tyabji, whose power of argument filled the judges with awe? He decided not to take up any more cases until he had the courage to conduct them, and in fact during the remaining months of his stay in India he never ventured to enter a court again.

But soon after the débâcle of the Mamibai case, he was approached by a poor native of Porbandar whose land had been confiscated. It was a weak case, but Gandhi consented to draft a memorial for him. He read out the memorial to some friends, they approved of it, and this gave him some confidence and satisfaction that he was qualified to draft a memorial.

In Bombay Dr P.J. Mehta had introduced him to several people, one of whom, Rajchandra, was the son-in-law of Dr Mehta's elder brother. Gandhi often met this amazing man, a Jain youth of nearly the same age as Gandhi. He wrote poetry and spoke with authority on matters not mundane, but obedient to a family calling, he had become a jewel merchant. Yet, however lovely the jewel before him might be, he was always willing to put it on one side and discuss religion. Gandhi found in him a man of great character and learning. He had a phenomenal memory and concentration and was also known as a *shatavadhani*, one who could attend to a hundred (*shata*) affairs simultaneously. He could play a game of chess, and at the same time solve an intricate mathematical problem, read from a book and play a musical

45

instrument. On one occasion, Gandhi wrote, 'I exhausted my vocabulary of all the European tongues I knew, and asked the poet to repeat the words.' He repeated the unfamiliar Latin and French words 'in the precise order in which I had given them'. But what impressed Gandhi most was Rajchandra's inexhaustible knowledge of the scriptures, his spotless character, his moral earnestness and his burning passion for self-realization. 'In my moments of spiritual crisis he was my refuge,' Gandhi would write in his autobiography. The three men who made the deepest impression on his mind were 'Rajchandra, by his living contact; Tolstoy through his book *The Kingdom of God is Within You*; and Ruskin through his *Unto This Last*.'

Presently, Gandhi came across an advertisement in a newspaper for the post of a part-time teacher, required to teach English for an hour a day at a well-known school, and offering a salary of seventy-five rupees a month. His command of English was good, and he liked the idea of teaching. It was not bad pay, and he needed the job. He was called for interview, but when the principal found that he was not a university graduate, he regretfully refused him. 'But I have passed the matriculation from London University, with Latin as my second subject,' Gandhi pleaded. 'True, but we want a graduate,' the principal ruled.

His stay in Bombay was proving very expensive, and there seemed little hope of a job. Laxmidas was also getting concerned. They both agreed that there was no point spending more time in Bombay, and Gandhi returned to Rajkot, where he set up his own office, taking up briefing cases for other lawyers. He earned in time a reasonable three hundred rupees a month by writing memorials and petitions. But this was also the time when the attitude of a British officer gave him 'the first shock of my life'.

Laxmidas was the secretary and adviser to a young prince, Bhavsingh who was to inherit the throne of Porbandar. It seemed at the time that Laxmidas would follow his father's and grandfather's footsteps and become *dewan* of the tiny state. It so happened that some jewels were found to be missing from the treasury, and it was reported that the prince had secretly and unlawfully removed them. The British political agent, Charles Ollivant, was also notified that the prince had acted on the advice of Laxmidas Gandhi. In any event, Laxmidas had failed to report the theft to the political agent, and on account of this alone he was considered an accessory to this irregularity. The prince was immune from punishment, but his adviser fell from grace and thus his ambition to rise to the top administrative post received a big jolt.

Mohandas had struck up an acquaintance with Charles Ollivant in London, and Laxmidas thought that his brother's friendship with the political agent could adjust matters. Mohandas could certainly put in a good word for him. But the young barrister was unwilling to intervene. If Laxmidas was innocent he should submit a petition in the proper course and face the result. 'You do not know [this region of] Kathiawar,' Laxmidas said, 'and you have yet to know the world. Only influence counts here. It is not proper for you, a brother, to shirk your duty, when you can speak favourably about me to an officer you know.'

Mohandas reluctantly sought an interview with the political agent. As soon as he was ushered into the office he noticed that the friendly man he had met on leave in England had now, sitting at his desk in Kathiawar, a different demeanour. The Englishman owned the acquaintance, and the reminder seemed to stiffen him. Mohandas weakly opened the case for his brother, but the political agent was already impatient. 'Your brother is an intriguer. I want to hear nothing more from you. I have no time. If your brother has anything to say, let him apply through the proper channels.'

Mohandas did not want to abandon this opportunity, however questionable, of being of some use to his brother, so he continued with his case. The political agent got up and said: 'You must leave now.' Mohandas was getting more anxious than ever to present his case. 'But please hear me out,' he pleaded. This infuriated Ollivant, who summoned the doorkeeper to remove the offending caller. Gandhi still reluctant to leave, felt the doorman's hands firmly placed on his shoulders, and was removed forthwith. He was so disturbed by this episode that he immediately rushed out a letter of protest: 'You have insulted me. You have assaulted me through your peon. If you make no amends, I shall have to proceed against you.'

The threatening letter did not in the least worry the political agent. He sent his *sowar* (messenger on horseback) to deliver the reply: 'You were rude to me. I asked you to go and you would not. I had no option but to order my peon to show you the door. Even after he asked you to leave the office, you would not do so. He therefore had to use just enough force to send you out. You are at liberty to proceed as you wish.'

Mohandas was crestfallen, and his good brother did not know how to console him. The young barrister spoke about the incident to every lawyer he met. Sir Pherozeshah Mehta, 'the lion of Bombay', was visiting Rajkot at the time, and Mohandas sent him details of the incident, along with copies of his own letter and the political agent's reply. 'Tell Gandhi,' Sir Pherozeshah said, 'such things are common experience of many *vakils* and barristers. He is still fresh from England, and hot-blooded. He does not know British officers. If he would earn something and have an easy time here, let him tear up the note and pocket the insult. He will gain nothing by proceeding against the *sahib*, but on the contrary will very likely ruin himself. Tell him he has yet to know life.'

Mohandas found Sir Pherozeshah's advice 'as bitter as poison'. Nevertheless he swallowed it, but not without profit. Never again would he place himself in such a clumsy position or seek to exploit a friendship this way. The officer could have politely asked him to leave, but 'power had intoxicated him to an inordinate extent'. The shock of his encounter with the British political agent, Gandhi wrote, 'changed the course of my life'.

Mohandas had been doing the odd legal job for the ruling prince. He and his brother hoped that he would eventually achieve a position in the government, which might lead to further advancement in the tradition of the family. But his encounter with the political agent stood in the way of any progress in his career, even as a barrister. He could now see more clearly the prevailing atmosphere of snobbery, palace pomp and petty intrigue. He was convinced that one had to be a fawning sycophant to get ahead, and he wanted to come out unscathed from the 'poisonous atmosphere'. Finally help came from a totally unexpected quarter.

Dada Abdulla & Co., shipowners and traders with important interests in South Africa, were at the time fighting a lawsuit there relating to a promissory note totalling £40,000 against another firm owned by a distant cousin of Dada Abdulla. It was an intricate case, and though European lawyers were working on it, they required someone who would be in a position to offer advice from an Indian standpoint, as well as look after the office correspondence, which was mostly in English. Dada Abdulla & Co., located at Porbandar, wrote to Laxmidas asking if his brother Mohandas might be interested in the job. Mohandas was not quite clear whether the position also entailed appearing in court. He travelled to Porbandar to discuss the offer with Abdul Karim Jhaveri. He asked how long they would require his services. 'Not more than a year,' Jhaveri said. 'We will pay you a first-class return fare and a sum of £105, all found.'

It was not a very attractive proposition, but he took it. He wanted somehow to leave India, and the offer also promised the opportunity of seeing a new country. He would leave his family behind in the care of Laxmidas, remitting the entire £105 toward the expenses of the household, since 'all found' meant that his own expenses would be paid by Dada Abdulla & Co. in South Africa. He felt no emotional turmoil at the thought of leaving his wife and two sons behind; on 28 October 1892, a second son, Manilal, had been born. 'We are bound to meet again in a year,' he consoled Kasturbai.

On arrival in Bombay, Gandhi discovered that the agent of Dada Abdulla & Co. was unable to arrange for his travel as scheduled. There were no cabins available. He could however travel as a deck passenger, but 'those were my days of first-class travelling, and how could a barrister travel as a deck passenger?' He was anxious to leave, for if he did not sail at that time he would be stranded in Bombay for a month. In his despair, he went aboard to see the chief officer. 'Could you not possibly squeeze me in?' he asked. The chief officer, a genial man, surveyed the young barrister and smiled. 'There is an extra berth in my cabin which is usually not available to passengers,' he said. 'But I am prepared to give it to you.' The agent arranged for the passage money, and Gandhi sailed from Bombay on the SS *Safari* on 19 April 1893.

# FIVE

# Unwelcome Visitor

The chief officer was fond of chess, but being a novice he preferred to play with inexperienced players. He therefore found in Gandhi an agreeable companion, so much so that soon after the ship anchored at Zanzibar he invited his young friend to go ashore and see the town – including a visit to a brothel. Suddenly Gandhi found himself alone in a room with a negro woman. 'I simply stood there dumb with shame,' he wrote. 'Heaven only knows what the poor woman must have thought of me.' He stayed there for a while, engrossed with mixed feelings of horror and shame, before he was rescued by the chief officer. What distressed him most was his lack of courage to refuse to go into the room.

The stopover at Zanzibar was of about a week's duration, so he took rooms, spent some time with the Indians living there and wandered through the town, admiring the luxuriant vegetation; he was amazed at the massive trees and the unusually large size of the fruit.

Gandhi left Zanzibar on the SS *Admiral*, disembarking at Durban, the chief port of the British Crown Colony of Natal, on 23 May 1893. He was wearing a starched white shirt, a black tie, a black frock coat, striped trousers, a black turban and black patent leather shoes. He landed with a full sense of his own importance and noticed at once that Indians were treated in a rather contemptuous manner – and this did not exclude Dada Abdulla, the merchant who had come to the port to receive him.

South Africa in 1893 consisted of four colonies – Natal, the Cape, the Transvaal and the Orange Free State. The Dutch or Boers, who first settled South Africa in the sixteenth century, had brought their slaves from Malaya, Java and other Pacific islands. They were fairly well established in the country for almost two hundred years before the British arrived on the scene and captured the Cape from them in 1806 and Natal in 1843. In Natal the British found that they could grow sugar cane, tea and coffee, but the negroes were unwilling to work for them, and were content to live on what they grew on their land. Arrangements were accordingly made with the British rulers of India for the shipment of Indian labourers under a contract.

The first Indian indentured workers landed in Natal on 16 November 1860. They were amongst the poorest class and, in accordance with the terms of the contract, were tied to a farm for a period of five years. They were given free board and lodgings for themselves and their families and ten shillings a month. After the expiry of the contract, the contractor would pay their passage back to India. Alternatively, they could remain in South Africa and renew their contract for a further period of five years, or settle as free working men on land allotted to them by the government equivalent in value to the cost of their return passage. In numerous cases, the indentured labourers chose to become permanent residents.

Following these workers were free Indians called 'passenger Indians' since they paid their own passage, who came as hawkers, tradesmen, artisans and, like Gandhi, members of the professions. British and Dutch businessmen alike found Indians formidable rivals in both agriculture and trade.

The Indian cultivator introduced new fruits and vegetables and produced them cheaply and in abundance, thus bringing down the prices of the white farmer. The Indian trader was a competitor in selling to the white population, and secured a near monopoly on dealing with the negroes, for he lived cheaply, spent little on equipment and staff, and could easily undersell the British and the Dutch. Initially this fed the whites' fear that they would be swamped by the Indians if the Indians were allowed to enter the country freely and establish themselves on land or in trade as they pleased.

Although the Indians entered Natal as Her Majesty's citizens, many Indians established themselves in the the Transvaal. Article 4 of the London Convention of 1884, between Her Majesty and the Transvaal Dutch Republic declared that all persons 'other than Natives' would have full liberty to enter, travel, reside, hold property and carry on business in any part of the Republic of the Transvaal, and that they would not be subject to any taxes other than those imposed on the Dutch citizens. The threatened 'Asiatic invasion', however, hit both the Dutch and the British, and over the years numerous restrictions were placed on Indians. The racial discrimination against the Indians intensified. The expression 'coolie', which was initially used to describe the bona fide farm labourers, came to be used in a derogatory sense for the Indians wherever they went, and the terms 'coolie doctor' and 'coolie barrister' were not unheard of. A good number of indentured Indians were from southern India. Among them the family name Ramaswamy was very common. In course of time this name would be distorted, and the expression 'Sami' was contemptuously used for the Indians. (*Swami*, paradoxically, means master.)

In 1894, notwithstanding the unfavourable conditions, some 250 free Indians in Natal, being subjects of Her Majesty Queen Victoria, and having met the wealth qualification, enjoyed the right to vote. Soon the Natal government's new approach in this regard would launch Gandhi on a remarkable political career.

Dada Abdulla, an elderly man, was virtually unlettered and had scant knowledge of English, but his vast experience stood him in good stead. He was considered one of the richest Indians in Natal. The merchant could not see exactly what work might be assigned to the dapper barrister and thought the people at Porbandar had made a wrong move in sending him over. On the second or third day after his arrival, he took Gandhi to the Durban Court to watch the proceedings. The English magistrate kept staring at Gandhi's turban and finally asked him to remove it, stating that he was merely enforcing a rule of the court. Gandhi demurred and walked out. The incident was reported in the *Natal Advertiser* of 26 May under the heading 'An Unwelcome Visitor'. The same day Gandhi wrote to the paper explaining that 'as it is a mark of respect amongst the Europeans to take off their hats, in like manner it is in Indians to retain one's headdress'. About his entering the court without bowing or *salaaming*, he wrote that he had simply observed the rule of the Bombay High Court: 'If an advocate enters the court after the judge has taken his seat on the bench he does not bow.' He sought his Lordship's pardon if he was offended at 'what he considered to be my rudeness, which was the result of ignorance and quite unintentional'. Gandhi pleaded with the paper to publish his letter, for 'if unexplained the incident would likely to do me harm'. In any event, as he reports in his autobiography, 'the incident gave me an unexpected advertisement in South Africa within a few days of my arrival'.

Dada Abdulla had his clerk fill Gandhi in on the details of the case, but the young barrister knew nothing about accounting or bookkeeping. He therefore bought a book on the subject and studied it. He also found time to establish contact with many Indians in Durban, including some Christians of Indian origin, widening his circle of acquaintances. In the meantime the merchant was asked by the firm's lawyers in Pretoria to see them in connection with the case. Since he was preoccupied with his business interests in Durban, he decided to send Gandhi instead. With detailed instructions about men, matters and places, the barrister now felt more confident that he could be of some assistance to the lawyers in Pretoria.

In those days there was no direct railroad link between Durban and Pretoria. The train went as far as Charlestown near the Transvaal border, and it was then necessary to board a coach to Johannesburg before taking another train to Pretoria. Gandhi was travelling first class, but when the train reached Maritzburg, the capital of Natal, at about 9 p.m., a passenger saw that he was dark-skinned and objected to his travelling in a first-class compartment. Two railway officials soon appeared on the scene. One of them ordered him to move to the van compartment (third class) reserved for coloured people in the rear of the train. Gandhi explained that he had a first-class ticket. 'That does not matter,' said the official. 'You must go to the van compartment, or else I shall have to call a police constable to push you out.' Gandhi was adamant and refused to get out voluntarily. The police constable deposited him and his bags on the station platform. Since the bags were taken into custody by the station master, he found himself without an overcoat in a cold, dark waiting room at an altitude of two thousand feet. He was too humiliated and confused to approach the station master to retrieve his overcoat. It was during this wintry night that he resolved that South Africa was, indeed, the country for him – if only he could learn to be the man for that country. He could see at the time the significance of the unpalatable experience. 'The hardship to which I was subjected was superficial – only a symptom of the deep disease of colour prejudice.' He resolved to 'try, if possible, to root out the disease and suffer hardships in the process'. This resolution somewhat pacified him and equipped him for future battles. Early in the morning he sent a strongly worded telegram to the general manager of the railroad and another to Dada Abdulla, who immediately rushed to see the manager. The manager justified the conduct of the railway authorities, but informed Dada Abdulla that he had already instructed the station master at Maritzburg to ensure that Gandhi reached his destination safely. A telegram was also sent from Durban to Indian merchants in Maritzburg, requesting them to provide any assistance to Gandhi. They came to the station and tried to comfort him by narrating their own hardships, explaining that Indians travelling first or second class had to expect trouble from railway officials and white passengers. The day was spent listening to their tales of woe, and when Gandhi boarded the train in the evening there was a reserved berth for him. At the time of leaving Durban Dada Abdulla had strongly advised him to pay five shillings for the bedding which he would receive at Maritzburg. Gandhi thought it was a waste of money. This time, however, he purchased the bedding ticket he had refused to book at Durban. The train reached Charlestown in the morning.

He already possessed a ticket for travel by stagecoach between Charlestown and Johannesburg. The coach's 'leader', a Dutchman, would not let Gandhi sit inside with other passengers, who all happened to be Europeans that day. There were three seats on the coachbox usually occupied by the driver and the leader in charge of the passengers. On this

53

occasion the leader decided to take a seat inside the coach, and bluntly asked Gandhi to sit with the driver and a Hottentot. There was space for Gandhi inside, but he did not want to make a fuss lest he should miss the coach.

When the stagecoach stopped at a town called Pardekop, the leader himself desired to sit on the coachbox for a while to have a smoke. He took a dirty sackcloth from the driver, spread it on the footboard and, addressing the first-class travelling barrister, said: 'Sami, you sit on this. I want to sit near the driver.' The insult was more than Gandhi could bear. He was shaking with fear, but managed to tell the leader: 'It was you who seated me here, though I should have been accommodated inside. I put up with the insult . . . and now you would have me sit at your feet. I will not do so, but I am prepared to sit inside.' As he was struggling through these sentences, the heavy-set Dutchman boxed his ears, seized him by the arm and tried to push him down on the footboard, cursing him and beating him, while Gandhi clung to the brass rails of the coachbox, determined to keep his hold though he felt that his wrists would break. The coach passengers took pity on him and were shouting: 'Leave him alone. He is not to blame.' Gandhi looked like a man who was determined to suffer. The Dutchman went on cursing, but finally let go of his victim and asked the Hottentot to sit on the footboard while he himself took the seat so vacated.

The whistle blew, the passengers re-entered the coach, and they drove off. From time to time the angry Dutchman would turn to Gandhi and growl: 'Wait till we get to Standerton, I will show you what I do.' Gandhi sat speechless and prayed to God for protection. 'I was wondering whether I would ever reach my destination alive.' He was received at Standerton by Indian friends of Dada Abdulla who had requested them to take care of the newly arrived barrister. The following morning a larger coach took him to Johannesburg. This time he sat inside with the other passengers, and the bullying Dutchman was nowhere in sight.

It had been arranged that someone would meet him at the Johannesburg railroad station, but for some reason Gandhi failed to recognize the man deputed to do so. After waiting he drove in a cab to the Grand National Hotel, which he was informed was full. Then he drove to one of Dada Abdulla's agents, Abdul Gani, and was well cared for. He told the merchant of his recent experiences, but the rich businessman had a hearty laugh. 'Only we can live in a land like this,' he said, 'because for making money we do not mind pocketing insults, and here we are . . . this country is not for men like you.' Abdul Gani reminded him that conditions in the Transvaal were far worse than in Natal and told him he would have to travel third class to Pretoria, a distance of thirty-seven miles. 'First- and second-class tickets are never issued to Indians.' Gandhi sent a note to the

Johannesburg station master, introducing himself.

Next day he appeared before the station master in immaculate English dress, wearing his frock coat, top hat and necktie. The station master smiled. 'I am not a Transvaaler. I am a Hollander,' he said. 'I do want to give you a first-class ticket – on one condition, however, that, if the guard should ask you to shift to the third class . . . you should not proceed against the railway company. I wish you a safe journey. I can see you are a gentleman.'

Gandhi took his seat in the first-class compartment, but when the train halted at Germiston, a guard, on seeing him, immediately displayed three fingers. Gandhi showed his ticket. 'That does not matter,' the guard said angrily. 'Go to the third class.' A friendly Englishman, the only other passenger in the compartment, intervened. 'Don't you see he has a first-class ticket?' he said. 'I do not mind in the least his travelling with me.' The Englishman then asked Gandhi to make himself comfortable. 'If you want to travel with a coolie, what do I care,' the guard grumbled and went away. At eight o'clock in the evening the train steamed into Pretoria Station. It was a Sunday, and there was no one to meet him.

Lights were burning dimly at the station and there were few travellers. Gandhi wanted to ask the ticket collector to direct him to a small hotel, but he was somewhat afraid of a rebuff. He waited till all the other passengers had left. The ticket collector was not much help, but a negro who was standing nearby, volunteered to take him to Johnston's Family Hotel, run by an American. The proprietor said he had no colour prejudice and accepted Gandhi on condition that he would eat in his room and not in the dining room where the European customers had their meals. Gandhi sat in his room musing. In the meantime, Mr Johnston, feeling rather uncomfortable about the way he had treated the dark-skinned stranger, spoke to the other guests. They said they had no objection to the Indian's staying there like any other guest. He went to Gandhi's room to break the good news: 'Please come to the dining room, if you will, and stay here as long as you wish.'

The following morning Gandhi went to see the firm's attorney, A.W. Baker, and was received warmly. Mr Baker spoke about the protracted and complicated lawsuit and the fact that the best counsel had already been secured. There was no work for Gandhi as a barrister, and his assistance would be useful only to the extent of assembling all the necessary information. Mr Baker made arrangements for his lodgings with a family of modest means at thirty-five shillings a week.

# SIX

# *Exposure to Christianity*

Mr Baker, besides being an attorney, was a staunch lay preacher, and during the very first interview with Gandhi he sought to ascertain the young man's religious views. 'I am a Hindu by birth but I do not know much about Hinduism,' Gandhi confessed. 'In fact I do not know where I am, and what is and what should be my belief. I intend to make a careful study of my own religion and, as far as I can, of other religions as well.'

Mr Baker was one of the directors of the South African General Mission and had built, at his own expense, a church where he met some co-workers at one o'clock every day for a few minutes and prayed for peace and enlightenment. Despite an inkling that the attorney-preacher saw in him a possible convert to Christianity, Gandhi readily accepted the invitation to attend the one o'clock prayer meeting the very next day. Mr Baker introduced him to several elderly spinsters and a Quaker, Michael Coates, together with some Plymouth Brethren. Everyone knelt to pray and Gandhi joined them. The prayers were supplications to God for various things according to each person's desire. This would be followed by supplications for something special every day. Thus on this day a prayer was added for Gandhi's welfare: 'Lord, show the path to the new brother who has come amongst us. Give him, Lord, the peace that Thou hast given us. May the Lord Jesus who has saved us save him too. We ask all this in the name of Jesus.' There was no singing of hymns or other music at these meetings, and the prayer did not take more than five minutes.

Tyeb Khan Mohammed, the defendant in the lawsuit, held the same prominent position in the Transvaal as was enjoyed by Dada Abdulla in Natal. With his help Gandhi, within a week of his arrival in Pretoria, called a meeting of all the Indians in town. The meeting was mainly attended by Muslim merchants – the Hindu population in Pretoria was very small. In this first political speech of his career, Gandhi dwelt on the subject of being truthful in business. He disagreed with the prevailing contention among most merchants that truth was inconsistent with business. 'Business, they say, is a very practical affair, and truth a matter of religion.' He stressed that their responsibility to be truthful was even greater in a foreign land, because 'the conduct of a few Indians was the measure of the millions of their countrymen'. He spoke to them about the lack of sanitary habits among them and the necessity of cultivating individual and corporate cleanliness. He appealed to them to dispense with all distinction between Hindus, Muslims and Christians, as also the differences of their provincial origins in India. There was hardly anything in this that the audience had not at one time or another previously heard. But never before had anyone spoken to them with such sincerity and fervour of conviction. His speech made a deep impression. He suggested the formation of an association to make representations to the authorities about the hardships suffered by the Indian settlers, and offered to place at its disposal as much of his time and service as possible. He was twenty-three.

Gandhi noted that very few among his audience knew English. Three young men expressed their desire to learn the language, on condition that he went to their places to teach them. Of these, two were Muslims, one a barber and the other a clerk and the third was a Hindu petty shopkeeper. Gandhi taught them for eight months, and two of them made fairly good progress.

Encouraged by the success of this meeting, future gatherings were held, more or less regularly. At these all matters of political importance to individuals or to the community were freely discussed. Gandhi made the acquaintance of the British agent in Pretoria, who had shown some sympathy for the Indians. The railway authorities also agreed to issue first- and second-class tickets to Indians 'who were properly dressed'.

With plenty of time on hand, he read voraciously, and during his stay in Pretoria in 1893 devoured numerous books on religion. Michael Coates was particularly persistent in his effort to convert Gandhi, who kept a 'religious diary' in which he recorded his impressions of Christianity. Once a week he would give the diary to Mr Coates, who would read it carefully and return it with his comments. They went for long walks together, discussing religion and the books he had read, and Coates would also recommend to Gandhi the books of his choice. The elderly spinsters, Miss Harris and Miss Gabb, entertained him with four o'clock tea every Sunday.

To Coates, as to Baker, Christianity was the truth – the only true religion. One day Coates noticed the sacred *tulasi* beads which Gandhi wore round his neck. *Tulasi*, or basil plant, is sacred to the Hindus. Many Hindus used to keep pots or tubs of *tulasi* plants in their homes and temples. They prayed in front of the plants, and considered the wearing of *tulasi* beeds auspicious. Coates was distressed at his new-found friend's Hindu superstition. 'This superstition does not become you,' he said. 'Come, let me break the necklace.'

'No, you will not. It is a sacred gift from my mother.'

'But do you believe in it?'

'I do not know its mysterious significance. I do not think I should come to harm if I did not wear it. But I cannot, without sufficient reason, give up a necklace that she put round my neck out of love and in the conviction that it would be conducive to my welfare.'

Gandhi promised, however, that when the necklace wore away with age, he would have no desire to replace it. In later years he did not wear beads.

As Gandhi's Christian friends proceeded to teach him the essence of Christianity, their efforts left him in a mood of disenchantment. They said that there was no escape from the belief that Jesus suffered and atoned for all the sins of mankind. 'Only he who accepts His great redemption can have eternal peace.' Gandhi sought to be redeemed 'from the sin itself, or rather from the very thought of sin'. Unless he attained that end, he would be content to be restless.

Mr Baker was getting anxious about Gandhi, who, despite a concerted effort on the part of his Christian friends, still seemed outside their influence. He took Gandhi to the famous Wellington Convention, hoping that the atmosphere of religious exaltation at the convention, and the enthusiasm and earnestness of the people attending it, would lead him into the Christian fold.

Baker ran into many difficulties in associating with an Indian. As the group would not travel on the Sabbath day, they had to break the journey en route. The manager of the station hotel accommodated the 'coloured man' only after an altercation. At Wellington the same problem cropped up. Many years later Baker recalled in his autobiography *Grace Triumphant*:

I had great difficulty in getting leave for him to travel in the same compartment of the train with me to the Convention at Wellington, and could get no separate accommodation for him there. My host, who was a Dutch Salvationist, put a double-bedded room at our service, and I had the great distinction of sleeping in the same bed with the now so highly esteemed Indian Philosopher.

It was an assemblage of devout Christians, and Gandhi was delighted at their faith but could see no genuine reason to change his belief – his Hindu religion. When he frankly communicated his ideas to some good Christian friends, they were appalled. Years later Gandhi wrote:

My difficulties lay deeper. It was more than I could believe that Jesus was the only incarnate son of God, and that only he who believed in Him would attain salvation. If God could have sons, all of us were his sons. If Jesus was like God, or God Himself, then all men were like God and could be God Himself. My reason was not ready to believe literally that Jesus by his death and by his blood redeemed the sins of the world. Metaphorically there might be some truth in it. Again, according to Christianity, only human beings had souls, not other living beings, for whom death meant complete extinction; while I held a contrary belief. I could accept Jesus as a martyr, an embodiment of sacrifice, and a divine teacher, but not as the most perfect man ever born. His death on the Cross was a great example to the world, but that there was anything like a mysterious or miraculous virtue in it my heart could not accept. The pious lives of Christians did not give me anything that the lives of men of other faiths had failed to give.

Thus Gandhi could not accept Christianity as the greatest religion, but nor did he advocate Hinduism as being such. He did not understand the multitudes of sects and castes, and the institution of untouchability. 'If the *Vedas* were the inspired word of God, why not also the Bible and the *Koran?*' he asked. He recoiled from the competitiveness of religions.

In an effort to allay his doubt and perplexity, he wrote to Rajchandra, his jeweller-philosopher friend in Bombay. He followed up with correspondence which continued off and on till Rajchandra's death in 1901. The questions related to the nature of the self and God: 'What is God? What is the soul? What is salvation? Do all Indian religions originate from the *Vedas?* Who wrote the *Vedas* and the *Bhagavad Gita?* Does any merit accrue from the sacrifice of animals to gods? Was Christ the incarnation of God? Were all the Old Testament prophesies fulfilled in Christ? What will finally happen to the world? Can we attain salvation through faith in Rama and Krishna ? If a snake were about to bite me, should I allow myself to be bitten or should I kill it?'

The last question had a special significance to Gandhi, for he was aware that without full control over the emotion of fear it was not possible to attain *moksha* – to be a true *sanyasi*. In response Rajchandra observed:

If you have realized the transitory nature of the perishable body and the eternal glory of the immortal soul and its boundless potentialities, you will not wish to barter the latter for prolonging the momentary existence of the former. The question, therefore, is not what *I* would wish you to do, but what *you* should wish your choice to be. That choice will depend on the degree of your illumination or enlightenment.

He asked Gandhi not to lose heart but patiently to make a deeper study of Hinduism. Relating to the Christian missionaries' exclusive claims in regard to Christianity and its founder, he wrote in one of his letters to this effect: 'On a dispassionate view of the question, I feel convinced that no other religion has the subtle and profound thought of Hinduism, its vision of the soul, or its clarity.'

Though his Christian friends were disappointed that he had not taken the path they had intended for him, Gandhi was highly indebted to them for the religious quest they had awakened in him. 'I shall always cherish the memory of their contact.'

# SEVEN

# Emerging Leader

Gandhi's association with Indians in Pretoria led him to study the so-called 'disability laws' directed against them in the Transvaal. Indians were prohibited from owning property except in designated locations, and even there they could not have freeholds. They were not allowed to vote and were required to pay a poll tax of £3 as fee for entry into the Transvaal. They could not use footpaths and were prohibited from being on the street after 9 p.m. unless they carried a pass stating the nature of the business.

A friend introduced Gandhi to the State Attorney, Dr Krause, who issued a letter, instead of a pass, authorizing him to be out of doors at all hours. 'The fact that I never had to make use of it was a mere accident.' But an incident did take place when he was out for a walk, committing the cardinal sin of walking on a footpath. Suddenly, without warning, a policeman descended on him, pushing and kicking him into the street. Michael Coates, his Quaker friend, happened to be in the area on horseback and saw it all. Coates pressed him to proceed against the policeman, but Gandhi had made it a rule not to go to court to get his personal grievances redressed. Coates reprimanded the policeman, who apologized to Gandhi, but this was not necessary, 'for I had already forgiven him'.

Prior to Gandhi's active involvement in South African Indian affairs, there were other Indians already engaged in the fight against racial discrimination, individually and collectively raising their voices against this vexatious problem. Gandhi's appearance on the scene added a new dimension to their fight. The Indian had become the *bête noire* and, as Gandhi commented, no word in the best English dictionary was 'strong enough to damn him with'.

In the press Indians were referred to only as 'Ramasamy', 'Mr Coolie' or the 'black man'. The Draconian measures adopted in the Transvaal and the Orange Free State were held up as a model that the two British colonies should also adopt if Natal and the Cape were not to become 'the asylum of all these outcastes from the Interior States'.

In an editorial, the *Natal Advertiser* of 15 September 1893 expressed the opinion that among the 'coolie' population, the Indian trader was 'the most dangerous and harmful of all'. The paper came out with measures to combat the 'coolie trader' problem: 'They must be expelled, if possible, and if that can not be effected forthwith, then at least they can be so taxed as not to make it worth their while to remain longer in the Colony.'

A week later, on 23 September, Gandhi wrote to the *Natal Advertiser* at some length:

But why all this outpouring of wrath on the poor Asiatic traders?

Now, granting that a majority of Asiatic traders do become insolvent, and pay very little to their creditors (which is not at all the case), is that a good reason for driving them out of the Colony or South Africa? Does it not rather show that there must be a defect in the Insolvency Law that they can thus ruin their creditors? If the law would give any latitude for such practices, people would take advantage of it. Do not the Europeans seek the protection of the Insolvency Court?. . . And does not the very fact that these traders do get credit from the European merchants show that they are not, after all, so bad as they are portrayed by you?

If the small European trader has been driven out, is it to be laid at their door? This shows, it would appear, a greater competency on the part of the Indian trader in commerce, and this very superior competency is to be a reason for his expulsion! . . . Is it a sound policy to stifle healthy competition? Should not the European trader take a leaf out of the book of the Indian trader, if that be not below his dignity, and learn how to trade cheaply, how to live simply? . . .

But you say these wretched Asiatics live a semi-barbaric life. It would be highly interesting to learn your views of a semi-barbaric life. I have some notion of the life they live. If a room without a nice, rich carpet and ornamental hangings, a dinner table (perhaps unvarnished), without an expensive table-cloth, with no flowers to decorate it, with no wines spread, no pork or beef *ad lib*, be a semi-barbaric life; if a white comfortable dress, specially adapted to a warm climate, which, I am told, many Europeans envy them in the trying heat of summer, be a semi-barbaric life; if no beer, no tobacco, no ornamental walking-stick, no golden watch chain, no luxuriously-fitted sitting-room, be a semi-barbaric life; if, in short, what one commonly understands by a simple frugal life be a semi-barbaric life, then, indeed, the Indian traders must plead guilty to the charge, and the sooner the semi-barbarity is wiped out from the highest Colonial civilization, the better . . .

But they spend nothing, says the leading article under discussion. Don't they? I suppose they live on air or sentiments. We know that Becky lived on nothing for a year in *Vanity Fair*. And here a whole class seems to have been found out doing the same. It is to be presumed they have to pay nothing for shop rents, taxes, butchers' bills, grocers' bills, clerks' salaries, etc. One would, indeed, like to belong to such a blessed class of traders, especially in the present critical condition of the trade all the world over.

It seems, on the whole, that their simplicity, their total abstinence from intoxicants, their peaceful and, above all, their businesslike and frugal habits, which should serve as a recommendation, are really at the bottom of all this contempt and hatred of the poor Indian traders. And they are British subjects. Is this Christian-like, is this fair play, is this justice, is this civilization? I pause for a reply.

Meanwhile the prolonged lawsuit continued to demand his attention, involving as it did sifting and marshalling all the facts, studying bookkeeping and looking up law cases. From the outset Gandhi had wished to bring about a compromise, for he felt that the interminable delays were profiting no one except the lawyers. He had obviously a very junior position among the lawyers working on the case, but because of the crusading community work he was involved in, he had become well known and respected and had established a good rapport with his employer, Dada Abdulla, as well as the defendant, Tyeb Khan Mohammed. He persuaded the two parties and the senior lawyers to take the time-consuming litigation to arbitration. They agreed, and a few days later the arbitrator handed down his decision, one which delighted Dada Abdulla. Tyeb Khan Mohammed had to pay £37,000 and all the court costs. The defendant was threatened with bankruptcy, but Gandhi persuaded Dada Abdulla to agree to accept payment by easy instalments. Both parties, having saved themselves from ruinous litigation, were satisfied with the result. For Gandhi the outcome was a milestone in his career. 'My joy was boundless,' he wrote in his autobiography. 'I had learnt the true practice of law.' He learned to see 'the better side of human nature and enter men's hearts. I realized that the true function of a lawyer was to unite parties riven asunder.' In his future practice as a lawyer, he was occupied with bringing about out-of-court settlements. 'I lost nothing thereby – not even money, certainly not my soul.'

The lawsuit having been concluded, Gandhi's year in South Africa had also come to a close. He returned to Durban to make preparations for his trip back home. Dada Abdulla gave him a farewell party in Durban, attended by all the Muslim merchants. That same day, as it happened, Gandhi picked up a newspaper, the *Natal Mercury*, and was shocked to read an article on a debate in the Natal Legislative Assembly over the Franchise Amendment Bill, which was about to be passed: it would disfranchise all the Indians in the Crown Colony. 'I was ignorant of the bill,' Gandhi wrote, 'and so were the rest of the guests who had assembled there.' This admission by Gandhi causes some confusion to his biographer. The proposed disfranchising of Indians should not have taken the avid scanner of newspapers by surprise, for he was well aware of the gravity of the

situation, and his own scrapbook includes the following extract from the
*Natal Mercury* of 18 October 1893:

> The *Gazette* contains four bills proposed to be introduced in the Legislative
> Assembly by Mr Henry Bale. One of these is a measure to amend the franchise
> so that no person who is of Indian, Asiatic, or Polynesian descent or origin shall
> be entitled to be placed on a voters' list or to vote at the elections.

It appears that Gandhi's priority of working on the lawsuit, as recorded in
his diary, throws some light on the subject. Referring to the wrongs to
which his compatriots were subjected in South Africa, he wrote:

> During 1893 I was merely a witness and a victim of these wrongs. I then awoke
> to a sense of my duty. I made up my mind to take some steps . . . I obtained full
> experience of the condition of Indians in South Africa. But I did nothing
> beyond talking on the subject with the Indians in Pretoria. It appeared to me
> that to look after the firm's case and to take up the question of Indian grievances
> at the same time would be to ruin both.

His contractual obligation to the company of Dada Abdulla over, was he
not now determined to jump into the fray? He warned his compatriots: 'It
is the first nail in our coffin. It strikes at the root of our self-respect.' He
explained to them the difficulties that lay ahead and urged them to form a
fighting committee and make representation to the government. The
Indians gathered at the farewell party said they were unlettered and helpless people and then clamoured for Gandhi to remain in Durban for some
time and help them launch a campaign against the bill. And Gandhi*bhai*, as
they then called him, agreed to stay for a month, turning the farewell party
into a working committee to plan the campaign.

A meeting was called the next day at the residence of Dada Abdulla and
volunteers were enrolled. Local Muslim merchants, Natal-born Indian
youths, mostly Christians, and others came forward. The first step was to
send letters to the Speaker of the Natal Legislative Assembly, the
Attorney-General and the Prime Minister protesting against the bill.
Consequently, the further reading of the bill was postponed by two days.

The petition to be presented to the Legislative Assembly was drawn up.
Merchant volunteers went out in their carriages, or carriages whose hire
they had paid for, to obtain signatures. Many volunteers with a knowledge
of English, and several others, worked through the night. The petition,
bearing five hundred signatures, was dispatched. There were at that time
about 250 free Indians in Natal who, having passed the wealth qualification,
were entitled to vote.

The agitation had infused a new life into the community. On 28 June 1894, in anticipation of the presentation of the Indian petition to the Assembly, the 'Strangers' Gallery' was, reported a correspondent, 'for the first time within the memory of man . . . invaded by Arabs [*sic*] and Hindus clothed head and foot'. They, to the chagrin of the Europeans, 'straight-away appropriated the front seats', so that when the ladies arrived later in the evening 'not being content to take a back seat – they had to retire'. In the speeches (it was the bill's third reading), the fact that the Indians had expressed no opposition to the stringent bill was urged as proof of their unfitness for the franchise. The bill was passed, but the community had managed to make its presence felt, and this, as Gandhi put it, 'gladdened our hearts'. The petition was published in the press and was on the whole favourably received. 'We must admit', wrote the *Natal Mercury*, 'that the Indians make a very good case from their point of view in the petition.'

The petition to the Legislative Assembly for the maintenance of the Indian franchise was emphasized with the persuasive argument that India had an ancient tradition of municipal and local government. Gandhi used the *panchayet* (village council), whose members were elected by the village, as an example. The following day he addressed the Prime Minister of Natal on the same subject. Petitions to the Governor and the Legislative Council followed in quick succession. Gandhi's next course of action was to send a 'monster petition' to Lord Ripon, the Secretary of State for the Colonies. It was a time-consuming exercise, and he ended up doing extensive research on the subject. He insisted that each signatory be made aware of the significance of the petition. In a matter of two weeks he succeeded in mobilizing Indians in Durban and the outlying villages, collecting about ten thousand signatures.

During this time Gandhi wrote to Dadabhai Naoroji, the 'grand old man of India', who was then a member of the British Parliament, and apprised him of the problems the Indian community was facing. In concluding the letter he put in 'a word for myself and what I have done'.

> I am inexperienced and young, and, therefore, liable to make mistakes. The responsibility undertaken is quite out of proportion to my ability. I may mention that I am doing this without any remuneration. So you will see that I have not taken the matter up, which is beyond my ability, in order to enrich myself at the expense of the Indians. I am the only available person who can handle the question. You will, therefore, oblige me very greatly if you will kindly direct and guide me, and make necessary suggestions which shall be received as from a father to his child.

Considering his letter to Naoroji, it appears unlikely that Gandhi was in any rush to leave South Africa. So when Dada Abdulla and his merchant friends pleaded with him to stay among them permanently and help them fight for their rights, he agreed, provided he could earn at least three hundred pounds a year, which would enable him to live in a style commensurate with his station in life. It was suggested that the sum could be raised annually through voluntary contributions, but Gandhi was of the opinion that no one should be paid for doing public work. He stressed that he must earn the three hundred pounds solely in his capacity as a barrister. This was readily accepted by about twenty principal traders, who collectively retained him as their counsel.

Beach Grove Villas, where Gandhi now took up residence, was a two-storey, five-bedroomed house, with a balcony overlooking the Durban Bay and a backyard equipped with a swing and parallel bars. Dada Abdulla bought the necessary furniture in lieu of some cash he had intended to give him as a gift on his departure. It was into this setting that Gandhi planned to bring his family. In the meantime he engaged domestic help and took some of his clerks as boarders.

Soon Gandhi was instrumental in founding the first major Indian political organization in South Africa, the Natal Indian Congress, whose secretary he became. He borrowed the name from the already well-established Indian National Congress. He was to conduct his future struggle for Indian rights in Natal under the auspices of the Natal Indian Congress. It was originally designed to serve the middle-class Indian, for each member was obliged to pay at least three pounds a year – the ordinary indentured labourer could not afford its annual subscription. Gandhi kept accounts meticulously, but 'the collection of subscriptions was an uphill task'.

He now decided that there were advantages in becoming an advocate in the Supreme Court of Natal. The Natal Law Society opposed his application in court, chiefly because he was an Indian. But when the matter came up before the Chief Justice, his application was approved. 'The law', the Chief Justice observed, 'makes no distinction between white and coloured people.' Gandhi took the oath, and was then gently reminded to remove his turban, so submitting to the rules of the court. This he did with good grace, but his Indian merchant friends maintained that as a matter of racial pride, he should not have given in. Gandhi granted that they had a point, but, as he wrote in his autobiography, 'I wanted to reserve my strength for fighting bigger battles.' The opposition of the Law Society, as it turned out, gave him more publicity, for most newspapers condemned its attitude, and 'the advertisement, to some extent, simplified my work'.

His commitment to the Natal Indian Congress and, consequently, the community it represented, was total. Natal's newspapers and government offices were flooded with correspondence on every subject. Gandhi maintained a very high standard of erudition, quoting the writings of Max Mueller, Schopenhauer and Victor Hugo, among others, in support of the Indian position. Some of the erstwhile critical newspapers were beginning to recognize his ability. The *Natal Witness* observed:

> There are many Indians of the stamp of Mr Gandhi who are doubtless eminently qualified to exercise the fullest possible franchise in any self-governing community. But with all possible deference to such authorities as Schopenhauer, Macaulay, and Max Mueller, the fact remains that for Natal to admit an equality which does not exist in fact and could not be safely admitted even if it did, would be foolish.

Although Gandhi's work kept him fully occupied, he would also find time whenever possible to propagate his ideas on vegetarianism, nurtured during his student days in England. He had read in Anna Kingsford's *The Perfect Way in Diet* about a colony of Trappists in South Africa who were vegetarians. One day in the spring of 1895 he, along with a companion, visited the settlement, and wrote a long account of his visit for *The Vegetarian*.

The Trappist settlement, on Mariann Hill near Pine Town, sixteen miles from Durban, consisted of about one hundred and twenty brothers, sixty nuns, and over one thousand Zulus, including women and children. Gandhi was enchanted by the serenity of the surroundings which was, however, occasionally broken by the noise of the instruments in the workshops or the native children. There were schools for the teaching of English and Zulu, and although most of the Trappists were Germans, they never attempted to teach German to their pupils, a fact which Gandhi considered 'highmindedness'. Zulu boys were trained to be blacksmiths, tinsmiths, carpenters, shoemakers and tanners, while the girls were taught sewing, knitting and straw-hat making. They had a printing press and a flour mill worked by a waterfall. There was also a machine for extracting oil from peanuts. The farm was well taken care of and they also grew tropical fruits there. The community was thus more or less self-supporting.

He was impressed, too, by the Trappists' austere and devotional life. They observed strict vows of silence and chastity. Only those inmates who had to look after visitors or go to town to make purchases were allowed to speak. They rose at two o'clock in the morning, devoting four hours to prayer and contemplation. They breakfasted at six on bread and coffee, and the midday meal consisted of soup, bread and fruits. Supper was at six in the evening, and by eight o'clock they were in bed. None of the brothers ate fish, fowl or meat, nor did they partake of eggs. However, the nuns had meat four days a week because, as the guide showing him around put it, 'the sisters were more delicate than the brothers'. This revelation somewhat distressed Gandhi, but he felt compensated by the Trappists' other habits of simplicity. No one drank alcohol, no one kept money for private use, no one left the confines of the community except on approved business, and there were no newspapers available. And yet everyone appeared happy, and visitors were received with humble bows. There was no race or class distinction. The Zulus ate the same food as the brothers, and slept in the same kind of large halls. There were no wardrobes, chests of drawers or portmanteaus. The dining tables, made on the settlement, were without any varnish and they used no tablecloths.

Gandhi was pleased about the existence of vegetarianism on Mariann Hill. 'They base it simply on the ground', he reported, 'that a vegetarian diet helps to crucify the flesh better.' They were 'a living testimony to the triumph of vegetarianism from a spiritual point of view'. He was moved by the religious atmosphere of the settlement. 'You see religion everywhere,' he wrote. 'I know from personal experience that a visit to the farm is worth a voyage from London to Natal.' He spent just a single day at Mariann Hill, but the brief visit left a deep impression.

Gandhi's approach to community work was that of a lawyer, not an agitator, and this brought him some appreciation from certain quarters, including the press. 'What we want,' wrote the *Natal Mercury*, 'is a European Mr Gandhi to come forward and put life and movement into the dry bones of our political ideas. It is all the more necessary that we should have something of the kind, when we have an example of the Indian Congress before us.' On another occasion the *Mercury* observed:

> Mr Gandhi writes with calmness and moderation. He is as impartial as any one could expect him to be, and probably a little more so than might have been expected, considering that he did not receive very just treatment at the hands of the Law Society which had opposed Gandhi's admission as an advocate to practise before the Supreme Court when he first came to the Colony.

While he was attracting attention in the colonial press, he was also collecting enemies in the legislature. During the assembly debate on the Franchise Law Amendment Bill, one representative remarked that Gandhi was opposing the bill for personal political advantage. 'He is a discredited person,' the honourable member added, 'among the class which he is seeking to benefit, and beyond that he loses if he fails to fight the battle, the direct personal gain of receiving reward for the battle which he fights, consequently whether he wins or loses, he has everything to gain by fighting.'

# EIGHT

# The Green Pamphlet

In the middle of 1896, Gandhi, now twenty-six years of age, returned to India as an official representative of the community, to inform his fellow countrymen about the indignities to which Indians were subjected in South Africa, and he also wanted to sound out the opinions of the leaders of the Indian National Congress.

He sailed on 5 June on the SS *Pongola*, studying Tamil and Telugu, two of the south Indian languages, during the journey. He landed at Calcutta on 4 July and took the train to Bombay. There was a forty-five-minute stopover at Allahabad, and he decided to drive to the town, which would also enable him to buy some medicine. The pharmacist was half-asleep and took more time than was necessary in dispensing the medicine, with the result that Gandhi returned to the train station a few minutes too late. Fortunately, the station master had ordered his luggage to be taken out of the train, and realizing that he had a whole day to spare in Allahabad before catching the next train, Gandhi called on the editor of *The Pioneer*. The editor gave him a patient hearing and promised to publish in his paper anything that Gandhi might write on the South African problem, but he could not promise to endorse all Indian demands, stating that he was obliged to give due weight to the viewpoint of the white colonists. Gandhi told him that all he expected of him was to make a careful, unbiased study of the issue and then act according to his lights.

Back in Rajkot Gandhi spent some weeks with his family, writing a pamphlet entitled *The Grievances of the British Indians in South Africa*. Bound in green, it was consequently known as the Green Pamphlet. Ten thousand copies were printed and sent to newspapers and prominent Indians, and it became necessary to print a second edition.

*The Pioneer* was the first to notice it editorially, and a summary of the paper's article was cabled by Reuters to England. The Reuters' London office sent a still briefer three-line summary to Natal: 'A pamphlet published in India declares that the Indians in Natal are robbed and assaulted, and treated like beasts, and are unable to obtain redress. *The Times of India* advocates an inquiry into these allegations.'

The *Natal Mercury* commented:

Mr Gandhi, on his part and on behalf of his countrymen, has done nothing that he is not entitled to do, and from his point of view, the principle he is working for is an honourable and legitimate one . . . We cannot honestly say, that his latest pamphlet is an unfair statement of the case from his point of view . . . He enumerates only a number of grievances, but these by no means justify anyone in stating that his pamphlet declares that the Indians in Natal are robbed and assaulted and treated like beasts . . .

The *Natal Advertiser* commented that the Reuters' message had distorted the issue: 'A perusal of Mr Gandhi's pamphlet, recently published in Bombay, leads to the conclusion that the telegraphic description of its objects and contents was considerably exaggerated.'

Several other newspapers, however, maintained the telegram's version of the contents of the pamphlet, and made some scathing comments. On his return to South Africa, Gandhi would have a taste of a much more hostile atmosphere than he had hitherto experienced.

The Green Pamphlet was in fact a summary of the several petitions, memorials, circulars and leaflets he had issued to the authorities in Natal, London and Calcutta, then the capital of India. It detailed the sufferings of the Indians in Natal:

The man in the street hates him, curses him, spits upon him, and often pushes him off the footpath. The Press cannot find a sufficiently strong word in the best English dictionary to damn him with. Here are a few examples: 'The real canker that is eating into the very vitals of the community'; 'these parasites'; 'wily wretched semi-barbarous Asiatics'; 'a thing black and lean and a long way from clean, which they call the accursed Hindoo'; 'he is chokeful of vice and he lives upon rice. I heartily cuss the Hindoo'; 'squalid coolies with truthless tongues and artful ways'. The Press almost unanimously refuses to call the Indian by his proper name. He is 'Ramysamy'. He is Mr 'Samy'. He is Mr 'Coolie'. He is the 'black man'. And these offensive epithets have become so common that they (at any rate, one of them, Coolies) are used even in the sacred precincts of the Courts, as if the Coolie were the legal and proper name to give to any and every Indian. The public men, too, seem to use the word freely. I have often heard the painful expression . . .

The tramcars are not for the Indians. The railway officials may treat the Indians as beasts. No matter how clean, his very sight is such an offence to every White man in the Colony that he would object to sit, even for a short time, in the same compartment with the Indian. The hotels shut their doors against them. Even the public baths are not for the Indians no matter who they are . . . The vagrant law is needlessly oppressive and often puts respectable

Indians in a very awkward position.

Gandhi quoted this because 'the statement has been before the South African public for nearly one year and a half, has been commented upon freely by almost every newspaper in South Africa and remains practically uncontradicted and because, during the interval that has elapsed, I have seen nothing to change that view'. The Green Pamphlet further reported:

In Dundee last year, during the Christmas time, a gang of White men set fire to the Indian stores without the slightest provocation, in order to enjoy themselves.

Mr Abdulla Haji Adam, a shipowner and one of the leading members of the Indian community in South Africa, was travelling with me as far as Krantzkloof Station. He alighted there to go by postal cart to Natal. No one there would sell him even bread. The hotel-keeper would not allow him a room in his hotel, and he had to sleep in the coach shivering the whole night with cold. And the winter in that part of Africa is no joke.

Mr Haji Mohamed, another leading Indian gentleman, was travelling in a coach, some time ago from Pretoria to Charlestown. He was forced out of the coach and had to walk a distance of three miles because he had not got a pass – whatever that may mean . . .

An Indian, about two years ago, took out a second-class ticket on the Natal railway. In a single night journey he was thrice disturbed and was twice made to change compartments to please European passengers. The case came before the Court and the Indian got £10 damages . . .

Such feeling of deep-seated hatred towards the Indians is reproduced all over South Africa, in special legislation for Indians . . . The Attorney-General of Natal wants to keep the Indians for ever 'hewers of wood and drawers of water'. We are classed with the natives of South Africa – Kaffir races. He defines the status of Indians in the followings words: 'These Indians were brought here for the purpose of supplying labour for development of local industries and were not intended to form a portion of the South Africa Nation which was being built up in the various States . . .'

A member of the Legislative Assembly said on the occasion of the passing of the Immigration Bill of 1894 that 'the intention of the Colony is to make the Indian's life more comfortable in his native land than in the Colony of Natal . . .'

Gandhi did not limit his comments to the situation in Natal; he also discussed the difficulties being faced by Indians in Cape Colony, the Orange Free State and the Transvaal. He expanded on the injustice of the pass system, the three-pound tax, restrictions in the purchase of property, and other inequities.

The method employed by Indians, Gandhi explained, was 'to conquer this hatred by love – that is our goal'. He added:

We would often fall short of that ideal, but we can adduce innumerable instances to show that we have acted in that spirit. We do not attempt to have individuals punished but, as a rule, patiently suffer wrongs at their hands. Generally our prayers are not to demand compensation for past injuries, but to render a repetition of those injuries impossible and to remove the causes. Our grievances have been laid before the Indian public in the same spirit. If we have quoted instances of personal injuries, that we have done, not for the purpose of seeking compensation, but for that of laying our position vividly before the public of India.

Gandhi finished mailing copies of the pamphlet with the help of the children of the neighbourhood.

There were other pressing matters on his mind, and he was anxious to meet prominent Indians who might be helpful to the cause of the Indians in South Africa. In Bombay he met Justice M.G. Ranade and Justice Badrudin Tyabji who were sympathetic but as officials could not arrange meetings or participate in political affairs. They advised him to talk to Sir Pherozeshah Mehta, whom he had planned to see in any case. Gandhi was prepared to be awed by Sir Pherozeshah, but the 'Lion of Bombay' met him 'as a loving father would his grown up son', and introduced him to some friends, amongst them the economist and statistician D.E. Wacha, who said to the young visitor: 'Gandhi, we must meet again.'

Sir Pherozeshah carefully acquainted himself with the South African problem. 'Gandhi,' he said, 'I see that I must help you. I must call a public meeting here.' In accordance with instructions, Gandhi reported to Sir Pherozeshah's office at 5 p.m. on the eve of the meeting.

'Is your speech ready, Gandhi?' he was asked.

'No, sir. I am thinking of speaking extempore.'

'This will not do in Bombay. Reporting here is bad, and if we would benefit by this meeting, you should write out your speech, and it should be printed before daybreak tomorrow.'

The meeting was held in the hall of the Sir Cowasji Jehangir Institute, and the presence of Sir Pherozeshah ensured that the place was fully packed. Gandhi was glad to be armed with a prepared speech, but he could barely make himself heard. His old friend Keshavrao Deshpande came to his rescue, but as Gandhi handed his speech to Deshpande the hall rang with cries of 'Wacha! Wacha!' whereupon, at a nod from Sir Pherozeshah, Mr Wacha stood up and read the speech. The audience listened with rapt attention. His recital of the indignities heaped on their brethren in Natal and their heroic struggle against heavy odds brought applause and frequent cries of 'Shame!'

This was Gandhi's first important public speech in India and, despite his nervousness, which had nearly brought about a disaster, he was delighted, for Sir Pherozeshah had pronounced that it was brilliantly prepared. Gandhi was only too well aware that he had much to learn from the intellectual giants in Bombay. With Sir Pherozeshah's assistance, all the doors of India would be opened to him.

He went to Poona to see Bal Gangadhar Tilak, a giant intellect and towering political leader, whose revolutionary cry '*Swaraj* [self-rule] is my birth right, and I shall have it' was heard all over India. Gandhi fell under his spell, but was even more drawn toward Gopal Krishna Gokhale, a quieter and more thoughtful scholar who believed that freedom could be achieved by constitutional means. Like Gandhi he was also a champion of Hindu-Muslim amity. Later Gandhi would say he regarded Sir Pherozeshah as the 'unscalable Himalayas'; Tilak was the ocean 'on which one could not easily launch forth'; while Gokhale was like the Ganges which 'invited one to its bosom'. Of all the Indians he encountered, Gokhale had the greatest influence on him.

Gandhi went on to Madras, where the editors of the *Madras Standard* and *The Hindu* were very sympathetic. Editor G.P. Pillay even gave him unobstructed access to the columns of the *Madras Standard*. Gandhi spoke at a crowded meeting and his speech, like the ones he delivered at Bombay and Poona, was mainly based on the information contained in the Green Pamphlet. He then went to Calcutta for a while, where he was interviewed by representatives of *The Statesman* and *The Englishman*, and the long interviews were published in full. Mr Saunders, editor of *The Englishman*, claimed Gandhi as his own, and placed his office and the paper at his disposal. The visit to the *Amrit Bazar Patrika* was quite uneventful, but the unsolicited advice offered by the busy editor of *The Bangabasi* had a rather sobering effect. 'Don't you see our hands are full?' the editor reminded the future Mahatma. 'There is no end to the number of visitors like you. You had better go. I am not disposed to listen to you.' His paper had no dearth of topics for discussion, and South Africa was hardly known at the time. While plans to arrange a public meeting in Calcutta were still afoot, Gandhi received a telegram from Durban, urging him to return.

The £75 that the Natal Indian Congress had sanctioned toward his expenses had by now been all spent. He had, indeed, used some £40 out of his own pocket. Very characteristic was the statement of expenses he prepared to be submitted on his return to South Africa, showing a total of Rs

1,766-12-7 (one thousand seven hundred and sixty-six rupees twelve annas and seven pies). Among the items entered in it were:

Barber, 4 annas; Washerman, 8 annas; Pickwick pens, 6 annas; Theatre, rupees 4; Tram fare, 4 annas; Charity, 8 annas; Carriage, 4 annas; Telegraph boy, 1 anna; Trick man, 6 pies; Poor man, 1 anna; Magician, 8 annas.

Gandhi left Calcutta for Rajkot to collect his family, while Dada Abdulla made travel arrangements for them on the SS *Courtland*, the newest ship in his fleet, which left Bombay on 30 November 1896, bound for Durban. Gandhi was accompanied by his wife and two sons, and by his widowed sister's only son, Gokuldas. Dada Abdulla gave the whole family a free trip. Another ship, the SS *Naderi*, sailed from Bombay about the same time.

Kasturbai, now twenty-seven, was about to become the mistress of the house at Beach Grove Villas, and Gandhi felt rather strongly that she should be suitably dressed. He was then of the opinion that in order to look civilized the entire family's dress and manner should be in close proximity to those of the Europeans because, he thought, 'only thus could we have some influence, and without influence it would not be possible to serve the community'. He decided that she should wear the Parsi *sari*, while his two sons and nephew wore the Parsi coat and trousers. The Parsi community in India, descendants of emigrants from Persia, belongs to the religious system known as Zoroastrianism. The Parsis were considered élite among Indians, and their formal and well-cut dress was admired by the Europeans. The boys complained – the shoes hurt their feet, and the trousers were not as comfortable as the old *dhoti* – but Gandhi's authority over them was complete. Kasturbai, who looked well in her Parsi *sari*, and the smartly dressed boys, pretending to be comfortable, boarded the ship.

The two vessels, reportedly with a total of about eight hundred Indian passengers, reached Durban on 18 December, and a peculiar kind of storm was awaiting them.

While in India, Gandhi had aroused public opinion with speeches and pamphlets which detailed the sufferings of the Indians in South Africa; he had said little, if anything, that he had not already told the South Africans, perhaps in stronger language, to their faces. But, with the publication of the Green Pamphlet and the distorted Reuters' telegram that followed, he had earned for himself the dubious distinction of being the most hated Indian in South Africa. When the Europeans in Natal learned that he was on one of these ships they accused him of leading an 'invasion' of Natal designed to swamp the colony with Indians. Word also went about that there was a printing press on board together with fifty trained printers to carry out a sustained campaign for Indian immigration. Many of the passengers were in fact old residents, and a good proportion of them were heading for the Transvaal, which in those days offered better prospects than Natal. There was no printing press on board, and no printers. The total number of passengers was close to six hundred, and apart from his family Gandhi had no hand or interest in the travel arrangement of any other passengers.

As there had been an outbreak of plague in Bombay in the recent past, the port authorities in Natal ordered the two ships to remain in quarantine until the twenty-third day of sailing. Consequently a five-day quarantine was imposed, but when the port medical officer was about to give the ships a clean bill of health, he was replaced. The new medical officer, Dr Birtwell, imposed an additional quarantine of eleven days. All old clothes had to be burned; other clothes had to be washed and disinfected; the holds and passenger quarters were fumigated. Water and provisions were running out, but no assistance appeared to be forthcoming.

There was some semblance of Christmas celebration on board. When the captain invited the saloon passengers to dinner, he, anticipating trouble for the Indians on landing, asked Gandhi what he would do if he were faced with a lynch mob. Gandhi replied that he hoped he would forgive them. In the days to come, he was given an opportunity to prove his Christian sentiments.

Dr Birtwell inspected the two ships once again and declared his satisfaction with the manner in which his orders had been carried out, but he placed the vessels under quarantine for a further period of twelve days. The captain of the *Courtland* signalled the need for clothing and asked for written instructions on how long quarantine was to last, 'as verbal time changes with every visit of quarantine officer'. The signal from the *Naderi* asked the government to supply at once 250 blankets, since the passengers were wet and could easily get sick. These signals remained unanswered, and therefore the Indian residents in Durban hastily organized a Quarantine Relief Fund. Blankets were supplied to all the passengers and the poor passengers were, in addition, provided with food, free of charge.

Meanwhile trouble was brewing up ashore. Harry Sparks, a butcher with a commission in the cavalry, inserted a notice in his capacity as 'chairman of preliminary meeting', in the *Natal Advertiser* of 30 December:

Wanted every man in Durban to attend a meeting to be held in the large room at The Victoria Café, on Monday the 4th January at 8 o'clock for the purpose of arranging a demonstration to proceed to the Point and protest against the landing of Asiatics.

This meeting was ultimately held in the Town Hall of Durban. Inflammatory speeches were made, and some commissioned officers besides Captain Sparks also participated in the animated proceedings. Most of the audience were of the artisan class. Dr MacKenzie, a prominent hardliner, spoke with some vehemence, and his speech was reported in the *Natal Advertiser* the following day:

> Mr Gandhi, (prolonged hissing and hooting) that gentleman came to Natal and settled in the borough of Durban. He was received here freely and openly; all the privileges and advantages which the Colony could afford him were at his disposal . . . In return, Mr Gandhi had accused the Colonists of Natal of having dealt unfairly with Indians, and of having abused and robbed and swindled them. (A voice, 'You can't swindle a coolie'). He (the doctor) quite agreed with that. Mr Gandhi had returned to India and dragged them in the gutters, and painted them as black and filthy as his own skin. (applause). And this was what they might call, in Indian parlance, an honourable and manly return for the privileges which Natal had allowed him . . . It was the intention of these facile and delicate creatures to make themselves proprietors of the only thing that the ruler of this country had withheld from them – the franchise . . . Their country had decided that they had enough Asiatics and Indians here, and they were going to treat them fairly and well, provided they behaved themselves; but, if they were going to associate themselves with such men as Gandhi, and abuse their hospitality, and act in the way he had done, they might expect the same kind of treatment that was to be meted out to him (applause). However great a misfortune it might be for those people, he could not get over the distinction between black and white.

At a subsequent meeting Dr MacKenzie generated laughter when he expressed the opinion that the Indian Ocean was the proper place for these Indians. He accused Gandhi of organizing 'an independent emigration agency in India to land his countrymen here at the rate of from 1,000 to 2,000 per month', and cautioned him that he had judged the European character badly in thinking that he would be allowed to work such a scheme with impunity:

> Our forefathers won this country at the point of the sword . . . we should be false to the trust we have received were we to allow this fair land to be overrun with a people alien to us in blood, in habits, in traditions, in religion, and in everything that goes to make up national life.

MacKenzie also spoke about half a million natives 'who look to the white man as the child looks to his father'.

A mass meeting in support of the demand for the return of the quarantined ships was held at Maritzburg. It was also moved that a special parliamentary session should consider the pressing issue. Several members of the Legislative Assembly (MLAs) were present at the public meeting, which the *Natal Witness* reported extensively:

. . . Mr Bale, MLA . . . The hon. member was received with much cheering. He said that although no resolution had been entrusted to him he desired to state that he entirely and cordially sympathized with the objectives of the promoters of the meeting. (Loud cheers). As one of their members it would be his privilege and his duty to do all that he possibly could to secure the enforcement of that which they had at heart. (Hear, hear.) He took it that the existence in the Colony of an Indian population equal to the European was a menace to the social, the moral and the material welfare of the colonists – (loud cheers) – and it was the bounden duty of a Government which was a Government of the people for the people by the people to give effect to that which would be demanded that day, and by the universal voice of colonists. (Cheers.). . . He did not desire on an occasion like that, by anything he might say, to unduly hamper the Government, but he could not understand a Government, face to face with a difficulty, refusing to face that difficulty and deal with it as Englishmen always faced difficulties. (Loud and prolonged cheers.) The greater the difficulty, the greater the need for those at the head of affairs to tackle it. A united, bold, manly front was required in connection with a very serious evil. Let them take care that it did not become a more serious evil . . .

Mr T.P. O'Meara, MLA, who was heartily cheered . . . said it was the duty of the white community to state to the Government through their representatives, in a legal and constitutional way, that they would no longer tolerate the introduction of an undesirable class of people to this country. (Loud cheers.) He assured them, from his knowledge of the Government, that the members of the Ministry were as much in sympathy with their objects as he was and as they were themselves. Their objects would not be gained by any violence. If the people of Durban were going to march to the Point and throw Gandhi, as they said, into the sea – (loud laughter, interruption and voices: 'Keep him outside') – they would make a martyr of that man, and he would receive the sympathy of the whole of the British people. (A voice: 'He is making a martyr of us.') The duty of every white man was to act legally and constitutionally and to bring pressure to bear upon the Government to do what they desired. (Cheers, and a voice: 'Do what you are told, Pat, when you go to the House.')

Mr Young, MLA, received with cheers, proposed: 'Every man at this meeting agrees and binds himself, with a view to assisting the Government . . .' Let them all fall into line, work together, bring their shoulder to the wheel, and he would tell them they would get what they desired from the Government. (A voice: 'We cannot wait for the Government.') They had got to wait. (A voice: 'Too late,' and interruption). They were Englishmen, and 5,000 men walking to the Point to throw two or three hundred miserable coolies into the water was – (interruption, and a voice: 'What about the tea in America?') Never mind, it would not help them – (interruption) – it would brand their cause for years and years. They might march to the Point with the very best intention to behave themselves, but who was to control the crowd when they got there? It was simply rot. (Interruption.) . . . They would begin fighting amongst themselves. (Laughter and a voice: 'We are not Irish.'). . . The hon. member proceeded to say that he believed the Government, or at any rate the majority of the Assembly would bring about the laws he indicated (a voice 'When?') He could not tell them when, but at any rate it was only the question of a few months. The Colony had a perfect right to object to the landing of these people. Their mouthpiece was a gentleman of the name of Gandhi (hooting, and a voice, 'Don't say a gentleman.') Mr Gandhi had taken upon himself to introduce along with his ideas a huge army of Indians, but they had to see that the term 'British subject' was defiled no longer. Don't let them, however, be such fools as to run down to Durban to try and drown a few miserable coolies.

Mr T.H. Harris (of the Pavilion Bar) responded to the general invitation for speakers to ascend the platform. He said: Boys, I am an American subject. It took £2 to get the Chinamen and niggers into California; it took about £40 to get them out. (Hear, hear, and loud cheers.) Boys, who's running your railways at the present moment? ('Coolies.') Who's bringing and brought disease into the Colony? ('Coolies.') Who's ruining the Colony? ('Coolies,' and cheers.) Boys, stand by – let no coolie into the country. (Loud cheers.) . . .

Mr Joseph Baynes, MLA, ascended the platform only after peremptory calls for 'Baynes'. There was no need to use anything but constitutional means . . . When he heard Mr O'Meara advocating constitutional legislation for the danger threatening the Colony, he began to doubt whether Mr O'Meara was an Irishman. (Loud laughter.) There had been many times in the history of the world where constitutional action would not meet the requirements of the case, and where even while constitutional agitation was proceeding the evil grew. As far as this agitation was concerned, he was thoroughly with them, but he was rather sorry that one of the speakers should have introduced the matter he did into his speech. There was no question of going to drown a few Indians. (Cries of 'No!') There was no need for it; and he thought it would be a calumny on that gathering to suppose it would ever do such a thing. (Cheers, and a voice: 'Good old Baynes.')

Cheers were also raised for Mr Baynes . . .

The chairman then read and put the resolutions, and on a show of hands for and against each, declared them carried unanimously.

Mr H. Curry expressed the hope that every European in the town would join the Association. (Cheers.)

An individual came forward on the platform and solemnly said: 'Gentlemen, we may all be curry(i)ed, but let us ric(s)e to the occasion.' The gathering did *not* remain solemn.

Mr Craddock, president of the Association, moved a hearty vote of thanks to the chairman, who said he might safely send a wire to Mr Harry Sparks about this splendid meeting. (Cheers.)

The meeting, which had lasted a little over an hour, and had been thoroughly enthusiastic, broke up with the singing of 'Rule Britannia'.

The prejudice sometimes exceeded all limits. A columnist of the *Natal Mercury* reported the instance of a socialite lady who was distressed at the idea of eating a 'coolie's hen's eggs'. 'What essential difference is there between an egg laid by a coolie hen, (by which I mean a hen owned by a coolie) and the similar product of a fowl owned by a European?' he impishly asked and further observed:

There are, I admit, eggs and eggs. There are, for instance, the platform and stage egg (addled), the pastry egg, the 'bad egg', the egg of the 'oof fowl, and the egg laid by Jameson's cackling hen (produced while you wait species). Each has its merits and its utility . . . But to return to the lady and the egg of the coolie hen. Probably she (the lady) never dreams while reposing that the pillowslip on which her dainty head rests has been washed and manipulated by the hands of her *dhobi* . . . that the vegetables she eats are cultivated by Sammy and that the fish she enjoys has been caught and handled and fondled by the same individual – yet all this, if I may be eggscused [*sic*] for saying it, seems to me much like straining at the egg of the unoffending hen and swallowing the rest of the coolie's stock-in-trade.

It was not until 11 January that the medical officer announced that all the provisions of the quarantine regulations had been completed. The government of Natal could not impose restrictions indefinitely, nor were they in a position to forcibly send the ships back. On the same day the captain of the *Courtland* received a letter from Harry Sparks, saying that any attempt to land the passengers would result in dire consequences, and it was therefore advisable that he should return to India forthwith, taking his passengers with him. It was Sparks's understanding that the Natal government was prepared to bear any expenses so incurred.

On the afternoon of 13 January, Mr Harry Escombe, the Attorney-General, and the port captain came on board the *Courtland* to announce that the passengers were free to land and would be given full protection. A similar communication was sent to the other steamer, and the Attorney-General was then rowed ashore where an excited crowd of about five thousand had gathered. Harry Escombe had earlier openly given his blessing to the militants, but he was now obliged to pacify them. He advised them not to forcibly restrict the landing of any Indian passengers. 'You will injure your own interests and place the government in an awkward position,' he said. 'I assure you, however, that the Government of Natal will obtain from the Legislative Council the requisite powers in order to restrict future immigration.' The militants were disappointed, but they reluctantly dispersed.

Escombe had earlier sent word that in view of the hostile atmosphere, Gandhi and his family should wait and land under the cover of darkness. Gandhi was agreeable to this suggestion,but Mr F.A. Laughton, Gandhi's friend and legal adviser to the firm of Dada Abdulla, was against it. He felt it was safe for Gandhi to land along with the other passengers. Moreover he did not like the idea of his friend sneaking into Durban like a fugitive. He offered to accompany him, and Gandhi accepted the offer. Kasturbai and the children were sent separately and reached the residence of Parsee Rustomji, a wealthy Indian friend.

As soon as Gandhi landed, some boys recognized him and raised the alarm. 'Gandhi, Gandhi!' they shouted. 'Thrash him, Surround him.' A few older Europeans joined the growing party of rioters, and Mr Laughton rushed to engage a nearby ricksha. Gandhi disliked the idea of sitting in a vehicle pulled by humans, but this time he had no option. However, the mob terrified the Zulu ricksha boy, and he took to his heels. 'I was thus spared the shame of ricksha ride.' The mob followed Gandhi and his companion till they reached West Street by which time the crowd had grown so large that it became almost impossible for the two men to proceed further. In the confusion and hustling, a strongly built man took hold of Mr Laughton and tore him away from Gandhi. The crowd was cursing and shouting, and Gandhi was in danger of his life. Stones, brickbats, mud and rotten fish were being hurled at him. Someone dislodged his turban; someone else struck him with a riding whip. A burly fellow came up to the Mahatma-to-be, slapped him in the face and then kicked him hard. He was gripping the railings of a house, nearly unconscious. 'I had almost given up the hope of reaching home alive,' he wrote. 'But I remember well that even then my heart did not arraign my assailants.' At that moment Mrs Alexander, the wife of the police superintendent, saw what was happening. She advanced into the fray with an open umbrella to keep off the flying missiles and stood between the crowd and Gandhi, protecting him at least against hard blows until the constables arrived to accompany him to the house where his family was waiting. He was bruised all over and received immediate medical attention.

The crowd had followed Gandhi, however, and now surrounded the house and threatened to burn it down. They demanded his extradition so that they could hang him. The police superintendent came and posted himself at the gate, lustily singing along with them a lynching chant:

And we'll hang old Gandhi
On the sour apple tree

While Alexander was employing the tactic of humouring the crowd, Gandhi put on the uniform of an Indian constable. Two detectives accompanied him, one of them disguised as an Indian merchant, his face suitably painted. The three men left through the back door unnoticed and walked to the sanctuary of the police station. Apparently Gandhi consented to sneak out of the house in disguise only for the sake of the families inside.

When the superintendent became certain of Gandhi's safe arrival at the police station, he stopped humouring the crowd and asked seriously:

'What do you want?'

'We want Gandhi.'

'What will you do with him?'

'We will burn him.'

'What harm has he done to you?'

'He has vilified us in India and wants to flood Natal with Indians.'

'What if he does not come out?'

'We will then burn the house.'

'His wife and children are also there. There are other men and women besides. Would you not be ashamed of burning women and children?'

'The responsibility for that will rest with you . . . We do not want to hurt anyone else. It would be enough if you hand over Gandhi to us.'

The superintendent smiled and informed the crowd that the man they were looking for had left Rustomji's house and already reached another place. There was huge laughter among the crowd and shouts of 'It is a lie, it is a lie.' They would not take the superintendent at his word. It was agreed that they would send a group of three or four men into the house, and if they failed to find Gandhi inside it, they would disperse peacefully. The superintendent had beaten them in the game. They kept their word and left, most of them admiring the superintendent's tactful handling of the situation, while others fretted, fumed and cursed.

Gandhi remained in voluntary police custody for a few days. News of the vicious attack on him disturbed London. Joseph Chamberlain, British Secretary of State for the Colonies, cabled the Natal authorities to prosecute the attackers. Gandhi could identify a few of his assailants, and Harry Escombe, the Attorney-General, was obliged to arrest and prosecute them. But Gandhi did not hold the assailants responsible for the attack. The blame rested on the community leaders and on the Natal government. 'The leaders and, if you permit me to say so, you are to blame,' he told the Attorney-General. 'You could have guided the people properly, but you also believed Reuter and assumed that I must have indulged in exaggeration. I do not want to bring anyone to book. I am sure when the truth becomes known, they will be sorry for their conduct.' Escombe requested him to put his decision in writing so that he could cable a reply to Chamberlain, and Gandhi consented without the least hesitation.

The press had now changed their stance and cleared him of the worst quotations attributed to him. He encountered no further threat and in fact acquired the image of a man with noble and nonviolent intentions. While speaking at a meeting in Bombay during his controversial trip to India, he complained that 'neither the traders nor the English-educated Indians are treated with any degree of respect' and 'You can easily imagine how difficult it must be for a respectable Indian to exist in such a country.' This was, of course, also the time when the élite Gandhi's concern for humanity at large had not yet fully manifested itself. He also told the Bombay meeting:

> Ours is one continual struggle against a degradation sought to be inflicted upon us by the Europeans, who desire to degrade us to the level of the raw Kaffir whose occupation is hunting, and whose sole ambition is to collect a certain number of cattle to buy a wife with and, then, pass his life in indolence and nakedness.

Though the Europeans' anger against Gandhi personally was assuaged, they were more than ever determined that the Indian community should be held in check. Two bills were introduced in the Natal Legislative Assembly, and although not expressly directed against the Indians, one of them was calculated to affect the Indian trader adversely, and the other to impose a stringent restriction on Indian immigration. Gandhi, working through the Natal Indian Congress, had the bills translated into Indian languages, explaining the real implications. The bills were passed by the local legislature. An appeal was made to the Colonial Secretary to reject them, but he declined to intervene and they became law.

The prevailing crisis involved Gandhi more fully in his community work, and he appealed on behalf of the Natal Indian Congress for larger membership and funds. As a result, sufficient capital was accumulated to acquire property, which was then leased out, yielding enough rent to meet the day-to-day expenses of Congress.

The *Courtland* episode brought him more publicity than he could handle. Large numbers of Indians began to descend on his law office, which had been kept open during his absence, and before long he was making more money than he needed. To his utter dismay, he was becoming a successful lawyer and spending much of his time in his office.

## NINE

# Self-reliance and War

The Gandhis had some difficulty in adjusting to their new life at Beach Grove Villas, their large house in Durban. Gandhi once again ensured that the children wore Western clothes, including shoes and stockings, although they complained constantly about discomfort. Yet he refused to send them to a local school for fear of them becoming Europeanized. It was difficult for him to get a suitable teacher who could teach them in their native Gujarati, so he engaged an English governess to teach them under his direction. This arrangement lasted just a few months. Gandhi then decided to send his son, Harilal, and Gokuldas, his widowed sister's son, back home to a boarding school, but they were soon recalled. He was beginning to feel that formal education of any kind was an impediment. Real education comprised learning self-reliance, simplicity and the spirit of service. 'Their artificial ways of living', he wrote, 'might have been a serious handicap in my public work.' Gandhi's idea of self-reliance was, however, somewhat different from that propounded by Smiles in his famous book *Self-Help* published in 1859. Samuel Smiles set out the message to 'stimulate youths to apply themselves diligently to right pursuits, sparing neither labour, pains, nor self-denial in prosecuting them, – and to rely upon their own efforts in life, rather than depend upon help or patronage of others'. Gandhi's concept of self-reliance underlined simplicity in day-to-day living, without depending on other people's service for personal comfort – in fact, serving others in a spirit of selflessness.

Both Gandhi and Smiles, however, recognized the spirit of self-help as being crucial for all genuine growth in the individual. They both felt that the worth and strength of a nation depended far more on the character of its individuals than on the form of its institutions. And Gandhi would certainly have agreed with Smiles's observation in his *Self-Help*: 'It may be of comparatively little consequence how a man is governed from without, whilst everything depends upon how he governs himself from within . . . No law, however stringent, can make the idle industrious, the thriftless prudent or the drunken sober.' And, any legislative reforms 'can only be effected by means of individual action, economy and self-denial, by better habits than by greater rights'.

Self-reliance was, indeed, becoming the rule of life at Gandhi's five-bed-roomed Beach Grove Villas, which was now filled to bursting, for, apart from the Gandhi family, there were a few of non-paying boarders – his law clerk and assistants – staying there in communal fashion, sharing the household tasks and eating with the family, irrespective of their religion or caste.

There was no running water in the Gandhi home. The only bathroom was downstairs, and accordingly chamber pots were provided in each of the upstairs bedrooms. Gandhi had dispensed with the services of the Untouchable sweeper who generally did the scavenging work, because it was beginning to dawn on him that untouchability was an excrescence of Hinduism and was akin to the racist attitude of Europeans toward Indians and native Africans. Everyone in the house, including Kasturbai, helped with the latrine work, but when a new clerk came to stay sometime in 1898, the peaceful atmosphere of the house was threatened.

The new arrival, a Christian, was earlier an Untouchable and had embraced Christianity in order to escape the wrath of Hindu orthodoxy. The new clerk was not yet aware of the practice relating to chamber pots, and Gandhi did not enlighten him. Kasturbai was assigned the task of cleaning his chamber pot. She had all along been opposed to Gandhi's idea of communal living, but her husband's insistence that she clean the cham-ber pot of the newly arrived, whom she still considered an Untouchable, brought things to a head. She rebelled. Gandhi would have readily per-formed the task himself, and was therefore shocked by her attitude. After all this was part of her 'education'. She came down the outside stairs with the pot in her hands, tears streaming down her cheeks. He was far from being satisfied by her merely carrying the pot; he would have her do it cheerfully. 'I will not tolerate this nonsense in my house,' he said, raising his voice. 'Keep this house to yourself and let me go,' she shouted back.

Being in an obliging mood, he caught her by the hand and dragged her to the gate, and was about to open it with the intention of pushing her into the street when she cried: 'Have you no sense of shame? Must you so far forget yourself? Where am I to go? I have no parents or relatives here to harbour me. Being your wife, you think I must put up with your cuffs and kicks? For Heaven's sake behave yourself, and shut the gate. Let us not be found making scenes like this.' Gandhi put on a brave face, but 'I was really ashamed, and shut the gate.' In his autobiography he explains this incident: 'It was a time when I thought that the wife was the object of the husband's lust, born to do her husband's behest, rather than a helpmate and a partner in the husband's joys and sorrows.'

As his law practice became more lucrative, the question of simplifying his life agitated him constantly. He wanted to be of some service to his compatriots, and notwithstanding his busy schedule he characteristically made it more crowded. His friend Parsee Rustomji had opened a small charitable hospital for Indians, and Gandhi worked there for two hours every morning as a male nurse. 'This work brought me some peace,' he wrote.

His efforts toward economy and self-reliance now took a serious turn. The household laundry bill was getting heavy and he discovered that the charge for washing a collar was as much as its price. He bought a book on washing, studied the art, and taught it to his wife. The first fruits of his experiment in washing proved disastrous, for he found himself in court wearing a collar dripping starch. His colleagues thoroughly enjoyed the spectacle, but 'even in those days I could be impervious to ridicule'. When an English barber contemptuously refused to cut his hair, he promptly bought a pair of clippers and ventured to cut it himself, with the aid of a mirror. The result proved equally disastrous. He had done a fairly good job of clipping the front of his head, but the quality of work at the back left a lot to be desired. His friends at court enquired if rats had been nibbling at it. 'The barber was not at fault in having refused to cut my hair,' Gandhi wrote. 'There was every chance of his losing his custom, if he should serve black men.' He regarded the experience as 'punishment for our sins', for in India 'we do not allow our barbers to serve our untouchable brethren'.

Gandhi, who had first thought of becoming a doctor, read popular health manuals and books on nature cure. (The nature cure treatment involved dispensing with medicines and using earth and water treatment, as well as regulating food intake and eating fruit and nuts.) He gave free advice to his Indian clients and friends. He also studied a popular work on childbirth, which constituted a full course in obstetrics and infant care. He assisted in the delivery of their son Ramdas, born in Durban in 1897. And when labour came too swiftly for professional help to be fetched, Gandhi himself delivered their last child; this was Devadas born in 1900, also in Durban.

Meanwhile the Boer War, which was waged in South Africa from 1899 to 1902 between the Dutch settlers and the British, afforded Gandhi an opportunity to demonstrate his loyalty to the British Empire, even though his personal sympathies 'were all with the Boers'. Although he considered the Boers of the Transvaal and the Orange Free State to be white-racist empire builders, his attitude was complicated by the degree of sympathy and admiration he felt for them. He liked their traditional and archaic society, their resistance to modern civilization. And he also liked their discipline and fighting spirit, and the fact that when the war broke out, 'among the Boers, the entire male population joined the war. Lawyers gave up their practice, farmers their farms, traders their trade, and the servants left their services.'

Gandhi nevertheless felt that Indians, who claimed the right to be regarded as British subjects, must accept the responsibility of fighting in time of war. In those days, though not unaware of the defects of British rule, he believed that it was 'on the whole beneficial to the ruled' and that 'India could achieve her complete independence only within and through the British Empire'. The Indians were despised in Natal, but Gandhi did not want them to look on with folded hands at a time when 'ruin stared the British in the face as well as ourselves . . . such criminal inaction could only aggravate our difficulties . . . and it would be no matter of surprise if then the English treated us worse than before and sneered at us more than ever'. He defended his noncombatant participation in the Boer War:

> If any class among the subjects considers that the action of a government is immoral from a religious standpoint, before they help or hinder it, they must endeavour fully and even at the risk of their lives to dissuade the government from pursuing such a course. We have done nothing of the kind. Such a moral crisis is not present before us, and no one says that we wish to hold aloof from this war for any such universal and comprehensive reason. Our ordinary duty as subjects, therefore, is not to enter into the merits of the war, but when war has actully broken out, to render such assistance as we possibly can.

There were many among Gandhi's compatriots who also held the view that they should do their bit in the war, but now the practical question arose: who would lend an ear to the weak voice of the Indians when the whirlwind of war was raging? None of them had ever wielded a weapon of war, and even the work performed by noncombatants in a war required training.

Gandhi offered to organize Indians as stretcher-bearers and medical orderlies. The Natal government rejected the offer. Nevertheless Gandhi and other Indians began, at their own expense, to train as nurses, and notified the authorities accordingly. They also forwarded certificates of physical fitness. Another rejection came on the grounds that they were not needed. The common sneer prevailed that 'if danger threatened the colony, the Indians would run away'. But the initial success of the Boers and the heavy casualties suffered by the British forces soon caused the Natal government to sanction the formation of an Indian Ambulance Corps.

There were about three hundred ex-indentured Indians in the corps, who had been recruited by the efforts of the free Indians. Of these, thirty-seven were looked upon as leaders, as the offer to the government had been sent under their signatures, and they had brought the others together.

86

These three hundred volunteered together with some eight hundred indentured labourers furloughed by their masters. Gandhi recorded with pride that 'a large and splendid corps composed of nearly eleven hundred Indians left Durban for the front'. A photograph taken at the time shows him in khaki uniform and broad-brimmed felt hat, seated in the centre of twenty-one similarly dressed men. He has a drooping moustache and, like others, wears a Red Cross armband. Next to him is Dr Booth, an English physician who trained the volunteers.

The corps members were African- and Indian-born Hindus, Muslims and Christians. They served the British Army for about six weeks, bringing the wounded from the battlefield, and sometimes walking twenty-five miles a day. In the fierce engagement at Spion Kop in January 1900 the British were forced to retire. Consequently General Buller, the commanding officer, sent through a message saying that although by the terms of enlistment the Indians were not to enter the firing line, he would appreciate it if they came up to remove the wounded. 'We were only too willing to enter the danger zone and had never liked to remain outside.' Gandhi led his men on to the battlefield. For days they worked under the fire of enemy guns, carrying the wounded to the field hospital until eleven o'clock at night, and then working again at the first dawn. Vere Stent, British editor of the *Pretoria News*, wrote about a visit to the front during the Spion Kop battle:

> After a night's work, which had shattered men with much bigger frames, I came across Gandhi in the early morning sitting by the roadside eating a regulation army biscuit. Every man in Buller's force was dull and depressed, and damnation was invoked on everything. But Gandhi was stoical in his bearing, cheerful, and confident in his conversations, and had a kindly eye. He did one good.

For their services Gandhi and several other Indian volunteers were awarded the War Medal, and the corps was mentioned in dispatches. The most important phase of the war was over in 1900 when reinforcements arrived from England.

Early in the New Year Queen Victoria died after a brief illness. Gandhi promptly sent a cable to London: 'British Indians Natal tender humble condolences to the Royal Family in their bereavement and join Her Majesty's other children in bewailing the Empire's loss in the death of the greatest and most loved Sovereign on earth.' He led a procession of Indian mourners through the streets of Durban, and sent telegrams to friends in other cities bidding them do likewise.

He had by now resumed his busy schedule as a lawyer and a politician, but suddenly in May there came a reminder that the spiritual world existed. He learned that his jeweller-philosopher friend Rajchandra had died after a protracted illness. Writing to a friend, he observed:

> It was hard to believe the news. I can't put it out of my mind. There is very little time in this country to dwell on any matter. I got the letter while I was at my desk. Reading it, I felt grieved for a minute and then plunged immediately into my office work. Such is life here. But whenever there is a little leisure, the mind reverts to it . . . I loved him deeply . . . So I mourn out of selfishness. What consolation then can I give you?

Gandhi now felt that as a result of Indians' war service their lot in South Africa would improve, and at the conclusion of the war many of their grievances be redressed. In any case, he could do more for them by going home and fighting the larger social and political battles of Indians in India. He consulted his co-workers, who were loath to see him leave South Africa but eventually gave their consent, on condition that he should return if, within a year, his services were required.

There were farewell meetings in several places in Natal and costly gifts were presented to him of silver, gold and diamonds, including a necklace worth fifty guineas meant for Kasturbai. The evening he was presented with the bulk of these gifts, he had a sleepless night. 'I walked up and down my room deeply agitated, but I could find no solution.' It would be improper to refuse the gifts; but how could he accept them when he had been training his family 'to a life of service and a belief that service is its own reward'? Knowing for certain that he would have difficulty in persuading his wife, he astutely convinced the children that these baubles would serve no purpose. He then confronted her with the unanimous view that to keep the gifts would be morally wrong. There followed a dialogue between husband and wife which Gandhi recorded in his autobiography:

KASTURBAI: You may not need these gold and silver ornaments. Your children may not need them. Cajoled, they will dance to your tune. I can understand you not permitting me to wear them. But what about my daughters-in-law? They will be sure to need them. . .. I would not part with the gifts so lovingly given.
GANDHI: The children are not yet married. We do not want to see them married very young. When they are grown-up, they can take care of themselves. And surely we shall not have for our sons brides who are fond of ornaments. And if, after all, we have to provide them with ornaments, I am there and you can ask me then.
KASTURBAI: Ask you? I know you by this time. You deprived me of my own ornaments. Fancy you offering to get ornaments for the daughters-in-law! What

right have you to the necklace meant for me?

GANDHI: Has the necklace been given you for your service or for mine?

KASTURBAI: I agree. But service rendered by you is as good as rendered by me. I have toiled and moiled for you day and night. Is that no service? You forced all and sundry on me, making me weep bitter tears, and I slaved for them.

He remained firm, and finally Kasturbai yielded. He had all the gifts put into a trust for the service of the community. 'I have never since regretted the step,' he observed, 'and as the years have gone by, my wife has also seen its wisdom. It has saved us from many temptations.'

Gandhi sailed with his family for India on 18 October 1901. It was a long journey, for he stayed three weeks on the island of Mauritius. The Indians there were aware of his community work in South Africa, and greeted him with affection.

# TEN

# Indian Interlude

Gandhi settled his family in Rajkot on 14 December and three days later rushed to Bombay to consult with Sir Pherozeshah Mehta. The Congress* session was due to open in Calcutta in the last week of the month, and he was keen to address the Congress and have a resolution passed on behalf of the Indians in South Africa. Although Sir Pherozeshah was busy and could not see him in Bombay, Gandhi came to know that he would be travelling in a private saloon to Calcutta, and arranged to be on the same train. That year Dinshaw Wacha was president of the Congress, and being the principal legal assistant of Sir Pherozeshah was travelling with him. Gandhi had instructions to travel in the saloon between stations. Dressed in a Parsi coat and trousers, he presented himself at the appointed time. Sir Pherozeshah's words were rather discouraging. 'Gandhi, it seems nothing can be done for you,' he said. 'Of course we will pass the resolution you want. But what rights have we in our own country? I believe that so long as we have no power in our own land, you cannot fare better in the colonies.' Gandhi was disappointed, but had the consolation that he would be allowed to move his resolution. 'You will of course show me the resolution,' said Wacha, to cheer him up.

The Congress was held in a massive tent, and the president was treated with the utmost respect and escorted to his camp with great pomp by the reception committee. The delegates were housed in the local colleges. Although he was not a delegate, Gandhi was accommodated in the same college as Bal Gangadhar Tilak, the veteran revolutionary. Tilak had succeeded in creating and popularizing a militant brand of nationalism, thus providing a basis for an extremist faction within the Congress party. He had won himself the popular title of Lokamanya – one revered by the people. For many years after its inception, the Congress had been an élitist group, fed by neo-Western liberalism, and it was Tilak who gave the nationalist movement a much broader basis; the identification of the teem-

---

*The Indian National Congress. Chapter 20 covers a brief history of Congress until the time Gandhi finally returned from South Africa in 1915.

90

ing millions of India with the struggle for its independence. Now, sitting up in bed, Tilak held court, receiving his throngs of visitors with majestic tolerance. Gandhi was awed in the presence of the Lokamanya, but never fell under his spell.

Gandhi made friends with a few volunteers and tried to bring home to them the value of service, but 'the Congress would meet three days every year and then go to sleep. What training could one have out of a three-day show?' And the delegates had no better or longer training. They were disinclined to shoulder any task themselves, continually clapping their hands and demanding that the Congress volunteers perform services for them. The sanitary arrangements in the college were atrocious, and Gandhi's attempt to give some object lessons to the Congress volunteers proved futile:

> There was no limit to insanitation. Pools of water were everywhere. There were only a few latrines, and the recollection of their stink still oppresses me. I pointed it out to the volunteers. They said point-blank: 'This is not our work, it is the scavenger's work.' I asked for a broom. The man stared at me in wonder. I procured one and cleaned the latrine.

Since the Congress would not officially be open for two days, he decided to gain some experience in Congress work. At the Congress office, a self-important minor functionary, surrounded by volunteers, proved quite obliging and assigned Gandhi some clerical work. 'Well, then, here is a heap of letters for disposal. Take that chair and begin,' he commanded. 'As you see, hundreds of people come to see me. What am I to do? Am I to meet them, or am I to answer these busybodies inundating me with letters? I have no clerks to whom I can entrust this work. Most of these letters have nothing in them, but you will please look them through. Acknowledge those that are worth it, and refer to me those that need a considered reply.'

Gandhi did not take long to finish his work, and when the functionary learned about his background he was apologetic for having assigned him clerical work. 'What am I before you?' Gandhi assured him. 'You have grown grey in the service of the Congress . . . I am but an inexperienced youth . . . I want to do Congress work, and you have given me the rare opportunity of understanding the details.' The functionary was delighted to hear this. 'That is the proper spirit,' he said. 'But young men of today do not realize it. Of course I have known the Congress since its birth. In fact I may claim a certain share with Mr Hume in bringing the Congress into being.' The functionary's incessant talk was quite revealing, and his charge was learning all the time. Gandhi met most of the leaders, and by the time the Congress opened he knew his way around it and could perceive the manner of its working better than most of the dignitaries who attended.

The Congress pavilion was decorated with coloured foliage, plants and palms, and was lit by electricity. The session opened on 23 December and the president began his address with a touching tribute to Mahadev Govind Ranade, an eminent judge, economist, historian and social worker, who had recently died. He then spoke gratefully of the late Queen Empress. After referring briefly to the new King Emperor, the president turned to the subject of famine. The presidential address was a lengthy one and only a few selected passages were read. The elders seated on the dais in the mammoth pavilion overwhelmed Gandhi.

Gandhi was taken by Gopal Krishna Gokhale to a meeting of the Subject Committee. He was somewhat discouraged to note that there were lengthy speeches on every resolution, and every resolution had some well-known leader to back it. 'Mine was but a feeble pipe amongst those veteran drums.' It was now getting late, and they were rushing mechanically through the resolutions. Gandhi drew near Gokhale's chair and whispered to him: 'Please do something for me.' Suddenly Sir Pherozeshah exclaimed with satisfaction that they had come to the end of them.

'No, no, there is still the resolution on South Africa,' Gokhale cried out. 'Mr Gandhi has been waiting for a long time.'

'Have you seen the resolution?' asked Sir Pherozeshah.

'Of course.'

'Do you like it?'

'It is quite good.'

'Well then, let us have it, Gandhi.'

He read the resolution rather nervously. Gokhale supported it. 'Unanimously passed,' cried out everyone. 'You will have five minutes to speak on it, Gandhi,' said Mr Wacha.

Gandhi was somewhat perturbed that no one had taken the trouble to understand the resolution. Since it was getting late, everyone was in a rush to leave, and just because Gokhale had seen the resolution, they did not deem it necessary to see what it was all about.

The morning dawned, and Gandhi found himself worrying about his speech. He had prepared himself well, but what could he say in five minutes? He decided to speak extempore. But when Mr Wacha called his name and he rose to face the delegates, the old affliction of stage fright once again overcame him, and 'the faculty of speaking that I had acquired in South Africa seemed to have left me for the moment'. After three minutes the president rang a bell. Gandhi was not aware that the bell was rung two minutes before the end of each speech, as a warning. Thinking that his time was up, he promptly sat down, thoroughly bewildered. In any event his resolution was passed, and 'the very fact that it was passed by the Congress was enough to delight my heart'. In those days there was hardly any difference between visitors and delegates. Everyone raised his hand, and all resolutions were passed unanimously.

The Calcutta Congress was over, but Gandhi had plans to extend his stay in the town to meet various people in connection with his work in South Africa. He arranged to stay at the India Club, for among the members were some prominent Indians whom he was keen to interest in South Africa. Gokhale frequently went to the club to play billiards, and when he learned about Gandhi's extended schedule in Calcutta, he invited him to stay in his house instead. Gandhi accepted the invitation joyfully. Gokhale having discovered his reserve, offered advice: 'Gandhi, you have to stay in the country, and this kind of reserve will not do. You must get in touch with as many people as possible. I want you to do Congress work.'

Gandhi had a crowded programme in Calcutta. He walked long distances to meet people, and occasionally would take the tramcar. Gokhale was impressed with his habit of fending for himself, his personal cleanliness, perseverance and regularity. He introduced Gandhi to all the distinguished people who called on him. Dr P.C. Ray, who lived next door, was a frequent visitor. Gandhi was highly impressed by the simple life of the scientist, who earned eight hundred rupees a month but kept only forty rupees for himself, devoting the balance to public purposes.

He divided his day between seeing leading people and studying the religious and public institutions of Calcutta. One day he went to visit Debendranath Tagore, but as no interviews with him were allowed then, he could not see him. However, he was welcomed to a musical celebration held at his residence by the Brahmo Samaj. 'Ever since I have been a lover of Bengali music.' Gandhi looked forward to meeting Swami Vivekananda, a dynamic spiritual leader and reformer. With great enthusiasm he went all the way to Belur Math on foot, but was disappointed to be told that the Swami was lying ill at his Calcutta house and could not be seen.

His visit to the temple of Kali was an unpalatable experience. On his way he saw a flock of sheep going to be sacrificed. He was shocked to see rows of beggars pestering the visitors for alms. He was opposed to giving alms to sturdy beggars. Near the temple he saw pools of blood of goats which were slaughtered to appease Kali. That very evening, at a dinner party, he spoke to a Bengali friend about this cruel form of worship. 'The sheep don't feel anything,' said the friend. 'The noise and the drum-beating there deadens all sensation of pain.' Gandhi was appalled. 'If the sheep had speech, they would tell a different tale,' he observed. The sight at the temple of Kali haunted him for days.

After a month with Gokhale in Calcutta, Gandhi paid a short visit to Rangoon. He was impressed by the independence and spirit of the Burmese women, but found their menfolk indolent. He disapproved of the countless candles burning in the Golden Pagoda and was disappointed to note that the Indian and British merchants combined to exploit the Burmese.

He had decided that before settling down he would make a tour across India, travelling third class. This way he would mingle with his country-men and would also familiarize himself with the hardships of the third-class passengers. Gokhale ridiculed the idea, but equipped him with a metal tiffin-box filled with food. Gandhi also carried a twelve-anna canvas bag, which contained a long coat made of coarse wool, a *dhoti*, a towel and a shirt. A blanket and a water jug completed his baggage. Gokhale and Dr Ray accompanied him to the railroad station. He had asked them both not to inconvenience themselves, but they insisted on seeing him off. 'I should not have come if you were travelling first class, but now I had to,' said Gokhale.

Gandhi planned to stop at Benares, Agra, Jaipur and Palanpur for one day each, before making his way to Rajkot. He was determined to travel like an ordinary pilgrim visiting holy places, staying for the night at *dharamsha-las* (low-cost philanthropic lodgings). He ended up spending only thirty rupees, and that included the train fare, but the discomfort experienced was substantial.

Third-class compartments in India were overcrowded, and the indiffer-ence of the authorities, coupled with the dirty and inconsiderate habits of the passengers, made 'third-class travelling a trial for a passenger of cleanly ways'. Third class in South Africa was usually reserved for the negroes, but it was much more comfortable than in India. The South African trains had cushioned seats and sleeping accommodation, and regulations against over-crowding were enforced. 'Third-class passengers [in India] are treated like sheep and their comforts are sheep's comforts,' wrote Gandhi. He urged educated men to make a point of travelling third class and reforming the habits of the people, never putting up with the infringement of rules on the part of anyone concerned. It was important that the authorities were not allowed to 'rest in peace' and were constantly reminded of the rights of third-class passengers.

In the holy city of Benares a priest made preparation for Gandhi's ablu-tion in the Ganges in the proper orthodox manner. He had told the priest beforehand that on no account could he give him more than one rupee four annas as *dakshina* (offering),and that he should therefore keep this in mind while making the preparations. The priest readily assented. The *puja* (worship) was over by noon, and soon after Gandhi visited the great Kashi Vishwanath temple, reaching it by way of narrow, slippery lanes. The swarms of flies and the noise made by the shopkeepers and pilgrims dominated the scene,and instead of pure, sweet and serene surroundings he found a bazaar where cunning shopkeepers were selling sweets and toys of the latest fashion.

He was greeted at the entrance to the temple by a stinking mass of rotten flowers. He went to the Well of Knowledge, and found its surroundings equally depressing. 'I searched here for God,but failed to find Him.' He offered a pie, the lowest-denomination coin existing in India, to a priest as a contribution, who cursed him and said: 'This insult will take you straight to hell.'

Gandhi was in full command of the situation. 'Maharaj,' he said, 'whatever fate has in store for me, it does not behove one of your class to indulge in such language. You may take this pie if you like, or you may lose that too.'

The priest's refusal was followed by a further volley of abuse. Gandhi pocketed both the insult and the coin.

But the priest was hardly the man to let the pie go. He called the young pilgrim back and said: 'All right, leave the pie here. If I refuse your pie, it will be a bad omen for you.'

Gandhi finally parted with his pie without any further ado.

He was still little known in India, and as he wandered from place to place, carrying his tiffin-box and canvas bag, he could hardly be distinguished from all the other wandering pilgrims. Before leaving Benares he called on Mrs Annie Besant, the theosophist and brilliant advocate of Indian freedom, who was convalescing there. 'I only wanted to pay my respects. I am thankful that you have been good enough to receive me in spite of your indifferent health.' So saying he took leave of her.

Back in Rajkot he settled down to practise law. Soon he had acquired considerable knowledge of Indian law, and the winning of a case gave him some confidence. He wanted to stay in Rajkot longer but Kevalram Dave, the lawyer who was chiefly responsible for his decision to study in England, insisted that he was wasting his talents in a small provincial town. Gandhi did not want to make a quick move to Bombay, since the unpleasant memories of the past failure were yet with him; the man who spoke so confidently in Durban was tongue-tied in India. But Gokhale strongly advised him to settle in Bombay, practise at the Bar and help him in Congress work. He eventually decided to take the plunge and, with the help of a remittance from friends in South Africa, took chambers in Payne, Gilbert and Sayani's offices, and rented a house at Girgaum. His South African connections brought him work, and though he secured no cases in the High Court, he did better than he expected. Writing to a friend, he observed: 'I do not despair. I rather appreciate the regular life and the struggle that Bombay imposes on one. So long, therefore, as the latter does not become unbearable, I am not likely to wish to be out of Bombay.'

Shortly after Gandhi took up chambers in Bombay, an American insurance agent visited him in his office. The smooth-talking agent discussed Gandhi's future 'as though we were old friends'. He stressed the need for insurance coverage for the family. Gandhi was impressed and took out an insurance policy for ten thousand rupees. Later, however, he became annoyed with himself for having fallen into the agent's trap, for he had earlier maintained that 'life insurance implied fear and want of faith in God'. He let the policy lapse. 'In getting my life insured I had robbed my wife and children of their self-reliance,' he reasoned. 'Why should they not be expected to take care of themselves? What happened to the families of numberless poor in the world? Why should I not count myself as one of them?'

Hardly had the family established itself in Bombay than Gandhi's second son, ten-year-old Manilal, who had been through an accute bout of smallpox some years earlier, came down with a severe attack of typhoid complicated by pneumonia. At night the boy had a dangerously high temperature. A Parsi doctor recommended chicken broth and eggs to build up the boy's strength. But Gandhi and his family were strict vegetarians. 'Your son's life is in danger,' the doctor cautioned him. For Gandhi it was part of his religious conviction that there were certain things which could not be done even to preserve life, and one of those things was the taking of life. He felt he could cure his son with a vegetarian diet and hydropathy. He would have liked to have the child make his own choice between the two cures, but reasoning that Manilal was too young to choose, Gandhi chose for him 'some hydropathic remedies which I happened to know'. Manilal was submitted to three-minute hip baths according to the formula devised by Dr Ludwig Kuhne of Leipzig, and starved on diluted orange juice for three days. But his temperature remained at 104°. His skin was dry, and there was no perspiration.

One night it occurred to Gandhi that his son might be cured with the aid of a wet sheet pack. He dipped a bedsheet in water, wrung it out, wrapped the feverish boy in it and then covered him with two blankets. It was a grave risk he had taken. Leaving his son in the care of Kasturbai, he walked out of the house to lessen the tension within him. He paced the streets with the name of Rama on his lips and prayed: 'My honour is in Thy keeping, O

Lord, in this hour of trial.' After a short while he returned, thoroughly exhausted, his heart beating furiously. But good news awaited him. 'Bapu, I am simply soaked. Do please take me out,' Manilal said. Gandhi felt his son's forehead. He was perspiring, and his temperature was going down. For forty days Manilal was permitted only diluted milk and fruit juices. He slowly regained his health and, as Gandhi wrote, 'God had saved my honour.'

The damp and ill-lit house at Girgaum had perhaps contributed to Manilal's illness. Gandhi felt he must find a better place to live. Finally he decided on a well-ventilated bungalow in suburban Santa Cruz and settled his family in it. 'I took a first-class season ticket from Santa Cruz to Churchgate, and remember having felt a certain pride in being the only passenger in my compartment.'

He began to make use of the High Court library, made new acquaintances, and felt that he should soon secure work in the High Court as well. From time to time Gokhale would call on him in his chambers, usually bringing some distinguished persons who might be useful in the furtherance of his professional career.

Just when he seemed to be settling down as he had intended, he received a telegram from Durban: 'Barrister Gandhi, Rajkot, Committee requests fulfil promise. Remitting.' It appears he had lost touch with his friends in Durban, who thought he was in Rajkot at a time when he had been practising law in Bombay for five months.

On receiving funds from Natal, he sailed for South Africa around the middle of November 1902, taking with him four or five educated young men who could speak English and might be able to continue his work in South Africa. Among them was Maganlal Gandhi, the son of a cousin. Thinking that he would not be detained there for more than a year, Gandhi left Kasturbai and the children in the rented bungalow at Santa Cruz.

# ELEVEN

# Phoenix

The Secretary of State for the Colonies, Joseph Chamberlain, was expected in South Africa to collect a 'gift' of £35 million – a sort of war debt from the defeated Boers, intended to repay the British Treasury for the cost of the war – and to pave the way for the union between the British colonies and the Boer territories. At the conclusion of the war, the restrictions imposed on the Indians, contrary to their expectations, became harsher, particularly in the Transvaal. The Indians wanted Gandhi to speak to Chamberlain on their behalf.

On arrival in Durban he was immediately required to draft a memorial for submission to Chamberlain on behalf of the Indians in Natal, and to accompany the deputation which would wait on him. He wrote a long petition regarding their grievances, emphasizing that they were law-abiding, orderly and respectable, a credit to any community. Chamberlain was sympathetic, but pointed out that the imperial government had little control over self-governing colonies. He promised, however, to do what he could, but 'you must try your best to placate the Europeans, if you wish to live in their midst'.

From Natal Chamberlain proceeded to the Transvaal. Gandhi was asked also to prepare a petition for the Indians residing there and accompany their deputation. Owing to the dislocation caused by the Boer War, a permit was required to gain entry into the Transvaal, but Europeans normally encountered no difficulty in this regard. On the other hand, the Transvaal government was refusing to allow many Indians, who had become refugees during the war, to return to their homes and businesses in the Transvaal. Guessing that he would be refused the necessary permit if he applied through the newly established Asiatic Department, Gandhi approached his old friend, the police superintendent Alexander. The superintendent prevailed upon the Permit Officer to issue him a permit without reference to the Asiatic Department. The officers of this department were puzzled at Gandhi's arrival in Pretoria, but they had no power to send him back. They did, however, decide to obstruct his work by disallowing his inclusion in the deputation that was to wait on the Secretary of State for the Colonies, on the grounds that he was not a local resident and that Chamberlain had already seen him in Natal. George Godfrey, an Indian barrister, led the deputation in his place. In his reply Chamberlain referred to Gandhi, and said it was better to hear a fresh local representative than the same one again, though he was aware of Gandhi's work in Natal and the Transvaal.

Realizing that the centre of struggle had now shifted to British Transvaal, Gandhi decided to forgo for the present the prospect of public life in the wider field of India. He wrote to Gokhale that he had found more work in South Africa than he had anticipated, and at once applied for admission as an attorney in the Supreme Court. Encountering no opposition, he opened an office in Johannesburg. Also here was the new Asiatic Department, manned exclusively by army officers stationed before the Boer War in India, and 'with the coming of the officers from Asia, came also its autocracy'. He believed that the Asiatic Department, far from protecting Indian interests in the Transvaal, was going to be 'a frightful engine of oppression'.

Gandhi now set about acquiring staff in his office. His first stenographer was a Miss Dick, who had recently arrived from Scotland. She announced that she wanted a salary of £17-10-0 and was accepted forthwith. She soon became his confidential assistant and was entrusted with large sums of money. She was engaged to be married, and Gandhi soon lost a woman who was 'the very picture of loyalty and purity'. He gave her away in marriage.

Miss Dick's replacement was the formidable Sonja Schlesin, seventeen years old, of Russian-Jewish origin. She was introduced to Gandhi by his friend Hermann Kallenbach: 'This girl has been entrusted to me by her mother. She is very clever and honest, but she is very mischievous and impetuous . . . You keep her if you can manage her.' She was highly efficient and dedicated, but grossly opinionated. She asked for little money, and when he urged her to take more, she scolded him: 'I am not here to draw a salary from you. I am here because I like to work for you and I like your ideals.'

Gandhi had in his employ some Indian law clerks, but their knowledge of the English language was limited. The employment of Louis Walter Ritch, an Englishman, therefore, was of considerable help. Most of Gandhi's European friends in Johannesburg were from theosophical and vegetarian circles. Gandhi had been attending meetings of the Johannesburg branch of the Theosophical Society, and it was at one of these meetings that he met Ritch, who at the time was the manager of a commercial company. He was married with a large family, and on Gandhi's suggestion, he left the firm and became an articled clerk in Gandhi's law office. He was delighted by law, stayed with Gandhi for about two years, and then sailed for England to continue his legal studies.

Hermann Kallenbach was the the closest among Gandhi's European friends. A tall, stoutly built and rather ponderous architect, he was rich, liked to wear expensive clothes, and lived in his own elegant house on a hill some distance from Johannesburg. Born in Poland, brought up in Germany, and taken to South Africa at an early age, he was singularly successful in his profession. He was unmarried, and had time and money to spare. Ten years after first coming under Gandhi's influence, his main ambition was to go to India and serve him in some humble capacity. For some reason this plan did not materialize, and Kallenbach spent his last days designing the houses of the wealthy.

Gandhi frequented vegetarian restaurants where he became acquainted with many fellow vegetarians. Among them was Albert West, who was unmarried, came from Louth, in Lincolnshire, and was equipped with only the rudiments of education. He had begun his career as a printer's devil and was now a partner in a none-too-profitable printing shop. He was a kindly, determined man, always ready to serve in a good cause.

Gandhi joined a group of theosophists called the 'Seekers' Club'. They often read the *Bhagavad Gita* together, and this revived his interest in it. He now began to study the *Gita* with the utmost regularity and devotion, and over a period of time memorized a good portion of it. He sought to go deeper into its message, and attempted once again to understand the Sanskrit original. The *Bhagavad Gita* became his 'dictionary of daily reference'. Words like *aparigraha* (nonpossession) and *samabhava* (equability) gripped him. Gandhi understood the *Gita* teaching of nonpossession to mean that one who desired salvation should act like a trustee who, though having control over great possessions, regards not an iota of them as his own. Nonpossession and equality to him presupposed 'a change of heart'.

He wrote to his brother Laxmidas that though he had in the past offered him his savings, henceforth his brother should expect nothing from him, for 'all future savings, if any, would be utilized for the benefit of the community'. Laxmidas was annoyed that his brother had chosen to consider the entire community as his 'family', and stopped communication with him. Gandhi was deeply distressed, but 'it would have been a greater distress to give up what I considered to be my duty, and I preferred the lesser'.

With the growing simplicity of his life, his dislike of medicines steadily increased. He suffered from frequent headaches, and constipation. He concluded that he overate. He took his cue from the recently established 'No-Breakfast Association' in Manchester, and decided to do without the morning meal. The headaches soon disappeared. Thereafter he dispensed with laxatives and medicines, and began to experiment with treatment offered by Adolf Just in his *Return to Nature*. Accordingly, he regularly applied a poultice of clean earth moistened with cold water to his abdomen. It proved a radical cure.

Gandhi's law practice began to progress well, as did his community work. He issued a spate of appeals and reports to the Transvaal, Natal and British authorities, and to prominent leaders in India. He wrote to newspapers in South Africa, India and England about the anti-Indian laws and bills which affected the Indian traders' licences, immigration, residential locations, bazaars, indentured labour, permits and franchise. He also referred these matters to the Viceroy of India. It was vain to expect that the Indians would receive in their struggle any cooperation or support from the white press in South Africa, which was virtually controlled by big finance. The issuing of pamphlets or brochures could hardly fill the gap. An acute need was therefore felt for an Indian newspaper that would voice the views and aspirations of the Indian community and serve as an organ of its struggle.

About this time Madanjit Vyavaharik, a Bombay schoolmaster, approached Gandhi with a proposal to start an Indian newspaper. A few years earlier, with Gandhi's help, he had set up a press in Durban called the International Printing Press. This printing press was now available. With Gandhi's blessing, Vyavaharik founded, on 4 June 1903, a weekly called *Indian Opinion*. Mansukhlal Nazar, an undergraduate but a trained journalist, became its first editor.

The early part of 1904 witnessed unusual rain. For seventeen days the clouds hung low over Johannesburg, and rain soaked the city. Hospitals began to get crowded with people suffering from a strange, unidentifiable disease. The Europeans and the negroes were affected, but the Indians, living as they did in crowded, unsanitary locations and having less resistance, suffered most. The disease originated at one of the gold mines, and when Gandhi received a message from Madanjit Vyavaharik, who happened to be at the location seeking subscribers for *Indian Opinion*, that twenty-three Indian workers were stricken with black plague, he sent a hurried note to the medical officer and promptly bicycled to the location. With the help of some Indian volunteers, he broke open an empty store, converted it into a hospital, and collected up the patients. Dr William Godfrey,who practised in Johannesburg, rushed to take charge of the improvised hospital, and became both nurse and doctor. But twenty-three patients were more than the three men could cope with. Louis Ritch, Gandhi's articled clerk, was ready to take the plunge, but he had the responsibility of a large family, and 'I had not the heart to expose him to the risk.'

The following morning the old custom house was provided by the municipal council as a temporary hospital. Volunteers cleaned the place and fitted it up as best as they could, before the patients were brought in. The municipality lent the services of a nurse, who came with brandy and hospital equipment. Only two patients were saved, the rest died in quick succession. The nurse also caught the contagion and died.

Gandhi regularly took his meals at a vegetarian restaurant, where he would usually have a word with Albert West, 'that sober, god-fearing, humane Englishman'. Since he was engaged in nursing the plague patients, he wanted to avoid the contact of friends as much as possible. West had learned about his nursing and not having seen him as usual at the restaurant, became concerned lest something should have happened to him. He called at Gandhi's apartment and was delighted to see him hale and hearty, then immediately offered his services: 'You know I have no one depending on me.' Gandhi was in no need of Europeans to nurse the Indian miners, but since Madanjit Vyavaharik was likely to be engaged in nursing for a while, he did need a capable manager with some experience of printing to take charge of the *Indian Opinion* press. Albert West was offered the position with a salary of £10 a month plus a share of the profits, if any. He gave himself a few hours to think it over and finally accepted it. The following day he left for Durban to take up his new duties.

Gandhi now helped the Johannesburg authorities to evacuate the 'coolie location', as the Indian settlement was called. Arrangements were made to resettle the evacuees in a camp under canvas cover, about thirteen miles outside the city. With his assistance, the Indians were persuaded to dig up silver and copper coins amounting to sixty thousand pounds which they had buried in the old settlement for safekeeping, because they knew nothing about banks. Gandhi became their banker and money started pouring in. The banks were by no means anxious to accept large amounts of copper and silver, and their employees were certain to refuse to touch money coming from a plague-affected area. But Gandhi's own bank manager proved helpful. The coins were sterilized and deposited in the bank in the names of their owners, with Gandhi as a sort of custodian.

When the plague broke out, Gandhi had written a strong letter to the press, accusing the municipal authorities of negligence in not providing adequate facilities for the Indian labourers. The letter caught the attention of Henry Polak, born in Dover, in England, in 1882, who had become a vegetarian after reading Count Leo Tolstoy. He patronized the same restaurant as Gandhi, and one evening seeing him there, he sent over his card. Gandhi invited him to his table. 'When I read your letter to the press about the plague, I felt a strong desire to see you,' Polak said. 'I am glad to have the opportunity.' They talked, found much in common, and became friends. Polak was assistant editor of *The Critic*, a weekly publication dealing mainly with Transvaal politics. The two men would meet often. Polak was somewhat surprised to see a picture of Christ above Gandhi's desk. There were also portraits of Dadabhai Naoroji, the 'grand old man of India', and Gokhale. Polak, who was an avid reader, observed that the small bookcase there included a Bible, Sir Edwin Arnold's *The Song Celestial*, some works by Tolstoy, and Max Mueller's *India: What Can It Teach Us?* Gandhi wrote of Polak: 'He had a wonderful faculty of translating into practice anything that appealed to his intellect. Some of the changes that he had made in his life were as prompt as they were radical.' Incidentally, the three Europeans closest to Gandhi in Johannesburg – Sonja Schlesin, Hermann Kallenbach and Henry Polak – were all Jews, but none of them practiced the Jewish faith in the traditional sense.

The weekly *Indian Opinion* was first published in four languages, English, Gujarati, Hindi and Tamil. Later, the Hindi and Tamil issues were discontinued for want of suitable editors and compositors. Technically, Gandhi was neither the owner nor the editor of the newspaper, but he single-handedly guided its conduct. Since Mansukhlal Nazar, the editor, found it difficult to venture to write on intricate South African problems, the responsibility of attending to the editorial columns fell on Gandhi.

Because the newspaper was so important to him as a political weapon rather than a commercial enterprise, he kept tight control over its policy, and poured nearly all his savings into it, at one time paying out £75 a month. Some help also came from the Natal Indian Congress and the British Indian Association. *Indian Opinion* was intended to expose the 'blemishes' of the South African Indians even as it insisted on their rights, and when he began to organize passive resistance it was the medium through which he issued instructions about tactics.

When Madanjit Vyavaharik began to entertain a keen desire to return to India to resume his career as a schoolmaster, he told Gandhi that he could not bring out *Indian Opinion* any longer, and expressed his intention to sell the newspaper and the printing press to him. Gandhi immediately accepted the offer.

In October 1904 Albert West sent an alarming report from Durban:

The books are not in order. There are heavy arrears to be recovered, but one cannot make head or tail of them. Considerable overhauling will have to be done. But all this need not alarm you. I shall try to put things right as best as I can. I remain on, whether there is profit or not.

Gandhi decided to go to Durban and investigate the situation. Henry Polak accompanied him to the railroad station and handed him a book, saying he might like to read it during the twenty-four-hour journey. It was John Ruskin's *Unto This Last*. 'The book was impossible to lay aside once I had begun it,' Gandhi writes. 'It gripped me . . . I could not get any sleep that night. I was determined to change my life in accordance with the ideals of the book.'

*Unto This Last* contains some essays on the principles of political economy. Published in a series of articles in the *Cornhill Magazine*, they appeared later as a book. Ruskin believed that the true basis of society was not wealth, as the classical economists had it, but the 'invisible gold' of human companionship. Social economists, in expounding their theories, invariably disregarded the principal motive that rules a man's life, his desire to maintain human relationships with his fellow men. Ruskin maintained that the relationship between the employer and the employee must be a human one deriving from 'social affections', otherwise it is meaningless. The rich should abstain from luxuries until all, the poorest too, should have enough, 'until the time come, and the kingdom, when Christ's gift of bread and bequest of peace shall be Unto this last as unto thee . . .'

Gandhi said the book was written with 'blood and tears', and he took from it what he wanted to take:

That the good of the individual is contained in the good of all; that a lawyer's work has the same value as a barber's inasmuch as all have the same right of earning their livelihood from their work; that a life of labour, i.e., the life of the tiller of the soil and the handicraftsman is the life worth living.

On arrival at the *Indian Opinion* press he discussed the book with Albert West, having already reached certain conclusions. He described to West the effect the book had produced on his mind, and proposed that they should remove the press to a farm where everyone would do farm work on the same basic living wage of £3 a month, and would attend to the press and publication of *Indian Opinion* in their spare time. Albert West readily agreed to take part in this enterprise. Most of the other workers were also agreeable.

Gandhi promptly inserted an advertisement in a newspaper for a piece of land near Durban and close to a railroad station. On receipt of a reply, Gandhi and West immediately went to inspect the land and succeeded in acquiring for £1,000 one hundred acres at Phoenix, fourteen miles from Durban and about three miles from the nearest railroad station. Several rich Indians helped with the money. The land contained a fine little spring, a dilapidated cottage, and plenty of fruit trees. But there were disadvantages. While only a few acres were under plough, the remaining fertile land was thickly overgrown with snake-infested wild grass. Nevertheless the land offered immense possibilities to hard-working cultivators. There was no scarcity of rain.

Gandhi took with him to Phoenix those relations and friends who had come from India with him. They had come to South Africa in search of wealth. It was therefore difficult to persuade them to stay, but some agreed and among those Gandhi singled out Maganlal Gandhi's name: 'He left his business for good to cast in his lot with me, and by ability, sacrifice and devotion stands foremost among my original co-workers in my ethical experiments. As a self-taught handicraftsman his place among them is unique.'

Apart from the run-down cottage there were no buildings on the farm, and the first priority was to procure building materials. The ever-helpful Parsee Rustomji placed at the pioneers' disposal some corrugated iron sheets from a disassembled warehouse. Within a month, with the help of some veterans from the ambulance unit in the Boer War, a neat-looking structure, seventy-five feet long and fifty feet wide, was erected to accommodate the printing press.

Before houses could be built, the settlers lived under canvas,and complained about the snakes they would encounter. Nonkilling was a fundamental principle at the farm, and yet a snake was killed without a complaint from Gandhi, although he said that man should fear nothing that God had created. Beyond the settlement no buildings were to be seen except for a few small Zulu farm huts about two miles away. There were no shopping facilities, and all articles had to be procured from Durban.

In the beginning the printing of *Indian Opinion* involved some difficulties, and the first number from Phoenix, though printed on the due date, 24 December 1904, was only a two-page edition. There were some regular paid compositors, but every member of the settlement was required to learn the typesetting work, and to help in dispatching copies of the paper. There were a few Zulu servants, two or three Tamils, two or three Hindi-speaking Indians, and about half a dozen Gujaratis, most of them distant relatives of Gandhi, all working at the press under the guidance of Albert West.

The settlers of Phoenix were divided into two classes – the 'schemers' and the paid workers. The 'schemers' were each granted three acres of the estate, together with a small house built of corrugated iron with rough wooden supports, which they would pay for when they could. No land was fenced in, and paths and narrow roads divided one holding from another. If a member vacated his house and holding, it was not sold but passed to another member. Each 'schemer' drew £3 a month from *Indian Opinion*, with the right to divide the profits. The rest were simply paid for their labour. The purpose behind the establishment of the settlement was stated by *Indian Opinion*: 'Living under such conditions and amidst the beautiful surroundings, the workers could live a more simple and natural life and the ideals of Ruskin and Tolstoy be combined with strict business principle.'

The settlers were now joined from India by Gandhi's eldest son, sixteen-year-old Harilal. His cousin, Gokuldas, also came to live there. Gandhi had hardly settled down at Phoenix when he realized that he could not afford to neglect his work at Johannesburg, where he had a lucrative law practice. He was well off by any yardstick, making around £5,000 a year, with a large, elegant eight-roomed house in the suburbs. As usual, he had some of his law clerks living with him. Soon Kasturbai and their three younger sons came to join him.

When he informed Polak of the important changes he had made, the young journalist was delighted that the loan of his book had been so fruitful. Polak resigned from *The Critic* to move to Phoenix, and took to the simple life there 'like a duck takes to water'. But Gandhi could not keep him there long. Louis Ritch had decided to sail for England to continue his legal studies, and since a suitable replacement was essential, Gandhi suggested that Polak join the office to qualify as an attorney. Polak was supremely happy with his lot at Phoenix, but he agreed to be articled. They both hoped that in the not too distant future they would retire from legal work and settle at Phoenix, earning their livelihood by manual work and editing *Indian Opinion*.

Meanwhile the Johannesburg house came in for much severe overhauling in the light of Ruskin's teaching. Gandhi introduced as much simplicity as was possible in a barrister's house. Physical labour was stressed. For health and economy reasons, he purchased a handmill to grind the wheat, and the flour was used in baking unleavened wholemeal biscuits after a recipe of Dr Ludwig Kuhne of Leipzig. Everyone took turns at this arduous task.

Gandhi's life was a well-regulated one. For a while he bicycled to his office in the centre of the town, a journey of about six miles, but soon he preferred to walk the whole distance. At seven-thirty in the morning he would leave his house without breakfast, reaching his office at about nine. He would spend a little over an hour reading his morning mail and dictating letters to Sonja Schlesin, and would then walk across the street to the law courts. At one o'clock he would lunch, accompanied by his law clerks, at a nearby vegetarian restaurant. He would leave the office after five o'clock, and was home by seven. Dinner would consist of some vegetable dishes, lentils, home-baked bread and nut butter followed by a dessert of raw fruit or milk pudding. Cereal coffee or lemonade rounded off the meal. Afterwards Gandhi would intone some verses from the *Bhagavad Gita* with Henry Polak, his frequent house guest, reading the English equivalent from Edwin Arnold's *The Song Celestial*. These evening prayer meetings were also a regular feature at Phoenix Farm.

Ever shaping the lives of others, Gandhi now strongly advised Henry Polak and Albert West to find wives for themselves. When West went to England to see his parents, Gandhi urged him to return married, if possible. West returned with both a wife and a mother-in-law, the widow of a shoemaker. Polak had been engaged to a young woman in England; he had postponed marriage for financial reasons. 'When there is a heart union, as in your case,' Gandhi told Polak, 'it is hardly right to postpone marriage for financial considerations . . . And then you are now staying with me. There is no question of household expenses.' So Polak sent for his future wife. Millie Graham was a Christian, Polak a Jew, but their real religion, Gandhi said, was 'the religion of ethics'. He also encouraged his Indian friends to summon their families from home. Phoenix thus developed into a small village. 'Phoenix was the common home,' Gandhi wrote, 'and as we were all supposed to have become farmers, we were not afraid of marriage and its usual consequences.'

Though outwardly Gandhi gave the impression of leading the life of a contented patriarch, maintaining unquestioned control at Phoenix, in his law office and in his house, his vastly complicated life was beset with considerable difficulties. He was doing pretty well as a lawyer and had reason to be satisfied professionally; however, he yearned to live the life of a peasant. In the area of public service, however, it was an altogether different story. He had been writing petitions to the government on behalf of the Indians at a feverish pitch; the government chose to appear blissfully oblivious to them. He had been writing editorials in *Indian Opinion*, and they were proving ineffective. He had been making speeches which were well attended, but no one acted on his utterances. He strove to demonstrate to the government that the Indians were hard-working, law-abiding and patriotic servants of the Crown, deserving to be assimilated in the mainstream of South African life, but the government kept reminding him, sometimes obliquely, that in fact their way of life made it necessary for the government to single them out and impose restrictive laws on them. As if his hands were not already full, he received an angry letter from his elder brother, Laxmidas, reminding him that he had been blatantly neglecting the Gandhi family back home, and accusing him of having severed links with the family. He added that even during Gandhi's stay in India he had wanted to separate from Laxmidas, as he seemed to dislike the joint family system. Laxmidas also made a demand for money.

Gandhi's reply, dated 27 May 1906, was addressed to Laxmidas Gandhi, 'respected brother'. 'I do not know what to say,' he wrote. 'You are prejudiced against me. There is no cure for prejudice.' He assured Laxmidas that he had no idea of separating from him or from any other member of the family and, at the same time, made no claim to any family property in India. In fact he did not claim anything as his own. All that he had was being utilized for public purpose, and was available to relations who devoted themselves to public work. Gandhi's two brothers had pooled their resources to finance his law studies in England in the hope that his earnings as a qualified barrister would be of benefit to the entire family. He had paid his brothers back more than they had spent. 'I could have satisfied your desire for money [as in the past] if I had not dedicated my all for public use . . . I am now not in a position to send you money as you desire.' But Laxmidas need have no financial insecurity. 'Rest assured that I will cheerfully assume the burden of supporting the family in case you pass away before me.'

Gandhi's eldest son, Harilal, now eighteen, who had returned to India to achieve personal independence, planned to get married; his father thought it was too early, and temporarily disowned him. Touching on the subject, he wrote to his brother: 'It is well if Harilal is married; it is also well if he is not. For the present at any rate I have ceased to think of him as a son.'

He did not remember having expressed a desire to separate from his brother when he was in India. 'But even if I did, my mind is now quite clear, my aspirations are higher and I have no desire for worldly enjoyments of any type whatever.' He looked upon the activity he was engaged in as 'essential to life', and was prepared to sacrifice his all, including his life, while thus engaged. 'I am now a stranger to fear.'

# TWELVE

# *Brahmacharya*

In the early part of 1906 the newspapers reported that the Zulus had come out in open rebellion in Natal. In the beginning Gandhi did not take serious note of the developments, and went about his legal and other work as usual. Suddenly, early in the summer, he decided to move to Natal, where he could organize the Indians against the Zulus. He still believed that the British Empire 'existed for the welfare of the world', and he wanted to take this opportunity of demonstrating his loyalty to the Crown. He gave his landlord the requisite notice, vacating the large suburban house never to return to it. He had, in the meantime, offered to raise, as in the Boer War, an Indian ambulance unit, and the offer was this time readily accepted by the authorities. He knew he would be away from Johannesburg for a long time, but decided to retain his law office. He had a trained staff who could more or less carry on the business in his absence. He took his family to Phoenix and then rushed to Durban to raise volunteers for his unit.

Through the medium of *Indian Opinion* Gandhi urged the Indians to fight on the side of the British. He insisted that the Europeans had always looked upon Indians as timid, devoid of any fighting prowess, and people who would run away at the slightest sign of risk. 'We cannot meet this charge with a written rejoinder,' he wrote in *Indian Opinion*. 'There is but one way of disproving it – the way of action.' He considered it sheer superstition that there was a greater risk to life in going to the battlefield. 'The Crimean War caused heavy casualties; yet it has been estimated that fewer men died from bayonet or bullet wounds than from sheer carelessness or perverse living,' he wrote. In the attack on Ladysmith 'more men died of fever than by Boer bullets'. Though Gandhi's ideas about war would undergo a sea change, he never lost his respect for the disciplined front-line soldier. He now made a clarion call to his compatriots to rise to the occasion and join the British in their campaign against the Zulus:

> Those who can take care of themselves and lead regular lives at the front can live in health and happiness. The training such men receive cannot be had elsewhere, that is, if they do not go to the front only to prove their valour or quench

their thirst for blood. A man going to the battle front has to train himself to endure severe hardship. He is obliged to cultivate the habit of living in comradeship with large numbers of men. He easily learns to make do with simple food. He is required to keep regular hours. He forms the habit of obeying his superior's orders promptly and without argument. He also learns to discipline the movement of his limbs. And he has also to learn how to live in limited space according to the maxims of health. Instances are known of unruly and wayward men who went to the front and returned reformed and able fully to control both their mind and their body.

For the Indian community, going to the battlefield should be an easy matter; for, whether Muslims or Hindus, we are men with profound faith in God. We have a greater sense of duty, and it should therefore be easier for us to volunteer. We are not overcome by fear when hundreds of thousands of men die of famine or plague in our country. What is more, when we are told of our duty, we continue to be indifferent, keep our houses dirty, lie hugging our hoarded wealth. Thus we lead a wretched life acquiescing in a long tormented process ending in death.

Why, then, should we fear the death that may perhaps overtake us on the battlefield? We have to learn much from what the whites are doing in Natal. There is hardly any family from which someone has not gone to fight the Kaffir rebels. Following their example, we should steel our hearts and take courage. Now is the time when the leading whites want us to take this step; if we let go this opportunity, we shall repent later. We therefore urge all Indian leaders to do their duty to the best of their ability.


Notwithstanding his professed loyalty to the Crown, it was not so much a call to wage a war against the Zulus as a cry against the Indians in South Africa – their lack of sense of duty, their indifferent attitude to sanitation, and their hoarded wealth. Discipline was a prerequisite for a man going to battle, and for this he received the proper training. It was in fact an appeal to the Indians to go to war even if only to acquire discipline, no matter if some lives were laid down in the process. He would have raised a contingent of Indian recruits for the Voluntary Force, but he could not convince the authorities that they would make good recruits. He contented himself with organizing a small ambulance corps consisting of twenty men. The Chief Medical Officer appointed him to the temporary rank of sergeant-major. There were three sergeants, one corporal, and fifteen privates under him.

When Gandhi and his corps got to Zululand, they discovered that the violent disturbances were the result of a no-tax campaign. The British had annexed Zululand in 1887, and the spirited Zulus – who were predominantly farmers – did not like the arrangement. The Natal government now mounted a punitive expedition to put down what it called the Zulu Rebellion. It was a strange little war against an unarmed people, and the British troops, mostly volunteers, behaved like amateurs. There were raids into Zulu territory, the kraals were set on fire, and there were public hangings and floggings of suspects. The Indians were for the most part attached to a swift-moving column of mixed cavalry and infantry which they had to follow on foot, sometimes forty miles a day, with stretchers on their shoulders. The wounded nursed by the corps were mostly Zulus, some of them 'friendlies' who had been inadvertently shot by the troops. In addition, Gandhi was required to compound and dispense prescriptions for the white soldiers. This brought him into close contact with many Europeans. But he derived special satisfaction from nursing the Zulus:

> It was no part of our duty to nurse the wounded after we had taken them to the hospital. But we had joined the war with the desire to do all we could, no matter whether it did or did not fall within the scope of our work. The good doctor [Dr Savage] told us that he could not induce Europeans to nurse the Zulus, that it was beyond his power to compel them and that he would feel obliged if we undertook this mission of mercy. We were only too glad to do this. We had to cleanse the wounds of several Zulus which had not been attended to for as many as five to six days and were therefore stinking horribly. We liked the work. The Zulus could not talk to us, but from their gestures and the expression of their eyes they seemed to feel as if God had sent us to their succour.

The 'rebellion' gave Gandhi a lot to think about. In contrast to the Boer War, this one was a man-hunt, 'not only in my opinion, but also in that of many Englishmen with whom I had occasion to talk'. Marching with or without the wounded through the hills and the dales of Zululand, Gandhi often fell into deep thought. Two ideas which had been floating in his mind became fixed: an aspirant after a life exclusively devoted to service must observe Brahmacharya, or celibacy, which was an ancient Hindu vow, and must accept voluntary poverty as a constant companion. Gandhi was determined to dedicate himself completely to public service, and 'I should find myself unequal to my task if I were engaged in the pleasures of family life and in the propagation and rearing of children.'

He discussed these matters with his stretcher-bearers, who gave him a sympathetic hearing, though none of them was eventually converted. He was getting impatient to take a final vow. The origin of his vow of celibacy goes back to 1900 when his son Devadas was born. He did not want any more children. Subsequently, Kasturbai began to keep indifferent health – she had anaemia – and another pregnancy might have endangered her life.

Despite these practical considerations the outstanding reason was the spiritual one. His concept of self-control can be traced to his student days in London. He was then greatly influenced by the ideas of A.F. Hills, president of the Vegetarian Society, who was a staunch opponent of birth control by artificial means. Gandhi reports in his autobiography:

> Mr Hill's opposition to those methods and his advocacy of internal effort as opposed to outward means, in a word, of self-control, had a great effect on me, which in due time came to be abiding. Seeing, therefore, that I did not desire more children I began to strive after self-control.

It was now Gandhi's deep conviction that 'without the observation of Brahmacharya service of the family would be inconsistent with service of the community. With Brahmacharya they would be perfectly consistent.' In essence, 'I could not live both after the flesh and the spirit.' On his return to Phoenix after four weeks of service in Zululand, he told Kasturbai of his pledge to forswear sex. An obedient wife, she accepted the decision as she had accepted all the other demands he had made on her. 'She was never the temptress,' Gandhi asserted; he determined the character of their intimate relations. The Brahmacharya, which Gandhi had been observing 'willy-nilly' since 1900, was sealed with a vow in the middle of 1906. 'The elimination of carnal relationship with one's wife seemed a strange thing,' he reports, 'but I launched forth with faith in the sustaining power of God.' He was thirty-six.

'I must confess that I had not then fully realized the magnitude and immensity of the task,' he wrote twenty years later. 'The difficulties are even today staring me in the face.' The control of senses 'in thought, word, and deed' – for that was what Brahmacharya meant to Gandhi – posed difficulties which appeared insurmountable. From time to time he would be assailed by agonizing conflicts, and his attitude toward the demanding physical body would be stern and unforgiving:

> God is striving for mastery over the body, and so is Satan engaged in a desperate struggle for it. When it is under the control of God, it is like a jewel. When it passes into the control of the Devil, it is a pit of filth. If engrossed in pleasure, gorging itself the whole day with all variety of putrefying food, exuding evil odours, with limbs employed in thieving, the tongue uttering unworthy words, and taking in unwholesome things, the ears hearing, the eyes seeing and the nose smelling what they ought not to, the body is worse than hell.

His vow of Brahmacharya was the most decisive break with his past. Without it he could not have practised his two principles: Satyagraha, or the force of truth and love, which was his own invention; and *ahimsa*, or nonviolence to all living things, which was an ancient Jain commandment. Gandhi summed up his conception of truth:

> This God whom we seek to realize is Truth. Or to put it another way, Truth is God. This Truth is not merely the Truth we are expected to speak. It is that which alone is, which constitutes the stuff of which all things are made, which subsists by virtue of its own power, which is not supported by anything else but supports everything that exists. Truth alone is eternal, everything else is momentary. It need not assume shape or form. It is pure intelligence as well as pure bliss. We call it *Iswara*, because everything is regulated by its will. It and the Law it promulgates are one. Therefore it is not a blind Law. It governs the entire universe.
>
> This Truth to be realized is also the God and the power that is the Satyagrahi's soul-force. Soul-force originates in that power. It attributes definite points of contact and linkage needed to bring that reality into practical relation with material life.

Gandhi's vow of Brahmacharya and his quest for truth led him to simplify further his style of living. In Johannesburg he took a small house in a distant suburb and furnished it with the minimum of furniture. There were two small bedrooms, a kitchen and an extra tiny room which was occupied by a young Indian worker. Soon the Polaks came to stay with him. There was no servant in the house, and everyone shared the housework. During these years in Johannesburg he continued his dietetic experiments, which initially of course were conducted mainly from a health and vegetarian's point of view. But once he took the vow, he pursued them purely from the standpoint of a Brahmachari, or celibate, partaking of such food as he believed was conducive to the maintaining of the vow. He found that complete fasting at regular intervals was an aid to self-restraint, and he thus began to accustom himself to such fasts.

# THIRTEEN

# A Mission to London

The Transvaal government considered that the existing laws did not provide adequately for preventing the surreptitious infiltration of Indians into the Transvaal and for deporting unauthorized residents. A draft Asiatic Law Amendment Ordinance was published in the *Government Gazette* on 22 August 1906, enjoining that all Indian men, women and children over eight years of age must submit to being fingerprinted, and should also receive a certificate of registration which they must carry with them at all times and produce on demand. Every Indian who failed to register would forfeit his right of residence in the Transvaal and render himself to fine, imprisonment or deportation, and failure or refusal to produce a certificate on demand by a police officer was also made a punishable offence. The police could enter any Indian house without a warrant and demand to see the certificate. Presentation of the certificate was a prerequisite for an Indian to establish any contact with a government office, even if he only wanted to apply for a bicycle licence.

At a small meeting of leading Indians, Gandhi said that he had never known legislation of this nature being directed against free men in any part of the world. 'If anyone came forward to demand a certificate from my wife,' exclaimed an irate Indian, 'I would shoot him on the spot and take the consequences.' Gandhi said it would not do to be hasty, impatient or angry. He explained that the ordinance was a deliberate attempt by the government to humiliate the ten or fifteen thousand Indians living in the Transvaal, and if it was passed into law, it would be the beginning of similar laws in other parts of South Africa. 'As it seems to me, it is designed to strike at the very root of our existence in South Africa,' he declared. 'It is not the last step, but the first step with a view to hounding us out of the country . . . But God will come to our help, if we calmly think over, and carry out in time measures of resistance, presenting a united front and bearing the hardship, which such resistance brings in its train.' All present at the meeting resolved to agitate publicly against the ordinance.

The Empire Theatre, popularly known as the 'Jewish Theatre', rented for the afternoon of 11 September 1906, was filled to the brim with about three thousand Indians from all over the Transvaal. There had never been a mass meeting like this in Johannesburg. It was organized largely through the efforts of H.O. Ally, a soda-water manufacturer, and the newly formed Hamida Islamic Society. An old and eminent Muslim businessman, Abdul Gani, the chairman of the Transvaal British Indian Association, presided.

The most important resolution passed by the meeting, the fourth, called for all present to 'vote' that they would rather suffer all penalties than submit to the 'Black Ordinance'. Gandhi explained the resolution to the meeting, and it was also explained in a variety of Indian languages. The crucial fourth resolution was moved by Haji Habib, another rich and influential businessman, speaking in Gujarati with English interpolations to assist the press. He then went on solemnly to declare with God as his witness that he would never submit to the law. The resolution was seconded by H.O. Ally. Another seconder was Dr. William Godfrey. The whole house took an oath with God as witness not to submit to the ordinance if it became law. Gandhi claimed later that he did not then understand 'all the implications of the resolutions I had helped to frame; nor had I gauged all the possible conclusions to which they might lead'. His moment came when Haji Habib, in Gandhi's words, 'imported the name of God into the resolution'. The 'vote' was thus in danger of becoming an oath, and an oath was, indeed, Gandhi's business, 'possessing as I did much experience of solemn pledges and having profited from them'. Haji Habib's solemn declaration had startled him and, accustomed as he was to tower above all other Indians in South Africa, he asked for the rostrum to explain to the meeting the implications:

We all believe in one and the same God, the differences of nomenclature in Hinduism and Islam notwithstanding. To pledge ourselves or to take an oath in the name of that God or with Him as witness is not something to be trifled with. If having taken such an oath we violate our pledge we are guilty before man and God . . . Everyone must only search his own heart, and if the inner voice assures him that he has the requisite strength to carry him through, then only should he pledge himself and then only will his pledge bear fruit . . .

We may have to go to jail, where we may be insulted. We may have to go hungry and suffer extreme heat or cold. Hard labour may be imposed upon us. We may be flogged by rude warders. We may be fined heavily and our property may be attached and held up to auction if there are only a few resisters left. Opulent today, we may be reduced to abject poverty tomorrow. We may be deported. Suffering from starvation and similar hardships in jail, some of us may fall ill and die. In short, therefore, it is not at all impossible that we may have to endure every hardship that we can imagine, and wisdom lies in pledging ourselves on the understanding that we shall have to suffer all that and worse.

If many of us fall back under storm and stress, the struggle will be prolonged. But I can boldly declare, and with certainty, that so long as there is even a handful of men true to their pledge, there can only be one end to the struggle, and that is victory . . . It is quite unlikely but even if everyone else flinched, leaving me alone to face the music, I am confident that I would never violate my pledge . . .

Gandhi often repeated this faith, and perhaps it is just a coincidence that at that time he was not familiar with Thoreau, who described civil disobedience in precise terms, as Gandhi understood it:

I know this well, that if one thousand, if one hundred, if ten men whom I could name – if ten *honest* men only – ay, if one *honest* man, in this state of Massachusetts, ceasing to hold slaves, were actually to withdraw from this copartnership, and be locked up in the county jail therefor, it would be the abolition of slavery in America. For it matters not how small the beginning may seem to be: what is once well done is done forever.

At the conclusion of Gandhi's speech, the chairman contributed his own sobering words and then the 'vote' was taken. All present raised their hands and took an oath with God as witness not to obey the proposed anti-Indian ordinance if it became law. Then they gave three cheers to the King Emperor Edward VII and sang 'God save the King'. A few hours later the Empire Theatre caught fire, and was completely destroyed.

The 'Black Ordinance' had not yet been enacted, and the Indian community, under Gandhi's guidance, decided to exhaust all legal and constitutional methods to prevent it from becoming law. Gandhi approached the government with memorials and petitions; a deputation waited on the Colonial Secretary, who in a formal reply vouchsafed that the government would consider its suggestion. The Legislative Council deleted the clause relating to women, but the rest of the ordinance was passed very much as originally drafted.

The Transvaal in 1906 was still a Crown Colony, and the royal assent to its legislative measures was by no means a formality. It was therefore decided to appeal directly to the British government. A delegation consisting of Gandhi and H.O. Ally was authorized to present a petition to Lord Elgin, the Secretary of State for the Colonies, urging that the assent to the ordinance be withheld. Ally had long experience of community work in South Africa, having been engaged in the defence of Indian rights before Gandhi set foot on the continent, and his Hamida Islamic Society was instrumental in making the Empire Theatre meeting a success. Ally was also the man who had seconded the crucial fourth resolution. He spoke

English and Dutch fluently.

Soon after boarding the SS *Armadale Castle*, Gandhi got on with the task of drafting the petition to be submitted to Lord Elgin. Ally was unable to assist much since he came down with a severe attack of rheumatism. Gandhi also experienced his own moments of pain – he had toothache.

Dr William Godfrey, an Indian Christian who had studied in Britain and had a British wife, was hopeful that he would he selected to accompany Gandhi to London. Godfrey, another seconder of the fourth resolution, took strong exception to Ally's selection and went to the extent of immediately conspiring with C.M. Pillay – an opponent of Gandhi – to instigate the Tamil and colonial-born resentment against the Gujarati leadership of Gandhi and the Muslims. A letter of protest bearing more than a hundred signatures was sent off to Lord Elgin on 1 October, before Gandhi had even left Johannesburg. It was followed two weeks later by another petition with two hundred and seventy signatures, The second petition declared:

> Mr Gandhi is a well-known professional political agitator whose mischievous political views upon the Indian question in South Africa has [*sic*] been productive of the greatest possible harm to the Indian community; and the anti-Asiatic Laws in the various colonies here has [*sic*] been the direct outcome of such views from which Mr Gandhi derived considerable financial advantage while the Indians in South Africa gained nothing . . . He is attempting to draw a sharp line of cleavage between Europeans and Indians . . . Mr Ally's Hamida Islamic Society is promoting the sovereignty of Abdul Hamid, Sultan of Turkey . . .

Gandhi was oblivious to the existence of this petition,but before he arrived in England the news of it had already reached the Colonial Office, registering a strong impression.

On 20 October 1906, Gandhi stepped ashore at Southampton, returning to England for the first time since leaving the country as a newly qualified barrister fifteen years before. It was during his student days that Dadabhai Naoroji had told him: 'You can come and have my advice whenever you like.' On the day of his arrival, Gandhi and some friends attended a meeting of the London Indian Society, where they met Naoroji, now eighty-one. Dadabhai Naoroji had been a past president of the Indian National Congress party and, in 1892, at the age of sixty-six, won election to the British Parliament as the Liberal member for Central Finsbury by a majority of three votes, thus earning for himself the nickname 'Narrowji'. He was now a member of the Indian National Congress's British Committee. Naoroji put Gandhi in touch with Sir William Wedderburn, the committee's chairman, and with Sir Henry Cotton, a fervent exponent in

Parliament of Indian nationalism. Wedderburn and Cotton were retired Indian Civil Service officials and former presidents of the Indian National Congress. Gandhi also met Sir Muncherjee Bhownaggree and Sir Lepel Griffin. Sir Muncherjee was the second Indian to sit in Parliament, and had held a seat for the Conservative Party from 1895 until the party's débâcle in the recent general election. Sir Lepel, a former administrator in India, had been for many years chairman of the East India Association in London. He was opposed to the political movements that were current in India, but loved India passionately, and was prepared to help Gandhi.

In London the delegation stayed at the prestigious and expensive Hotel Cecil, which has long since been pulled down. Located on the Strand just half a mile from Parliament and government offices, it was considered a good address from which to engage in political work involving high government officials and influential English politicians. Since it was imperative that the delegation should elicit as much attention as possible, an incessant stream of letters, requests for interviews and pronouncements on the detested ordinance were sent out. English friends and Indian students helped in dispatching, during a period of six weeks, some five thousand letters. Gandhi was so busy that he did not have the time to have his tooth extracted.

On 7 November Gandhi and Ally addressed a meeting of Liberal, Labour and other sympathetic Members of Parliament in the Committee Room of the House of Commons. Gandhi explained the grievances of the British Indians and the stand taken by them. Sir Henry Cotton, chairman of the meeting, protested against the treatment meted out to the British Indians in South Africa and claimed that the question had become one of imperial importance. The meeting unanimously supported the objectives of the delegation.

The following day a distinguished committee accompanied the delegation to present a petition to Lord Elgin at the Colonial Office. Gandhi felt confident that his success in getting together a group of such eminent gentlemen was bound to lend weight to the petition, for his committee included Sir Lepel Griffin, Sir Henry Cotton, Sir Charles Dilke, Dadabhai Naoroji, Sir Muncherjee Bhownaggree, Lord Stanley of Alderley, Sir Charles Schwann and Sir George Birdwood.

Lord Elgin made a short speech of welcome, and Sir Lepel Griffin introduced the delegates from the Transvaal. Sir Lepel outlined the case of the Indians, and explained that contrary to expectations the position of the Indians after the Boer War had worsened under British rule. Legislation of this sort was unheard of under the British flag. 'Indeed, with the exception of the Russian legislation against the Jews, there is no legislation comparable to this on the continent and England. If we want a similar case, we shall have to go back to the Plantagenets.' Then, rather surprisingly, Sir Lepel proceeded to blame the Jewish traders in the Transvaal, refugees from Russia and Germany, for the wretched condition of the Indians with whom they were in competition. He blamed these Jews and Syrians – 'the very offscourings of the international sewers of Europe' – for having provoked the government to introduce the legislation. The Indians, he asserted, were 'the most orderly, honourable, industrious, temperate race in the world, people of our own stock and blood'.

It is very likely that Gandhi felt embarrassed at Sir Lepel's virulent denunciation of the Jewish and Syrian refugees, but he deemed it fit not to make any comment on it. In his own short speech he urged that the British Indians ought to be treated as British subjects. He concluded by saying that the least that was due to the British Indian community was to appoint a commission which would consider the principle involved, the adequacy of the existing and the necessity for further legislation.

H.O. Ally made a brief appeal for justice. The Indians as loyal subjects were entitled to full protection. 'We have not asked for and we do not now ask for, political rights,' he said. 'We are content that the white man should be predominant in the Transvaal, but we do feel that we are entitled to all the other ordinary rights that a British subject should enjoy.' One by one all the members of the committee presented their views.

Lord Elgin, in his reply, reaffirmed the government's commitment to look after the interests of its subjects, but said it was his understanding that the registration of the Indians was being introduced for the benefit of the Indians themselves. He then touched on the subject of the thumb mark. Most of the Indians in South Africa at the time were illiterate and did not object to the practice of a thumb mark in lieu of signature. Elgin added that the previous pass had borne the thumb mark and therefore he could not see why the present requirement of fingerprints should be considered debasing. This statement drew Gandhi into a brief discussion:

GANDHI: It is the ten-finger mark.
ELGIN: Is it more debasing with ten fingers?
HENRY COTTON: It is required in the case of criminals.
ELGIN: I do not want to argue it.

Then Lord Elgin let Dr Godfrey's bombshell make its appearance. He said he had received telegrams from the Transvaal relating to a petition from British Indians that gave a completely different picture, for it was 'in opposition to the views which have been placed before me today'. He would, however, give the best consideration to the delegation's representation. Gandhi spoke briefly again, and concluded by saying that some of Lord Elgin's information was not correct and therefore 'nothing short of a commission would place our position accurately before your Lordship'.

Some days later a large deputation headed by Gandhi and Sir Lepel Griffin waited on John Morley, Secretary of State for India. Gandhi asked that a royal commission be appointed to enquire into the grievances of the Indians in South Africa. Morley, in his reply, pointed out that he could not recall an instance when a commission had solved a problem. He added that soon the Transvaal would have self-government, and it would then no longer be bound by any decisions made by the Secretary of State for the Colonies. Gandhi was aware of this, but still hoped that if the British government put enough pressure on the rulers of the Transvaal things might improve for the Indians. John Morley was sympathetic, and offered 'as much support as I find myself able to give'.

A second meeting of the Members of Parliament was held on 26 November, and the following day a deputation called on the Prime Minister, Sir Henry Campbell-Bannerman, to apprise him of the gravity of the situation in the Transvaal. The Prime Minister assured the parliamentarians that he 'did not approve of the ordinance, and would speak to Lord Elgin'. That day Gandhi had an appointment to see Winston Churchill, who was then the Under Secretary of State for the Colonies. It was a friendly meeting and Churchill promised to do all he could, but he cautioned Gandhi that on achieving self-governing status, the new government in the Transvaal would pass an ever harsher law. It was the only meeting between Churchill and Gandhi.

Two days later Gandhi invited friends and well-wishers of the British Indians in South Africa to a farewell breakfast. He had done everything possible to present the case before the responsible authorities, and 'truth and justice are on our side'. The delegation left England on 1 December, full of hope.

# FOURTEEN

# Birth of Satyagraha

When the RMS *Briton* touched at Madeira, two telegrams, one from Louis Ritch in London, the other from Johannesburg, awaited Gandhi, with the news that the ordinance had been refused assent by Lord Elgin. 'This was more than we had hoped for,' he wrote in his notebook. 'But God's ways are inscrutable. Well-directed efforts yield appropriate fruit.' In this mood of euphoria, the delegation arrived at Cape Town on 20 December.

It soon became evident that Lord Elgin had employed a 'trick'. He had notified the Transvaal Commissioner in London that the King would disallow the registration ordinance. But since Transvaal would cease to be a Crown Colony on 1 January 1907, it could re-enact the ordinance, and royal approval would then be no more than a formality. In fact the self-government of the Transvaal would be in a position to legislate without royal assent. Gandhi condemned this as a 'crooked policy'.

In the general election in the Transvaal on 20 February, the *Het Volk* party, led by Louis Botha, emerged victorious. On 21 March the Transvaal Parliament was formally opened, and Botha sworn in as the colony's first Prime Minister. J.C. Smuts was the Colonial Secretary in the new government, thus becoming responsible for the 'Asiatic question'. At the first session of the newly constituted legislature, the government introduced an Asiatic law amendment bill which was in essence the same piece of legislation disallowed by the British government a few months earlier. The bill was rushed through all its stages within twenty-four hours. The law was passed on 22 March, received the royal assent, which was a pure technicality, in May, and took effect from 1 July. Thereafter all Indians were required to register under it by 31 July.

In the meantime Gandhi's brother Laxmidas wrote to him after a long silence. He reminded his younger brother that he was failing in his duty towards the family. Mohandas should not 'aspire to be wiser than our father' and must support the family as Laxmidas did. Gandhi's long letter to his brother, written in the last week of April 1907 should be quoted at length, since it clearly indicates the crystallization of his ideas, particularly his concepts of the word 'family', nonpossession and service. In this letter he no longer addresses Laxmidas as 'respected brother'.

Respected Sir,

I have received your letter. I wish to answer it with the utmost calmness and as fully as possible. I shall first put my thoughts before you as they come to my mind, and then answer your questions.

I am afraid our outlooks differ widely and I see no possibility, for the present, of their being reconciled. You seek peace and happiness through money. I don't depend on money for my peace; and for the moment at any rate my mind is quite calm and able to stand any amount of suffering.

Like you, I too believe in the old traditions, but there is a difference in our beliefs. For you believe in age-old superstitions, while I not only do not but consider it sinful to believe in them.

You desire to attain *moksha*, so do I. Nevertheless, your notion of that state seems to be widely different from mine. Though I have the highest regard for you, untainted by any mean or selfish thought, you harbour hatred for me in your mind. The reason for this, as I see it, is that you are overcome by attachment and maintain relationships for selfish ends. Though you do this unconsciously, the result is practically the same as I have indicated. If you have really got to the stage of striving for *moksha*, you should remain calm and unperturbed and forget all about me, even if I am extremely sinful and may be deceiving you. But you are not able to do so because of your excessive attachment. This is what I believe; but if I am wrong in holding this belief, I prostrate myself at your feet and beg to be forgiven.

I fail to understand what you mean by the word 'family'. To me, the family includes not only the two brothers but the sister as well. It also includes our cousins. Indeed, if I could say so without arrogance, I would say that my family comprises all living beings: the only difference being that those who are more dependent on me, because of blood relationship or other circumstances, get more help from me. Hence it was that I took out an insurance policy in my wife's favour. And this I did because of your bitter letters to me when I was in Bombay and in order to escape your imprecations in case the responsibility for [supporting] my wife and children fell on you, as I was at the time engaged in helping the plague-stricken. Though I am myself against insurance, I took out an insurance policy for these and other reasons. If by any chance you die before me, you may be sure that I shall myself [serve as] an insurance policy for your wife and children. I beseech you to feel secure on this account. I would cite the case of Raliatbehn in this context.

If [sister] Raliat does not stay with you, I do not consider that to be due to any fault of mine, but hold your nature responsible. I would humbly remind you that mother was not happy with you, nor at any time were any of the other relatives.

As to your demand for a hundred rupees a month, I must say that I see neither the means at present nor the need of meeting it. I run the Phoenix Press with borrowed money. Moreover, I may have to go to gaol in the course of the struggle here against the new Ordinance. In that case I may become poorer still. This will come about in a month or two. If, however, the condition here improves during the next few months and I am free from trouble, I shall try to send you the money you have asked for by money order with the sole intention of pleasing you.

I do agree that you and Karsandas have [the right to] a share in my earnings. But I spend much less on my personal enjoyment than you do [on yours]. My object in staying here was not to make money but to serve the people; hence I deem it my duty to use for the benefit of the people whatever is left over after meeting the expenditure on the family here. So please don't think that I am making money here. At this point I would remind you that between you two brothers I have already paid nearly Rs. 60,000. I cleared all the debts while I was there; and you told me that no more money was wanted. It was only after this that I began spending money here. I handed over all my savings in Natal to you; and I have not kept a penny for myself either from that amount or from my sub-sequent earnings. From this you will see that I have paid back much more than the Rs. 13,000 spent on me during my stay in England. In saying this I do not mean to suggest that I have done you a favour. I only state the bare facts to pacify your anger.

I shall now answer your questions. These I return herewith.

1. The object of sending me to England was that we, all the three of us, might thereby maintain the status of our father more or less, be well off and enjoy the good things of life.

2. The risk was indeed great as we had decided to stake whatever we had on my education.

3. As those who had promised to help us did not keep their word, you worked hard, and even at the cost of your health, ungrudgingly gave me as much money as I asked for. This shows your magnanimity and your affection for a younger brother . . .

4. I must say with deep sorrow that, on account of your extravagant and thoughtless way of life, you have squandered a lot of money on pleasures and on pomp and show. You kept a horse and carriage, gave parties, and spent money on selfish friends; and some money was spent in what I consider immoral ways.

5. I do not remember to have sold [the ornaments] secretly without your knowledge; even if I had done so, I do not mind it . . .

6. As for getting the jewellery made afresh, I will not do so, as I consider it a sin. When I refuse to get the jewellery made, it means that my ideas about such things have substantially changed.

7. I am not the master of my earnings, since I have dedicated my all to the people. I do not suffer from the illusion that it is I who earn; I simply believe that God gives me the money for making good use of it.

8. I do recognize your [right to a] share in all my earnings; but since there is no such thing as an income for me now, what can I send you?

9. I am not spending your share [on myself]; but I use all the money that God gives me for the public good. If anything is left over after what has been used for this purpose, I would like to send you all of it, not just your share of it.

I revere you as you are my elder brother. Our religion bids us treat our elders with veneration. I implicitly believe in that injunction. But I have greater regard for truth. This too is taught by our religion. If you find anything objectionable in what I say, please accept my assurance that I have answered all your questions with the greatest regard for truth, and not in order to hurt you or be rude. Formerly, there was no difference of opinion or misunderstanding between us, hence you had affection for me. Now you have turned away from me because my views have changed, as I have said. Since you consider this change has been for the worse, I can quite understand that some of my answers will not be acceptable to you. But as the change in my ideas is due to my pursuit of truth, I am quite helpless. My devotion to you remains the same as before; it has simply assumed a new form. All this I shall explain to you most humbly and at length some day when we meet and if you want me to tell you about it. But I am unable to say when I can leave this country because of the peculiar circumstances and my several obligations here.

Do please believe me when I say that I have written all this with the best of intentions. If you do that, your displeasure will cease. Wherever you think that I am erring, please bear with me . . .

On the political front, Gandhi and his followers, stigmatizing the recently passed law as the 'Black Act', formed the Passive Resistance Association (later called the Satyagraha Association), and refused to register under its auspices. Public meetings were held, and at every meeting the political situation was explained and the oaths of resistance were administered afresh.

The government had definite plans to carry out the registration, district by district. On 1 July a permit office was opened in Pretoria. The Indian pickets went from house to house and explained to the people the precise meaning of registration. All over Pretoria posters, screaming protest, made their appearance: 'Boycott the permit office – By going to jail we do not resist, but suffer for our common good and self-respect – Loyalty to the King demands loyalty to the King of Kings – Indians be free!' The boycott was more or less complete.

Permit offices were opened, one after another, in all the Indian locations – Germiston, Pietersburg, Krugersdorp, Volksrust, Johannesburg and elsewhere. Volunteers assigned the job of picketing the registration offices were provided with badges, and each group of pickets was under the command of a captain. They were strictly instructed not to be impolite to any Indian taking out a permit. These volunteers, mostly boys aged between twelve and eighteen years, were to obey the police and, if arrested, go to the police station quietly and peacefully. And if an occasion arose when they were subjected to police brutality, they would suffer in silence.

On 31 July, the last day of registration, a mass meeting was held outside the mosque in Pretoria where two thousand resisters, representing Indians all over the Transvaal, sat on the ground and listened to speakers who were seated on a small platform. Yusuf Ismail Mian, acting chairman of the British Indian Association, presided. On the advice of General Botha, William Hosken, a member of the Transvaal Assembly, and considered to be a friend of the Indian community, met Gandhi in the morning and expressed his desire to address the meeting. 'You know I am your friend, I need scarcely say that my feelings in this matter are with you,' Hosken told the meeting. 'General Botha entertains a feeling of respect for you and understands your sentiments, but he says he is helpless. All the Europeans in the Transvaal unanimously ask for such a law, and he himself is convinced of the necessity for it . . . Now that the Indians' opposition has failed and the law has been passed, the community must prove their loyalty and love of peace by submitting to it . . . My own advice to you also is, that you should comply with the general's message. I know the Transvaal government is firm regarding this law. To resist it will be to dash your head against a wall.'

Gandhi translated Hosken's speech to the audience, then put them on their guard on his own behalf: 'If we submit to the law, there is no guarantee that this legislation will be final. The natural consequences of such legislation would be segregation in locations and finally expulsion from the country.' Gandhi was loudly applauded, and Mr Hosken retired amid cheers.

There were some bitter speeches to come. Ahmed Kachalia, a Muslim trader, said that the Transvaal government, however powerful, could not do more than enact this law. They could imprison the resisters, confiscate their property and deport them. 'All this we will bear cheerfully, but we cannot simply put up with the law.' Red-faced and shaking with anger, he proclaimed: 'I swear in the name of God, that I will be hanged, but I will not submit to this law!' Gandhi smiled. He thought Kachalia was overacting. Later he came to realize that he had meant what he said.

As the struggle advanced, Gandhi found the name 'passive resistance' inadequate to express its real meaning, since it was being looked upon as a 'weapon of the weak'. Moreover, he wanted an Indian name for this basically Indian movement. He offered a prize in *Indian Opinion* for the best suggestion. Maganlal Gandhi, who lived on Phoenix Farm, suggested 'Sadagraha,' or 'Firmness in a good cause'. But Gandhi adopted a slightly different word, 'Satyagraha': 'Truth (*satya*) implies love, and firmness (*agraha*) engenders and therefore serves as a synonym for force. I thus began to call the Indian movement "Satyagraha", that is to say, the Force which is born of Truth and Love or non-violence.'

The registration officers moved from town to town, which in fact was an exercise in futility. A mere five per cent of the Indian community took out 'the bond of slavery', though the limit for registration was extended again and again.

On 8 November, three weeks before the extended last day for registration, one Pandit Ram Sundara was arrested at Germiston for 'unlawfully entering and remaining in the Transvaal' after expiry of his temporary permit. The real reason for his arrest became clear during his trial – he was the captain of the Indian pickets in Germiston and had made a number of spirited speeches urging Indians to disobey the law. He 'wore a brave look and was endowed with some gift of the gab'. He knew a few Sanskrit verses by heart, and this had earned him the title of 'Pandit' (learned man). He refused to be bailed out, though several of his compatriots had offered to stand security for him, and for this reason he was hailed as a hero. He was sentenced to one month's imprisonment. The government meant his sentence as a warning, but he was led to jail by a a celebrating crowd.

The propaganda advantages to be derived from Ram Sundara's sentence were enormous. It was marked by the closure of all stores for a day. Telegrams were sent to people in high places against the travesty of justice. Gandhi could not praise him enough in the pages of *Indian Opinion*. 'Panditji has opened the gate of our freedom.' Ram Sundara was given a separate cell in the European wing of the prison and was permitted to receive visitors and to discuss the prevailing situation. When Gandhi came to interview him in his cell, he said that his only sorrow was that he had not been sentenced to hard labour. After his release he was garlanded and fêted. He became the envy of his community and famous all over South Africa. The government lost no time in issuing an order that he must leave the Transvaal within seven days or face further imprisonment. Suddenly he decided that he did not want to be part of the struggle any more, and taking his family with him he left for Natal. The Indian community was appalled.

Gandhi had regarded Ram Sundara as the embodiment of courage and sacrifice and a comrade who would give him a helping hand in the struggle ahead. The manner of his departure was certainly not conducive to the strength of the resistance movement. Gandhi was furious, and delivered an uncharacteristically venomous attack on Ram Sundara in the columns of *Indian Opinion*:

As far as the community is concerned, Ram Sundara is dead as from today. He lives to no purpose. He has poisoned himself by his own hand. Physical death is to be preferred to such social death. He would have enjoyed undying fame if he had been killed in an accident at Germiston before the critical moment when he entrained for Natal. Having meanly betrayed the people of Germiston, his community, himself, and his family, he has fled like a coward in fear of imprisonment.

Gandhi's colleague, H.O. Ally, also left the Transvaal with his family when the time for the actual struggle came. Later Gandhi revealed: 'Ally could not continue to trust me fully because I was a Hindu.' Ally had written to Syed Ameer Ali, a member of the South Africa British Indian Committee, that Gandhi's campaign against the registration 'would ruin thousands of his [Ally's] co-religionists who are all traders while Hindus are mostly hawkers'.

Gandhi was well aware of the universal meaning of his crusade. 'Indians in the Transvaal will stagger humanity without shedding a drop of blood,' he wrote to the Johannesburg *Star*. 'It is because I consider myself to be a lover of the Empire for what I have learnt to be its beauties that, seeing, rightly or wrongly, in the Asiatic Law Amendment Act seeds of danger to it, I have advised my countrymen at all costs to resist the Act in the most peaceful, and shall I add, Christian manner.'

Meanwhile the Indians were determined to refuse to obey the Black Act. An exasperated Lord Selborne, the British High Commissioner, wrote to General Smuts: 'Mr Gandhi ardently desires martyrdom, and when a man ardently desires such a thing . . . one's natural instinct is to give it to him.'

Presently Gandhi was arrested and brought before the magistrates' court in Johannesburg; he asked for the heaviest penalty provided by the law, which was six months' hard labour and a fine of £500. The magistrate, however, not fully sharing Selborne's feelings, decided that an appropriate punishment would be two months' imprisonment without hard labour. Gandhi was promptly locked up in a cell in the courtroom. There for a moment he lost heart. What if his followers failed to fill the prisons in order to make the government's position untenable? In that situation 'two months would be as tedious as an age'. But he reprimanded himself for entertaining such thoughts:

How vain I was! I, who had asked the people to consider the prisons as His Majesty's hotels, the suffering consequent upon disobeying the Black Act as perfect bliss, and the sacrifice of one's all and of life itself in resisting it as supreme enjoyment! Where had all this knowledge vanished today? This second train of thought acted upon me as a bracing tonic, and I began to laugh at my own folly.

At the Johannesburg prison he changed into, for the first time, a soiled prison uniform and was locked up in a large cell – in the 'Negro Block'. Before long, laughing Satyagrahi prisoners began to descend on the prison – 150 of them, including a few Chinese, for they were also covered by the Black Act and fought side by side with the Indians.

There were many things about prison life in Johannesburg that annoyed and disturbed Gandhi– the food, overcrowding and poor ventilation - but on the whole he found it quite satisfactory, because there were few distractions and he had ample leisure for reading. He read the *Bhagavad Gita* in the morning and the Koran, in English translation, at noon. In the evening he read the Bible to a Chinese Christian fellow prisoner who wanted to improve his English. He also read Ruskin, Socrates, Tolstoy, Huxley, Plato's *Dialogues*, Carlyle's *Lives*, and Bacon's *Essays*. He had started translating a book by Carlyle and Ruskin's *Unto This Last* into Gujarati.

His pursuit of study was interrupted, however, when his friend Albert Cartwright, editor of the *Transvaal Leader*, came as an emissary from General Smuts, armed with a document spelling out, though vaguely, terms of settlement. The draft proposed that the Indians should register voluntarily, and not under any law, and that the details to be entered in the certificates should be settled by the government with the Indian community. It was also proposed that if the majority of Indians underwent voluntary registration, the government would repeal the Black Act and take steps to legalize the voluntary registration.

Gandhi consulted his fellow prisoners who too did not like the language of the draft, but agreed to the settlement if Smuts would accept his amendment. The draft was quite vague as to the condition which required the government to repeal the Black Act. Gandhi's amendments sought clarity on this point. Thambi Naidoo, a Tamil Satyagrahi with keen intelligence, and Leuing Quinn, president of the Chinese Association, joined Gandhi in signing the slightly amended draft, which was then handed to Cartwright.

A few days later, on 30 January 1908, Johannesburg's chief of police personally guided Gandhi from his prison cell to Pretoria for a meeting with General Smuts. The general received Gandhi with courtesy and congratulated him on the Indian community having remained firm even after his imprisonment. 'I could never entertain a dislike for you people,' he said. 'But I must do my duty.' He reiterated that all Europeans wanted the law and added, according to Gandhi: 'I have consulted General Botha also, and I assure you that I will repeal the Asiatic Act as soon as most of you have undergone voluntary registration.'

The meeting had begun at noon, and lasted about two hours. In the afternoon there was a cabinet meeting, and Gandhi waited in an anteroom.

It was a long wait. At about seven o'clock he was summoned to the general's office to learn that the agreement had received the cabinet's approval. Smuts rose. 'Where am I to go?' Gandhi asked. The general laughed and assured him: 'You are free this very moment. I am telephoning to the prison officials to release the other prisoners tomorrow morning. But I must advise you not to go in for many meetings or demonstrations.'

Gandhi explained that it would be necessary to hold meetings to explain the new regulations to the Indian community. 'Of such meetings,' said Smuts, 'you may have as many as you please. It is sufficient that you have understood what I desire in the matter.'

It was evening, and Gandhi had no money on him. Smuts's secretary gave him the train fare to enable him to catch the last train to Johannesburg.

Immediately on arrival in Johannesburg that evening, Gandhi called on Yusuf Mian, chairman of the British Indian Association, apprised him of the discussion he had had with General Smuts, and asked him to call a meeting to discuss the situation. Volunteers went out to summon all the Indians, and the meeting was held late that night outside a mosque, not far from Yusuf Mian's house. Despite the short notice, about a thousand people were present. A solitary hurricane lamp, placed on the speaker's platform, was considered sufficient to provide light.

Before the meeting, Gandhi explained the terms of the settlement to the leaders present at Yusuf Mian's residence. A few of them were not convinced about the wisdom of registering voluntarily before the Act was repealed. Gandhi reminded them that a Satyagrahi was different from the generality of men in this regard:

> A Satyagrahi bids good-bye to fear. He is therefore never afraid of trusting the opponent. Even if the opponent plays him false twenty times, the Satyagrahi is ready to trust him the twenty-first time, for an implicit trust in human nature is the very essence of his creed . . . If he submits to a restriction, he submits voluntarily, not because he is afraid of punishment, but because he thinks that such submission is essential to the common weal.

Gandhi told the small gathering of leaders that it did not matter whether or not there was any law in force. 'The government can't exercise control over us without our cooperation . . . We are fearless and free, so long as we have the weapon of Satyagraha in our hands.'

At the late-night meeting itself, he explained the nature of his agreement with General Smuts. It was a victory for the community; in future all registration would be on a voluntary basis. The Black Act would be repealed as soon as the Parliament met; and the freedom they had been yearning for would be granted to them. The responsibility of the community was, at the same time, enhanced by the settlement:

> We must register voluntarily in order to show that we do not intend to bring a single Indian into the Transvaal surreptitiously or by fraud . . . And it is only when we have thus worthily fulfilled our part that we shall reap the real fruit of our victory.

The majority of the Indians raised their hands and pledged to register. But one Pathan, Mir Alam, who had been Gandhi's client and had often gone to him for advice, made a great fuss about the fingerprints, saying that they were only required of criminals 'and that the struggle centred round them'. Yet now they were expected to give them. Gandhi replied that it would have been a sin to give them under the Black Act, but to do so under the altered circumstances was 'the hallmark of a gentleman'. The martial Pathan would have nothing to do with these Hindu subtleties. He accused Gandhi of selling out to General Smuts for £15,000. 'I swear with Allah as my witness,' he roared, 'that I will kill any man who takes the lead in applying for registration.' Gandhi calmly said that it was his 'clear duty' to take the lead in giving the fingerprints and added:

> Death is the appointed end of all life. To die by the hand of a brother rather than by disease or in some other way cannot be for me a matter of sorrow. And if even in such a case I am free from the thoughts of anger or hatred against my assailant, I know that that will redound to my eternal welfare, and even the assailant will later on realize my perfect innocence.

On 3 February 1908 Gandhi saw General Smuts in the presence of Mr Chamney, the registrar of Asiatics, and appealed to him to repeal the Transvaal Asiatic Registration Act. Afterwards Gandhi said that Smuts had agreed in Chamney's presence that he would do it if the Asiatics abided freely and frankly by the terms of the compromise.

A week later, Gandhi, accompanied by Yusuf Mian and Thambi Naidoo, set out from his office for the registration office, less than a mile away. Mir Alam and a few other Pathans were waiting for him. Asked where he was going, he offered them a true Bania deal: 'If you will go with me, I will first arrange that you receive a certificate with only two thumb-prints, and then I will take one for myself with all my finger-prints.'

He had scarcely finished speaking when Mir Alam, 'fully six feet in height and of a long and powerful frame', hit him on the head, knocking him unconscious, then, with his companions, proceeded to kick and beat him. Gandhi was finally rescued by passing Europeans, who managed to apprehend the fleeing Pathans and handed them over to the police. He was picked up and carried to a nearby office where he regained consciousness and agreed to be taken to the home of a friend and staunch supporter, the Reverend Joseph Doke, a Baptist minister. (Doke, with the publication a year later of *M.K.Gandhi – An Indian Patriot in South Africa*, became Gandhi's first biographer.) He was stitched up and forbidden to speak, but he insisted on being the first to register. Mr Chamney, the registrar, brought the papers to the house, and the patient, in considerable pain, gladly allowed himself to be fingerprinted. The gesture proved too much for Mr Chamney, who began to weep. 'I had often to write bitterly against him, but this showed me how man's heart may be softened by events.' Having performed the duty of getting himself fingerprinted, Gandhi's other concern was Mir Alam. He refused to testify against his assailants, but since there had been European witnesses to the assault, the Pathans were sentenced to hard labour. 'In my mind there was not the slightest anger or hatred for the assailants.'

Gandhi spent ten days at Doke's house recovering from his injuries. 'I never so much as felt that it was not my home, or that my nearest and dearest could have looked after me better than the Dokes.' They were good enough to extend 'uniform courtesy and consideration' to hundreds of people who dropped in to enquire after his health. Doke's little daughter, Olive, would stand at the door of his room and sing one of his favourite English hymns, 'Lead, Kindly Light'. 'The whole scene passes before my eyes,' he wrote years later, 'and the melodious voice of little Olive reverberates in my ears.'

After recovering, Gandhi tirelessly preached loyalty to his registration settlement. He stayed for a while with Henry Polak, and early in March took the train to Durban in order to explain the situation in the Transvaal to the Indians of Natal. He spoke at public meetings where, at times, he faced hostile audiences. He visited Kasturbai and the boys on Phoenix Farm, and spent most of his time there writing for *Indian Opinion*, justifying his settlement with Smuts for voluntary fingerprinting. But another shock was in store for him.

General Smuts introduced into legislature a bill validating the voluntary certificates, but not repealing the Black Act itself. Gandhi accused him not only of a breach of promise but also of behaviour unbecoming to a gentleman. Smuts flatly dismissed the accusation. Gandhi's critics taunted him for being credulous. He replied that what they called credulity was trust – the trust we must have in our fellow men. True, the trust had proved misplaced in this instance, but instead of brooding about the whole episode, the community must now consider calmly how to resume the struggle if the government persisted in its refusal to repeal the Black Act.

Gandhi met with Albert Cartwright, the mediator. 'Really I cannot understand this man [Smuts] at all,' said the shocked Cartwright. 'I perfectly remember that he promised to repeal the Asiatic Act. I will do my best, but you know nothing can move General Smuts when he has once taken up a stand.' Nothing could, indeed, move the general. In this extremely tense situation Gandhi wrote articles in *Indian Opinion* under the caption 'Foul Play', and called Smuts 'a heartless man'. A few months later Gandhi criticized the registrar of Asiatics in no uncertain terms for making a statement on oath, which Gandhi considered false:

> Mr Chamney has been less than a man in putting his signature before a Justice of the Peace to an affidavit that was made on oath to the effect that he was present on the interview on the 3rd day of February and General Smuts never promised repeal of the Act. I say that that affidavit is untrue. He not only listened to the promise made by General Smuts as to the repeal of the Act, but he repeated that promise to me; he mentioned that promise to me, if once, twelve times, and each time he said that General Smuts was going to play the game, that he was going to repeal the Act.

Writing of these events two decades later, however, he added a question mark to a chapter headed 'General Smuts's Breach of Faith?' and said:

> Even today, I look upon the incident as a breach of faith from the Indian community's standpoint. Nevertheless I have placed a mark of interrogation after the phrase, as in point of fact the general's action did not perhaps amount to an intentional breach of faith. It could not be described as a breach of faith if the intention was absent.

It appears probable that Smuts hoped and intended to repeal the Black Act and, without making any firm promise, said so to Gandhi, but later found himself unable to carry out his intention.

Gandhi at that time, however, was in no doubt at all that Smuts had deceived him and thereby given him good cause for resuming the struggle. The weekly *Indian Opinion* kept Indians fully informed of current events, and warned them of the almost certain failure of the voluntary registration. In view of the recent introduction of the new Asiatic bill through the legislature, a petition on behalf of the Indians was presented to the government. Smuts called the petition an 'ultimatum' because it prescribed a time limit for a reply, and it was made quite explicit that the only acceptable reply was the repeal of the Asiatic Act, failing which there would be a mass burning of certificates of voluntary registration. The ultimatum was to expire on the same day that the new Asiatic bill was to be carried through the legislature. On 16 August 1908, about three thousand Indians from all over the Transvaal gathered outside the Hamida Mosque in Johannesburg to hear their leaders, who included Yusuf Mian, Leuing Quinn, and, of course, Gandhi. A message was sent to the government saying that the burning of the certificates would be called off if the government would stop the passage of the new Asiatic bill. Members of the Transvaal Assembly, 'reddened with rage,' promptly 'unanimously' and 'enthusiastically' passed Smuts's new version of the bill. Shortly after four o'clock, as the business of the meeting was about to commence, a volunteer on a bicycle arrived with a telegram from the government announcing that the new Asiatic bill would be passed into law. The news was greeted with cheers.

In a long fighting speech, Gandhi told the assembled Indians that the burning of the certificates would possibly bring 'untold sufferings' on them, but it should be preferable to submitting to the new legislation. Had they not taken a solemn oath not to submit to the Asiatic Act? Whatever the suffering that might result, the dignity of Indians must be upheld. It was going to be a long struggle and they must be absolutely determined to face the difficult times ahead. If there was any Indian who had handed in his certificate to be burnt but wanted it to be returned to him, he could step forward and have it, and in so doing would be exhibiting 'a certain kind of courage'. He declared:

> I did not come out of the gaol before my time was up in order that I might leave the hardships that I was suffering there – personally, I was not undergoing any hardships whatever. It would be a far greater hardship to me to have to submit to indignity or to see a fellow-countryman trampled underfoot or his bread, to which he is justly entitled, taken away from him. I would pass the whole of my lifetime in gaol, and I say that in the House of God, the House of Prayer, and I repeat it that I would far rather pass the whole of my lifetime in gaol and be perfectly happy than to see my fellow-countrymen subjected to indignity and I should come out of the gaol.
>
> No, gentlemen, the servant who stands before you this afternoon is not made of that stuff, and it is because I ask you to suffer everything that may be necessary than break your oath, it is because I expect this of my countrymen, that they will be, above all, true to their God, that I ask you this afternoon to burn all these certificates.

Gandhi repeated his speech in Gujarati, then about two thousand registration certificates were heaped into a huge three-legged African cauldron which had been conspicuously placed on a raised platform. Paraffin was poured in and Yusuf Mian set the certificates ablaze amid a scene of wild enthusiasm. The crowds roared themselves hoarse, hats and caps were thrown in the air, and whistles were blown. For a considerable time it was impossible for any of the leaders on the platform to make themselves heard. The London *Daily Mail* correspondent in Johannesburg compared the scene with the Boston Tea Party. A party, indeed, it was, and Mir Alam, the Pathan who had tried to kill Gandhi, apologized publicly and received a warm handshake and assurance that there was no ill feeling. The burning of the registration certificates was the first of a series of public symbolic acts which Gandhi used throughout his life to further his causes.

The Asiatic Registration Amendment Act was gazetted on 2 September 1908. In the early months of its life, the colony passed an Immigration Restriction Act (Act 15 of 1907), which was ostensibly of general application, but was chiefly aimed at Indians. The Asiatic Act and the Immigration Act provided three penalties: fine, imprisonment and deportation. There was a provision in the Immigration Act to the effect that any person who was not conversant with a European language should be treated as a prohibited immigrant. It was decided by the Satyagraha Committee to test the right of educated Indians to enter the Transvaal. There were many Indians in Natal who possessed ancient rights of domicile in the Transvaal and who also had some knowledge of English.

On 18 August two prominent Natal traders, Sheth Daud Mohamed and Parsee Rustomji, arrived on the frontiers of the Transvaal and were arrested. However, after having been warned, they were deported without trial. Two weeks later they re-entered the Transvaal and were finally fined £50. The two Satyagrahis cheerfully elected to go to jail instead. More Indians from Natal followed and courted arrest. Some Transvaal Indians began to hawk without licences, resulting in many arrests in Johannesburg. Jails began to be filled, 'invaders' from Natal getting three months while the Transvaal hawkers' sentences varied from four days to three months.

Gandhi's eldest son Harilal had also, at his father's urging, plunged into the struggle against the government. Now about twenty, he had got married in India against his father's wishes. He was summoned to come to South Africa alone to begin his life of service to the people, but he brought his wife Gulab with him. Harilal had earlier spent a year in prison, and soon after his release he was given a sentence of seven days with hard labour for publicly hawking fruit without a licence. He was represented in court by his father, who offered no defence and characteristically asked the magistrate to hand down a severe sentence, adding that if a light sentence was passed his son would repeat the offence. The magistrate chose not to oblige Gandhi, and Harilal received a light sentence. On coming out of prison he repeated the offence, and was finally deported from the Transvaal.

Harilal missed his wife immensely. He was participating in the struggle because his father insisted upon it and because he considered it his duty, but soon he began to lose the will to continue any longer. He wrote to his father accordingly. Gandhi was furious: 'I see that you will have to undergo imprisonment for a long time.' He told Gulab that she should expect a long separation from her husband, for he would have to live in Johannesburg either in prison or actively participating in the Satyagraha movement. He assured her, however, that the separation from her husband offered some advantages:

> Be sure that if you give up the idea of staying with Harilal for the present, it will be good for both of you. Harilal will grow by staying apart and will perform his other duties. Love for you does not consist only in staying with you. At times one has to live apart just for the sake of love. This is true in your case. From every side, I see that your separation is for your benefit. But it can be a source of happiness only if you do not become restless owing to separation.

Before events could proceed further, Gandhi, while returning from Natal on 7 October, was unable to produce his registration certificate and refused to be fingerprinted on demand. He was arrested and a week later brought before a magistrate at Volksrust. He asked for the maximum possible punishment, which was three months' hard labour, but the magistrate handed down a £25 fine or two months' imprisonment with hard labour. Gandhi determined upon the latter alternative, considering himself 'the happiest man in the Transvaal'. In a message to *Indian Opinion* he wrote: 'Keep absolutely firm to the end. Suffering is our only remedy. Victory is certain.'

His first impression of the Volksrust jail was favourable. He approved of the tidy cells, the adequate lighting and ventilation. As part of the hard labour, he was forced to dig pits, break stones and work with road gangs, but as a true Satyagrahi he was content to suffer. Yet two weeks later when he was taken to Johannesburg jail to testify in a case that was coming up in the courts, he was horrified. All round him in the jail were Kaffirs and Chinese, the dregs of Johannesburg society, haggard and murderous, their gestures reeking of obscenity. He felt his life was in danger, and since they were all staring at him he reached for the *Bhagavad Gita* and began to read the passages that provide solace at difficult times. He had to make frequent appearances at the court, and thus ended up spending ten days in the Johannesburg jail. There was one incident when he was actually manhandled. After he had been a few days in this dreadful place, he was moved to another cell full of Indians, and this comforted him; but the Indians and the Kaffirs shared the same doorless lavatories. As soon as he occupied one of them there appeared a massive and fierce Kaffir who started abusing him and told him to get out. He answered that he would be out very soon, but the Kaffir did not accept this reply and promptly seized him, lifted him high in the air, and would have dashed him to the ground if he had not managed to get hold of the doorframe. 'I was not in the least frightened by this,' Gandhi wrote, narrating his jail experiences. 'I smiled and walked away; but one or two Indian prisoners who saw what had happened started weeping.'

He was glad to return to Volksrust, but a few days later he received disturbing news. Albert West telegraphed from Phoenix that Kasturbai had been taken ill again and was haemorrhaging. Some days before Gandhi's arrest she had undergone a gynaecological operation at Durban. The doctor and his wife had nursed her and allowed Gandhi to go to Johannesburg.

Gandhi, however, felt that his political duty was far greater than his duty to his wife. He calmly put aside the idea of paying the fine and walking out of the prison. He asked West to keep him informed, and wrote to Kasturbai a most touching but courageous letter:

I have received Mr West's telegram today about your illness. It cuts my heart. I am very much grieved, but I am not in a position to go there to nurse you. I have offered my all to the Satyagraha struggle. My coming there is out of the question. I can come only if I pay the fine, which I must not. If you keep courage and take the necessary nutrition, you will recover. If, however, my ill luck so has it that you pass away, I should only say that there would be nothing wrong in your doing so in your separation from me while I am still alive. I love you so dearly that even if you are dead, you will be alive to me. Your soul is deathless. I repeat what I have frequently told you and assure you that if you do succumb to your illness, I will not marry again. Time and again I have told you that you may quietly breathe your last with faith in God. If you die, even that death of yours will be a sacrifice to the cause of Satyagraha. My struggle is not merely political. It is religious and therefore quite pure. It does not matter much whether one dies in it or lives. I hope and expect that you will also think likewise and not be unhappy.

Although the hard labour schedule at Volksrust stretched to nine hours a day, there was still time, more so on Saturdays and Sundays, for reading and meditation. He completed the Gujarati translation of Ruskin's *Unto This Last* – the task which he had commenced during his first jail term – and read for the first time Thoreau's essay, *Civil Disobedience*, which reinforced the ideas he had already arrived at himself. 'From Thoreau and Ruskin,' he wrote, 'I could discover arguments in favour of our fight.' Gandhi glorified life in prison, emphasizing that one should consider oneself fortunate to be in jail where 'there is only one warden, whereas in ordinary life there are many . . . The prisoner has no anxiety to earn his daily bread . . . there is enough work to keep the body healthy . . . He is freed from vicious habits. His soul is thus free. He has time to pray to God. His body is restrained, but not his soul . . . The real road to happiness lies in going to jail and undergoing sufferings and privations there in the interest of one's country and religion.'

Gandhi, who had borrowed *Civil Disobedience* from the prison library, was delighted with the essay. For many years it was believed that he took the idea of Satyagraha from Thoreau. In a letter dated 10 September 1935, addressed to Mr P. Kodanda Rao of the Servants of India Society, Gandhi denied this claim. He wrote:

The statement that I had derived my idea of Civil Disobedience from the writings of Thoreau is wrong. The resistance to authority in South Africa was well advanced before I got the essay of Thoreau on Civil Disobedience. But the movement was then known as passive resistance. As it was incomplete I had coined the word Satyagraha for the Gujarati readers. When I saw the title of Thoreau's great essay, I began to use his phrase to explain our struggle to the English readers. But I found that even 'Civil Disobedience` failed to convey the full meaning of that struggle. I therefore adopted the phrase Civil Resistance. Non-violence was always an integral part of our struggle.

Henry David Thoreau (1817–66), poet and essayist, believed that it was more honourable to be right than to be law-abiding; that every individual ought to resist a tyrannical government; that a very small minority, even a single individual, could bring about a change in the government. He was opposed to the traditional concept of democracy. 'Why does [the government] not cherish its minority?' he asked. 'Why does it always crucify Christ?' He was a staunch opponent of negro slavery and individual 'slavery' to the church, and turned away from the polite artificiality of materialistic civilization to a life of simplicity in natural surroundings. In 1845 he commenced his experiment in 'extraordinary simplicity' of living, building with his own hands a hut at Walden Pond outside Concord, Massachusetts. He lived there a self-contained and joyous life, and gave in his *Walden* an account of his experiments.

Two years at Walden instilled in Thoreau much courage and inner strength to be free in isolation. When he returned to Concord, he could savour no freedom whatsoever inside the community, but he was determined not to 'lend myself to the wrong which I condemn'. He had negro slavery and Mexican invasion in mind when, in 1849, he refused to pay taxes and was jailed. He spent barely twenty-four hours inside, for a friend paid the tax for him, but the experience led him to present his provoking political essay, *Civil Disobedience*. Gandhi cherished the following excerpt from Thoreau:

> I saw that, if there was a wall of stone between me and my townsmen, there was a still more difficult one to climb or break through before they could get to be as free as I was. I did not feel for a moment confined, and the walls seemed a great waste of stone and mortar. They plainly did not know how to treat me, but behaved like persons who are underbred. In every threat and in every compliment there was a blunder; for they thought that my chief desire was to stand on the other side of the stone wall. I could not but smile to see how industriously they locked the door on my meditations which followed them out again without let or hindrance, and they were nearly all that was dangerous.
>
> As they could not reach me, they had resolved to punish my body; just as boys, if they cannot come to some person against whom they have a spite, will abuse his dog. I saw that the state was half-witted, that it was timid as a lone woman with her silver spoons, and that it did not know its friends from its foes, and I lost all my remaining respect for it and pitied it.

Thoreau had read the *Bhagavad Gita* and the Hindu *Upanishads*. The noted American reporter, Webb Miller, a long-time admirer of Thoreau asked Gandhi in 1931 while the Mahatma was in London for the Round Table Conference, if he had ever read Henry D. Thoreau. 'Why, of course, I read Thoreau,' replied Gandhi. 'I read *Walden* first in Johannesburg in South Africa in 1906, and his ideas influenced me greatly. I adopted some of them and recommended the study of Thoreau to all my friends who were helping me in the cause of Indian independence . . . There is no doubt that Thoreau's ideas greatly influenced my movement in India.'

Miller noted that Gandhi, a 'Hindu mystic', adopted from Thoreau the philosophy which was to affect millions of Indians and inspire them to defy the powerful British Empire. 'It would seem', Miller concluded, 'that Gandhi received back from America what was fundamentally the philosophy of India after it had been distilled and crystallized in the mind of Thoreau.' In a preface to *Hind Swaraj* printed in *Indian Opinion*, Gandhi stated: 'While the views expressed in *Hind Swaraj* are held by me, I have but endeavoured humbly to follow Tolstoy, Ruskin, Thoreau, Emerson and other writers, besides the masters of Indian philosophy.'

Gandhi came out of Volksrust prison on 12 December and found himself too engrossed in his work to rush to Kasturbai's bedside. But when her doctor telephoned and asked whether she could be permitted to have beef tea, he was so alarmed that he took the first train to Durban. The doctor calmly told him that he had already given her beef tea, and insisted that as long as Kasturbai was under his care he had the right to give her whatever food or medicines she needed: 'I cannot see her die under my roof.' Gandhi could not accept this explanation, but felt that Kasturbai must be consulted. She could have beef tea if she so chose. When she learned about the argument between her husband and the doctor, the emaciated patient settled it, saying to Gandhi: 'I will not take beef tea. It is a rare thing in this world to be born as a human being, and I would far rather die than pollute my body with such abominations.' She pleaded with him to remove her at once.

Gandhi was delighted, but was not fully aware of the risk of moving her to Phoenix in her present condition. 'I trusted in God, and proceeded with my task.' It was drizzling,and the ricksha journey to the railroad station gave him some anxious moments. She, however, reassured her husband: 'Nothing will happen to me. Don't worry.' At Phoenix, Albert West was waiting with a hammock, six bearers to carry her the two miles to the settlement, and a bottle of hot milk. Gandhi put her under his own hydropathic treatment, yet the haemorrhages persisted. He then asked her to give up salt and lentils. Kasturbai had not much faith in his remedies, but when he himself offered to give them up too, if that would help her, she agreed, for she knew that he could not be dissuaded. 'You are too obstinate,' she said. 'You will listen to no one.' Kasturbai's health began to pick up, the haemorrhages completely stopped, and Gandhi commented rather humorously, 'I added somewhat to my reputation as a quack.'

On his return to Johannesburg he was arrested again for failure to produce a registration certificate and sentenced on 25 February 1909, to a fine of £50 or three months' imprisonment with hard labour. He went back to Volksrust prison, but a week later, carrying a few possessions on his head and walking in torrential rain, was led to a train for Pretoria, where he spent the rest of his term in the recently built local penitentiary. Here again he managed to do much reading in his spare time. He received a gift of two religious books from General Smuts; he also read Stevenson's *Dr Jekyll and Mr Hyde*, Carlyle's *French Revolution*, some Emerson, Thoreau, Mazzini, Ruskin, Tolstoy and many Indian religious volumes.

Letters were few and far between in prison. Gandhi was allowed to write and receive one letter per month. On 25 March he chose to write to his second son, Manilal, 'because you have been nearest my thoughts in all my reading'. At seventeen, with virtually no formal education, Manilal worried about his future prospects. Now he was his father's agent on the farm and in *Indian Opinion*, and probably under considerable pressure. Gandhi wrote to his son that if he practised the three virtues of truth, *ahimsa* and Brahmacharya and if these virtues became part of his life, he would have completed his education as far as his father was concerned. He added:

Although I think that you are well able to bear all the burden I have placed on your shoulders and that you are doing it quite cheerfully, I have often felt that you required greater personal guidance than I have been able to give you. I know too that you have sometimes felt that your education was being neglected. Now I have read a great deal in the prison. I have been reading Emerson, Ruskin and Mazzini. I have also been reading the Upanishads. All confirm the view that education does not mean a knowledge of letters but it means character building. It means a knowledge of duty. Our own [Gujarati] word literally means training. If this is the true view, and it is to my mind the only true view, you are receiving the best education-training possible. What can be better than that you should have the opportunity of nursing mother and cheerfully bearing her ill temper, or than looking after Chanchi [the nickname of Harilal's wife, Gulab] and anticipating her wants and behaving to her so as not to make her feel the absence of Harilal or again than being guardian to Ramdas and Devadas? If you succeed in doing this well, you have received more than half your education . . . This does not mean that you should not receive instruction in letters. That you should and you are doing. But it is a thing over which you need not fret yourself. You have plenty of time for it and after all you are to receive such instruction in order that your training may be of use to others.

Remember please that henceforth our lot is poverty. The more I think of it the more I feel that it is more blessed to be poor than to be rich. The uses of poverty are far sweeter than those of riches . . . Do give ample work to gardening, actual digging, hoeing, etc. We have to live upon it in future. And you should be the expert gardener of the family. Keep your tools in their respective places and absolutely clean . . . I hope you are keeping an accurate account as it should be kept of every penny spent for the household.

# FIFTEEN

# The Petitioner and the Terrorists

Having completed his three-month sentence, Gandhi was released from Pretoria jail at 7.30 a.m. on 24 May 1909. Usually prisoners were released at 9 a.m., but the government hoped to prevent a demonstration. He told a crowd of about a hundred Indians waiting outside that he would rather suffer imprisonment for the sake of the cause and, therefore, could derive no pleasure from being released. At Park Town, on his way to Johannesburg, he was greeted at a meeting with a new slogan: 'Salute to the King of Hindus and Muslims'. Gandhi said he was their servant and added: 'My aspirations will be fulfilled only if I have to lay down my life in the very act of serving the community.'

Meanwhile it was becoming increasingly difficult for Gandhi to hold his followers. The deportations, imprisonments, confiscation of properties and a number of other difficulties had blunted the edge of the Satyagraha movement. The worst setbacks did not shake his faith in victory, but now a bigger danger loomed: the governments of Natal, the Transvaal, the Cape Colony and the Orange Free State all became preoccupied with the establishment of the federal Union of South Africa. General Botha and General Smuts were expected in London shortly. It was felt that the Union would incorporate the anti-Indian tendencies of the individual colonies and that consequently the Indians would be in a far worse situation than ever before. Since the new Union was to have dominion status within the British Empire, it was resolved that a two-man deputation, composed of Gandhi and a Muslim, Sheth Haji Habib, should be sent to London to voice the interests of South African Indians, though Gandhi feared that 'their small voice [would be] drowned in the loud roar of British and Boer lions'. Gandhi and Habib were given first-class tickets on the SS *Kenilworth Castle*, which sailed from Cape Town on 23 June.

The sending of the deputation was not Gandhi's idea. It was virtually a concession to other elements in the community, who believed that he was relying too much on passive resistance and not making use of the constitutional methods of petition. Gandhi's own feeling on the subject was that the prisoners would provide more strength to the community than the deputation. The names of Ahmed Kachalia, chairman of the British Indian Association, and V.A. Chattiar, chairman of the Tamil Benefit Society, were also originally proposed to be included in the deputation but in the meantime they were arrested. 'I am sure Mr Kachalia and Mr Chattiar will speak for us more eloquently from gaol than they could have done in England,' wrote Gandhi. In any event Gandhi was this time going to London with far more impressive credentials than before, and the world was becoming increasingly conscious of the plight of the Indians because of the dramatic nature of the Satyagraha movement.

Gandhi and Habib arrived at Southampton on 10 July. Apart from a Reuters' man, there was no one to receive them there or in London. Leaving their baggage at the Hotel Cecil, they called on a surprised Louis Ritch at his office. He had heard of the arrest of Kachalia and Chattiar, the other two members of the deputation, and had assumed that nobody would be coming for a while. They all set to work immediately, calling on Sir Muncherjee Bhownaggree and writing to Lord Ampthill. The next day Gandhi and Habib moved into rooms in the Westminster Palace Hotel, one of the older luxury hotels, opposite Westminster Abbey, and close to the Houses of Parliament.

On the way to London, when pressed for details of his plans, Gandhi repeated that 'we shall naturally be very largely guided by Lord Ampthill's committee in London'. To speak of 'Lord Ampthill's committee' was somewhat deceptive, since the South Africa British Indian Committee had been established by Gandhi himself. Moreover, Lord Ampthill, its present president, who appears to have been recruited to the committee by Bhownaggree, much preferred to work alone behind the scenes, resisting most suggestions to call the members together.

Arthur Oliver Russell, the second Baron Ampthill, was born in the same year as Gandhi, and at the age of thirty was appointed Governor of Madras. Five years later he became the acting Viceroy of India. Now he had returned from India, and his activities were confined to the House of Lords and the family estate in Bedfordshire. During his visits to London he would act as Gandhi's intermediary with powerful men in the Foreign Office and the Colonial Office. He was no supporter of the Indian National Congress or any form of Indian nationalism, and from 1909 to 1935 used his seat in the Lords to oppose any reforms for India in the direction of self-government. However, in 1909 he wholeheartedly helped Gandhi, as evidenced by some sixty letters exchanged between the two.

Two weeks after their first meeting, Lord Ampthill reported to Gandhi that he had had long talks with Lord Crewe, the Secretary of State for the Colonies, and Lord Selborne, the High Commissioner for South Africa, and that he had 'approached' Lord Morley, the Secretary of State for India, General Smuts and others. He also said that Lord Curzon, the former Viceroy, was working with him. During his last visit to England in 1906 Gandhi had established contacts with men in high positions, but Lord Ampthill suggested that all talks with General Botha, General Smuts and the British government should be held in private, with the two ex-Viceroys acting as the deputation's spokesmen, for such meetings permitted greater scope for diplomacy. There should be no newspaper articles and no public discussions. But after meeting Lord Morley and Lord Curzon, it became quite clear to Gandhi that nothing concrete would ever come out of these private meetings.

In the following few weeks Gandhi met many British journalists, Members of Parliament and powerful men in the government, but there was little to show for his continued presence in London. In a letter to a friend he said:

> Everyone seems to be wrapped in his own thoughts. Those in power have scarcely any sense of justice for its own sake. They care for maintaining and magnifying their position. Had it been a question of justice, pure and simple, it would have been decided long ago. To drudge in this way, to waste one's whole precious day in trying to see at the most one or two persons, to spend money on all this, goes against the grain of a Satyagrahi. Far better to go to jail and suffer. If our demand is granted, it would be more on account of the hardships endured by those who have gone to jail than as a result of the labours of the deputation; and if we fail, the reason would clearly be that we have not suffered enough.

Ampthill's diplomatic activity continued but, in the circumstances, proved unproductive. Smuts told Ampthill that he could grant some minor concessions, which included the entry of up to six 'approved Asiatics' per year on temporary permits only, but was unwilling to repeal the Asiatic Act or the Immigration Act. He refused to remove the racial bar from the law. In a communication to Lord Crewe on 26 August, Smuts observed:

> We cannot recognize in our legislation the equal rights of all alike to emigrate to South Africa. Under our special circumstances we leave the door as wide as possible to white immigrants, but we could never do the same to Asiatic immigrants.'

Ampthill strongly advised the delegation to accept the minor concessions offered by General Botha and General Smuts. 'We cannot have everything that we desire,' he said. 'This is their final offer. If you ask for more you will only be inviting trouble for yourself as well as for your people . . . If you wish to fight for principle's sake, you could do so later.'

Haji Habib found it proper to accept the offer 'on behalf of the concili-
ation party'. The fight for the principle could be taken up later. 'The party
I represent constitutes the majority of the community, and it also holds the
major portion of the community's wealth.' Habib spoke in Gujarati and
Gandhi translated the statement. He thanked Ampthill for his efforts, and
then speaking on behalf of the Satyagrahis, said:

> The Indians for whom I speak are comparatively poor and inferior in numbers,
> but they are resolute unto death. They are fighting not only for practical relief
> but for principle as well. If they must give up either of the two, they will jettison
> the former and fight for the latter.

In his reply, Lord Ampthill said:

> Yours is a righteous struggle, and you are fighting with clean weapons. How can
> I possibly give you up? But you must recognize my delicate position. The suf-
> fering, if any, must be borne by you alone, and therefore it is my duty to advise
> you to accept any settlement possible in the circumstances. But if you, who have
> to suffer, are prepared to undergo any amount of suffering for principle's sake,
> I must not only not come in your way but even congratulate you. I will there-
> fore continue as President of your Committee and help you to the best of my
> ability.

Henry Polak had been sent to India to familiarize the public there with the
South African situation. After all, 'it is for India that we have been suffering'. Every week Gandhi wrote to him, but the letters were chiefly about
Polak's relatives in London and the deputation's uneventful meetings with
the British authorities. 'We will be having a brief meeting with Lord
Crewe; Lord Ampthill is still at work; I am tired of repeating that there is
nothing to report,' he wrote in despair.

By the end of August, Gandhi had started feeling that there was no purpose in staying in London any longer, and he let his friends know that the
deputation would soon return to South Africa. However, encouraged by
Ampthill, he made another appointment with Lord Crewe, the Secretary
of State for the Colonies, for 16 September. Gandhi suggested entry of a
limited number of educated Indians but stressed that he objected to the
stated limit of six which, in fact, incorporated racial discrimination into the
law. He proposed that the numerical limit, even of six Indians, should be
set by the Governor, administrative control being the responsibility of the
immigration officers, thus keeping it out of the law books. After the meeting Gandhi wrote to Ampthill that Crewe would press his proposal on

Smuts, but pointed out that his own and Crewe's minutes as to what Crewe was to cable Smuts were at variance with each other. It would be some seven weeks before the situation would be clarified, and during this time Gandhi was effectively immobilized. The negotiations, which had been taken out of his hands, were presumably under way, and he could not therefore launch a campaign through the press, public meetings or Parliament. As it turned out, Crewe had decided not to present Gandhi's proposals to the Colonial Office. His proposed solution was based on the Australian Acts and Regulations and these, it should be noted, became the basis of South Africa's Immigration Regulation Act of 1913.

Crewe, whose encounters with Gandhi must have caused him some difficult moments, spoke of Gandhi as 'a quite astonishingly hopeless and impracticable person for any kind of deal, but with a sort of ardent, though restrained honesty which becomes the most pigheaded obstinacy at the critical moment'.

On 10 July, when Gandhi arrived in London, the newspapers were still discussing the assassination of Sir Curzon Wyllie nine days before. The murdered man, who had been the government's prosecutor in the cases against some terrorists in Bengal, was presently a senior official in the office of the Secretary of State for India, and was shot by a young Indian at the Imperial Institute in South Kensington. A Parsi doctor who had flung himself between the assassin and the victim also died instantly. Gandhi, like other moderate Indian leaders, felt that the killing of Sir Curzon Wyllie had done India much harm, and he thought that his deputation's efforts too had received a setback.

The murderer, Madanlal Dhingra, a Punjabi engineering student in London, was arrested on the spot. He represented himself as an Indian patriot who had committed the murder to avenge the rule of terror perpetrated by the British in India, and insisted that he had acted alone.

In fact Dhingra belonged to a revolutionary group led by a student at Gray's Inn, Vinayak Damodar Savarkar, a short, slender man, with broad cheekbones. Savarkar, who was then twenty-six, managed a private hostel for Indian students called India House, in the London suburb of Highgate. Most of the approximately thirty students who lived there were under his strong influence. It was widely suspected that he was behind the recent assassination. When a few days after the event leaders of the Indian community held a memorial meeting to pass a resolution condemning Dhingra, one voice shouted, 'No!' It was Savarkar, who claimed that the meeting had no right to pass the resolution in advance while the case was *sub judice*. Pandemonium broke out as someone attacked Savarkar, and the meeting ended in utter confusion.

Gandhi had visited the hostel in Highgate several times in 1906 and knew its benefactor, Shyamji Krishnavarma, well. The *Times* pointed out that Dhingra was at one time a resident of India House, and had 'imbibed with disastrous effect the teaching of Mr Krishnavarma and others who more or less directly favour and command political assassination'. Krishnavarma was a scholar of several Indian and European languages, and despite his sound financial position he lived like an ascetic, spending his money on scholarships, supporting his revolutionary magazine, *The Indian Sociologist*, and obtaining weapons for the terrorists. He wrote in the July issue of the magazine: 'Political assassination is not murder.' Since the author could not be apprehended – he was then in France – the authorities arrested his English printer for seditious libel.

Gandhi was deeply disturbed by the assassination. He recognized the courage in Dhingra but said he had acted as if in a state of intoxication, under the overwhelming pressure of an idea. 'A man's own courage consists in suffering deeply and over a long period of time. That alone is a brave act which is preceded by careful reflection.' He warned those who sought to glorify Dhingra's act:

> I must say that those who believe and argue that such murders may do good to India are ignorant men indeed. No act of treachery can ever profit a nation. Even should the British leave in consequence of such murderous acts, who will then rule in their place? The only answer is: the murderers . . . India can gain nothing from the rule of murderers – no matter whether they are black or white.

Much later it became known that Dhingra had been under Savarkar's training for several months before he was deemed fit to lay down his life for the cause. To test his courage, a needle was driven through the palm of his hand; he remained unperturbed. Training at a rifle club equipped him to accomplish the task. The initial target was the former Viceroy, Lord Curzon, who was mainly responsible for the partition of Bengal in 1905, but the attempt failed since Curzon slipped through a door just when Dhingra was about to pull the trigger. Savarkar was thoroughly annoyed with Dhingra. On the morning of the assassination of Sir Curzon Wyllie, he gave Dhingra a nickel-plated revolver and said curtly: 'Don't show me your face if you fail this time.' It was Savarkar who prepared a final militant statement for Dhingra, proclaiming that 'the only lesson required for India at present is to learn how to die, and the only way to teach it is by dying ourselves. Therefore I die, and glory in my martyrdom.' Concluding his speech from the dock, Dhingra said: 'My only prayer to God is may I be born of the same Mother, and may I redie in the same sacred cause till the cause is successful and she stands free for the good of humanity and to the glory of God.'

He was sentenced to death and hanged in Brixton prison on 17 August. 'Those who believe that India has gained by Dhingra's and other similar acts in India make a serious mistake,' Gandhi wrote. 'Dhingra was a patriot, but his love was blind. He gave his body in a wrong way, its results can only be mischievous.'

The revolutionaries disliked intensely Gandhi's methods of petition and his close contacts with the Conservatives and they considered passive resistance humiliating. But they could not fail to admire his ongoing campaign in the Transvaal for the rights of the Indians there.

On 24 October he attended a dinner hosted by the extremist group so that, as he confessed to Polak, 'I might speak to those who might assemble there on the uselessness of violence for securing reforms.' Gandhi's terms to attend were that no controversial politics would be touched upon. Savarkar was also invited to speak.

The occasion of the dinner was Dussera festival, or *Vijay Dashami*, celebrating the victory of the hero-god Rama over the evil King Ravana and the rescue of his Queen Sita.

Presiding over the function, Gandhi, resplendent in starched shirt and swallowtail coat, welcomed the guests and made a vigorous speech. He maintained that Rama was a historical figure and could thus be honoured by all Indians as a hero and become a symbol of unity. He went on to describe the personal qualities of the leading characters in the great epic the *Ramayana*. Rama suffered fourteen years' exile, Sita endured suffering and remained the personification of purity, while faithful brother Lakshmana practised austerities. Such personal qualities of devotion, sacrifice and suffering would liberate India and be the source of a new victory of Truth over Falsehood.

Savarkar shared with Gandhi the view that all Indians, irrespective of their religion, could live together peacefully, but he no doubt said so to please the audience which consisted of both Hindus and Muslims. 'Hindus are the heart of Hindustan,' he declared somewhat condescendingly. 'Nevertheless, just as the beauty of the rainbow is not impaired but enhanced by its varied hues, so also Hindustan will appear all the more beautiful across the sky of the future by assimilating all that is best in the Muslim, Parsi, Jewish and other civilizations.' After his pleasant opening remarks, Savarkar continued with a speech which was as heavily burdened with politics as Gandhi's had been. Savarkar spoke of the greatness of the *Ramayana* and said that every Indian ought to be aware of the significance of the fact that *Vijay Dashami* was preceded by *Navratri*, a nine-day fast observed to propitiate the fierce goddess Durga; but whereas Gandhi emphasized the significance of fasting, Savarkar spoke of Durga the avenger and asked the audience to recall that it was only after slaying Ravana, the symbol of oppression and injustice, that Rama had established his ideal kingdom. Using the language of religious mythology, both Gandhi and Savarkar spoke obliquely, in a sort of dialogue in code. Gandhi mentioned Sita, the pure, long-suffering, while Savarkar's talk of Durga and Ravana implied that nonviolence had no relevance in securing justice and independence for India.

The meeting had a powerful impact on Gandhi, and he was distressed to note that he had hardly met any Indian in London who believed that 'India can ever become free without resort to violence'. Gandhi's encounters with the extremists would be the theme in the writing of the dialogue in *Hind Swaraj* or 'Indian Home Rule', on his homeward voyage.

Savarkar's conspiratorial days in London came to an end when Mr A.M.T. Jackson, the district magistrate at Nasik, was shot dead while attending a farewell party given in his honour. The assassin was apprehended and the police soon established that the Browning pistol used to kill Mr Jackson had originally been sent by Savarkar to his accomplices, possibly via some friendly sailors on a ship travelling to India. The government of Bombay issued a warrant for his arrest, but when the warrant was presented at Bow Street Court, Savarkar had already left London for Paris where he was staying with Shayamji Krishnavarma. A few weeks later, however, for some unexplained reason, he decided to give himself up and was promptly arrested when he got off the boat-train at Victoria Station.

It was decided to send him to Bombay to face the charges against him. On 1 July 1910, he boarded the SS *Morea* under heavy guard. A week later, when the ship anchored half a mile off Marseilles, Savarkar made a daring escape through a porthole. He swam ashore and climbed on to the quay, a free man, but the French authorities would have nothing to do with him, and he was handed over to the British detectives who had given chase in a boat. There was some commotion in French political circles and the press about the arrest of an Indian by British detectives on their own soil, but the controversy soon subsided.

The three-month trial of Savarkar and his co-conspirators ended on 23 December 1910. Savarkar was sentenced to transportation for life to the Andaman Islands and forfeiture of all his property. Years in jail shattered his health, and in 1924 he was released on parole and confined to the district of Ratnagiri. In the 1930s he became leader of the Hindu Mahasabha, a party of right-wing Hindu nationalists bitterly opposed to the ideas of Gandhi. At one time he possessed a vast following running into millions, but the dominance of Gandhi on the Indian political scene blunted his efforts to wrest power from the British by force of arms.

Forty years later, ironically, Savarkar's name would figure in the plot to assassinate the Mahatma.

# SIXTEEN

# The New Outlook

The long and uncertain stay in London had given Gandhi much food for thought. His view of his younger days of 'dear London', which to him was 'the land of the philosophers and poets' was showing a marked change, although a few weeks prior to his arrival he had felt that 'even now, next to India, I would rather live in London than in any other place in the world'.

But when Gandhi set out for London in 1909 he carried with him a new outlook. The dismal outcome of the 1906 deputation had resulted in the struggle, and the terms of imprisonment that followed proved to be days of spiritual retreat and renewal. Nurtured by his inner discipline (Brahmacharya), his confidence in the validity of Indian civilization was strengthened. The impact of Ruskin's *Unto This Last* which he first read in 1904 had inspired him to establish the Phoenix Farm. He published his Gujarati translation of Ruskin's work, and he now highlighted in his writings Ruskin's condemnation of commercialism and industrialism, stressing that his words had more validity in India, where industry and arms were seen by some nationalists as the effective means to force the British out of India. He wrote:

> It is wrong normally for one nation to rule over another. British rule in India is an evil but we need not believe that any very great advantage would accrue to the Indians if the British were to leave India. The reason why they rule over us is to be found in ourselves; that reason is our disunity, our immorality and our ignorance.
>
> Many people exult at the prospect of using arms against the British . . . this only shows ignorance and lack of understanding. If all the British were to be killed, those who kill them would become the masters of India, and as a result India would still continue in a state of slavery. Their fresh targets will now be their own fellow-Indians . . .
>
> Just as we cannot achieve real *swaraj* (independence) by following the path of evil – by killing the British – so also will it not be possible for us to achieve it by establishing big factories in India. Accumulation of gold and silver will not bring *swaraj*. This has been convincingly proved by Ruskin.

He sought to differentiate between Western civilization and Christian progress. During the weeks when he was held up in his negotiations, he had long talks with leaders of the movement for women's suffrage. He was also drawn to the Tolstoyan critics of industrial civilization, and other groups, such as followers of Thoreau, advocating a simple life. He noted with dismay that during the all-night budget session of Parliament early in August, the members, in blissful slumber on their benches, were awakened only to record their votes. And when the Union Bill, with its prohibition of non-white office-holding was passed, he observed that many members who had voted for it expressed regret in private. 'Why do they not give up their office?' he demanded. 'They express regret but their actions are just the same.' His new outlook was only fortified by the low expectations of political accomplishment in London.

At this juncture Gandhi read with delight Edward Carpenter's *Civilization: Its Cause and Cure.* Carpenter put forward the view that so-called civilization 'is a kind of disease which the various races of man have to pass through – as children pass through measles or whooping cough'. He found it quite discouraging that he knew of 'no single case in History in which a nation has fairly recovered from and passed through it to a more normal and healthy condition'. Pre-civilized man, he argued, was more free from disease and had a social life 'more harmonious and compact'. Amplifying on the ills brought about by civilization, he observed:

[Even] the savage races of the earth do not escape the baneful influence. Wherever Civilization touches them, they die like flies from the small-pox, drink, and worse evils it brings along with it, and often its mere contact is sufficient to destroy whole races.

But the word Disease is applicable to our social as well as to our physical condition. For as in the body disease arises from the loss of the physical unity which constitutes Health, and so takes the form of warfare or discord between the various parts, or of the abnormal development of individual organs, or the consumption of the system by predatory germs and growths; so in our modern life we find the unity gone which constitutes true society, and in its place warfare of classes and individuals, abnormal development of some to the detriment of others, and consumption of the organism by masses of social parasites. If the word disease is applicable anywhere, I should say it is – both in its direct and its derived sense – to the civilised societies of to-day.

Again, mentally, is not our condition most unsatisfactory? . . . A strange sense of mental unrest which marks our populations, and which amply justifies Ruskin's cutting epigram: that our two objects in life are, 'Whatever we have – to get more; and wherever we are – to go somewhere else.' . . . All down the Christian centuries we find this strange sense of inward strife and discord developed, in marked contrast to the naive insouciance of the pagan and primitive world; and, what is strangest, we even find people glorying in this consciousness – which, while it may be the harbinger of better things to come, is and can be in itself only the evidence of loss of unity, and therefore of ill-health, in the very centre of human life.

Carpenter maintained that the only cure for this malady would be to move 'towards a return to nature and community of human life', including a simplification of domestic life and clothing. Among its signs would be open air (coming out of 'boxes with breathing holes which Man calls houses') and a clean and pure diet of fruits and grains. Carpenter stressed the importance of a vegetarian diet, for animal foods inflamed the passions and brought on a condition of internal disunity and disease.

Gandhi's imagination was stimulated by an article written by G.K. Chesterton in the *Illustrated London News* of 18 September 1909. Chesterton, who was in love with the Middle Ages, insisted that the Indians were doing themselves a big disfavour by being enamoured of Western thinkers. He was critical of *The Indian Sociologist* for propagating ideas which, in his opinion, prevented the Indians from living their own lives. Gandhi translated Chesterton's article, entitled 'What is Indian Nationalism?' into Gujarati, and then retranslated it into English for *Indian Opinion*. Some passages in the article inevitably delighted him:

> When young Indians talk of independence for India, I get a feeling that they do not understand what they are talking about. I admit that they who demand *swarajya* are fine fellows; most young idealists are fine fellows. I do not doubt that many of our officials are stupid and oppressive. Most such officials are stupid and oppressive. But when I see the actual papers and know the views of Indian nationalists, I get bored and feel dubious about them. What they want is not very Indian and not very national. They talk about Herbert Spencer's philosophy* and other similar matters. What is the good of the Indian national spirit if they cannot protect themselves from Herbert Spencer? I am not fond of the philosophy of Buddhism, but it is not as shallow as Spencer's philosophy. It has some noble ideals, unlike the latter. One of their papers is called *The Indian Sociologist*. Do the Indian youths want to pollute their ancient villages and poison their kindly homes by introducing Spencer's philosophy into them?

---

*Herbert Spencer (1820–1903), English sociologist and philosopher, was a leading figure in the intellectual revolution of the nineteenth century. His education was haphazard and essentially in scientific subjects. He was impatient with the books of his predecessors, and thus relied on getting knowledge wherever he could. He did acquire, however, a remarkable intellectual self-reliance.

Spencer was greatly influenced by Charles Darwin's idea of evolution (gradual develop-

There is a great difference between a people asking for its own ancient life and a people asking for things that have been wholly invented by somebody else. There is a difference between a conquered people demanding its own institutions and the same people demanding the institutions of the conqueror. Suppose an Indian said: 'I wish India had always been free from white men and all their works. Everything has its own faults and we prefer our own. Had we our own institutions, there would have been dynastic wars; but I prefer dying in battle to dying in hospital. There would have been despotism; but I prefer one king whom I hardly even see to a hundred kings regulating my diet and my children. There would have been pestilence; but I would sooner die of the plague than live like a dead man, in constant fear of the plague. There would have been religious differences dangerous to public peace; but I think religion more important than peace. Life is very short; a man must live somehow and die somewhere; the amount of bodily comfort a peasant gets under your way of living is not so much more than mine. If you do not like our way

ment), although in 1852, seven years before the publication of Darwin's *On the Origin of Species*, he had already brought out an essay, *The Development Hypothesis*, elaborating an earlier version of evolutionary theory by Von Baer. It was Spencer who coined the phrases 'struggle for existence' and 'survival of the fittest', later attributed to Darwin.

Spencer attempted to work out a comprehensive philosophy based on the scientific discoveries of his day. This was the basis of his life work, the multi-volume *System of Synthetic Philosophy* (1862–96) which first set forth a set of general evolutionary principles and then applied them to social development. He endeavoured to combine the contemporary ideas of *laissez-faire* individualism and evolutionary theory. Societies, he argued, were like organisms, evolving 'from a state of relatively indefinite, incoherent, homogeneity to a state of relatively definite, coherent, heterogeneity'. They may organize and control their own processes of adaptation, and thereby develop into militaristic states; or they may permit free and plastic adaptation, and thereby develop into industrial states.

Aside from being an advocate of the theory or evolution, the other theme dominating Spencer's philosophy was the individualistic doctrine of utilitarianism. He advocated pre-eminence of the individual over society and of science over religion. In *The Man Versus the State*, he wrote: 'The function of liberalism in the past was that of putting a limit to the power of the kings. The function of true liberalism in future will be that of putting a limit to the power of parliaments.'

Spencer's advocacy of individualism and *laissez-faire* led him to champion the philosophy of social Darwinism. He stressed that it would benefit the race biologically if the unfit person was allowed to be eliminated from society through natural selection – the state should not attempt to alleviate the condition of the poor, whom he assumed to be less fit. Spencer also believed that in an ideal economic system each individual should be allowed to seek his own private interests, the state intervening only to enforce contracts and to ensure that no one infringes upon 'the equal freedom of any other man'. He maintained that in the resulting competition, the fittest business enterprises and economic institutions would survive. He put forward these views at length in *Social Statics* (1850) and *The Man Versus the State* (1884).

Spencer's philosophy can be summed up by saying that it was 'individualistic, anti-military and anti-coercive, evolutionary, and materialistic'.

of living, we never asked you to do so. Go, and leave us with it.'

Suppose an Indian said that, I should call him an Indian nationalist. He would be an authentic Indian, and I think it would be very hard to answer him. But the Indian nationalists whose works I have read go on saying: 'Give me a ballot box. Give us power, give me the judge's wig. I have a natural right to be Prime Minister. I have a right to introduce a Budget. My soul is starved if I am excluded for the editorship of the *Daily Mail*', or words to that effect. Now this is not so difficult to answer. Even the most sympathetic person may say in reply: 'What you say is very fine, my good Indian, but it is we who invented all these things. If they are so good as you make out, you owe it to us that you have ever heard of them. If they are indeed natural rights, you would never even have thought of your natural rights but for us.' If voting is such a very important thing (which I am inclined rather to doubt myself) then, certainly we have some of the authority that belongs to founders. When Indians take a haughty tone in demanding a vote, I imagine to myself the situation reversed . . .

Perhaps you think that in writing this I am opposing Indian nationalism. But that will be a mistake; I am only letting my mind play round the subject. This is desirable when there is a conflict between two complete civilizations. I also admit the existence of natural rights. The right of a people to express itself, to be itself in action, is a genuine right. Indians have a right to be and to live as Indians. But Herbert Spencer is not Indian; his philosophy is not Indian philosophy; all this clatter about the science of education and other things is not Indian. I often wish it were not English either. But this is our first difficulty, that the Indian nationalist is not national.

Gandhi, no doubt, found Carpenter and Chesterton exceedingly interesting, but their importance was limited in comparison with his direct communication with Leo Tolstoy, for it was around this time that he began a correspondence that would continue until Tolstoy's death a year later.

*War and Peace* and other works had brought Tolstoy considerable success and universal recognition, but he could find no inner peace. The discrepancy between Christ's message and man's way of life deeply tormented him. He was born in 1828 into a wealthy and titled family, but at the age of fifty-seven he chose to lead the simple life. Developing a strong aversion to the use of money, he often travelled among the poorest on the railroad and on one occasion walked the one hundred and fifteen miles from Moscow to Yasnaya Polyana, a nameless old man, dressed in peasant clothes, with a rough stick in his hand, making new acquaintances and talking endlessly to the people he met. These journeys brought him great solace. He refused the Nobel Prize because he did not accept money.

Gandhi came to know Tolstoy through *The Kingdom of God is Within You*, a volume that persuaded Gandhi that the core of the Christian gospel was not any different from the *ahimsa* or harmlessness taught in Hinduism and Jainism. Later he read more of Tolstoy's writings on religion, poverty, vegetarianism and peace.

Over the years Tolstoy had been obsessed with questions concerning the meaning and purpose of life. The resulting spiritual crisis changed him completely, and he now rejected the authority of the Russian Orthodox Church. He developed his own version of Christianity, which he detailed in *The Kingdom of God is Within You*. In this work, Tolstoy carried his Christian anarchism to its furthest development. While giving an account of his belief in Christ's teaching he accused churchmen of teaching contrary to Christ's commandments clearly and definitely expressed in the Sermon on the Mount, and especially contrary to his command concerning nonresistance to evil, thus depriving Christ's teaching of its significance: 'Our present conception of the Church – with its sacraments, its hierarchy, and especially its claim to infallibility – is to be found neither in Christ's words nor in the conceptions of men of his time.'

Tolstoy was equally critical of governments, and reached the conclusion that they were all essentially immoral since they existed primarily for furthering the interests of the rich and powerful, persecuting the masses of mankind and murdering them in the violence of war. He preached peaceful, painful refusal to serve or obey evil power structures (governments) using force, internally for oppression, externally for war. He was specific about refusal to serve or obey evil governments: no oath of allegiance, no oath in court, 'for an oath is distinctly forbidden by the Gospel', no police duty, no military duty, no payment of taxes.

> Think of your duties – not your imaginary duties as a landowner to your estate, as a merchant to your capital, as an emperor, minister, or official to the State – but those real duties which follow from your real position as a being called to life and endowed with reason and love. Let a man but realize that the purpose of his life is to fulfil the law of God, and that law will dominate him and supplant all other laws, and by its supreme dominion will in his eyes deprive all human laws of their right to command or restrict him.

Tolstoy conceded that one might not have the strength to free oneself from the shackles of man-made laws, 'but to recognize the truth as a truth and avoid lying about it is a thing you can always do . . . because in this alone – in freeing yourself from falsehood and confessing the truth – lies the sole welfare of your life'.

The prime meaning of human life lay in serving the world by promoting the establishment of the Kingdom of God. A better life was only possible when man's consciousness changed for the better: 'The Kingdom of God cometh not with outward show; neither shall they say, Lo here! or lo there! for, behold, the Kingdom of God is within you.'

Gandhi's first personal contact with Tolstoy was in the form of a letter which he wrote from London on 1 October 1909, in which he described his campaign in South Africa and asked for the master's blessing. He also sought his permission to publish and distribute 20,000 copies of a tract written by Tolstoy called *Letter to a Hindu*. This tract was written in reply to Tarak Nath Das, the young editor of *Free Hindustan*, a revolutionary paper published in Vancouver, British Columbia. Das had asked Tolstoy whether the Indian people had not the right to throw off the yoke of British rule by force and terrorism.

Tolstoy replied that it was wrong to blame the British for their presence in India. They were there because the Indians had accepted enslavement with good grace and connived with their enslavers. Das had written that the British held the people of India in subjugation because the Indians had not resisted resolutely enough and had not met violence with force. 'But the case is just the opposite,' Tolstoy replied. 'If the English have enslaved the people of India it is just because the latter recognized, and still recognize, force as the fundamental principle of the social order. In the name of this principle they submitted to their little Tsars, the Princes, in the name of it they struggled with each other, fought with Europeans, with the English, and, at present , are preparing to struggle with them again.'

Tolstoy found it preposterous that the British who originally established contact in India as a commercial company could enslave a nation of 200 million. 'Tell this to a man free from superstition and he will fail to grasp what these words mean,' he wrote. ' What does it mean that 30,000 people, not athletes, but rather weak and ill-looking, have enslaved 200 millions of vigorous, clever, strong, freedom-loving people? Do not the figures alone make it clear that not the English, but the Hindus themselves are the cause of their slavery?'

For the Indians to complain that the English had enslaved them was like villagers addicted to drink complaining that the winesellers who had settled in their midst were the cause of their drinking habit. 'Is that not the case with all the people, the millions of people, who submit to thousands or even hundreds of individuals of their own nation or those of foreign nations?'

If the Indians had been enslaved by violence, it was 'because they themselves have lived, and continue to live by violence, and fail to recognize the eternal law of love inherent in humanity. If man only lives in accord with the law of love which includes nonresistance, and does not participate in any form of violence, not only will hundreds not enslave millions, but even millions will be unable to enslave one individual. Do not resist evil, but also do not participate in evil yourselves.' If the Indians truly wanted to free themselves from the foreign yoke, they should refuse to cooperate with the 'violent deeds of the administration, of the law courts, of the collection of taxes and what is most important, of the soldiers. Then no one in the world can enslave you.'

Tolstoy conveyed his thoughts in the tract in both a particular and a general way. He felt that these 'dreadful calamities' had arisen because there were encumbrances which prevented man from understanding the meaning of the law of love. Superstitions, sciences, religions were all impediments to achieving freedom and happiness. He dwelt on the subject at some length:

In order to save a sinking ship it is necessary to throw overboard the ballast which, though it might have been indispensable at one time, would cause destruction. It is exactly the same with religious and scientific superstitions which hide this salutary truth from men. If people are to embrace the truth, not with the vagueness of childhood, nor with the one-sided uncertainty of inter-pretation given to them by religious and scientific teachers, but in such a man-ner that it should become the highest law of human life, they must effect the complete liberation of this truth from *all* those superstitions, pseudo-religious as well as pseudo-scientific, which now obscure it. Not a partial, timid liber-ation, which considers tradition sanctified by antiquity and the habits of the people, but a complete deliverance of the religious truth from all the ancient religions as well as the modern scientific superstitions.

If people only freed themselves from beliefs in all kinds of Ormuzds, Brahmas, Sabbaoths, their incarnation in Krishnas and Christs, from beliefs in paradise and hell, in angels and demons, in reincarnation, resurrections and the idea of the *interference of God in the life of the Universe*; freed themselves, chiefly, from the belief in the infallibility of the various Vedas, Bibles, Gospels, Tripitakas, Korans, etc. If people only freed themselves also from blindly believing all sorts of scientific doctrines about infinitesimally small atoms, molecules, about all kinds of infinitely great, and infinitely remote, worlds, about their movements and their origin, about forces; from the implicit faith in all manner of theoretical scientific laws to which man is supposed to be sub-jected; the historic and economic laws, the laws of struggle and survival, etc. – if people only freed themselves from this terrible accumulation of the idle exer-cise of our lower capacities of mind and memory which is called the sciences, from all the innumerable divisions of all sorts of histories, anthropologies, homiletics, bacteriologies, jurisprudences, cosmographics, strategies, whose name is legion: if only people would unburden themselves from this ruinous intoxicating ballast – that simple, explicit law of love, accessible to all, which is so natural to mankind, and which solves all questions and perplexities, would, of its own accord, become clear and obligatory.

To escape from the self-inflicted calamities which have reached the highest degree of intensity men do not require new explanations and justifications of old religious superstitions . . . formulated in your country, and an infinite number of similar new interpreters and expounders of whom no one stands in need in our Christian world; nor do they require the innumerable sciences about matters which not only are not essential but mostly harmful (in the spiritual realm there is nothing indifferent; what is not useful is always harmful). The Hindu, as well as the Englishman, the Frenchman, the German, the Russian, do not require constitutions, revolutions, conferences, congresses, or any new ingenious devices for submarine navigation, aerial navigation, powerful explosives, or all kinds of conveniences for the enjoyment of the rich ruling classes; nor new schools and universities with instruction in innumerable sciences, nor the augmentation of papers and books, and gramophones and cinematographs, nor those childish and, mostly corrupt stupidities which are called arts: one thing only is needful: the knowledge of that simple lucid truth which can be contained in the soul of every man who has not been perverted by religious and scientific superstitions – that the law of human life is the law of love which gives the highest happiness to every individual as well as to all mankind.

If people would only free their consciousness from those mountains of nonsense which hide from them the indubitable eternal truth inherent in mankind, one and the same in all the great religions of the world. The truth would then reveal itself at once in spite of the mass of pseudo-religious nonsense which now conceals it. And as soon as this truth is revealed to the consciousness of people, all that stupidity which now conceals it, will disappear of its own accord and, with it, also that evil from which humanity now suffers.

'Children, look upwards with your beclouded eyes, and a world full of joy and love will disclose itself to you, a rational world made by my wisdom, the only real world. Then you would know what Love has done with you, what Love has bestowed upon you, and what Love demands from you.' – (Krishna)

In his letter to Tolstoy, Gandhi stated that he would like, when publishing the tract, to omit the word 'reincarnation' among the religious ideas denounced by Tolstoy. 'I do not know whether (if it is not impertinent on my part to mention this) you have specially studied the question,' Gandhi wrote. 'Reincarnation or transmigration is a cherished belief with millions in India, indeed, in China also. With many, one might almost say, it is a matter of experience, no longer a matter of academic acceptance. It explains reasonably many mysteries of life.'

Gandhi's letter to Tolstoy reached Yasnaya Polyana a week later and in his diary entry for 24 September 1909 (the Russian calendar was then thirteen days behind the Western), Tolstoy noted: 'Received a pleasant letter from a Hindu of the Transvaal.' In his reply dated 7 (20) October, Tolstoy wrote:

I have just received your most interesting letter, which has given me great plea-sure. May God help all our dear brothers and co-workers in the Transvaal. The struggle of the gentle against the harsh, of humility and love against conceit and violence, is making itself felt more and more among us also.

He had no objection to Gandhi publishing the *Letter to a Hindu* with the omission of the word 'reincarnation' but he, on his part, would certainly retain it, for, in his opinion, 'belief in reincarnation can never be as firm as belief in the soul's immortality and in God's justice and love'.

At this point in time, the progress of the political negotiations seemed as well as could be expected, but the influence of G.K. Chesterton's article and Tolstoy's *Letter to a Hindu* represented an important stage in the development of Gandhi's ideas. Now he spoke about the evils arising from the British occupation of India. He argued that modern civilization had brought nothing good to India. Railroads, telephones, the telegraph had impeded the moral elevation of the nation. Large cities were symbols of slavery. He spoke about the affinity between East and West, and considered that Kipling's line about 'East is East and West is West, and never the twain shall meet' was based on a lack of clear understanding of the real nature of the relations between East and West.

Although the profound change in Gandhi's thinking had resulted partly from his reading of Thoreau and Tolstoy, its principal source could be found in India, in the great epics and the simple feudal life of Indian vil-lages. The concept that India had an older, deeper and more spiritual civil-ization than the West was being explained by such spokesmen of the emerging Hindu consciousness as reformer-philosopher Vivekananda and poet laureate Tagore, and confirmed by Western admirers such as the theosophists and many others. Gandhi had shared this awareness for many years and as far back as 1894 there were signs that he was not satisfied by 'the dazzling and bright surface of modern civilization'. Fifteen years later he was evidently more emphatic:

Looking at this land [England], I at any rate have grown disillusioned with Western civilization. The people whom you meet on the way seem half-crazy. They spend their days in luxury or in making a bare living and retire at night thoroughly exhausted. In this state of affairs, I cannot understand when they can devote themselves to prayers ... While Western civilization is still young, we find things have come to such a pass that, unless its whole machinery is thrown overboard, people will destroy themselves like so many moths.

Now that all hope of successful negotiations had faded in London, Gandhi booked passage for South Africa. On 10 November 1909, a few days before his departure, he wrote a second letter to Tolstoy, in which he referred to the Indians' struggle in the Transvaal as 'the greatest of modern times'. If the struggle succeded, 'it will be not only a triumph of religion, love and truth over irreligion, hatred and falsehood but should hopefully serve as an example to the millions in India and to the downtrodden in other parts of the world'. With the letter he enclosed a copy of *M.K. Gandhi: An Indian Patriot in South Africa* by Joseph Doke. 'This book has a bearing on the struggle with which I am so connected, and to which my life is dedicated,' he wrote. 'As I am very anxious to engage your active interest and sympathy, I thought that it would not be considered by you as out of the way for me to send you the book.' Tolstoy was in poor health, and a period of several months elapsed before he had the time and inclination to read the book. When he finally read it during the following April, he was delighted by it.

Lord Crewe had informed Gandhi that General Smuts was unable to accept the claim that Asiatics should be placed in a position of equality with Europeans in respect of entry or otherwise. Gandhi issued a statement to the British press about the failure of the negotiations. On 12 November, at a farewell meeting, he reiterated that as subjects of the Empire Indians should have equal rights. In resisting the law they were rendering a service not only to British India but to the whole British Empire. Indians, he concluded, wanted equality in the eyes of the law, which General Smuts refused to grant. So they were determined to tear off the bonds of slavery.

On the voyage home the forty-year-old Gandhi worked incessantly, catching up with his correspondence, writing a book and translating Tolstoy's *Letter to a Hindu* into Gujarati. He gave it a subtitle: *The Subjugation of India – Its Cause and Cure*, reflecting Carpenter's words. The most intense and imaginative of Gandhi's writings, *Hind Swaraj*, was composed during the voyage. In this book he proclaimed his total rejection of the West. The disillusionment of the recent weeks in London, intensified by the impact of Carpenter, Chesterton and above all Tolstoy, and brought to a fine edge by his encounters with the extremists, took shape in the work. The eighty-page book was originally written in his native Gujarati and was only later translated, somewhat hastily, he affirms, into English.

Gandhi describes *Hind Swaraj* as being 'in answer to the Indian school of violence' which had appeared in London, and years later he declared that it was a record (not necessarily verbatim) of actual conversations with workers in London, 'one of whom was an avowed anarchist'. In *Hind*

*Swaraj* Gandhi adopted a dialogue form which permitted him to state both sides of the debate. The book consists of twenty chapters, and the dialogues are between the Editor, Gandhi, and the Reader, who is contemptuous of the Indian National Congress and its leaders, whom he regards as merely perpetuating British rule. The Reader is, no doubt, modelled on Savarkar.

EDITOR: . . . Why do you want to drive away the English?

READER: Because India has become impoverished by their Government. They take away our money from year to year. The most important posts are reserved for themselves. We are kept in a state of slavery. They behave insolently towards us and disregard our feelings.

EDITOR: If they do not take our money away, become gentle, and give us responsible posts, would you still consider their presence to be harmful?

READER: That question is useless. It is similar to the question whether there is any harm in associating with a tiger if he changes his nature. Such a question is sheer waste of time. When a tiger changes his nature, Englishmen will change theirs. This is not possible . . .

EDITOR: Supposing we get Self-Government similar to what the Canadians and the South Africans have, will it be good enough?

READER: That question also is useless. We may get it when we have the same powers; we shall then hoist our own flag. As is Japan, so must India be. We must own our navy, our army, and we must have our own splendour, and then will India's voice ring through the world.

EDITOR: You have well drawn the picture. In effect it means this: that we want English rule without the Englishman. You want the tiger's nature, but not the tiger; that is to say, you would make India English. And when it becomes English, it will be called not Hindustan but *Englistan*. This is not the *swaraj* that I want.

READER: . . . If the education we have received be of any use, if the works of Spencer, Mill and others be of any importance, and if the English Parliament be the Mother of Parliaments, I certainly think that we should copy the English people, and this to such an extent that just as they do not allow others to obtain a footing in their country, so we should not allow them or others to obtain it in ours . . .

EDITOR: The condition of England at present is pitiable . . . that which you consider to be the Mother of Parliaments is like a sterile woman and a prostitute. Both these are harsh terms, but exactly fit the case. The Parliament has not yet, of its own accord, done a single good thing. Hence I have compared it to a sterile woman. The natural condition of the Parliament is such that, without outside pressure, it can do nothing. It is like a prostitute because it is under the control of ministers who change from time to time. Today it is under Mr Asquith, tomorrow it may be under Mr Balfour.

READER: You have said this sarcastically. The term 'sterile woman' is not applicable. The Parliament, being elected by the people, must work under public pressure. This is its quality.

EDITOR: . . . Its members are hypocritical and selfish. Each thinks of his own little interest. It is fear that is the guiding motive. What is done today may be undone tomorrow. One cannot recall a single instance in which finality can be predicted for its work. When the greatest questions are debated, its members have been seen to stretch themselves and to doze . . . Carlyle has called it the 'talking shop of the world'. Members vote for their party without a thought. Their so-called discipline binds them to it. If any member, by way of exception, gives an independent vote, he is considered a renegade. . . . It has remained a baby after an existence of seven hundred years. When will it outgrow its babyhood?

READER: . . . Now will you tell me something of what you have read and thought of modern civilization?

EDITOR: Let us first consider what state of things is described in the word 'civilization.' Its true test lies in the fact that people living in it make bodily welfare the object of life . . . The people of Europe today live in better-built houses than they did a hundred years ago. This is considered an emblem of civilization . . . Formerly, they wore skins and used spears as their weapons. Now they wear long trousers, and . . . instead of spears, they carry with them revolvers containing five or more chambers. If the people of a certain country . . . adopt European clothing, they are supposed to have become civilized out of savagery. Formerly, in Europe, people ploughed their lands mainly by manual labour. Now one man can plough a vast tract by means of steam engines and can thus amass great wealth . . . Formerly, the fewest men wrote books that were most valuable. Now anybody writes and prints anything he likes and poisons people's mind. . . . Formerly, when people wanted to fight with one another, they measured between them their bodily strength; now it is possible to take away thousands of lives . . . Formerly, men worked in the open air only so much as they liked. Now thousands of workmen meet together and . . . work in factories or mines. Their condition is worse than that of beasts. They are obliged to work, at the risk of their lives, at most dangerous occupations, for the sake of millionaires. Formerly, men were made slaves under physical compulsion, now they are enslaved by the temptation of money and of the luxuries that money can buy . . . What more need I say? All this you can ascertain . . . This civilization takes note neither of morality nor of religion . . . Civilization seeks to increase bodily comforts and it fails miserably even in doing so . . . This civilization is such that one has only to be patient and it will be self-destroyed . . .

READER: I should now like to know your views about the condition of our country.

EDITOR: When I give you my views on the poverty of India, you will perhaps begin to dislike me because what you and I have hitherto considered beneficial for India no longer appears to me to be so.

READER: What may that be?

EDITOR: Railways, lawyers and doctors have impoverished the country so much so that, if we do not wake up in time, we shall be ruined.

READER: Very well, then, I shall hear you on the railways.

EDITOR: But for the railways, the English could not have such a hold on India as they have. The railways too have spread the bubonic plague, for without them the masses could not move from place to place . . . Formerly, we had natural segregation. Railways have increased the frequency of famines because, owing to facility of means of locomotion, people sell out their grain and send it to markets where they get the maximum price . . . Railways accentuate the evil nature of man. Bad men fulfil their evil designs with greater rapidity. The holy places of India have become unholy. Formerly, people went to these places with very great difficulty. Generally, therefore, only the real devotees visited such places. Nowadays rogues frequent them to practise their roguery.

READER: Good men can also visit these places . . . Why can not they take advantage of the railways?

EDITOR: Those who want to do good are not selfish, they are not in a hurry, they know that to instil goodness in people requires a long time. But evil has wings . . . It may be debatable whether railways spread famine, but it is beyond dispute that they propagate evil.

READER: . . . [Now, talking about the lawyers], you tell me that when two men quarrel they should not go to a law court. This is astonishing.

EDITOR: . . . It is within my knowledge that [the lawyers] are glad when men have disputes. Petty pleaders actually manufacture them. Their touts, like so many leeches, suck the blood of the poor people. Lawyers are men who have little to do. Lazy people, in order to indulge in luxuries, take up such professions . . . But the greatest injury they have done to the country is that they have tightened the English grip. Do you think that it would be possible for the English to carry on their government in India without law courts? . . . The English could not rule India without Indian judges and Indian lawyers . . . If the latter were to abandon their profession . . . English rule in India would break up in a day . . .

READER: I now understand the lawyers; the good they may have done is accidental. I feel that profession is certainly hateful. You, however, drag in the doctors also, how is that?

EDITOR: Their business is really to rid the body of diseases that may afflict it. How do these diseases arise? Surely by our negligence or indulgence. I overeat. I have indigestion, I go to a doctor, he gives me medicine, I am cured. I overeat again, I take his pills again. Had I not taken the pills in the first instance, I would not have suffered the punishment deserved by me and I would not have overeaten again. The doctor intervened and helped me to indulge myself. My body thereby certainly felt more at ease; but my mind became weakened. A continuance of a course of medicine must, therefore, result in loss of control over the mind . . .

READER: You have denounced railways, lawyers and doctors. I can see you will discard all machinery. What, then, is civilization?

EDITOR: The answer to that question is not difficult. I believe that the civilization India has evolved is not to be beaten in the world . . . Rome went. Greece shared the same fate, the might of the Pharaohs was broken, Japan has become Westernized, of China nothing can be said, but India is still somehow or other sound at the foundation . . . What we have tested and found true on the anvil of experience we dare not change . . .

Civilization is that mode of conduct which points out to man the path of duty . . . To observe morality is to attain mastery over our mind and our passions . . . We notice that the mind is a restless bird; the more it gets the more it wants, and still remains unsatisfied. The more we indulge our passions the more unbridled they become. Our ancestors, therefore, set a limit to our indulgences. They saw that happiness was largely a mental condition. A man is not necessarily happy because he is rich, or unhappy because he is poor . . . Millions will always remain poor. Observing all this, our ancestors dissuaded us from luxuries and pleasures. We have managed with the same kind of plough as existed thousands of years ago. We have retained the same kind of cottages that we had in former times and our indigenous education remains the same as before. We have had no system of life-corroding competition. Each followed his own occupation or trade and charged a regulation wage . . . This [ancient] nation had courts, lawyers and doctors but they were all within bounds. Everybody knew that these professions were not particularly superior; moreover, [they] did not rob people, they were considered people's dependents, not their masters. Justice was tolerably fair. The ordinary rule was to avoid courts . . . The common people lived independently and followed their agricultural occupation. They enjoyed true Home Rule.

. . . The tendency of Indian civilization is to elevate the moral being, that of the Western civilization is to propagate immorality . . .

READER: What then . . . would you suggest for freeing India?

EDITOR: When we are slaves we think that the whole universe is enslaved. Because we are in an abject condition, we think that the whole of India is in that condition . . . But if we bear in mind the above fact, we can see that if we become free, India is free. And in this thought you have a definition of *swaraj*. It is *swaraj* when we learn to rule ourselves. It is, therefore, in the palms of our hands . . . But such *swaraj* has to be experienced, by each one for himself. One drowning man will never save another. Slaves ourselves, it is mere pretension to think of freeing others. Now you will have seen that it is not necessary for us to have as our goal the expulsion of the English. If the English become Indianized, we can accommodate them. If they wish to remain in India along with their civilization there is no room for them . . . If we keep our house in order, only those who are fit to live in it will remain. Others will leave of their own accord. Such things occur within the experience of all of us.

READER: But it has not occurred in history.

EDITOR: To believe that what has not occurred in history will not occur at all is to argue disbelief in the dignity of man . . .

READER: I cannot follow this. There seems little doubt that we shall have to expel the English by force of arms . . .

EDITOR: We brought the English, and we keep them. Why do you forget that our adoption of their civilization makes their presence in India at all possible? Your hatred against them ought to be transferred to their civilization. But let us assume that we have to drive them away by fighting, how is that to be done?

READER: In the same way as Italy did it. What was possible for Mazzini and Garibaldi is possible for us. You cannot deny that they were very great men.

EDITOR: Mazzini was a great and good man. Garibaldi was a great warrior. Both are adorable; we can learn much from their lives. But the condition of Italy was different from that of India . . . Mazzini has shown in his writings on the duty of man that every man must learn how to rule himself . . . Garibaldi simply wanted Italy to be free from the Austrian yoke . . . [and to him] Italy meant the King of Italy and his henchmen. To Mazzini it meant the whole of the Italian people . . . The Italy of Mazzini still remains in a state of slavery . . . Again, India can fight like Italy only when she has arms. You have not considered this problem at all. The English are splendidly armed; that does not frighten me, but it is clear that, to pit ourselves against them in arms, thousands of Indians must be armed. If such a thing be possible, how many years will it take? Moreover, to arm India on a large scale is to Europeanize it. Then her condition will be just as pitiable as that of Europe . . . But the fact is that the Indian nation will not adopt arms, and it is well that it does not.

READER: You are overstating the facts. All need not be armed. At first we shall assassinate a few Englishmen and strike terror; then, a few men who have been armed will fight openly. We may have to lose 200,000 or 250,000 men, more or less but we shall regain our land. We shall undertake guerrilla warfare, and defeat the English.

EDITOR: That is to say, you want to make the holy land of India unholy. Do you not tremble to think of freeing India by assassination? What we need to do is to sacrifice ourselves. It is a cowardly thought, that of killing others. Whom do you suppose to free by assassination? The millions of India do not desire it. Those who are intoxicated by the wretched modern civilization think of these things. Those who will rise to power by murder will certainly not make the nation happy . . .

READER: . . . You know what the English obtained in their own country they obtained by using brute force . . . why should we not achieve our goal, which is good, by any means whatsoever, even by using violence? . . .

EDITOR: It is perfectly true that [the English] used brute force and that it is possible for us to do likewise, but by using similar means we can get only the same thing that they got . . . Your reasoning is . . . saying that we can get a rose through planting a noxious weed . . . We reap exactly as we sow . . .

Commenting on *Hind Swaraj* a decade later, Gandhi said: 'Except for withdrawing the word "prostitute" used in connection with the British Parliament which annoyed an English lady, I wish to make no change at all.'

# SEVENTEEN

# Tolstoy Farm

When Gandhi arrived back at Cape Town, he was more determined than ever about his plans to go ahead with the Satyagraha movement. Nevertheless he was aware of some tangible problems. He had no source of income and there was no likelihood of any in the future, for he wanted to give up his law practice completely. The funds of the Satyagraha Association were dwindling and it was unlikely that the Indians would continue to court imprisonment unless some money was available for their families at least at a subsistence level while they were in prison. But shortly after he stepped off the boat at Cape Town, he was pleasantly surprised to receive a telegram from Gokhale, saying that R. J. Tata, the industrialist and philanthropist, had donated the sum of twenty thousand rupees for the Satyagraha movement in the Transvaal. It was a rather healthy gift, amounting to £1500 in the currency of the time, and could not have come at a more suitable moment, for there was a pressing need for a place where the wives and children of the imprisoned Satyagrahis could take refuge. The Phoenix settlement was thirty hours away by train, and it seemed imperative that another settlement was established. Gokhale had promised to afford all possible assistance to the Satyagraha movement, and he was as good as his word. Gandhi sent a telegram of appreciation, asking Gokhale to convey his thanks to Mr Tata for the timely help. Years later Gandhi wrote:

But this or even the largest possible gift of money could not by itself help forward a Satyagraha struggle, a fight on behalf of Truth consisting chiefly in self-purification and self-reliance. A Satyagraha struggle is impossible without capital in the shape of character. As a splendid palace deserted by its inmates looks like a ruin, so does a man without character, all his material belongings notwithstanding.

In any event more gifts from India followed, including some from former princely states. A thousand rupees came from the Maharajah of Bikaner, two thousand from the Maharajah of Mysore, and two thousand five hundred from the nizam of Hyderabad, the southern Muslim-ruled state. Gandhi preferred to ignore what the industrialists and maharajahs stood for, and accepted the gifts gratefully. At the Indian National Congress session at Lahore, Gokhale moved a resolution on the South African situation and described Gandhi as 'a man among men, a hero among heroes, a patriot among patriots, and we may well say that in him Indian humanity at the present time has really reached its high-water mark.' G.A. Natesan, editor of *Indian Review*, spoke movingly on South Africa. Women tore off their gold rings and bangles and, in addition, eighteen thousand rupees were collected on the spot.

A more important gift came from Gandhi's rich architect friend, Hermann Kallenbach, who bought a 1,100-acre farm at Lawley, twenty miles from Johannesburg, and gave it to him rent free for his second community. There were about a thousand orange, apricot and plum trees on the farm, and a small house at the foot of the hill, and two wells and a spring provided an adequate supply of water. The Lawley train station was about a mile away. Gandhi called this settlement Tolstoy Farm, not after the Tolstoy of *War and Peace* but after the later, awefully detached and radically religious Tolstoy of *The Kingdom of God is Within You*.

For two months the settlers lived in tents while the buildings, planned by Kallenbach, were under construction. The structures were all of corrugated iron and did not take long to raise. Some skilled workers were hired, but the settlers did all the unskilled work. Gandhi and his family came to live on the farm, and so did Kallenbach. The population of the farm consisted initially of forty young men, three elderly men, five women and between twenty and thirty children. The number would later vary with arrests and other circumstances. There were Hindus, Muslims, Christians and Parsis among the settlers. The community grew their own food and ground their own wheat. 'I prepare the bread that is required on the farm,' Gandhi wrote to a friend in India. 'The general opinion about it is that it is well-made. We put in no yeast and no baking powder.' Some of the wheat was toasted to make caffeine-free caramel coffee according to a recipe provided by Gandhi. They prepared marmalade from the oranges grown on the farm and made their own groundnut butter. Small workshops were started to help make the community self-supporting. Kallenbach went to stay in the Trappist monastery at Mariann Hill to learn the art of sandal making. This he then taught to Gandhi, who in turn taught it to others. Surplus sandals were sold to friends. Kallenbach, who knew something of carpentry, was in charge of the woodwork department. Gandhi learned to make school benches, chests of drawers and other items. There were no beds on the farm; all slept on the floor.

Each person was given two blankets and a wooden pillow.

Life on the farm was kept extremely simple. Men shaved and cut one another's hair. Since they all had become labourers, they wore working men's trousers and shirts, which were immitations of prison uniforms. These garments were made out of coarse blue cloth, and were stitched by women settlers.

The food served on the farm was strictly vegetarian. There were three meals a day: bread and wheaten 'coffee' at six in the morning, rice, lentils and vegetables at eleven, and wheat pap and milk, or bread and 'coffee' at half past six in the evening. The food was served in the kind of bowl supplied to prisoners in jail. The wooden spoons were made on the farm. There was chanting of prayers after the evening meal. They sang *bhajans* (devotional songs) and sometimes heard passages from the *Ramayana* or books on Islam. Everyone retired at nine o'clock.

Gandhi still had legal cases to work on, and this necessitated travelling to Johannesburg. Occasionally, Kallenbach would also have business in town. The community could ill afford to spend money on train fares. The rule was that anyone going to town for shopping or other work for the commune could travel by train, third class. But if one went for personal reasons, or if children were going on a picnic trip, the journey had to be made on foot. Gandhi would often get up at two o'clock in the morning, walk the twenty-one miles to Johannesburg, attend to his law practice, and walk back to the farm the same night.

The children were kept busy with work on the farm. Gandhi regarded character building as the proper foundation for their education; however, he felt that some literary training, in addition, was essential. He and Kallenbach shared the task of teaching the children religion, geography, history, arithmetic, etc. School could be held only in the afternoons, when both the teachers and the taught were already thoroughly exhausted by several hours of hard work. Moreover, when business would take Gandhi or Kallenbach to Johannesburg, there would be inevitable interruptions. Gandhi's ideas on co-education were based on his own improvisation. He encouraged boys and girls, some of them adolescents, to bathe at the spring at the same time. He was certainly concerned about the girls' safety and 'my eyes followed the girls as a mother's eye follows a daughter'. At night everyone slept on an open veranda. The young folk would take up their sleeping places around Gandhi, with the beds hardly three feet apart. Gandhi had, no doubt, explained the duty of self-restraint to them.

One day, when he learned that some of the youngsters on the farm were making light-hearted advances to two girls, he was visibly shaken. He wondered where he had gone wrong. The youngsters were summoned and reprimanded; the girls, too, were called to his presence and reprimanded. But Gandhi had to search for a method 'to sterilize the sinner's eye'. The quest kept him awake all night. In the morning the girls were again summoned and he informed them of an exemplary form of punishment he had devised, which would certainly warn off their admirers and protect their purity. He would cut off their long fine hair. The girls objected firmly; so did the older women at the farm. But he had an irresistible way, and finally the girls agreed to have their heads shaved.

Years later he would not consider the type of liberty which he had granted the co-educational class at Tolstoy Farm. 'I have often felt that my mind then used to be more innocent than it is now, and that was due perhaps to my ignorance,' he wrote. 'Since then I have had bitter experiences, and have sometimes burnt my fingers badly . . . My faith and courage were at their highest at Tolstoy Farm . . . I have been praying to God to permit me to reattain that height, but the prayer has not yet been heard . . . '

On 4 April 1910, about two months prior to receiving the gift of the farm from Hermann Kallenbach, Gandhi wrote another letter to Leo Tolstoy and accompanied it with a copy of his little book, *Hind Swaraj*. 'I am most anxious not to worry you,' he wrote, 'but, if your health permits it and if you could find the time to go through the booklet, needless to say I shall value very highly your criticism of the writing.'

On 19 April (2 May), Tolstoy noted in his diary: 'This morning two Japanese arrived. Wild men in ecstasy over European civilization. On the other hand, the book and the letter of the Hindu reveal an understanding of all the shortcomings of European civilization and even of its total inadequacy.' A few days later he wrote a letter to his friend Vladimir Chertkov in which he referred to Gandhi as 'a person very close to us, to me'.

Writing from Yasnaya Polyana on 25 April (8 May), Tolstoy acknowledged Gandhi's letter and the book. He had read the book with great interest 'because I think that the question you treat in it: the passive resistance – is a question of the greatest importance not only for India but for the whole of humanity'. He found Gandhi's biography by Joseph Doke interesting too, and it 'gave me the possibility to know and understand you better.' Tolstoy wrote that he was not quite well and therefore could not write much about the two books, but he promised to do so as soon as he felt better.

In his letter of 15 August, Gandhi acknowledged, with thanks, Tolstoy's letter and expressed his gratitude for his general approval of his booklet: 'I shall look forward to your detailed criticism of the work which you have been so good as to promise in your letter.' He also informed Tolstoy of the establishment of Tolstoy Farm by Kallenbach and himself. 'I should not have burdened you,' he concluded, 'but for the fact of your taking a personal interest in the passive resistance struggle that is going on in the Transvaal.'

Tolstoy was then in a state of serious spiritual depression and physically ill. There were quarrels with his wife and children, and sudden reconciliations were followed by even more disturbing outbreaks. His days were filled with despair and feverish efforts to wriggle out of the stranglehold of his family. Nevertheless he replied to Gandhi's communication on the day he received it, with the longest letter in the whole correspondence. His was an anguished mind and he had not long to live, but he summoned the energy to write with utmost calmness and kindliness. This was his last testament, his laying of hands on the head of his young disciple, blessing him to continue with the message of universal love and brotherhood:

> The longer I live, and especially now, when I vividly feel the nearness of death, I want to tell others what I feel so particularly clearly and what to my mind is of great importance, namely, that which is called 'passive resistance', but which is in reality nothing else than the teaching of love uncorrupted by false interpretations. That love, which is the striving for the union of human souls and the activity derived from it, is the highest and only law of human life; and in the depth of his soul every human being – as we most clearly see in children – feels and knows this; he knows this until he is entangled by the false teachings of the world. This law was proclaimed by all – by the Indian as by the Chinese, Hebrew, Greek and Roman sages of the world. I think this law was most clearly expressed by Christ, who plainly said, 'In love alone is all the law and the prophets.'

> But seeing the corruption to which this law may be subject, he straightaway pointed out the danger of its corruption, which is natural to people who live in worldly interests – the danger, namely, which justifies the defence of those interests by the use of force, or, as he said, 'with blows to answer blows, by force to take back things usurped', etc. He knew, as every sensible man must know, that the use of force is incompatible with love as the fundamental law of life; that as soon as violence is permitted, in whichever case it may be, the insufficiency of the law of love is acknowledged, and by this the very law of love is denied. The whole Christian civilization, so brilliant outwardly, grew up on this self-evident and strange misunderstanding and contradiction, sometimes conscious but mostly unconscious.

> In reality, as soon as force was admitted into love, there was no more love; there could be no love as the law of life; and as there was no law of love, there was no law at all except violence, the power of the strongest. So lived Christian humanity for nineteen centuries. It is true that in all times people were guided by violence in arranging their lives . . .

> The question now evidently stands thus: either to admit that we do not rec-

ognize any Christian teaching at all, arranging our lives only by the power of the stronger, or that all our compulsory taxes, court and police establishments, but mainly our armies, must be abolished.

Therefore, your activity in the Transvaal, as it seems to us, at this end of the world, is the most essential work, the most important of all the work now being done in the world, wherein not only the nations of the Christian, but of all the world, will unavoidably take part.

Tolstoy's letter, dated 7 September (20 September 1910), written in Russian, was translated into English by Vladimir Chertkov and then sent to an intermediary in England for posting to Gandhi. The intermediary was ill at the time and the letter was not mailed until 1 November, so that Gandhi received it in the Transvaal several days after Tolstoy's death.

# EIGHTEEN

# Glimmer of Hope

The government of India, on the advice of Gopal Krishna Gokhale, the Indian nationalist leader and a member of the Viceroy's Imperial Council, had made a strong recommendation to Downing Street that the recruitment of indentured labour in India for the colony of Natal be forthwith prohibited. Meanwhile Lord Ampthill and the South African Committee also put substantial pressure on the British government, urging it to take the necessary action. Consequently, in October 1910 the Imperial government sent a dispatch to the Union government, recommending the repeal of Act 2 of 1907. It demanded the removal of the racial bar and the substitution of nonracial legislation, effectively limiting future Indian immigration in the Union to an annual minimum number of highly educated men.

On 2 January 1911, Lord Hardinge, the Viceroy, telegraphed the Secretary of State that on 1 April a notification would be published prohibiting indentured emigration to Natal as of 1 July 1911. This seemed to be a triumph for Gandhi and Gokhale.

The South African government introduced into Parliament in February 1911 a new bill which sought to repeal Act 2 of 1907. Under its provision, the exclusion of Asiatics was to be brought about not by naming and specifically prohibiting the entry of such people but by subjecting them to a rigorous education test. The bill seemed to concede the basic demands of the Indians for the removal of the racial bar from the immigration law of the Union. But the racial bar was retained in the Orange Free State. Furthermore, the new bill attempted to take away the rights of the Cape and Natal Asiatics which they had hitherto enjoyed without interference. For a time, however, it appeared that all problems would be solved by speedy alteration of the bill during its passage through Parliament. Amendments were proposed to allow the under-age children and wives of legal immigrants to enter the Union.

The diehards in the Union Parliament strongly objected to Smuts's declaration that 'as a limited number of Asiatics would be allowed, under the bill, to enter the Union, every year, there could be no limitation of their right to travel about or settle in any part of the Union territory.' Gandhi warned his compatriots that 'there can be no playing with the snake of racial legislation. The virus of racial legislation in the Orange Free State will speedily attack the whole Union.'

Telegrams and letters were exchanged between Smuts and Gandhi. On 27 March Gandhi went to Cape Town and spent virtually the whole of April discussing the new bill and canvassing support for the modifications he proposed. On 19 April he met with Smuts in an interview of which he kept notes. The general was his most friendly self. 'You will insist on enjoying yourself in Cape Town,' he commented. In this interview the general did most of the talking:

SMUTS: . . . You as a lawyer will understand when I tell you that it is difficult to carry out your alternative suggestion . . . Gandhi, my boy, I am sorry for you. You know I want peace . . . Parliament will not pass such a bill. I therefore want to pass my bill, which I like and which I consider is fair. I shall try, but I may fail to pass it during this session. All the members want to go away. And the Free State members are still opposed to admitting any Asiatic. I think I can beat them in the Assembly, but the Senate will throw out the bill. I therefore want to pass the measure during the next session, if I cannot carry it this session. But meanwhile I want peace. I do not want to harass your people. You know that. And I do not want you to bring people from India and elsewhere to fight. I want to help the Imperial Government and they want to help me. I want to help you and you want to help me. Will you not see our point of view?

GANDHI: I emphatically do.

SMUTS: I know you have many leaders. I know you to be high-minded and honest. I have told [the] Imperial Government so. You have a right to fight in your own way. But this country is the Kaffirs', where whites are a handful. We do not want Asia to come in. Now that Natal won't have immigration, I am hopeful of solving this question. But how can we hold out against you? I have read your pamphlet. You are a simple-living and frugal race, in many respects more intelligent than we are. You belong to a civilization that is thousands of years old. Ours, as you say, is but an experiment. Who knows but that the whole damned thing will perish before long. But you see why we do not want Asia here. But, as I say, the Natal difficulty being out of the way, I shall cope with the problem here. But I want time. I shall yet beat the Free Staters. But you should not be aggressive. The whole question, as you know, will be discussed before the Imperial Conference. You should therefore wait. Now just think it over and let me know. [Pause.]

I do not know how your people spread. They go everywhere. I have now more petitions against dealers. My difficulty of the future will be regarding them. I do not want to disturb them. I want to let things remain as they are. But I do not know what will happen. You are too hard.

Gandhi, what are you doing for a living?

GANDHI: I am not practising at present.

SMUTS: But how then are you living? Have you plenty of money?

GANDHI: No. I am living like a pauper, the same as other passive resisters on Tolstoy Farm.

SMUTS: Whose is it?

GANDHI: It is Mr Kallenbach's. He is a German.

SMUTS: [laughing] Oh, old Kallenbach! He is your admirer, eh? I know.

GANDHI: I do not know that he is my admirer. We are certainly very great friends.

SMUTS: I must go and see the Farm. Where is it?

GANDHI: Near Lawley.

SMUTS: I know, on the Vereeniging line. How far is it from the station?

GANDHI: About twenty minutes. We shall be pleased to see you there.

SMUTS: Yes, I must go one day . . . [So saying he got up to say goodbye. Gandhi did likewise].

GANDHI: You say you cannot amend the Transvaal Immigration Act. I must confess I do not see any difficulty.

SMUTS: Yes there is. The whites won't have it unless you adopt my suggestion.

GANDHI: And that is . . .

SMUTS: To give the Governor the power to make regulations setting a different test for different people. The regulations must only refer to Indians. And this I know you won't like. But you think the whole thing over and let me know what you think. You know I want to help you. If there are any individual cases of hardship, you can always come to me . . .

In view of the implacable opposition of the Free State members, any progress in the matter seemed impossible. Smuts now started thinking in terms of withdrawing the bill so that a more acceptable measure could be worked out the following year. He was confident that he could arrange a truce with Gandhi till a fresh bill was introduced. On 25 April Prime Minister Botha announced the dropping of the first attempt under the Union to settle the immigration question to the satisfaction of the Indians and the various segments of the white population in South Africa. At the same time, Smuts and Gandhi sat down to serious negotiations and a provisional settlement was arrived at following Smuts's assurance that the Transvaal Asiatic Registration Act would be repealed. At a public meeting held in Johannesburg on 28 April the Indian community ratified the 'settlement', and for a time at least the struggle was over. A few days later the Indian prisoners were released.

In October a fresh immigration bill was introduced in the Union Parliament. The bill was in some respects more satisfactory than the old one, but was still resented by the Indians as they felt it did not seek to ful-

fil Smuts's promise. It was dropped for the time, and the period of the provisional settlement was extended by one year. Gokhale was expected to
arrive in South Africa soon, and it was hoped that with his involvement a
formula acceptable to all would be worked out.

With the suspension of the struggle, life on Tolstoy Farm was quiet. The
settlers were enjoying themselves in the fruit garden, away from the din
and roar of the cities. They did not know, not did they care, when the
struggle would end. Nevertheless they were determined to keep the pledge
they had taken – to refuse submission to the Black Act and to suffer whatever such refusal might bring.

In the autumn of 1912, in response to repeated urging by Gandhi, Gopal
Krishna Gokhale arrived in South Africa for a month in order to assess
the Indian community's condition and assist Gandhi in ameliorating it.
Gokhale, formerly a professor of English literature, history, economics and
mathematics, was the president of the Servants of India Society, a close
friend of Lord Hardinge, the Viceroy, a skilful negotiator and a highly cultivated man. He had initiated debate in the Legislative Council of India and
moved a resolution in favour of prohibiting the recruitment of indentured
labour for Natal, which was carried. Gokhale had kept in close touch with
Gandhi and the Indian situation in South Africa for many years. He was
certainly the most prominent Indian ever to visit South Africa, and he came
with the blessing of both the British and the Indian governments. Gandhi
had framed an exhausting itinerary, forgetting that Gokhale was in poor
health, suffering from diabetes. However, the eminent visitor accepted the
busy schedule with good grace. On the advice of the wily Smuts, the Union
government made Gokhale a state guest, and showered him with flattery
and adulation with a view to dulling the edge of his resentment. From the
time of his arrival in Cape Town on 22 October, a private state railroad car
was placed at his disposal, and for the whole of the month-long tour red
carpets and illuminations greeted him at every stop. Decorations by
Indians at the principal railroad stations added to the glitter.

Gandhi and Kallenbach welcomed him at the ship and acted as his secretaries and personal attendants throughout the tour. From Cape Town
they took the train to Johannesburg, making stops at several places where
Indians were living. There were welcoming speeches for Gokhale at each
stop, with mayors and local dignitaries in attendance. In Johannesburg
there were elaborate celebrations, with the mayor of the city receiving his
distinguished visitor at the railroad station on a raised dais covered with
carpets. The civic address presented to Gokhale was engraved on a solid
plate of gold from the Rand mounted on Rhodesian teak. He was then taken
to Kallenbach's elegant hilltop house five miles away. A spacious office had

been hired for Gokhale to receive visitors; there was a private chamber for him, a drawing room and a waiting room for visitors. He was introduced to many eminent citizens. A private meeting of leading Europeans was organized so as to give him a thorough understanding of their standpoint. There were mass meetings, banquets and continual celebrations.

Despite Gokhale's failing health, Gandhi could not resist the temptation of bringing him to Tolstoy Farm, where there were hardly any creature comforts. It did not occur to him that the mile and a half walk from the Lawley railroad station could prove trying for the honoured guest. It rained. Gokhale was drenched and caught a bad cold. Arrangements were made for him to stay in Kallenbach's room where a cot was specially installed for him. When he learned that everyone else at the farm slept on the floor, he dispensed with the cot and had his bed spread on the floor.

The next morning Gokhale decided to write a letter. To think the subject out, he was in the habit of walking up and down the room. This *modus operandi* appeared strange to Gandhi, who himself was never at a loss for a word, and he conveyed his feelings on this to his friend. A sharp homily was in store for Gandhi, and it is questionable whether he took it to heart. Gokhale replied:

> You do not know my way of life. I will not do even the least little thing in a hurry. I will think about it and consider the central idea. I will next deliberate as to the language suited to the subject and then set to write. If everyone did as I did, what a huge saving of time there would be. And the nation would be saved from the avalanche of half-baked ideas which now threaten to overwhelm her.

After a few days at Tolstoy Farm Gokhale continued his triumphal procession through South Africa. There were more public dinners, reception committees, gifts, scrolls and addresses. At Pretoria he saw most of the prominent members of the government, and on 12 November had lunch with the Governor-General. His interview with General Botha and General Smuts lasted about two hours and covered the entire field of government policy. Gandhi decided to take no part in the meeting, for being a controversial figure, his presence would not be conducive to a friendly atmosphere. Nor did Gokhale insist on his participation, although the day before the meeting was held he asked Gandhi to prepare for him a summary of the Indians' history in the four colonies. The two men spent the entire night discussing various aspects of the struggle. At one stage Gandhi politely protested against the responsibility Gokhale had assumed, for he feared Gokhale might make errors of fact or fail to answer a question raised by one of the ministers or make a commitment which he himself would not have made. Gandhi would rather continue with the struggle a little longer, but Gokhale was determined to carry out his mission to its logical conclusion.

When the talks were over, Gokhale reported to Gandhi that everything had been satisfactorily settled. The Black Act was to be repealed, the £3 poll tax on ex-indentured Indians was to be abolished, and the restriction of Asian immigration was to be based explicitly on social and economic grounds and not on race. Gandhi inevitably did not share Gokhale's optimism:

> You do not know the ministers as I do. I am not as hopeful in the matter as you are. It is enough for me that you have obtained this undertaking from the ministers. The promise given to you will serve as a proof of the justice of our demands and will redouble our fighting spirit if it comes to fighting at all.

To Gokhale's urging that he should return to India in a year, Gandhi replied that it was unlikely that the prevailing circumstances would permit him to do so. 'I do not think I can return to India in a year and before many more Indians have gone to jail.'

On 15 November, while making a farewell speech at the Pretoria Town Hall, Gokhale told his compatriots:

> Your future is largely in your own hands . . . If the struggle has to be resumed, or if you have to enter struggles of like nature for justice denied or injustice forced upon you, remember that the issue will largely turn on the character you show, on your capacity for combined action, on your readiness to suffer and sacrifice in a just cause. India will no doubt be behind you.

Three days later, Gokhale, Gandhi and Kallenbach took the train to Delagoa Bay and boarded the SS *Kronprinz*, which would take Gokhale back to India. Gandhi and Kallenbach accompanied him as far as Zanzibar. As they said farewell, Gokhale again insisted that Gandhi should return to India within the year. Gandhi refused, but soon after Gokhale had sailed away, he apologized for his imperfections in a letter written from Dar es Salaam:

> Will you forgive me for all my imperfections? I want to be a worthy pupil of yours. This is not mock humility, but Indian seriousness. I want to realize in myself the conception I have of an Eastern pupil. We may have many differences of opinion, but you shall still be my pattern in political life.

Notwithstanding Gandhi's utmost respect for Gokhale and for other towering personalities of India, he lived his own life, experimented with his own truth and never let anyone have intellectual dominance over him. All through his career he would have utter confidence in his own improvised ideas and would rather find his resources in himself than look upon anyone as his political *guru*. 'You will always have your way. And there is no help for me as I am here at your mercy,' Gokhale told Gandhi during his visit to South Africa.

# NINETEEN

# Satyagraha: A Moral Victory

When Gandhi returned to Delagoa Bay after saying farewell to Gokhale, he was detained on the ship by an immigration officer, who refused to give him a landing permit. Gandhi had earlier noted that a group of Greek immigrants, after brief cross-examination, were all permitted to land, mainly due to the fact that they had the requisite £20 on their persons. Kallenbach, being a European, was given a landing permit without fuss, but refused to leave his friend. While Gandhi sat glued to a chair, awaiting disposal of his case, Kallenbach looked, as Gandhi wrote later, 'like a lion caught in a cage'. Gandhi was equally disturbed. It was only rarely that he had such feeling of intense despair, what had distressed him even more was the sight of deck-class Indian passengers living in squalor, having no regard for sanitation. Many spat right where they happened to be sitting. 'One of them spat over Mr Kallenbach's head where he sat,' Gandhi reported in *Indian Opinion*. He blamed the Indians themselves for the treatment meted out to them.

While the memories of Gokhale's triumphal tour were still fresh, General Smuts announced in the House of Assembly that the Europeans of Natal, who were the original employers of Indian contract labour, would not permit the lifting of the £3 annual poll tax on ex-indentured Indians. That was the signal for the renewal of civil disobedience. When Gandhi wrote to Gokhale about the breach of the pledge, the latter was evidently pained. He asked Gandhi to provide him with more information about the strength of the 'army of peace' that he intended to throw against the Union government. Gokhale was not impressed with the reply.

Gandhi now wanted to conduct the campaign himself, without interference from abroad or monetary help from India. He told Gokhale to ensure that no funds were raised in India for the South African cause. Gokhale felt that Gandhi was beginning to exceed his proper limitations. In a stern reply he observed:

We in India have some idea of our duty, even as you understand your obligations in South Africa. We will not permit you to tell us what is or is not proper for us to do. I only desired to know the position in South Africa, but did not seek your advice as to what we may do.

Gandhi's belief that there had been a breach of pledge was, indeed, genuine, and Gokhale's own statements in this regard strengthened that belief. But Gokhale does not appear to have categorically stated that Botha and Smuts actually pledged themselves to abolish the tax. W.K. Hancock, Smuts's biographer, contends that although the ministers aroused expectations which they failed subsequently to fulfil, they stopped short of giving a binding pledge, and that Gokhale himself, as he left his interview with them, merely 'supposed' that the tax would be abolished.

Gandhi's tactics in the final campaign showed ample astuteness. He was aware that the number of Satyagrahis he could really rely on was very small. Thus far Satyagraha had not even been mentioned among the indentured labourers, nor had they been educated to participate in it. Being illiterate they could not read *Indian Opinion* or other newspapers. And yet Gandhi reckoned that his demand for the abolition of the burdensome £3 tax had a considerable appeal for the many thousands of Indians of the labouring class who had to pay it. They could therefore be considered potential recruits to his 'army'. He had always been sympathetic toward these poor people and had helped them as a lawyer for little or no fee; he had voluntarily worked as a dispenser at their hospital; he was widely known to be their well-wisher. Accordingly, he could possibly count on them to follow his leadership. Other events proved favourable, 'as if unseen by anyone God was preparing the ingredients for the Indians' victory'.

In March 1913, a case involving the right of one Bai Mariam to join her husband, a Muslim immigrant to the Cape, came before Justice Malcolm Searle, of the Cape provincial division of the Supreme Court. The justice ruled that only those marriages celebrated according to Christian rites and recorded by a registrar of marriages were valid. Hindu, Muslim and Parsi marriages, which had never been registered anywhere and were solely subject to religious traditions, were deprived overnight of their official sanction, and Indians all over South Africa learned to their horror that their wives had acquired the status of concubines and their children were rendered illegitimate.

When Gandhi told Kasturbai about her changed status as a result of the Searle judgment, she was incensed and asked: 'Then I am not your wife according to the laws of the country?' Gandhi replied that this was true, and added that their children were not their heirs any more. 'Then let us go to India,' she suggested. 'No,' he answered, 'that would be cowardly and would not solve the difficulty.' Despite being unwell, Kasturbai offered to take part in the forthcoming struggle,

Gandhi had so far restricted women's participation in Satyagraha, but 'this insult offered to Indian womanhood' provided him with a simple, basic moral issue that touched the lives of Indian men and women throughout South Africa.

Meanwhile the publication of the new immigration bill provided little respite to the Indians. Although it conceded some of the points for which Satyagraha had been launched, it did not seek to carry out the provisional settlement as it took away some of the existing rights. On 21 July Gandhi telegraphed Gokhale: 'Going Transvaal to present final letter to Minister. If reply satisfactory and fresh settlement made, no passive resistance. The act appears to contain four fatal objections. Not very hopeful. Failing settlement, passive resistance starting . . . July.'

The new immigration act came into operation on 1 August. The failure of the British government to disallow it and the Union government's apparent satisfaction relating to the Orange Free State racial bar, the £3 tax, and the Searle judgement led Gandhi once more to ask his followers to withdraw their support from certain of the laws of the Union of South Africa. On 13 September he announced in *Indian Opinion* that the negotiations had failed. He added:

> A settlement without a settlement is not settlement . . . It is much better to have an open fight than a patched-up truce. The fight this time must be for altering the spirit of the government and European population of South Africa. And the result can only be attained by prolonged and bitter suffering that must melt the hearts alike of the government, and of the predominant partner.

On 15 September a group of twelve men and four women, including Kasturbai, left Durban for Volksrust to cross the border into the Transvaal. The authorities at Volksrust did not have adequate accommodation for all the resisters at the police station; they were therefore asked to find shelter at the houses of their friends. Three days later they were summoned and charged under the new act as prohibited immigrants. The whole party was then deported to the Natal border, and when they attempted to cross back into the Transvaal they were sentenced to terms of hard labour ranging from one to three months.

Soon a group of eleven women from Tolstoy Farm crossed the border without the required immigration permits, this time from the Transvaal into Natal. For some reason the police refused to arrest them, and so, in accordance with Gandhi's strategy, they marched on thirty-six miles to Newcastle, the state's mining centre. There the women Satyagrahis persuaded some three thousand indentured Indian miners to go out on strike to protest against the £3 tax and the Searle judgement. Gandhi, 'as much perplexed as pleased', immediately proceeded to Newcastle. The women from Tolstoy Farm were arrested and sentenced to three months' hard labour. Their arrest caused a considerable stir in India. Sir Pherozeshah Mehta, who had hitherto been totally indifferent to the Satyagraha in South Africa, said that 'his blood boiled at the thought of these women lying in jails herded with ordinary criminals, and India could not sleep over the matter any longer'.

In the meantime the mineowners cut off the light and water supply in the strikers' company houses, and some of the strikers were beaten up. Gandhi fearlessly advised them to leave their houses and 'fare forth like pilgrims'. More indentured labourers now downed tools in sympathy with the rebellious Newcastle miners.

Gandhi was staying in Newcastle with an Indian Christian couple, Mr and Mrs D.M. Lazarus, who owned a house and a plot of land. This small 'establishment' was now receiving an incessant stream of pilgrims who had 'retired from the household life to the houseless one'. The strikers slept under the sky. Luckily the weather was favourable, and the traders of Newcastle provided cooking pots and bags of rice and *dal*. Before long over two thousand men, women and children, outfitted with only the clothes on their bodies and blankets for bedding, were camped within sight of the Lazarus house. Never before had Gandhi possessed so many willing followers.

He was at a loss to know how he could feed such a large number of people. In consultation with Kallenbach, Polak, and his secretary, Sonja Schlesin, Gandhi resolved to lead this multitude from Natal into the Transvaal in order to 'safely deposit them in jail'. If the authorities should fail to intercept them and in the unlikely event of the strikers completing their journey successfully, he intended to settle them in the Tolstoy Farm establishment. He warned the strikers of the horrors of being an Indian prisoner in a European-run jail, and urged the waverers to return to the mines. None did. He insisted on hygienic and social restraints and also stressed the basic ethical rules for the forthcoming march: no one was to touch anyone's property on the way; they were to welcome arrest and bear patiently with abuse and even flogging.

On 28 October 1913, Gandhi set out with his 'army of peace' – 2,037 men, 127 women and 57 children – on a daily ration of a pound and a half of bread and an ounce of sugar. The thirty-six miles from Newcastle to the small border town of Charlestown were covered in two days. Commenting on the march, the *Sunday Post* observed:

The pilgrims which Mr Gandhi is guiding are an exceedingly picturesque crew. To the eye they appear most meagre, indeed emaciated; their legs are mere sticks but the way they are marching on starvation rations shows them to be particularly hardy. Of the two thousand, some 1,500 walk together in a fairly compact body, the rest following in little groups of stragglers within two or three miles. Mr Gandhi is looked upon with absolute veneration and is habitually addressed as *Bapu* (father).

The Indian merchants of Charlestown provided rice, vegetables, kitchen equipment, etc; they also contributed toward affording shelter to the marchers. Women and children were accommodated in houses; the men slept in the grounds of the local mosque.

Before marching on Gandhi telegraphed the authorities that if the government repealed the £3 tax the strike could be called off and the labourers would return to work as he did not want them to join the general struggle for the rest of the Indians' grievances. There was no reply from the government for a week, nor were the marchers arrested. Gandhi had by now an inkling that the authorities might not stop the marchers even if they got well into the Transvaal. In that case he had tentative plans to descend on Tolstoy Farm in about a week, covering some twenty-five miles each day. Kallenbach had made arrangements for supplies along the way.

In a bid to make one last appeal to the government, Gandhi telephoned Pretoria and told Smuts's secretary that he was prepared to stop the march if General Smuts would promise to abolish the £3 tax. After a short pause the secretary returned with news for Gandhi: 'General Smuts will have nothing to do with you. You may do just as you please.'

The next morning as he led his 'army' to the border, just a mile away, a large detachment of mounted police was on emergency duty at the border gate on the main road. Apart from the gate, the border was unprotected and there were no fences of any description. Gandhi went up to the mounted police after leaving instructions with the 'army' to cross over when he signalled to them. But while he was still talking to the police, the marchers made a sudden rush and crossed the border. The police, vastly outnumbered, proved quite ineffective. The procession then advanced on Volksrust, expecting trouble, as some of the local jingoes had threatened to shoot them like rabbits. But, perhaps as a result of the meeting Kallenbach had earlier had with the locals, all were out to witness the novel sight, while, as Gandhi put it, 'there was even a friendly twinkle in the eyes of some of them.'

That day, the marchers got as far as Palmford, a town eight miles beyond

Volksrust, where they had a meagre meal of bread and sugar. Gandhi surveyed his slumbering multitude under the sky and was about to lie down when he heard footsteps and moments later saw someone approaching, lantern in hand. It was a police officer, who told Gandhi he was under arrest. Gandhi woke P.K. Naidoo, a faithful lieutenant, and instructed him to ensure that on no account should the news of his arrest be given to the pilgrims during the night. They should commence marching before sunrise, and be told of his arrest when they halted for breakfast. He then walked off with the policeman to the railroad station.

The next morning he was taken before the magistrate at Volksrust. The public prosecutor needed time to prepare the case, and Gandhi applied for bail, as he was anxious to be with the Indian 'army'. He was released on bail of £50. Kallenbach, stationed in Volksrust to send on stragglers and new recruits, had a car ready and promptly drove Gandhi back to the marchers.

On the following day, at Standerton, while he was handing out bread and marmalade, a gift from friendly storekeepers in town he noticed that the local magistrate was waiting patiently for him till the distribution was over. Gandhi knew the magistrate and thought perhaps that he wanted to talk with him. 'You are my prisoner,' said the friendly magistrate. 'It seems I have been promoted,' Gandhi responded, 'as magistrates take the trouble to arrest me instead of mere police officials.' He was again released on bail on the same grounds as in Volksrust. The Indian merchants had kept a carriage ready and Gandhi quickly rejoined the pilgrims. The next day, on 9 November, as Gandhi and Polak were walking at the head of a long column through Teakworth, Gandhi was arrested for the third time in four days. He passed the command to Polak. This time there was no question of being released on bail. He was found guilty of the charge of having induced indentured labourers to leave the province of Natal, and was sentenced to a £60 fine or nine months' imprisonment with hard labour. He elected to go to prison and was sent to the Bloemfontein jail in the Orange Free State. Soon, Polak and Kallenbach were also arrested and sentenced to three months' imprisonment with hard labour.

The pilgrims continued to march in the direction of Tolstoy Farm, but when they reached the town of Balfour, near Johannesburg, they were stopped and herded on to three special trains bound for Natal. The indentured Indians were sent back to the mines at Newcastle, after being sentenced to various terms of imprisonment, with the mine compounds designated as outstations of the Dundee and Newcastle jails. The mineowners' European staffs were appointed warders, and work in the mines was made part of the sentence. The prisoners refused to descend to the coal face even though they were whipped and beaten. As the news of these excesses became generally known, Indian workers all over Natal came out on strike in sympathy with their fellow countrymen, only to be set upon by the mounted military police. In one place the military killed and wounded several.

The passive resistance campaign soon made 'the South African question' the burning topic of the day in India and throughout the Empire. Lord Hardinge, the Viceroy, took the unprecedented step of publicly criticizing the Union government and expressing the 'sympathy of India, deep and burning . . . for their compatriots in South Africa in their resistance to invidious and unjust laws'.

The resistance movement picked up, and before long tens of thousands of indentured labourers were on strike; several thousand free Indians were in prison. It was arranged that a number of leading Indians, Albert West, who edited *Indian Opinion*, and Sonja Schlesin, Gandhi's secretary, would avoid arrest so that they could keep the organizational, financial and propaganda aspects of the resistance in order. West was, however, arrested.

At this dismal hour, the Union government, under pressure from the Viceroy and the British authorities in Whitehall, announced its intention to establish an 'Indian Enquiry Commission' to investigate the causes of the strike and the disturbances that had occurred in connection with it. One of the commission's first actions was to recommend the release of Gandhi, Polak and Kallenbach, and on 18 December the three prisoners were brought to Pretoria and unconditionally set free.

Gandhi was most dissatisfied with the composition of the commission. 'It is considered that the commission has been appointed to give fair play,' he wrote to Gokhale, 'but it is a packed body intended to hoodwink the public in England and India.' The Indian community was not represented and two of the three members of the commission were noted for their anti-Indian bias.

A few days after leaving prison, Gandhi appeared at a mass meeting in Durban, wearing *kurta, dhoti,* and sandals. He had abandoned Western clothing, he told the meeting, in honour of comrades killed during the miners' strike. The thought of his own responsibility in their deaths haunted him. He felt how 'glorious' it would have been if one of those bullets had struck him.

He wrote to Smuts condemning the choice of the two anti-Asiatic commission members, but reconstruction of the commission was nowhere in sight. Despite the opposition of both the Viceroy and Gokhale, Gandhi resolved to boycott its proceedings and to urge his followers not to give evidence. Gokhale was particularly peeved: 'Gandhi had no business to take a vow and tie himself up . . . This is politics and compromise is the essence.'

The situation in South Africa persuaded Lord Hardinge to send there his special envoy, Sir Benjamin Robertson. Gokhale also sent his emissaries – Charles Freer Andrews and William Pearson, both missionaries, both possessing immense knowledge of India, and both closely associated with Rabindranath Tagore and Santiniketan, the residential school maintained by him. Santiniketan, meaning 'the abode of peace', had been founded by Tagore with a view to enlarging the creative gifts of its pupils. Andrews, who taught at Santiniketan, would soon make it his permanent residence, and would live there for the rest of his life.

Charles Freer Andrews was born in 1871 at Newcastle upon Tyne. Some years later the family moved to Birmingham. From King Edward VI School he went to Pembroke College, Cambridge, where he took firsts in Classics and Theology.

For some years Andrews did clerical and teaching work with devotion, and in 1904 went out to India with the Cambridge Mission. As an Anglican priest and lecturer at St Stephen's College, Delhi, his voice came increasingly to be heard and respected within both Indian nationalist and official British circles. Andrews made no secret of his desire to see India achieve freedom. Inevitably, he incurred the displeasure of the Church authorities on this account, and had to give up the clerical robes so dear to him.

Andrews loved the poor, the lowly and the downtrodden. He frequently toured the United States, England, Australia, New Zealand, Fiji, Ceylon, Africa and other areas to take stock of the conditions of the Indians settled there, and to take up their cause.

On 2 January 1914, when Andrews and Pearson reached Durban after a week of storms in the Indian Ocean, there was a small reception committee at the dockside to greet them. Andrews was anticipating Gandhi possessing the same impressive spiritual presence as Tagore and Mahatma Munshi Ram, the prominent Hindu nationalist leader later known as Swami Shraddhanand. As he surveyed the waiting group, he spotted Henry Polak, whom he had met at Delhi, and hastily asked him whether Gandhi was present. Writing of their first encounter, Andrews observed:

> He [Polak] pointed to an ascetic figure with head shaven, dressed in a white *dhoti* and *kurta* of such coarse material as an indentured labourer might wear, looking as though in mourning, and said: 'Here is Mr Gandhi.' I stooped at once instinctively, and touched his feet [in the traditional Hindu gesture of reverence], and he said in a low tone: 'Pray do not do that, it is a humiliation to me.'

Gandhi at once recognized something extraordinary in Andrews and readily saw in him the confidant who would assist him in deciding on future policy and tactics. The unassuming Andrews had contacts in high places: he knew personally the Governor-General of South Africa, Lord Gladstone, the scholarly son of William Ewart Gladstone.

There now seemed to be a stalemate: Gandhi was not prepared to give evidence before a stacked commission without prior assurance from the government. He was not disposed to disregard the £3 tax, the statutory insult to Indian women, the murders and the beatings that were fresh in his mind. Andrews asked Gandhi whether his opposition to the commission was not a question of Indian honour. 'Yes,' Gandhi responded vigorously. 'That is it, that is it. That is the real point at issue.' 'Then,' said Andrews, 'I am sure you are right to stand out. There must be no sacrifice of honour.' Andrews and Gandhi were friends from that moment forth, within two or three days they were 'Mohan' and 'Charlie' to each other.

Against the backdrop of the impending resumption of Satyagraha, Gandhi, accompanied by Andrews, travelled to Pretoria to see Smuts. The Indian controversy was now overtaken by a conflict which Smuts considered far more serious: a strike by white workers which brought all the South African railroads to a standstill. If the railroad workers, in seizing this moment, were deliberately exploiting the government's predicament, the Satyagrahis would not do likewise. Gandhi was not at all anxious to take advantage of the government's embarrassment, and announced that passive resistance would be suspended for the duration of the railroad strike. It was a unique experience for the Union government to be the recipient of such a magnanimous gesture. One of Smuts's secretaries, in a jocular strain, told Gandhi:

> I do not like your people, and do not care to assist them at all. But what am I to do? You help us in our days of need. How can we lay hands upon you? I often wish you took to violence like the English strikers, and then we would know at once how to dispose of you. But you will not injure even the enemy. You desire victory by self-suffering alone and never transgress your self-imposed limit of courtesy and chivalry. And that is what reduces us to sheer helplessness.

Charlie Andrews believed that the commission might provide a way out, but in the event that it failed to achieve its objectives, he was clear about his role. 'If the march of the sufferers to Pretoria takes place, I must join it,' he wrote to Munshi Ram. 'There is nothing else to be done, and this may mean arrest.'

The Archdeacon of Natal, F.S.K. Gregson, invited Andrews to the pulpit of the cathedral to deliver his message to the people of Natal. Willy Pearson took Gandhi along to hear him out, but Gandhi was not permitted to enter the church, which was for whites only. Commenting on the incident, Andrews told Tagore: 'Christianity in its present unholy alliance with the white race is utterly unable to cope with the evil [of racism].' He had no doubt as to where the 'meek and lowly' Christ was in South Africa: he was, Andrews declared, making his presence felt among the Indian Satyagrahis, 'the humblest and the lowliest and lost'. Speaking of the incident many years later, Andrews said: 'If Christ had gone to that church, he also would have been turned away because he was an Asiatic.'

Meanwhile the strike by European railroad workers took a serious turn – martial law had been declared – threatening the survival of Botha's government. Gandhi's decision not to capitalize on the government's difficulties led to a more congenial atmosphere, and through a number of letters and conversations he negotiated an agreement with General Smuts. With Andrews acting as the mediator and the witness in the agreement, and Sir Benjamin Robertson representing the government of India, there was very little likelihood of the agreement being subsequently repudiated.

Smuts was quite anxious to settle the Indian question. He told Gandhi that the government had decided to grant his demands but it was politically necessary that such a recommendation must come from the enquiry commission. He was certain it would be forthcoming. He would have no objection if Gandhi decided to boycott the commission, but he should not prevent others from tendering evidence before it. In addition, Satyagraha should be suspended.

On 21 January 1914, a provisional agreement was arrived at between General Smuts and Gandhi, and Satyagraha was suspended. Satyagrahis were gradually released from jail. In the meantime the commission set to work, but only a few witnesses on behalf of Indians appeared before it. This virtual boycott of the commission shortened its work and the report was published at once. It recommended that the main Indian demands should be accepted.

Meetings were held in various places and Gandhi was able to persuade the Indians to approve the terms of the agreement. Smuts, for his part, pleaded with Members of Parliament to approach the problem 'in a non-controversial spirit'. On 30 June, Gandhi and Smuts finally exchanged letters confirming the terms of a complete agreement. This document was then incorporated into the Indian Relief Bill and submitted to the Union Parliament.

Under the new legislation, all monogamous Indian marriages solemnized by Hindu, Muslim and Parsi traditions were recognized as valid, and the £3 tax was abolished and arrears cancelled. A domicile certificate bearing the holder's thumbprint was made sufficient evidence of right to enter the Union, although the main provisions of the Black Act still remained in force – Indians were not permitted to move freely from one province to another, and the entry of Indian labourers into South Africa was to stop totally after 1920. The Union Immigration Restriction Act also remained in force, except that as a gesture the government allowed six educated Indians to immigrate to South Africa every year. Gandhi now felt that a substantial victory had been won. Consequently, he did not insist on an enquiry into the police brutality toward Indians, nor did he raise the crucial issue of the 'locations' (ghettos) in which Indians were forced to live. He felt that this was not the time to press his advantages. The Satyagraha campaign was called off and among the Indians Gandhi emerged as a hero.

It was no easy task for a European to conduct negotiations with Gandhi. Lord Gladstone, the Governor-General, certainly echoed General Smuts's thoughts when, in a letter to the Secretary of State, he referred to Gandhi as 'an unusual type of humanity, whose peculiarities, however inconvenient they may be to the Minister, are not devoid of attraction to the student . . . His [Gandhi's] ethical and intellectual attitude, based it appears on a curious compound of mysticism and astuteness, baffles the ordinary process of thought.' Lord Hardinge's emissary Robertson felt that Gandhi 'has a terrible amount of conscience and is very hard to manage'.

The peaceful march had made a good impression on the public, and this was undoubtedly responsible for the compromise settlement that ensued. Despite limited gains Gandhi regarded the agreement as the 'Magna Carta' of South African Indians. He asserted that the victory, however limited, certainly sought to remove the racial taint in the law and was a vindication of civil resistance.

Just as the intricate and time-consuming negotiations were coming to an end, Gandhi's joy in his triumph was dimmed, for Kasturbai's health was deteriorating rapidly. The steep decline in her health had begun during her recent prison term, and though Gandhi was finalizing his plans to return to India, he was not too certain that Kasturbai, in her present condition, would survive the journey. He cared for her as best as he could.

There was another illness in the family at that time. Gandhi's erstwhile estranged brother, Laxmidas, had been ailing for a while and it was Gandhi's ardent wish to return to India and nurse him, but Laxmidas died long before he could reach India. His second brother, Karsandas, had died a year before. In a letter to Kallenbach, Gandhi expressed his innermost thoughts on the passing away of his eldest brother:

The greatest grief imaginable has befallen me. My brother died yesterday, I suppose simply thinking up to his last breath of me. What a passionate wish it

189

was on his part to meet me. I was hurrying everything on so that I could go to India with the quickest despatch and fall down at his feet and nurse him. But it was not to be. Now I must go to a family of widows with my poor self as the head. You who do not know the Indian patriarchal cause do not quite realize what this may mean. Anyway my desire to get to India is keener than ever. And yet who knows? I doubt very much whether I shall ever realize that desire. However, I must prepare for the pilgrimage and then leave it calmly in the hands of Him who wields the almighty power. These shocks make in me still more intense fearlessness of death. Why should the event agitate one! The grief itself has a selfish touch about it. It is no calamity that my brother is dead if I am ready to meet death and consider it as the supreme and welcome crisis in life. It is because we fear death so much for ourselves that we shed tears over the deaths of others. How can I who know the body to be perishable and soul to be imperishable mourn over the separation of body from soul? But it is a condition attached to a real belief and consoling doctrine. He who believes in it must not pamper the body but must be its ruler. He must regulate his wants so as to make it serve the dweller within and not allow the body to master him. Not to grieve over the death of others is to accept a state almost of perpetual grief. For this connection between body and soul is itself grievous.

There was another shock in store for Gandhi, and the resultant grief was far more than he had experienced at the death of Laxmidas. At Phoenix a young female pupil twice committed a moral lapse, and when Gandhi heard the news he was visibly shaken and hurried from Johannesburg to Phoenix. He was in such a disturbed state of mind that Kallenbach insisted on going with him. As a penance he imposed on himself a fast for seven days and a vow to have only one meal a day for four months. When Kallenbach failed to dissuade him, he himself fasted with Gandhi. The girl involved also fasted, took off all her jewellery, put on the garb of mourning and had her hair cropped short as a sign of guilt and remorse. This episode led Gandhi into a deep depression. In a letter to an unknown correspondent he wrote about ending his life as a penitential sacrifice; he also pointed out that he had a strain of cruelty in him which manifested itself in his determination to dominate others against their will:

> Never before have I spent such days of agony as I am doing now. I talk and I smile, I walk and eat and work, all mechanically these days. I can do no writing whatever. The heart seems to have gone dry. The agony I am going through is unspeakable. I have often wanted to take out the knife from my pocket and put it through the stomach. Sometimes I have felt like striking my head against the wall opposite, and at other times I have thought of running away from the world.
>
> I do not know what evil there is in me. I have a strain of cruelty in me, as

others say, such that people force themselves to do things, even to attempt impossible things, in order to please me. Lacking the necessary strength, they put on a false show and deceive me. Even Gokhale used to tell me that I was so harsh that people felt terrified of me and allowed themselves to be dragged against their will out of sheer fear or in the attempt to please me, and that those who found themselves too weak assumed an artificial pose in the end. I put far too heavy burdens on people.

About this time Gandhi's second son, Manilal, got involved with a married woman. Gandhi found it fit to make the affair a public scandal, and he also fasted and proclaimed that he would never allow Manilal to marry. He only relented under Kasturbai's pressure – in 1927 when Manilal was thirty-five.

In this strangely mixed mood of despondency and satisfaction derived from political achievement, Gandhi was preparing to leave South Africa to start a new life in India. He felt that his work in South Africa was over. Although South Africa had laid the political and spiritual foundations with which he was to combat British imperialism in India, he foresaw his future in India: 'For me there can be no deliverance from this earthly life except in India. Anyone who seeks such deliverance . . . must go to the sacred soil of India. For me, as for everyone else, the land of India is the "refuge of the afflicted".'

As Gandhi left South Africa for the final time, his supporters swamped him with testimonials and farewell banquets. Even his former adversaries were not ungenerous in praise, but that did not imply their acceptance of Indians into the mainstream of South African life. Smuts exclaimed, with obvious relief: 'The saint has left our shores, I sincerely hope for ever.' Yet in 1939, when invited to contribute to a volume on the occasion of the Mahatma's seventieth birthday, Smuts, by then a world-famous statesman and war leader, graciously complied, writing:

It was my fate to be the antagonist of a man for whom even then I had the highest respect . . . He never forgot the human background of the situation, never lost his temper or succumbed to hate, and preserved his gentle humour even in the most trying situations. I must admit that his activities at that time were very trying to me. Together with other South African leaders I was then busily engaged on the task of welding the old Colonies into a unified State . . . It was a colossal work which took up every moment of my time. Suddenly in the midst of all those engrossing preoccupations Gandhi raised a most troublesome issue. We had a skeleton in our cupboard . . .

His method was deliberately to break the law, and to organize his followers into a mass movement of passive resistance in disobedience to the law objected to. In both provinces a wild and disconcerting commotion was created, large numbers of Indians had to be imprisoned for lawless behaviour, and Gandhi himself received – what no doubt he desired – a short period of rest and quiet in gaol. For him everything went according to plan. For me – the defender of law and order – there was the usual trying situation, the odium of carrying out a law which had no strong public support, and finally the discomfiture when the law had to be repealed. For him it was a successful coup. Nor was the personal touch wanting, for nothing in Gandhi's procedure is without a peculiar personal touch. In gaol he had prepared for me a very useful pair of sandals which he presented to me when he was set free! I have worn these sandals for many a summer since then, even though I may feel that I am not worthy to stand in the shoes of so great a man!

Anyhow it was in this spirit that we fought out our quarrels in South Africa. There was no hatred or personal ill-feeling, the spirit of humanity was never absent, and when the fight was over there was the atmosphere in which a decent peace could be concluded. Gandhi and I made a settlement which Parliament ratified, and which kept the peace between the races for many years.

Gandhi's work in South Africa had helped to return to the Indians their honour, but some of the objectionable laws were still on the statute books and Indians continued to remain in an unenviable position. He was aware that the efficacy of Satyagraha as a solution to the problems of mankind was questionable. 'There is a law of nature that a thing can be retained by the same means by which it has been acquired,' he wrote. 'A thing acquired by violence can be retained by violence alone, while one acquired by truth can be retained only by truth. The Indians in South Africa, therefore, can ensure their safety today if they can wield the weapon of Satyagraha. Satyagraha is a priceless and matchless weapon and those who wield it are strangers to disappointment or defeat.'

In an essay, 'The Soul as it is, and How to Deal with it', in *Hibbert Journal*, Professor Gilbert Murray of Oxford wrote of Gandhi:

Persons in power should be very careful how they deal with a man who cares nothing for sensual pleasures, nothing for riches, nothing for comfort or praise or for promotion, but is simply determined to do what he believes to be right. He is a dangerous and uncomfortable enemy, because his body, which you can always conquer, gives you so little purchase on his soul.

When Gandhi, accompanied by Kasturbai and Kallenbach, boarded the RMS *Kilfauns Castle* at Durban on 18 July 1914, war clouds were racing across the skies of Europe, but he had no inkling of their coming. Gokhale was in England at the time, and they were scheduled to go there first and return to Indian with him. In his third-class cabin Gandhi spent his days quietly, doing some writing work and nursing Kasturbai, who was still quite weak. Gandhi himself was not in the best of health, for his recent fast and two weeks of banquets and speeches had exhausted him. He would often have earnest discussion with Kallenbach on moral principles, with Gandhi doing most of the talking. Kallenbach's possession of a pair of expensive binoculars prompted Gandhi to give him a lecture on the subject of personal possession and simplicity. Kallenbach was finally persuaded to throw his binoculars, worth £7, into the sea. After all, this possession which the German valued so intensely was not in keeping with the ideal of simplicity that they aspired to reach.

Gandhi had spent twenty-one 'sweet and bitter' years in South Africa, in which time he had 'realized my vocation in life'. When he arrived in London on 6 August, he entered a world where violence had become commonplace, for war had already broken out. Gokhale had instructed Gandhi to see him in London, but there was no sign of him there – he had gone to France in an effort to cure his diabetes by drinking Vichy water. Communications between Paris and London were cut off and it was not certain when he would return to London. However, he had asked his poetess friend, Sarojini Naidu, to look after Gandhi.

Mrs Sarojini Naidu (née Chattopadhyay) (1879–1949) was a leading nationalist who did much for the social uplift of her people. She inherited her poetic instinct from her parents. 'One day when I was eleven, I was sighing over a sum of algebra: it would not come right; but instead a whole poem came to me suddenly. I wrote it down . . . From that day my poetic career began.'

She was a brilliant student and was only twelve when she matriculated. Upon graduation she was awarded a Nizam of Hyderabad scholarship to study in England, where she attended King's College, London, and Girton College, Cambridge.

She soon made her presence felt in English society, which found the young Indian scholar intellectually mature and talented in literature. In the circles in which Sarojini moved, she met Thomas Hardy, Henry James and other prominent persons of the time.

She wrote Western poetry, her verses the product of her extensive reading of the romantic English poets. Edmund Gosse, the poet and anthologist, found her writing 'totally without individuality'. He advised her to dispense with everything in this 'falsely English vein', and to present some revelation of the heart of India. Thereafter, Sarojini mainly used Indian subjects and backgrounds. In 1898 her health broke down, and she returned to India.

Her first volume of verse, *The Golden Threshold*, was initially published in 1905 and reprinted in London in 1906. Her poems, wrote Arthur Symons in his introduction, 'hint in a delicately evasive way at a rare temperament of a woman of the East'. The second volume, *The Bird of Time*, published in England in 1913 and in the United States in 1916, was also well received, and Edmund Gosse, now more admiring, observed in his introduction to this volume that Sarojini Naidu's poetry 'springs from the very soil of India, her spirit, although it employs the English language as its vehicle'.

As instructed by Gokhale, Mrs Naidu promptly went out in search for Gandhi, finding him in an old lodging-house in Kensington. She took charge of him and Kasturbai, organized a reception in his honour, invited numerous people of importance, including Mohamed Ali Jinnah, the Muslim nationalist leader, and Ananda Coomaraswamy, the authority on Indian art, who paid rich tributes to the 'hero' of the South African struggle. In his reply, Gandhi spoke of the great crisis and hoped his Indian friends would 'think imperially in the best sense of the word and do their duty'.

He was at the time still hopeful of improving the status of Indians through the help and cooperation of the British, and concluded that it was the duty of Indians 'to win the help of the British by standing by them in their hour of need'. There were some Indians who felt that this was a fitting time to make a bold declaration of the Indian demand. Gandhi pleaded that England's need should not be turned into India's opportunity. He volunteered to raise and head an ambulance corps. Eighty Indian volunteers, mostly university students in London, were given some training. But they fell out with their commanding officer, who was rather dictatorial in manner and decided to offer what Gandhi described as 'miniature Satyagraha',. Consequently some of the corps refused to proceed to Netley Hospital where their services had been requisitioned. The differences were patched up, but this time Gandhi himself was confined to bed, having been afflicted with pleurisy.

His participation in the war inevitably provoked criticism in certain quarters. He had obviously no delusions: 'Those who confine themselves to attending to the wounded in battle cannot be absolved from the guilt of war.' But the same line of argument that had persuaded him to take part in the Boer War weighed with him again on this occasion. He argued that while he had accepted the benefits and protection of the British Empire, he had not tried to destroy it. Now that the very existence of the Empire was threatened, it was his duty not to allow it to be destroyed. 'It was quite clear to me that participation in war could never be consistent with *ahimsa*,' he wrote years later. 'But it is not always given to one to be equally clear about one's duty. A votary of Truth is often obliged to grope in the dark. He may not do anything in deference to convention. He must always hold himself open to correction, and whenever he discovers himself to be wrong he must confess it at all costs and atone for it.'

Meanwhile Gokhale returned to London. Gandhi and Kallenbach often visited him and talked about the war. Gandhi's health also became a topic of regular discussion. Gokhale was distressed to know that his obstinate disciple, in spite of pleurisy, was continuing with his dietetic experiments. Gandhi's diet then mainly consisted of groundnuts, ripe and unripe bananas, lemons, tomatoes, grapes and olive oil. His physician strongly recommended the inclusion of milk in his diet, but he was adamant. 'I had before me a picture of the wicked processes the *govals* in Calcutta adopted to extract the last drop of milk from their cows and buffaloes,' he wrote. 'I also had the feeling that, just as meat was not man's food, even so animal's milk could not be man's food.'

He consulted Dr Allinson, the vegetarian doctor who had been forced to leave the Vegetarian Society for advocating birth control. Dr Allinson, to Gandhi's delight, agreed that it was not necessary to take milk. He recommended brown bread, fresh fruit and raw vegetables such as beet, radish, onion and other tubers and greens. The doctor also recommended fresh air, daily walks and oil massage as a cure for pleurisy. Winter was now approaching and Gandhi wondered if he would survive the inclement London weather. Kasturbai's health was not showing any sign of improvement either. He was still directing the ambulance corps and conducting a voluminous correspondence, but the pain in his chest was growing worse. 'Just now my own health seems to have been completely shattered,' he wrote late in November. 'I feel that I hopelessly mismanaged my constitution in the fast.' It was one of his rare admissions of failure. He wondered whether he had been right in forming the Indian Ambulance Corps, and as he struggled back to health, he found himself conscience-stricken. Thousands had already been killed in the war. 'Everything appears so artificial, so materialistic and immoral that one's soul almost becomes atrophied,' he wrote to a friend in South Africa.

Gandhi was attended in his sickness by some of the most distinguished women of the time. Olive Schreiner, the South African novelist, nursed him with devotion. Lady Cecilia Roberts, the wife of the Under-Secretary of State for India, often visited him. Sarojini Naidu cheered him up with her inexhaustible humour, until she left for India.

He himself was in no hurry to return to India and in fact had been planning to take charge of the Indian Ambulance Corps at Netley as soon as he recovered. But when one day in November Charles Roberts, the Under-

Secretary of State, visited the emaciated Gandhi, who was living on a handful of groundnuts and dry bananas, he strongly urged him to go back to India. 'You cannot possibly go to Netley in this condition. There is still severe cold ahead of us,' he said. 'It is only in India that you can be completely cured. If, after your recovery, you should find the war still going on, you will find many opportunities there of rendering help. As it is, I do not regard what you have already done as by any means a small contribution.' Gandhi felt that the advice given by Charles Roberts was sound.

A farewell reception was organized at the Westminster Palace Hotel. Speeches were made in his honour, and he replied that he considered his work in South Africa purely a matter of duty which thus carried no merit with it. His raising of the ambulance corps was the least he could do in England's hour of need. If he should be restored to health, and hostilities still continued, it would be his desire to return to England to continue with his work there.

The following day, 19 December, Gandhi and Kasturbai sailed as second-class passengers on the SS *Arabia*, bound for Bombay. Kallenbach had plans to accompany them, but being a German citizen (he had not taken out South African citizenship), he was not permitted to travel to India. They carried with them enough groundnuts, dates and dried fruit to last the entire journey. At times Gandhi despaired; the prospect of an uncertain future haunted him. 'I have been so often prevented from reaching India that it seems hardly real that I am sitting in a ship bound for India,' he wrote to Albert West. 'And having reached there what shall I do with myself? However, "Lead, Kindly Light, amid the encircling gloom, lead Thou me on." That thought is my solace . . .'

# TWENTY

# The Moderates and the Extremists

Notwithstanding Gandhi's professed uncertainty about his future, his return to India heralded a new era in Indian politics. Through the medium of the already established Indian National Congress, he worked incessantly to leave an indelible mark on history. In fact under his leadership Congress passed through a metamorphosis from a body of upper-class Anglicized Indians to one of the masses. But it would also be interesting to discuss the changes that Congress underwent from its inception to the time when Gandhi appeared on India's political horizon.

Various 'Indian Associations', the forerunners of Congress, were formed during the second half of the nineteenth century, and were the product of the Indian Renaissance, which was essentially a synthesis of Hindu traditon and the Western spirit of enquiry. The dormant forces of ancient Indian culture thus began to reassert themselves after centuries of decay.

The Indian National Congress, or the Congress, as Indians call it, was launched in Bombay on 28 December 1885. Most of the first Congress representatives were high-caste Hindus and Parsis – lawyers, journalists, teachers and businessmen. There were also a few wealthy landowners and merchants, and some Englishmen too. Seventy-three men were found ready to serve as representatives.

Allan Octavian Hume, an Englishman who had retired from the Indian Civil Service, was instrumental in bringing the Congress into being. He was its first general secretary, and he retained this position, sometimes jointly with Indian colleagues, until 1907. During the first twenty-five years of its existence, Congress would elect an Englishman as president on five occasions.

The first Congress was composed of self-appointed leaders, the second of elected delegates. In the beginning Congress was no more than an élitist debating society, and its loyalty to the Crown was unquestionable. Although Congress asked for political reforms, its members would not wish to endanger the imperial edifice, for its stable existence was conducive to their prominence in public life. Moreover, Congress was aware of the social and religious implications involved and avoided the possibility of any conflict in these areas that any assertive demands might cause. Under these conditions, Congress provided 'a new public forum in which Indians could become influential and in which the discourse was in terms of an Indian nation'. These leaders of new India wanted less of India's wealth spent on military expenditure, and stressed the need to allocate more funds for education and internal development. They emphasized the development of self-government, the separation of judicial and executive functions, and the employment of a larger number of Indians in the higher ranks of the Civil Service.

In the early years of Congress – when its appeal was confined to the English-speaking middle class – its Anglophile members would not hesitate to demonstrate their loyalty to the Crown. In his 'confession of faith of a devout and irreclaimable Congressman', Sir Pherozeshah Mehta said:

> I am a robust optimist . . . I believe in divine guidance through human agency . . . I accept British rule . . . as a dispensation so wonderful, a little island set at one end of the world establishing itself in a far continent as different as could be, that it would be folly not to accept it as a declaration of God's will.

W.C. Bonnerjee, who presided at the first Congress session, spoke thus at the second:

> It is under the civilizing rule of the Queen and the people of England that we meet here together, hindered by none, freely allowed to speak our minds, without the least fear and hesitation. Such a thing is possible under British rule, and under British rule only.

As late as 1902 Surendranath Banerjea, presiding at the annual session of Congress at Ahmedabad, observed: 'We plead for the permanence of British rule in India.'

In order that these leaders' words are not taken as gospel, it may be noted that although British rule had brought about general stability in the country at the time, the treatment of the natives by individual Englishmen was often domineering and at times even brutal, thereby staining England's record.

In January 1872, during a minor rising among a sect called the Kookas, a fort was attacked. It turned out to be a freak encounter, for the Kookas just managed to tie up a few soldiers, and did not resort to any violence. Fifty Kookas were, however, taken prisoner and the English official in charge took it upon himself to have them all blown from a cannon's mouth. He was dismissed from the service, but no other action was taken.

Another shocking occurrence was described by William Bonnar in 1895 in *Contemporary Review*:

Not so very long ago I heard a civil surgeon gaily tell at a mess dinner how the other day he had felt constrained to teach a native somewhat forcibly his respectful duty to the 'Ruling Race'. The 'nigger', as he put it, had his whiskers and beard tied up, as all natives like to have them when travelling, when he met him on a country road. The doctor pulled him up and demanded to know why he had not undone his face cloth when he saw a *Sahib* coming. Then suddenly remembering that he had a pair of forceps in his pocket, he dismounted, and taking the poor man's head under his powerful arm extracted two of his teeth, saying, 'Now tie up your mouth, my man. You have some excuse now.'

Such cases were, however, very uncommon. As a rule, British officers were hard-working, just and honourable. Although their attitude towards the natives was condescending, they invariably set examples, even at the peril of their lives, to combat epidemics such as cholera and plague. There were also innumerable instances of life-long close friendships between Englishmen and Indians.

Even though the loyalty of India's new political leaders pleased the government of India, their demands for any tangible reforms were virtually ignored. This indifference on the part of the government would lead to growing nationalism. The government's approval of Congress thus could not continue for long. On the eve of his departure in 1888, Lord Dufferin, the Viceroy, scornfully referred to Congress as a 'microscopic minority' which had no claim to represent Indian opinion. In the years to come, Congressmen would start asserting that they were the legitimate spokesmen of the poor and illiterate millions, the natural custodians of their interests.

Notwithstanding the sharp tone of speeches and the increasing number of resolutions passed annually by Congress, the grip of the Crown remained firm from 1885 through to 1904. During these years, religious fervour was used for the first time for political purposes. In Maharashtra, western India, in 1895 Bal Gangadhar Tilak inaugurated the Shivaji Festival, which became a platform for preaching nationalism. (Shivaji, the seventeenth-century Maratha warrior king, who fought against the Mughal Empire in India, is revered by Hindus). The British government strongly suspected the motive behind the religious overtones in such a celebration and used all means to suppress it. Tilak and other like-minded leaders spoke with passion and made their presence felt.

The first real threat to the British in India was felt in 1905 when, under the viceroyalty of Lord Curzon, the province of Bengal was partitioned, ostensibly for administrative reasons, the predominantly Muslim region of eastern Bengal separating from the Hindu-dominated western part. National leaders, however, saw it as a move to create a rift between the Bengali Hindus and Muslims. The movement against the partition of Bengal swiftly assumed a national character. People took to the streets, demonstrating against what they considered to be the British policy of divide and rule. At a spirited demonstration organized in Calcutta Town Hall on 7 August 1905, Surendranath Banerjea, a leading Congressman, drafted a boycott pledge and appealed to the people to sign it: 'I hereby pledge myself to abstain from the purchase of all English-made goods for at least a year from this date, so help me God.'

As anti-partition passions gained momentum and the sale of *swadeshi* (Indian-made goods) boomed, the government resorted to large-scale criminal prosecutions against the most vocal leaders. Police wielded metal-tipped *lathis* to contain the demonstrators.

In the wake of the partition of Bengal, Bipin Chandra Pal emerged as the most popular leader of Bengal's radical youth. In August 1906 he started a journal called *Bande Mataram*, ably assisted by Aurobindo Ghosh, first principal of Bengal's National College. Through the medium of this journal they propagated the boycott of British goods and institutions, including schools, colleges, law courts and government services, with a view to making the British administration in India ineffective. Soon their spirit of boycott gained the support of Bal Gangadhar Tilak in Poona, and Lala Lajpat Rai, the leader of the popular Hindu revivalist organization Arya Samaj which led the Punjab nationalist awakening.

In this climate of growing political unrest, the economic policies of the British government added to the discontent: unemployment was on the increase, prices were rising and the masses were becoming impoverished further. These and many other factors helped the nationalist movement acquire a militant character. Many terrorist organizations sprang up. The government inevitably adopted stern measures to combat lawlessness, and in the process many nationalists were detained or deported without trial. The press was muzzled, civil liberties were curtailed and the police were given a free hand in dealing with the situation.

The net result of the frustrations following partition was the emergence of the revolutionary wing of Congress under the firebrand leadership of Bal Gangadhar Tilak, Bipin Chandra Pal and Lala Lajpat Rai, who came to be collectively known as Bal-Pal-Lal, their names thus chanted by students all over the subcontinent. The conflict between the extremists and the moderates in Congress now came to the surface.

At the Congress session held in Calcutta in 1906, there was a serious rift between the two wings. The moderates were committed to employing petitions, appeals and memoranda to achieve their goals, whilst the extremists were becoming restive and wanted to start a vigorous movement to achieve *swaraj*. When Tilak's name was proposed for president of the Calcutta Congress of 1906, the outgoing president, Gopal Krishna Gokhale, a staunch moderate, refused to agree, and Sir Pherozeshah Mehta was equally firm.

Things came to a head at the 1907 session held at Surat. When the name of Lajpat Rai was proposed for president, Gokhale and Sir Pherozeshah found him as unacceptable as they had done Tilak the previous year. Dr Rash Behari Ghosh, an eminent Bengali, was nominated to serve as president at Surat, but he was unable to deliver the address due to the pandemonium that had broken out. G.S. Khaparde, a member of the extremist group, reported in his diary dated 27 December 1907:

When the Congress sitting commenced again, Surendra Babu [Surendranath Banerjea] resumed his speech and was patiently heard. Then Tilak, who had given notice of amendment, got up to the platform to move it. The Chairman ruled it out of order. Tilak wished to appeal to the delegates. This the Chairman and the Moderates would not allow. A Moderate threw a chair at Tilak. This enraged all our party. A shoe thrown by a Moderate at Tilak struck Surendra Babu on the back and Sir Pherozeshah Mehta on the cheek. There arose a tremendous uproar and many young men got on the platform. There was a free fight. The police took possession of the *pandal* (convention enclosure).

The split at Surat had ensured that India's foremost nationalist organization would remain a house divided for the next nine years.

While impassioned youth took to violent means – including the use of bombs – to win freedom, Tilak tried to argue in his journal *Kesari* that the way to bring about peace was the immediate granting of *swaraj* to the people. A short while later he wrote of the bomb as 'magic', calling it a 'sacred formula' and an 'amulet'. Soon he was arrested and charged with sedition. He was tried in Bombay, and was sentenced to six years' imprisonment. He was taken to the prison at Mandalay, Burma.

There was a nationwide protest against Tilak's incarceration. Students stayed away from schools and colleges. There were *hartals*, and the textile workers of Bombay absented themselves from work. This was the first political strike by workers in India.

While Tilak languished in his Burmese prison, Bipin Chandra Pal moved to London, where he lived in penury in a small dingy room, and Lajpat Rai travelled to the United States, subsisting on the meagre royalties from his writings. The leaderless terrorists, deprived of any semblance of guidance, kept up their acts of murder, arson and suicide. The government, under the stress of its policy of repression against the extremists and terrorists, tried to win over the moderate wing of Congress, which culminated in the legislative reforms of 1909. The moderates who controlled the Congress offered their cooperation in the working of the government's new scheme. As elected members they were thus in a position to offer constructive criticism of the government in the legislative councils and make valuable suggestions and proposals for further reforms. The reforms were however halting, and were always in the form of some concession and never a willing surrender of power.

In November 1910 Lord Hardinge of Penshurst, a Liberal, took over as viceroy. His first significant official act was to propose the unification of Bengal, which was approved by Whitehall. The information was, however, kept top secret till King George V made it public on 12 December 1911 at his coronation (*durbar*) in Delhi. The King also announced that the government of India's capital was to be moved from Calcutta to the ancient capital of Delhi, where a new city, New Delhi, would be born.

Neither the reforms nor the repressive measures brought any reduction in the terrorist activities in India. In December 1913, as Lord Hardinge made his state entry into the new capital, a bomb was thrown at the viceregal elephant in Old Delhi's Chandni Chowk. The explosion killed one of the Viceroy's attendants and wounded some others. Lord Hardinge was slightly hurt.

The revolutionary movement reached its peak during 1913–16, in both Bengal and the Punjab. The outbreak of World War I in 1914 added a new dimension to the situation. Indians thought that at the end of the war there could be a change of heart on the part of the British. The All-India Muslim League (which was formally founded in 1906) would be another factor in the national context. In the meantime, the pan-Islamic movement had gained strength in India, and as a consequence of Britain's attitude towards Turkey, Muslims and Congress became closer, anticipating the mutual benefit emanating from such unity. Accordingly, a new constitution was adopted at the annual sesson of the Muslim League at Karachi in 1913, the League accepting the attainment of self-government for India as its goal. The Congress placed on record 'its appreciation to the adoption by the All-India Muslim League of the idea of self-government'. In 1915 the Congress and the Muslim League held their annual sessions in Bombay simultaneously. Gandhi, Mrs Annie Besant, Madan Mohan Malaviya and

Surendranath Banerjea all attended the Muslim League session. The Muslim League, under the persuasive leadership of Mohamed Ali Jinnah, set up a committee to frame, in consultation with the Congress, a scheme of reforms. The Congress-League plan of reforms was ratified by both the parties at their annual sessions held at Lucknow in December 1916. It was at the Lucknow Congress that a compromise between the moderate and the extremist wings of the party was approved. But the compromise lasted only two years, and the moderates, now calling themselves Liberals, walked out of the Congress.

At this juncture in Indian history, the younger generation had lost nearly all confidence in the elder statesmen, including Sir Pherozeshah Mehta and Surendranath Banerjea, whose tenacity had once earned him the nickname 'Surrender Not'. Gopal Krishna Gokhale, though still highly respected, was dangerously ill in Poona. Bal Gangadhar Tilak had reently been released from Burma's Mandalay jail after six years' imprisonment, and being still busy with his famous rendering of the *Bhagavad Gita*, had not yet resumed his fiery involvement in politics. Lala Lajpat Rai was in America, doing propaganda work, and Aurobindo Ghosh had chosen to remain aloof in Pondicherry. Mrs Annie Besant, who had become more Indian than the Indians, was now planning her Home Rule agitation, but had not yet begun active work. The way was thus clear for a new leader. And Gandhi could not have stepped in at a more favourable psychological moment.

# TWENTY-ONE

# Return of the Native

Gandhi arrived back in India on 9 January 1915. His reputation no doubt preceded him, for his novel Satyagraha campaign had aroused the keenest interest and admiration in India, and he was already marked out as one of the political leaders of the future. Gokhale, his political mentor, had sent him a message saying he should spend a year touring India as an observer and a student. After all, he had been out of the country so long that he could not safely form any definite conclusion about matters essentially Indian. Gandhi promised to obey, but found it impossible to keep his promise.

On arrival in Bombay, he was accorded the privilege of landing at the Apollo Bunder – an honour shared with royalty by the viceroys and the most distinguished of India's sons. A deputation consisting of several prominent people met him on board and there was a large gathering at the quay to greet him.

Several receptions were arranged in his honour. On 12 January he was welcomed by the Imperial Citizenship Association of India at Mount Petit, the sumptuous residence of Jehangir Petit, who had been a sympathizer with the South African Indians' cause and had contributed liberally towards it. Over six hundred of the élite of Bombay, representing all communities in the city, had accepted an invitation. In those surroundings of dazzling splendour, Gandhi was conspicuous by his simple attire. Jehangir Petit's cousin, Raihana, then in her teens, recalls:

> I caught a glimpse of him in the midst of silks and brocades, frills and sparkling jewels. He was dressed in a coarse *khadi dhoti* and looked like a small-town tailor who had wandered in by mistake. I lost my heart to him. He became my father, my mother, my girlfriend, my boyfriend, my daughter, my son, my teacher, my *guru*.

Sir Pherozeshah Mehta spoke of Gandhi's courage and his great moral qualities, his incessant hard work and his sufferings in the cause of the Indians in South Africa. Gandhi, in his reply, said he had felt that he would be more at home in his own motherland than he used to be in South Africa among his countrymen. But during the past few days that they had spent in Bombay, they had felt – and he thought he was voicing the feelings of his wife too – that they had been much more at home among those indentured Indians, who were the truest heroes of India. They felt that they were indeed in strange company in the city of Bombay.

The Gujarati community, to which Gandhi belonged, received him at a garden party, and the chairman of its association, M.A. Jinnah, delivered the welcome speech in English. Jinnah praised Gandhi's struggle in South Africa and frankly added that the Indians in South Africa were not at the end of their difficulties. Most of the other speeches were also in English. Gandhi expressed his thanks in Gujarati and registered 'a humble protest against the use of English at a Gujarati gathering'.

He was invited to an audience with Lord Willingdon, the governor of the Bombay Presidency, who said: 'I would like you to come and see me whenever you propose to take any steps concerning government.' Gandhi replied that he could easily give the promise, inasmuch as it was his rule, as a Satyagrahi, to understand the viewpoint of the party he proposed to deal with. Lord Willingdon was pleased. 'You may come to me whenever you like,' he said, 'and you will see that my Government do not wilfully do anything wrong.' 'It is that faith that sustains me,' answered Gandhi, implying his faith in the goodness of British rule.

From Bombay he journeyed to Kathiawar to see his relatives. At Wadhwan train station, Motilal, a noted worker and a tailor by vocation, met him and complained about the customs cordon at Viramgam (between Kathiawar and British Indian territory) and the hardships the railway passengers had to suffer on account of it. 'Are you prepared to go to jail?' Gandhi asked rather abruptly. 'We will certainly go to jail, provided you lead us,' Motilal replied. 'You will be delighted to see the work and spirit of our youths, and you may trust us to respond as soon as you summon us.' Wherever he went about in Kathiawar, Gandhi heard complaints about the Viramgam customs cordon. He collected and read the literature available on the subject and was convinced about the genuineness of the complaints. He opened a correspondence with the Bombay government and called on the private secretary to the governor. He also waited on His Excellency to discuss the matter. 'If it had been in our hands, we would have removed the cordon long ago,' replied the governor, and advised Gandhi to approach the government of India.

The private secretary to the governor strongly objected to Gandhi's reference in a speech which he had delivered at Bagasra, in Kathiawar, to the launching of Satyagraha.

'Is not this a threat?' the private secretary asked. 'And do you think a powerful government will yield to threats?'

'This was no threat,' Gandhi replied. 'It was educating the people . . . A nation that wants to come into its own ought to know all the ways and means to freedom. Usually they include violence as the last remedy. Satyagraha, on the other hand, is an absolutely non-violent weapon. I regard it as my duty to explain its practice and its limitations. I have no doubt that the British Government is a powerful government, but I have no doubt also that Satyagraha is a sovereign remedy.'

Gandhi communicated with the government of India, but got no reply beyond an acknowledgement. It was only when he had the occasion to meet Lord Chelmsford, the Viceroy, later in 1917, that redress could be had. Within a few days of the interview the customs cordon between Kathiawar and British Indian territory was removed. Gandhi regarded this episode as the advent of Satyagraha in India.

Meanwhile there were more speeches, presents and testimonials. He was now getting anxious to go to Poona to pay his homage to Gokhale. Despite ill-health, Gokhale summoned all members of the Servants of India Society to meet Gandhi. The society, founded in 1905, was dedicated to nation-building in India, within the British Empire, in a true missionary spirit aimed at spiritualizing public life. The objectives of the society were to Gandhi the message by which he wished to be guided in life. He had been looking forward to joining it on his arrival in India. But it soon became apparent that not all members of the society shared Gokhale's judgement of Gandhi. They in fact feared that if they accepted him as a member he would before long be laying down new laws, announcing new goals and taking full control. Gokhale strongly vouched for him, but at the last moment Gandhi withdrew his candidacy.

Whether he was admitted to the Servants of India Society or not, Gandhi was very keen to have an ashram where he could settle down with a small community around him. He informed Gokhale of his intention. Gokhale liked the idea and asked a colleague to open an account for Gandhi in the society's books, and to give him whatever he might require for the ashram and for public expenses. Several of the young Indians who had earlier been at Phoenix Farm were now in Bengal as guests of the school founded by Rabindranath Tagore at Santiniketan. Since Gandhi wanted to establish them elsewhere in an ashram of his own, the offer of financial help was most welcome.

On the eve of Gandhi's departure for Santiniketan, Gokhale gave a farewell party for him. Refreshments consisting of fruit, groundnuts and dates were served. Gokhale was too ill to leave his bed, but he was determined to pay his tribute to Gandhi. Soon he was seen staggering about the gathering but the effort proved too much. He fainted and had to be carried back to his sickbed. As he recovered he sent word that the party must go on.

When Gandhi reached Santiniketan, Tagore was away on tour. Gandhi was welcomed by the teachers and students, and the former inmates of Phoenix Farm were delighted to see him. Tagore had written to Charles Andrews, who along with Willy Pearson was once more teaching at the school, that the Mahatma should be accorded a fitting welcome. But he had hardly been two days at Santiniketan when a telegram from Poona arrived. Gokhale was dead.

Gandhi hurriedly left for Poona to pay homage to his dead mentor. He did his travelling third class, and as he now wore only a shirt, a *dhoti*, and a cheap Kashmiri cap, having dispensed with Western dress during the Satyagraha campaign, he could mingle with third-class passengers and experience their difficulties without attracting attention. He was not yet as widely known in India as he soon was to be. The journey to Poona proved to be quite an ordeal.

With the death of Gokhale, there was a deep void in Gandhi's life. 'Launching on the stormy sea of Indian public life, I was in need of a sure pilot,' he wrote years later. 'I had one in Gokhale and had felt secure in his keeping. Now that he was gone, I was thrown on my own resources.'

He once again sought membership of the Servants of India Society. But when he left Poona a few days later after attending the memorial meeting in the company of Lord Willingdon, it was obvious that most members of the society did not want to admit him into the fold. His track record had certainly caused some fear in them.

When Gandhi returned to Santiniketan, Rabindranath Tagore was waiting for him. Tagore, India's great novelist and poet laureate, had won the Nobel Prize for literature two years earlier. It was Andrews who introduced the two men. Tagore, with his tall, stately figure, silver hair, white beard and rich gown, stood magnificently against the lean Gandhi, dressed in simple shirt and *dhoti*. One was in love with poetry and youth, the other was a man of action. Although their paths and temperaments were different, they were spiritually inheritors of India's ancient culture and traditions. Despite their strongly divergent views on certain matters, they had much affection and admiration for each other.

Two days after their meeting Tagore left for Calcutta. Gandhi, during his remaining stay at Santiniketan, persuaded the entire community of students and teachers to accept from the point of view of their physical and moral health the concept of self-help.

About this time the great fair called the Kumbh Mela, held every twelve years at Hardwar, a city in the United Provinces in the foothills of the Himalayas, was about to open. Gandhi was by no means eager to attend the fair, but he was anxious to meet Mahatma Munshi Ram, later known as Swami Shraddhanand, who had opened a school called the Gurukul in nearby Kangri. Mahatma Munshi Ram, a huge, heavily built man, was a prominent nationalist leader and a man of great sanctity. He asked Gandhi to consider founding his ashram around this area situated in the foothills of the Himalayas. Gandhi was so enchanted by the beauty of the place that he sometimes spoke of remaining there. While the Phoenix boys, led by Maganlal, were doing voluntary work at the Kumbh Mela, Gandhi divided his time between the Gurukul and the sacred city of Hardwar. Since he was not so well-known at the time, it was possible for him to move about without creating much fuss. At Hardwar he came to observe more of the pilgrims' hypocrisy and slovenliness than of their piety. Even the so-called *sadhus* were not any different, and 'seemed to have been born to enjoy the good things of life'. Spectacles such as the five-footed cow, meant to persuade the ignorant into handing over their money, revolted him. He was so disturbed by the prevailing licence at the fair that he took a vow that he would henceforth eat only five articles of food every day, and no food after sunset. The vow was a new addition to his regimen of austerity. Only a few weeks before, when Gokhale had died, he made a vow that he would walk barefoot for a year.

Leaving his Phoenix family at the Gurukul, he took a train for Delhi. Dressed like a poor peasant, he was once again travelling in crowded third-class railroad carriages, indistinguishable from all the other poor passengers on the train. When he reached Madras in April 1915, the welcoming committee searched through the first- and second-class sections, and finally found him emerging in a dishevelled condition from a third-class carriage. Looking thin and emaciated, he was wearing a loose shirt and trousers, soiled by four days of continuous travelling across the country. There were cries of 'Long live Mr and Mrs Gandhi!' and 'Long live the hero!' The students who had been waiting with a horse and carriage were persuaded by his appearance to unyoke the horse and themselves pull the carriage in triumph through the streets. When Gandhi and Kasturbai were shown their sparsely furnished apartment – with two cots, a chair, table and desk – Gandhi asked for the removal of these emblems of luxury. He preferred the bare, unfurnished rooms.

The Madrasis welcomed him with open arms, for the majority of the indentured labourers in South Africa had come from southern India. Several functions were arranged in his honour where he was fêted, garlanded and eulogized. Replying to the address at the Victoria Hall he spoke movingly of the heroism of the Indian labourers. He did not accept the proposition that he had inspired those men and women. 'It was they, the simple-minded folk who worked away in faith, never expecting the slightest reward, who inspired me . . . to do the work that I was able to do.'

At the annual dinner of the Madras Bar Association, an exalted ceremony among the local members of his old profession, he was seated next to the Advocate-General, and was asked to propose a toast to the British Empire. His admiration for the empire had not yet begun to dampen, and he declared:

> I know that a passive resister has to make good his claim to passive resistance, no matter under what circumstances he finds himself, and I discovered that the British Empire had certain ideals with which I have fallen in love, ('Hear, hear.') and one of those ideals is that every subject of the British Empire has the freest scope possible for his energies and efforts and whatever he thinks is due to his conscience. I think that this is true of the British Empire as it is not true of any other Government that we see . . . I feel as you have perhaps known that I am no lover of any Government and I have more than once said that Government is best which governs least, and I have found that it is possible for me to be governed least under the British Empire.

It was after much travelling and much soul-searching that Gandhi decided to settle on the outskirts of Ahmedabad, where he, his family, friends and nearest co-workers would live in an atmosphere of renunciation and service. His friend Jivanlal Desai, a barrister, offered him the use of a bungalow in the neighbouring village of Kochrab where on 25 May 1915, an ashram was founded. Two more properties were soon acquired to house all the ashramites, now consisting of twenty-five men and women. Ahmedabad's textile merchants provided funds to keep the ashram going. Handweaving was the principal industry, and there was some carpentry. No outside help was provided; everyone worked. The running of the ashram was largely in the hands of Maganlal, who had done yeoman service at the Phoenix settlement. The name selected for it, Satyagraha Ashram, reflected Gandhi's desire 'to acquaint India with the method I had tried in South Africa and . . . to test in India the extent to which its application might be possible'.

He lost no time in drawing up a draft constitution incorporating the rules and observances which the ashramites were obliged to adhere to. It was a formidable list, for all had to make the vows of truth-telling, *ahimsa*, celibacy, control of the palate, nonstealing, nonpossession, use of handspun and handwoven *khadi* and refusal to use foreign cloth, acceptance of

Untouchables, fearlessness. Each vow was explained in its various aspects. Fearlessness to Gandhi was 'freedom from the fear of kings, people, caste, families, thieves, robbers, ferocious animals, such as tigers, and even death'. Those who took the vow of fearlessness promised that they would never resort to force, but would defend themselves always with soul-force – the weapon of a person who is trained to practise Satyagraha, which is the force of truth and love.

A few months after the Satyagraha Ashram was founded, its peace was suddenly disturbed when a teacher named Dudabhai, his wife Danibehn and baby daughter Lakshmi, belonging to the Untouchable class of Dheds, were admitted to the community. There was much resentment, and some ashramites, however much they thought to follow Gandhi's precepts, found the family's presence humiliating and defiling, and shunned their company. They gave up their evening meal as a protest against the admission. It was a traumatic experience for Kasturbai, who threatened to leave the ashram. Gandhi insisted she must observe the rules or leave, and added that they would part as good friends. His diary of 8 October reads: 'Got excited again and lost temper with Ba. I must find a medicine for this grave defect.' Notwithstanding this regret, another shock was in store for Kasturbai. Gandhi announced that he had adopted Lakshmi as his own daughter. Kasturbai became the mother of an Untouchable!

These developments caused quite a commotion in Ahmedabad, and the textile merchants who had helped to finance the ashram now began to withdraw their support, until the time came when the ashram had been depleted of all its funds. Along with the stoppage of all financial assistance, a rumour had gained currency that the 'polluted' ashram would be socially boycotted. Gandhi was unperturbed and told the ashramites that if the situation warranted they would all move to the Untouchable quarter of Ahmedabad and live on whatever they could earn by manual labour.

One morning a rich man drove up to the ashram and placed into Gandhi's hands an envelope containing thirteen thousand rupees in banknotes. The social boycott of the ashram never materialized, and the presence in it of an Untouchable family 'proclaimed to the world that the ashram would not countenance untouchability'.

# TWENTY-TWO

# A Speech to Remember

The Satyagraha Ashram continued to have its share of problems, but Gandhi was not confined to it. The ashram was his home, and he would travel across India and return to it. Though he was continually being invited to speak at various functions, he made no political speeches during the year, but instead gave expression to his views on social reform. The year saw Gandhi mentioned in the King's birthday honours list, in which the Kaiser-i-Hind medal was conferred on him for his public services. When a friend congratulated him, Gandhi replied that there need be no congratulations. 'One may get it and also lose it,' he added. 'I do want a medal, but of a different kind altogether. There is no knowing when I shall get it, if ever.'

With the raging of World War I, the struggle in Congress between the liberal and revolutionary wings became more intense, and even moderate Congressmen began to ask for Home Rule. In September 1915 Mrs Annie Besant announced the formation of a Home Rule League and raised the cry: 'The moment of England's difficulty is the moment of India's opportunity.'

Mrs Besant, a distinguished Englishwoman, was a theosophist, socialist and women's rights advocate. She was then approaching seventy, and had over the years become an accepted and respected leader of India. In 1892 she had founded the Central Hindu College at Benares, the holy city on the Ganges, and now, at last, with the guidance of Madan Mohan Malaviya, educationalist and Hindu Mahasabha leader, it was officially granted the status of a university. Members of the academic world, aristocrats and dignitaries of state attended the three-day opening ceremonies. Lord Hardinge, the Viceroy, arrived under strict security. A galaxy of ruling princes, bedecked and bejewelled, presented a dazzling scene. Gandhi was among those invited to speak, but the forthright, unvarnished speech he delivered on 6 February 1916 was to end in utter confusion.

The Maharajah of Darbhanga took the chair. Gandhi spoke in English and addressed himself primarily to the students. All the speeches delivered at the university had been in English, and this disturbed him. Wearing a short white *dhoti* and a white Kathiawari cloak, he spoke extemporaneously and bluntly, sparing no one, least of all those present. And he did so with abandon:

> It is a matter of deep humiliation and shame for us that I am compelled this evening, under the shadow of this great college in this sacred city, to address my countrymen in a language that is foreign to me . . . our language is the reflection of ourselves, and if you tell me that our languages are too poor to express the best thoughts, then I say that the sooner we are wiped out of existence the better for us . . .The charge against us is that we have no initiative. How can we have any if we are to devote the precious years of our lives to the mastery of a foreign tongue? We fail in this attempt also. Was it possible for any speaker yesterday and today to impress his audience as was possible for Mr Higginbotham?

The fact that the previous speakers could not engage the audience was not, Gandhi pointed out, due to lack of substance in their addresses. He was critical of the popular notion that it was only English-educated Indians who were leading and doing things for the nation:

> But suppose that we have been receiving, during the past fifty years, education through our vernaculars, what should we have today? We should have today a free India, we should have our educated men, not as if they were foreigners in their own land but speaking to the heart of the nation, they would be working among the poorest of the poor, and whatever they would have gained during the past fifty years would be a heritage for the nation. . .

He asked the indulgence of his audience for speaking without reserve. He was allowing himself to think 'audibly' that evening, and 'if you think that I seem to transgress the limits that courtesy imposes on me, pardon me for the liberty I may be taking'.

Congress had lately passed a resolution about self-government, but he frankly confessed that he was not interested in what they would be able to produce as he was interested in what the student world was going to produce or the masses were going to produce. 'No amount of speeches will ever make us fit for self-government,' he declared. He wanted action, not speeches. As he spoke of the dirt and squalor he had seen in the streets of Benares when visiting the famous Vishwanath temple, his speech became progressively more vigorous:

> If a stranger dropped from above on to this great temple and he had to consider what we as Hindus were, would he not be justified in condemning us? Is not this great temple a reflection of our own character? I speak feelingly as a Hindu. Is

it right that the lanes of our sacred temple should be as dirty as they are? The houses round about are built anyhow. The lanes are tortuous and narrow. If even our temples are not models of cleanliness, what can our self-government be? Shall our temples be abodes of holiness, cleanliness and peace as soon as the English have retired from India, either of their own pleasure or by compulsion, bag and baggage?

He had not yet finished his lecture on cleanliness and civic sense. He described Indian cities as 'stinking dens', and added: 'It is not comforting to think that people walk about the streets of Indian Bombay, under the perpetual fear of dwellers in the storeyed buildings spitting upon them.' Many Indians felt uncomfortable in their seats. Was it proper for him to admonish them in the presence of the Englishmen? No other Indian leader had ever touched on the subject so pointedly before. And what had spitting to do with Benares University and independence?

Having damned the English language, Indian temples and Indian cities, he dwelt on the behaviour of railroad passengers in the third-class compartment. 'We do not trouble ourselves as to how we use it; the result is indescribable filth.' He could observe the difficulty of third-class passengers, but the railway administration was by no means completely to blame for their hard lot. Indians spat where others had to sleep. The behaviour of students on the train left a lot to be desired. 'They can speak English,' he commented sarcastically, 'and they have worn Norfolk jackets and therefore claim the right to force their way in and command seating accommodation . . . I am setting my heart bare. Surely we must set these things right in our progress toward self-government.'

Having addressed himself to the students, he turned the spotlight on the princes who sat with Mrs Besant on the dais. He minced no words in insisting that they had extracted their wealth from the poor:

His Highness the Maharajah, who presided yesterday over our deliberations, spoke about the poverty of India. Other speakers laid great stress upon it. But what did we witness . . . in . . . the foundation ceremony . . . performed by the Viceroy? Certainly a most gorgeous show, an exhibition of jewellery which made a splendid feast for the eyes of the greatest jeweller who chose to come from Paris. I compare with the richly bedecked noblemen the millions of the poor. And I feel like saying to these noblemen: 'There is no salvation for India unless you strip yourselves of this Jewellery and hold it in trust for your countrymen in India.' I am sure it is not the desire of the King-Emperor or Lord Hardinge that in order to show the truest loyalty to our King-Emperor, it is necessary for us to ransack our jewellery-boxes and to appear bedecked from top to toe. I would undertake at the peril of my life to bring to you a message from

King George himself that he expects nothing of the kind. Sir, whenever I hear of a great palace rising in any great city of India, be it in British India or be it in India which is ruled by our great chiefs, I become jealous at once and I say: 'Oh, it is the money that has come from the agriculturists.'

The maharajahs, no doubt, took strong exception to Gandhi's utterings. This was what they were receiving in return for making large donations to the university fund. The students had listened to Gandhi's sermon about character building in stony silence, but when he came out with his scathing criticism of the maharajahs and their jewels, some of them shouted their approval. The tension in the hall was gaining momentum and no one knew in which direction he would turn next. He now spoke of the superabundance of detectives stationed in the streets of Benares for the safety of the Viceroy, Lord Hardinge, when he arrived for the university opening. The government was in great fear of a bomb-thrower. This was something not to be talked about in public. But Gandhi had no hesitation in doing so:

Why was it necessary to impose these detectives on us? Why this distrust? Is it not better that even Lord Hardinge should die than live a living death? But a representative of a mighty Sovereign may not. He might find it necessary even to live a living death.

We may foam, we may fret, we may resent, but let us not forget that India of today in her impatience has produced an army of anarchists. I am myself an anarchist, but of another type. But there is a class of anarchists amongst us, and if I was able to reach this class, I would say to them that their anarchism has no room in India if India is to conquer the conqueror. It is a sign of fear. If we trust and fear God, we shall have to fear no one, not Maharajahs, not Viceroys, not the detectives, not even King George.

I honour the anarchist for his love of the country. I honour him for his bravery in being willing to die for his country; but I ask him: Is killing honourable? Is the dagger of an assassin a fit precursor of an honourable death? I deny it. There is no warrant for such measures in any scriptures. If I found it necessary for the salvation of India that the English should retire, that they should be driven out, I would not hesitate to declare that they would have to go, and I hope I would be prepared to die in defence of that belief. That would, in my opinion, be an honourable death. The bomb-thrower creates secret plots, is afraid to come into the open, and when caught pays the penalty of misdirected zeal.

It was only two days earlier that a smiling Mrs Besant, in her moment of glory, had received the foundation deeds from the hands of the Viceroy. That she should now be a witness to Gandhi's freewheeling speech was more than she could bear. 'Please stop it,' she exclaimed. As she explained later, this was an appeal to the chairman to stop Gandhi, but Gandhi thought she meant to shut him up. He interrupted his speech and, turning to the Maharajah of Darbhanga, asked for his orders. 'I think what I am saying is necessary,' announced Gandhi. 'If you consider that by my speaking as I am, I am not serving the country and the empire, I shall certainly stop.' Many in the audience cried: 'Go on.' The Maharajah of Darbhanga said: 'Please explain your object', and Gandhi offered the stereotyped explanation that he was merely attempting to purge India of the prevailing atmosphere of suspicion, then added:

Is it not better that we talk under the shadow of this college than that we should be talking irresponsibly in our homes? . . . I know that there is nothing that the students are not discussing. There is nothing that the students do not know. I am therefore turning the searchlight towards ourselves. I hold the name of my country so dear to me that I exchange these thoughts with you and submit to you that there is no reason for anarchism in India. Let us frankly and openly say whatever we want to say to our rulers and face the consequences if what we have to say does not please them.

He went on to tell how he had recently met an Englishman in the Indian Civil Service who complained that the Indians considered all civil servants oppressors. Since Gandhi did not think that they were all such a bad lot, the Englishman asked him to put in a good word for the much-abused Civil Service. There could not be a better opportunity. Gandhi now addressed himself to the 'civilians' present:

Yes, many members of the Indian Civil Service are most decidedly overbearing, they are tyrannical, at times thoughtless. Many other adjectives may be used . . . But what does that signify? They were gentlemen before they came here, and if they have lost some of their moral fibre, it is a reflection upon ourselves. (Cries of 'No.') Just think out for yourselves, if a man who was good yesterday has become bad after having come in contact with me, is he responsible that he has deteriorated or am I? The atmosphere of sycophancy and falsity that surrounds them on their coming to India demoralizes them, as it would many of us . . . The Indians by not taking power in their own hands have become the willing victims of oppression . . . If we are to receive self-government, we shall have to take it. We shall never be granted self-government.

The audience could sense that although he did not approve of the bomb-throwing anarchists, he was now suggesting the use of force to achieve independence. People were urging Gandhi to go on while others shouted to him to leave the platform. Some of the princes and other dignitaries were already descending from the dais. In the midst of the uproar Gandhi declared: 'Look at the history of the British Empire and the British nation; freedom-loving as it is, it will not be a party to give freedom to a people who will not take it themselves.' As he continued, the Maharajah of Darbhanga suddenly left the meeting: 'Learn your lesson if you wish to from the Boer War. Those who were enemies of the British Empire only a few years ago have now become friends.' With the departure of the chairman, Gandhi was obliged to end his speech abruptly.

Late that night, the police commissioner wrote out an order asking Gandhi to leave Benares immediately, but soon after, at the insistence of Madan Mohan Malaviya, the order was withdrawn. Gandhi, however, left Benares the following morning.

Mrs Besant strongly condemned his speech, but he commented that but for her interruption, 'I would have concluded my speech in a few minutes and no possible misconception about my views on anarchism would have arisen.' When asked about the strong views he had expressed relating to the measures to protect Lord Hardinge, an attempt on whose life had earlier been made, Gandhi explained that only his sympathy for 'one of the noblest of viceroys, an honoured guest in this sacred city' had made him utter those words.

Benares was soon relegated to the past. Gandhi would not agree to discuss something of so 'little importance.' From all over India there came invitations to speak, and he would talk about the ashram, the pursuit of truth and *ahimsa*, the benefits of handweaving, and control of the palate. Again and again he would protest vigorously against stimulating condiments and warn against the dangers of tea-drinking, insisting that it was Lord Curzon who had set this fashion. 'That pernicious drug now bids fair to overwhelm the nation, and it has already undermined the digestive apparatus of hundreds of thousands of men and women,' he said at a missionary conference.

Gandhi was of the view that handicrafts and cottage industries, particularly handloom weaving and hand-spinning, were the most effective corrective measures to control India's grinding poverty. They could yield to villagers a supplementary income during the dead months when there was little work for them to do in the fields. By reviving the spinning wheel Gandhi was seeking to encourage village industries and to reduce the import of British cloth, which he reckoned would loosen the grip of British capitalism.

There was so much poverty in India at the time that in tens of thousands of villages men did not earn more than two and a half rupees a month. Wearing *khadi* meant providing employment for the poor. India produced cotton that was exported to Britain and Japan, and bought back the finished textile product. Gandhi charged that the British had annihilated India's village industries to help the textile mills of Lancashire, resulting in Indian wealth flowing to the British Isles as profit.

In his speeches on the *khadi* movement, Gandhi would remind his listeners that before the advent of the British, every village was self-sufficient. Women would weave their own cloth, thus practising a trade that kept them usefully employed and gave dignity to their lives.

Some of Gandhi's close associates were not in agreement with him over his firm views on *khadi* and felt that he was overstating the benefits that might accrue even if he was successful; notwithstanding his lofty ideal, it would be unwise to lose sight of the fact that it was the machine age, and reverting to the old methods of production would impede the country's development. Nevertheless, *khadi* was Gandhi's contribution to bringing political consciousness to the people of India. The wearing of *khadi* was the only visible and tangible tie that bound the educated Indians to the masses. The spinning wheel was thus the bond of brotherhood that united all Indians; *khadi* became the uniform of the national movement.

# TWENTY-THREE

# The Stain of Indigo

Gandhi had not forgotten about his compatriots in South Africa. The abolition of the indentured system was, in fact, again in the forefront of his mind. In 1916, in response to Indian pressure, the Viceroy promised its abolition as soon as alternative arrangements could be made for emigrant Indian labour. Gandhi considered this as a vague promise, and early in 1917 he expressed his intention to work up an all-India agitation against this system of 'semi-slavery'. Resolutions were passed at meetings held in Bombay, Calcutta and other cities for its abolition 'by July 31'. The Viceroy, with whom he discussed the matter, kept his promise and the ending of the indentured system was announced before 31 July. Gandhi felt that 'potential Satyagraha hastened the end'.

Meanwhile his attention had been turned to the plight of the tenants of indigo planters in the province of Bihar, in eastern India. Under the ancient *tinkathia* system, they were bound by long-term contract to plant three-twentieths of their land with indigo, and surrender the entire indigo harvest as part payment of rent. But they were also subjected to bullying by the landlords. During World War I the price of indigo went up considerably. Since the synthetic dyes from Germany were in short supply, the value of indigo exported from India soared, and as a result of this the landlords, who had hitherto reduced their production of indigo, now insisted that more land should be made available for its plantation, without offering any incentive to the peasants.

In December 1916, at the annual session of Congress at Lucknow, an obscure cultivator, Rajkumar Shukla, approached Gandhi and urged him to visit Bihar and see for himself the hardships faced by the indigo workers. Shukla kept talking in his native dialect about a place called Champaran, which Gandhi had never heard of, and about indigo plants, which he had never seen in his life. The peasant ran off to find Braijkishore Prasad, an official delegate from Bihar, who was better equipped to familiarize Gandhi with the problem. Braijkishore Prasad was a lawyer with a large practice, Gandhi was not overly impressed by him and finally said: 'I cannot give you my opinion without seeing it with my own eyes.' He thought the matter would end there, but Champaran was destined to afford him the opportunity for his first conspicuous entry on to the political stage in India.

Shukla was a determined man, and when Gandhi travelled to Cawnpore, he followed him there. 'Champaran is very close,' he said. 'Please spend a day there.' He was so persistent that Gandhi promised to visit Bihar in the near future. Then he returned to his ashram near Ahmedabad. Shukla followed him to the ashram. 'Please fix a date,' he begged. Gandhi had a busy schedule, but impressed by the peasant's story he said he would be able to spare a day or two after his projected visit to Calcutta in April. He asked Shukla to meet him there, and they would travel together to see Champaran. The weeks passed. When Gandhi reached his host's place in Calcutta, Shukla had already established himself there. On 9 April, looking like two peasants, they took the train for Patna, the capital of Bihar, and on arrival Shukla led his companion to the house of a lawyer named Rajendra Prasad, who later became the first president of the Republic of India. Prasad was out of town, and the servants at his house refused to allow Gandhi to use the lavatory inside the house or to draw water from the well while they themselves were doing so, for his general appearance in no way revealed his caste; how did they know that he was not an Untouchable?

Worn out by a long journey, without even a smattering of the local language, Gandhi had no clear idea what he could achieve in this remote place. He wondered if the whole exercise was a waste of time, and even considered abandoning the project.

Shukla, for his part, though he had no idea how to go about attending to the peasants' grievances, was trying to help Gandhi as best as he could, making him as comfortable as possible, running down to the bazaar to buy dates for him, and performing other errands. As Gandhi was reviewing the situation, it suddenly struck him that Maulana Mazharul Haq, the Muslim leader, was also living in Patna. The two had been friends during their student days in London. Haq now advised Gandhi to proceed to Muzaffarpur, where he would find leaders who were aware of the problem and capable of offering assistance. Gandhi accordingly sent a telegram to J.B. Kripalani, who had recently resigned from his teaching post at the local Government College. The two men had briefly met at Tagore's school at Santiniketan. When the train arrived at Muzaffarpur at about midnight, Kripalani was waiting at the station with a large group of students. Arrangements had been made for Gandhi's stay in the home of a certain Professor Malkani.

The following morning Muzaffarpur lawyers, who frequently represented peasant groups in court, called on Gandhi to brief him. Gandhi was appalled to learn about the exorbitant fees they charged the peasants. 'I have come to the conclusion that we should stop going to law courts,' he said. 'Taking such cases to the courts does little good. Where the peasants are so crushed and fear-stricken, law courts are useless. The real relief for them is to be free from fear.'

He needed the lawyers' assistance, but he had little use for their legal knowledge. 'I require clerical assistance and help in interpretation,' he said. He could not fully understand the local dialect and was unable to read papers written in Kaithi or Urdu. He could not afford to pay the lawyers for their translation and other work; moreover, in the course of their voluntary work involving compilation of testimony by peasants in full view of the police and government officers, it might be necessary to face imprisonment, and 'much as I would love you to run that risk, you would go only so far as you feel yourselves capable of going'. Above all there must be no violence.

At first, Gandhi's proposed method of work surprised his listeners, but they said they would do as much as they could. The idea of accommodating oneself to imprisonment was a novelty, but that too, they said, they would endeavour to assimilate. Rajendra Prasad, whom Gandhi had failed to meet in Patna, soon came to Muzaffarpur and offered his services to the cause. Having met several lawyers and teachers, Gandhi was certainly convinced Rajkumar Shukla's story about the plight of indigo workers was after all an authentic one, and the young peasant thus returned to his good graces.

The news of Gandhi's advent and his fact-finding mission spread quickly throughout Bihar. Crowds began to follow him wherever he went. Before setting out for Motihari, the headquarters of the Champaran district, he found it proper to seek interviews with the secretary of the planters' association and the commissioner of the Tirhut division, but was rebuffed. The Champaran police were perturbed about his impending visit, and on enquiring of their superiors as to how they should handle the possibly volatile situation, they received a forthright reply:

> We quite agree with you that his mere presence in Champaran is most undesirable. Unfortunately this gentleman has in the past been allowed to speak pretty freely in other provinces on the question of indentured labour for the abolition of which he is a champion. He is not on any list of agitators . . . He has a biggish following and one needs to be very careful in dealing with men of his notoriety.

On 15 April 1917, Gandhi, accompanied by two interpreters, left for Motihari by the midday train, reaching his destination three hours later. He was taken to the house of one Gorakh Prasad and, using it as his headquarters, continued his investigation. That very day a report came in that a peasant in a nearby village had been mistreated. Gandhi decided to go and see him the following morning. Starting out on the back of an elephant, he had not proceeded far when a police sub-inspector riding a bicycle caught up with him and asked him to return to town in the hired carriage he had brought along. Immediately on arrival in Motihari, Gandhi was served with a notice signed by Mr W.B. Heycock, the district magistrate, ordering him to quit Champaran. He acknowledged receipt of the notice and added a note to the magistrate that he was unable to leave the district. 'My desire is purely and simply for a genuine search for knowledge,' he wrote. 'And this I shall continue to satisfy so long as I am left free.'

Anticipating a summons at any moment, he spent the rest of the day and night writing letters, preparing a plan for the guidance of those who were to carry on the work in his absence. He telegraphed Rajendra Prasad to come from Patna with influential friends. In a letter to the Viceroy's secretary, he explained that he would refuse to submit to the expulsion order so long as the peasants were living 'under a reign of terror, and their property, their persons, and their minds were all under the planters' heels'.

On 17 April a large number of peasants descended on Motihari and the work of recording their statements went on for the whole day. Gandhi notified the district magistrate of his intention to visit a village sixteen miles from Motihari. Shortly the summons came, calling upon him to appear in court the following day.

In the morning the town of Motihari witnessed unprecedented scenes. Several thousand peasants had assembled in the court compound. When Gandhi entered the small courtroom, he was followed by some two thousand men, who attempted to make their way in. The glass panels of the doors were smashed, and the officials were helpless until Gandhi helped them to regulate the crowd.

He pleaded guilty and read out to the magistrate a statement explaining his reasons for coming to the district and for disobeying the order to leave it:

I have entered the country with motives of rendering humanitarian and national service. I have done so in response to a pressing invitation to come and help the peasants who urge they are not being fairly treated by the indigo planters. I could not render any help without studying the problem . . . As a law-abiding citizen, my first instinct would be, as it was, to obey the order served upon me. I could not do so without doing violence to my sense of duty to those for whom I have come. I feel that I could just now serve them only by remaining in their midst . . . I have disregarded the order served upon me not for want of respect for lawful authority, but in obedience to the higher law of our being, the voice of conscience.

The magistrate told Gandhi that his statement did not contain a clear plea of guilty. 'I do not wish to waste the time of the court and I plead guilty,' said Gandhi. 'If you leave the district now and promise not to return, the case against you would be withdrawn,' the magistrate said. 'That cannot be,' replied Gandhi. 'Not to speak of this time alone, I shall make Champaran my home even after my return from jail.'

The magistrate pronounced a two-hour recess. When Gandhi returned shortly before three o'clock the magistrate told him that he would pass orders on 21 April, but in the meantime would release him on a bail of one hundred rupees. Gandhi said he could not offer bail in good conscience, and none of his followers, understandably, would stand bail for him. He even declined to be released on personal recognizance. The magistrate finally allowed him to remain at liberty and asked him to return on 21 April to hear the verdict.

Gandhi's devoted follower, Charles Freer Andrews, the English pacifist, arrived for a short visit. He had come to see Gandhi before going on a tour of duty to the Fiji Islands. This tall, thin, horse-faced man was in a position to hob-nob with people in high places, including the Viceroy and the governors of many provinces, and Gandhi's lawyer friends thought that he could thus be of great service to them. He was willing to stay a little longer if Gandhi agreed, but Gandhi admonished the lawyers for making such a suggestion, and could not resist the temptation of pointing a moral:

> You want Mr Andrews to stay because you have fear in your hearts. You think the fight is with European planters. Mr Andrews is an Englishman, and in a fight with Englishmen he could act as a shield. You must get rid of your fear . . . I had half a mind to let him stay, but now that I read your minds, I think he will do more harm than good to the cause by staying, and so my decision is that he will leave tomorrow morning.

Rajendra Prasad, Braijkishore Prasad, Maulana Mazharul Haq and other prominent lawyers of Bihar conferred with Gandhi. He asked them what they would do if he was sentenced to imprisonment. They had come to advise and help him. If he was sent to prison there would be nobody to advise and help, and the senior lawyers therefore replied that in that event they would go home. Gandhi could not accept the lawyers' attitude and reminded them that they were losing sight of the injustice to the peasants. The lawyers withdrew to consult. It soon dawned on them that a total stranger was prepared to go to prison for the sake of the peasants; if they, not only residents of the adjoining districts but also those who claimed to serve the peasants, should go home, it would be disgraceful. They returned to Gandhi to inform him that they were ready to shoulder their responsibility in the struggle and would follow him into jail. 'The battle of Champaran is won,' he exclaimed.

Meanwhile batches of tenants kept pouring in, and Gandhi and his co-workers recorded their statements. To help in this work a number of volunteers had arrived. A day before he was to reappear in court, Gandhi unexpectedly received a written message from Mr Heycock, the district magistrate, that the Lieutenant-Governor of Bihar, Sir Edward Gait, had ordered the case against him to be withdrawn and that the local officials had been asked to assist him in his enquiry. To his surprise, Gandhi had won a total victory. 'The country thus had its first direct object-lesson in civil disobedience,' he wrote later.

On 22 April, after first notifying the authorities, he set out by slow train for Bettiah – a three-hour journey. Crowds of peasants waiting at each station to receive his *darshan* pelted him with flowers. At Bettiah the crush of peasants on the platform caused a near stampede and it was decided to stop the train some distance away to avoid an accident. When Gandhi got down from a third-class compartment and entered a carriage, the peasants unharnessed the horses and insisted on pulling the carriage by the shafts until he threatened to leave it if they persisted. It was Rajkumar Shukla's day in the sun. He had, after all, been instrumental in bringing Gandhi to his own people.

Shukla lived in the remote village of Murali Bharahwa, eight miles from the nearest railroad station, and accessible only by a dusty narrow footpath. A month earlier his house had been looted by the agents of the local factory owners, who considered him a troublemaker. Several of the villagers who had witnessed the looting gave evidence, which Gandhi recorded. He also interviewed the manager of the factory, a man noted for his brutality, and spent the rest of the day with the villagers. The following morning he returned to Bettiah.

Gandhi continued with the far-flung enquiry into the grievances of the farmers. Depositions by over ten thousand peasants were written down and notes made on other evidence. Persons responsible for taking down the statements were strictly instructed to observe certain rules. Each peasant had to be cross-examined, and anyone who failed to satisfy the test was rejected. This exercise called for a considerable amount of extra time, and most of the statements thus rendered were indisputable. Some officers of the police Criminal Investigation Department (CID) would invariably be present when these statements were recorded. Gandhi not only raised no objection to their presence but extended them courtesy and furnished them with information they would require. The presence of the officers exercised a definite restraint on exaggeration by the peasants.

The planters had kept up their efforts to malign Gandhi and his associates through the newspapers, and to dislodge them from Champaran. 'I can only say that nothing but physical force from the government or an absolute guarantee that the admitted or proverbial wrongs of the *ryots* [peasants] are to stop for ever, can possibly remove us from the district,' he declared. 'What I have seen of the condition of the *ryots* is sufficient to convince me that if we withdraw at this stage, we would stand condemned before man and God and, what is more important of all, we would never be able to forgive ourselves.'

His rapport with the peasants, he wrote in his autobiography, brought him 'face to face with God, *ahimsa* and Truth'. Mr W.A. Lewis, the Indian Civil Service officer in Bettiah, wrote after his first meeting with Gandhi:

We may look on Mr Gandhi as an idealist, a fanatic, or a revolutionary according to our particular opinions. But to the *ryots* he is their liberator, and they credit him with extraordinary powers. He moves about in the villages asking them to lay their grievances before him, and he is transfiguring the imaginations of masses of ignorant men with visions of an early millennium. I put the danger of this before Mr Gandhi, and he assured me that his utterances are so carefully guarded that they could not be construed as an incitement to revolt. I am willing to believe Mr Gandhi, whose sincerity is, I think, above suspicion, but he cannot control the tongues of all his followers.

Gandhi was summoned to see Sir Edward Gait, the Lieutenant-Governor. For three days he had long interviews with Sir Edward and his executive council, as a result of which it was decided that a commission of inquiry should be appointed and that Gandhi should be one of its members. Sir Frank Sly, the Commissioner of the Central Provinces and an experienced negotiator, was made chairman of the commission. The official inquiry assembled voluminous evidence against the big planters, and the result was a foregone conclusion. Keeping in view the innumerable taxes and exactions imposed on the peasants in the indigo fields, the planters feared that Gandhi would demand repayment in full of the money they had illegally exacted. But he asked only for fifty per cent and later agreed to the planters' offer to refund to the extent of twenty-five per cent. He did not attribute much importance to the amount of the refund, explaining that the fact that the landlords had been obliged to surrender part of the money was a moral victory for the peasants.

The inquiry commission submitted its report, recommending clearly the abolition of the hated *tinkathia* system and several other inequities which had plagued the tenant-planter relationship. Consequently, the Champaran Agrarian Bill was passed on 29 November and became law. 'What I did', Gandhi commented about the Champaran episode, 'was a very ordinary thing. I declared that the British could not order me around in my own country.'

# TWENTY-FOUR

# Sabarmati

During his stay in Champaran, Gandhi kept himself informed about matters relating to the running of the ashram. He sent regular instructions by mail and asked for financial accounts. Occasionally he would pay a flying visit to the community. The ashram was about to develop into a much larger one when plague broke out in the village. Notwithstanding the observance of strict sanitation within the community walls, the safety of the ashramites was threatened, for the villagers were too ill or too obstinate to accept Gandhi's offer to organize their sanitation. He took this as sufficient notice to quit Kochrab, choosing instead a site on the banks of the Sabarmati River, about four miles north of the city of Ahmedabad, not far from the Central Jail. 'As jail-going was understood to be the normal lot of the Satyagrahis,' he wrote, 'I liked this position. And I know that the sites selected for jails have generally clean surroundings.'

Gandhi bought the twenty-acre plot with the help of an Ahmedabad merchant, and pitched tents in the middle of it. The place was infested with snakes, but the general rule was not to kill them. Work to construct small houses soon began, trees were planted, brick roads and pathways were laid. The ashram was managed by Maganlal, as Gandhi himself was preoccupied with pressing problems elsewhere.

While he was winding up his work at Champaran, his friends wrote to him about the failure of crops in the Kheda district, asking him to guide the peasants, who were unable to pay claiming exemption from payment of that year's land tax. But unrest among textile workers brought him instead back to Ahmedabad.

The mill hands of Ahmedabad were full of grievances, demanding a fifty per cent increase in their meagre wages and better conditions. Gandhi felt their demands were justified. He urged Ambalal Sarabhai and other prominent millowners, whom he knew well, to arbitrate the dispute. They rejected arbitration. Gandhi accordingly advised the workers to go on strike, and exacted from them the solemn pledge that they would not go back to work unless the employers accepted their demands or agreed to arbitration. They must not resort to violence. They must remain united and earn bread, during the strike, by any other honest labour. Ambalal Sarabhai's sister, Anasuyabehn, gave Gandhi her active support. She would spend some time in the ashram and was well known for her charities.

Every day Gandhi met the strikers under a spreading *babul* (acacia) tree near the Sabarmati River. Thousands came to hear him. He called for discipline, determination and the acceptance of suffering. From these meetings, they marched off into town carrying banners which read: *EK TEK* (KEEP THE PLEDGE). Gandhi kept himself in regular communication with the millowners, who still refused to submit to arbitration. As the strikers were beginning to starve, he wrote to Ambalal Sarabhai, the millowners' leader:

> If you succeed, the poor, already suppressed, will be suppressed still more, will be more abject than ever and the impression will have been confirmed that money can subdue everyone. If, despite your efforts, the workers succeed in securing the increase, you and others with you will regard the result as your failure. Can I possibly wish you success in so far as the first result is concerned? Is your desire that the arrogance of money should increase? Or that the workers be reduced to utter submission? Would you be so unkindly disposed to them as to see no success for you in their getting what they are entitled to, may be even a few pice more? Do you not see that in your failure lies your success, that your success is fraught with danger for you?
>
> My success everyone will accept as success. My failure, too, will not harm anyone, it will only prove that the workers were not prepared to go farther than they did. An effort like mine is Satyagraha. Kindly look deep into your heart, listen to the still small voice within and obey it, I pray you.

As the strike dragged on the almost destitute mill hands began to waver. The crowd under the *babul* tree was getting smaller, and this alarmed Gandhi. He was beginning to feel that the strike would collapse unless an entirely new approach was discovered. In his autobiography he explains how the spontaneous thought to undergo the first of his political fasts came about:

> One morning – it was at a mill-hands' meeting – while I was still groping and unable to see my way clearly, the light came to me. Unbidden and all by themselves the words came to my lips: 'Unless the strikers rally,' I declared to the meeting, 'and continue the strike until a settlement is reached, or until they leave the mills altogether, I will not touch any food.'
>
> The labourers were thunderstruck. Tears began to pour down Anasuyabehn's cheeks. The labourers broke out: 'Not you, but we shall fast. It would be monstrous if you were to fast. Please forgive us for our lapse, we shall now remain faithful to our pledge to the end.

On the first day of the fast, Anasuyabehn Sarabhai and several strike leaders fasted too. Gandhi persuaded them to give it up and instead look after the mill hands and help them keep their pledge.

The fact that he had cordial relations with the millowners raised a doubt in his own mind whether the fast was flawed, for 'my fast could not but affect their decision'. He pleaded with them to appraise the situation fully and act in a manner they considered proper. 'Be guided by your sense of justice rather than your desire to see that I break my fast,' he wrote to Ambalal Sarabhai. Despite Gandhi's knowledge that his fast was bound to put pressure upon the millowners, as in fact it did, he felt he could not help it. 'The duty to undertake it seemed to me to be clear,' he wrote.

On the third day of the fast when Gandhi addressed the mill hands, he had a feeling of much satisfaction. 'I am at present overflowing with joy,' he said . 'My mind is filled with profound peace. I feel like pouring forth my soul to you all, but I am beside myself with joy.' He told the mill hands that he wanted them to go to the millowners and say that they were prepared to go back to work if they were offered a thirty-five per cent increase in their wages. The millowners were agreeable, and the strike ended on the following day. And yet the feeling that his fast was flawed disturbed him greatly, and he bitterly said that if such a feeling came over him again, 'I would go where they would never be able to seek me out'.

Meanwhile Gandhi had kept himself informed about the situation in the Kheda district, where the crop failure had caused a near-famine condition. A few days after the fast, with a haste signifying a long-delayed obligation, he took over in Kheda. He felt that since petitions and agitation in the Bombay Legislative Council had proved ineffective, only large-scale civil disobedience would bring the matter to the government's notice. Under the land revenue rules, if the crop yield was less than twenty-five per cent of the normal figure, the cultivators could claim exemption from payment of land tax for the year. According to the official figures, the yield was said to be over twenty-five per cent. The cultivators, however, contended that this was an exaggeration.

In the course of his investigation, Gandhi travelled through numerous villages and it became quite clear to him that the peasants were not overstating their plight. He favoured the appointment of an impartial inquiry committee to look into the matter, but the government turned down his suggestion. He now impelled the cultivators to refuse to pay the taxes, notwithstanding the consequences. The government sent its attachment officers out into the villages; they sold people's cattle and whatever movables they could get hold of. At times they even seized standing crops.

Gandhi's principal workers in this struggle included Vallabhbhai Patel,

Shankarlal Banker, Anasuyabehn Sarabhai, Indulal Yajnik and Mahadev Desai. As the movement advanced, Patel emerged as its chief organizer. It was only in the recent past that he was an Anglicized lawyer and clubman, and when Gandhi first spoke at the Ahmedabad Club, of which Patel was a member, he did not even interrupt his card game to stroll into the adjoining room to listen. This stocky, gruff man had studied law at the Middle Temple and had already entered into notable confrontation with the British authorities in Ahmedabad over the appointment of a British engineer in preference to better qualified Indians. At forty-two, he was an eminently successful lawyer and a devastating cross-examiner. He was no doubt aware of Gandhi's career in South Africa, but had some reservations about his method. Gandhi's campaign for the indigo workers in Champaran, however, influenced him so deeply that within a year he had forsworn his Western ideas and garments to join Gandhi and the Congress party; he also renounced his personal wealth. Wearing a shirt and a *dhoti*, Patel walked from village to village, exhorting and encouraging the villagers to remain firm and refuse to pay up. 'They cannot grab your land and ship it to England,' he said good-humouredly.

As a result of the government's coercive measures, the resolution of some of the Satyagrahis was beginning to break. Although the majority of the peasants were determined to hold by their pledge, Gandhi himself realized after some three months that people were showing signs of exhaustion. The struggle had, however, put enough pressure on the government, which was now anxious to arrive at some settlement. Orders were issued that the land tax should be collected only from the well-to-do who could afford to pay. All attempts to tax the poor peasants were abandoned. Gandhi was somewhat distressed, for there was no clear-cut ending of the Kheda agitation, and it 'lacked the grace with which the termination of every Satyagraha campaign ought to be accompanied'. Nevertheless he recognized that the campaign marked the beginning of an awakening among the peasants of Gujarat, making them conscious of their strength and imprinting on the public mind that 'the salvation of the people depends upon themselves, upon their capacity for suffering and sacrifice'. Here, as at Champaran, educated public workers established contact with the actual life of the peasants, signifying the first beginnings of a mass movement.

In the spring of 1918, the war in Europe was entering its final phase and the Allies needed help. Since massive additional manpower was required, Britain turned towards India, hoping to harness her manpower to the war effort. The Viceroy, Lord Chelmsford, invited a number of Indian leaders, including Gandhi, to a war conference in Delhi. Gandhi raised certain objections, one being the non-inclusion in the conference of leaders like

Tilak, Mrs Besant, Mohamed Ali and Shaukat Ali, whom Gandhi regarded as 'the most powerful leaders of public opinion'. He accordingly wrote to the Viceroy, expressing his inability to attend. Lord Chelmsford invited him to discuss the matter, and pleaded with Gandhi that he could raise whatever moral issues he liked and challenge the government as much as he pleased after the conclusion of the war. 'If you agree that the empire has been, on the whole, a power for good, if you believe that India has, on the whole, benefited by the British connection, would you not admit that it is the duty of every Indian citizen to help the empire in the hour of its need?' asked the Viceroy. The argument was familiar. Gandhi had himself taken a similar line in the past. It appealed to him and he finally agreed to attend the conference. He supported 'with a full sense of my responsibility' the resolution calling for the immediate recruitment of 500,000 Indians for the British Army. After the conference, Gandhi, in a letter to Lord Chelmsford published with the Viceroy's consent, wrote that the Indians' response was 'due to the expectation that our goal will be reached all the more speedily . . . we aspire in the near future to be partners of the empire in the same sense as the dominions overseas'. And to the Viceroy's private secretary Gandhi wrote: 'I have an idea that if I become your recruiting agent-in-chief, I might rain men on you.'

He made a quick trip to Bihar, and at a meeting in Patna addressed an audience of ten thousand people whose enthusiasm waned as his speech progressed. Presenting himself as the government's devoted recruiting agent and yet also as a leader in Bihar, he advised his audience to enlist in the army and 'to go with him and to wherever the government directed'. A large number of people quietly slipped away. On his return to Kheda he offered the same message to the peasants whom, only a short while earlier, he had urged to be nonviolent even against the most brutal British officers. The peasants were dumbfounded. The logic of numbers in the recruitment leaflet only proved to add insult to injury:

> There are 600 villages in Kheda district. Every village has on an average a population of over 1,000. If every village gave at least twenty men, Kheda district would be able to raise an army of 12,000 men. The population of the whole district is 700,000 and this number will then work out at 1.7 per cent, a rate which is lower than the death rate.

In his speech at Nadiad Gandhi called upon people 'to learn the use of arms with the greatest possible despatch'. Accordingly they must enlist themselves in the army. 'There can be no friendship between the brave and the effeminate,' he asserted. 'We are regarded as a cowardly people. If we want to become free from that reproach, we should learn the use of arms.'

His oft-repeated plea was that the easiest and straightest way to win *swaraj* was to participate in the defence of the empire. 'If the empire perished, with it perishes our cherished aspirations.'

His friend Charlie Andrews criticized his recruiting campaign, saying that he was deluding himself, and his activity might injure the service to the cause of *ahimsa*. Gandhi sought to justify himself:

> There was a danger of those who put faith in my word becoming or remaining utterly unmanly, falsely believing that it was *ahimsa*. We must have the ability in the fullest measure to strike and then perceive the inability of brute force and renounce the power.

Early in July he was writing to friends that so far he had not been able to obtain even a single recruit. But he would not take no for an answer. He worked even more desperately, until he was 'recruiting mad. I do nothing else, think of nothing else, talk of nothing else.' But the bitter experiences that the people of Kheda had of the officials were still fresh in their minds, and they were in no mood to pay heed to Gandhi for his 'inglorious' work. They denied him transportation and food which they had gladly afforded during the Satyagraha campaign. He was unable to get a cart even on hire. Gandhi and Vallabhbhai Patel, carrying their food in their satchels, trudged as much as twenty miles a day. He addressed several meetings where he was asked the inevitable questions: 'You are a votary of *ahimsa*, how can you ask us to take up arms? What good has the government done for India to deserve our cooperation?'

Still Gandhi's intensive recruiting campaign yielded negligible results. Moreover, on account of his exertions and inadequate diet – he was living merely on groundnut butter and lemons – he fell ill with extremely painful dysentery and a high fever. He rejected all medical treatment and refused to partake of any restorative foods, including milk.

Ambalal Sarabhai and his wife, Sarladevi, came with a comfortable car to take him to their mansion near Ahmedabad and, a month later, on his insistence, to the ashram. Soon he treated himself with hydropathy which gave some relief but contributed little in building up his strength. His poor health bothered him a great deal. One night, as he was struck by a feeling of utter despair, he proclaimed to the ashramites that his end was round the corner. Anasuyabehn Sarabhai insisted on calling a 'real' physician. The doctor told Gandhi in no uncertain terms that his pulse was entirely normal and that he was suffering from a nervous breakdown due to exhaustion and extreme weakness. The doctor's reassurance proved ineffective, and

Gandhi, having convinced himself that he was 'at death's door', began to devote all his waking hours to listening to the ashramites reciting verses from the *Bhagavad Gita*. While he was preoccupied with the notion that his days were numbered, he agreed to undergo the treatment recommended by a 'doctor' which consisted of the application of ice all over the body. 'While I am unable to endorse his claim about the effect his treatment had on me,' Gandhi wrote, 'it certainly infused in me a new hope and a new energy.' As he began to feel a little better, Kasturbai managed to persuade her husband to take goat's milk. 'The will to live proved stronger than the devotion to truth, and for once the votary of truth compromised his sacred ideal by his eagerness to take up the Satyagraha fight.'

Meanwhile news was received that Germany had been defeated. That recruiting was no longer necessary was a great relief to Gandhi, but he was still irked by the feeling that not one of his Satyagrahis had refused to go to war because of a reluctance to kill – they simply did not wish to die. Writing to Charlie Andrews, he observed:

When friends told me here that passive resistance was taken up by the people as a weapon of the weak, I laughed at the libel, as I called it then. But they were right and I was wrong. With me alone and a few other co-workers it came out of our strength and was described as Satyagraha, but with the majority it was purely and simply passive resistance that they resorted to, because they were too weak to undertake methods of violence. This discovery was forced on me repeatedly in Kheda.

Although Gandhi's recruitment campaign proved ineffective, soldiers of the regular Indian Army represented a massive force in Britain's battle in Europe, with large contingents being sent by the princely states. Meanwhile Bal Gangadhar Tilak had been interned again. Mrs Besant was under arrest. Civil liberties were withdrawn and the press was muzzled by wartime censorship. There were a number of small-scale terrorist plots which the government regarded with alarm. The war had also caused a sharp increase in the cost of living and the peasants were finding themselves under added strain.

During the war the government of India had appointed a committee headed by an English judge, Sir Sidney Rowlatt, to investigate and report on the conspiracies connected with the revolutionary movement in India. In July 1918 the committee known as the Sedition Committee recommended, in effect, a continuation of the wartime rigours. The Congress party, at a special session held in Bombay bitterly criticized the Rowlatt findings. With the coming of peace, the country expected the restoration of civil liberties. Instead, in February 1919, a bill embodying the recommendations of the Rowlatt Committee was introduced by the government in the Central Legislative Council. The majority of the council consisted of British government officials, and thus the passage of the bill was a certainty.

Gandhi, not fully recovered from dysentery and from an operation for fissures necessitated by it, declared that the provisions of the bill were 'unjust, subversive of the principle of liberty, and destructive of the elementary rights of individuals on which the safety of the community as a whole and of the State itself is based'. He concluded from the study of the Rowlatt report that secret violence was confined to isolated and very small parts of India. The introduction of the legislation, designed to affect the whole of the country, reflected 'an unmistakable symptom of a deep-seated disease in the governing body'. Anticipating enactment of the bill, he began preparations for a campaign of nonviolent resistance, travelling across India with his message. Since his voice was still weak and his body still frail, somebody had to read his speeches.

On 18 March 1919, the Rowlatt Bill, despite the united opposition of all sections in the country, was passed into law. Several Indian leaders, Surendranath Banerjea and Mohamed Ali Jinnah among them, spoke vigorously against the legislation. On that fateful day Gandhi was in Madras, where he discussed the situation with his host, C. Rajagopalachari, and other friends, and wondered how an entire nation could be expected to embrace the strict code of Satyagraha. At night an idea came to him, as if in a dream, in that twilight condition between sleep and consciousness. He would call on the country to observe a general *hartal* (that is, the closing-down of all places of business and work) and observe the day as one of fasting and prayer. The date was first fixed for 30 March, but was subsequently changed to 6 April. The telegram notifying the postponement reached Delhi late and consequently the city fasted and demonstrated on 30 March. Contrary to Gandhi's expectation, the *hartal* led to violence. There were parades, and speeches in the mosques and the temples. Hindus and Muslims seemed in perfect harmony. Swami Shraddhanand, the Hindu scholar, was invited to speak in Jumma Masjid, the largest mosque in India, and later headed the vast procession which marched along Chandni Chowk, the main street in Old Delhi. In their attempt to break up the procession, Gurkha troops opened fire. The tall and stately Shraddhanand, clothed in the orange robe of a *sanyasi*, bared his breast and dared them to shoot him. Instead, nine others were killed, five Hindus and four Muslims.

On the morning of 6 April people assembled in their thousands on Bombay's Chowpati beach, having begun the day's programme with a 'purifying' sea bath. Gandhi was one of the first arrivals at Chowpati, together with several volunteers, and soon took his seat on one of the stone benches with about a hundred Satyagrahis around him. The gathering steadily increased in size until it became one huge mass of people. In his speech Gandhi criticized the state violence exhibited in Delhi a week previously, but reminded his followers that their noisy protest in response to the government's action was not desirable. He impressed upon his followers that they must acquire the requisite discipline and other qualities expected of a Satyagrahi:

> When we have acquired habits of discipline, self-control, qualities of leadership and obedience, we shall be better able to offer collective civil disobedience, but until we have developed these qualities, I have advised that we should select for disobedience only such laws as can be disobeyed by individuals . . . And then when we have reached the necessary standard of knowledge and discipline, we shall find that machine-guns and all other weapons, even the plague of aeroplanes, will cease to afflict us.

Then a massive procession moved slowly from the seashore to Madhav Baug Temple compound for prayers. There was a complete cessation of business activity in the city. In the evening, driving in a slow-moving automobile with Sarojini Naidu by his side, Gandhi sold copies of his own works, *Hind Swaraj* and *Sarvodaya*, the Gujarati translation of Ruskin's *Unto This Last*, because they were proscribed, making the distributor liable to punishment under the Rowlatt Act. People paid up to fifty rupees for copies normally priced at four annas. The authorities turned a blind eye to the sale of the forbidden literature, and this caused some disappointment to those seeking arrest and imprisonment for civil disobedience.

The *hartal* made a profound impact throughout the length and breadth of India. Two days later, on the invitation of Swami Shraddhanand, the well-known Hindu nationalist leader, Gandhi left Bombay for Delhi, but he was pulled off the train near the little railroad station of Palwal where he was served with a written order prohibiting him from entering the Punjab and Delhi, as his presence there was 'likely to result in a disturbance of peace'. Accompanied by a police party, he boarded a Bombay-bound train. 'You are now free,' the officer told him when the train reached Bombay.

In Bombay he was greeted by crowds gone wild with joy, for the news of his arrest had been reported and a rumour had gained currency that he had been removed to an unknown destination. The hastily formed procession had barely moved when mounted police charged, swinging iron-tipped *lathis*, cutting their way through the dense crowd, trampling and mauling whoever came their way, until finally the people dispersed. Gandhi drove straight to the police commissioner's office. The commissioner, Mr Griffith, did not agree with him that the police charge was unnecessary. 'We police officers know better the effect of your teaching on the people,' he said. 'If we did not start with drastic measures the situation would pass out of our hands.' The commissioner felt certain that Gandhi would be unable to control the people. 'Disobedience of law will quickly appeal to them; it is beyond them to understand the duty of keeping peaceful.' Gandhi said that the people were by nature peaceful and not violent. When Mr Griffith enquired what Gandhi would do if he was convinced that his teaching had been lost on the people, he replied that he would suspend civil disobedience. The commissioner informed him of disturbances reported from Ahmedabad, Amritsar and other places, and insisted that the news of his arrest had led to these riots. Gandhi took leave of the commissioner and a few hours later, addressing a large gathering on the Chowpati sands, he spoke at length on the significance of nonviolence. 'Satyagraha is essentially a weapon of the truthful,' he said. 'A Satyagrahi is pledged to non-violence, and unless people observe it in thought, word and deed I cannot offer mass Satyagraha.'

He rushed back to Ahmedabad only to find it in the grip of martial law. A mob of mill hands had killed a British officer, attempted to tear up the railroad lines, and set fire to a number of government buildings. Gandhi asked for permission to hold a mass meeting at the Sabarmati ashram, where he reproached the people for their violence:

Now, instead of going to Delhi, it remains to me to offer Satyagraha against our own people, and as it was my determination to offer Satyagraha even unto death for securing the withdrawal of the Rowlatt legislation, I think the occasion has arrived when I should offer Satyagraha against ourselves for the violence that has occurred. And I shall do so at the sacrifice of my body, so long as we do not keep perfect peace and cease from violence to person and property.

He announced that he would undertake a penitential fast for three days. Immediately after the Sabarmati meeting, Gandhi left for Nadiad, a town in the Kheda district, where he discovered that violence had spread to small towns as well. This proved too much for him to bear and he announced publicly the suspension of Satyagraha, confessing that he had made a 'Himalayan miscalculation' in calling upon the people to offer civil disobedience before they were trained to do so. This admission excited a good deal of ridicule, but Gandhi was characteristically impervious to criticism. 'I have always held', he wrote in his autobiography, 'that it is only when one sees one's own mistakes with a convex lens, and does just the reverse in the case of others, that one is able to arrive at a just relative estimate of the two.'

When Gandhi was speaking of his 'Himalayan miscalculation,' he was blissfully unaware of the developments in the holy city of Amritsar, in the north, for the authorities had imposed a complete news blackout. There a British officer in command of a small detachment of soldiers had staged a massacre that would leave an indeliable mark on history.

# TWENTY-FIVE

# Massacre

In the Punjab, the 6 April *hartal* passed off peacefully. Amritsar, a city of 150,000 inhabitants, had also observed the *hartal* on 30 March but unlike in Delhi, here there was no collision with the police and no resort to violence. The Punjab government, however, objected to the utterances of two Congress party leaders, Dr. Saiffudin Kitchlew, a Muslim, and Dr Satyapal, a Hindu. The authorities were also getting alarmed at the demonstration of communal amity. (The term 'communal' or 'community' as used in India has political implications, pertaining to 'religion' or 'sectarian', unlike its broader connotation in the West.) On 9 April, the day of the Hindu festival Ram Naumi, Muslims also participated, shouting '*Mahatma Gandhi ki jai* (Long live Mahatma Gandhi)' and '*Hindu-Musalman ki jai* (Long live Hindu-Muslim unity).' Noting that the people were getting bolder, which he feared could lead to a more volatile situation, the district magistrate asked for a single company of troops stationed at Amritsar to be reinforced. Meanwhile he received orders from the Punjab government to arrest and deport from the district the two leaders. Accordingly, he summoned them both to his bungalow on the morning of 10 April, and notified them of their arrest under the Defence of India Act.

As the news of the arrests spread through the city, *hartal* was declared. Large crowds gathered and attempted to make their way across the railway into the Civil Lines, where the British officially lived, to demand the release of Dr Kitchlew and Dr Satyapal. They were held up at the bridge over the railway by a small military picket which had orders to prevent them at all costs from entering the Civil Lines. Finding themselves unable to contain the agitators the soldiers opened fire. Infuriated by the sight of their dead and wounded, the mob rushed back to the city, set fire to government buildings and attacked any European they could find. Three British bank officials were dragged out of their offices, beaten to death and their bodies thrown into the street and burned. Miss Sherwood, a missionary schoolteacher, was knocked off her bicycle, brutally attacked and left for dead. The civil authorities, having failed to grapple with the situation, now formally abdicated.

Brigadier General Reginald Dyer, an Englishman born in Simla and well known for his war record – he had fought on the North-West Frontier, in Burma and Persia – arrived from Jullundur on the evening of 11 April to assume command. The following day a proclamation was issued, forbidding all public meetings and processions, and the people were warned by beat of drum that defiance of orders would be dealt with under martial law. During the morning of 13 April the exercise of reading the proclamation was repeated. However, when the police later drew up a map showing where the announcements had been made, it became evident that in many parts of the city the proclamation was not read. No steps were taken to post it up on the walls.

In any event, the populace of Amritsar was not particularly awed by the presence of the troops in the city. When on the afternoon of 13 April General Dyer learned that a mass meeting had been called in the Jallianwala Bagh for half past four, he was determined to inflict exemplary punishment on those defying his orders.

The word Bagh means garden, but the Jallianwala Bagh was no more than a dusty, sunken courtyard, about the size of Trafalgar Square, surrounded by houses and low walls, with only a few narrow exits. Soon after the meeting opened, two resolutions were passed. One called for the repeal of the Rowlatt Act, the other condemned the firings by soldiers three days earlier and expressed profound sympathy for the dead and bereaved. A number of speeches were made. Suddenly the sound of heavy boots was heard in the Bagh. General Dyer arrived in an armoured car at the head of a column of twenty-five Gurkhas and twenty-five Baluchi troops armed with rifles, and forty Gurkhas armed with only *kukris*, the curved Nepalese daggers. One other armoured car accompanied the column, but General Dyer soon discovered that none of the entrances to the Bagh were sufficiently wide to allow the vehicles to pass and they were therefore abandoned in the street outside.

As soon as General Dyer entered the Bagh he found himself on rising ground, where he stationed fifty troops and promptly ordered them to fire into the crowd below until all their ammunition was exhausted. The panic-stricken multitude of about ten thousand people broke at once. For ten minutes the Gurkha and Baluchi riflemen fired accurately and deliberately, carefully selecting their targets. From his vantage point, General Dyer continued to direct the fire towards people trying to scale the walls and scrambling blindly for the few narrow exits. In all, 1,650 rounds were fired, killing 379 persons and wounding 1,137. 'You people know well that I am a soldier and a military man,' Dyer warned the leading citizens of Amritsar after the massacre. 'For me the battlefield of France or Amritsar is the same.'

Dyer did not rest content with firing 1,650 rounds into a defenceless crowd. He issued a series of humiliating orders, one of which, the 'crawling order', required Indians to go on all fours if they wished to pass down the lane in which Miss Sherwood, the missionary schoolteacher, had been assaulted. Any Indians who refused to crawl were flogged. It did not matter to the general that many of the people living there were entirely innocent and ignorant of the assault, or that some of them had attempted to rescue Miss Sherwood. Public floggings were also ordered for offences like disregarding the curfew order, refusing to salaam to British officers, and tearing down of official proclamations. An entire marriage party was rounded up and summarily flogged. Thousands of students were ordered to go on sixteen-mile route marches in scorching heat; six of the biggest boys in a high school were flogged simply because they were big schoolboys. General Dyer used numerous other methods to bring the people of Amritsar to their knees. Two days after the massacre at the Jallianwala Bagh he proclaimed martial law. As a result of the strict censorship imposed it was weeks before the news reached the rest of India.

Dyer's action at the Jallianwala Bagh – but not his subsequent 'crawling order' – was approved by the divisional commander and by the governor of the Punjab, Sir Michael O'Dwyer. The governor and his supporters were determined to convince the Indians that the British were there to stay – by military might and by the negation of democracy. Some British officials were of the view that the gravity of the situation warranted an immediate enquiry. But it was not till the late summer that an official commission was appointed by the government of India. The commission consisting of seven members – four British and three Indian, with Lord Hunter, a senior judge of the College of Justice of Scotland, as chairman – investigated the Punjab disturbances for many months and then published its report.

Under cross-examination before the Hunter Commission, Dyer admitted that, if he could have got the armoured cars into the Bagh, he would have opened fire with machine-guns. He could have dispersed the crowd perhaps without firing, but 'they could have come back again and laughed, and I would have made what I consider to be a fool of myself'. He was determined to punish them and his idea was to 'produce a sufficient moral effect from the military point of view not only on those who were present, but more especially throughout the Punjab'. He confessed that he had decided to fire into the crowd long before he arrived on the scene. 'I had made up my mind,' Dyer testified, 'I would do all men to death . . .' On being questioned if he had taken any measures after the firing for the relief of the wounded, Dyer replied: 'No, certainly not. It was not my job.'

During the Hunter Commission investigations Jawaharlal Nehru happened to be travelling from Amritsar to Delhi by the night train. In his autobiography Nehru wrote:

The compartment I entered was almost full and all the berths, except one upper one, were occupied by sleeping passengers. I took the vacant upper berth. In the morning I discovered that all my fellow-passengers were military officers. They conversed with each other in loud voices which I could not help overhearing. One of them was holding forth in an aggressive and triumphant tone and soon I discovered that he was Dyer, the hero of Jallianwala Bagh, and he was describing his Amritsar experiences. He pointed out how he had the whole town at his mercy and he had felt like reducing the rebellious city to a heap of ashes, but he took pity on it and refrained. He was evidently coming back from Lahore after giving his evidence before the Hunter Committee of inquiry. I was greatly shocked to hear his conversation and to observe his callous manner. He descended at Delhi station in pyjamas with bright pink stripes, and a dressing-gown.

Dyer was censured by the Hunter Commission and subsequently relieved of his command. Edwin Montague, the Secretary of State for India, in an official dispatch to the Viceroy, Lord Chelmsford, observed: 'His Majesty's Government repudiate emphatically the doctrine upon which Brigadier General Dyer based his action at Jallianwala Bagh . . . The crawling order offended against every canon of civilized government.' And yet Dyer was not long in finding allies. People in high places spoke on his behalf and a major section of the British public appeared to approve his action. A substantial fund was raised for his benefit, while a group calling itself 'The Women of England' solemnly presented him with a sword of honour.

As a result of the tight censorship imposed on Amritsar it was not until June that Gandhi became aware of the extent of the massacre. He, no doubt, felt the shooting was frightful, the loss of innocent life deplorable, but he was more infuriated by the 'crawling order' and other indignities that followed. 'The actors who performed these deeds deserve greater condemnation than General Dyer for the Jallianwala Bagh massacre,' he wrote. 'Dyer merely destroyed a few bodies, but the others tried to kill the soul of a nation.' The Amritsar massacre was a tremendous shock to Indian opinion and proved a turning point. Gandhi was no longer a loyalist, for he could now see the extent to which British rule had 'emasculated the people of India'. The episode had a far-reaching effect on moderate Congressmen and nationalists, so outraging them that almost all became ready to swing into line behind Gandhi in the course of action he was soon to advocate.

Although Gandhi was appalled by the widespread rioting that followed his announcement of the *hartal*, he did not subscribe to the view that the Satyagraha movement was responsible for it. Since Satyagraha must be peaceful, and men capable of being peaceful under all circumstances were difficult to find, it would be better to have a Satyagraha campaign localized in time and place, with only a few chosen ones taking part. He spoke about his new approach to offering civil resistance, claiming that even 'one real Satyagrahi is enough for victory'.

The Viceroy had assured him of the appointment of a strong and impartial committee to investigate the Punjab disturbances. Gandhi was prepared to pay attention to this assurance, 'for a civil resister never seeks to embarrass the government'. But he warned:

> If my occasional resistance be a lighted match, the Rowlatt legislation and the persistence in retaining it on the statute book is a thousand matches scattered throughout India. The only way to avoid civil resistance altogether is to withdraw that legislation.

About this time the government took very serious note of the writings of B.G. Horniman, editor of the *Bombay Chronicle*, and deported him to England. The directors of the *Chronicle*, Umar Sobani and Shankarlal Banker, asked Gandhi to take up the responsibility of conducting the paper, but soon the government ordered its publication to be suspended. These directors, who also controlled *Young India*, then offered Gandhi the editorship. Gandhi was anxious to expound the inner meaning of Satyagraha to the public, and he readily accepted the offer. In order that his message should reach the general public, a Gujarati journal, *Navajivan*, published from Ahmedabad and controlled by Sobani and Banker, was placed at Gandhi's disposal and at his suggestion the publication of *Young India* was moved to Ahmedabad. Later, a Hindi edition of *Navajivan* was also brought out.

Gandhi was under orders not to travel outside the Bombay Presidency, and during the suspension of Satyagraha he devoted himself more and more to the *khadi* campaign, giving innumerable speeches on the benefits of homespun cloth. By reviving the spinning wheel he hoped to encourage village industry and to reduce the import of British cloth, thus providing income, however meagre, to countless millions living in dire poverty.

Meanwhile Congress had boycotted the Hunter Commission for various reasons, and had set up a parallel inquiry committee of its own. At last, in October, Gandhi was permitted to visit the Punjab, where he received a rousing reception and was promptly appointed a member of this alternative committee. The main responsibility for direction rested with Motilal Nehru, a veteran Congressman and father of Jawaharlal, and C.R. Das, the Bengal nationalist; but much of the actual inquiry and the task of drafting the report was entrusted to Gandhi.

Chitta Ranjan Das (1870–1925) was a leading barrister who attained eminence as a politician. On many occasions he clashed with Gandhi on the question of nonviolence, as well as on constitutionalism. But, in response to the Mahatma's call for noncooperation at the Congress session at Nagpur in 1920, he announced that he was giving up his prosperous legal practice.

Though Das took part in the noncooperation movement, he later argued that confronting the bureaucracy in the councils would 'be the most effective boycott'. At the Congress session at Gaya in December 1922, when the resolution for council entry which he supported was lost, he resigned from the Congress presidentship.

Motilal Nehru (1861–1931) belonged to a well-to-do Brahmin family from Kashmir. After studying law at Muir College in Allahabad, he built up a lucrative legal practice and adopted an affluent Western style of life. Politically, he was a moderate at first. For some years he was president of the United Provinces Congress Committee, and in 1910 became a member of the UP Legislative Council.

Motilal was elected president of the 1919 Congress, and the following year, in response to Gandhi's appeal, gave up his large legal practice and opulent way of living. Like Das, he advocated entry into councils. He led the nationalist opposition within the Legislative Assembly that the British had established, but after Congress's decision on council entry he would resign from the Legislative Assembly.

# TWENTY-SIX

# Leader of the Nation

The annual session of Congress was held at Amritsar in the last week of December. Gandhi himself considered his participation in its proceedings as his real entrance into Congress politics. Jawaharlal Nehru referred to the Amritsar Congress as 'the first Gandhi Congress'. 'There could be no doubt about it,' Nehru observed, 'that the majority of the delegates and even more so the crowds outside, looked to Gandhi for leadership. The slogan '*Mahatma Gandhi ki jai*' began to dominate the Indian political horizon.'

The much-heralded Montague-Chelmsford reforms which had, by design or coincidence, received the Royal Assent a day before the Congress was convened were the main subjects for consideration at the Amritsar session. The Government of India Act of 1919, incorporating these reforms, set up a new constitution on a basis described as dyarchy, the Rule of the Two – Great Britain and India. Indians, however, had no power in the federal government and none was envisaged. In the provinces most of the government departments would be entrusted to Indian ministers, but the British governor retained a veto and controlled finance and police. The royal proclamation announcing these changes included promises of amnesty for many political prisoners, and increased Indian participation in the Civil Service.

Gandhi trusted Britain's good intentions and wanted the Amritsar Congress to accept the intended constitutional changes. Tilak and C.R. Das, the two prominent Congress leaders, wished however to reject them as wholly inadequate, and Gandhi found it 'unbearable' having to differ from such seasoned and revered leaders. 'I tried to run away from the Congress,' he wrote in his autobiography. He was persuaded to stay, for he had become one of its pillars. Many of the 7,031 delegates, an unprecedented number, supported him. The president, Motilal Nehru, knew that a motion rejecting the Montague-Chelmsford plan would not be easy to press against Gandhi's opposition. Frantic discussions followed to avoid a possible split. Gandhi turned to Tilak who was sitting on the dais. Gandhi was wearing a white homespun cap, the original of the 'Gandhi Cap' which became a badge of nationalism. In a dramatic moment, he tossed his cap at Tilak's feet in token of obeisance, and entreated him to consent to a compromise. Tilak said he would if Das did, and Das gave an indication, but before he could pronounce a definite yes, it was announced to the noisily joyous audience that a formula had been found. The compromise resolution, while condemning the Montague-Chelmsford reforms as unsatisfactory and disappointing, expressed the hope that people would work them so as to secure the establishment of full responsible government. However, Lord Chelmsford was censured for mismanaging Indian affairs, and his recall was demanded. Other resolutions demanded the repeal of the Rowlatt Act and condemned excesses in the Punjab, Indian as well as British – a gesture by Gandhi indicating impartiality.

In those days the Muslims of India were preoccupied with a somewhat far-flung movement. The end of World War I had marked the decisive defeat of Turkey, and of the Turkish sultan, who, in addition to being a temporal ruler, bore the title of caliph and was regarded as the religious head of all Islam. The Sultan had sided with the Germans and now had to take the consequences. The threatened dissolution of the Turkish Empire and the fate of the Caliph, though of no lasting significance to the Muslims of India, had begun to be perceived as Britain's anti-Muslim approach. A group of Muslims headed by the brothers Shaukat and Mohamed Ali, who had been interned during the war, were planning a sustained agitation against Britain's 'betrayal of Islam'. This led to a powerful Caliphate or, as it is always known in India, Khilafat movement. It was primarily an Indian Muslim movement, for there was no concerted effort on the part of Muslim countries to restore the authority of the Caliph. In fact, the smaller nations, crushed under the heel of the Turkish Ottoman Empire, were struggling to throw off the Turkish yoke.

The Khilafat movement had from its inception attracted Gandhi's sympathy. Indeed, it was not of much interest to him in itself, but his mind was fixed on the Muslims of India. Here was a genuine moral issue on which the Hindus could make common cause with the Muslims. He did not profess to go into the merits of the Khilafat, but it certainly seemed to him to afford 'such an opportunity of uniting the two communities as would not arise in a hundred years'.

The Muslims of the Khilafat Committee were also eager to attract Hindu support. At their conference in Delhi in November 1919, which Gandhi attended, many Hindus were present. The letter of invitation notified Gandhi that cow protection – the prevention of slaughtering of cows – as well as the Caliph would be discussed. For centuries Hindus have regarded the cow as sacred, and for this reason they do not eat beef. The cow, according to Gandhi, is the poem of pity. One reads pity in the gentle animal. Through the cow, man 'is enjoined to realize his identity with all that lives'. Cow protection signifies 'protection of the whole dumb creation of God'.

Soon after Gandhi's arrival at the Khilafat conference, it became quite apparent to him that the Muslims, in deference to Hindu regard for the cow as a sacred animal, were prepared to desist from slaughtering it in return for the Hindus supporting the Khilafat movement. Gandhi brushed the Muslims' offer aside. If their cause was right, it was right, and there should be no question of driving bargains. The cow, therefore, faded from the agenda.

The conference debated what to do if their pressure failed and the impending treaty between the victorious Allies and the government of Turkey took the form predicted. Some speakers suggested boycotting British textiles, while others expressed the opinion that it would be difficult to make such a ban complete. On the platform, Gandhi groped for a plan of action and a slogan that would summarize it. It darted into his head spontaneously, and when he was called on to speak he said: 'Non-cooperation.' When presenting his scheme to the conference he was careful to stress its hypothetical nature. He used phrases like 'in case of betrayal' in the context of a possible situation where the Sultan of Turkey was not favourably treated.

In the early part of the year Gandhi was ill. He would have severe pain in his left leg, and this at times depressed him. He entertained the idea that his power to make everyone listen to him and follow him had waned. 'My best time is over,' he wrote to Maganlal Gandhi. 'People may take now what they can from my ideas. I have ceased to be the ideal man of action that I used to be.' Two years earlier, when he was in high spirits and everything looked promising, he had written to this devoted disciple: 'I feel that, while my star is in the ascendant, I should do all I can to spread my ideas.' In any event, his 'best time' was far from over, for he would soon lead a bold and stirring campaign against the British Raj.

Gandhi wrote a stream of letters in defence of his position on the Caliphate. He took part in a Khilafat deputation to the Viceroy, without result. Another deputation that was sent to Europe was bluntly told that Turkey would not be allowed sway over non-Turkish lands. As the first few months of 1920 passed, it grew increasingly plain that Turkey's position would remain unenviable. On 14 May the peace terms presented by the Allies to Turkey were published in India in the *Gazette of India Extraordinary*, causing deep indignation among the Muslims.

Just two weeks later the publication of the Hunter Commission's findings on the Punjab roused intense resentment throughout India. 'The report,' Gandhi commented, 'is a laboured defence of every official act of inhumanity.' It confirmed the horrors, yet the conclusions drawn were unconvincing. According to the report, Dyer had 'committed a grave error of judgement which exceeded the reasonable requirements of the case' and had acted under an 'honest but mistaken conception of duty'. The general was shorn of his command, but kept his pension. However, the minor persecutors came through unscathed. Although Montague found Dyer's conduct very embarrassing and harmful to the empire, the House of Lords passed a vote of approval. 'The present representatives of the empire have no real regard for the wishes of the people of India,' Gandhi wrote, 'and they count the honour of India as of little consequence.'

It was five months since Gandhi had approved the Montague-Chelmsford dyarchy reforms at the Amritsar Congress session. These legislative reforms under the Government of India Act of 1919 could be seen as a stepping stone towards responsible government at the centre at a later date. But Gandhi now proposed that as a protest against the Turkish peace treaty and the decision of the government relating to the Punjab, as indicated in the Hunter Report, Congress should recommend a pro-gramme of noncooperation. On 30 June, guided by Gandhi, the Khilafat Committee sanctioned noncooperation as the only means left now to the Muslims. The Muslim leaders had no belief in nonviolence, or any of the other principles and policies that Gandhi advocated, but in their eagerness to secure his support and the mass influence that he could command, they were prepared to enter into an opportunist alliance. Those were the days of the honeymoon of the Hindu-Muslim political friendship. Gandhi believed that he was laying the foundations of Hindu-Muslim unity.

As he made it a rule of Satyagraha to warn one's opponent, he wrote to the Viceroy: 'I have advised my Muslim friends to withdraw their support from your Excellency's Government, and advised the Hindus to join them.' Lord Chelmsford replied that noncooperation was 'the most foolish of all foolish things'. Gandhi rejoined: 'Unfortunately for His Excellency the movement is likely to grow with ridicule as it is certain to flourish on repression.'

Gandhi's plan of noncooperation had by now taken a definite shape. He envisaged a strategy whereby a systematic war would be waged against the government. Initially he proposed the return of decorations and honours awarded by the British, the withdrawal of children and students from government-supported schools and colleges, the boycott of law courts by lawyers and litigants, and the boycott of elections to new legislative coun-cils under the Montague-Chelmsford reforms. If these steps did not yield the desired results, all government officials would be asked to leave their offices, and soldiers would be called upon to lay down their arms. A massive refusal to pay taxes would take care of the rest of his programme of 'progressive non-violent non-cooperation'. Gandhi felt that noncooperation would be less liable than direct civil disobedience to provoke clashes, and therefore less dangerous as a mass technique. But if carried out properly, the machinery of government would gradually grind to a halt. For several months he travelled across the country, usually with Shaukat Ali, propagating these ideas whenever he addressed a meeting, criticizing the British betrayal of Islam and the massacre at Amritsar. At times he would speak with an uncharacteristic vehemence:

> Where a tyrant reigns a prison is a palace and a palace a prison . . . Proclaim to the Government: 'You may hang us on the gallows, you may send us to prison, but you will get no cooperation from us. You will get it in jail or on the gallows, but not in the regiments of the army. You will not get it in legislatures or in any department of Government service.

> The British Empire today represents Satanism and has been guilty of such terrible atrocities that, if it did not apologize for them to God and to the country, it would certainly perish. I will go further and say that, unless it so apologized, it was the duty of every Indian to destroy it.

When he spoke of the duty of Indians to destroy the 'Satanist' British Empire, he clearly was not contemplating the use of force and violence. *Swaraj* was to be won by peaceful noncooperation. In an article in *Young India* entitled 'The Doctrine of the Sword', he wrote:

> Where there is only a choice between cowardice and violence, I would advise violence . . . But I believe that non-violence is infinitely superior to violence, forgiveness more manly than punishment. Forgiveness adorns a soldier. But abstinence is forgiveness only when there is the power to punish; it is meaningless when it pretends to proceed from a helpless creature . . . Let me not be misunderstood. Strength does not come from physical capacity. It comes from an indomitable will.
>
> We in India may in a moment realize that one hundred thousand Englishmen need not frighten three hundred million human beings. A definite forgiveness would mean a definite recognition of our strength. With enlightened forgiveness must come a mighty wave of strength in us, which would make it impossible for a Dyer . . . to heap affront on India's devoted head.
>
> Non-violence is the law of our species as violence is the law of the brute. Non-violence in its dynamic condition means conscious suffering. It does not mean meek submission to the will of the evil-doer, but it means the putting of

one's whole soul against the will of the tyrant. Working under this law of our being, it is possible for a single individual to defy the whole might of an unjust empire to save his honour, his religion, his soul, and lay the foundation for that empire's fall or its regeneration.

I am not pleading for India to practise non-violence because she is weak. I want her to practise non-violence being conscious of her strength and power. No training in arms is required for realization of her strength. We seem to need it, because we seem to think that we are but a lump of flesh. I want to recognize that she has a soul that cannot perish and that can rise triumphant above physical weakness.

When Gandhi announced that noncooperation would commence on 1 August 1920, he was running ahead of Congress. By that date it had not been accepted or even considered by Congress. It was on this very day that Tilak died in Bombay. 'My strongest bulwark is gone,' exclaimed Gandhi on hearing the news. With the passing away of Tilak, his position as a leader became much more identifiable.

Soon Gandhi made his first move in noncooperation. Writing to the Viceroy he returned his two South African war medals and his Kaiser-i-Hind gold medal for humanitarian work in South Africa. The British government, he declared, had handled the Khilafat matter 'in an unscrupulous, immoral and unjust manner, going from wrong to wrong, in order to defend its immorality. I can retain neither respect nor affection for such a government.' Its attitude on the Punjab atrocities was also a cause of great dissatisfaction. No doubt the mob excesses were unacceptable. The killing of five innocent Englishmen and the cowardly attack on Miss Sherwood were most deplorable. But the punitive measures taken by General Dyer and other officers were 'out of proportion to the crime of the people and amounted to wanton cruelty and inhumanity almost unparalleled in modern times'. Gandhi criticized the Viceroy for his light treatment of the official crime, leading to the exoneration of Sir Michael O'Dwyer, the Governor of the Punjab. Furthermore, the dispatch on the Khilafat agitation of the Secretary of State for India, Mr Montague, and the 'callous disregard of the feelings of Indians betrayed by the House of Lords' signified 'shameful ignorance of the Punjab events'. These developments, he wrote, 'have filled me with the greatest misgivings regarding the future of the empire and have estranged me completely from the present government'.

Most prominent Congress leaders of the elder generation were not in agreement with Gandhi on his noncooperation programme. But the younger members of Congress were behind him, and when a special session of the party met in Calcutta in September his battle cry of 'Khilafat and

Amritsar' was put to the test. Gandhi moved his resolution of noncooperation, and in the debate that followed it was pointed out that if the entire exercise of noncooperation was to be undertaken merely to compel British rethinking about the Khilafat and the Punjab, it seemed excessive. The situation was transformed by Motilal Nehru, who declared that the proper aim was *swaraj* itself. The others were necessary but secondary. A noisy debate ensued, but finally Gandhi emerged to lead noncooperation, with *swaraj* or self-rule as its goal, by 'peaceful and legitimate means' (the word 'constitutional' was deleted), 'within the British Empire if possible, or outside it if necessary'.

A few stalwarts broke from Congress after the Calcutta session established Gandhi's ascendancy and accepted his policy of noncooperation, among them Jinnah, a staunch nationalist, who had only joined the Muslim League in 1913 on condition that this would not prejudice his Congress membership. In the past few years he had done much to bring the Muslim League into line with Congress politics and had been acclaimed the 'ambassador of Hindu-Muslim unity'. He had been a great admirer of Gopal Krishna Gokhale and it was his 'one ambition to become the Muslim Gokhale.' Following the passing of the noncooperation resolution Jinnah resigned from the Home Rule League. Gandhi wrote to him to return to the national fold and take his share in the 'new life' that had opened up before the country, but Jinnah replied:

If by 'new life' you mean your methods and programme, I am afraid I cannot accept them, for I am fully convinced that it must lead to disaster . . . Your methods have already caused split and division in almost every institution that you have approached hitherto . . . People generally are desperate all over the country and your extreme programme has for the moment struck the imagination mostly of the inexperienced youth and the ignorant and the illiterate. All this means complete disorganization and chaos. What the consequences of this may be, I shudder to contemplate.

The annual session of Congress was held in the last week of October at Nagpur, central India, where the noncooperation movement approved at Calcutta awaited confirmation. When Jinnah, denouncing Gandhi's programme of noncooperation, made a reference to 'Mr Gandhi' the entire assembly roared 'MAHATMA GANDHI'. Cold, cultivated and Westernized, Jinnah did not take kindly to the new breed of Congressmen.

Among the delegates at Nagpur was Diwan Chaman Lall, the distinguished barrister, who recalled the scene when Jinnah protested against Gandhi's programme. Jinnah said: 'Your way is the wrong way. Mine is the right way – the constitutional way.' It was Maulana Mohamed Ali, the Khilafat movement leader, who secured the cheers of the assembly by jumping to his feet and repudiating Jinnah:

> You talk too much of the constitutional way. It reminds me of a story – of a young Tory who came out of the Carlton Club one evening and walked up to Piccadilly Circus, where there was a Salvation Army meeting in progress. The speaker was saying, 'Come this way – it is God's way.' The young Tory interrupted him and said, 'How long have you been preaching this?' 'Twenty years,' said the Salvationist. 'Well,' was the answer, 'if it's only got you as far as Piccadilly Circus, I don't think much of it.'

According to Diwan Chaman Lall, 'Jinnah sat down with a hurt look on his face. He just lapsed into silence.' Gradually Jinnah drifted away from Congress. It was only several years later that the significance of his departure became apparent.

Fourteen thousand delegates were in attendance at the Nagpur session, among them a massive block of Muslims and over a hundred women. Apart from Jinnah's criticism there were other mutterings at a high level. Gandhi was accused of aspiring to a moral dictatorship but managed to convince the opposition of the merits of his programme and the doubters were more or less won over. The main resolution was passed amidst scenes of excitement. Other resolutions called for the removal of untouchability, the revival of spinning and handweaving, and the collection of ten million rupees as a Tilak Memorial Fund. Gandhi promised that if India noncooperated nonviolently, self-government would come within a year. This was the advent of the Gandhian era in Congress, when the party was being converted from a Westernized into an essentially Indian institution. Jawaharlal Nehru described the swift change in the look of the Congress:

> European clothes vanished and soon only *khadi* was to be seen; a new class of delegates, chiefly drawn from the lower middle-class, became the type of Congressman; the language used became increasingly Hindustani . . . and a new life and enthusiasm and earnestness became evident in Congress gatherings.

The Nagpur session adopted a new constitution for Congress drafted by Gandhi which transformed it from little more than an upper middle-class debating society into a closely knit and effective political organization with a Working Committee, an All-India Committee and provincial committees with roots reaching down to districts, towns, and even villages instead of being confined, as previously, to the more important cities. Gandhi was fully aware that a well-organized Congress machinery was a prerequisite for the success of any agitation against the government which he would launch in future. He himself had no official role in the organization, but this very fact helped him over the years to strengthen his position in Congress, for he was not subject to too many rules.

At the beginning of 1921 many Indians renounced their British titles and decorations. Motilal Nehru, C.R. Das, Vallabhbhai Patel and thousands of others abandoned their law practices and quit the British courts for ever. Students, teachers and professional men and women left the cities to go into villages and teach literacy and noncooperation.

About this time Subhas Chandra Bose, following his patriotic resignation from the Indian Civil Service, met with Gandhi. Bose describes his first encounter with the Mahatma:

> I was ushered into a room covered with Indian carpets. Almost in the centre, facing the door, sat the Mahatma surrounded by some of his closest followers. All were clad in homemade *khadi*. As I entered the room, I felt somewhat out of place in my foreign costume and could not help apologizing for it. The Mahatma received me with his characteristic hearty smile and soon put me at ease and the conversation started at once. I desired to obtain a clear understanding of the details – the successive stages – of his plan, leading on step by step to the ultimate seizure of power from the foreign bureaucracy.

Gandhi failed to satisfy Bose on these points, but he found it fit to send Bose to C. R. Das and the two became very close. Bose would ultimately openly defy Gandhi's authority and then run into armed conflict with Great Britain.

Gandhi was now touring the country extensively, addressing mammoth meetings where, in those pre-microphone days, many would be content just to have a glimpse of the Mahatma. Wherever he went he had to endure the tyranny of people's enthusiasm and devotion about which he complained to an audience:

> Last night I went to a place where everybody was busy shouting *'Mahatma Gandhi ki jai'* and was trying to fall at my feet; but no one was willing to listen to me. I was feeling disgusted with myself and all around me . . . If only I thought for a moment that these shouts could bring *swaraj* for you, I could reconcile myself to my misery. But when I find that people's time and energy are wasted in mere useless shouting at the cost of real work, how I wish that instead of shouting my name they prepared and lighted up a funeral pyre for me so that I might leap into it, and once and for all extinguish the fire that is scorching up my heart.

In the first few weeks of his seven-month tour, he laid stress on the boycott of law courts and schools and colleges. Later, however, the emphasis was on nonviolence, Hindu-Muslim unity and the constructive programme. It was a tour of mass conversion to the new creed. Unprecedented scenes were witnessed. The prostitutes of Barisal, Marwari merchants of Calcutta, Oriya coolies, railway strikers, all claimed his attention. The inhabitants of an obscure area sent word that if Gandhi's train did not halt at their tiny station, they would lie down on the tracks and let it run over them. About midnight, amid roars, the train was sighted. It did stop. Gandhi was asleep but he staggered up and showed himself. The din died away and the crowd knelt on the platform, weeping.

Rabindranath Tagore, the great novelist and poet laureate, admired Gandhi for the moral force which he represented, but he condemned the element of negation contained in the noncooperation movement. From Europe Tagore expressed his anxiety to friends in India and three of his letters appeared in the *Modern Review*. 'It is criminal to transform moral force into force,' he wrote. 'Unity is truth, and division evil . . . unity cannot be attained through negation. The present attempt to separate our spirit from that of the Occident is tentative of spiritual suicide . . . The present age has been dominated by the Occident, because the Occident has a mission to fulfil. We of the Orient should learn from the Occident. The problem is a world problem. No nation can find its own salvation by breaking away from others. We must all be saved or we must all perish together.'

Gandhi commented that the struggle was being waged against compulsory cooperation, against one-sided combination, against armed imposition of modern methods of exploitation masquerading under the name of civilization. 'Non-cooperation is the nation's notice that it is no longer satisfied to be a tutelage,' he added. 'The nation has taken to the harmless, natural and religious doctrine of non-cooperation in the place of the unnatural and irreligious doctrine of violence.'

Meanwhile Lord Chelmsford had returned to England. When Lord Reading, the new Viceroy, arrived in India on 2 April 1921, he was well aware that the political cauldron was boiling over. A Jewish fruit-broker's son, Reading was a self-made statesman of varied talents and had earlier held the positions of Lord Chief Justice in England and Ambassador to Washington. Soon after his arrival in India he made it a point to send for Gandhi, and during May they had several talks totalling thirteen hours. The Viceroy, in a letter to Montague, the Secretary of State for India, described their first meeting:

There is nothing striking about his appearance. He came to visit me in a white *dhoti* and cap, woven on a spinning wheel, with bare feet and legs, and my first impression on seeing him ushered into my room was that there was nothing to arrest attention in his appearance, and that I should have passed him by in the street without a second look at him. When he talks, the impression is different. He is direct, and expresses himself well in excellent English with a fine appreciation of the value of the words he uses. There is no hesitation about him and there is a ring of sincerity in all that he utters, save when discussing some political questions. His religious views are, I believe, genuinely held, and he is convinced to a point almost bordering on fanaticism that non-violence and love will give India its independence and enable it to withstand the British Government. His religious and moral views are admirable and indeed are on a remarkably high altitude, though I must confess that I find it difficult to understand his practice of them in politics.

Lord Reading did not have to wait long to realize that his difficulties were on the increase. Gandhi's espousal of the Khilafat movement had brought about a Hindu-Muslim entente, regarded by the British as the greatest danger to them in India. He was becoming more and more critical of the government. Noncooperation was extended to cover a boycott of foreign cloth and the picketing of liquor shops; plans were afoot to add to it a fresh campaign of civil disobedience, confined initially to only one limited territory. But a growing number of people were becoming impatient to embark on mass civil disobedience.

Gandhi's appeal to boycott foreign cloth aroused great enthusiasm. He firmly believed that a successful boycott would produce an atmosphere 'that would enable us to inaugurate civil disobedience on a scale that no government can resist'. On 31 July, in commemoration of Tilak's death, a huge bonfire was made of foreign cloth. Some of the finest *saris*, shirts and jackets were consigned to the flames to the accompaniment of shouts of joy. 'Untouchability of foreign cloth ought to be as much a virtue with Indians of all religions as untouchability of suppressed classes must be a sin with every devout Hindu,' Gandhi declared at a meeting on the Chowpati sands the following day. The bonfire ritual soon spread all over the country, though Gandhi's action evoked severe criticism from even some of his close associates. Charlie Andrews, who wore homespun himself, protested at the destruction of the 'noble handiwork of one's fellow men and women abroad'. Gandhi replied that the love of foreign cloth had brought 'foreign domination, pauperism and, what is worse, shame in many a home'. For the next few weeks holocausts of the same kind were a feature of his tour. It was Gandhi's firm conviction that the destruction of foreign cloth was a sound proposition from the highest moral standpoint. Monsieur Richard, a Frenchman, wrote to a friend in India on this subject and the letter was published in 1921. If Gandhi saw it he would certainly have been delighted.

I know you are distressed at the burning of foreign clothes as directed by Mr Gandhi . . . But consider that by these bonfires material goods are being transmuted into dynamic moral forces for the nation's awakening, just as material food in ourselves is transformed into vital and mental forces for our work and for our progress. Destruction of clothes is not to be regretted more than consumption of – combustion of – beautiful plants and fruits for the sake of a high ideal life. Let the spiritual body of the nation be fed by this sacrificial holocaust . . . These foreign fabrics are the winding sheets of the nation. When Lazarus resuscitates, when the nation rises from the dead, his shroud has to be burned.

While Gandhi preached burning of the imported fabric, he urged the people not to substitute it with Indian mill products; they must learn to spin and weave themselves. He took to spinning half an hour a day and expected his associates to do likewise. He continued to stress the practical aspect of using the spinning wheel – that it would give families work and income in the dead months, and help in escaping the clutches of British capitalism. Spinning was a means to self-reliance and self-respect. It forged a bond between those who did it. 'Daily spinning is a sacrament and would take the spinner's mind Godward.'

As he continued with the preaching of his gospel, a fierce revolt of the Moplahs, a Muslim peasantry of partly Arab descent, rudely disturbed the prevailing concept of Hindu-Muslim unity. Influenced by the Khilafat agitation, they declared a holy war, designed to set up a Caliphate kingdom. In their fanatical fervour they murdered a number of Europeans and Hindu moneylenders and landlords, and then directed their rebellion against the Hindus. A long campaign of terror, murder, arson, rapine, looting, desecration of Hindu temples and forcible conversions to Islam resulted. Gandhi, minimizing the first reports of the uprising, spoke of the 'brave God-fearing Moplahs fighting for what they consider as religion, and in a manner which they consider religious'. But when dismay and alarm spread through the Hindu community, Gandhi's whole policy of alliance with extremist Muslims on a religious issue began to be questioned.

Meanwhile the Ali brothers, Mohamed and Shaukat, who had been instrumental in starting the Khilafat movement, were arrested and charged with attempting to detach Muslims from the armed forces. On 5 October 1921, the Congress Working Committee approved all the Ali brothers had done, and resolved that Indians ought not to remain in the employ, civil or military, of 'a system of government which has brought India's economic, moral and political degradation'. Congress thus reiterated the seditious statement for which the Ali brothers had been arrested.

The trial of the Ali brothers took place at Karachi, where on 1 November they were both sentenced to two years' imprisonment with hard labour. Three days later the All-India Congress Committee authorized provincial branches to prepare for civil disobedience, including refusal to pay taxes. Gandhi announced that he would make an experimental start in Bardoli, a district in Gujarat with a population of about eighty thousand.

On 17 November the Prince of Wales, subsequently King Edward VIII and the Duke of Windsor, arrived in Bombay on a ceremonial visit, to be greeted by an impressive silence, for all over India the people, in response to a call by Congress, had observed a complete *hartal*. In Bombay there were Parsis, Christians, Anglo-Indians and many others who felt it was only proper that the heir to the throne be accorded a welcome, but the demonstration by noncooperators against those who participated in welcoming him ended in mob violence. Several policemen were beaten to death. The *khadi*-clad demonstrators looted shops, burned foreign cloth and wrecked automobiles, shouting, as Gandhi himself witnessed, '*Mahatma Gandhi ki jai.*' 'Never', he wrote later, 'has the sound of these words grated so much on my ears.' He felt that what he saw was the failure of nonviolent noncooperation. Any confrontation with the government had to cease forthwith, and accordingly he suspended preparations for civil disobedience in Bardoli. With murder and arson still raging, he sternly rebuked those who had broken the pledge of nonviolence:

> The *swaraj* that I have witnessed during the last two days has stunk in my nostrils. Hindu-Muslim unity has been a menace to the handful of Parsis, Christians and Jews . . . With non-violence on our lips, we have terrorized those who have differed from us, and in so doing we have deceived our God . . . I invite every Hindu and Musalman citizen to retire to his house, ask God for forgiveness, and to befriend the injured communities from the very depth of his heart.

He began a penitential fast, and the violence gradually died down. A deputation representing all communities waited on him, gave a pledge of good conduct and persuaded him to end the fast, but he took a vow 'to observe every Monday a twenty-four-hour fast till *swaraj* is attained'. In the three days of violent disturbances fifty-eight Bombay citizens were killed and four hundred injured.

While Congress continued to snub the royal traveller with *hartals* and boycotts, the provincial governments of Bengal, the Punjab and the United Provinces declared all Congress and Khilafat volunteer organizations to be unlawful bodies and ordered the suppression of political meetings. Early in December the long-anticipated wave of arrests began. C.R. Das, Motilal Nehru, Lajpat Rai and hundreds of other top Congressmen were arrested. When Congress met for its annual session in the last week of December, twenty thousand Indians had been jailed for civil disobedience and sedition. The six thousand delegates, workers and leaders who were in attendance at Ahmedabad all wore *khadi*, with one exception. M.A. Jinnah was dressed immaculately in his Savile Row suit. Gandhi entered the *pandal* (makeshift enclosure) wearing only a loincloth.

There were some Congressmen, Jinnah and Madan Mohan Malaviya among them, who were in favour of calling a round table conference to discuss with the government the uneasy situation. A resolution to this effect was introduced, but it was defeated by an overwhelming majority. Referring to a peace proposal, Gandhi said: 'I am a man of peace but I do not want peace that you find in the grave.' The Muslim leader, Hazarat Mohani, introduced a resolution for a change of the Congress creed in favour of complete independence. He proposed proclaiming an Indian republic and marshalling the forces around it. Gandhi, opposing the resolution, said:

Let us first gather up our strength . . . Let us not go into waters whose depth we do not know. Our creeds are not such simple things as clothes which a man changes at will . . . they are creeds for which people die, for which people live for ages and ages.

The delegates passed Gandhi's resolution calling for civil disobedience to all the government laws and constitutions, for nonviolence, for the continuance of public meetings throughout India despite the government prohibition, and for all Indians to offer themselves peacefully for arrest by joining the banned volunteer corps.

Gandhi accepted a resolution investing him with 'sole executive authority' on the understanding that he would resume preparations for civil disobedience. He appealed to the British government 'in all humility' to 'take care what you are doing, and see that you do not make the three hundred millions of India your eternal enemies'. The pages of *Young India* were full of reports of repression. Gandhi observed:

The massacre of Jallianwala Bagh though atrocious was the cleanest demonstration of the government's intentions and it gave us the needed shock. What is now going on is being done inside the cold prison walls or in little unknown villages and, therefore, has no theatrical value. Our duty, therefore, clearly is to invite martial law and no 'damned nonsense' and evolve the courage to draw the rifle fire not in our backs as in 1919, but in our open and willing breasts and without resentment.

The year 1921 had passed. The *swaraj* or self-rule Gandhi had promised was nowhere in sight. Many questioned the logic of his declaration a year ago, but he attributed more importance to moral principles and moral character; political forms and constitutional issues were secondary. *Swaraj* for him meant self-government not only in the political sense, but in the moral sense of individual and national self-control. 'I do not work for freedom of India. I work for non-violence in the world,' he had said. 'I am ready to sacrifice even the freedom of my country for the sake of truth.' To the critics who complained about the absence of any concrete results, Gandhi replied:

I am unable to accept any blame for having set the time-limit. I would have been wrong not to do so, knowing as I did that if the people fulfilled the conditions which were not difficult to fulfil, *swaraj* was possible inside of twelve months. The time-limit was not set in order to rouse the teeming milions, but it was fixed in order to rivet the attention of Congressmen and Congresswomen on their sense of immediate duty and on the grand consequence of its fulfilment. Without the time-limit we would not have collected the one *crore* [rupees], nor would we have introduced so many *charkhas*, nor manufactured large quantities of hand-spun *khadi* . . . It is not a sign of bad soldiery to find Bengal, the United Provinces and the Punjab supplying prisoners as fast as the government can take them. And when the word is passed round the other provinces for repression of a violent type, I doubt not that they will shine as brilliantly as the three fortunate ones I have mentioned.

As thousands more Indians were thrown into prisons for political offences, Gandhi announced that mass civil disobedience in Bardoli, postponed earlier, would now commence. On 1 February 1922, he sent Lord Reading an open letter saying that he proposed to lead a vast civil-disobedience movement in the Bardoli district unless various demands were met. The 'official lawlessness' in the form of repression of 'virulent types' was continuing, therefore it was necessary to seek redress. Freedom of speech, freedom of association and freedom of the press had been suspended, and it was imperative that they were restored. Since innocent people had been jailed, it was necessary to release them. The government must declare in unambiguous terms 'a policy of absolute non-interference with all non-violent activities in the country, whether they be regarding the redress of the Khilafat or the Punjab wrongs or *swaraj* or any other purpose'.

It was a tall order for the Viceroy who evidently considered that its acceptance would mean the abject surrender of the government. If the government adopted the policy of absolute noninterference with all nonviolent activities, it would inevitably help Gandhi in building up his counter-establishment with a prior guarantee against hindrance of any description – even if he persuaded three million of Britain's customers to forgo her products; even if his reasoning caused the troops to desert to him; even if he declared India a republic. The Viceroy promptly rejected Gandhi's ultimatum.

There were many Indians who questioned Gandhi's plan to paralyse the British administration in only one limited territory, for they thought he might have done the same thing on a massive scale – in all the provinces – thus making the country unmanageable and perhaps even bringing the government to terms. But Gandhi felt India was not yet ready to launch nonviolent civil disobedience on a wider scale. He believed that only civil disobedience confined to a limited territory could be properly conducted and he could see immense possibilities in such a movement. The government feared that if Bardoli's lead in refusing to pay taxes were followed and the stoppage became prevalent the Raj would soon be rendered bankrupt. Gandhi too anticipated some such trend:

When the *swaraj* flag floats victoriously at Bardoli, then the people of the district next to Bardoli, following in the steps of Bardoli should seek to plant the flag of *swaraj* in their midst. Thus in district after district, in regular succession, throughout the length and breadth of India, should the *swaraj* flag be hoisted.

Bardoli was due to launch civil disobedience on 8 February. The country was agog. Then something happened in a remote part of the United Provinces. In the small village of Chauri Chaura in the Gorakhpur district, eight hundred miles from Bardoli, a procession of noncooperators marched past the local police station in good order. Some stragglers were taunted by the police, trouble started, and the police opened fire, without apparently killing anybody. Having exhausted their scant ammunition, and driven back by the weight of numbers, the twenty-three constables took refuge in the police station, which was set on fire. 'The self-imprisoned constables had to come out for dear life,' Gandhi reported in *Young India* of 16 February, 'and as they did so they were hacked to pieces and their mangled remains were thrown into the raging flames.'

The news of this violence reached Gandhi on the morning of 8 February. Struck by grief and remorse, he suspended the campaign in Bardoli and discontinued defiance of the government everywhere in India. He fasted for five days in penance. 'Suppose,' he asked, 'the non-violent disobedience of Bardoli was permitted by God to succeed and the government had abdicated in favour of the victors of Bardoli, who would control the unruly elements that must be expected to perpetrate inhumanity upon due provocation?' He was painfully aware that India's masses had not yet absorbed his teaching.

He summoned members of the Congress Working Committee to Bardoli, and they gloomily yielded to his insistence that the campaign be suspended. The Bardoli decision caused considerable dismay among the Congress leaders most of whom were in prison, and left the rank and file disgruntled. Motilal Nehru, Lajpat Rai and others sent indignant letters from prison. Why should, asked Motilal, a town at the foot of the Himalayas be penalized if a town at Cape Comorin failed to observe nonviolence? Subhas Chandra Bose, who was in jail with C.R. Das, wrote afterwards that Gandhi's move had angered Das. The chance of a lifetime, he said, had been lost.

Gandhi saw the justice of his colleagues' viewpoint. 'The drastic reversal of practically the whole of the aggressive programme may be politically unsound and unwise,' he affirmed, 'but there is no doubt that it is religiously sound.' He was critical of those who joined the volunteer corps knowing well that they were not nonviolent and did not intend to remain nonviolent. 'We are thus untruthful as we hold the government to be untruthful,' he wrote. 'We dare not enter the kingdom of liberty with mere lip-homage to truth and non-violence.' Those who were disappointed by the suspension of the campaign should 'feel relieved of the burden of unreality and of national sin'. Nevertheless they should not consider this as a defeat. 'The movement had drifted from the right path. We have come back to our moorings, and we can again go straight ahead.'

With the suspension of civil disobedience the noncooperation campaign also began to weaken and soon collapsed. Students resumed their studies and lawyers their practice. The Khilafat movement also began to wilt as the Turks themselves abolished the Caliphate. The Moplahs had given the Hindu-Muslim alliance a jolt; and the decision of the Turks caused the shaky foundations of the Hindu-Muslim alliance, based on the Khilafat issue to crumble.

# TWENTY-SEVEN

# The Great Trial

Although developments had temporarily discomfited Gandhi, he had by now gained a hold on the population greater than any earlier nationalist leader. His decision to suspend the Bardoli civil disobedience led the government to believe that he was no longer in command of a powerful movement; he could therefore be arrested with impunity.

On the night of 10 March, a police car drew up to the ashram at Sabarmati. Dan Healey, the superintendent of police at Ahmedabad, sent word that Gandhi should consider himself under arrest and come along when he was ready. After singing the Vaishnava song with a group of ashramites, the prisoner collected a spare loincloth, two blankets, and a few books, including the *Bhagavad Gita*. He was driven the short distance to prison.

Gandhi had expected arrest and in an article entitled 'If I am Arrested', published in *Young India* of 9 March, had declared: 'Rivers of blood shed by the government cannot frighten me.' The only thing he feared was that the people might be carried away by the news of his arrest. He strongly urged them to remain calm and consider the day of his arrest as 'a day of rejoicing'.

At the preliminary hearing Gandhi gave his occupation as 'farmer and weaver,' and pleaded guilty to the charge of sedition on the basis of three of his more challenging articles in *Young India*. The publisher, Shankarlal Banker, was arraigned at the same time. In the first of the articles, called 'Tampering with Loyalty', which appeared in on 29 September 1921, Gandhi openly preached sedition:

I have no hesitation in saying that it is sinful for anyone, either soldier or civilian, to serve this Government which has proved treacherous to the Muslims of India and which has been guilty of the inhumanities of the Punjab.

Sedition has become the creed of Congress . . . Non-cooperation, though a religious and strictly moral movement, deliberately aims at the overthrow of the Government, and is therefore legally seditious . . . We ask for no quarter; we expect none from the Government. We did not solicit the promise of immunity from prison so long as we remained non-violent. We may not now complain if we are imprisoned for sedition. Therefore, our self-respect and our pledge require us to remain calm, unperturbed and non-violent. We have our appointed course to follow.

Lord Reading was 'puzzled and perplexed', for he could not see what purpose was served by flagrant breaches of the law for the mere sake of challenging the government and compelling arrest. Gandhi was quite happy to clarify with the utmost simplicity. In an article, 'A Puzzle and Its Solution', in *Young India* of 15 December 1921, he declared:

We seek arrest because the so-called freedom is slavery. We are challenging the might of this Government because we consider its activity to be wholly evil. We want to overthrow the Government. We want to compel its submission to the people's will. We desire to show that the Government exists to serve the people, not the people the Government. Free life under the Government has become intolerable, for the price exacted for the retention of freedom is unconscionably great. Lord Reading must clearly understand that the non-cooperators are at war with the Government. They have declared rebellion against it . . . Lord Reading is entitled therefore to put them out of harm's way.

In the third seditious article, 'Shaking the Manes', in *Young India* of 23 February 1922, Gandhi made his most scathing attack on British power:

How can there be any compromise while the British lion continues to shake his gory claws in our faces? No empire intoxicated with the red wine of power and plunder of weaker races has yet lived long in the world, and this British Empire, which is based upon organized exploitation of physically weaker races of the earth and upon a continuous exhibition of brute force, cannot live if there is a just God ruling the universe . . . It is high time that the British people were made to realize that the fight that was commenced in 1920 is a fight to the finish, whether it lasts one month or one year or many years and whether the representatives of Britain re-enact all the orgies of the [1857] Mutiny days with redoubled force or whether they do not.

These highly charged statements, made over a period of five months were, as Gandhi himself realized, merely contributory causes of his arrest. In fact it was a surprise to him that he had not been arrested after the first or the second of the articles. The government had all along been aware of his growing power and the tremendous influence he could exercise over the Indian people. But now that he spoke of 'a fight to the finish, whether it lasts one month or one year or many years', and the government was of the opinion that he had, in the wake of the suspension of civil disobedience, rendered himself disarmed, a decision was made to arrest him.

The brief trial, which came to be known as 'The Great Trial', was held in the heavily guarded Government Circuit House at Ahmedabad on 18 March 1922, before Mr Justice Robert Broomfield. Gandhi and Shankarlal Banker, the co-accused, had no lawyers. The little courtroom was jammed with well-wishers.

The advocate-general, Sir J.T. Strangman, read the indictment and stated the Crown's case. The judge then asked Gandhi whether he wished to make a statement. Gandhi had a written statement ready, but before reading it he made some extemporaneous comments, offering no defence, and enlarging on his plea:

I have no desire whatsoever to conceal from this court the fact that to preach disaffection towards the existing system of government has become almost a passion with me ... I wish to endorse all the blame which the learned Advocate-General has thrown on my shoulders in connection with the Bombay occurrences, Madras occurrences, and the Chauri Chaura occurrences. Thinking over these deeply and sleeping over them night after night, it is impossible for me to disassociate myself from the diabolical crimes of Chauri Chaura or the mad outrages of Bombay. He is quite right when he says that as a man of responsibility, a man having received a fair share of education, having had a fair share of experience of this world, I should have known the consequences of every one of my acts. I knew that I was playing with fire ...

I want to avoid violence. Non-violence is the first article of my faith. It is also the last article of my creed. But I had to make my choice. I had either to submit to a system which I considered had done irreparable harm to my country, or incur the risk of the mad fury of my people bursting forth, when they understood the truth from my lips. I know that my people have sometimes gone mad. I am deeply sorry for it, and I am, therefore, here to submit not to a light penalty but to the highest penalty. I do not ask for mercy. I do not plead any extenuating act. I am here, therefore, to invite and cheerfully submit to the highest penalty that can be inflicted upon me, for what in law is a deliberate crime and what appears to me to be the highest duty of a citizen.

The only course open to you, the Judge, is, as I am just going to say in my statement, either to resign your post, or inflict on me the severest penalty, if you believe that the system and the law you are assisting to administer are good for the people. I do not expect that kind of conversion, but by the time I have finished with my statement, you will perhaps have a glimpse of what is raging within my breast, to run the maddest risk which a sane man can run.

Gandhi then read his written statement, tracing the series of disillusionments which had turned him from a staunch supporter of the Empire into a rebel. It was a carefully reasoned explanation of his actions. The import of the document warrants that it should be quoted extensively.

I owe it perhaps to the Indian public and to the public in England, to . . . explain why from a staunch loyalist and co-operator I have become an uncompromising disaffectionist and non-co-operator. To the Court too I should say why I plead guilty to the charge of promoting disaffection towards the Government established by law in India.

My public life began in 1893 in South Africa in troubled weather. My first contact with British authority in that country was not of a happy character. I discovered that as a man and an Indian, I had no rights. More correctly I discovered that I had no rights as a man because I was an Indian. But I was not baffled. I thought that this treatment of Indians was an excrescence upon a system which was intrinsically and mainly good. I gave the Government my voluntary and hearty co-operation, criticizing it freely where I felt it was faulty but never wishing its destruction.

Consequently when the existence of the Empire was threatened in 1899 by the Boer challenge, I offered my services to it, raised a volunteer ambulance corps and served at several actions that took place for the relief of Ladysmith. Similarly in 1906, at the time of Zulu 'revolt', I raised a stretcher-bearer party and served till the end of the 'rebellion'. On both the occasions I received medals and was even mentioned in despatches. For my work in South Africa I was given by Lord Hardinge a Kaisar-i-Hind gold medal. When the war broke out in 1914 between England and Germany, I raised a volunteer ambulance corps in London, consisting of the then resident Indians in London, chiefly students. Its work was acknowledged by the authorities to be valuable. Lastly, in India when a special appeal was made at the War Conference in Delhi in 1918 by Lord Chelmsford for recruits, I struggled at the cost of my health to raise a corps in Kheda, and the response was being made when hostilities ceased and orders were received that no more recruits were wanted. In all these efforts at service, I was actuated by the belief that it was possible by such services to gain a status of full equality in the Empire for my countrymen.

The first shock came in the shape of the Rowlatt Act . . . Then followed the Punjab horrors beginning with the massacre at Jallianwala Bagh and culminating in crawling orders, public flogging and other indescribable humiliations . . . The Punjab crime was whitewashed and most culprits went not only unpunished but remained in service, and some continued to draw pensions from the Indian revenue and in some cases were even rewarded. I saw too that not only did the reforms not make a change of heart, but they were only a method of further draining India of her wealth and of prolonging her servitude.

I came reluctantly to the conclusion that the British connection had made India more helpless than she ever was before, politically and economically. A disarmed India had no power of resistance against any aggressor if she wanted to engage in an armed conflict with him. So much is this the case that some of our best men consider that India must take generations before she can achieve Dominion Status. She has become so poor that she has little power of resisting famines. Before the British advent India spun and wove in her millions of cottages, just the supplement she needed for adding to her meagre agricultural resources. This cottage industry, so vital for India's existence, has been ruined by incredibly heartless and inhuman processes as described by English witnesses. Little do town dwellers know how the semi-starved masses of India are slowly sinking to lifelessness. Little do they know that their miserable comfort represents the brokerage they get for the work they do for the foreign exploiter, that the profits and brokerage are sucked from the masses. Little do they realize that the Government established by law in British India is carried on for this exploitation of the masses. No sophistry, no jugglery in figures, can explain away the evidence that the skeletons in many villages present to the naked eye. I have no doubt whatsoever that both England and the town dwellers of India will have to answer, if there is a God above, for this crime against humanity, which is perhaps unequalled in history. . . .

The greatest misfortune is that Englishmen and their Indian associates in the administration of the country do not know that they are engaged in the crime I have attempted to describe. I am satisfied that many English and Indian officials honestly believe that they are administering one of the best systems devised in the world and that India is making steady though slow progress. They do not know that a subtle but effective system of terrorism and an organized display of force on the one hand, and the deprivation of all powers of retaliation or self-defence on the other, have emasculated the people and induced in them the habit of simulation.

I have no personal ill-will against any single administrator, much less can I have any disaffection towards the King's person. But I hold it to be a virtue to be disaffected towards a Government which in its totality has done more harm to India than any previous system. India is less manly under the British rule than she ever was before. Holding such a belief, I consider it to be a sin to have affection for the system. In fact, I believe I have rendered a service to India and England by showing in non-co-operation the way out of an unnatural state in which both are living. In my humble opinion, non-co-operation with evil is as much a duty as is co-operation with good. But in the past, non-co-operation has been deliberately expressed in violence to the evil-doer. I am endeavouring to show to my countrymen that violent non-co-operation only multiplies evil, and that as evil can only be sustained by violence, withdrawal of support of evil requires complete abstention from violence.

Gandhi asked again for the 'severest penalty'. When the prisoner sat down, Mr Justice Broomfield bowed to him and pronounced sentence.

The judge noted that Gandhi had made his task easy by pleading guilty to the charges. But this was no ordinary trial. 'The determination of a just sentence', the judge declared, 'is perhaps as difficult a proposition as a judge in this country could have to face. The law is no respecter of persons. Nevertheless it would be impossible to ignore the fact that you are in a different category from any person I have ever tried or am likely to have to try. It would be impossible to ignore the fact that in the eyes of millions of your countrymen you are a great patriot and a great leader . . . But it is my duty to judge you as a man subject to law.' Judge Broomfield proposed to follow the precedent of the case against Bal Gangadhar Tilak several years before when he was sentenced for sedition to six years' imprisonment. He said: 'You will not consider it unreasonable, I think, that you should be classed with Mr Tilak.' The judge then sentenced Gandhi to six years' imprisonment, and added that if the government later deemed it fit to reduce the term 'no one would be better pleased than I'. The co-accused, Shankarlal Banker, received one year in jail and a fine of one thousand rupees.

On hearing the sentence, Gandhi rose and said that he regarded it as the 'proudest privilege and honour' to be associated with the well-revered name of Lokamanya Tilak. 'So far as the sentence itself is concerned,' he added, 'I certainly consider that it is as light as any judge would inflict on me, and so far as the whole proceedings are concerned, I must say that I could not have expected greater courtesy.'

The 'farmer and weaver' had for a short while reverted to his old profession and it appeared as if he had indicted the Empire. As the judge left the courtroom, he bowed once more to the prisoner in the coarse and scanty loincloth, who bowed in return. Suddenly the Mahatma found himself surrounded by the spectators in the room. Looking round at the familiar faces of men and women who had travelled far to offer him their homage, he commented: 'This is like a family gathering and not a law court.' He took his leave with a benign smile. This was the last time the authorities ever put him on trial. After 1922 they imprisoned him without trial.

# TWENTY-EIGHT

# The 'Silent' Years

On 20 March, two days after their trial and sentencing, Gandhi and Banker were removed from Sabarmati jail and taken by special train to Kirkee, a suburb of Poona, where a waiting police van took them to Yeravda jail. As they entered the prison, the jail superintendent announced that they must leave their spinning wheel behind. Gandhi had earlier taken a vow that he would spin for at least half an hour a day unless he was ill or travelling. He was allowed to spin in Sabarmati jail and had told his companion that he would refuse food if they tried to forbid him. Gandhi notified the superintendent of his vow. 'Yeravda is not Sabarmati,' came the curt reply. His first impression of Yeravda was thus 'rather unfavourable'. The following day, however, Gandhi's spinning wheel was restored to him.

The cell at Yeravda did not displease him. It was clean and provided with adequate ventilation. Outside there was a rather dingy courtyard which was however better than no courtyard at all. At first the jail staff imposed some restrictions. He could have no access to books. They kept him apart from other prisoners. He was forbidden to sleep outdoors (a hardship in hot weather) and was provided with no pillow – he rested his head on the clothes he was not wearing. His penknife was in safe custody, for according to the jail manual it was a 'lethal weapon'. Gandhi needed it to prepare his toasted bread and to cut up his lemons. He gave the superintendent the option of withdrawing bread and lemons or giving him the use of a knife. After a great deal of fuss his own penknife was made available to him, but it had to remain in the custody of his 'convict warder' when not in use. Such warders were 'trustees', usually murderers undergoing long sentences, who, by their good behaviour, were, under supervision, entrusted with light responsibilities. The warders went through the ritual of a daily search which Gandhi no doubt found petty and unpleasant. However, most of the rigours were soon relaxed. As well as the books in the jail library he could procure at his own expense books and periodicals from outside, though the newspapers were not allowed, for they were too political. Gandhi stated that a newspaper was a periodical. The superintendent seemed to agree, but the matter was outside his jurisdiction. Later Gandhi complained that he was not permitted to receive some journals of his choice.

He enjoyed being an isolation prisoner. 'By nature I like solitude,' he wrote. 'Silence pleases me. And I am able to indulge in studies which I prize, but which I was bound to neglect outside.' Prison life also afforded him the opportunity to spend more time on the spinning wheel. He rose at four o'clock each morning and spent the hours before sunrise in prayer and meditation. When there was sufficient light, he would start his work, reading and writing. He spent six hours on literary work and devoted four hours to spinning and carding. There was a well-stocked library with books in most of the Indian languages. He drew up an extensive programme of study, as though he was trying to make up for the lack of time for literary pursuit outside the prison. The list of what he read, as recorded in his jail diary, is quite formidable. Aside from the intensive study of Hindu religion and philosophy, he probed further into other religions, and also read numerous works of general interest. Sometimes he read without choice or discrimination. Christian friends in England and America were continually sending him books and he felt he should at least peruse them. But he had his reservations about works of the orthodox type. 'The orthodox books on Christianity do not give me any satisfaction,' he wrote in *Young India*. 'My regard for the life of Jesus is indeed very great. His ethical teaching, his common sense, his sacrifice command my reverence. But I do not [subscribe to] the orthodox teaching [about] Jesus . . . in the accepted sense . . . I do not believe in the doctrine of appropriation of another's merit. His sacrifice is a type and example for us. Everyone of us has to be "crucified" for salvation.'

The rich assortment of a hundred and fifty books he studied included commentaries on the *Bhagavad Gita* by several Indian writers, *Manusmriti* and the *Upanishads* in English translations by Buhler and Max Mueller, Tulsidas's *Ramayana*, Iyer's *Vedanta*, Woodroffe's *Shakta and Shakti*, Abbott's *What Christianity Means to Me*, James's *The Varieties of Religious Experience*, Moulton's *Early Zoroastrianism*, Washington Irving's *The Lives of Mahomet and His Successors*, Paul Carus's *Gospel of Buddha* and Hopkins's *Origin and Evolution of Religions*.

In social sciences, he read Gibbon's *Decline and Fall of the Roman Empire*, Bacon's *Wisdom of the Ancients*, Buckle's *History of Civilization*, Motley's *Rise of the Dutch Republic*, Wells's *Outline of History*, Lecky's *European Morals*, Geddes's *Evolution of Cities* and Roseberry's *Life of Pitt*.

He also read Goethe's *Faust*, Tagore's *Sadhana*, Shaw's *Man and Superman* and Kipling's *Barrack-Room Ballads*.

While Gandhi was stimulating his intellectual appetite, outside Yeravda a movement was set going under the leadership of C.R. Das and Motilal Nehru, who had recently been released from prison, to withdraw the boycott and to participate in the general elections which were due to be held at the end of 1923. The municipal, provincial and national legislative councils, it was asserted, afforded the most suitable arena in which to obstruct, discredit and change the government. However, several Congress leaders, such as C. Rajagopalachari and Vallabhbhai Patel, vehemently opposed this non-Gandhian policy. In the teeth of strong opposition to their proposed strategy, C.R. Das and Motilal Nehru, along with a few followers, seceded from Congress at the beginning of 1923 to form a separate and temporary Swaraj Party. In the ensuing months support for the Swarajists increased more than they had expected, and at a special session of Congress held in Delhi in September a resolution was passed permitting Congressmen to enter the legislatures if they had no conscientious objection against doing so. The Swarajists built up an efficient party machine of their own and their candidates achieved considerable success.

Gandhi was evidently not in favour of council entry, but there was not much he could do to oppose it. In fact he was quite happy with his lot and did not feel that he was accomplishing less inside than outside the prison.

Suddenly, on the evening of 12 January 1924, his prison life came to an end. He developed acute appendicitis, and was promptly carried to Sassoon Hospital in the city of Poona, where it was decided that he should be operated on. Indian doctors from Bombay were awaited, but about midnight, Colonel Maddock, the British surgeon, informed Gandhi that he would have to operate without any further delay. Gandhi knew that if the operation went badly India might go through a period of violent turmoil. He summoned Srinivasa Sastri, head of the Servants of India Society, and Dr Phatak, a close friend residing in Poona, and dictated a public statement which Sastri took down in pencil. In it he acknowledged the kindness and attention he had received from the surgeon, other medical officers and the attendants, and stated that he had full confidence in Colonel Maddock. He proceeded to thank the government for their consideration in allowing him to send for his own doctors and stated that the urgency of the situation did not leave much time for such an arrangement. As Gandhi signed the statement, he remarked to Colonel Maddock, with a laugh: 'See how my hand trembles.' The surgeon replied: 'Oh we will put tons and tons of strength in you.' A few minutes later the operation began, and it was still going on when a thunderstorm cut off the electricity. Then the flashlight which one of the nurses had been holding went out. The last stages of the operation were conducted by the light of a hurricane lamp.

The operation was successful, but an abscess slowed the patient's recovery. As soon as his illness became known, a strong agitation was started for his release. The Viceroy was aware that Gandhi's return to jail would revive the danger of martyrdom. Moreover, with the changes that had taken place in Congress over the past year or so, a free Mahatma could not immediately regain his former hold on the party. On 5 February Colonel Maddock brought Gandhi the news that the government had decided to release him unconditionally. The following month he was well enough to go to the beach at Juhu, near Bombay, to recuperate in the home of Shantikumar Morarji, an industrialist.

He was not particularly pleased about his unconditional release, for he had settled down into routines of study and spinning and carding. Besides, he had not reached any conclusions about the next stage in the war against the Raj; and he was too ill and too weak to take an active role in politics. From his point of view the situation in India had sadly deteriorated during his two years of imprisonment. First the Hindu-Muslim alliance, the firm rock on which Gandhi hoped to build a united, free India, was in shambles. The Khilafat Committee had virtually succumbed to events in Turkey. There Kemal Pasha (Ataturk), the secular-minded master of Muslim Turkey, had deprived the Sultan of all his titles, including that of Caliph, and allowed him to flee to the island of Malta. The Khilafat movement had fizzled out. The spurious Hindu-Muslim amity of Khilafat days had steadily given place to hostilities more pronounced than ever. The non-cooperation movement had ground to a halt. The spinning wheels were idle. Anxious to make a start, Gandhi resumed the burden of his two week-lies, *Young India* and *Navajivan*. 'Our non-cooperation', he wrote in *Young India*, 'has taken the form of non-cooperation in practice with each other instead of with the government.'

C.R. Das and Motilal Nehru approached Gandhi at Juhu and tried to get his blessing for their policy of entry into the legislatures. He was opposed to the Swarajists' methods, for he had faith in his own, but with a view to preventing further breaches he would not throw his weight behind the No-Changers, who continued to uphold his nonviolent noncooperation. Instead he gave his blessing to a pact recognizing the right of both groups to freedom of action.

Das and Motilal Nehru were dominating Congress, and Gandhi now felt impelled to put his authority to the test. Accordingly, at a meeting of the Congress Working Committee in June he put forward, at the risk of defeat, a number of resolutions designed to reveal the level of support for the two vital elements in his programme – *khadi* and nonviolence. One resolution proposed that office-bearers in the Congress party should spin at least half an hour a day and send in the prescribed self-spun yarn every month,

failing which they should cease to remain in office. Another resolution condemned a recent terrorist outrage in Bengal, in which a European had been
murdered in mistake for the commissioner of police. These resolutions
caused noisy scenes and at one stage the Swarajists, led by Das and Nehru,
walked out of the meeting. The first resolution was eventually passed with
an amendment withdrawing the penalty clause. The second, condemning
the incident of violence in Bengal, was passed by a bare majority of eight,
which disappointed Gandhi immensely. Finding that some of his closest
colleagues had voted against the resolution, he broke down and shed tears
in public. He touched on this traumatic experience in *Young India*:

> I sank within me . . . My grief consisted in the doubt about my own ability to
> lead those who would not follow . . . I felt that God was speaking to me through
> them and seemed to say, 'Thou fool, knowest not thou that thou art impossi-
> ble? Thy time is up.'
>
> I saw that I was utterly defeated and humbled. But defeat cannot dishearten
> me. It can only chasten me. My faith in my creed stands immovable. I know that
> God will guide me. Truth is superior to man's wisdom.

Meanwhile the Hindu-Muslim amity had waned. Gandhi's writings and
speeches were widely discussed, but few seemed to have profited by them.
He was shocked at the publication of a book that had thoroughly offended
the Muslims. Its Hindu author was eventually murdered for it. The publication of this highly controversial book had far-reaching repercussions. As
it circulated, riots broke out in several cities, till at Kohat in the North-
West Frontier, thirty-six Hindus were killed and a hundred and forty-five
injured. Thousands were driven from the town. On 18 September 1924, a
week after the Kohat massacre, Gandhi imposed on himself a three-week
purificatory fast. 'It seems', he said, 'as if God had been dethroned. Let us
reinstate Him in our hearts.' The fast was undertaken in the Delhi house of
the Khilafat leader, Mohamed Ali, and soon a conference of Hindus and
Muslims, with Christian bishops attending, assembled in the capital. The
fast lasted the full three weeks and ended in a scene of holy amity. Passages
from the *Upanishads* and the *Koran* were read. Charles Freer Andrews sang
'When I survey the wondrous Cross', one of Gandhi's favourite Christian
hymns. Das, Motilal Nehru, the Ali brothers and many others sat on the
floor, and watched the exhausted Mahatma sip orange juice.

Despite the country-wide interest and concern Gandhi's fast had
evoked, he could not, for the time being at least, dominate Congress. And
yet at the annual session of Congress at Belgaum in December 1924 he had
no objection to being elected president for the coming year. 'The develop-

ments, both internal and external, have necessitated my acceptance of the burden,' he told the gathering. At Belgaum noncooperation was formally suspended, for 'at this hour of disunion and weakness' the nation was not ready for it. However, refusal to wear foreign cloth remained and Gandhi exacted a price: the wearing of *khadi* as a strict condition of membership in the Congress party. It was also resolved at Belgaum that the Swaraj party's work relating to central and provincial legislatures would be carried out as an integral part of Congress. This was a clear victory for the Swarajists.

Lord Reading, the Viceroy, gave his impression of Gandhi's position at this time:

Gandhi is now attached to the tail of Das and Nehru, although they try their utmost to make him and his supporters think that he is one of the heads, if not *the* head. It is pathetic to observe the rapid decline in the power of Gandhi and the frantic attempts he is now making to cling to his position as leader at the expense of practically every principle he has hitherto advocated . . . I have always believed in his sincerity and his devotion to high ideals, but I have always doubted the wisdom of his political leadership and have felt that personal vanity still played far too important a part in his mental equipment.

While the Swarajists confronted the government in the central and provincial legislative assemblies, Gandhi concentrated on his own constructive programme, travelling across India spreading the gospel of *khadi*, Hindu-Muslim unity and anti-untouchability.

The campaign against untouchability, particularly in the south, had all along been beset with difficulties. 'I may talk glibly of the Englishman's sin in Jallianwala,' he wrote to C.F. Andrews. 'But as a Hindu, I may not talk about the sin of Hinduism against the Untouchables. I have to deal with the Hindu Dyers'. He had to deal with the 'Hindu Dyers', responsible for perpetrating atrocities against the Untouchables. The Hindus must realize that they were guilty of having suppressed their own weaker brethren. 'We make them crawl on their bellies,' he said at a meeting. 'We have made them rub their noses on the ground; with eyes red with rage, we push them out of the railway compartments – what more than this has British rule done?' *Swaraj* was an utter impossibility unless the offenders had purged themselves of the sin. 'Supposing *swaraj* was a gift descending from Downing Street to India, that gift would be a curse upon the land, if we do not get rid of this curse of untouchability.'

His faith in *khadi* remained unabated despite discouragement and even a certain amount of ridicule. He maintained that for industrializing rural India there was nothing better than the spinning wheel. Once as he sat spinning in public, he said: 'It is my certain conviction that with every thread that I draw, I am spinning the destiny of India.' In the small town of Bogura, in Bengal, Gandhi was delighted to see a seven-year-old Muslim girl pulling away yarn at a great speed. He stood before her, but she would not look up. He pulled her ear and asked: 'Do you know Mahatma Gandhi?'

At a meeting of the All-India Congress Committee in September 1925, he was able to persuade Congress to establish an All-India Spinners' Association, with a branch in every district. He had a definite political objective in the establishment of such an organization, for it would provide training and keep employed an exclusive corps of political workers who could be effectively mobilized in any future nonviolent campaign of civil disobedience. The following year about a million rupees were distributed through this association to about fifty thousand spinners, weavers and carders. Measures were taken to create the necessary market for the *khadi* that was produced.

For several months during 1925 Gandhi was travelling in indifferent health, and *khadi* was his main theme. He was on a tour of Assam when news came of the sudden death of C.R. Das on 16 June. He hurriedly travelled to Calcutta where he led the funeral procession of two million people. 'When the heart feels a deep cut the pen refuses to move,' he wrote. 'I am too much in the centre of grief to be able to send much for the readers of *Young India*.' It was only recently that Gandhi and Das were together for several days and had had long discussions. That gave Gandhi an opportunity to 'realize not only how great Das was, but also how good he was. India has lost a jewel. But we must regain it by gaining *swaraj*.'

Meanwhile Gandhi's attention was drawn to a family matter. Harilal's affairs were doing badly. Father and son had quarrelled in South Africa, Harilal complaining of parental callousness towards himself and his brothers. Tension continued and Harilal, in the hope of achieving personal independence, went back to India where, at eighteen, he got married against his father's wishes. He suffered inner trauma, but while his wife lived was outwardly normal. When she died in the influenza epidemic of 1918, and Gandhi frowned on his remarriage, Harilal's whole personality degenerated. He got drunk in public, kept company with dubious women, and took to many other ways that would hurt his father. Furthermore, he exploited his parentage to raise cash for a shady business venture. Gandhi received a lawyer's letter on behalf of a swindled client, a Muslim 'whose respect for Mahatmaji led him to become a shareholder'. There was no way for Gandhi to return the lost investment, but he published the letter in *Young India* and appended his reply:

I do indeed happen to be the father of Harilal M.Gandhi. He is my eldest boy, is over thirty-six years old and is father of four children, the eldest being nineteen years old. His ideals and mine having been discovered over fifteen years ago to be different, he has been living separately from me and has not been supported by or through me. It has been my invariable rule to regard my boys as my friends and equals as soon as they completed their sixteen years . . . I do not know Harilal's affairs. He meets me occasionally, but I never pry into his affairs. I do not know how his affairs stand at present except that they are in a bad way . . . There is much in Harilal's life that I dislike. He knows that, but I love him in spite of his faults. The bosom of a father will take him in as soon as he seeks entrance . . . Let the client's example be a warning against people being guided by big names in their transactions. Men may be good, not necessarily their children.

This last sentence, proclaiming a general law based on his own experiences, demonstrates his unusual attitude, tormented by memories. He blamed himself for Harilal having gone astray. 'I was a slave of passion when Harilal was conceived,' he said. 'I led a carnal and luxurious life during his childhood.' He had wanted a perfect son; instead he adopted perfect daughters, whom he welcomed into his ashram.

Miss Madeleine Slade, daughter of Sir Edmund Slade, a British admiral, landed at Bombay in November 1925. In her early thirties, she had a passion for music which led her to Romain Rolland, who had written a life of Beethoven. When the conversation drifted from music, Rolland happened to mention Gandhi as 'another Christ'. Miss Slade sent Gandhi £20 and wrote a letter so utterly sincere that he invited her to India, to live and study by his side. Immediately after her arrival at the ashram she was shown into the room where Gandhi was. As he rose from a mattress on the floor, she hurried to kneel before him. Gandhi gently lifted her up and said: 'You shall be my daughter.' He gave her the Indian name of Mirabehn.

Gandhi's year as president of Congress was now ending and at the annual session at Cawnpore, in December 1925, he handed over the presidency to Mrs Sarojini Naidu and announced to Congress that he would withdraw for a year from active participation in politics. Throughout 1926 he would remain at Sabarmati, concentrating on matters relating to the ashram there and on the work of the All-India Spinners' Association. He observed complete silence on Mondays, when he would confine his communications to short notes. He would go no further than Ahmedabad but kept himself occupied writing articles in *Young India* and the instalments of his autobiography, which began to appear in that journal, resulting in innumerable questions from correspondents.

Meanwhile Gandhi's attention was directed to his second son, Manilal, who was at the time living in South Africa, in charge of *Indian Opinion*. Manilal had plans to marry a Muslim girl named Fatima. 'What you desire is contrary to *dharma*,' Gandhi wrote to his son. 'If you stick to Hinduism and Fatima follows Islam it will be like putting two swords in one sheath.' Manilal's intermarriage, he warned, would not be in the interests of society and would have a powerful impact on the Hindu-Muslim question. 'If you enter into this relationship,' he added, 'you may not be able to render any service. I fear you may no more be the right person to run *Indian Opinion*.' Manilal eventually came to India and married twenty-year-old Sushila, the niece of a close associate of Gandhi. Manilal was thirty-five. A few days prior to the wedding, he received a few words of advice from his father, who had apparently not forgotten about Manilal's involvement with a married woman several years earlier:

> The more I think the more I feel that you are going to have a jewel. My only fear is whether you would be able to take care of her.
>
> Please keep your passion under control; let her study. The girl would be helpful in many of your activities. She can even learn composing. If she tries she can improve her Gujarati but it all depends upon you whether you would make a doll or a companion out of her. After all, she is just a child. She does not know the ways of the world. If, henceforth, you will observe more restraint than hitherto I see a blissful future for both of you. . . .
>
> You should start from there on the 4th [March] and meet me in Bombay on the morning of 5th.
>
> I am writing to Ramdas and Devadas that they may come along if they want to.
>
> Blessings from
> BAPU
>
> [PS] I have sent your letter to Sushila. Write nothing to Harilal.

During 1926 and most of 1927 India was politically rather quiet. 'Political India', Gandhi wrote, 'is disrupted and demoralized. It seems a good time for silence.' He had for the time being ceased to intervene in Hindu-Muslim disputes, because he was aware that his involvement at that stage could only do harm.

There were numerous communal riots in 1926, and the year closed with the assassination in Delhi of Swami Shraddhanand, the founder of Gurukul, the residential school at Kangri, and the man who had welcomed Gandhi after his return to India. A young Muslim named Abdul Rashid called on the Swami and announced that he wished to discuss religion with him. The Swami, who was ill in bed, told the insistent caller that he would be glad to talk to him as soon as he felt stronger. The Muslim asked for a drink of water, and when the servant was sent out to fetch it, stabbed Swami Shraddhanand to death.

Gandhi was on his way to Gauhati, in north-east India, to attend the annual session of Congress there when he learned about the assassination, which horrified India. Over ten thousand people were in attendance at Gauhati. Addressing the Congress Gandhi referred to the assassin as his 'brother'. Abdul Rashid was not guilty. The guilty were 'those who excited feelings of hatred against one another'. Paying his tribute to the slain leader, he said: 'Let us not shed tears, but chasten our hearts and steel them with some of the fire and faith that were Shraddhanandji's.'

Around this time Lord Reading was replaced as viceroy by Lord Irwin, the future Viscount Halifax. Gandhi did not mention this change in *Young India*, nor did he seem to have noted it in any other way. He was still a non-cooperator. Moreover, this was a time for him of withdrawal, of meditation and consolidation. He deliberately avoided controversies, although the one involving dogs confronted him for several weeks.

Ambalal Sarabhai, the textile magnate of Ahmedabad, had ordered the rounding up of some sixty stray dogs that frequented his sprawling industrial estates, and in the absence of any guidance from the municipality had had them killed. The distressed Sarabhai called on Gandhi the next morning and asked his opinion about his action. 'What else could be done?' said Gandhi.

The Ahmedabad Humanitarian Society learned about this conversation, and in a letter to Gandhi demanded whether he had in fact said such a thing. If so, what had he meant by it? 'When Hinduism forbids the taking of life of any living being,' the letter continued, 'when it declares it to be a sin, do you think it right to kill rabid dogs for the reason that they would bite human beings and by biting other dogs make them also rabid?'

Gandhi published the letter in *Young India* and appended his reply. Yes, he had said, 'What else could be done?' and he added that having thought over the matter he felt that his reply was proper. 'Imperfect, erring mortals as we are,' he reasoned, 'there is no course open to us but the destruction of rabid dogs. At times we may be faced with the unavoidable duty of killing a man who is found in the act of killing people.' He was no doubt turning away from the doctrine of absolute *ahimsa* which he had imbibed from his religious background.

Gandhi's article evoked a howl of rage from the readers of *Young India*. 'Angry letters', some of them close to being insulting, began to arrive, and a few 'friends' invaded the ashram and engaged him in a discussion on the subject. Gandhi was quite clear in his mind. In the following issue of *Young*

*India* he reiterated that the multiplication of dogs was unnecessary. 'A roving dog without an owner is a danger to society and a swarm of them is a menace to its very existence,' he wrote. 'If people were really religious, dogs would have owners . . . There is a regular science of dog keeping in the West . . . We should learn it.'

The dog mail continued to pour in, but Gandhi stood his ground. 'I do not mind their outburst of anger,' he said. 'I appreciate the motive behind it. I must try to reason with them patiently.' When the state did not care for stray dogs and people themselves were equally indifferent to this menace, Gandhi asserted, the suffering dogs should be 'relieved from a lingering death. This is a bitter dose, I agree. But it is my innermost conviction that true love and compassion consist in taking it.' There were moments when his reasoning would have a touch of anger:

> Cows we cannot protect, dogs we kick about and belabour with sticks, their ribs are seen sticking out, and yet we are not ashamed of ourselves and raise a hue and cry when a stray dog is killed. Which of the two is better – that five thousand dogs should wander about in semi-starvation, living on dirt . . . and drag on a miserable existence, or that fifty should die and keep the rest in a decent condition? It is admittedly sinful always to be spurning and kicking the dogs. But it is possible that the man who kills the dogs that he cannot bear to see tortured thus may be doing a meritorious act. Merely taking life is not always *himsa*, one may even say that there is sometimes more *himsa* in not taking life.
>
> It is a sin, it should be a sin to feed stray dogs. It is a false sense of compassion. It is an insult to a starving dog to throw a crumb at him. Roving dogs do not indicate the civilization or compassion of the society; they betray on the contrary the ignorance and lethargy of its members.

Many correspondents accused Gandhi of condoning the killing of lower beings for the sake of man because he was under the Western influence. 'It is better for you to confess your error and apologize to the world,' one correspondent demanded. 'You should have made up your mind in this matter after exhaustive sifting. Instead you have passionately taken sides and discredited yourself.'

Gandhi urged India to ponder over the gravity of the situation. In one Ahmedabad hospital, he reported, 1,117 cases of hydrophobia had been treated in 1925 and 990 in 1926. There was nothing wrong in learning from the West in this matter. Responding to the comment that he was under the Western influence, he declared:

> I do not think that everything Western is to be rejected. I have condemned the Western civilization in no measured terms. I still do so . . . but I have learnt a

great deal from the West and I am grateful to it. I should think myself unfortun-
ate if contact with and the literature of the West had no influence on me. But I
do not think I owe my opinion about the dogs to my Western education or
Western influence.

If any one thinks that the people in the West are innocent of humanity he is
sadly mistaken. The ideal of humanity in the West is perhaps lower, but their
practice of it is very much more thorough than ours. We rest content with a lofty
ideal and are slow or lazy in its practice. We are wrapped in deep darkness, as is
evident from our paupers, cattle and other animals. They are eloquent of our
irreligion rather than of our religion.

My opinions should be considered as they are, irrespective of whether they
are derived from the West or the East. Whether they are based on truth or
untruth, *himsa* or *ahimsa*, is the only thing to be considered. I firmly believe that
they are based on truth and *ahimsa*.

Some time later Gandhi was involved in a far more bitter controversy over
the killing of a calf in the ashram premises. The calf had been maimed and
was suffering from an incurable disease. It lay in agony, making terrible
sounds and kicking out its legs in paroxysms of pain, while the ashramites
discussed what action should be taken. The animal appeared to have only a
day or two to live, and Vallabhbhai Patel expressed the opinion that it
would be more appropriate to let nature take its course. There was also the
question of collecting money in Bombay on behalf of the ashram: no one
would contribute if it was learned that the calf had been killed. Gandhi said
it would be very cruel to let the calf writhe away its last moments in agony,
and added that there was no reason why a fellow creature should be denied
'the last and most solemn service we can render it'. His will prevailed. A
Parsi doctor was summoned to put the animal out of its agony. The doctor
injected poison into the calf's veins, and it died immediately.

All over India, people wrote to the newspapers attacking the Mahatma
for abandoning *ahimsa*. A large number of them said that the killing of the
calf was wrong and an act of violence, as the cow was sacred. Some of the
letters received by Gandhi were more virulent than those about the dog
incident. A Jain correspondent angrily wrote: 'Gandhi, you killed that calf.
You killed that cow, and if I do not kill you in return, I am no Jain.'

Gandhi's health was failing, for he suffered from high blood pressure,
but he embarked on a fresh series of tours after attending the Gauhati session of Congress. He was still hesitant about saying much about his old
theme of Hindu-Muslim amity. 'I must not touch the problem of Hindu-
Muslim unity,' he said. 'It has passed out of human hands . . . Let us ask
God in all humility to give us sense, to give us wisdom.' Instead he laid
more stress on the untouchability question and the *charkha*. He had an

exhausting schedule, addressing meetings and collecting funds and finally at Kolhapur, late in March 1927, he suffered a mild stroke. There was a numbness in the left side of his body and his vision was temporarily blurred. Doctors forbade him to continue his tour and ordered him to bed. After a while he felt better and resumed his work, but he suffered another slight stroke, and this time the doctors' advice prevailed. 'Well, my cart has been stuck in the mire,' he wrote to the ashramites.

While Gandhi was recuperating at Nandi Hills, near Bangalore, Congress leaders were in the process of deciding on the choice of the next party president. Jawaharlal Nehru had lately made a fine impression at the Brussels Congress of Oppressed Nationalities, and his name now began to figure for the top party job.

Jawaharlal Nehru (1889–1964), the son of the eminent lawyer Motilal Nehru, was born at Allahabad. Until he was fifteen, he was educated at home by British tutors. In 1905 his father took him to England and enrolled him at Harrow. From there he went to Trinity College, Cambridge, where in 1910 he took a science degree. He read law at the Inner Temple and was called to the Bar. On his return to India in 1912, he practised law for some time, but his political activities eventually absorbed his interest.

Nehru first met Gandhi at a session of the Congress party in Lucknow in 1916. They apparently did not make much impression on each other at that time. Recalling this first meeting, Nehru wrote: 'All of us admired him for his heroic fight in South Africa, but he seemed very distant and different and unpolitical to many of us young men.'

In 1918 Nehru was elected a member of the All-India Congress Committee. After the Jallianwala Bagh massacre in April 1919, both he and his father Motilal were drawn towards Gandhi and joined his activity.

Nehru's participation in the 1920 noncooperation movement gave him ample opportunity to work with Gandhi, to whom he remained close throughout his life. As a Congress worker, Nehru travelled through the Indian countryside, speaking to the peasants. The levels of poverty that existed in rural India left a lasting impression on his mind. Henceforth, he saw India largely in terms of oppressed peasantry. Both Motilal and Jawaharlal gave up their legal practice so that they could give their full attention to Gandhi's freedom movement. That was for Jawaharlal the beginning of a meteoric political career.

From 1923 to 1925 Nehru was a general secretary of the Indian National Congress. In the first week of May Motilal Nehru unhesitatingly wrote to Gandhi, recommending his son for the presidentship of Congress. On 25 May 1927, Gandhi wrote to Jawaharlal, who was then in Europe, where his wife was undergoing medical treatment, and asked him to cable his wishes.

Gandhi aged seven.

Karamchand Gandhi (father).

Putlibai Gandhi (mother).

Gandhi aged seventeen (*right*), with his brother Laxmidas.

Gandhi as a law student in London.

Gandhi (*bottom row, right*) with members of the Vegetarian Society, 1890.

Kasturbai Gandhi with Gokuldas (nephew of Gandhi) and sons Manilal, Ramdas and Harilal in Durban, 1898.

Gandhi in London, 1909.

Gandhi with his office staff in Johannesburg, 1907.

Gandhi, Sonja Schlesin and Kallenbach, before the historic march of 1913.

Gandhi in 1915.

Kasturbai Gandhi in
1915.

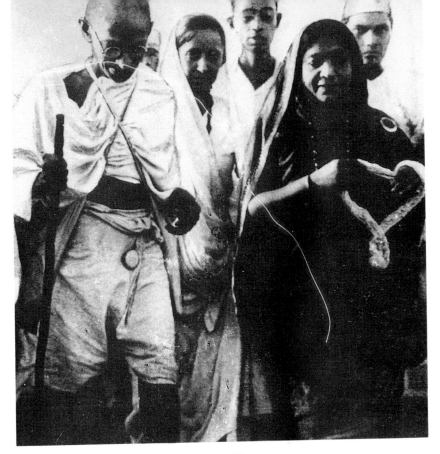

Gandhi and Sarojini Naidu at Dandi, 5 April 1930.

Round Table Conference, 1931. To Gandhi's right: Lord Sankey, Sir Samuel Hoare, Ramsay MacDonald.

(*Top*) Gandhi arriving at a friend's flat in London, 1931.
Gandhi in London. Seated on his right is Charlie Chaplin.

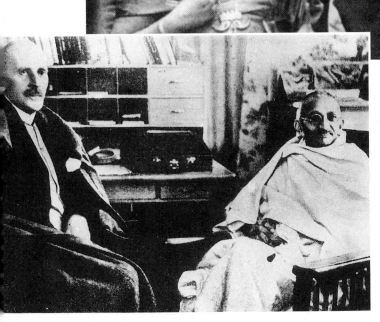

(*Top*) Gandhi among employees of a Lancashire mill, 1931. (*Above*) Gandhi with Mrs Naidu on their way to Buckingham Palace to meet King George V. (*Left*) Gandhi with Romain Rolland in Villeneuve, Switzerland.

Gandhi discussing a draft resolution with Nehru, 1938.
Gandhi with Subhas Bose at the Haripura Congress, 1938.

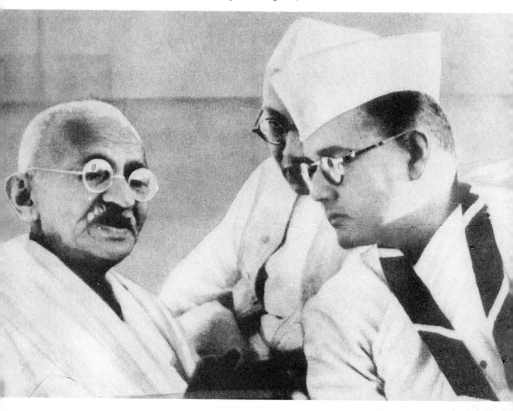

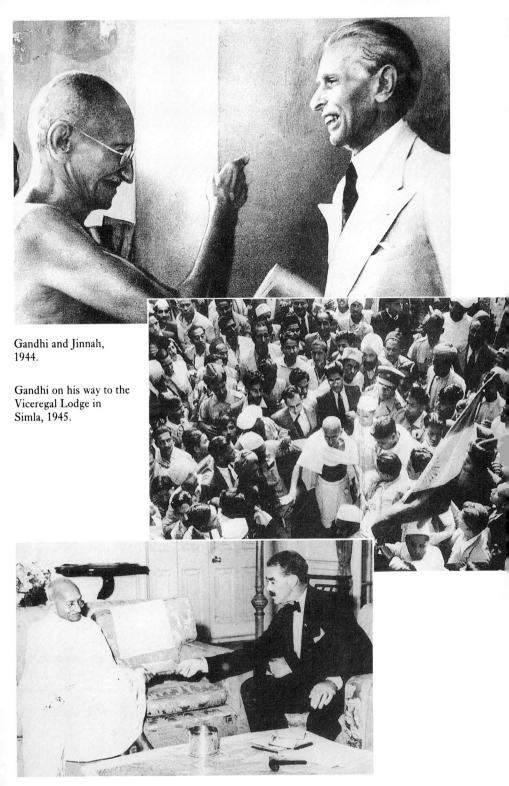

Gandhi and Jinnah,
1944.

Gandhi on his way to the
Viceregal Lodge in
Simla, 1945.

Gandhi with Mr Casey, Governor of Bengal. 'Notes passed to me by M K
Gandhi during our "talk" on 3 December 1945 – one of his silence days –
during which I talked to him for 1½ hours; he said nothing.'

Gandhi with Lord Pethick-Lawrence (*above*), and with Lord and Lady Mountbatten.

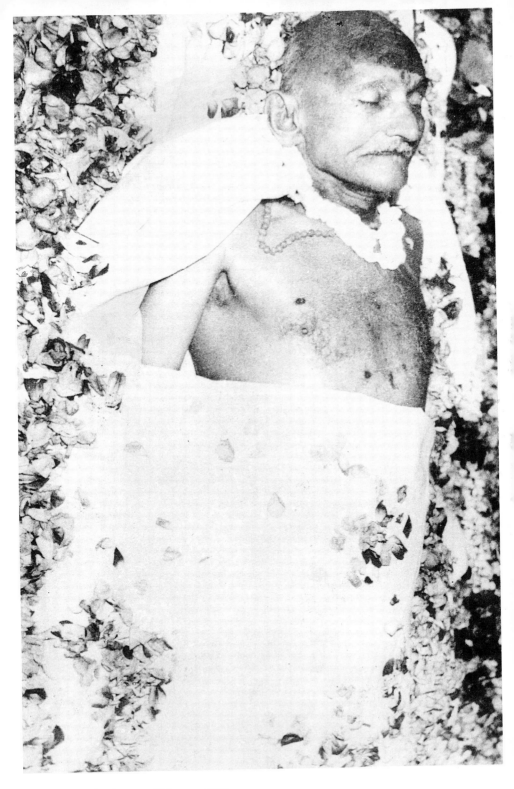

Gandhi lying in state, 30 January 1948.

The cremation, 31 January 1948.

(*Opposite*) The funeral cortege.

The assassin.

"THE ODD THING ABOUT ASSASSINS, DR. KING, IS THAT THEY THINK THEY'VE KILLED YOU."

Gandhi was in fact not in favour of Jawaharlal taking up the Congress presidentship: 'We have lost hold upon the masses, and it seems to me that if you become president, you will be lost for one year at any rate to the masses. That, however, does not mean that Congress work has to be neglected.' Motilal continued to put pressure on Gandhi to place the crown of Congress on his illustrious son's head, but Srinivas Iyengar, the current president, preferred Dr Ansari. Gandhi yielded, and informed Motilal accordingly. The Mahatma had kept away from Congress, but it was considered imperative to seek his approval in nominating a candidate for the presidency. Singly, he was a major force, but jointly the Swarajists and the nationalists dominated the field.

By the end of June Gandhi was able to continue with his tour in easy stages. To his familiar sermons on the *charkha* and untouchability he now added a sermon on the necessity of having a definite form of Hindustani – the fusing together of Hindi and Urdu languages, which would bridge the gap between the Hindus and Muslims. He wrote in *Young India* on an 'All-India Script', pointing out that 'the Hindu-Muslim madness no doubt stands in the way of a thorough reform'.

The lull in politics was broken at the end of 1927, when Gandhi was invited by the Viceroy to come and see him. Lord Irwin, who had succeeded Lord Reading in April 1926, was known to be a deeply religious man. On landing in Bombay on Good Friday he postponed the ceremonies that accompanied the arrival of a new viceroy and went to church. But it took him nineteen months to indicate any desire to discuss the Indian situation with the most influential leaders of this religious country. It was in Mangalore, in the far south, that Gandhi received a message that the Viceroy wished to see him in Delhi on 5 November. The meeting was attended by several other Indian leaders. Irwin handed out a memorandum announcing that a parliamentary commission headed by Sir John Simon was coming to report on dyarchy and the readiness of India for further constitutional progress. Gandhi asked whether that was all the business. Lord Irwin said: 'Yes.' Subsequently, Gandhi commented that the Viceroy had brought him twelve hundred miles just to give him a piece of paper where a postcard should have sufficed. In fact they had an informal chat afterwards and Gandhi inevitably made his views known. 'The English', he said, 'had no moral claim to be judges of Indian progress.' What the English ought to do, therefore, was 'to recognize that India should be accorded Dominion Status, and then to meet Indians and discuss the precise methods . . . by which this could be accomplished'. Deeply puzzled, Lord Irwin looked at the Mahatma as if he had dropped from another planet.

Shortly before the announcement of the Simon Commission, a best seller entitled *Mother India*, by Katherine Mayo, was published in England. The author, an American, had spent a few months in India, and in compiling her book had used the material churned out by hospitals, cases of inhuman cruelties picked up from criminal trial reports, and her own observation of isolated happenings. These she sought to fortify with quotations taken completely out of context. Equipped with such dubious information, she proceeded to formulate a general indictment against Hindu social life. 'She is interested in Indian society only when it is unhealthy,' commented a Labour party candidate to the British Parliament. In her book, Mayo absolved the British of any responsibility for India's ills, including political backwardness. This certainly delighted the British officials in India. On 29 September 1927, John Coatman, the Director of Public Information in the Home Department of the government of India, wrote to Mayo: 'What you say [in your book] about our work in this country has cheered us a lot. Now that the people in the Empire and in the USA realize what we are up against, we shall get a lot more support which will stand us in good stead in the hard days to come.' So it was not for nothing that a few months earlier Coatman was begging Mayo to 'take pity on us and get your book out as soon as possible'.

The Home Member, when heckled in the Central Assembly, denied that the government of India and the India Office had any connection 'with the production of the book', but they had extended to the writer 'the facilities that are usually extended to the students of social, economic, political and other subjects, whether Indians or foreigners, who can present satisfactory credentials'. Almost every newspaper in India criticized the book severely, and it was said that Katherine Mayo had been subsidized to write it in order to degrade Indians in the eyes of the world, and to prejudice the country's case for self-government. Gandhi, who had helped the author with her researches, reviewed the book in *Young India* under the caption 'Drain Inspector's Report':

> The book is cleverly and powerfully written. The carefully chosen quotations give it the appearance of a truthful book. But the impression it leaves on my mind is, that it is the report of a drain inspector sent out with the one purpose of opening and examining the drains of the country to be reported upon, or to give a graphic description of the stench exuded by the opened drains. If Miss Mayo had confessed that she had gone to India merely to open out and examine the drains of India, there would perhaps be little to complain about her compilation.
>
> The book is without doubt untruthful, be the facts stated ever so truthful. If I open out and describe with punctilious care all the stench exuded from the drains of London and say 'Behold London', my facts will be incapable of chal-

lenge, but my judgement will be rightly condemned as a travesty of truth. Miss Mayo's book is nothing better, nothing else . . . It is untruthful in that she condemns a whole nation or in her words 'the peoples of India' (she will not have us as one nation) practically without any reservation as to their sanitation, morals, religion, etc. It is also untruthful because she claims for the British Government merits which cannot be sustained and which many an honest British officer would blush to see the Government credited with. I hope that Miss Mayo will not take offence if she comes under the shadow of a suspicion that she is subsidized by the Government. If she is not subsidized, Miss Mayo is an avowed Indophobe and Anglophil, refusing to see anything good about the Indians and anything bad about the British and their rule.

She has done me the honour of quoting me frequently in support of her argument . . . But in her hurry to see everything Indian in a bad light, she has not only taken liberty with my writings, but she had not thought it necessary even to verify through me certain things ascribed by her or others to me.

But why am I writing this article? Not for the Indian readers but for many American and English readers who read these pages from week to week with sympathy and attention . . . that a book like Miss Mayo's can command a large circulation furnishes a sad commentary on Western literature and culture.

Whilst I consider the book to be unfit to be placed before Americans and Englishmen (for it can do no good to them), it is a book that every Indian can read with some degree of profit. We may repudiate the charge as it has been framed by her, but we may not repudiate the substance underlying the many allegations she has made . . . Let us not resent being made aware of the dark side of the picture wherever it exists. Overdrawn her pictures of our insanitation, child marriages, etc., undoubtedly are. But let them serve as a spur to much greater effort than we have hitherto put forth in order to rid society of all cause of reproach.

Our indignation which we are bound to express against the slanderous book must not blind us to our obvious imperfections and our great limitations. Our anger will leave Miss Mayo absolutely unhurt and it will only recoil upon ourselves. We too have our due share of thoughtless readers as the West has, and in seeking to disprove everything Miss Mayo has written, we shall make the reading public believe that we are a race of perfect human beings against whom nothing can be said, no one can dare say one word. The agitation that has been set up against the book is in danger of being overdone. There is no cause for fury.

When the Simon Commission landed in Bombay on 3 February 1928, it was greeted with black flags. Both the Hindus and the Muslims boycotted the commission. Processions chanting 'Simon go back' appeared in every city. Even Indians who knew no English learned that slogan.

About this time the peasants of Bardoli, in Bombay province, were confronted with a twenty-two per cent increase in taxes, decreed by the British government. At Gandhi's suggestion Vallabhbhai Patel, who was Mayor of Ahmedabad that year, resigned his mayorship and went to Bardoli to lead a peaceful revolt against the government.

Patel conducted the no-tax campaign with such efficiency that soon the Bombay government found itself at loggerheads with over eighty thousand peasants. The government brought in burly Pathans from North-West Frontier Province to drive families off their farms and confiscate their meagre belongings for delinquency. The peasants' cattle and lands were attached, but buyers could not be found for them. The peasants responded wholeheartedly to the leadership of Vallabhbhai Patel, who declared: 'Challenge the government to take your land, if they can, to England.' Week after week, in the face of mass arrests, the peasants remained firm, and when the coercive methods proved ineffective, the Bombay government proposed to move in troops and seize the whole cotton crop.

Funds poured in from the rest of India for the maintenance of the struggle. On 12 June Indians observed 'Bardoli Day' with a *hartal*. From all over the country Gandhi was urged to start civil disobedience in other provinces. He appealed for patience. 'The time has not yet come for even limited sympathetic Satyagraha. Bardoli has still to prove its mettle.'

On 2 August, anticipating Patel's arrest, Gandhi moved to Bardoli. Four days later, however, the government yielded and reached an agreement with Patel, restoring the property and releasing the prisoners. Soon an enquiry board set up to look into the matter cut the tax increase to 5.7 per cent. 'Bardoli has shown the way,' Gandhi wrote, 'if the sanction to be applied against the British Government is to be non-violent.'

While the civil disobedience in Bardoli was going on, Gandhi experienced an immense personal loss when Maganlal, whom he had singled out as his heir, suddenly died. Paying an emotional tribute to him, Gandhi wrote:

He closely studied and followed my spiritual career and when I presented to my co-workers Brahmacharya as a rule of life even for married men in search of Truth, he was the first to perceive the beauty and the necessity of the practice, and though it cost him to my knowledge a terrific struggle, he carried it through to success, taking his wife along with him by patient argument instead of imposing his views on her.

He was my hands, my feet and my eyes . . . With each day I realize more and more that my mahatmaship, which is a mere adornment, depends on others. I have shone with the glory borrowed from my innumerable co-workers. However, no one has done more to add to this glory than Maganlal.

As I am penning these lines, I hear the sobs of the widow bewailing the death of her dear husband. Little does she realize that I am more widowed than she. And but for the living God, I should become a raving maniac for the loss of one who was dearer to me than my own sons, who never once deceived me or failed me.

Gandhi had tentative plans to go to Europe, but the death of his best comrade kept him in close proximity to the ashram. In any case, he was not very eager to visit Europe or America. 'Not that I distrust the people of these great continents any more than I distrust my own, I distrust myself,' he wrote. 'I feel that I have as yet no message to deliver personally to the West. I believe my message to be universal but, as yet, I feel that I can best deliver it through my work in my own country.'

The Simon Commission returned to India in October on its second visit, which lasted six months. Though the Central Committee and the provincial committees appointed by the government helped by submitting their reports, the commission faced social and political boycott by the public everywhere. At a huge anti-Simon rally at Lahore, Lajpat Rai, the chief political figure of the Punjab, now aged sixty-three and popularly known as the 'Lion of the Punjab,' was struck over the heart with a *lathi* by a policeman, and died soon afterwards. Gandhi praised his life of service and sacrifice. Some weeks after Lajpat Rai's death, Assistant Police Superintendent Saunders of Lahore was assassinated, an occurrence which Gandhi denounced as a 'dastardly act'. Bhagat Singh, the suspected assassin, managed to evade arrest and quickly attained the status of hero.

At another anti-Simon demonstration in Lucknow, a policeman's *lathi* descended on Jawaharlal Nehru, causing a minor injury. Gandhi wrote to him: 'My love to you. It was all done bravely. You have braver things to do. May God spare you for many a long year to come and make you His chosen instrument for freeing India from the yoke.' Though Maganlal had been Gandhi's nonpolitical heir, the Mahatma, now nearing sixty, realized that to go further he would have to extend himself through alliance with a younger leader; and his choice was Jawaharlal. Soon, however, a crisis threatened to divide them.

At its session held at Calcutta in December 1928, Congress was to consider a draft constitution for a federal Dominion of India. Motilal Nehru had drawn this up in consultation with members of all parties. The Calcutta Congress witnessed a sharp division of opinion over the document, known as the Nehru Report. Motilal Nehru, who was the Congress president, wanted it to be accepted without controversy. But Jawaharlal, Subhas Chandra Bose, Srinivas Iyengar and other younger Congressmen were against its moderate demand for a government. They wanted a declaration of immediate independence and a complete break with Britain. To enable Congress to present a united front, Gandhi stepped in and produced a compromise formula which was adopted with amendments. Britain should be given a year in which to accept the constitution as recommended by the Nehru Report, failing which Congress would revive nonviolent noncooperation. Gandhi now rebuked the younger leaders. 'Independence is a thing made of sterner stuff,' he said. 'It is not made by the juggling of words.'

The Nehru Report provoked an unfavourable response from the Muslims. The Ali brothers had long since parted with Gandhi and were now accusing the Mahatma of trying to set up a Hindu Raj. Even the section of the Muslim League led by Jinnah rejected the Nehru Report. Jinnah had demanded some modifications in the report, but received no encouragement from the Congress leaders, and for him this was 'the parting of the ways'. Soon the two wings of the Muslim League would reunite and press their demands with vigour. Thus, contrary to the intentions of its authors, the Nehru Report had the effect of widening the gulf between the Hindus and the Muslims.

Once again Gandhi was thinking of a tour of Europe, but under the prevailing political situation it was now out of the question. Instead he began another tour of India, preparing the masses for a possible future struggle. While he was keeping speaking engagements and lighting bonfires of foreign cloth, political terrorism and industrial strife were rampant in the country. On 8 April 1929, Bhagat Singh, already guilty of the assassination condemned by Gandhi, and his companion, Batukeshwar Dutt, took up positions in the visitors' gallery of the Legislative Assembly, from where they hurled two bombs into the Assembly chamber filled with its British and Indian members. The bombs exploded with a mighty impact, generating suffocating smoke, but only one legislator was seriously hurt. The two young men were arrested. Sir John Simon witnessed the outrage from the President's gallery and went home carrying that picture with him.

Gandhi publicly condemned the incident, but also told the government that they were 'in no small measure to blame for the madness of the bomb-throwers. By their indifference to the popular feeling, they are exasperating the nation and the exasperation is bound to lead some astray.' At their trial, held in Delhi on 12 June, Bhagat Singh and Dutt were sentenced to transportation for life.

Motilal Nehru was again pressing the claim of his son on Gandhi, saying that Gandhi was the head and Jawaharlal the voice of the hour. Jawaharlal, however, wrote to Gandhi that his name should not be considered for Congress presidentship, for he lacked the politician's flair for forming groups and parties, though if it was thrust upon him he would not reject it.

He finally became Congress president, but since he was not elected in the ordinary way, he later observed in his autobiography that he did not come to it 'by the main entrance or even by a side door but by a trap-door'. By saddling Nehru with the responsibility, Gandhi astutely drove a wedge between him and Subhas Chandra Bose, and the younger Congressmen would now find it extremely difficult to dominate the next Congress at Lahore.

Meanwhile, national elections in Britain restored Labour to power, and Ramsay MacDonald became prime minister with a minority government. A few weeks later, in June 1929, MacDonald summoned Irwin home for consultations with himself and the Secretary of State for India, Wedgwood Benn. In October the Viceroy at last returned, having conferred with the Labour cabinet and with Baldwin, Churchill, Lloyd George, Simon and many more. He issued a statement on 31 October affirming the goal of dominion status, although the Simon Commission had not yet reported. A round table conference in London to be attended by the representatives of British India and the princely states together with the British government was also proposed. The Viceroy's statement raised a storm in England. MacDonald and Benn had considerable difficulty in explaining to the Tories and Liberals in the House of Commons that there was in fact no change of policy, or any speeding up of dominion status. Lord Reading led the attack in the House of Lords.

The Congress Working Committee met in Delhi to discuss Irwin's announcement. Gandhi and the elder statesmen found it favourable, but there was a strong protest against this conciliatory attitude especially from Jawaharlal Nehru, the president-elect of the Congress party for 1930, and Subhas Chandra Bose. Gandhi, however, persuaded Jawaharlal not to withdraw from the presidency.

On the eve of the Lahore Congress session, a meeting was arranged with Irwin. On the morning of the meeting, 23 December, the Viceroy returned from a tour of south India. As the viceregal train approached New Delhi station a bomb explosion on the railway track damaged a section of the train. Only one person was hurt, and Irwin was unaware of the incident until informed by a military aide. A few hours later Jinnah, Gandhi, Motilal Nehru, Vithalbhai Patel and Tej Bahadur Sapru entered the Viceroy's office. Gandhi congratulated him on his escape. A short discussion on the bomb explosion followed and then the Viceroy enquired: 'How shall we start? Shall we take up the question of the release of the prisoners?' Gandhi put the pertinent question: would the round table conference proceed on the basis of full dominion status? Irwin could not give this assurance. The Opposition parties at Westminster had shown that his October offer could not mean much, for they were in a position to combine forces to throw MacDonald out. The Indian leaders' audience with the Viceroy lasted two and a half hours; Irwin and Gandhi did most of the talking. 'As they anticipated,' observed the Viceroy in his *Fulness of Days*, 'I was unable to give them the kind of understanding they wanted.' About Gandhi he wrote: 'It was like grappling with a wrestler whose body had been greased and on whom no purchase could be gained.'

# TWENTY-NINE

# A Pinch of Salt Rocks an Empire

Congress assembled at Lahore in the last week of December 1929. His waverings over, Jawaharlal presided. In his presidential address he said that Congress would not acknowledge the right of the British Parliament to dictate to Indians. He was warmly supported by Subhas Chandra Bose, who wanted to set up a rival government on the spot. But that was seen as going too far. Gandhi moved a resolution in favour of unabridged independence. '*Swaraj*', he declared, 'is now to mean complete independence.' The Congress convention advised its members to resign from the legislatures and disassociate themselves from the proposed Round Table Conference. It authorized the launching of civil disobedience in such form as its leaders might determine. But no one was in any doubt that the duty devolved primarily on Gandhi.

At midnight on New Year's Eve thousands of delegates and spectators assembled on the banks of the Ravi, and against the sky rose the tricolour of free India amid deafening roars of '*Inquilab zindabad*', (Long live the revolution).

At Lahore Gandhi capitalized on the opportunity to tighten his hold on Congress. He dropped Bose and Srinivas Iyengar from the Congress Working Committee despite noisy protest from the members and delegates. Moreover, the decision of Congress to boycott the legislatures ensured that the Swaraj party was given a decent burial.

Soon Tagore came to Sabarmati. He was keen to know what exactly Gandhi planned to place before the country next. 'I am furiously thinking night and day,' Gandhi answered, 'and I do not see any light coming out of the surrounding darkness.' Gandhi was aware of the ominous tensions. The world economic crisis had resulted in a steep drop in the prices which peasants got for their produce. The hardship was reflected in a decline in their consumption of staples – cloth, oil, sugar. Owing to mounting debts farms were beginning to break up.

But even if Gandhi felt that his programme of effective resistance lacked clarity, it could not stop Indians from declaring the country's objective to mean independence, especially 'when Dominion Status is said to mean what we have never understood it to mean'. In accordance with the appeal of Congress, he asked the nation to observe 26 January as Independence Day. The national response was enormous. In every town and innumerable villages throughout India the flag of independence was hoisted and Gandhi's manifesto read. In his manifesto he declared:

> We believe it is the inalienable right of the Indian people, as of any other people, to have freedom and to enjoy the fruits of their toil and have the necessities of life, so that they may have full opportunities for growth. We believe also that if any government deprives a people of these rights and oppresses them, the people have a further right to alter it or abolish it. The British Government of India has not only deprived the Indian people of their freedom but has based itself on the exploitation of the masses, and has ruined India economically, politically, culturally and spiritually. We believe, therefore, that India must sever the British connection and attain *Purna Swaraj* or Complete Independence.

Only a few days later Gandhi suddenly announced an eleven-point pro-gramme, the acceptance of which by Britain, he felt, would be tantamount to the granting of independence. They were a startlingly miscellaneous assortment of demands, shrewdly chosen so as to appeal to almost every section of the population – reduction of land revenue by fifty per cent; abol-ition of salt tax; total prohibition of alcohol; a protective tariff against foreign cloth; enactment of a coastal reservation bill in favour of Indian shipping; revaluation of the rupee; reduction of military expenditure by at least fifty per cent; reduction of the salaries of civil servants by half; release of all political prisoners not condemned for murder or attempted murder; abolition or control of the Criminal Investigation Department, whose prin-cipal target was Congress; and issue of firearms for self-defence, subject to popular control.

'Let the Viceroy,' declared Gandhi, 'satisfy us with regard to these very simple but vital needs of India. He will then hear no talk of civil disobedi-ence.' However, Gandhi had not yet decided as to the precise issue on which he would possibly launch civil disobedience. Soon his 'inner voice' would prompt him towards a decision, and at the beginning of March his mind was made up. He would call upon Indians to shake off the burden of the salt tax by making salt for themselves. In a hot climate the intake of salt is essential for man and beast. The £25 million netted from the levy of salt tax was only about three per cent of the £800 million pounds collected by the British from India. But these revenues were obtained, literally, from the sweat of the poorest and from a commodity abundantly available along the thousands of miles of Indian coastline.

Gandhi's choice of the salt laws for defiance was characteristically original, but it was not for the first time that the imposition of the laws had been questioned. The manufacture of salt in India had long since been a government monopoly, and the British laws made it a punishable crime to possess salt not obtained from government sources. The tax on salt had given rise to a good deal of political controversy in the past, and at several sessions of the Indian National Congress it was subjected to severe criticism. In his speech in the House of Commons as early as 14 August 1894, Dadabhai Naoroji, 'the grand old man of India', had described the salt tax as a burden on the poor 'drawn from the wretchedness of the people'. Even Ramsay MacDonald, before coming to power, had denounced the Salt Act in his writings and public statements. But it was left to Gandhi to defy the laws as a method of challenging British authority in India.

On 2 March 1930, he wrote a long letter to Lord Irwin, reviewing the grievances covered by his Eleven Points. It was the most unusual type of communication the head of a government ever received.

Dear Friend,

Before embarking on Civil Disobedience and taking the risk I have dreaded to take all these years, I would fain approach you and find a way out.

My personal faith is absolutely clear. I cannot intentionally hurt anything that lives, much less fellow human beings, even though they may do the greatest wrong to me and mine. Whilst, therefore, I hold the British rule to be a curse, I do not intend harm to a single Englishman or to any legitimate interest he may have in India.

I must not be misunderstood. Though I hold the British rule in India to be a curse, I do not, therefore, consider Englishmen in general to be worse than any other people on earth. I have the privilege of claiming many Englishmen as dearest friends. Indeed much that I have learnt of the evil of British rule is due to the writings of frank and courageous Englishmen who have not hesitated to tell the unpalatable truth about that rule . . .

And why do I regard British rule as a curse?

It has impoverished the dumb millions by a system of progressive exploitation and by a ruinous expensive military and civil administration which the country can never afford. It has reduced us politically to serfdom. It has sapped the foundation of our culture. And by the policy of cruel disarmament, it has degraded us spiritually.

In common with many of my countrymen, I had hugged the hope that the proposed Round Table Conference might furnish a solution . . . I fear . . . there never has been any intention of granting . . . Dominion Status to India in the near future.

It seems as clear as daylight that responsible British statesmen do not

GANDHI

contemplate any alteration in British policy that might adversely affect Britain's commerce with India . . . If nothing is done to end the process of exploitation India must be bled with an ever increasing speed . . .

Let me put before you some of the salient points.

The terrific pressure of land revenue, which furnishes a large part of the total, must undergo considerable modification in an Independent India . . . the whole revenue system has to be so revised as to make the peasant's good its primary concern. But the British system seems to be designed to crush the very life out of him. Even the salt he must use to live is so taxed as to make the burden fall heaviest on him, if only because of the heartless impartiality of its incidence. The tax shows itself still more burdensome on the poor man when it is remembered that salt is the one thing he must eat more than the rich man . . . The drink and drug revenue, too, is derived from the poor. It saps the foundations both of their health and morals.

The iniquities sampled above are maintained in order to carry on a foreign administration, demonstrably the most expensive in the world. Take your own salary. It is over 21,000 rupees per month, besides many other indirect additions . . . You are getting over 700 rupees a day against India's average income of less than two annas per day. Thus you are getting much over five thousand times India's average income. The British Prime Minister is getting only ninety times Britain's average income. On bended knee, I ask you to ponder over this phenomenon. I have taken a personal illustration to drive home a painful truth. I have too great a regard for you as a man to wish to hurt your feelings. I know that you do not need the salary you get. Probably the whole of your salary goes for charity. But a system that provides for such an arrangement deserves to be summarily scrapped. What is true of the Viceregal salary is true generally of the whole administration . . . Nothing but organized nonviolence can check the organized violence of the British Government . . .

This non-violence will be expressed through Civil Disobedience, for the moment confined to the inmates of Satyagraha [Sabarmati] Ashram, but ultimately designed to cover all those who choose to join the movement. I know that in embarking on non-violence I shall be running what might be termed a mad risk. But the victories of truth have never been won without risks, often of the gravest character. Conversion of a nation that has consciously or unconsciously preyed upon another, far more numerous, far more ancient and no less cultured than itself, is worth any amount of risk . . .

My ambition is no less than to convert the British people through non-violence, and thus make them see the wrong they have done to India. I do not seek to harm your people. I want to serve them even as I want to serve my own people . . . If the [Indian] people join me as I expect they will, the sufferings they will undergo, unless the British nation soon retraces its steps, will be enough to melt the stoniest hearts.

The plan through Civil Disobedience will be to combat such evils as I have sampled out. I respectfully invite you to pave the way for the immediate removal of those evils, and thus open a way for a real conference between equals . . . But if you cannot see your way to deal with these evils and if my letter makes no appeal to your heart, on the eleventh day of this month I shall proceed with such co-workers of the Ashram as I can take, to disregard the provisions of the Salt Laws . . . It is, I know, open to you to frustrate my design by arresting me. I hope that there will be tens of thousands ready, in a disciplined manner, to take up the work after me . . .

I have no desire to cause you unnecessary embarrassment, or any at all, so far as I can help . . . If you will care to discuss matters with me, and if to that end you would like me to postpone publication of this letter, I shall gladly refrain on receipt of telegram . . .

This letter is not in any way intended as a threat but is a simple and sacred duty, peremptory on a civil resister. Therefore I am having it specially delivered by a young English friend who believes in the Indian cause and is a full believer in non-violence and whom Providence seems to have sent me, as it were, for the very purpose.

Your sincere friend,
M.K. GANDHI

The young English friend was Reginald Reynolds, a Quaker, then staying at Sabarmati ashram. Clad in *khadi*, he entered the Viceroy's house and presented the letter to the Viceroy's private secretary. Lord Irwin's reply was a mere expression of regret that Gandhi proposed to embark on a course of action which would inevitably involve violation of the law and disturb the public peace. Gandhi commented: 'I repudiate the law, and regard it as my sacred duty to break the mournful monotony of the compulsory peace that is choking the heart of a nation.'

As the days passed India bubbled with excitement and curiosity. The excitement spread abroad and foreign reporters followed Gandhi in the ashram, waiting to see exactly what he would do. A large number of onlookers gathered at the ashram gate and in the adjacent fields, waiting, watching. Day after day, Gandhi explained his programme, answered questions, and gave his message at prayer meetings. On the evening of 11 March he addressed a vast audience on the sands of the Sabarmati. 'This will be', he said calmly, 'my last speech on the sacred banks of the Sabarmati. Possibly these may be the last words of my life here.' He felt it was the opportunity of a lifetime.

On the morning of 12 March 1930, Gandhi set out from his ashram, accompanied by seventy-eight chosen followers, to march the two hundred and forty miles to the sea at Dandi. There were no women marchers. 'I must be considerate to the opponent,' Gandhi explained. 'We want to go in for suffering, and there may even be torture. If we put the women in front, the Government may hesitate to inflict on us all the penalty that they might otherwise inflict. A delicate sense of chivalry is what decides me against including the women in the first batch.' Not all the marchers were ashramites, and their names were printed in *Young India* for the benefit of the police. They included two Muslims and one Christian. The rest were Hindus, including two Untouchables. At their head Gandhi appeared with an iron-tipped bamboo walking staff. His steps were firm and his look serene and shining. The procession marched through the heat and dust from village to village, where crowds of eager onlookers waited, hoping for the Mahatma's *darshan*. Some Satyagrahis became fatigued and footsore and found it necessary to do part of their journey in a bullock cart. A horse was kept in readiness for their leader, but he never mounted. 'Less than twelve miles a day in two stages with not much luggage,' he said. 'Child's play!'

Whenever he stopped at villages, he would exhort the people to wear *khadi*, to treat the Untouchables with brotherly affection, to improve their sanitation, to abjure alcohol and drugs, to break the salt monopoly, and to join the ranks of the Satyagrahis. At Aslali, where he spent the first night, he told his followers that he would not return to the ashram at Sabarmati until the Salt Act was repealed, until the *swaraj* was won. 'The soldiers of the first batch had burnt their boats the moment the march began,' he declared. The following day the Viceroy, in a communication to the Secretary of State for India, said: 'Most of my thought at the moment is concentrated upon Gandhi. I wish I felt sure what the right way to deal with him is.'

The march commenced every morning at six-thirty. At sunrise and sunset Gandhi held prayer meetings in the open. He spun every day for an hour, kept a diary, prepared speeches and wrote for *Young India*. He retired at nine, still talking to people and giving interviews until he fell asleep. Long before his comrades were up he awoke to attend to his work. At four in the morning he was seen writing letters by moonlight as his little lamp had gone out for want of oil.

Gandhi marched at the head of the procession like a conqueror. Behind him the administration was silently crumbling as scores of village headmen resigned. On his arrival at Borsad on 18 March, large-scale resignations by village administrators were announced. Gandhi reiterated the significance of this noncooperation to the assembled crowd:

Today we are defying the salt law. Tomorrow we shall have to consign other laws to the waste-paper basket. Doing so we shall practise such severe non-cooperation that finally it will not be possible for the administration to be carried out at all. Let the government then, to carry on its rules, use guns against us, send us to prison, hang us. But how many can be given such punishment? Try and calculate how much time it will take of Britishers to hang three hundred million of persons.

The spectacle of this sixty-year-old man, staff in hand, striding vigorously along the dusty roads of India with his *khadi*-clad followers, to challenge peacefully the mighty British Empire aroused the interest and sympathy of millions all over the world. 'For me there is no turning back, whether I am alone or joined by thousands,' he declared. 'I would rather die a dog's death and have my bones licked by dogs than that I should return to the ashram a broken man.' In the course of his speech at Navsari a few days later, he proclaimed: 'I shall return with what I want or my dead body will float in the ocean.'

At first the authorities expected the salt march to fizzle out but when the tempo began to increase and the movement to spread, the Bombay government sought to persuade Lord Irwin to take action against Gandhi. The Viceroy was not in favour of Gandhi's arrest, though he knew he would have to act eventually. He was marking time, for he was more inclined to rely on the reports of his agents and advisers than on those in the world press, which was being fed by Indian nationalist sources. 'The will-power of the man must have been enormous to get him through his march,' he wrote to the Secretary of State for India a few days later. 'I was always told that his blood pressure is dangerous and his heart none too good, and I was also told a few days ago that his horoscope predicts that he will die this year, and that is the explanation of this desperate throw. It would be a very happy solution.' This was a rather harsh verdict, coming from a Viceroy who regarded himself as a man of principle. In any event Lord Irwin's sources of information were grossly inaccurate since they were primarily based on rumours.

Meanwhile villagers joined the column as it surged on, and when on 5 April, after a march of twenty-four days, it reached the sea coast at Dandi, the original group of seventy-nine had swelled to thousands. Among them were many women – not only the poor, but wealthy ladies from the cities. Asked what he hoped to achieve by breaking the salt laws, Gandhi answered: 'I want world sympathy in this battle of Right against Might.'

The Satyagrahis camped near the water and all through the night of 5 April they prayed. The next morning Gandhi, along with a large number of his followers, waded into the sea for a ceremonial bath of purification. After a short while he paced over the sand to a spot where the salt lay thick. As he bent down to scoop up a small portion of natural salt, Sarojini Naidu, who was among the pilgrims standing nearby, shouted excitedly: 'Hail, Deliverer!' Gandhi declared:

> Our path has been chalked out for us. Let every village manufacture or fetch contraband salt. Sisters should picket liquor shops and foreign cloth shops . . . Young and old in every home should ply the spinning wheel . . . Foreign cloth should be burnt . . . Hindus should eschew untouchability. Hindus, Muslims, Sikhs, Parsis and Christians should all achieve heart unity . . . Let the students leave government schools, and government servants resign their service and devote themselves to service of the people, and we shall find that *purna swaraj* will come knocking at our doors.

On that eventful morning in Dandi no policemen were present, and there were no arrests. But within a week the storm had swept across India and everybody seemed to be gathering salt, or reading Congress leaflets on how to make it, or picketing liquor shops, or burning foreign cloth. The police now began to inflict blows, attacking the peasants with *lathis* and rounding up Congress volunteers peddling salt in the streets. In Karachi the police fired at a demonstration, killing two young Congress volunteers. At Congress headquarters in Bombay they discovered salt being made in pans on the roof. During the raid sixty thousand people jammed the neighbouring streets, and hundreds were dragged off handcuffed or bound with ropes. Jawaharlal Nehru was arrested in Allahabad under the Salt Acts and sentenced to six months' imprisonment, nominating his father to be acting president of Congress. Vallabhbhai Patel had been arrested even before the commencement of the march. Presently his brother, Vithalbhai, resigned from the speakership of the Legislative Assembly. Other resignations followed. In Calcutta the Mayor, J.M. Sengupta, read seditious literature in public and soon landed in jail. At Patna a vast crowd moved out of the city toward one of the new salt depots. The police blocked the road, but the crowd would not go back. Rajendra Prasad, the leading Congressman of Bihar, was told to disperse the crowd. He refused. The police officer in command announced that he would charge with cavalry, but the crowd stayed where they were. As the mounted police galloped forward, the demonstrators threw themselves flat on the ground. The horses pulled up and would not trample the crowd; the demonstrators were finally lifted into trucks for transportation to prison.

With the spread of the salt movement, teachers, professors and students made salt at the sea and inland, and were marched to jail in batches. Civil resisters never resisted arrest; but they resisted the confiscation of bags containing the salt they had made, and were beaten and kicked. 'If we are to stand the final heat of the battle,' Gandhi declared, 'we must learn to stand our ground in the face of cavalry or baton charges and allow ourselves to be trampled under the horses' hoofs or be bruised by baton charges.'

Events soon played into the government's hands. On the night of 18 April a band of terrorists belonging to an organization known as the Hindustan Republican Association raided the police arsenals at Chittagong in East Bengal, and after murdering six guards escaped into the jungle. A few days later an even more serious event occurred at Peshawar in the North-West Frontier Province where, following the arrest of Khan Abdul Ghaffar Khan, known as the 'Frontier Gandhi', who was the leader of the organization called the Red Shirts, armoured cars were sent to disperse angry demonstrators. One armoured car was set on fire, its occupants escaping. Another, with the deputy police commissioner aboard, first drove full tilt into a crowd and then opened up with machine-guns, killing seventy and wounding almost one hundred. The police then retreated and left the city to the Red Shirts. Three days later two platoons of the Second Battalion of the 18th Royal Garhwali Rifles were ordered to quell the disturbances, but they refused to fire on crowds of unarmed Muslims. All the soldiers in the Garhwali Rifles were Hindus. From 25 April to 4 May there was no governmental authority in Peshawar. The British then sent loyal Gurkha troops with air support, and the city was retaken. Seventeen of the mutineers of the Garhwali Rifles were in due course court-martialled and given severe sentences. The Viceroy sought to hush up the Peshawar episode, and at the same time took measures to muzzle the Indian press ,which Gandhi felt constituted 'a veiled form of martial law'. He wrote to Lord Irwin still beginning 'Dear Friend', but protesting strongly at the police violence. 'You may condemn civil disobedience as much as you like,' he wrote. 'Will you prefer violent revolt to civil disobedience? . . . I shall hope that God will give the people of India wisdom and strength to withstand every temptation and provocation to violence.' If the Viceroy could not see his way clear to removing the salt tax, Gandhi proposed, 'God willing', to march with his companions to the government-owned Dharasana Saltworks and take possession of it in the name of the people.

On the night of 4 May he was sleeping peacefully in a cot under a mango tree at his camp at Karadi, a village some three miles from Dandi. Several disciples slept near him. Soon after midnight the British district magistrate of Surat, accompanied by two Indian officers and thirty heavily armed constables, invaded the leafy compound. The magistrate woke Gandhi by turning a flashlight on his face, and said he had come to arrest him. Soon all the sleepers in the compound had crowded near their leader. Gandhi needed time for his ablutions, and while brushing his few teeth he asked the magistrate to read out the warrant. He was arrested under the famous Regulation XXV of 1827, which was passed when the East India Company, the forerunner of the British Raj, was the dominant power. This regulation enabled the government to detain him without trial and with no fixed sentence. After the morning ritual of prayer with his followers the prisoner left. He was taken again to Yeravda, where the prison authorities noted some personal particulars: height, five feet five; a scar on the right thigh; a scar below the left elbow; a mole on the lower right eyelid.

Following Gandhi's arrest, the leadership fell to Sarojini Naidu, the poetess, who led about 2,500 members of Congress to to Dharasana Saltworks, 150 miles north of Bombay. Mrs Naidu cautioned the volunteers: 'You must not even raise a hand to ward off blows.' With Manilal Gandhi, the Mahatma's second son, in the forefront, the Satyagrahis approached the salt pans, which were surrounded by ditches and guarded by four hundred Indian policemen commanded by six British officers. A selected column of Satyagrahis advanced, wading through the ditches and approaching the barbed-wire stockade. The police officers ordered them to disperse. The column silently ignored the warning and walked slowly forward. Webb Miller, the well-known United Press correspondent who had managed to be on the scene, described the events:

> Suddenly, at a word of command, scores of native policemen rushed upon the advancing marchers and rained blows on their heads with their steel-shod *lathis*. Not one of the marchers even raised an arm to fend off the blows. They went down like ten-pins. From where I stood I heard the sickening whack of the clubs on unprotected skulls. The waiting crowd of marchers groaned and sucked in their breath in sympathetic pain at every blow. Those struck down fell sprawling, unconscious or writhing with fractured skulls or broken shoulders . . .

When the first column was laid low, another marched forward without any sign of wavering or fear, until itself struck down. There were not enough stretcher-bearers to carry off the wounded. The blankets used as stretchers were sodden with blood.

After a while tactics were changed, and twenty-five men would advance and sit down. The police continued to lash out at the sitting men with their *lathis*. Miller continued:

> Group after group walked forward, sat down, and submitted to being beaten into insensibility without raising an arm to fend off the blows. Finally the policemen became enraged by the non-resistance . . . They commenced savagely kicking the seated men in the abdomen and testicles. The injured men writhed and squealed in agony, which seemed to inflame the fury of the police,

and the crowd again almost broke away from their leaders. The police then began dragging the sitting men by their arms or feet, sometimes for a hundred yards, and then throwing them into ditches. One was dragged into the ditch where I stood; the splash of his body doused me with muddy water. Another policeman dragged a Gandhi man to the ditch, threw him in, and belabored him over the head with his *lathi*. Hour after hour stretcher-bearers carried back a stream of inert, bleeding bodies . . .

By eleven in the morning, at a temperature of 116° in the shade, activity slackened. Miller, the only foreign correspondent present, went to the improvised hospital and counted 320 wounded Satyagrahis. Many were unconscious, others in agony from the body and head blows. Two were already dead. For days these events were repeated. 'In eighteen years of reporting in twenty-two countries, during which I have witnessed innumerable civil disturbances, riots, street fights, and rebellions, I have never witnessed such harrowing scenes as at Dharasana,' wrote Miller.

Mrs Naidu and Manilal Gandhi were placed under arrest. Vithalbhai Patel, the former speaker of the Legislative Assembly, came and surveyed the scene. 'All hope of reconciling India with the British Empire is lost for ever,' he said quietly. 'I can understand any government taking people into custody and punishing them for breaches of the law, but I cannot understand how any government that calls itself civilized can deal as savagely and brutally with non-violent, unresisting men as the British have this morning.'

It is highly unlikely that the Viceroy was unaware of the treatment meted out to the Satyagrahis, but he found it necessary to write a breezy letter to King George V, informing him about the situation:

Your Majesty can hardly fail to have read with amusement the accounts of the several battles for the Salt Depot at Dharasana. The police for a long time tried to refrain from action. After a time this became impossible, and they eventually had to resort to sterner measures. A good many people suffered minor injuries in consequence, but I believe those who suffered injuries were as nothing compared with those who wished to sustain an honourable contusion or bruise, or who, to make the whole setting more dramatic, lay on the ground as if laid out for dead without any injury at all. But of course, as Your Majesty will appreciate, the whole business was propaganda and, as such, served its purpose admirably well.

If the Viceroy and the King were amused, there were many others who were not amused at all. Webb Miller's dispatch was circulated by United Press to over a thousand papers throughout the world. Raids on more of the salt depots followed, and the raiders managed to carry off some salt. At one depot near Bombay fifteen thousand volunteers took part. Nagley Farson, special correspondent of the Chicago *Daily News*, eye-witnessed a mass beating:

> In a few seconds that field was a shambles of reeling, bleeding men; men holding their heads with blood oozing down between their fingers, men trying to ward off blows with their bare forearms . . . women shrieking and tearing at the policemen's clothes . . . throwing themselves before the swishing *lathis*.

Farson saw one woman hold up her baby and endeavour to secure for it a crack on the head. When he expressed his horror to her through an interpreter she remained unmoved, anxious only to sacrifice her babe to the cause.

Farson then watched the *jatha*, or group, of Sikhs:

> The Sikh leader was like that statue of the gladiator in Rome; a Herculean man, with his beard tied to his ears. He was being struck on the head. I stood about six feet from him and watched. He was hit until his turban came undone and his topknot was exposed. A few more blows and his hair came undone and fell down on his face. A few more and blood began to drip off his dangling black hair. He stood there with his hands on his sides. Then a particularly heavy blow and he fell forward on his face.
>
> I could hardly hold myself back. I wanted to grab that white sergeant's *lathi*. I stood next to him. He was so sweaty from his exertions that his Sam Browne had stained his white tunic. I watched him with my heart in my mouth. He drew back his arm for a final swing . . . and he dropped his hands down by his side. 'It is no use,' he said turning to me with half an apologetic grin. 'You can't hit a bugger when he stands up to you like that.' He gave the Sikh a mock salute and walked off . . .
>
> No other Sikhs had tried to shield him, but now, shouting their defiance and their determination to die rather than move, they wiped away the blood streaming from his mouth. Hysterical Hindus rushed to him bearing cakes of ice to rub the contusions over his brown eyes. The Sikh gave me a bloody smile – and stood up for more.

# THIRTY

# Truce

In the calm of Yeravda jail Gandhi sat at his spinning wheel, read volum-
inously and, in the absence of any restrictions, wrote a stream of letters.
George Slocombe, an English journalist who witnessed the raid on the saltworks near Bombay, obtained, with the Viceroy's tacit approval, an interview with Gandhi in jail. 'The imprisoned Mahatma', he wrote, 'now
incarnates the very soul of India.' Slocombe pleaded that the government
should negotiate. In July, with the Viceroy's consent, Sir Tej Bahadur
Sapru and M.R. Jayakar, leaders of the moderates, met Gandhi in Yeravda
for discussions. Gandhi could not reply to their overtures without consulting the Congress Working Committee which, a few weeks before, had been
declared an unlawful association, leading to the arrest of the acting president Motilal Nehru and other Congress leaders.

The Nehrus, father and son, and Syed Mahmud, the acting secretary of
Congress, were accordingly brought from Naini jail to Yeravda. There
with Gandhi, Mrs Naidu and Vallabhbhai Patel, they met Sapru and
Jayakar, representing the Viceroy. The Working Committee members still
at liberty were not allowed to participate in these jail conversations. The
two-day talks at Yeravda were followed by other communications, with
Sapru and Jayakar acting as intermediaries. The government would make
no concession to conditions laid down by Congress about the transfer of
authority and the right to secede. The diehards felt that the whole exercise
was undesirable. 'The Government of India', said Churchill, 'had imprisoned Gandhi and they had been sitting outside his cell door, begging him
to help them out of their difficulties.'

Meanwhile Congress committees all over India were declared illegal
and, according to one estimate, as many as one hundred thousand
Satyagrahis, including most of the major and minor leaders, were in jail.
Civil disobedience nevertheless continued, with a no-tax campaign an
important feature of the programme. It was against the background of these
developments that the first Round Table Conference was convened in
London on 12 November 1930, to deliberate on the future of India. Sapru,
Jayakar, Jinnah, the Maharajah of Bikaner and Ambedkar were among the

Indian members. No Congress representatives attended. The conference lasted about two months and made some progress towards a constitution. When it adjourned, Prime Minister Ramsay MacDonald voiced a hope that Congress would participate in the second conference. Gandhi and many other Congress leaders were accordingly released from jail; a week later Motilal Nehru died in Lucknow. The Mahatma wrote to his 'Dear Friend' in New Delhi asking for an interview.

On 17 February 1931, there began the long series of talks between Irwin and Gandhi. At half past two in the afternoon, Gandhi walked up the steps of the Viceroy's newly built palace, designed by the British architect Sir Edwin Lutyens. The first session of talks continued for three and a half hours. 'So the stage was set', wrote Irwin's biographer, 'for the most dramatic personal encounter between a Viceroy and an Indian leader in the whole seething history of the British Raj.' From London Churchill, whose views on India appeared to belong to some bygone period of the world history, thundered his scorn of Gandhi:

It is alarming and also nauseating to see Mr Gandhi, a seditious Middle Temple lawyer, now posing as a *fakir* of a type well-known in the East, striding half-naked up the steps of the viceregal palace, while he is still organizing and conducting a defiant campaign of civil disobedience, to parley on equal terms with the representative of the King-Emperor.

Gandhi and Irwin conferred eight times over a period of three weeks. During this time Irwin was cabling the India Office in London, while Gandhi held long talks with Congress Working Committee members in New Delhi. Lord Irwin was determined to bring an end to civil disobedience. Gandhi was firm in his resolve to advance the cause of complete independence. Their talks were evidently not devoid of difficulties, and at one stage Gandhi was not sent for by the Viceroy for several days and it seemed that deadlock had been reached. When they met again on 27 February, the interview lasted three hours. They were both exhausted by the end and Irwin suggested a further meeting. 'Good night, Mr Gandhi, and my prayers go with you' were his parting words, as Gandhi, staff in hand, set out on foot for his five-mile journey to Dr Ansari's house, where he was staying. The Viceroy described his visitor in a letter to King George V:

I think that most people meeting him would be conscious, as I was conscious, of a very powerful personality, and this, independent of physical endowment, which indeed is unfavourable. Small, wizened, rather emaciated, no front teeth, it is a personality very poorly adorned with the world's trimmings. And yet you cannot help feeling the force of character behind the sharp little eyes and immensely active and acutely working mind.

One of the main stumbling blocks in the talks was Gandhi's insistence that there should be an inquiry into police brutality. The Viceroy refused, on the grounds that such an inquiry would simply exacerbate tempers on both sides. The Viceroy reported:

> This did not satisfy him at all, and we argued the point for two or three days. Finally, I said that I would tell him the main reason why I could not give him what he wanted. I had no guarantee that he might not start civil disobedience again, and if and when he did, I wanted the police to have their tails up and not down. Whereupon his face lit up and he said, 'Ah, now Your Excellency treats me like General Smuts treated me in South Africa. You do not deny that I have an equitable claim, but you advance unanswerable reasons from the point of view of the Government why you cannot meet it. I drop the demand.'

Finally, a kind of a truce was reached between the two men. It looked like a compromise to Gandhi's disadvantage, but in the Mahatma's estimation the signing of the Irwin-Gandhi Pact – or the Delhi Pact as Irwin's biographer calls – established, in principle, a position of equality between England and India.

The pact made provision for constitutional matters to be discussed at a Round Table Conference in London, and agreed that the civil disobedience campaign should be called off. People living in coastal areas would be permitted to collect salt for their own use; political prisoners, other than those involved in violent activities, would be released. Irwin reluctantly agreed to the peaceful picketing of shops but there was to be no compulsion on those traders who earned their living by selling foreign cloth.

The meeting between the two men on the night of 4 March seemed to present more hurdles, and when Gandhi left the Viceroy's house with a draft copy of the settlement it was past midnight. When the Mahatma reached Dr Ansari's house at 2 a.m., members of the Working Committee were waiting anxiously for him. Gandhi was aware of their objections. Vallabhbhai Patel disagreed with the formula on the question of confiscated lands. Jawaharlal Nehru was critical of acceptance on the basis of discussion short of complete independence. None of the members thought the undertaking to release prisoners was sufficiently comprehensive. But reluctantly the Working Committee accepted the settlement. Gandhi went back to Irwin rather depressed and said that Nehru was unhappy about the agreement to the extent that he had wept over 'this tragedy of the betrayal of India'. 'I exhorted him,' observed Irwin later, 'not to let this worry him unduly, as I had no doubt that very soon I should be getting cables from England telling me that in Churchill's opinion I had sold Great Britain.' Indeed, it was not long before Churchill thundered again:

> I am against this surrender to Gandhi. I am against these conversations and agreements between Lord Irwin and Mr Gandhi. Gandhi stands for the expulsion of Britain from India. Gandhi stands for the permanent exclusion of British trade from India . . . You will never be able to come to terms with Gandhi . . . In running after Gandhi and trying to build on Gandhi, in imagining that Mr Ramsay MacDonald and Mr Gandhi and Lord Irwin are going to bestow peace and progress upon India, we should be committing ourselves to a crazy dream, with a terrible awakening.

At noon on 5 March 1931, the Delhi Pact was formally signed at the Viceroy's house. Both the Mahatma and the Viceroy were in a cheerful mood. Irwin suggested that they should drink to each other's health. 'Thank you,' said Gandhi, taking a paper bag out of a fold in his shawl, 'I will put some of this salt in my tea to remind us of the famous Boston Tea Party.' Both laughed. They joked freely over Churchill's references to the 'half-naked *fakir*'. When it was now time for Gandhi to depart, he forgot to take his shawl. Lord Irwin at once picked it up, remarking with a gentle smile: 'Gandhi, you haven't so much on, you know, that you can afford to leave this behind.' The Mahatma laughed uproariously.

Years later, in his *Fulness of Days*, Irwin wrote of Gandhi:

> There was a directness about him which was singularly winning, but this could be accompanied by a subtlety of intellectual process which could sometimes be disconcerting. To appreciate what was passing in his mind it was necessary, if not to start from the same point, at least to understand very clearly what was the starting point for him; and this was nearly always very human and very simple.

The Congress Working Committee was evidently disturbed by the terms of the settlement, but an emotional issue was now looming large. Bhagat Singh who, along with two others, had shot dead in Lahore the young English police officer Saunders, was due to be executed. Public opinion demanded that the sentence be commuted but, as Irwin put it, 'I could not conceive anyone who had more thoroughly deserved capital punishment than Bhagat Singh.' On 23 March Singh was executed. The Mahatma had earlier cautioned the Viceroy that unless he could do something to save Singh's life, the effect would be to destroy their settlement. Irwin explained to Gandhi that from his point of view it was possible neither to grant Bhagat Singh a reprieve nor to postpone a decision on his sentence and thus encourage people to have a false notion that there was a chance of remission. Irwin reported:

Mr Gandhi thought for a moment, and then said: 'Would Your Excellency see any objection to my saying that I pleaded for the young man's life?' I said that I had none, if he would also add that from my point of view he did not see what other course I could have taken. He thought for a moment, then finally agreed, and on that basis went off to Karachi.

The cry of '*Bhagat Singh Zindabad!*' resounded throughout India. Angry demonstrators clashed with the police in many cities, resulting in about one hundred and fifty deaths. This was followed by bloody communal rioting in Cawnpore, where Muslims refused to participate in the *hartal* observed in Singh's memory.

The Congress session at Karachi was convened under the shadow of Bhagat Singh's execution. Gandhi and Vallabhbhai Patel (who had succeeded Motilal as president of Congress) were greeted on arrival with black flags and shouts of 'Gandhi, go back. Your truce has sent Bhagat Singh to the gallows.' He bore it all patiently. 'You must know that it is against my creed to punish even a murderer, a thief or a dacoit,' he told a mammoth gathering of fifty thousand. 'There can be therefore no excuse for suspicion that I did not want to save a brave man like Bhagat Singh. But I want you also to realize Bhagat Singh's error. If I had an opportunity of speaking to him and his comrades, I should have told them that the way they pursued was wrong and futile.' As a concession to his opponents, Gandhi got Congress to pass a resolution appreciating the courage and sacrifice of Bhagat Singh and his comrades while at the same time deploring political violence in any shape or form. Writing in *Navajivan* a few days later he admonished the government for having demonstrated 'its own brute nature' by ignoring public opinion. The government had the right to execute Singh, but 'if a person exercises all his rights on all occasions, in the end they are destroyed'. The controversy over Bhagat Singh's execution raged for some time and led to more terrorist activities. Sir Ernest Hotson, the acting Governor of Bombay, was shot at by a student while visiting the Ferguson College at Poona, but had a miraculous escape. A few days later Mr Garlick, the District Judge of Alipore, was shot dead. 'The Bhagat Singh worship has done and is doing incalculable harm to the country,' said Gandhi. Warning the Congressmen, he wrote in *Young India*:

The deed itself is being worshipped as if it was worthy of emulation. The result is *goonda*ism and degradation wherever this mad worship is being performed. The Congress is a power in the land, but I warn Congressmen that it will soon lose all its charm if they betray their trust and encourage the Bhagat Singh cult whether in thought, word or deed. If the majority do not believe in the Congress policy of non-violence and truth, let them have the first article altered. Let us understand the distinction between policy and creed. A policy may be changed, a creed cannot. But either is as good as the other whilst it is held. Those therefore who hold non-violence only as a policy may not, without exposing themselves to the charge of dishonourable conduct, use the Congress membership as a cover for violence. I cannot get rid of the conviction, that the greatest obstacle to our progress towards *swaraj* is our want of faith in our policy.

The main resolution at the Karachi session of Congress related to the Delhi Pact, which was duly ratified. However, it was clarified that the Congress goal of *purna swaraj* remained intact. Gandhi was authorized to attend the Round Table Conference in London as the sole representative of Congress. He made preparations to go, but lack of rapport with the new Viceroy, Lord Willingdon, led to the announcement that he could not attend. Following hectic negotiations at Simla, the summer capital of India, a new settlement was produced on 27 August, and a special train had to be arranged to take him to Bombay in time to catch the SS *Rajputana* on the 29th. 'I go to London with God as my only guide,' declared Gandhi. 'The horizon is as black as it possibly could be. There is every chance of my returning empty-handed. But believing as I do that God has made the way to London clear to go through the second settlement, I approach the visit with hope.'

# THIRTY-ONE

# Round Table Conference

Gandhi's personal party consisted of Pyarelal Nayyar, a secretary and disciple, his own son Devadas, Mirabehn (Madeleine Slade) and Mahadev Desai, his secretary and chronicler who, according to Gandhi, had 'outBoswelled Boswell'. Also travelling on the *Rajputana* were Pandit Madan Mohan Malaviya of the Hindu Mahasabha party and Mrs Sarojini Naidu, both of whom were delegates, and the industrialist G.D. Birla, who was soon appointed delegate at Gandhi's suggestion. Mrs Naidu, although a Congresswoman, was included in the conference, but as a representative of Indian women. Lord Willingdon had refused to accept a nationalist Muslim, Dr M.A. Ansari, as part of the Congress team which now consisted of Gandhi alone. Britain would have allowed more but the Working Committee preferred to stay at their posts in the event of trouble. If an agreement was reached they could be sent for.

At the Mahatma's insistence he and his party travelled second class, the lowest class available. When he discovered how much luggage they had brought he took them to task and saw to it that seven suitcases and cabin trunks were sent back from the first port of call. Throughout the passage he kept to his normal routine of early rising, prayer, spinning, reading and writing and open-air life.

His meals consisted mainly of fruit and goat's milk. He chose a corner of the second-class deck, where he received visitors, wrote for *Young India*, dictated letters and slept under the stars. On one occasion a number of passengers came to him and asked him whether they could hold a dance on the deck where he slept. 'Can we dance near you?' they asked. 'By all means,' Gandhi assured them, 'you can dance not only near me but all round me so long as you don't dance on me.' Throughout the noisy party the Mahatma slept peacefully.

On 11 September the ship anchored in Marseilles, where Gandhi was greeted by Madeleine Rolland, sister of Romain Rolland, the Mahatma's biographer. When a French customs officer asked Gandhi if he had anything to declare, he replied: 'I am a poor mendicant. My earthly possessions consist of six spinning wheels, prison dishes, a can of goat's milk, six homespun loincloths, one towel, and my reputation which cannot be worth much.'

It was pouring with rain when he landed at Folkestone. Wearing a loincloth and a shawl, he was escorted by police officers to a waiting automobile. He travelled to London by road, while the rest of the party took the train. The authorities were afraid that traffic would be blocked at Victoria Station if he arrived there, and they were not agreeable to the prospect of his getting a hero's welcome. Gandhi was taken directly to the Friends' Meeting House, where over a thousand representatives from the churches, the Labour Party, trade unions and women's organizations were waiting to greet him. Laurence Housman, the distinguished playwright, welcomed him in the name of the British people. 'You are strange to many, even in your own country,' he said. 'You are strange to the people of my country. You are so sincere that you make some of us suspicious, and you are so simple that you bewilder some of us.' In his reply to the address, Gandhi briefly spoke of Congress's aims and appealed on behalf of the 'dumb and starving millions of India'.

It was still raining heavily as he continued on to Kingsley Hall, a settlement house in the working-class district of Bow in the East End, where he had arranged to stay with Miss Muriel Lester. Gandhi had received many invitations to stay in the fashionable West End, near St James's Palace, the conference venue, but Miss Lester, who a few years earlier had been his guest at Ahmedabad, encountered no difficulty in convincing him that he would be more at home among the poor, and that he would be able to live more in the style to which he was accustomed. Five tiny rooms at the top of Kingsley Hall were reserved for Gandhi and his party. Gandhi's own room was seven or eight feet long, simple and scantily furnished. In this room, reminiscent of a prison cell, he felt at home. During the next three months Kingsley Hall would be jammed with reporters, as well as eminent people, and crowds of the curious.

The day after his arrival, the Columbia Broadcasting System brought their apparatus into Kingsley Hall to enable the Mahatma to speak to America. They were on the air at 6.30 and as Miss Lester was halfway through her five-minute introduction, describing Kingsley Hall to American listeners, Gandhi was just finishing his supper. The harassed Miss Lester stammered the rest of her description with an eye on the door Gandhi was supposed to come through; presently the door opened and he composedly entered the room. As she announced the concluding words introducing the Mahatma, she turned the microphone to face him. 'Do I talk into this?' he enquired in a low voice which was nevertheless heard by millions of listeners. Then he shut his eyes and bent his head and for a moment sat silent.

He spoke for half an hour. The means adopted by the Indians in their fight for liberty, he said, had no parallel in history. 'We have adopted not violence, not bloodshed, not diplomacy as one understands it nowadays but purely and simply truth and non-violence. No wonder that the attention of the world is directed towards this attempt to lead a successful bloodless revolution.' He would wait for ages rather than seek to attain the freedom of his country through bloody means. 'The world is sick unto death of blood-spilling. It is seeking a way out, and I flatter myself with the belief that perhaps it will be the privilege of the ancient land of India to show that way out to the hungering world.' He then dwelt on the internal problems confronting the country, referring to India as 'a house divided against itself'. Hindus and Muslims were at each other's throats. Much more painful was the fact that 'we Hindus regard several millions of our own kith and kin as too degraded even for our touch . . .' He spoke of the curse of drink and drugs, a huge source of revenue to the government, and the destruction by the East India Company, the forerunner of the British Raj, of village industries for the benefit of British manufacturers, rendering the peasants without work for six months in the year.

He concluded his broadcast by appealing, on behalf of the semi-starved millions, 'to the conscience of the world to come to the rescue of a people dying for regaining its liberty'. His voice was clear, but in the background were tiny staccato noises caused by swings and seesaws in a playground close by. Almost immediately the broadcast was finished, Gandhi addressed a Kingsley Hall audience on prayer, and then drove off to the West End to a reception, where he was to meet the Prime Minister and other dignitaries.

After a few days it was felt that the eight-mile trip through London to Bow was rather time-consuming, and a house was rented at 88 Knightsbridge, which Gandhi used as an office. Mahadev, Pyarelal and Devadas were accommodated there while Gandhi, despite an extremely busy schedule, preferred to return to Kingsley Hall for his brief sleep. Mirabehn woke him at three each morning for prayers. He would take an hour's pre-dawn morning walk, and women and men going to work would smile and greet him. Some would join him for conversation. Children would run beside him and call him 'Uncle Gandhi', and he would joke with them. On one occasion a mischievous youngster yelled: 'Hey, Gandhi, where's your trousers?' The Mahatma had a hearty laugh.

Miss Lester brought Gandhi and the people together at little evening sessions where neighbourhood residents would greet their guest. Children were also invited into the Hall, quite informally, to meet Gandhi. They listened to his argument with rapt attention. 'When a boy hits you, what do you do? What happens then? Is there a better way?' There was no hesitation in the children's answers and they could see his argument with clarity. There was a spark of humour and challenge in all he said. And when he visited the dwellings of the poor, he would say: 'Here I am doing the real round table work, getting to know the people of England.' One day he explored Eagling Road, a typical slum street in Bow. Muriel Lester gives a vivid description of that visit:

> This street Mr Gandhi chose to explore early one morning in November. His movements always created excitement. A large crowd was very soon accompanying us as we crossed Bruce Road and made our way to Eagling Road. In and out of the houses he went, on both sides of the street. The women were inordinately proud. They had had no idea he was coming, some were at their ironing, some cleaning, but all were ready to display every corner of their little domain for him to inspect, to ask about and to admire. He wanted to know what work the men round about did, the rent of the houses, the work of the sanitary authorities so far as drains and cleanliness were concerned, what provision was made for the care of the family during unemployment. Upstairs they took him and out into the backyards. They showed him their pets, their rabbits and their chickens; occasionally there was a piano to be proud of, and always it was obvious how the best was being made of everything and how anything that possessed any sort of beauty was cherished.
>
> Mr Gandhi enjoyed that morning more than any other spent in London, and those whose homes he visited will hold it always memorable.

From his first day in London, Gandhi set about the business of the conference. A few days earlier he had told a Reuters' special correspondent aboard the *Rajputana* that he would 'strive for a constitution, which will release India from all thraldom and patronage and give her, if need be, the right to sin'. But the composition of the conference ensured that the British reserved the 'right to sin' for themselves. The Round Table Conference consisted of 112 delegates: 20 representatives from the United Kingdom, 23 from the princely states, 69 from British India. The Viceroy had selected the princes and, with the exception of Gandhi, Mrs Naidu and a few others, appointed the delegates from British India, who consisted mainly of landlords, titled gentry, leaders of communal groups, businessmen and millionaires. None, of course, had been selected by any process of democratic election, and Gandhi in his second speech before the conference challenged the representation. 'The first feeling of oppression that has been coming upon me', he remarked, 'is that we are not the chosen ones of the nation which we should be representing, but we are the chosen ones of the government.'

If Gandhi had any hope of wringing concessions from the British government, it must have faded by the time he reached England. British politics were working against him, for when he landed on 12 September, the Labour party was already out of office and a coalition National Government headed by Ramsay MacDonald but of predominantly Conservative complexion was installed in power. Britain was going through such an acute economic crisis that it was hard to arouse much concern for India. Churchill and many other Conservatives argued that the loss of control over such a large portion of the Empire would be a deadly blow to hopes of recovery.

The purpose of the conference was 'constitution-building' for India, but at the outset the British intention was made apparent by Lord Reading, a member of the British delegation, when he observed:

I believe that the true policy between Britain and India is that we should in this country strive all we can to give effect to the views of India while preserving at the same time our own position, which we must not and cannot abandon.

The chief work of the conference was mainly done by the Federal Structure Committee and the Minorities Committee. Gandhi was a member of both and attended every session from beginning to end. On the way to the first session G.D. Birla asked him if he had thought of what he wanted to say. Gandhi is said to have replied:

I am absolutely blank. But perhaps God will help me in collecting my thoughts at the proper time. After all, we have to talk like simple men. I have no desire to appear extra intelligent. Like a simple villager all I have to say is: 'We want independence.'

In his speech before the Federal Structure Committee he put forward the claim of Congress that it represented all sections of the Indian nation, especially 'the dumb, semi-starved millions scattered over the length and breadth of the land in its 700,000 villages'. He read out the Karachi Congress resolution to remind the committee what Congress was seeking to achieve – complete independence, which meant control over the army, external affairs, finance, fiscal and economic policy. He had carefully studied the government's policy statement which, he warned, 'falls far short of what is aimed at and claimed by the Congress'. He declared:

If we are intent upon complete independence, it is not from any sense of arrogance; it is not because we want to parade before the universe that we have now severed all connection with the British people. Nothing of the kind. On the contrary, you find in this mandate itself that the Congress contemplates a partnership – the Congress contemplates a connection with the British people – but that connection to be such as can exist between two absolute equals. Time was when I prided myself on being, and being called, a British subject. I have ceased for many years to call myself a British subject; I would far rather be called a rebel than a subject. But I have aspired – I do aspire – to be a citizen, not of the Empire, but in a Commonwealth; in a partnership if possible – if God wills it, an indissoluble partnership – but not a partnership superimposed upon one nation by another.

While Congress claimed to speak for all India, the British government maintained that each minority – Muslims, Sikhs, Untouchables, Christians, Parsis, Europeans – must be protected and satisfied before self-rule could be granted. It was this issue, the representation of minorities, which provided some of the most difficult discussions at the conference. The Minorities Committee met, and Gandhi moved a week's adjournment with a view to having informal discussions with the parties concerned; but at the end he had to report 'with deep sorrow and deeper humiliation . . . utter failure to secure an agreed solution of the communal question'. He refused to accept Dr B.R. Ambedkar's claim to represent the Untouchables as a minority, for the Mahatma maintained that untouchability was a problem of Hinduism which the Hindus must heal, and that special representation would divide the communities. Ambedkar and Gandhi could not see eye to eye with each other throughout the conference, and after.

It was the Hindu-Muslim issue, however, that dominated the conference, and not surprisingly the British government could see immense possibilities in the chequered nature of the gathering, for it made it rather easy to set Hindu against Muslim, complicating the tangle by the intrusion of the Sikhs and the Untouchables. A Muslim League leader came near the truth when he said at the conference: 'It is the old maxim of "divide and rule". But there is a division of labour here. We divide and *you* rule.' Discussions in the Minorities Committee broke down over the question of separate electorates. With the exception of the Sikhs, all the other minorities, including the Untouchables, demanded them.

When Ramsay MacDonald in his speech on 13 November officially blessed the Minorities Pact and the Depressed Classes' demand for separate electorates as embodied in it, Gandhi refused to have anything to do with it. 'The Congress', he declared, 'will wander, no matter how many years, in the wilderness rather than lend itself to a proposal under which the hardy tree of freedom and responsible government can never grow.' He was particularly unhappy about the demand of the Untouchables for separate electorates outside the Hindu register which to him was the 'unkindest cut of all'. This, he pointed out, would make it certain that the Untouchables remained Untouchables in perpetuity, 'a perpetual bar sinister'. He would far rather that 'Hinduism died than that untouchability lived'.

During his three-month stay in London Gandhi spoke twelve times before the conference. In addition, he participated in its numerous lengthy proceedings. Outside St James's Palace his days were crowded, for there were speeches and interviews to be given, and correspondence to attend to. His interviews to the press alone totalled thirty-four. The following summary from the Mahatma's diary is indicative of a typical day's work:

|  | October 16, 1931 |
|---|---|
| 1:00 a.m. | Reach Kingsley Hall |
| 1:45 a.m. | Finish the spinning quota of 160 yards |
| 1:50 a.m. | Write up the diary |
| 2:00 a.m. to 3:45 a.m. | Sleep |
| 3:45 a.m. to 5:00 a.m. | Day begins with wash and prayer |
| 5:00 a.m. to 6:00 a.m. | Rest |
| 6:00 a.m. to 7:00 a.m. | Walk and give interview while walking |
| 7:00 a.m. to 8:00 a.m. | Morning ablutions and bath |
| 8:00 a.m. to 8:30 a.m. | Breakfast |
| 8:30 a.m. to 9:15 a.m. | Kingsley Hall to Knightsbridge |
| 9:15 a.m. to 10:45 a.m. | Interview with a journalist, an artist, a Sikh member of the delegation, and a merchant |
| 10:45 a.m. to 11:00 a.m. | To St James's Palace |
| 11:00 a.m. to 1:00 p.m. | At St James's (conference) |
| 1:00 p.m. to 2:45 p.m. | Luncheon with American journalists |
| 3:00 p.m. to 5:30 p.m. | With the Mohammedans |
| 5:30 p.m. to 7:00 p.m. | With the Secretary of State for India |
| 7:00 p.m. to 7:30 p.m. | Rush home for prayer and evening meal |
| 8:00 p.m. to 9:10 p.m. | Conference of Temperance Workers. Talk on the drink problem in India |
| 9:10 p.m. | Leave for an engagement with the Nawab of Bhopal |
| 9:45 p.m. to midnight | With the Nawab of Bhopal |

Despite the sort of politics he heard at the Palace, Gandhi was far from downcast. He knew that little was to be expected from the conference and that if his visit was to be of value it would be through a grass-roots dialogue with the people of England. His stay at Kingsley Hall and his rapport with the press went a long way to providing a touchstone of reality amidst the abstractions of diplomacy. At times, however, the press would exasperate him. George Slocombe, the well-known British journalist, whose coverage of the Salt Satyagraha movement had earned him kudos, wrote a story about Gandhi's generosity and said that when the Prince of Wales had visited India the Mahatma prostrated himself before 'the future Emperor of India'. The next time Gandhi saw Slocombe, he smiled and said: 'Well, Mr Slocombe, I should have expected you to know better. This does not even do credit to your imagination. I would bend the knee before the poorest Untouchable in India for having participated in crushing him for centuries. I would take the dust off his feet. But I would not prostrate myself, not even before the King, much less before the Prince of Wales, for the simple reason that he represented insolent might.'

In his intensive efforts to meet and understand the British people, he made several trips out of London, seeing more of England than ever before. He lived among the poor, but his fame and position assured him encounters with a wide range of British society.

He availed himself of an early opportunity of visiting Lancashire, a textile area, which was in the midst of a great depression partly because of the Indian boycott on foreign cloth. Despite this fact he was keen on discussing with the mill workers the conditions of the poor in India. The authorities were somewhat apprehensive about the trip and security measures were taken.

Gandhi spent two days in Lancashire and everywhere he listened with obvious attention and sympathy to those who were jobless before elaborating on the case for India. While Britain had three million unemployed, the vast majority of India's peasants were without work for half the year. The average Indian income was a tenth of what the British unemployed workers received as welfare benefit from the government. If England faced unemployment, India experienced starvation. 'If you went to the villages of India,' he explained, 'you would find utter despair in the eyes of the villagers, you would find half-starved skeletons, living corpses.' If India could revive them by putting life and food into them in the shape of work, it would help the world at large. Cheap British cloth was one of the causes of the decline of the cottage industries of India. A humane method, Gandhi added, was to give the peasants work with which they were familiar, which they could do in their cottages, which required no great investment in implements and the product of which could be easily sold. 'This is a task which is worthy of the attention even of Lancashire.'

Everywhere the reception accorded to Gandhi was friendly and at times even enthusiastic. 'We were prepared for courtesy,' he said afterwards. 'We were even prepared for a little bitterness which distress and misunderstanding often create; but we found instead a warmth of affection for which we were not prepared. I shall treasure the memory of these days to the end of my earthly existence.' Mirabehn, who accompanied him, described the scene which registered its culmination in the famous photograph of mill hands cheering the Mahatma:

> One of the most remarkable episodes was at a mill where Bapu was shown around by the manager, who, at the end of the inspection, asked Bapu if he might have the leave bell rung so that the mill hands, mostly women, might come out and meet Bapu.
> 'Of course, by all means,' Bapu said, and the bell was rung.
> Immediately the machinery was stopped and the building was filled with the sound of running feet. Across the rooms, along the passages, down the stairs they went, patter patter patter, and by the time we ourselves got outside, there was a large crowd of workers waiting. Bapu said a few words, then two of the women workers suddenly hooked him by the arms, one on each side, and throwing up their unengaged arms shouted, 'Three cheers for Mr Gandeye, hip, hip–.'
> 'Hurrah!' shouted the whole crowd, and then again, and once more, for the third and loudest time.

Gandhi did not limit himself to the poor; he spoke to the boys at Eton asking them to make, when they grew up, 'a unique contribution to the glory of your nation, by emancipating it from its sin of exploitation, and thus contribute to the progress of mankind'. At Oxford Dr A.D. Lindsay, the Master of Balliol College, invited leading scholars to have several discussions with Gandhi. The Mahatma was inevitably subjected to severe questioning. Professor Edward Thompson, the host of one of these gatherings, compared Gandhi to Socrates for his self-control and composure. 'For three hours', Thompson said, 'he was sifted and cross-examined by a group of trained minds, yet not for a moment was he rattled or at a loss.'

His encounters with intellectuals continued at Cambridge, and he spoke at the London School of Economics. He visited Canterbury at the invitation of its dean, Dr Hewlett Johnson. Asked whether he was hoping to convert Mr Gandhi to Christianity, the Dean replied: 'To convert him! He is one of the most Christ-like lives that I have yet come across.' Gandhi also had a talk on spiritual matters with Bishop Bell at Chichester. He valued these contacts with academics and learned clergy, for they gave him 'an insight into the working of the British mind which I could have got through no other means'. He spoke before such groups as the Temperance Council of Christian Churches, the Postal Workers' Union, the American Journalists' Association, the London Vegetarian Society, the School

Students' Union and the Indian Residents of London. When he spoke of British–Indian relations, his message was invariably the same. He wanted an honourable partnership with India in the Commonwealth, but by choice and not compulsion. 'I want to disabuse your minds of the notion', he declared at a meeting with a group of Members of Parliament, 'that the masses of India are enamoured of *Pax Britannica*. The truth is that they are anxious to throw off the British yoke simply because they do not want to starve.'

Although Gandhi, during his twelve-week stay in England, met people with a wide spectrum of political opinions, he was somewhat disappointed at not being able to have any communication with his most powerful political adversaries – Winston Churchill, Lord Rothermere and Lord Beaverbrook. They had not attempted to meet him, though he felt certain that if only he could talk with them alone they would appreciate his point of view. One day, as he was about to leave St James's Palace, a visiting card was brought to him. It was from Randolph Churchill but, to Gandhi's dismay, he had not come as his father's emissary but on a journalistic errand.

Gandhi's meeting with General Smuts was full of nostalgic memories of South Africa. 'I did not give you such a bad time as you gave me,' Smuts remarked. David Lloyd George, Britain's wartime prime minister, invited the Mahatma to his farm where they talked for several hours. George Bernard Shaw dropped in for a visit one day, referring to himself as the 'Mahatma Minor' and to Gandhi as the 'Mahatma Major'. When Shaw asked if the conference did not try his patience, Gandhi replied: 'It requires more than the patience of a Job. The whole thing is a huge camouflage, and harangues that we are treated to are meant only to mark time. Why not, I ask them, announce your policy and let us make our choice? But it does not seem to be in the English political nature to do so.' Another who desired a meeting was Charlie Chaplin. Gandhi was not a filmgoer and could not place the name, but when he learned that Chaplin had been born of a poor family in the East End of London, he gladly agreed to meet the actor. They had a pleasant discussion on the machine age and the Mahatma's attitude to it possibly inspired one of Chaplin's subsequent films.

An important social event of the season was the afternoon tea party on 5 November at Buckingham Palace to which all the Round Table Conference delegates were to be invited. Sir Samuel Hoare, the Secretary of State for India, wondered how King George V would receive the leader of the civil disobedience movement, so he had an audience with the King and cautiously touched on the subject. 'What! Have the rebel *fakir* in the Palace after he has been behind all these attacks on my loyal officers?' protested the King. He was equally averse to the prospect of having 'this little man' in the

Palace 'with no proper clothes on, and bare knees'. However, the helpless constitutional monarch had no option but to comply. Gandhi, for his part, had some qualms about the tea party, since he was feeling so 'heartsick and sore about the happenings in India' that he would rather not attend such function. But he accepted the invitation since it was essentially a courtesy extended to him as a guest.

He attended the party wearing his torn woollen shawl which had been mended with *khadi* cloth, and Sir Samuel Hoare presented him to the King. They had a gracious chat, but the King let the visitor know of his displeasure at his organization of the boycott of the Prince of Wales. 'Why did you boycott my son?' he finally asked. 'Not your son, Your Majesty, but the official representative of the British Crown,' Gandhi answered. The King proceeded to declare that he would not allow the stirring-up of any trouble in his empire. 'My government won't stand for it.' Gandhi maintained a dignified silence. He then said calmly: 'I must not be drawn into a political argument in Your Majesty's Palace after receiving Your Majesty's hospitality.'

From the strictly business point of view, Gandhi's visit to England was not productive at all but, as the *Manchester Guardian Weekly* observed, 'from the point of view of those who desire to promote understanding and sympathy between the peoples of the world, it was abundantly successful . . . he created wherever he went an atmosphere of friendship'. There were, however, people who felt otherwise. 'He is a perfect master of subtlety and has a greater passion for inconsistency than any other man I have ever met or heard of,' observed Sir Robert Craddock in the House of Commons. On alternate days he was Jekyll and Hyde, and 'on his day of silence, no one on earth knew whether he was Dr Jekyll or Mr Hyde'. Viscount Burnham remarked that 'Mr Gandhi has left our shores and carried his tortuosities with him, I sincerely hope, never to try our tempers and our patience again.'

The Round Table Conference accomplished very little toward constitution-building. The British capitalized on the communal tangle and very conveniently agreed to settle the question, if the Indians could not do it themselves. With tentative plans to meet again, the delegates appointed three committees to continue work until the next session. Charlie Andrews, who had done so much to get Gandhi around to meet the shapers of British opinion, called the conference a 'magnificent failure', but most of the magnificence had been provided by Gandhi, whose personal effect was enormous. 'No serious-minded man or woman,' observed Andrews, 'could any longer take the view, which had been widely held before, that Mahatma Gandhi was only an impossible fanatic after all.'

In his final speech before the conference, addressed to 'Prime Minister and Friends', Gandhi's main theme, as on previous occasions, was India's independence. He conceded that without the problem of minorities being solved there could be no *swaraj* for India, but he attributed this difficulty to the wedge in the shape of foreign rule. Economically, eighty per cent of the country's resources were mortgaged irretrievably for the benefit of the ruling power, resulting in the 'complete cramping of India'. Gandhi's speech lasted seventy minutes. He declared:

Speaker after speaker [in this conference] has got up and said that India should achieve her liberty through negotiation, by argument, and that it will be the greatest glory of Great Britain if Great Britain yields to India's demands by argument. But the Congress does not hold that view, quite. The Congress has an alternative which is unpleasant to you . . . For the sake of liberty people have fought, people have lost their lives, people have killed and have sought death at the hands of those whom they have sought to oust. The Congress then comes upon the scene and devises a new method not known to history, namely, that of civil disobedience . . . and I am told that that is a method that no government in the world will tolerate. Well, of course, the government may not tolerate, no government has tolerated open rebellion. No government may tolerate civil disobedience, but governments have to succumb to even these forces . . . It is this thing which weighs me down . . . the choice that lies before Indians, the parting of the ways . . . Whilst there is yet a little sand left in the glass, I want you to understand what this Congress stands for . . . But so long as there is not that one mind, that one definition, not one implication for the same word that you and I and we may be using, so long there is no compromise possible.

I do not want to revive civil disobedience. I want to turn the truce that was arrived at, at Delhi, into a permanent settlement. But for heaven's sake give me, a frail man, sixty-two years gone, a little bit of a chance. Find a little corner for him and the organization which he represents . . . If you will work the Congress for all it is worth, then you would say goodbye to terrorism; then you will not need terrorism. Today you have to fight the school of terrorists which is there with your disciplined and organized terrorism, because you will be blind to the facts or the writing on the wall.

I ask you not to try the patience of a people known to be proverbially patient . . . A nation of 350 million people does not need the dagger of the assassin, it does not need the poison bowl, it does not need the sword, the spear or the bullet. It needs simply a will of its own, an ability to say 'No', and that nation is today learning to say 'No' . . . This is, perhaps, the last time that I shall be sitting with you at negotiations. It is not that I want that. I want to sit at the same table with you and negotiate and plead with you and to go on bended knees before I take the final leap and final plunge.

No matter what befalls me, no matter what the fortunes may be of this Round

Table Conference, one thing I shall certainly carry with me – that is, that from high to low I have found nothing but the utmost courtesy and the utmost affection. I consider that it was well worth my paying this visit to England in order to find this human affection . . . I am carrying with me thousands upon thousands of English friendships. I do not know them, but I read that affection in their eyes as early in the morning I walk through your streets. All this hospitality, all this kindness will never be effaced from my memory no matter what befalls my unhappy land.

He was invited all over England, Scotland, Wales and Ireland, but had to refuse far more invitations than he could accept. There had been serious plans for an extensive lecture tour, and there were also numerous urgent requests for an American visit, which, however, he was obliged to decline, for he had work to do in India. On the morning of 5 December Gandhi boarded a train at Victoria Station. His entourage included his son, Devadas, Mirabehn, Muriel Lester, his secretaries Mahadev Desai and Pyarelal, and two powerfully built British detectives, Sergeant Evans and Sergeant Rogers. Evans and Rogers who had guarded Gandhi throughout his stay in London were now, at his request, accompanying him on the journey across Europe. 'They are part of my family,' said the Mahatma. His plan was to spend the night in Paris and then proceed to Villeneuve in Switzerland for a visit to Romain Rolland, the author of *Mahatma Gandhi*, the book that had made him a household name all over Europe. After a few days in Switzerland he would travel on to Rome, and after meeting Mussolini and the Pope would take ship to India.

When the party reached Boulogne after the short sea voyage from Folkestone they were treated with the utmost courtesy by French officials, who found it unnecessary to check their passports and waived examination of their numerous unwieldy parcels tied up with string. Large crowds gathered at the Gare du Nord in Paris to welcome Gandhi and there was pandemonium when he emerged from the train. A few hours later he addressed a public meeting organized in a cinema theatre, and the following morning took the train for the onward journey.

It was cold and wet when Gandhi arrived at Villeneuve, and since Romain Rolland had just recovered from bronchitis he could not go down to the railroad station to greet the Mahatma. Rolland, who wrote his biography in 1923, had never actually met Gandhi. He knew the Mahatma from long conversations with Tagore and C.F. Andrews, and had also read Gandhi's works. Rolland describes the meeting at Villa Olga, one of the two villas he possessed on the lake shore:

The little man, bespectacled and toothless, was wrapped in his white burnous, but his legs, thin as a heron's stilts, were bare. His shaven head with its few coarse hairs was uncovered and wet with rain. He came to me with a dry laugh, his mouth open like a good dog panting, and flinging an arm round me leaned his cheek against my shoulder. I felt his grizzled head against my cheek. It was, I amuse myself thinking, the kiss of St Dominic and St Francis.

The next day being a Monday was a day of silence for Gandhi, and while Rolland delivered a long talk on the tragic moral and social state of Europe since 1900, his guest listened and scribbled notes. On Tuesday they conversed. On the following two days Gandhi made short excursions to Lausanne and Geneva where he addressed public meetings. At each of the two meetings organized by Swiss pacifists he was subjected to prolonged heckling by atheists and others, but he answered them calmly. He also expounded Truth-Force (Satyagraha) to Pierre Ceresole, the founder of the International Voluntary Service for Peace. 'Tell us what qualities you think a leader of this age would need?' Ceresole asked. 'Realization of God every minute of the twenty-four hours,' the Mahatma replied.

Rolland and Gandhi resumed their discussions on the state of Europe, and art, and nonviolence, and God – an eternal principle, Gandhi said, not a person in the anthropomorphic sense. 'This is why I say that Truth is God. Even the atheists do not doubt the necessity of truth.' On the subject of art, he expressed the view that art and truth ought to be synonymous. 'I am against the formula, "Art for art's sake". For me all art must be based on truth. I reject beautiful things if, instead of expressing truth, they express untruth.' He agreed with Rolland that 'Art brings joy and is good', but he would accept this only on the condition he mentioned. 'To achieve truth in art,' Gandhi added, 'I do not expect exact reproductions of external things. Only living things bring joy to the soul and must elevate the soul.' Rolland was inclined to agree but he stressed the pain of searching for truth and for God. Rolland later said that he thought Gandhi's God found pleasure in man's sorrows.

After a few days' absorbing discussions Rolland observed in his diary:

I have a feeling today that Gandhi's path is so sharply marked out, and in many things so distinct from mine, that we have little to discuss with one another. Each knows exactly where he is going, and Gandhi's path is perfect for himself and his people. I would not wish that it were different, I admire and love him like that.

In a letter to a friend in America, Rolland said:

His mind proceeds through successive experiments into action and he follows a straight line, but he never stops, and one would risk an error in attempting to judge him by what he said ten years ago because his thought is in constant revolution.

On his last evening in Switzerland Gandhi asked his host to play him some Beethoven. Accordingly Romain Rolland played a piano transcription of the *andante* of the Fifth Symphony representing, as he explained, the triumph of the heroic will over the deepest gloom, for it came closest to his concept of Gandhi's personality. He also played, as an encore of his own accord, the Dance of the Blessed Spirits from Gluck's *Orphée et Eurydice*. The Mahatma revealed an expert knowledge of Indian religious chants, but Rolland's rendering of tender dream-like compositions left him unmoved and detached. 'He does not understand Beethoven, but he knows that Beethoven has been the intermediary between Mira [Madeleine Slade] and me, and consequently between Mira and himself,' Romain Rolland wrote a few days later.

Rolland was still weak as a result of his recent illness, but he insisted on taking Gandhi and his party to the railroad station. 'What would you like me to do in grateful memory of your visit?' he asked. 'Come and meet India,' Gandhi replied, and then they embraced as they had done when they first met.

From Villeneuve Gandhi went to Rome. Politely declining an invitation to be the guest of the Italian government, he stayed with General Moris, a friend of Rolland, but had an audience with Mussolini. It was the usual custom for visitors to walk straight from the guarded doorway into a huge hall to the massive desk at the farthest end, where Mussolini sat in stately eminence. On this occasion, however, Il Duce walked down the hall to receive and escort the visitor. They spoke about India, without coming to any conclusions. Mussolini asked Gandhi's opinion of the Fascist state, and he replied: 'You are building a house of cards.' The interview lasted about fifteen minutes. In another unusual gesture Mussolini accompanied Gandhi to the door. Some time later, when asked what impression Il Duce had made on him, Gandhi answered: 'He has the eyes of a cat . . . they move about in every direction as if in constant rotation . . . He looks so menacing even when he smiles.'

Gandhi was taken to the Rome–Naples rugby match and to a parade of well-drilled Balilla, the military organization of Fascist youth. When a Fascist official called upon him to address them, he said: 'I am glad to see you all hale and hearty.' His words were then translated for the armed youth. He would not say any more, for he was appalled by the sight of a gun carriage being dragged along by boys ten or eleven years old.

Tolstoy's daughter was in the city, and Gandhi sought her out for a long talk about Tolstoy. The seventeen-year-old Princess Maria came with an offering of figs which had been carefully wrapped and placed in the basket by the Queen of Italy. The Pope would not see him, probably for political reasons. But on a day when all other visitors were excluded he made the round of the Vatican, savouring the library and spending two happy hours in St Peter's. In the Sistine Chapel he stood before a life-size Christ on the Cross and was moved to tears.

As he was about to step aboard the SS *Pilsna* at Brindisi, Gandhi was offered milk from a cup dating from the fifth century BC. 'Is it goat's milk?' he asked. 'It is goat's milk,' several voices testified. He bade goodbye to the two British detectives, Evans and Rogers. Later he sent the detectives presents of their choice – silver watches with Gandhi's name engraved on them.

# THIRTY-TWO

# Crusade Against Untouchability

When the SS *Pilsna* docked in Bombay on the morning of 28 December 1931, Gandhi was accorded a hero's welcome. It was another of his silent Mondays, but he had to make an exception. Following his press conference, he joined the Working Committee in private, and heard what had been happening while he was at sea. Delhi was already using its Emergency Powers Ordinances in the North-West Frontier Province, the United Provinces and Bengal to deal with a widespread no-rent movement and minor terrorist outbreaks. The new ordinances empowered the military to seize buildings, impound bank accounts, confiscate wealth, arrest suspects without a warrant, suspend court trials, and prohibit picketing and boycotting. The Irwin-Gandhi Pact was badly bruised. Lord Willingdon found it rather unpalatable that Congress should aspire to become an alternative government. On the day of Gandhi's return, Jawaharlal Nehru and Abdul Ghaffar Khan were already in prison. That evening Gandhi addressed a mammoth crowd of two hundred thousand, reaching all of them through loudspeakers. Referring to the arrests and ordinances he said with an uncharacteristic touch of bitter humour: 'I take it these are all Christmas gifts from Lord Willingdon, our Christian Viceroy.' He spoke about the government's attempt to 'unman a whole race'. He would not flinch from 'sacrificing a million lives for India's liberty'. Yet he would spare no effort to continue his dialogue with the government. In any case Gandhi was all the more likely to be arrested, for during his voyage, the *Giornale d'Italia* had published an interview, purported to have been given by him, in which he was said to have announced the immediate resumption of the struggle to free India from the British yoke. This was quoted in the *Times*, and although Gandhi cabled from Aden to Sir Samuel Hoare, the Secretary of State for India, a categorical denial of the report, the harm had been done.

The day after his arrival, Gandhi sent a telegram to the Viceroy, apprising him of the Congress viewpoint on the prevailing situation. Referring to the new repressive ordinances, he wrote:

I do not know whether I am to regard these as an indication that friendly relations between us are closed, or whether you expect me still to see you and receive guidance from you as to the course I am to pursue in advising the Congress. I would esteem a wire in reply.

In his reply two days later, Lord Willingdon stressed that the ordinances were justified by the activities of Congress against the government, and that therefore there was very little to discuss. Nevertheless, if Gandhi insisted on a meeting, he was prepared to give his views 'as to the way in which you can best exert your influence to maintain the spirit of cooperation, which animated the proceedings of the Round Table Conference'. Gandhi replied that in his opinion, the constitutional issues had dwindled into insignificance in the face of the ordinances and action taken thereunder. Cooperation from Congress could not be demanded 'without returning any on behalf of the government'. He wrote about the possibility of another non-violent noncooperation campaign. 'I believe that civil disobedience is not only the natural right of a people, especially when they have no effective voice in their own government, but that it is also a substitute for violence and armed rebellion.' The Viceroy could not discern much difference between an armed rebellion and its substitute, and consequently could not invite Gandhi 'with the hope of any advantage, to an interview held under the threat of the resumption of civil disobedience'. Gandhi could not see the Viceroy's viewpoint, for had not Lord Irwin negotiated under a similar threat? There were veiled threats and counterthreats in their exchange of carefully worded telegrams. In a public statement on 2 January 1932, Gandhi declared that the government had banged the door in his face. He spent the following day working on messages to various groups and writing letters, including one to Tagore whom he urged to give his best 'to the sacrificial fire that is being lighted'.

In the small hours of 4 January, Devadas woke his father with the news that two police cars were waiting outside. Gandhi smiled, but said nothing; it was Monday again, another day of silence. Mirabehn collected the belongings he would need in prison – a pair of sandals, a mattress, a portable spinning wheel, extra clothing and food. He was arrested, as after the Salt March, under Regulation XXV of 1827, which permitted him to be detained during the pleasure of the government.

Gandhi was taken to Yeravda jail with Vallabhbhai Patel as his fellow prisoner. Subhas Chandra Bose and Mahadev Desai were arrested about the same time, and after several weeks Mahadev was allowed to join the Mahatma. Soon after Gandhi vanished into Yeravda, the Viceroy struck at his followers with much force, the result of long and meticulous planning. Congress organizations were closed and leading Congressmen all over

India put behind bars. Soon more ordinances empowered the government still further, covering, as the Secretary of State for India put it, 'almost every activity of Indian life'. Sir Samuel Hoare told the House of Commons that there would be 'no drawn battle this time'. Churchill praised the new measures as 'more drastic than any that were required since the Mutiny of 1857'. Despite the repression, large-scale boycott and civil disobedience movement were desperately renewed. In January and February the authorities, armed with a 'Civil Disobedience Manual', convicted over thirty thousand people of political offences. Many more arrests followed as the movement gained momentum. The police were ordered to use their *lathis* without restraint. Firing was resorted to in a number of towns and cities, some persons were killed and thousands were injured. Romain Rolland, in a letter to an English friend, wrote: 'If the India of Satyagraha were to go down in the battle, it is Christ himself who would be pierced by it, with a supreme lance-thrust, on the Cross. And this time there would be no resurrection.'

At Yeravda, as during his previous terms, Gandhi devoted a great deal of his time to reading, writing and spinning. He was pleased to have Patel as a companion. Patel had a distinct authoritarian streak which, in prison in the company of the Mahatma, he had little opportunity to exhibit. On occasions, however, he would not fail to display his wit, and in so doing he could be utterly frank. Once Gandhi said: 'I give you permission to fast.' Patel shrugged his shoulders. 'What is the use of giving me permission?' he replied. 'If I fast, they will let me die. If you fast, they will go to no end of trouble to keep you alive.'

Meanwhile the British government announced that it was drawing up its new scheme for a communal electorate. At the Round Table Conference, when the claims of the minorities were presented, Gandhi had declared that he would 'resist with all my life' the granting of separate electorate to the Untouchables, the Depressed Classes or Scheduled Castes. He was not against their representation in legislature, but held that their separate identity would 'vivisect and disrupt Hinduism'. In a letter to the Secretary of State for India he asserted that 'the separate electorate is neither a penance nor any remedy for the crushing degradation they have groaned under'. He took the opportunity of informing His Majesty's Government that 'in the event of their decision creating a separate electorate for the Depressed Classes, I must fast unto death'.

The Secretary of State replied that Gandhi's views would be fully taken into account before the final decision was taken. 'I can only say that we intend to give any decision that may be necessary, solely and only upon the merit of the case,' he added.

It appeared to be a satisfactory reply, and the threat of a fast unto death was thus held in abeyance for some months. Gandhi kept himself occupied with his routine and made full use of his special privileges to write and receive correspondence, but when the jail superintendent, Major Martin, bought for him furniture and other creature comforts, he was not too happy. Major Martin explained that he had permission from the central authorities to spend a minimum of three hundred rupees a month on such an honoured guest 'But this money comes from the Indian treasury,' Gandhi protested, 'and I do not want to increase the burden of my country. I hope my boarding expenses will not exceed thirty-five rupees a month.' Martin had no option but to remove the special equipment.

About this time Mahadev Desai, Gandhi's first secretary and disciple, was transferred from another jail to Yeravda. Gandhi had asked for his companionship. Desai and the Mahatma would have long discussions on various subjects – God, religion, Brahmacharya, birth control. Desai kept a diary and rarely failed to record anything relating to his master. 'Birth control has no place in India,' Gandhi declared. 'Millions are physically and mentally enfeebled, and if sex is given a loose rein, it will constitute an impossible bar to progress.' He spoke of children as a burden, a punishment for the sins of their parents. 'As a man sows so should he be ready to reap,' he said. 'If he gratifies his instinct, let him bear the burden of children.'

In Yeravda Gandhi received a particularly taunting letter from Harilal, his eldest son, who drank heavily, chased women and appeared to enjoy the prospect of displeasing his father. For many years Gandhi had felt that his own lustful life in the past was the cause of Harilal's conduct. In his reply to Harilal he expressed hope of his reformation 'even as I do not despair of myself'.

On 17 August 1932, Ramsay MacDonald, the British Prime Minister, published a provisional scheme of minority representation, commonly known as the Communal Award, defining separate electorates for Muslims, Sikhs, Europeans, Christians and the Untouchables. The weightage allowed to their representation would reduce the majority Hindu community to a minority in the Central Assembly. But Gandhi's prime objection to the scheme was the suggestion of separation of the Untouchables from the Hindu fold. He promptly informed 'Dear Friend' Ramsay MacDonald of his resolve to resist the scheme of a separate electorate for the Depressed Classes by resorting to a perpetual fast unto death, which he would commence on 20 September:

It may be that my judgement is warped and that I am wholly in error in regarding separate electorate for Depressed Classes as harmful to them or Hinduism. If so, I am not likely to be in the right with reference to other parts of my philosophy of life. In that case my death by fasting will be at once a penance for my error and a lifting of a weight from off those numberless men and women who have childlike faith in my wisdom. Whereas if my judgement is right, as I have little doubt it is, the contemplated step is but due to the fulfilment of the scheme of life, which I have tried for more than a quarter of a century, apparently not without considerable success.

The Prime Minister replied that the Award did not separate the Untouchables completely. Each of them would have two votes, one in his special group, the other with the Hindus. He added that the alternative method of reserving a number of seats for Untouchable legislators within the larger block of Hindu seats had been rejected because 'in practically all cases, such members would be elected by a majority consisting of higher caste Hindus', and consequently they might not be 'in a position to speak for themselves', MacDonald said he could not understand why Gandhi should starve himself to death 'solely to prevent the Depressed Classes, who admittedly suffer from terrible disabilities today, from being able to secure a limited number of representatives of their own choosing in the legislatures . . .'

Gandhi answered that he objected to the whole communal scheme, but the Untouchable question was one of religious principle. 'In the establishment of a separate electorate for the Depressed Classes,' he wrote, 'I sense the injection of poison that is calculated to destroy Hinduism and to do no good to the Depressed Classes. You will please permit me to say that no matter how sympathetic you may be, you cannot come to a correct decision on a matter of such vital and religious importance to the parties concerned.' Gandhi was not even against over-representation of the Untouchables whom he had started calling Harijans, or 'Children of God'. What he objected to was their statutory separation from the Hindu fold, so long as they chose to belong to it. Moreover, their outcaste status would be written into the constitution, which would certainly undo all the work of Hindu reformers. Therefore he must proceed with his fast.

MacDonald was puzzled and offended. Many Indians were equally perplexed and critical of Gandhi's decision to fast unto death. 'I felt angry with him,' Nehru wrote in his autobiography, 'at his religious and sentimental approach to a political issue, and his frequent references to God in connection with it.' Bose commented that all rational thinking had been suspended. Ambedkar, leader of the Depressed Classes, described the fast as a 'political stunt'.

Gandhi could clearly see the Untouchables' bitter opposition to a joint electorate. 'They have the right to distrust me,' he said. Did he not belong to a so-called superior caste which had over the centuries despised and shunned them? 'The marvel is that they have remained nevertheless in the Hindu fold.' He explained that the fast was not meant to coerce the British, but to sting Hindu consciences and inspire action.

The announcement of Gandhi's decision to fast to death resulted in a countrywide demand for the revision of the Communal Award. The caste Hindus now became concerned, not because they felt ashamed of their record of having treated the Untouchables like lepers but mainly because the life of Gandhi, their great political emancipator, was in danger. Sir Tej Bahadur Sapru, the eminent constitutional leader, appealed to the government to release Gandhi; Rajendra Prasad suggested that Hindus save the Mahatma by letting the Untouchables into their temples and schools; Pandit Madan Mohan Malaviya summoned a conference of Hindu leaders for 19 September. Over one hundred delegates attended; Rajagopalachari asked the country to pray and fast on 20 September.

Before that fateful day dawned, Gandhi wrote to Tagore saying he would enter the 'fiery gates' at noon, and asking for his blessing. Tagore, who was critical of Gandhi's *khadi* programme, had more respect for his efforts on behalf of the Untouchables. While Gandhi's letter still waited to be dispatched, a telegram from the poet was received: 'It is worth sacrificing precious life for the sake of India's unity and her social integrity. Our sorrowing hearts will follow your sublime penance with reverence and love.'

On 20 September Gandhi said his morning prayer and took his usual breakfast of milk and fruit. This was followed between 6.30 and 8.00 by the recital from the *Bhagavad Gita*. At 11.30 he took his last meal, of lemon juice and honey, and at noon, as the jail clock struck the hour, he reclined on a cot in the shade of a low mango tree in the quiet prison yard. Patel and Mahadev Desai sat near him. Mrs Sarojini Naidu had been transferred from the women's section of Yeravda jail to take care of him. He read and wrote and sipped water with a dash of salt or soda bicarbonate. In the evening, breaking all precedent, he was permitted to give his first interview to the press since entering the prison. In a low voice he spoke of himself as a touchable by birth, but an 'untouchable by choice'. It was his ambition to represent and identify himself with people on the lowest rung of society.

What I want, and what I am living for, and what I should delight in dying for, is the eradication of untouchability root and branch ... I believe that if untouchability is really rooted out, it will not only purge Hinduism of a terrible blot but its repercussion will be world-wide. My fight against untouchability is a fight against the impure in humanity.

Millions of Indians fasted for twenty-four hours. Throughout the country prayers were sung. Hindu leaders gathered at the Bombay residence of G.D. Birla, Gandhi's wealthy industrialist friend, for talks with Ambedkar, who appeared adamant. MacDonald had implied that Britain would accept an alternative solution if Hindus and Untouchables could agree on it. On the morning of 21 September a meeting was held in the prison office, attended by Sapru, Jayakar, Birla, Rajendra Prasad, Rajagopalachari, Gandhi, Patel and Mahadev Desai. Terms to be offered to Ambedkar were discussed. Gandhi had not yet seen Ambedkar and was therefore unable to ascertain whether they were acceptable. He was already feeling weak. To avoid further strain, it was decided to let him stay in his cot under the mango tree. Soon the Hindu leaders again hurried off to Bombay for further discussions with Ambedkar.

Dr B.R. Ambedkar, a brilliant lawyer, was a hard bargainer and his intense dislike for the caste-ridden Hindu society made negotiations all the more difficult. In his opinion, the outcaste was the by-product of the caste system. 'There will be outcastes as long as there are castes,' he said. 'Nothing can emancipate the outcaste except the destruction of the caste system. Nothing can help to save Hindus and ensure their survival in the coming struggle except the purging of the Hindu faith of this odious and vicious dogma.'

When Ambedkar and Gandhi met at Yeravda for a brief discussion, several of the Hindu leaders involved in the earlier talks were present. Ambedkar now had second thoughts about the legislators who would be elected jointly by the Hindu and Harijan votes. If a Harijan denounced Hindus too severely, the Hindus might defeat him in the next election and elect a more docile Untouchable. As the Hindu leaders parleyed with Ambedkar, occasionally consulting with the sinking Mahatma, an agreement appeared nowhere in sight. On the fourth day of the fast Gandhi's condition took a dangerous turn. His blood pressure was alarmingly high, he could no longer walk and had to be carried to the bathroom. His wife was hastily transferred from Sabarmati jail to be with him. As the Hindu leaders groped for a formula, it was becoming apparent that Sapru's suggestion, made at an earlier meeting, might be more acceptable to Ambedkar. On this basis, the Hindu leaders proposed that the number of seats reserved for the Depressed Classes in the provincial legislatures should be raised to 171 (MacDonald had proposed 71). The Hindus and the Depressed Classes would vote together, but the Harijans would first choose in primary elections a panel of four candidates for each seat, from which final selection would be made by the general body of Hindu voters. Accordingly, the Hindus would have no option but to vote for one of them. This plan would also prevent the caste Hindus from keeping the bold ones out of politics; the system of joint electorates would thus be retained as well.

While Ambedkar accepted the proposed formula in principle, there still remained some technicalities relating to the time period in which the separate primaries were to be abolished. Gandhi had by now entered the dangerous phase of his fast, and it was feared that paralysis might set in. When Ambedkar called on him, the Mahatma made an impassioned appeal for mutual trust and goodwill. 'You have a perfect right to demand cent per cent security by statutory safeguards,' he told Ambedkar. 'But, from my fiery bed I beg of you not to insist upon the right. I am here today to ask for a reprieve of my caste Hindu brethren.'

Ambedkar insisted that the question of reserved seats should be settled by referendum of the Depressed Classes after twenty-five years – he was not too hopeful of untouchability disappearing in a hurry. 'Five years or my life,' Gandhi said. Ambedkar returned to his Harijan colleagues and later informed the Hindu leaders that a period of less than ten years would not be acceptable. At this stage Rajagopalachari, the famous Madras lawyer, managed to secure Ambedkar's agreement that the timescale for abolition of the primaries would be determined in further discussion. This might make a referendum unnecessary. When the new arrangement was explained to Gandhi he found it satisfactory. As usual, he would yield unexpectedly on details, so long as he saved the principle.

On 24 September 1932, the agreement known as the Yeravda Pact was drafted and signed by all the chief Hindu and Harijan negotiators except Gandhi. It was ratified the following day at a joint conference. The British government had next to be persuaded to modify their Communal Award in accordance with this agreement. The text of the Yeravda Pact was therefore cabled to London, where C.F Andrews and Henry Polak were to submit it to the Prime Minister and get prompt action from the government. The Mahatma's life was ebbing away fast It was Sunday and ministers had left town, while MacDonald was at a funeral in Sussex. On hearing of the Yeravda agreement, the Prime Minister hurried back to 10 Downing Street and conferred with Sir Samuel Hoare till midnight. A few hours later the British government announced simultaneously in London and New Delhi that it had approved the Yeravda Pact.

Gandhi lay still on his cot in the courtyard. Patel, Mahadev Desai, Kasturbai and Mrs Naidu sat near him, saying nothing, for they were afraid to weaken him further. He was in no mood to end the fast without seeing the official document. Tagore, who had hurried across the whole width of India to Poona, was overcome with emotion when he visited Gandhi at noon. He had heard the news about the signing of the Yeravda Pact. 'I have come floating on the tide of good news,' he said. They talked for a while, very softly, and at last seeing that the strain of conversation was proving too much for the Mahatma, the poet moved away.

At four o'clock on Monday afternoon Colonel Doyle, the Inspector General of Prisons, arrived and having handed over the long-awaited document to Gandhi, promptly slipped away. Gandhi went through it carefully and then passed it on to the leaders present. He felt it was only proper that the document should first go to Ambedkar for approval. His friends protested that this could mean another conference. 'Then a conference it must be,' he replied. Finally, realizing that the document contained as complete an acceptance of the Yeravda Pact as could be expected, he agreed, though with misgivings, to break the fast A large audience surrounded Gandhi as the poet Rabindranath Tagore led the prayers by singing one of the Bengali hymns from his *Gitanjali*:

> When my heart is dry and parched,
> come with a merciful shower.
> When grace is lost from life, come
> with a burst of song.
>
> When tumultuous work raises its din
> on all sides shutting me out from beyond,
> come to me, my lord of silence, with
> thy peace and rest.
>
> When my beggarly heart sits crouched,
> shut in a corner, break open the door,
> my king, and come with the ceremony
> of a king.
>
> When desire blinds the mind with
> delusion and dust, O thou holy one,
> thou wakeful, come with thy light and
> thy thunder.

Then everyone sang Gandhi's favourite hymn, 'Vaishnava Jana', and the Mahatma broke his fast by accepting a glass of orange juice from Kasturbai.

The fast had focused caste Hindu attention on the Untouchables to such an extent that all across the country Hindus opened their temple doors to the Harijans, allowed them to use village water wells, and, in some cases, even touched them and broke bread with them. Resolutions against discrimination were rushed to Yeravda and piled five feet high in Gandhi's prison yard. During the six days of fast most Hindus were swept by a spirit of reform, penance and self-purification. This was followed by the observance of Untouchability Abolition Week. Soon the temple doors would be closed again; the work required to bring about an end to untouchability in India had only just begun. The fast could not result in the demise of untouchability, but it would never be the same again. Orthodox Hinduism was shaken.

Three days after the end of the fast, the authorities at Yeravda jail were given new instructions that Gandhi should no longer be entitled to special facilities. He could receive no more visitors. This did not upset him, but he could not bear the thought of being unable to contribute to the welfare of Untouchables. In November, after a lengthy correspondence with the government, some of the facilities were restored on the understanding that they would be used for work for the Untouchables. He founded, with the financial backing of G.D. Birla, an eight-page weekly, *Harijan,* which replaced *Young India,* suspended by the government. Through the columns of the new journal he began propagating his views on untouchability and answering numerous critics who complained that he was allowing himself to neglect the national struggle for freedom. The British authorities were, no doubt, delighted that his present work had taken his mind off *swaraj,* and nonviolent noncooperation. The civil disobedience movement was now continuing at a low ebb.

Gandhi was soon dissatisfied with the progress of his anti-untouchability work. 'A tempest has been raging within me for some days,' he said, 'and I have been struggling against it.' He announced that he would undertake a twenty-one-day fast as a 'heart prayer for purification of self and associates, for greater vigilance and watchfulness' in connection with the Harijan cause. His associates implored him not to refuse the gift of life, but the Mahatma could not go against 'God's peremptory command'.

At noon on 8 May 1933, the fast began under the mango tree in the prison yard. A few hours later the government published a communiqué stating that considering the nature and object of the fast, it had decided to set him at liberty. They did not want to be held accountable for his death. The release put Gandhi under a tremendous burden and strain, for he characteristically felt morally bound, at least for some time, not to prosecute the civil disobedience. Accordingly, he suspended the movement for six weeks. Many Congress leaders found this decision quite disagreeable, particularly when the communiqué had clearly stated that 'the release of Gandhi had no connection with the government's general policy'. The ordinances still remained and there were no plans for the release of other political prisoners. Vithalbhai Patel and Bose, who were abroad at this time, issued a vigorous statement, declaring that Gandhi had failed as a political leader and that the time had come for a radical reorganization of Congress 'on a new principle, with a new method, for which a new leader is essential'. Vithalbhai Patel soon died of heart trouble in a Swiss clinic near Geneva. Bose would have a protracted confrontation with the Mahatma.

Meanwhile Gandhi's health deteriorated. The famous 'epic fast' had lasted only six days, and it seemed unlikely that he could survive twenty-one days. He looked like a skeleton and at times was lost in a trance. Yet he handled it calmly. At noon on 29 May he broke the fast with the usual ritual of prayers, a hymn and a glass of orange juice. He announced that on the expiry of the present suspension, the civil-disobedience movement would be suspended for another six weeks. As soon as he had sufficiently recovered, he called an informal meeting of leading Congressmen at Poona and received their authority to seek an interview with the Viceroy to explore the possibilities of honourable peace. He wanted to 'take up the thread at the point where I was interrupted on my return from England'. Lord Willingdon declined to see him unless civil disobedience was definitely withdrawn. 'If I resort to non-cooperation or civil disobedience,' Gandhi wrote to the Viceroy, 'it is for establishing true and voluntary cooperation, in obedience to laws in the place of forced cooperation and forced obedience.' He expressed the hope that his request for an interview would be granted. The Viceroy replied that in his opinion civil disobedience was a movement 'intended to coerce the government by means of unlawful activities' and, therefore, there could be no question of holding a conversation with a representative of an association which had not abandoned that movement. Peace efforts having failed, it was decided to continue the struggle in another form. All those willing and able to offer individual civil disobedience were invited to do so. About this time Gandhi announced to his followers that he proposed to disband the Sabarmati ashram, which had been his home for eighteen years. The most compelling reason for this decision was the realization that the time had now come when the constructive programme of the ashram could no longer be carried on with any measure of certainty unless the community ceased to have anything to do with the campaign. 'To accept such a position', Gandhi observed, 'will be to deny its creed.' He handed over its land and buildings to a recently established Untouchable group called Harijan Sevak Sangh.

On 1 August he set out with the departing ashramites, Kasturbai and Mahadev Desai among them, to preach civil resistance to the Gujarati peasants. The marchers had not gone far when they were arrested. Gandhi was promptly taken back to Poona and lodged in Yeravda jail, only to be released three days later and ordered to remain within the limits of Poona. He rejected the restraint order, was arrested again, sentenced to one year's imprisonment and confined once more in Yeravda jail. During the brief trial he gave his occupation as 'a spinner, weaver and farmer', and his permanent address as 'Yeravda Jail'.

Now that he was a convict, not a mere detainee, the government refused to extend to him the unrestricted facilities which he had enjoyed previously for carrying on Harijan work. 'The strain of deprivation of this is becoming unbearable,' he wrote to the government of Bombay. 'Life ceases to interest me, if I may not do Harijan work without let or hindrance.' In the absence of a favourable response from the government, he embarked on another fast unto death on 16 August 1933. This time, after just a few days' fasting, he was a physical wreck. He seemed to have lost all will to live, refused to sip water, and was removed to the Sassoon Hospital in so precarious a condition that the government unconditionally released him.

In September he was well enough to be removed to Wardha, a small town in the Central Provinces, where he set up his new base in a small ashram established by his follower, Vinoba Bhave. Once more Gandhi was in a dilemma. He visualized the scenario of going to jail again, the government denying him the privileges to do Harijan work, leading to another fast. He felt that he ought not to be a party to such an 'undignified cat-and-mouse game' with the government. The problem was solved by his decision to devote the remaining period of his one-year sentence exclusively to Harijan work – 'the breath of life for me, more precious than daily bread'.

From Wardha, in November, he set out on a ten-month tour for Harijan welfare, in which he travelled over twelve thousand miles: from town to town, from village to village, holding meetings, preaching against untouchability, and collecting money for the Harijan cause. 'Mere money will not avail,' he would say. 'I must have your hearts also.' He organized informal dinners and concerts bringing Harijans and caste Hindus together. Gandhi's visit would herald the ceremonial opening of temples to the Harijans, though when he had gone on to the next town, the temples were sometimes closed again. There were always large crowds to greet him. They would listen to him politely, but usually seemed to be more interested in having his *darshan* than in following his teachings.

On 15 January 1934, a large section of Bihar province suffered a devastating earthquake. In a matter of a few minutes whole towns were razed to the ground, rivers changed their courses, bridges were twisted, railroad tracks damaged and the rails suspended in mid air. An area of thirty thousand square miles was affected. Fifteen thousand people lay dead; many more were injured. In March Gandhi interrupted his tour to visit the stricken area. He walked from village to village, inspecting the relief work and asking people to put all their energies into reconstruction, reminding them all the while of the curse of untouchability. He spoke of the earthquake in Bihar as a divine judgement on untouchability. The earthquake, he told the public, 'is a chastisement for your sins', chiefly 'the sin of untouchability'. Enlightened Indians were not in agreement with the Mahatma's interpretation of the devastation. Tagore denounced it as an unscientific view of things. 'Physical catastrophes have their inevitable and exclusive origin in certain combinations of physical facts,' he declared in a statement to the press, which he first sent to Gandhi. 'If we associate ethical principles with cosmic phenomena then we shall have to admit that human nature is morally superior to the Providence that preaches lessons in good behaviour in orgies of the worst behaviour possible . . . As for us, we feel perfectly secure in the faith that our sins and errors, however enormous, have not enough force to drag down the structure of creation to ruins . . . We who are immensely grateful to Mahatmaji for inducing by his wonder-working inspiration a freedom from fear and feebleness in the minds of his countrymen, feel profoundly hurt when any words from his mouth may emphasize the elements of unreason in those very minds.'

In his reply, in *Harijan* , Gandhi wrote with characteristic calmness:

I confess my utter ignorance of the working of the laws of nature. But even as I cannot help believing in God though I am unable to prove His existence to the sceptics, in like manner, I cannot prove the connection of the sin of untouchability with the Bihar visitation even though the connection is instinctively felt by me. If my belief turns out to be ill-founded, it will still have done good for me and those who believe with me. For we shall have been spurred to more vigorous efforts towards self-purification, assuming, of course, that untouchability is a deadly sin.

I have not the faith that Gurudev [Tagore] has that 'our own sins and errors, however enormous, have not enough force to drag down the structure of creation to ruins'. On the contrary, I have the faith that our own sins have more force to ruin that structure than any mere physical phenomenon . . . The connection between the cosmic phenomena and human behaviour is a living faith that draws me nearer to God.

During his Harijan tour orthodox Hindus would sometimes protest at his meetings, and when he toured earthquake-afflicted Bihar they were still following him with their waving black flags. On 26 April, at a place called Jassidi in south Bihar, they smashed the rear window of his car and prevented it from moving any further. Gandhi stepped out and began to walk while the protesters jeered at him. In June, when he and his small party reached Poona, he was on his way to the town hall to receive an address when an attempt was made on his life. A bomb was thrown at the car which the assailant believed to be carrying Gandhi. Seven people, including two police constables, were injured, but Gandhi was unscathed, for he was in the following car. He was willing, if the need arose, to 'die in the attempt to eradicate untouchability'. He urged those involved in Harijan work to redouble their efforts to rid the country of this deadly evil.

The most vocal among the orthodox Hindu demonstrators was Pandit Lalnath who, while addressing a meeting at Ajmer condemning the Harijan movement, was struck on the head with a *lathi*. Gandhi, shortly afterwards, rebuked the audience and in a statement issued to the press that day expressed his intention to embark on a seven-day penitential fast as soon as he reached Wardha. 'This is the least penance I owe to Pandit Lalnath and those he represents,' he said. 'Let it also be a warning to those who are in, or will join, the movement that they must approach it with clean hands and hearts, free from untruth and violence in thought, word and deed.' A month later, having completed an extensive tour and raised 800,000 rupees for the Harijan Fund, he commenced the fast. He had now regained his health and there were no ill effects.

Many Congressmen were now beginning to feel that civil disobedience had outlived its utility. Their representatives met Gandhi to secure his support for the tentative decision taken at a conference in Delhi to renew parliamentary activity and revive the Swaraj party. Gandhi had already made up his mind, for he was convinced that the masses had not yet appreciated the full message of Satyagraha. 'The indifferent civil resistance of many . . . has not touched the hearts of the rulers.' Even the change from mass to individual civil disobedience had proved ineffective. Personal conversations with ashramites helped him see things more clearly and led him to the extraordinary conclusion that 'I must advise all Congressmen to suspend civil resistance for *swaraj* as distinguished from specific grievances. They should leave it to me alone.' Gandhi clarified that this was mere advice to those who looked to him for guidance in matters of Satyagraha. 'I am in no way usurping the function of the Congress.' Many Congress leaders hailed Gandhi's statement but to Nehru, who was in prison at the time, the news was so disturbing that he felt 'the cords of allegiance that had bound me to him for many years had snapped'.

There was always a deep bond of affection between Nehru and Gandhi, but ideologically they appeared to be at variance with each other. Nehru was brought up in a family which was indifferent to religion. He was distressed by Gandhi's mixing of religion with politics, and was averse to some of the Mahatma's phrases, such as 'his frequent reference to Rama Raj as a golden age which was to return'. But he followed Gandhi because politically the Mahatma was uncompromising in his mission to secure freedom for India. Nehru considered Gandhi's method of peaceful resistance as 'a most civilized form of warfare'. But he also agreed with Gandhi's observation that it was 'better to fight than to be afraid. It is better to indulge in violence than to run away.' At one stage, during World War II, he thought of forming a national militia as well as resorting to guerrilla warfare to combat the Japanese aggression. Nehru spoke of science, economics and socialism, and Gandhi of truth, God and religion. But Gandhi said that while Nehru always disclaimed belief in religion or God, he was nearer to God than many who professed to be His worshippers.

In May 1934 the All-India Congress Committee was permitted by the government to meet at Patna to endorse Gandhi's statement of policy. Consequently civil disobedience was called off, but it was left open to Gandhi to offer it himself when he deemed it necessary. Shortly afterwards the government withdrew the ban on Congress. It had, however, become amply clear to Gandhi that a very large body of Congress intelligentsia were tired of his methods and views, that he was a hindrance rather than a help to the natural growth of the organization. The spread of *khadi* through personal handspinning and handweaving was of no interest to Congressmen any more. Nonviolence, after fourteen years of trial, remained only a policy with the majority of Congressmen, whereas it was a 'fundamental creed' with Gandhi. On the question of untouchability, his method of approach was considered to have disturbed the course of civil resistance struggle. 'For me, this is a deeply religious and moral issue . . . I feel that I would have been untrue to myself if I had taken any other course.' Notwithstanding these differences, Congressmen showed loyalty and devotion to Gandhi, though this exercise was putting them under strain. 'Their loyalty cannot blind my eyes to what appear to me to be fundamental differences between the Congress intelligentsia and me.' On 28 October 1934, at the Bombay session of Congress, Gandhi formally resigned from membership of the organization, but at his instigation several resolutions designed to promote his 'constructive programme' were passed.

His retirement was more nominal than real. He continued to be in close contact with senior Congress leaders and was always 'available for consultation' – no major decision was in fact taken without his advice. In order to be in close proximity to him, the Working Committee often met at Wardha.

He now threw himself with redoubled zeal into his 'constructive programme' and toured all over the country. His frequent writings in *Harijan* and his press interviews were devoted mainly to such topics as sanitation, hygiene, *khadi*, village industries and untouchability. He had seen the poverty of Indian villages at close quarters and felt that the development of modern industry was making the situation worse. With the advent of modern cotton mills, rice mills, flour mills, oil mills and sugar factories, the traditional village industries were falling into a state of decay and creating widespread rural unemployment. The only remedy, Gandhi felt, was the revival of village industries and handicrafts.

His views on the introduction of machinery underwent some changes over the years, but his opposition rested basically on the adverse effect of machinery on employment in an overpopulated country such as India:

Mechanization is good when the hands are too few for the work intended to be accomplished. It is an evil when there are more hands than required for the work, as is the case in India. The problem with us is not how to find leisure for the teeming millions inhabiting our villages, but how to utilize their idle hours, which are equal to working days of six months in the year. Today machinery merely helps a few to ride on the backs of millions. The impetus behind it all is not philanthropy to save labour, but greed.

I am not against all machinery. But, I am against its indiscriminate multi-plication. I refuse to be dazzled by the seeming triumph of machinery. I am uncompromisingly against all destructive machinery. But simple tools and instruments, and such instruments and such machinery as saves individual labour and lightens the burden of the millions of cottagers, I should welcome.

Machinery has its place; it has come to stay. But it must not be allowed to dis-place necessary human labour. I would welcome every improvement in the cot-tage machine, but I know that it is criminal to displace hand labour by the introduction of power-driven spindles, unless one is at the same time ready to give millions of farmers some other occupation in their houses.

Dead machinery must not be pitted against the millions of living machines represented by the villagers scattered in the seven hundred thousand villages of India. Machinery, to be well used, has to help and ease human effort. The pre-sent use of machinery tends more and more to concentrate wealth in the hands of a few, in total disregard of millions of men and women whose bread is snatched by it out of their mouths.

The central idea is . . . to utilize the idle hours of the nation and thus by natural process to help it get rid of its growing pauperism . . . The entire foundation of the spinning wheel rests on the fact that there are *crores* of semi-employed people in India, and I should admit that if there were none such, there should be no room for the spinning wheel . . . I would favour the use of the most elaborate machinery if thereby India's pauperism and resulting idleness could be avoided.

# THIRTY-THREE

# In Turmoil

While Gandhi immersed himself in Harijan and village reconstruction work, he continued to preach the observance of Brahmacharya as a prerequisite to personal elevation. In his opinion, people in India were getting more and more obsessed with sex.

> Sex complex is today steadily gaining ground in India. And what is more, those who fall under its sway feel as if there is something meritorious about it. When a slave begins to take pride in his fetters and hugs them like precious ornaments, the triumph of the slave-owner is complete . . . The conquest of lust is the highest endeavour of a man or woman's existence. And without conquering lust, man cannot hope to rule over self; without rule of self there can be no *swaraj*.

In the middle of January 1936 a solemn American visitor arrived at the Wardha ashram to argue with Gandhi about birth control. Mrs Margaret Sanger was an authority on the subject and her mission was to bring birth control to India. She half hoped to receive the seal of Gandhi's approval. There could be no discussion on the day of her arrival, it being Monday, the Mahatma's day of silence. For a while they smiled and nodded pleasantly to one another, and then Mrs Sanger was escorted to an old, sparsely furnished guest house.

The following morning she accompanied him on his daily walk, and on return to the ashram settled down to the task of convincing him of the necessity of birth control. His guiding principles, reinforced over a long period of time, ensured that each of her arguments was demolished. In Gandhi's eyes, though birth control was necessary, artificial aids led to self-indulgence and were therefore demoralizing and enfeebling. Sexual union was sinful except for the sake of offspring, and it was imperative that prevention against excess of offspring was strictly observed.

Mrs Sanger found him friendly and hospitable. He spoke in a low, carefully modulated voice, but she felt somewhat uneasy at his fluency and wondered whether he was really comprehending the argument. 'I felt his registering of impressions was blunted,' she wrote in her autobiography.

'While you were answering a question of his, he held to an idea or a train of thought of his own, and as soon as you stopped, continued as though he had not heard you.'

Gandhi's attitude toward birth control was, indeed, influenced by the storm of emotions he had weathered in South Africa, which culminated in his adoption of Brahmacharya in 1906. When Mrs Sanger suggested that there were several easily available contraceptives, he objected strongly, claiming that they all interfered in the process of nature, and that only continence was natural. Women must learn the primary right of resisting their husbands. He claimed to know women well and spoke of his association with them in South Africa:

> My wife I made the orbit of all women, and in her I studied all women. I came in contact with many European women in South Africa, and I knew practically every Indian woman there. I tried to show them they were not slaves either of their husbands or parents, not only in the political field but in the domestic as well. But the trouble was that some could not resist their husbands.
>
> The remedy is in the hands of women themselves. The struggle is difficult for them. I do not blame them. I blame the men. Men have legislated against them. Man has regarded woman as his tool. She has learnt to be his tool and in the end found it easy and pleasurable to be such, because when one drags another to his fall the descent is easy. I have felt that during the years still left to me if I can drive home to women's minds the truth that they are free we will have no birth control problems in India. If they will only learn to say 'no' to their husbands when they approach them carnally, I do not suppose that all husbands are brutes and if women only know how to resist them all will be well. I have been able to teach women who have come in contact with me how to resist their husbands. The real problem is that many do not want to resist them.

Mrs Sanger then put forth the issue of 'irritations, disputes, and thwarted longings' that Gandhi's advice would bring into the home, the absence of 'loving glances' and 'tender good-night kisses' and 'words of endearment'. In an effort to fortify her argument, she cited cases of nervous and mental breakdowns caused by the practice of self-control. Gandhi, who spoke with a knowledge gleaned from the numerous letters he often received, responded: 'The evidence is all based on examination of imbeciles. The conclusions are not drawn from the practice of healthy-minded people . . . who have lived a life of even tolerable continence.' Inevitably he would not accept Mrs Sanger's contention that 'sex love is a relationship which makes for oneness, for completeness between husband and wife and contributes to a finer understanding and a greater spiritual harmony'. Gandhi sought to differentiate between love and lust: 'When both want to satisfy the animal passion, without having to suffer the consequences of the act, it is not love, it is lust. But if love is pure, it will transcend animal passion and it will regulate itself.' He went on to say that 'we have not had enough education of the passions'. Mrs Sanger pointedly asked if two people happily in love were expected to unite sexually only when they wanted a child. Did he really think it was possible? Gandhi replied: 'I had the honour of doing that very thing, and I am not the only one.' He was speaking of his youngest son, whose conception was deliberately willed. The three others he considered to have been born of lust, and he was vehemently critical of himself for it.

Mrs Sanger could not concede that sexual union for the purpose of having children was love, while when they were not desired it was lust. 'I know from my own experience', Gandhi explained, 'that as long as I looked upon my wife carnally, we had no real understanding. Our love did not reach a high plane. Very often my wife would show restraint, but she rarely resisted me. The moment I bade good-bye to a life of carnal pleasure, our whole life became spiritual. Lust died and love reigned instead.'

Mrs Sanger was unconvinced by Gandhi's personal witness. 'Must the sexual union then take place only three or four times in an entire lifetime?'

'Exactly so,' Gandhi replied. 'People should be taught that it is immoral to have more than three or four children, and after they have had these children they should sleep separately. If people were taught this, it would harden into custom.'

And yet Mrs Sanger's 'dreadful earnestness' caused Gandhi to mention a remedy which eliminated the use of contraceptives: the performance of the sexual act during 'safe periods'. This warranted from the married couple a measure of self-control during the 'unsafe periods'. However, their views were so divergent that they parted without agreement. She had read his autobiography, and she concluded that his attitude to sex had emanated from the profound sense of guilt experienced at the time of his father's death.

Gandhi was suffering from high blood pressure. The interview proved quite strenuous for him and his condition got worse. He was in a state of collapse when he arrived at a Bombay hospital. A few days' rest improved his health, and then the doctors decided to remove his remaining teeth, which had been troubling him for some time. This was a major operation, and it left him very weak. It was while he was recovering from the operation that he experienced the agony of his 'darkest hour'. Writing in *Harijan* of 26 December 1936, the sixty-seven-year old Gandhi described his trauma:

My darkest hour was when I was in Bombay a few months ago. It was the hour of my temptation. Whilst I was asleep I suddenly felt as though I wanted to see a woman. Well, a man who had tried to rise superior to the instinct for nearly forty years was bound to be intensely pained when he had this frightful experience. I ultimately conquered the feeling, but I was face to face with the blackest moment of my life and if I had succumbed to it, it would have meant my absolute undoing.

The tension of 1936 had been aggravated by family trouble. Harilal's life was as unhappy as ever. In a supreme act of defiance against his father he embraced Islam in the midst of a large congregation in a Bombay mosque, assuming the name of Abdulla. Gandhi was aware that the problem was beyond solution, but in the hope of convincing the Muslims of Harilal's insincerity, he published in *Harijan* an article entitled 'To My Numerous Muslim Friends':

If this acceptance was from the heart and free from any worldly considerations, I should have no quarrel. For, I believe Islam to be as true as a religion as my own.

But I have the gravest doubt about this acceptance being from the heart or free from selfish considerations. Every one who knows my son Harilal knows that he has been for years addicted to the drink evil and has been in the habit of visiting houses of ill fame. For some years he has been living on the charity of friends who have helped him unstintingly. He is indebted to some Pathans from whom he has borrowed on heavy interest. Up to only recently he was in dread of his life from his Pathan creditors in Bombay. Now he is the hero of the hour in that city. He had a most devoted wife who forgave his many sins including his unfaithfulness. He has three grown up children, two daughters and one son, whom he ceased to support long ago . . .

My views on Islam are well known to the Musalmans, who are reported to have enthused over my son's profession. A brotherhood of Islam has telegraphed to me thus: 'Expect like your son, you a truth-seeker to embrace Islam, truest religion in the world.'

I must confess that all this has hurt me. I sense no religious spirit behind this demonstration. I feel that those who are responsible for Harilal's acceptance of Islam did not take the most ordinary precautions they ought to have in a case of this kind. Harilal's apostasy is no loss to Hinduism and his admission to Islam a source of weakness to it, if, as I fear, he remains the same wreck that he was before.

Surely conversion is a matter between man and his Maker who alone knows His creatures' hearts. And conversion without a clean heart is a denial of God and religion. Conversion without cleanness of heart can only be a matter for sorrow, not joy, to a godly person.

My object in addressing these lines to numerous Muslim friends is to ask them to examine Harilal in the light of his immediate past and if they find that his conversion is a soulless matter, to tell him so plainly and disown him, and if they discover sincerity in him, to see that he is protected against temptations, so that his sincerity results in his becoming a god-fearing member of society. Let them know that excessive indulgence has softened his brain and undermined his sense of right and wrong, truth and falsehood. I do not mind whether he is known as Abdulla or Harilal, if by adopting one name for the other he becomes a true devotee of God, which both the names mean.

Neither Gandhi nor Kasturbai was properly equipped to deal with their son. While Gandhi could turn his mind quickly from one subject to another, Kasturbai could not prevent herself from brooding. Now one of his adventures had gone into the newspapers. Deeply anguished, she dictated a letter to Devadas – a pathetic appeal to her eldest son:

Dear Son, Harilal,

I have read that recently in Madras for some disorderly behaviour in a state of drunkenness at midnight, you were taken into custody. Next day you were produced before a Magistrate, and he fined you, though only one rupee. This shows that the Magistrate was merciful to you and had also regard for your father. But I have been deeply pained by what you did. I do not know what to say to you. For years I have been pleading with you to lead a good life, but you have gone from bad to worse.

Alas! we, your father and I, have to suffer so much on your account in the evening of our life. What a pity that you, our eldest son, have turned our enemy! But what has grieved me greatly is your criticism of your father, in which you have been indulging nowadays. Of course, he remains silent and calm. Only if you knew how his heart is full of love for you. That is why he has again and again offered to keep you with him and me, and cater, too, to your creature comforts, but only on condition that you mend your present ways.

You are so ungrateful. Your father is no doubt bearing it all so bravely, but I am an old weak woman, who finds it difficult to suffer patiently the mental torture caused by your regrettable way of life. I cannot move about with ease among friends and all those who know us. Your father has always forgiven you, but God will never forgive you.

Every morning I open the daily newspaper in fear, lest it might have some further report of your evil doings. And often when I have sleepless nights, I think of you and wonder where you are these days, what you are eating, where you are staying, etc. Sometimes I even long ardently to meet you. But I do not know your whereabouts. But even if any time I chanced to meet you, I am afraid you might insult me.

Further, I fail to understand why you have changed your ancestral religion. However, this is your own personal affair. But why should you lead astray the simple and the innocent who, perhaps, out of regard for your father, are inclined to follow you? You consider only those people as your friends who give you money for drink. And what is worse, [even speaking from the platform] you ask the people to walk in your footsteps. This is a self-deception at its worst. But you cannot mislead the people for long. So I beseech you to mend your ways calmly and courageously. When you accepted Islam, you wrote to me that you did so to make yourself better. And willy-nilly, I reconciled myself to it. But some of your old friends, who saw you recently in Bombay, tell me that your present condition is worse than before.

It was during this phase of acute personal tension that Jamnalal Bajaj, the financial sponsor of Wardha ashram, gave Gandhi the farm and orchard which he owned in the village of Segaon, located just five miles east of Wardha. The village had no shops and no post office, only a dirt road linked it with the rest of the world. Many of its six hundred inhabitants were Harijans. Before long Segaon became virtually another ashram, which governed the life of the small community.

# THIRTY-FOUR

# The Rift Widens

While Gandhi was establishing himself at Segaon, Congress was grappling with the Government of India Act, the constitution framed by the British government. It had been wholly rejected at the Congress session in Bombay in 1934. But Congress, by participating in the elections to the old Legislative Assembly at the end of 1934, was virtually committed to constitutionalism. At a session in Lucknow in 1936, the new constitution was again condemned. In his presidential address Nehru described it as 'a Charter of Slavery, designed to perpetuate the hold of the British imperialism in India'. However, with Gandhi's blessing, it was decided to contest the elections under it. 'The boycott of the legislatures', Gandhi explained later, 'is not an eternal principle like that of truth and non-violence.'

The election results which were out in February 1937, showed that Congress had secured an absolute majority in six of the eleven provinces, and in three others it was the largest single party. Gandhi urged Congressmen to shoulder the burden of office. He was aware of the views of Nehru and Bose on this issue, and when they demurred, he was not surprised. However, he persuaded them to agree if the British governors would promise not to interfere with administration. Serving as an intermediary with the new Viceroy, Lord Linlithgow, it took Gandhi weeks to extract the required undertaking, leading to a gentleman's agreement. In order to play an effective part in bringing about this result, Gandhi found it necessary to secure the support of the right-wing parliamentarians against the left-wing socialists in Congress. Finally, in July Congress ministries were formed in six provinces (Bombay, Madras, United Provinces, Bihar, Central Provinces and Orissa), and shortly afterwards in a seventh, the North-West Frontier Province.

The elections of 1937 were destined to have a far-reaching effect on the history of India. The poor showing by the Muslim League and the attitude of the triumphant party ensured that the seeds of discord were sown and nurtured, contributing to the country's partition a decade later.

In dealing with the subject it is important to trace, however briefly, the rise and growth of Hindu-Muslim disunity. From ancient to modern times, India had been invaded numerous times, the British invasion being the last. The Muslims (Mughals) had been the immediate forerunners of the British as rulers of India, and just before British power in India began to expand, they had held many positions of power and privilege. The new rulers, in their efforts to have a firmer hold on the country, began to employ means to crush the Muslims and bring about their economic ruin. The education and economic policies of the British government benefited the Hindus but increased unemployment among the Muslims, impoverishing them. The Muslims were inevitably full of resentment against the new rulers. They were, however, too weak for rebellion.

In the latter part of the nineteenth century, at the time when Indian nationalism was growing, the British rulers felt that the time had come to take the Muslims into alliance rather than continue to antagonize them.

An Englishman, Mr Beck, principal of the Mohammedan Anglo-Oriental College, Aligarh, who was one of the secretaries of the Mohammedan Defence Association formed in 1893 to prevent Muslims from joining the Congress, proved the value of his empire-building activities when he persuaded Sir Syed Ahmed Khan, an educationalist who dominated Muslim public life in India from 1858 till his death in 1898, that 'while Anglo-Muslim alliance would ameliorate the condition of the Muslim community, the nationalist alignment would lead them once again to sweat, toil and tears . . .' Consequently Sir Syed Ahmed's unique influence was used to keep the Muslims, particularly in northern India, away from the Indian National Congress, though earlier he had been an ardent believer in Hindu-Muslim unity and had felt the justice of the Congress demands. In his last days he was obsessed by the thought of increasing domination of Muslims by Hindus in the educational, economic and political fields.

When the prospect of constitutional reform became apparent, the Muslims for the first time initiated a demand for a separate electorate. This development no doubt suited the British. The Morley-Minto reforms of 1909 managed to sow the seeds of political disunity in India by introducing separate electorates for Muslims. Nevertheless the façade of national unity was basically maintained till 1936 because the earlier constitution had not stated explicitly the amount of power which each community, Hindu and Muslim, might be able to acquire in comparison with the other. The Act of 1935, however, gave Indians limited but real power in the governance of their country. But the League had expressed no special anxiety at the prospect of a Hindu majority at the centre.

The relations between the Congress (the largest political party and predominantly Hindu) and the Muslim League before the elections of early

1937 appeared cordial. The political and economic programmes of the two parties were more or less on similar lines. Although the Muslim League professed to be an all-India party, its following was confined mainly to Hindu-majority provinces. In the Muslim-majority provinces of the Punjab and Bengal, the League candidates had been defeated in the 1936 elections by Muslims belonging to the local parties. In the North-West Frontier Province the Muslims led by Abdul Ghaffar Khan, had joined hands with Congress, and the League was virtually unknown. Its claim to represent the Muslims of India, therefore, could not be upheld. Till early 1937, Mohamed Ali Jinnah, though he was the president of the Muslim League, was known to be a true nationalist. He had hoped that in the Hindu-majority provinces, the Congress, if successful in elections, would join in alliance with the League in forming coalition governments. He envisaged the formation of similar coalitions at the centre when the federal part of the new constitution became operative. But Congressmen, jubilant over their success in the provincial elections, found themselves on cloud nine. They felt that there was no reason to form coalitions with the League; and in the United Provinces, where the League was the strongest, its members were promptly notified that only 'one or two' Muslim Leaguers would be taken into the cabinet. The condition for inclusion, the Congress leaders stressed, was that the League Assembly party must join Congress and 'cease to function as a separate group'.

In the Bombay Legislative Assembly the Muslim League had formed a fairly large group. And when B.G. Kher, the Congress party leader in the province, was preparing to form government he clearly had in mind the League joining his ministry. The Congress high command sternly cautioned Kher and ruled out the possibility of a coalition government. It was now left to M.A. Jinnah to appeal directly to Gandhi for his personal intervention in the interest of Hindu-Muslim unity. In response to Jinnah's request, Kher personally carried his message to Gandhi at Tithal, a seaside town in Gujarat. Gandhi's reply of 22 May 1937 reads:

Dear Mr Jinnah,
    Kher has given me your message. I wish I could do something, but I am utterly helpless. My faith in unity is as bright as ever; only I see no daylight out of the impenetrable darkness, and in such darkness and in such distress, I cry out to God for light.
    Yours sincerely,
    M.K. GANDHI

Jinnah now sought a meeting with Gandhi to discuss the problem with him personally. Gandhi's disinclination to have anything to do with Jinnah was evident in his reply, which amounted to a rebuff:

> So far as I am concerned, just as on the Hindu-Muslim question I was guided by Dr Ansari, now that he is no more in our midst, I have accepted Maulana Abul Kalam Azad [like Ansari a Muslim Congressman] as my guide. My suggestion, therefore, to you is that conversation should be opened in the first instance with the Maulana Sahib.

The Congress leaders, including Gandhi, had no inkling of the difficult situation they were getting into. Nehru in his speeches tried to ignore even the presence of the Muslim League when he said that in India there were only two parties – Congress and the British government – 'and the rest must line up'. At his command, Congress began with a great fanfare a programme of mass contact with the Muslims. Jinnah, in a statement to the press, said: 'What can I say to that busybody president [of Congress] . . . He seems to carry the responsibility of the whole world on his shoulders and must poke his nose into everything except minding his own business.'

Soon Jinnah would switch his tactics from seeking protection for the Muslim minority within a federal constitution to declaring that Congress was a Hindu organization which was now determined to deprive the Muslims for ever of a share in the governance of the country. 'The Congress attempt under the guise of establishing mass contact with the Muslims', he insisted, 'is calculated to divide and weaken and break the Muslims and is an effort to detach them from their accredited leaders.' His message was favourably received in the Muslim-majority provinces, and in the autumn of 1937 the Muslim premiers of the Punjab and Bengal came forward to join the League with all their Muslim followers, accepting Jinnah as their leader because they understood it to be a period of crisis for Muslims in India. Jinnah, greatly strengthened, began a campaign of vilifying the Congress, whipping up Muslim feeling against it and organizing the League to fight it. 'The Muslims can expect neither justice nor fair play under Congress Government,' he declared. He found the prospect of a Congress Raj at the centre quite discouraging. In 1938 Jinnah and the League denounced the federal part of the constitution. The idea of a separate homeland for the Indian Muslims – 'Pakistan' – had already gained wide acceptance in League circles.

Meanwhile Nehru was in communication with Jinnah, but there was no meaningful outcome, which depressed Gandhi. He now sought a meeting with Jinnah. A few days prior to the meeting, on 28 April 1938, Gandhi issued a statement:

For the first time in my public and private life I seem to have lost self-confidence. I seem to have detected a flaw in me which is unworthy of a votary of truth and *ahimsa*. I am going through a process of self-introspection, the result of which I cannot foresee. I find myself for the first time in the last fifty years in a slough of despond. I do not consider myself fit for the negotiations or any such thing for the moment. It must now be clear that if I regarded the forthcoming interview as between two politicians, I should not entertain it in my present depression. But I approach it in no political spirit. I approach it in a prayerful and religious spirit, using the adjective in its broadest sense.

Jinnah told Gandhi in no uncertain terms that he should accept the Muslim League as the one authoritative organization of the Muslims in India and should not look for guidance on Hindu-Muslim questions to Congress Muslims like Abul Kalam Azad. Both Gandhi and Congress found this suggestion unacceptable. The talks proved unproductive, but they added to Jinnah's prestige. Soon the newly sought power would carry him on the crest of a wave which no one, not even Jinnah himself, could stop.

Jinnah was six feet tall and exceedingly thin. Dressed in Savile Row suits, coupled with his style of living, he gave the impression of being a highly Westernized cosmopolitan aristocrat. His clothes remained European until the last years of his life, when he adopted the *sherwani* and *shelwar* of a Muslim. English had become his principal language, for he never mastered Urdu, and he was both fluent and colloquial in the tongue.

A highly successful lawyer, Jinnah's intense ego sustained his emaciated body. Suave and ruthless, he could be arrogantly and infuriatingly wrong, but his honesty of purpose was unquestionable and he was 'incorruptible by any outside agency'. He looked with disdain upon any minds less intricate than his own. Quick, clever and sarcastic, his greatest delight was known to be to confound the opposing lawyer with confidential asides and to outwit the presiding judge in repartee. When a wealthy Hindu landowner objected to the amount of Jinnah's fee, he replied: 'You can't travel in a pullman on a third-class ticket.' On one occasion a lawyer colleague, collecting for charity, approached him in the Bar library and handed him the subscription list. He placed his monocle in his eye, read the list, handed it back to the lawyer and said: 'I am not interested.' Years later when some members of the Muslim League suggested that it would be politically beneficial if he travelled third class on the railways, as Gandhi did, he was very annoyed. 'Do not dictate to me what I should do or should not do,' he told them. 'It is not your money I am spending, and I shall live and act as I choose.' After the creation of the Dominion of Pakistan in 1947, when one among many supplicants for rewards for services rendered approached Jinnah, who was then Governor-General, he enquired rather contemptuously: 'You helped to create Pakistan? My dear man, I got you Pakistan with a typist and a typewriter.' This was more or less a statement of fact.

There was romance with high drama in Jinnah's life when, at the age of forty, he met a Parsi girl, the sixteen-year-old daughter of Sir Dinshaw Petit. Ruttenbai was extremely beautiful and charming and was as patriotic as she was self-willed. She had a great admiration for Jinnah's role in politics and shared with him the hobby of horse-riding. The dreamy-eyed Ruttenbai's mind was immediately set on marriage. Jinnah (whom she called 'J') tried to talk her out of it for various reasons, stressing the difference in their age as an important one. But Ruttenbai considered these objections to be flimsy and declared that she would marry no one else. When Jinnah contacted Ruttenbai's father with a view to discussing the subject, all his tact and persuasiveness proved ineffective. Sir Dinshaw was so perturbed to hear of the proposal that he obtained a court order restraining Jinnah from meeting his minor daughter. They, however, got married when she came of age. The husband and wife eventually reached a very difficult stage in their relationship, with the difference in their ages and habits adding to the incompatibility. Eventually Ruttenbai left their Bombay house in Mount Pleasant Road, and took up residence in the Taj Mahal Hotel, where she became dangerously ill. Two months later she died. She was twenty-eight. The tragic end to their marriage possibly influenced the course of Jinnah's political career by leaving him lonely in an unsympathetic world.

Jinnah's daughter, Dina, married Neville Wadia, a Parsi-born Christian, a match of which Jinnah did not approve. In an effort to dissuade her, he went almost to the same lengths as Dinshaw Petit had done with his daughter. Jinnah hardly spoke to Dina after she married, and although they did correspond occasionally, he always addressed her formally as 'Mrs Wadia' and never talked of her to his friends.

Born of a family of moderate means in Karachi, Mohamed Ali Jinnah attended schools in his native province before going to England at the age of sixteen to study law. The year was 1892 and he had arrived in London in time to watch – perhaps to help – the election of the first Indian, Dadabhai Naoroji, to the British Parliament. Young Jinnah prospered under the influence of Naoroji, whom he was to serve as secretary fourteen years later. When Jinnah returned to Bombay as a qualified barrister, he spoke, thought and had his being in politics. As a lieutenant of Pheroze Shah Mehta in the Indian National Congress and a colleague of Gokhale in the old Imperial Legislative Council, he was among the foremost Congressmen of his time. His efforts to bring about harmonious cooperation between Hindus and Muslims were widely recognized. Gopal Krishna Gokhale said of Jinnah in those days: 'He has true stuff in him and that freedom from all sectarian prejudice which will make him the ambassador of Hindu-Muslim unity.' Jinnah himself declared that it was his 'one ambition to become the Muslim Gokhale'. Commenting on the fear harboured by some Muslims of Hindu domination, Jinnah told a Muslim League meeting in 1917: 'Fear not. This is a bogy which is put before you to scare you away from the cooperation and unity which are essential to self-government.' And at a convention ten years later, he declared:

If we do not settle this [minority] question today we will settle it tomorrow. We are sons of this land, we have to live together. We have to work together and whatever our differences may be let us not arouse bad blood. If we cannot agree let us agree to differ, but let us part as friends. Nothing will make me more happy than to see Hindus and Muslims united. I believe there is no progress for India until Muslims and Hindus are united. Let not logic, philosophy and squabbles stand in the way of your bringing that about.

But Congress's launch of the noncooperation movement under Gandhi's guidance marked the parting of the ways for Jinnah, since he was essentially a constitutionalist and a parliamentarian. The wearing of *khadi*, the boycott of courts and councils and the seeking of imprisonment did not appeal to him. He was averse to the Mahatma's call to Indian students to leave their schools and colleges and participate in the civil-disobedience movement. He considered the involvement of students to be a wasteful sacrifice which could lead to indiscipline in future.

Thus at the Nagpur session of Congress in 1920 when the noncooperation programme was approved, his was the solitary voice raised in opposition. For many more years he would seek to persuade Indian Muslims to accept the ideal of Indian nationalism, till they refused to follow him any longer because of his nationalistic views. The efforts of Congress to resolve the minority question did not prove to be of much help either. Finally, in 1931, Jinnah withdrew from the Indian political scene to settle in London, where he took up law practice. 'Not that I did not love India,' he said, 'but I felt so utterly helpless.' He had no intention of returning, though each year friends came from India and told him of conditions there, impressing upon him how much he could do. While he still hesitated, Liaquat Ali Khan, the Muslim leader, repeated to him that Nehru had indiscreetly said at a private dinner party that 'Jinnah is finished.' An infuriated Jinnah packed up and sailed back to India just to 'show Nehru . . .' His self-imposed exile had lasted about three years.

The situation following the provincial elections of 1937 led Jinnah to appeal to Muslims to develop their own national consciousness. 'Gandhi', he complained, 'had destroyed the very ideals with which Congress started its career and converted it into a communal Hindu body.' Even granting that it was not the intention of Gandhi to convert the organization into a Hindu body, Jinnah's complaint was not entirely baseless. Gandhi's political aims nevertheless were so closely bound up with his ideas of Hindu reform that in this respect his message contributed toward the blame levied against him for 'Hinduizing politics'. In his speeches and writings he put as much stress on the reform of Hinduism as on the achievement of freedom. His basic concepts, his moral values and ideals were unmistakably of Hindu origin. Duty-bound only by his goodwill toward the Muslims, he chose not to perceive the unfavourable effects on Muslim opinion of his pronounced Hinduism. As a result the Muslims, notwithstanding his impeccably earnest intentions, had been baffled over the years and wondered if Congress really represented their interests and aspirations. And when the time came for Jinnah to mobilize his co-religionists, he skilfully fed their suspicions. Gandhi and Congress found it impossible to allay them.

# THIRTY-FIVE

# Subhas Chandra Bose

Early in 1939 a storm was brewing up in the Congress party. Although the principal part of the new constitution of 1935 provided possibilities for popular government, the federal part was unanimously rejected by Indian public opinion, in particular by Congress, for it was a scheme not for self-government but for maintaining British rule in the new political conditions. However, the British were inclined to think that Congress, as in the case of the provinces, would compromise and agree to work the federal scheme. In fact some influential Congress leaders had been advocating conditional acceptance of the federal scheme. Meanwhile, word went round the left-wing Congress circles that another surrender was in the offing. Efforts now began to thwart the possible acceptance of the federal scheme by Congress. Subhas Chandra Bose who, with Gandhi's approval, had held the office of president in 1938, resolved to seek re-election since it was 'imperative to have a Congress president who will be an anti-federationist to the core of his heart', and able to give a lead to the country in resisting its imposition. The Congress high command was displeased with Bose's decision to contest for a second term. Gandhi was also opposed to the idea, but he did not explicitly give any reason for his opposition to Bose's candidature.

Gandhi's resignation from formal membership of the Congress party in 1934 did not result in any lessening of his power in the organization. He did not love power in as much as he had no attraction for the mere holding of high office. He was quite content to watch the election of smaller men to the presidency of the Indian National Congress; but he certainly needed power in the sense that he would not accept a position from which he could not impose his own political ethics and weapons of moral warfare. He endeavoured to be democratic and tolerated dissent, but if his leadership was challenged in the process the politician in him would make him act as ruthlessly as any party boss in a democratic set-up ever did. Jawaharlal Nehru had realized this early in his political career, and therefore, despite differences with Gandhi on several points, he chose to avoid an open con-frontation. This was in sharp contrast to Bose's approach. Gandhi, no doubt, was partial to Nehru, but their political rapport was in essence based on the latter's less rigid attitude, as well as his deep respect for Gandhi. A situation arose as late as 1942 when Gandhi informed Nehru in no uncertain terms that he was not indispensable. Years earlier when Nehru displayed a somewhat spirited defence of his action in sponsoring a resolution concerning the objectives of Congress which Gandhi had described as 'hastily conceived' and 'thoughtlessly passed', Nehru inevitably received a piece of the Mahatma's mind:

> If any freedom is required from me I give you all the freedom you may need from the humble, unquestioning allegiance that you have given to me for all these years and which I value all the more for the knowledge I have now gained of your state . . . The differences between you and me appear to me to be so vast and radical that there seems to be no meeting ground between us. I can't conceal from you my grief that I should lose a comrade so valiant, so faithful, so able and so honest as you have always been; but in serving a cause, comradeships have got to be sacrificed.

Gandhi even offered to publish the correspondence relating to their differences, but Nehru decided to avoid an open break. He assured Gandhi that the differences between them related only to some minor points and that they were in agreement on most issues.

When Gandhi decided to sponsor the election of his most vocal critic, Bose, as Congress president for 1938, his aim was to forge unity between the left and right wings of the party. It may well be that it was done also to take the wind out of the sails of the leftists as he had done earlier by sponsoring Nehru. But it did not work in the case of Bose, and soon their deep differences would come to the fore. They differed in their approaches as to the method for securing freedom for their country. Bose felt that what India needed was a modern, combative and optimistic outlook. He opposed Gandhi's doctrine of nonviolence and espousal of the spinning wheel which, he asserted, generated passive, backward-looking tendencies. India would have to fight her enemies with modern weapons and the country could not afford to adhere to the principle of nonviolence. At times, Bose expressed the view that nonviolence would have to be supplemented by diplomacy and international propaganda, but Gandhi had no use for either.

Before Bose made known his intention to seek re-election, Gandhi discussed the question of the presidency with Vallabhbhai Patel and other members of the Working Committee. Patel later spoke of this meeting:

> At informal consultations at one stage or the other at which Maulana Azad, Jawaharlal Nehru, Rajendra Prasad, Bhulabhai Desai, Kripalani, Mahatma Gandhi and myself were present, not by design but by accident, it was agreed

that if perchance Maulana Azad remained adamant . . . then, according to the constitution Dr Pattabhai Sitaramayya was the only choice left, since we were clearly of the opinion that it was unnecessary to re-elect Subhas Bose.

The names of Azad, Bose and Sitaramayya were now prominently mentioned, and it was hoped that two of them would withdraw, leaving the result to be unanimous. The election was to be held on 29 January 1939. On 20 January Azad stated that for reasons of health he could not agree to shoulder the burden of the high office, and recommended Sitaramayya's name for the presidentship of Congress. Bose promptly issued a statement to the press notifying his intention to seek re-election:

The issue is not a personal one. The progressive sharpening of the anti-imperialist struggle in India has given birth to new ideas, ideologies, problems and programmes. People are consequently veering round to the opinion that, as in other countries, the Congress Presidential election in India should be fought on the basis of definite problems and programme so that the contest may help the clarification of issues and give a clear indication of the working of the public mind . . .

There is a prospect of a compromise on the federal scheme between the right-wing of the Congress and the British Government during the coming year. Consequently the right-wing do not want a leftist president who may be a thorn in the way of compromise and may put obstacles in the path of negotiations . . .

A few days later, from Bardoli, seven members of the Working Committee, including Patel, issued a statement, at Gandhi's behest, questioning the validity of the reasons for a contest given in Bose's statement. Patel wrote to Nehru urging him to sign it as Gandhi had asked him to, or issue a different statement independently. Nehru did it independently, which displeased Gandhi. 'The election, as befits the dignity of this high office, has always been unanimous,' the group of seven declared. 'Any controversy over the election, even on the score of the politics and programmes is, therefore, to be deprecated.'

In his reply Bose expressed regret at the Working Committee members taking sides in an organized manner. It was news to him that the decision to advocate Sitaramayya's name was taken with much deliberation. 'Neither I, nor some of my colleagues on the Working Committee, had any knowledge or idea of either the deliberation or the decision.' He would much rather that the signatories had issued the statement not as members of the Working Committee but as individual Congressmen. 'And if the presidential election is to be an election worth the name, there should be freedom of voting without any moral coercion. Otherwise why not end the elective system and have the president nominated by the Working Committee?' Bose added that he had suggested to his numerous friends that a new candidate from the left should be put up, but that could not be done and his name was proposed from various provinces. 'I am prepared to withdraw from the contest if a genuine anti-federationist like Acharya Narendra Dev, for instance, be accepted as president for the coming year.'

On the eve of the elections Gandhi wrote an article in *Harijan* under the title 'Internal Decay', in which he said that indiscipline and corruption were seeping through the Congress party and he saw 'nothing but red ruin and anarchy' in the future. But he added rather fervently that if God willed it, 'I feel that I have enough strength and energy in me to lead a battle much more strenuous than any I have fought'. He clearly had Bose in mind when he wrote this.

Notwithstanding Gandhi's opposition, Bose was confident he would win. 'I am mathematically certain that I shall beat Sitaramayya,' he told a journalist on the day of the elections. Out of the total number of 2,957 votes polled in the provinces Bose got 1,580 and Sitaramayya 1,377. The margin confounded Bose's critics and staggered the Old Guard.

Being instrumental in opposing Bose, Gandhi termed Sitaramayya's defeat 'more mine than his' and confessed that from the very beginning he had been decidedly against Bose's re-election 'for reasons into which I need not go'. He had been solely responsible for inducing Sitaramayya not to withdraw his name as a candidate when Maulana Azad declined to enter the contest. 'I rejoice in this defeat,' he said somewhat untruthfully, for his anger was quite obvious when he complained that Congress had become a 'corrupt organization' in the sense that it contained a large number of 'bogus members'. Gandhi and the Working Committee would now proceed with a ruthlessness and cunning more in keeping with his character as a politician than as a saint. Of all the participants only Gandhi had a clear and consistent object – to oust Bose.

Bose regretted that Gandhi should have taken the result of the elections as a personal defeat. 'I would respectfully differ from him on this point. The voters were not called upon to vote for or against Mahatma Gandhi.' Bose tried to dispel the apprehension in some quarters about a split between the leftists and the rightists. 'Let me make it quite clear that there will be no violent break with the past, parliamentary or in the extra-parliamentary sphere.'

In an effort to win Gandhi's support, Bose met him at Segaon on 15 February, three weeks before the Congress session at Tripuri was scheduled to be held. Although certain tentative conclusions were reached, nothing definite came out of the three-hour meeting. Bose was aware of the disunity among his leftists and he knew about Nehru's opposition. It had become apparent to him that he could not function without the support of Gandhi.

It was decided to hold a meeting of the Working Committee at Segaon on 22 February to discuss the agenda for the Tripuri session. Soon after, Bose was taken seriously ill. Accordingly, he sent a telegram asking for a postponement of the meeting and forbidding it to transact any business in his absence. This was conveniently construed by his colleagues as an expression of the president's lack of confidence in them. Consequently twelve of the fifteen members, including such luminaries as Patel, Azad, Prasad, Mrs Sarojini Naidu and Sitaramayya, resigned from the Working Committee with the knowledge and concurrence of Gandhi. Nehru, feeling somewhat uneasy in having left his old comrade, prefaced his resignation with a covering letter. The size of the Working Committee was now reduced to two members – the president and his brother, Sarat Chandra Bose.

Gandhi was determined not to attend the Tripuri session. He wrote to Nehru: 'After the election and the manner in which it was fought, I feel that I shall serve the country better by absenting myself from the forthcoming session of Congress.'

He had other plans. On 28 February he arrived at his boyhood habitat in the princely state of Rajkot to make certain that the pledge made by the ruler to the people was redeemed. Here Vallabhbhai Patel led civil disobedience aimed at extracting a political amnesty and reforms. Gandhi and Patel could not gain their object by negotiations with the ruler and his prime minister, or with the British political agent, and so on 3 March Gandhi resorted to a fast unto death to achieve his aims. Nehru and Bose were alarmed: by his fast, Gandhi had attracted public attention to Rajkot, and Tripuri was thus side-lined.

The president-elect defied his doctors and travelled from Calcutta to Tripuri. He had broncho-pneumonia, with liver and intestinal complications. This illness, coinciding with a period of political crisis, caused him much anxiety. He had no rest, physical or mental, working in bed even with a high fever. On 7 March, lying on an invalid's chair and attended by doctors, Subhas Chandra Bose presided over the All-India Congress Committee meeting at Tripuri. Three days later when the annual session of Congress opened, he was too ill to attend, and Maulana Azad took the chair. The president's address was read by Sarat Bose, raised the issue of *swaraj* and proposed that 'we should submit our National Demand to the British Government in the form of an ultimatum and give a certain time limit. If no reply is received within this period or if an unsatisfactory reply is received, we should resort to such sanctions as we possess in order to enforce our National Demand.'

Bose's proposal was opposed by the right wing and Nehru, and was thrown out. Many delegates who had voted for Bose in the presidential election had now changed their views due to Gandhi's opposition. It had become obvious to them that there was a definite conflict between Gandhi and Bose, even though neither of them would say so. When the issue came to deciding between the two leaders, Gandhi emerged supreme.

There was to follow a more serious defeat for Bose on the last day of the session. The right-wing leaders, without any opposition from Gandhi, sponsored and got adopted a resolution asking Bose to constitute the new Working Committee 'in accordance with the wishes of Mahatma Gandhi', although according to the constitution of Congress the Working Committee was to consist of the president's nominees. The passing of this resolution with an overwhelming majority was a clear indication that the president's hands were tied. Bose left Tripuri bitter and disappointed. Gandhi advised him to resign if he was not keeping good health. Bose replied:

> I have not the slightest desire to stick to office, but I do not see any reason for resigning because I am ill. No [Congress] president resigned when he was in prison for instance; I may tell you that great pressure is being brought to bear on me to resign. I am resisting because my resignation will mean a new phase in Congress politics which I want to avoid till the last.

Bose's prolonged correspondence with Gandhi to win the Mahatma's support in forming the Working Committee produced no result. 'Assuming that your policy has the backing of the All-India Congress Committee,' Gandhi wrote to Bose, 'you should have a Working Committee composed purely of those who believe in your policy.' But he did not empower Bose to appoint an exclusively leftist cabinet. Feeling utterly discouraged, Bose wrote to Gandhi:

> I have been pondering deeply over the advice you have given me regarding the formation of the Working Committee. I feel that your advice is a counsel of despair. It destroys all hope of unity . . . You are against the idea of a composite Cabinet. Is your opposition due to grounds of principle (viz., joint work is impossible in your view), or is it because you feel that the 'Gandhi-ites' (I am using this expression in the absence of anything better, and you will please pardon me for doing so) should have a larger representation on the Cabinet? In the latter case, please let me know, so that I may have an opportunity of reconsid-

ering the matter. In the former case, please reconsider the advice you have already tendered in the light of what I am submitting in this letter. At Haripura, when I suggested inviting the socialists to serve on the Cabinet, you told me distinctly that you were in favour of my doing so. Has the situation changed so materially since then as to induce you to insist on a homogeneous Cabinet?. . .

Then, again, what is the president's position regarding appointing the Working Committee after the Tripuri resolution was passed? I am again asking this question because the present constitution is practically your handiwork and your opinion in the matter will carry great weight with me. There is another question, in this connection, which I have been asking you. Do you regard this resolution as one of no-confidence in me? If so, I shall resign at once and that too unconditionally. Some papers have criticized this question of mine in my Press statement on the ground that I should decide for myself what the significance of the resolution is. I have sense enough to give my own interpretation, but there are occasions when personal interpretations would not be one's sole guide. Speaking quite frankly, I feel that my stand has been justified by the result of the Presidential election. I have now no desire whatsoever to stick to office for one day, unless I can thereby advance the public cause, as I understand it . . . I wanted to appeal to you to come forward and directly and openly conduct the affairs of the Congress. This will simplify matters. Much of the opposition against the Old Guard – and opposition there certainly is – will automatically vanish.

If you cannot do this, then I have an alternative suggestion to make. Please resume the national struggle for independence, as we have been demanding, and begin by delivering the ultimatum to the British Government. In that event, we shall all gladly retire from our official positions, if you so desire. We shall gladly hand over these positions to whomsoever you like or trust But only on one condition – the fight for independence must be resumed. People like myself feel that today we have an opportunity which is rare in the lifetime of a nation. For that reason we are prepared to make any sacrifice that will help the resumption of the fight.

Nehru made a half-hearted effort to resolve the differences between Gandhi and Bose. He wrote to Gandhi: 'I think you should accept Subhas as president. To try to push him out seems to me to be an exceedingly wrong step.' Gandhi was unmoved. He was, however, persuaded by Nehru to visit Calcutta at the time of the All-India Congress Committee meeting. On Gandhi's advice, Vallabhbhai Patel, the party chief, did not attend the meeting as it was 'in the best interests of the country to absent himself from Calcutta'.

Soon after Gandhi's arrival in Calcutta Bose called on him and the two leaders discussed matters in detail. As he had repeated in his letters, Gandhi advised Bose to have discussions with the former members of the

Working Committee in order that a settlement might be reached. His advice was contained in a letter which was handed over to Bose. But when Bose discussed the matter with his old colleagues, they failed to come to any agreement.

At the Congress Committee meeting, which Gandhi did not attend, Bose read out the Mahatma's letter. He then gave a detailed account of his efforts to come to a settlement. He regretted that he was unable to announce the members of the new Working Committee, and then tendered his resignation. Gandhi had thus succeeded in disposing of the only real opposition to his leadership. Rajendra Prasad was now installed as president and he, according to Gandhi's wishes, renominated all the old members of the Working Committee. Lord Linlithgow, the Viceroy, admired the ability which Gandhi had shown in ousting Bose although his methods were 'of questionable constitutional validity'. Rabindranath Tagore wrote to Bose: 'The dignity and forbearance which you have shown in the midst of the most aggravating situation has won my admiration and confidence in your leadership.'

Bose proceeded to form a new party within Congress called the Forward Bloc, whose aim was to be 'to rally radical and anti-imperialist elements within Congress'. The All-India Congress Committee at its meeting in Bombay, which Gandhi attended, adopted two resolutions: one stressed that no Congressman might offer or organize any form of Satyagraha in the administrative provinces of India without the sanction of the provincial Congress committee concerned; the other defined the relation between the Congress ministries and the provincial Congress committees. The resolutions were opposed by Subhas Bose and the socialists, but were passed by a large majority after full discussion. Two weeks later the left consolidation group staged protests against the Congress Committee's resolutions, and Bose also took the opportunity of criticizing some policies of the Bombay government.

On 9 August 1939, the Working Committee began its three-day session at Wardha. One of the more important matters that came up for consideration related to the conduct of Bose and other office-bearers and members of the executive committees on 9 July, when they organized protest meetings against the two resolutions of the All-India Congress Committee. The Working Committee had before it the explanation of Bose, who argued that it was his constitutional right to express his views on any resolution adopted by the Congress Committee. The Working Committee gave the matter its 'most anxious consideration' and was of the view that if every member was free to interpret the Congress constitution as he liked, there would be 'perfect anarchy' in the organization. The committee concluded that it would fail in its duty if it condoned 'the deliberate and flagrant breach of discipline by Shri Subhas Bose'. The Working Committee disqualified him from being the president of the Bengal Congress Committee and from holding any office in Congress for a period of three years.

The resolution censuring Bose led to a public outcry. A week after the event Gandhi wrote:

I continue to receive letters, mostly abusive, about what may be called the Subhas Babu resolution of the Working Committee. I also saw a letter addressed to Rajendra Prasad, which can hardly be surpassed in the use of filthy language.

I owe it to the public to make my position clear about this matter. I must confess that the Subhas Babu resolution was drafted by me. I can say that the members of the Working Committee would have shirked the duty of taking action, if they could have. They knew that there would be a storm of opposition against their action. It was easier for them to have a colourless resolution than to have one which was no respecter of persons. Not to take some action would have amounted to abdication of their primary function of preserving discipline amongst the Congressmen.

Subhas Babu knew that he could not be hurt by the Working Committee ... He had pitted himself against the Working Committee, if not the Congress organization. The members of the Working Committee, therefore, had to perform their duty...It has been suggested that Subhas Babu has done what I would have done under similar circumstances. I cannot recall a single instance in my life of having done what Subhas Babu has done, that is, defied an organization to which I owe allegiance. I could understand rebellion after secession from such an organization. That was the meaning and secret of the non-violent non-cooperation of 1920 ...

Bose's difficulties, no doubt, started with the showdown at Tripuri which was virtually a defeat for him and the leftists. It was, as an associate put it, 'a case of one sick man lying in bed fighting (1) twelve stalwarts of the Old Guard, (2) Jawaharlal Nehru, (3) seven provincial ministries (who were convassing for the Old Guard), and (4) the name, influence and prestige of Mahatma Gandhi'.

What appeared surprising to Bose at this critical time was the attitude of Nehru, whom he had always held in respect for his radical socialistic views. He had hoped that Nehru would support him in his conflict with the Old Guard. But Nehru had decided to sever his connections with the radical elements. 'No one has done more harm to me personally than Pandit Jawaharlal Nehru,' Bose wrote to his nephew Amiyanath, who was then in England. 'If he had been with us, we would have a majority. Even his neutrality would have probably given us a majority. But he was with the Old

Guard at Tripuri. His open propaganda against me has done me more harm than the activities of the twelve stalwarts [put together]. What a pity!'

Years later, Nehru confessed to Taya Zinkin, the British journalist, that he had let Bose down:

> I had realized that, at that stage, whatever one's views might be about the way India should develop, Gandhi was India. Anything that weakened Gandhi, weakened India. So I subordinated myself to Gandhi although I was in agreement with what Bose was trying to do. I suppose it is right to say that I let him down.

Bose was now shorn of any authority in Congress, but he was still a member of the party. Although he had earlier written to Gandhi about having felt 'such a loathing and disgust for Congress politics', he was still in fighting mood. After he was arrested under the Defence of India Rules, he observed  to his brother, Sarat, in a letter from the Presidency Jail, Calcutta:

> The more I think of Congress politics, the more convinced I feel that in future we should devote more energy and time to fighting the High Command. If power goes into the hands of such mean, vindictive and unscrupulous persons when *swaraj* is won, what will happen to the country? If we don't fight them now, we shall not be able to prevent power passing into their hands. Another reason why we should fight them now is that they have no idea of national reconstruction. Gandhiism will land free India in a ditch – if free India is sought to be rebuilt on Gandhian, non-violent principles. India will then be offering a standing invitation to all predatory powers.

Despite their vast differences, there existed between Gandhi and Bose mutual regard and affection. In fact Gandhi was incapable of disliking any person, though his self-righteousness knew no bounds. It was just that his personality and views were diametrically opposed to Bose's and consequently there could be no provision for an agreement. When his leadership was threatened by Bose, the politician in Gandhi responded in a way appearing to be democratic but in reality not devoid of intrigue.

In June 1940 Bose called on Gandhi at the Sevagram ashram. This was the last time they met and Gandhi listened to Bose at great length. Fortunately a full record of the talks was kept by Nathalal Parikh, a close associate of Bose whom Bose asked to be present.

GANDHI: Subhas I have always loved you. You are keen on launching some mass movement. You thrive when there is fight. You are terribly emotional, but I had to think of several factors. I am an old man now and must not do anything in haste. I have the greatest admiration for you. Regarding your love for the country and determination to achieve its freedom, you are second to none. Your sincerity is transparent. Your spirit of self-sacrifice and suffering cannot be surpassed by anybody. But I would like these qualities to be used at a more opportune moment.

BOSE: This is the most opportune time and it is impossible to think of any other situation in which India could start the struggle.

GANDHI: Why do you think we cannot get better opportunities later on? I am sure we will have many such opportunities. Whether England wins or loses this war, she will be weakened by it; she will not have the strength to shoulder the responsibilities of administering the country, and with some slight effort on our part she will have no alternative but to recognize India's independence. Both politically and morally, I feel, we should not be hasty in launching a movement at the present juncture. My conscience tells me to wait for better times.

BOSE: Bapu, if you give a call, the whole nation will respond to it.

GANDHI: Even if the nation is ready at a moment like this, I must not do anything that is inopportune.

BOSE: If you think that this moment is inopportune, I want your blessings for starting such a movement.

GANDHI: You don't need my blessings, Subhas. How can I bless a movement which I consider inopportune, and which I feel is morally unjustifiable now? You have got the qualities of a great leader, and if your conscience tells you that this is the best time for striking out, go ahead and do your best. If you come out successful, I shall be the first to congratulate you. But my advice to you is not to be hasty. You are too emotional, and you must realise that everyone who talks of supporting you will not do so when the testing time comes. So be careful in whatever you do. You can always write to me and consult me. My heart is entirely with you, my love for you and for your family is great, and therefore I would not like you to do anything that will inflict any unnecessary suffering. I would like to tell you again that India will get better opportunities in future, and will be in a better position to give a fight to England than it is now . . .

# THIRTY-SIX

# Descent into War

While efforts to strip Bose of any authority in the Congress organization were in full progress, the international situation had greatly worsened. The threat of war loomed over Europe, with Hitler giving an ultimatum to Poland and signing a pact with Stalin. On 3 September 1939, the day World War II started, the Viceroy proclaimed without consulting any Indians that India was at war with Germany. He knew that consultations relating to Indian involvement in an 'imperialist' war would be beset with difficulties and might end in deadlock. The Viceroy also knew that he would arouse widespread opposition, but he hoped that once the decision was announced some opponents could be persuaded to accept it and the remainder would be isolated.

Lord Linlithgow promptly invited Gandhi to see him. On receiving the telegraphic message Gandhi boarded the first available train to Simla, the summer capital. The crowd gathered at the station chanted: 'We do not want any understanding' as the Mahatma walked to the train. It was Monday, his day of silence, so he simply smiled and departed.

Gandhi explained to the Viceroy that he had no instructions from the Working Committee to represent the national mind because of his 'irrepressible belief in non-violence which others did not share'. But he said that his personal sympathies were with England and France from the purely humanitarian standpoint. As he was picturing to himself the House of Parliament and Westminster Abbey, the thought of their possible destruction proved too much to bear, and he wept. 'Hitler knows no God but brute force,' he said later.

Yet concerning events which took place outside India, South Africa or England, Gandhi sometimes betrayed a surprising lack of knowledge. For instance, he made a statement that the Jews 'called down upon the Germans the curses of mankind and they wanted America and England to fight Germany on their behalf'. When some Englishmen criticized him for this allegation, the Mahatma readily withdrew his statement without any reservation. Notwithstanding his acute moral sense, Gandhi's apparent 'prejudice' against the Jews, whom the Muslims regarded as their enemies, stemmed from the fact that he was still functioning in a political field in which Hindu-Muslim amity and cooperation remained the fulcrum of his policy, however disappointing the results had been so far. Then in the middle of May 1940 he wrote to Rajkumari Amrit Kaur, a Christian princess and an ardent disciple: 'I do not consider Hitler to be as bad as he is depicted. He is showing an ability that is amazing and he seems to be gaining his victories without much bloodshed.'

In any event Gandhi firmly believed that dictators like Mussolini and Hitler were not beyond redemption. In this context his counsel to the Jews to follow the path of nonviolence provoked discussions of considerably challenging character. Writing in *Harijan* of 26 November 1938, he said:

My sympathies are all with the Jews . . . They have been the untouchables of Christianity. The parallel between their treatment by Christians and the treatment of untouchables by Hindus is very close. Religious sanction has been invoked in both cases for the justification of the inhuman treatment meted out to them . . . But the German persecution of the Jews seems to have no parallel in history. The tyrants of old never went so mad as Hitler seems to have done . . . If there ever could be a justifiable war in the name of and for humanity, war against Germany to prevent the wanton persecution of a whole race, would be completely justified. But I do not believe in any war.

Germany is showing to the world how efficiently violence can be worked when it is not hampered by any hypocrisy or weakness masquerading as humanitarianism. It is also showing how hideous, terrible and terrifying it looks in its nakedness.

Can the Jews resist this organized and shameless persecution? Is there a way to preserve their self-respect, and not to feel helpless, neglected and forlorn? I submit there is . . . If I were a Jew and were born in Germany and earned my livelihood there, I would claim Germany as my home even as the tallest gentile German might, and challenge him to shoot me or cast me in the dungeon; I would refuse to be expelled or to submit to discriminating treatment. And for doing this, I should not wait for the fellow Jews to join me in civil resistance but would have confidence that in the end the rest were bound to follow my example. If one Jew or all the Jews were to accept the prescription here offered, he or they cannot be worse off than now. And suffering voluntarily undergone will bring them an inner strength and joy which no number of resolutions of sympathy passed in the world outside Germany can. Indeed even if Britain, France and America were to declare hostilities against Germany, they can bring no inner joy, no inner strength. The calculated violence of Hitler may even result in a general massacre of the Jews by way of his first answer to the declaration of such hostilities. But if the Jewish mind could be prepared for voluntary sacrifice, even the massacre I have imagined could be turned into a day of thanksgiving and joy that Jehovah had wrought deliverance of the race even at the hands of a tyrant. For to the God-fearing, death has no terror . . .

The Jews of Germany can offer Satyagraha under infinitely better auspices than the Indians of South Africa. The Jews are a compact, homogeneous community in Germany. They are far more gifted than the Indians of South Africa. And they have organized world opinion behind them. I am convinced that if someone with courage and vision can arise among them to lead them in non-violent action, the winter of their despair can in the twinkling of an eye be turned into the summer of hope. And what has today become a degrading man-hunt can be turned into a calm and determined stand offered by unarmed men and women possessing the strength of suffering given to them by Jehovah . . . The German Jews will score a lasting victory over the German gentiles in the sense that they will have converted the latter to an appreciation of human dignity . . .

The Jews have a record of enriching the world's literature, art, music, drama, science, medicine, agriculture, etc. They can add to their many contributions the surpassing contribution of non-violent action.

The Jewish press vehemently criticized Gandhi for what he felt 'in the innermost recesses of my heart to be one hundred per cent sound advice'. To be truly nonviolent one must love one's adversary even if he becomes violent. Gandhi went to the extent of advising the Jews to pray for Hitler. 'Even if one Jew acted thus, he would save his self-respect and leave an example which, if it became infectious, would save the whole of Jewry and leave a rich heritage to mankind besides.' But the Jews were being annihilated and even Gandhi's old friend from South Africa, Hermann Kallenbach, who was staying at Sevagram at the time, could not find it in his heart to pray for Hitler.

The journalist Hayim Greenberg had long been an admirer of Gandhi, but now he questioned the Mahatma's statements. Writing in *Jewish Frontier*, a New York magazine, Greenberg rejected Gandhi's comparison between the Indians and the German Jews. He argued that Gandhi's Satyagrahis had never faced the sheer bestiality and 'moral anaesthesia' of Nazi Germany. It was neither fair nor psychologically understanding of Gandhi to demand heroism from Indians but super-heroism from the Jews. Gandhi agreed with Greenberg that 'a Jewish Gandhi in Germany, should one arise, could function for about five minutes, and would be promptly taken to the guillotine'. But that, he said, did not disprove his case or shake his belief in the efficacy of *ahimsa*. 'I can conceive the necessity of the immolation of hundreds, if not thousands, to appease the hunger of dictators,' he wrote in *Harijan* of 27 May 1939. He argued for the long-term effectiveness of non-violent resistance: 'Sufferers need not see the result during their lifetime. They must have faith that, if their cult survives, the result is a certainty.' In any case the method of violent opposition gave no greater guarantee of success than nonviolent resistance. Some years later Gandhi said he was convinced that if the Jews in Germany had offered themselves to the butchers' knives and thrown themselves from the cliffs into the sea, they would have aroused the world and the people of Germany. Through Satyagraha they would have achieved a moral triumph which would have been remembered for all the ages to come. 'As it is they succumbed anyway in their millions . . . '

When the war had been raging for about two years and Hitler was at the height of his power, with the whole of Europe under his domination and his armies deep in Russia, Gandhi wrote an open letter to the dictator, acquainting him with the advantages of nonviolence and censuring him for actions which were 'monstrous and unbecoming of human dignity especially in the estimation of men like me who believe in universal friendliness'.

Dear Friend,

That I address you as a friend is no formality. I own no foes. My business in life for the past thirty-three years has been to enlist the friendship of the whole of humanity by befriending mankind, irrespective of race, colour or creed.

I hope you will have the time and desire to know how a good portion of humanity who have been living under the influence of that doctrine of universal friendship, view your actions . . . your humiliation of Czechoslovakia, the rape of Poland and the swallowing of Denmark. I am aware that your view of life regards such spoliations as virtuous acts. But we have been taught from childhood to regard them as acts degrading to humanity. Hence we cannot possibly wish success to your arms.

But ours is a unique position. We resist the British imperialism no less than Nazism. If there is a difference, it is in degree. One-fifth of the human race has been brought under the British heel by means that will not bear scrutiny. Our resistance to it does not mean harm to the British people. We seek to convert them, not to defeat them on the battlefield. Ours is an unarmed revolt against British rule. But whether we convert them or not, we are determined to make their rule impossible by non-violent non-cooperation. It is a method in its nature undefeatable. It is based upon the knowledge that no spoliator can compass his end without a certain degree of cooperation, willing or compulsory, from the victim. Our rulers may have our land and bodies but not our souls. They can have the former only by complete destruction of every Indian – man, woman or child. That all may not rise to that degree of heroism and that a fair amount of frightfulness can bend the back of revolt is true; but the argument would be beside the point. For, if a fair number of men and women can be found in India who would be prepared, without any ill-will against the spoliators, to lay down their lives rather than bend the knee to them, they will have shown the way to freedom from the tyranny of violence. I ask you to believe me when I say that you will find an unexpected number of such men and women in India. They have been having that training for the past twenty years.

In non-violent technique, as I have said, there is no such thing as defeat. It is all 'do or die', without killing or hurting. It can be used practically without money and obviously without the aid of the science of destruction which you have brought to such perfection. It is a marvel to me that you do not see that it is nobody's monopoly. If not the British, then some other power will certainly improve upon your method and beat you with your own weapon. You are leaving no legacy to your people of which they would feel proud. They cannot take pride in a recital of cruel deeds, however skilfully planned. I therefore appeal to you in the name of humanity to stop the war . . .

On the Indian political front, while Gandhi at his Simla meeting with the Viceroy could offer only his unconditional moral support, the members of the Working Committee and most Congressmen, as the Mahatma soon discovered, were unprepared to join him in 'non-violent defence' against armed invasion. They were agreeable to fighting against Hitler on terms. But the manner of the Viceroy's declaration of war made it certain that their terms would not be easy. On 14 September 1939, after four days of discussion, the Working Committee adopted a resolution drafted by Nehru, asking for 'the right of the Indian people of framing their constitution through a constituent assembly' and a sharing of power. If this was granted they would contribute toward the war effort. 'India cannot associate herself in a war said to be for democratic freedom when that very freedom is denied to her, and such limited freedom as she possesses taken away from her.' Gandhi was present during the Working Committee discussions as a guest. 'I was sorry', he commented, 'to find myself alone in thinking that whatever support was given to the British should be given unconditionally' and nonviolently. Nevertheless he loyally backed the resolution and commended it to the country: 'I hope the statement will receive the unanimous support of all the parties among Congressmen. The strongest among them will not find any lack of strength in it.' But how could he appeal for support for a view he had opposed? It appears the saint had to co-exist with the politician.

But had he not changed his mind since 1918? some critics chided. And how could he with his nonviolent activity associate with and help Congress 'whose policy is based on violence in the present crisis'? Gandhi explained:

At the time of writing, I never think of what I have said before. My aim is not to be consistent with my previous statements on a given question, but to be consistent with truth, as it may present itself to me at a given moment. The result has been that I have grown from truth to truth . . . Whenever I have been

obliged to compare my writing of even fifty years ago with the latest, I have discovered no inconsistency, between the two. But friends who observe inconsistency will do well to take the meaning that my latest writing may yield, unless
they prefer the old. But before making the choice, they should try to see if there
is not an underlying and abiding consistency between the two seeming incon-
sistencies . . .

There are degrees of violence as of non-violence. The Working Committee
has not wilfully departed from the policy of non-violence. It could not honestly
accept the real implications of non-violence. It felt that the vast mass of
Congressmen had never clearly understood that, in the event of danger from
without, they were to defend the country by non-violent means. All that they
had learnt was that they could put up a successful fight, on the whole non-
violent, against the British Government . . . I would not serve the cause of non-
violence, if I deserted my best co-workers because they could not follow me in
an extended application of non-violence. I, therefore, remain with them in the
faith that their departure from the non-violent method will be confined to the
narrowest field and will be temporary.

The Viceroy now invited over fifty Indian leaders of all shades of opinion,
including Gandhi, Nehru, Bose, Patel and Jinnah, for an interview.
Consequently, on 17 October 1939, he issued an uninspiring statement that
dominion status was the goal of the British policy in India, and and that the
Act of 1935 would be open to modification at the end of the war 'in the light
of the Indian views' and with due regard for the opinions of the minorities.

'The Viceregal declaration is profoundly disappointing,' Gandhi commented. 'It simply shows that the policy of "divide and rule" is to continue.' The Working Committee promptly rejected the Viceroy's
statement and affirmed that they would not give any support to Great
Britain. By 15 November all the Congress provincial ministries resigned,
leaving the governors in charge.

Jinnah could hardly believe his good fortune. He proclaimed Friday 22
December 'as a day of deliverance and thanksgiving, as a mark of relief that
the Congress regime had at last ceased to function'. The Muslim League
passed resolutions and offered prayers, thanking God for 'deliverance from
tyranny, oppression and injustice during the last two and a half years'. But
the British governors said that the Congress ministers had acted with
impartiality and catholicity. Withdrawal from office at this critical juncture
put Congress at a great disadvantage with the Muslim League, which could
now manoeuvre more freely without the obstacles of the Congress ministries. Being out of office, there was also a marked lessening of its influence
with the British government. Consequently, for the next eight years it
would function in the wilderness.

Meanwhile, relieved of the arduous task of confronting Congress ministries, Jinnah could devote his undivided attention to the challenging problem of formulating his party's constitutional goal. In March 1940, at a session in Lahore, the Muslim League voted for a separate state of Pakistan. Addressing an audience of about one hundred thousand Muslims, Jinnah declared:

> It is extremely difficult to appreciate why our Hindu friends fail to understand the real nature of Islam and of Hinduism. They are not religions in the strict sense of word, but they are, in fact, different and distinct social orders, and it is a dream that the Hindus and the Muslims can ever evolve a common nationality. This misconception of one Indian nation has gone far beyond the limits and is the cause of most of our troubles and will lead India to destruction, if we fail to revise our notions in time.
>
> The Hindus and the Muslims have two different religious philosophies, social customs and literatures. They neither intermarry, nor interdine together, and indeed they belong to two different civilizations which are based mainly on conflicting ideas and conceptions. Their aspects on life and of life are different. It is quite clear that the Hindus and the Muslims derive inspiration from different sources of history. They have different episodes. Very often the hero of one is a foe of the other and, likewise, their victories and defeats overlap. To yoke together two such nations under a single state, one as a numerical minority and the other as a majority, must lead to growing discontent and final destruction of any fabric that may be so built up for the government of such a state.

The Pakistan resolution demanded that India be partitioned and 'the areas in which the Muslims are numerically in a majority as in the northwestern and northeastern zones of India should be grouped to constitute "Independent States", in which the constituent units shall be autonomous and sovereign.'

Gandhi was 'deeply hurt' by the Lahore Resolution. 'The "two-nation" theory is an untruth,' he wrote in *Harijan*. 'The vast majority of Muslims of India are converts to Islam or are the descendants of converts. They did not become a separate nation as soon as they became converts.' He did not believe that the Muslims would ever want a separate homeland. However, as a man of nonviolence, he could not forcibly resist the proposed partition if the Muslims of India really insisted upon it. But he would never be a willing party to the vivisection.

> My whole soul rebels against the idea that Hinduism and Islam represent two antagonistic cultures and doctrines. To assent to such a doctrine is for me denial of God, for I believe with my whole soul that the God of the *Koran* is

also the God of the *Bhagavad Gita*.

Gandhi's sincerity of purpose was unquestionable, but this fact alone could not lead to a better understanding with Jinnah and the Muslim League. There were times when Gandhi's political astuteness would baffle even the most intricate minds, but on some other occasions, in his pursuit of truth, he would be content to be tactless, sidelining the ramifications of a profound political situation. Despite Jinnah's rhetoric at Lahore there was sufficient scope for negotiation and compromise, for Muslims as a whole, including Jinnah himself, were not yet committed to partition. But there were no feelers forthcoming from the Congress side with a view to allaying Muslim fears of a 'Hindu Raj'. Some positive, concrete effort in this regard could have saved Gandhi and Congress the exercise of leaning over backwards to please Jinnah in their future negotiations with him. An important step in promoting greater harmony would have been to work toward Congress-League coalition governments in the provinces and the expansion of the Viceroy's Executive Council so as to include leaders of both the Congress and the League. But these possibilities were hampered by Congress's refusal to, directly or indirectly, be a party to the war and by its insistence on the plan for a Constituent Assembly which Jinnah summarily rejected.

In the war arena, Hitler had overrun Norway, Denmark, Holland and Belgium. France was next. Britain's position was extremely vulnerable. To many Indians this seemed to be the most appropriate time to launch civil disobedience. 'We do not seek our independence out of Britain's ruin,' Gandhi wrote. 'That is not the way of non-violence.' Indeed at this time he was imbued more than ever before with 'the utmost non-violence' and issued an appeal to every Briton to accept the method of nonviolence and fight Nazism without arms:

> I do not want Britain to be defeated, nor do I want her to be victorious in a trial of brute strength . . . I hope you do not wish to enter into such an undignified competition with the Nazis . . . I want you to fight Nazism without arms or, if I am to retain the military terminology, with non-violent arms. I would like you to lay down the arms as being useless for saving you or humanity. You will invite Herr Hitler and Signor Mussolini to take what they want of the countries you call your possession. Let them take possession of your beautiful island with your many beautiful buildings. You will give all these, but neither your souls nor your minds. If these gentlemen choose to occupy your homes, you will vacate them. If they do not give you free passage out, you will allow yourself, man, woman and child, to be slaughtered, but you will refuse to owe allegiance to them.

The Congress Working Committee did not share the Mahatma's pacifism and felt that Britain's difficulties could afford a favourable opportunity for a fresh beginning. On 21 June 1940, it categorically stated that it could not go 'to the full length with Gandhiji' on nonviolence. 'So, for the first time,' Nehru wrote in his autobiography, Gandhi 'went one way and the Congress Working Committee another.' Commenting on the Working Committee's decision, Gandhi wrote:

> For the Congress, non-violence has always been a matter of policy; for me it is a creed . . . Since propagation of non-violence is the mission of my life, I must pursue it in all weathers . . . I am both happy and unhappy over the result. Happy, because I have been given the strength to stand alone. And unhappy because my word seems to have lost the power to carry with me those whom it was my proud privilege to carry these many years.

Despite the Working Committee's snub, Gandhi went to see the Viceroy on its behalf, and returned with an offer to broaden Indian participation in the government. He had no use for the offer, but Rajagopalachari (Rajaji) and Patel favoured further discussion. On 3 July the Working Committee adopted Rajaji's resolution, which stated that if India were given complete independence and a central government Congress would throw its full weight 'in the efforts for the effective organization of the defence of the country'. Gandhi was wholly opposed to the programme. Only Abdul Ghaffar Khan, the 'Frontier Gandhi', sided with the Mahatma. All acknowledged that Gandhi could have persuaded Rajaji to withdraw the resolution, but he chose not to dictate. 'I therefore encouraged Rajaji to persist in his effort, though all the time I held him to be hopelessly in the wrong.'

The British government had fresh plans of its own. In response to the Working Committee's offer, the Viceroy made a statement on 8 August. The constitutional issues could not be decided at 'a moment when the Commonwealth is engaged in a struggle for existence'. He would, however, invite a number of Indians to join his Executive Council and establish a War Advisory Council, but 'the British obligations must be fulfilled'. He spoke of safeguards for minorities, in a tone reassuring to the Muslim League but like a red rag to a bull as far as Congress was concerned. With Churchill's War Cabinet having replaced Chamberlain's discredited government and the crisis of the German war continuing, British policy was to tighten up. Even before making his 8 August statement the Viceroy had prepared secret contingency plans to curtail freedom of speech and other liberties, directed basically against nationalism.

The Congress leaders were disappointed at the Viceroy's statement. Gandhi at first refrained from making comment, but under pressure from friends in England and India, he responded:

> The Viceregal pronouncement is deeply distressing. It widens the gulf between India, as represented by Congress, and England . . . Britain cannot claim to stand for justice if she fails to be just to India. India's disease is too deep to yield to any make-believe or half-hearted measures.

The Working Committee declared that the British government had bolstered the minority issue to impede India's progress and its rejection of the Congress proposals suggested its 'determination to hold India by the sword'.

Congressmen who had so recently rejected Gandhi's leadership now felt that they could ill afford to be deprived of the Mahatma's guidance. So they again asked him to give them a lead. A resolution adopted at the All-India Congress Committee meeting in Bombay on 15 September affirmed the party's allegiance to Gandhi. The 21 June resolution had been a great obstacle in his way. The offer having been rejected by the government, he could now have no objection to accepting the leadership of Congress. 'The responsibility I am assuming', he told the meeting, 'is perhaps the greatest I have ever assumed in my life.' He continued to explain the new position:

> I do not want England to be defeated or humiliated. It hurts me to find St Paul's Cathedral damaged . . . It is not because I love the British nation and hate the Germans. I do not think the Germans as a nation are any worse than the English or the Italians . . . We are all members of the vast human family. I decline to draw any distinction. I cannot claim any superiority for Indians . . . I can keep India intact and its freedom intact only if I have goodwill towards the whole of the human family and not merely the human family which inhabits this little spot of the earth called India.
>
> Let there be no mistake as to what I am about. I want my individuality to remain unimpaired. If I lose it, I would be of no service to India, much less to the British people, still less to humanity . . . I claim the liberty of going through the streets of Bombay and say that I shall have nothing to do with this war and in this fratricide that is now going on in Europe. I admire the bravery. But what is the use of this bravery? I deplore the foolishness and the crass ignorance. These people do not know what they are fighting for. That is how I look at this war that is going on across the seas. I cannot possibly take part in it, nor do I want Congress to participate.
>
> I will approach the Viceroy in your name and our position, in essence, is this: 'We do not want to embarrass you and deflect you from your purpose in regard to the war effort. We go our way, and you go yours . . . If we carry the people

with us, there will be no war effort on the part of our people. If, on the other hand, without using any but moral pressure, you find that the people help the war effort, we can have no cause for grumbling. If you get assistance from the princes, the landlords, from anybody high or low, you can have it, but let our voice also be heard. If you accept my proposal . . . it will certainly be a feather in your cap. It will be honourable of you, although you are engaged in a life and death struggle, that you have given us this liberty.'

The Viceroy may say: 'You are visionary.' I may fail in my mission, but we will not quarrel. If he says he is helpless, I will not feel helpless . . . I will place my argument before him . . . in the confidence and hope that he will understand the reasonable request of Congress for full liberty to preach that we cannot aid imperialism, we cannot help spoliation . . .

Gandhi discussed his claim to this liberty with Lord Linlithgow at the end of September, but the Viceroy said no, orally and in a confirming letter. The Mahatma now proceeded to launch his campaign of civil disobedience which was at the outset individual and symbolic, for he wanted to ensure that the British were subjected to the minimum of anxiety and inconvenience. Having given the Viceroy advance notice, he called upon Vinoba Bhave, one of his earliest disciples, to defy the official ban on propaganda against the war. On 17 October 1940, Bhave set out from Wardha, inviting arrest. For three days he made anti-war speeches in the neighbouring villages, before he was arrested and sentenced to three months in prison. Nehru notified the police of his intention to follow in Bhave's footsteps, and ten days later he too was arrested before he had time to make a single speech. The judge gave him four years for some speeches he had delivered earlier in the year. Patel was chosen next, followed by Sarojini Naidu and Maulana Azad. They all disappeared behind prison bars. Vinoba Bhave was released on expiry of his three-month prison term, but he again courted arrest. Soon many prominent Congressmen, including former ministers, were selected to make anti-war statements and were sentenced to varying terms of imprisonment. A short while later provincial and local Congress committees started submitting to Gandhi lists of potential resisters, and by May 1941 about fifteen thousand persons were in prison. The protest against the Raj was generally nonviolent. In Bengal, however, the terrorist movement was revived following the house arrest of Subhas Bose in 1940 and the banning of his Forward Bloc party.

With the outbreak of war Bose started thinking in terms of achieving the liberation of India with the help of an organized army of support made up from anti-British foreign powers. His creed as a freedom fighter was simple: to wage war against the British imperialism by every means on every front, till freedom was won. In a dramatic move he escaped from

India and joined the Axis powers. On the question of whether it was morally right to seek help from foreign powers he would point out that 'if a powerful empire like the British Empire could go round the world with the begging bowl, what objection could there be to an enslaved, disarmed people like ourselves taking help from abroad?' It is unlikely that he had fascist leanings, but he had suggested that if, say, 50,000 men, Italians, Germans or Japanese, could reach the frontiers of India, the Indian army would desert, the masses would rise up and the end of English domination could be achieved in a very short time.

The individually based civil disobedience campaign was dull compared with its predecessors, purely because under wartime rules reports of it in the press could be suppressed. Gandhi temporarily suspended the publication of *Harijan* and advised his followers to become 'walking newspapers', carrying information from place to place. The individual civil disobedience lasted about a year, and by early December 1941 the government, anxious to win popular support in view of the possible involvement of the Japanese in the war, began to free the prisoners. Nehru and Azad were released on 3 December. Reacting to the government's gesture, Gandhi commented: 'This has not evoked a single responsive or appreciative chord in me.'

On 7 December the bombing of Pearl Harbor brought Japan and America fully into the war. Shortly afterwards the hostilities acquired a further dimension when the swift advance of the Japanese through Malaya and Burma brought the war to the gates of India. The Congress Working Committee was again inclined to barter support of the war effort for an Indian National Government, but Gandhi considered it wrong that India should obtain independence at a price and under the shadow of war. This was not in keeping with his doctrine of nonviolence. The Mahatma, accordingly, withdrew once more from the Congress leadership.

Meanwhile President Roosevelt and Winston Churchill met aboard the cruiser *Augusta* with a view to committing the United States and Great Britain jointly to peace aims. The resultant document, which came to be known as the Atlantic Charter, proclaimed the right of all people to choose the form of government under which they would live and expressed the 'wish to see sovereign rights and self-government restored to those who have been forcibly deprived of it'. Indians were delighted by this new charter of freedom, but Churchill hastened to declare in the House of Commons that the Atlantic Charter did not apply to 'India, Burma and other parts of the British Empire'. Later, in an exchange of cablegrams and in transatlantic telephonic conversations, Roosevelt discussed India with Churchill and urged him to make an acceptable offer to the Indian people. Churchill's reaction was not devoid of a certain amount of irritation, so the

President said no more on the subject. However, in a move calculated to impress the British government with America's concern, he sent Colonel Louis Johnson as his personal envoy to India. Under the pressure of American opinion and Britain's own military defeats, with Japan at India's eastern door, India had attained such an importance as an Allied base that even Winston Churchill felt the urgency of seeking some constitutional settlement.

# THIRTY-SEVEN

# 'Quit India' Movement

With the fall of Rangoon on 7 March 1942, Japan was knocking at the gates of India. Four days later Churchill announced the decision of the War Cabinet to send Sir Stafford Cripps on a mission to New Delhi. The plan that Cripps was bringing had the unanimous approval of the War Cabinet, which included Churchill's Labour and Liberal colleagues in the Coalition.

Cripps, who was then Leader of the House of Commons, was a good choice on several grounds – as a Socialist contemporary with Nehru, and as a vegetarian of austere habits like Gandhi. Jinnah knew him as a successful lawyer who donated a large part of his huge professional income to political causes. He was personally sympathetic to Indian aspirations for freedom.

Sir Stafford arrived in New Delhi on 22 March and stayed there for three ill-fated weeks, during which time he met many Indian leaders representing various shades of political opinion. Congress was mainly represented by Azad and Nehru. On 27 March, at 2.15 p.m., Gandhi arrived at 3 Queen Victoria Road, where Cripps was staying, and remained with him for about two hours. Sir Stafford showed the Mahatma the as-yet-unpublished proposals of His Majesty's Government. The offer embodied a clear pledge of full dominion status for an Indian Union, under a constitution to be framed by Indians themselves, with the power to secede from the Commonwealth. This ostensibly met the Congress's plea for a unified India. The proposals were, however, hedged with clauses. Any provinces or Indian princely states that preferred not to belong to that Union would have the right to opt out, and British rule would remain virtually unchanged throughout the duration of the war. 'Why did you come if this is what you have to offer?' Gandhi asked Cripps. 'I would advise you to take the first plane home.' Gandhi described the offer as 'a post-dated cheque on a failing bank'. Cripps continued his negotiations with other Indian leaders while the Mahatma took the first train to Sevagram.

The Working Committee admitted that 'the self-determination for the people of India is accepted in principle', but stated that 'the novel principle of non-accession' was a 'severe blow' to the conception of Indian unity.

Nevertheless the main hurdle turned out to be Article E of the offer, which dealt with India's war effort. Regarding the immediate wartime arrangement, Article E stated: 'His Majesty's Government must inevitably bear the responsibility for and retain control and direction of the defence of India as part of the total war effort', but invited leaders of the Indian people to participate in it. Article E was obviously unacceptable to Gandhi. Congress, however, wished not only to contribute toward the war, but, paradoxically, to expand the responsibility and activity of Indians in the war effort, whereas the British sought to limit them. The Congress demand for an Indian Defence Minister was conceded on the British side, but it was held that the Commander-in-Chief could not transfer his major duties to any civilian colleague in the middle of the war. Congress insisted that the Viceroy was to treat his new council as a cabinet and accept its decisions. Sir Stafford rejected this and left Delhi for London empty-handed. The Cripps negotiations had broken down on the question of defence alone.

While the creation of Pakistan was not clearly stated, the possibility of partition through the non-accession of some of the Muslim-majority provinces was for the first time publicly acknowledged by the British. Jinnah and the Muslim League were prepared to accept the offer since it embodied, though implicitly, their Pakistan demand; however, in view of Congress's rejection they were left with no political option but to do likewise in order that they might compete more effectively for mass support.

Many critics blamed Gandhi for his uncompromising attitude which, they said, led to Congress's rejection of the offer. Others blamed Cripps and Churchill. Some years later Nehru observed in his book, *The Discovery of India*: 'After Gandhiji left Delhi there was no consultation with him of any kind and it is entirely wrong to imagine that the rejection was due to his pressure.' Azad in an interview reaffirmed Nehru's contention and said that Mahatma Gandhi made it explicit to the Working Committee members that they were free to come to their own decisions on the merits of the proposals. Azad reiterated that the negotiations failed solely on the question of defence. On whether he had influenced the Cripps negotiations after he left Delhi for Sevagram, Gandhi responded: 'That is a lie.' But Leopold S. Amery, Secretary of State for India, was convinced that the negotiations were demolished by Gandhi. Writing to Lord Linlithgow, the Viceroy, on 9 July 1942, Amery observed:

I see Gandhi is suffering from high blood pressure. The pity is that it was not high enough three months ago to prevent him from talking for two hours on the telephone from Wardha to Delhi and definitely wrecking the Cripps Mission . . . One can only hope that the present bout of high blood pressure may have weakened his power for mischief at this week's meeting of the Congress Working Committee.

In the event that such a vital telephone conversation did take place, it would certainly have been tapped. But in the confidential records, which are now available to researchers, there is no trace of a transcript relating to the alleged conversation.

Among the critics of Congress for its rejection of Cripps's offer was Rajagopalachari, himself a member of the Working Committee since 1921. On 23 April he addressed a small gathering of his old Congress supporters in the Madras legislature and received their approval to submit to the forthcoming meeting of the Congress Committee a resolution recommending the acceptance of Pakistan in principle. The basic reason behind the move was explained by the resolution itself, which asserted that 'to sacrifice the chances of the formation of a national government for the doubtful advantage of maintaining a controversy over the unity of India is the most unwise policy and that it has become necessary to choose the lesser evil'.

On the eve of the Congress Committee meeting Gandhi wrote to Patel that if an unequivocal resolution about nonviolent noncooperation was not accepted by the committee, he should resign from Congress. 'The wrong sort of action is being taken,' he said. 'We cannot go on just watching it, but must speak out even at the cost of popularity.'

When the Congress Committee met at Allahabad on 29 April, the feeling of resentment over the Madras meeting was so intense that Rajagopalachari found his position in the Working Committee very uncomfortable. He at once resigned from the committee, and having freed himself submitted the Madras resolution to the Congress Committee. He was heavily defeated. A counter-resolution was adopted, stating that Congress could not agree to such proposals as would 'disintegrate India by giving liberty to any component State or territorial unit to secede from the Indian Union'.

It was only two weeks earlier that Nehru had been advocating guerrilla warfare against the Japanese. He now accepted that resistance must be nonviolent, and sought to justify on practical grounds what Gandhi demanded on principle. Gandhi had sent from Wardha a draft resolution for the consideration of the Working Committee. The resolution, modified by Nehru, called for a nonviolent noncooperation form of resistance in case an invasion of India took place. It added that 'not only the interests of India, but also Britain's safety and the world peace and freedom, demand that Britain must abandon her hold on India'. Gandhi's resolution was carried almost without opposition in the Congress Committee. Now that Indian participation in the war effort had once again been ruled out, Gandhi was back in full command. Although it was a compromise resolution, Gandhi had triumphed and Nehru had surrendered.

The Mahatma was now seventy-two. He had been promising *swaraj* in a year or in a day for the past twenty-three years. Disillusionment with Cripps had destroyed the last vestige of his loyalty. He suddenly felt that this was the beginning of the ultimate crisis with nothing beyond it. Writing in *Harijan* of 7 June 1942, he said, somewhat desperately:

> I waited and waited, until the country should develop the non-violent strength necessary to throw off the foreign yoke. But my attitude has now undergone a change. I feel that I cannot afford to wait. If I continue to wait, I might have to wait till doomsday. For the preparation that I have prayed for and worked for may never come, and in the meantime I may be enveloped and overwhelmed by the flames that threaten all of us. That is why I have decided that even at certain risks which are obviously involved I must ask the people to resist the slavery.

He first expressed the idea of immediate British withdrawal in an article, 'Foreign Soldiers in India', which he wrote on 19 April, published in *Harijan* a week later. 'If the British left India to her fate as they had to leave Singapore,' Gandhi observed, 'the Japanese would most likely leave India alone.' It was his feeling that Japan and Germany would win. He had this aspect in mind when he prepared his draft resolution for the Allahabad Congress. 'India's participation in the war is a purely British act,' he said in the draft. 'Japan's quarrel is not with India. She is warring against the British Empire . . . If India is freed her first step would probably be to negotiate with Japan.' India harboured no enmity against her, the draft assured Japan, but should she attack India all Indians who looked to Congress for guidance would be expected to offer nonviolent noncooperation to the Japanese.

There was a new urgency and passion in his speech and writing. Some readers asked him if he was not inviting the Japanese to attack India by asking the British rulers to withdraw. He maintained that the British presence was 'the incentive for the Japanese attack'. When asked by reporters to whom the British should relinquish their authority, Gandhi answered: 'Leave India to God. If that is too much, then leave her to anarchy.'

He was fully aware that India as a whole had never been and had never claimed to be nonviolent. 'And what is decisive', he wrote, 'is that India has not yet demonstrated the non-violence of the strong, such as would be required to withstand a powerful army of invasion. If we had developed that strength, we would have acquired our freedom long ago.'

In an article entitled 'To Every Briton', he appealed to the British 'to retire from every Asiatic and African possession and at least from India':

The British statesmen talk glibly of India's participation in the war. Now, India was never even formally consulted on the declaration of war. Why should it be? India does not belong to Indians. It belongs to the British. It has been called a British possession. The British practically do with it as they like. They make me, an all-war resister, pay a war tax in a variety of ways . . . If I was a student of economics, I could produce startling figures as to what India has been made to pay towards the war, apart from what are miscalled voluntary contributions. No contribution made to a conqueror can be truly described as voluntary. [The British conqueror] is well saddled in his seat. I do not exaggerate when I say that a whisper of his wish is promptly answered in India. Britain may, therefore, be said to be at perpetual war with India, which she holds by right of conquest and through an army of occupation. How does India profit by this enforced participation in Britain's war? The bravery of Indian soldiers profits India nothing . . .

My people may or may not approve of this loud thinking . . . When slavery was abolished in America, many slaves protested, some even wept . . . The abolition was the result of a bloody war between the south and the north . . . I am asking for something much higher. I ask for a bloodless end of an unnatural domination and for a new era, even though there may be protests and wailings from some of us.

Gandhi was inclined to believe that as the Japanese thundered at the gates of India the British would come to terms as soon as his movement against them was started. But he admitted to the representative of the *News Chronicle* that despite a British withdrawal the invading Japanese would possibly use Indian ports for strategic purposes. In that case, he said, free India would allow Allied troops to operate from India. 'For Britain her defeat in Indian waters may mean only the loss of India but if Japan wins, India loses everything.' He now saw no reason why the presence of British troops in India should affect the feeling of real freedom:

Did the French feel differently when during the last war the English troops were operating in France? When my master of yesterday becomes my equal and lives in my house on my own terms, surely his presence cannot detract from my freedom. Nay, I may profit by his presence which I have permitted.

In any event, British imperialism was on its last legs. 'Whether Britain wins or loses, imperialism has to die,' he wrote. 'It is certainly of no use now to the British people, whatever it may have been in the past'

Gandhi argued for several days with the Working Committee at Wardha and finally, on 14 July, the committee declared that Congress was agreeable to the stationing of Allied armed forces in India, should they so desire, in order to ward off and resist Japanese or other aggression, and to protect and help China. But, the Working Committee affirmed, British rule in India must end immediately, 'not merely because foreign domination, at its best, is an evil in itself and a continuing injury to the subject people, but because India in bondage can play no effective part in defending herself and in affecting the fortune of the war that is desolating humanity'. The committee held that India must contribute to the safety of the world and the ending of Nazism, fascism, militarism and other forms of imperialism. It regretted that Cripps's proposals clearly showed that British hold on India was in no way to be relaxed. The frustration left by Cripps' mission 'has resulted in a rapid and widespread increase of ill will against Britain and a growing satisfaction at the success of Japanese arms. The Working Committee views this development with grave apprehension, as this, unless checked, will inevitably lead to a passive acceptance of the aggression. The committee holds that all aggression must be resisted . . . The Congress would change the present ill will against Britain into goodwill and make India a willing partner in a joint enterprise . . . This is only possible if India feels the glow of freedom.'

Congress, the resolution added, had no intention whatsoever of embarrassing the Allied powers; it was therefore 'agreeable to the stationing of the armed forces of the Allies in India . . .' If this appeal for withdrawal of the British power from India failed, the resolution concluded, Congress would 'be reluctantly compelled to utilize all the non-violent strength' to start a widespread civil disobedience movement which 'would inevitably be under the leadership of Mahatma Gandhi'.

In view of the far-reaching importance of the resolution, it required the approval of the All-India Congress Committee, which was summoned to meet in Bombay early in August. Meanwhile, in an open letter 'To every Japanese', Gandhi expressed his intense dislike for Japan's imperial designs, although he had no ill feeling against the Japanese people. 'You will be sadly disillusioned,' he warned Tokyo, 'if you believe that you will receive a willing welcome from India.' It was no doubt imperative that Britain performed the just and righteous act of freeing India. 'Our appeal to Britain', he added, 'is coupled with the offer of free India's willingness to let the Allies retain their troops in India. The offer is made in order to prove that we do not in any way mean to harm the Allied cause, and in order to prevent you from being misled into feeling that you have but to step into the country that Britain has vacated.'

Edgar Snow, an American journalist, asked Gandhi if he desired to have India's freedom in order to help the Allies. Would a free India carry out total mobilization and adopt the methods of total war?

'That question', said Gandhi, 'is legitimate, but it is beyond me. I can only say free India will make common cause with the Allies. I cannot say that free India will take part in militarism or choose to go the non-violent way. But I can say without any hesitation that if I can turn India to non-violence, I will certainly do so . . . it will be a tremendous thing, a wonderful transformation.'

The Working Committee's resolution of 14 July was evidently passed with Gandhi's approval. Rajagopalachari was critical of the proposal in that while civil power might be withdrawn, the British and the Allied forces could continue in India in anticipation of a treaty with a provisional Indian government. In a letter to Gandhi he pointed out that this would lead to the exercise of all government functions by the military forces, if only for their own safety and effective functioning. 'This would be the reinstallation of the British Government in a worse form.' But Gandhi said he believed in Britain's honesty. However, while the Working Committee at Wardha was discussing the programme of the 'Quit India' movement, the War Cabinet authorized the Viceroy to take stringent measures against Congress.

Jinnah, not surprisingly, took strongly against the Congress Working Committee's resolution, considering it to be an attempt 'to coerce the British Government to surrender to a Congress Raj'. He described the Quit India campaign as 'a manifestation of an angered and desperate mentality', and asked if this was the best contribution that Gandhi could make to India in the evening of his life. He declared that he would summon the Working Committee of the Muslim League to discuss the 'most dangerous and serious situation' created by Gandhi's challenge to the British government and to Muslim India.

Leopold S. Amery, Secretary of State for India, warned the Congress leaders that there would be no compromise with rebellion. Sir Stafford Cripps, in a broadcast to the Americans, criticized Gandhi for his ultimatum to Britain to leave India without any constitutional form of government, and insisted on keeping India as 'a safe and orderly base for our joint operations against the Japanese.' Gandhi, nevertheless, continued to justify the Congress Working Committee's demand for the ending of British rule and the moment chosen for enforcing its resolution. 'India is not playing any effective part in the war,' he told a correspondent of the *Daily Herald*. 'Some of us feel ashamed that it is so . . . We feel that if we were free from the foreign yoke, we should play a worthy, nay, a decisive part in the World War.'

About this time General Smuts was on a visit to London. His opinion about Gandhi now was far different from what it had been when they confronted each other in South Africa. During dinner a dialogue ensued between Smuts and Winston Churchill. It was Smuts who raised the subject; the Prime Minister was just not interested. Smuts expressed the view that big changes were coming.

PM: As I get older I begin to see a pattern of things.
SMUTS: There is a pattern in history, though it is not easy to see or follow.
SMUTS (of Gandhi): He is a man of God. You and I are mundane people. Gandhi has appealed to religious motives. You never have. That is where you have failed.
PM (with a grin): I have made more bishops than anyone since St Augustine. (But Smuts did not smile. His face was very grave.)

The Congress Committee duly met in Bombay on 7 August 1942. On the following day it ratified with little opposition the 14 July resolution of the Working Committee, calling for a nonviolent mass struggle. On the subject of India's independence the resolution provided that a provisional government acceptable to all sections of the people would be formed, and a free India would become an ally of the United Nations in the defence of the country, 'with all the armed as well as the non-violent forces at its command'.

On 8 August after the Quit India resolution was passed, Gandhi addressed the committee. He spoke at length about his endeavours to bring about Hindu-Muslim unity. 'The Qaid-e-Azam [Great Leader] himself was at one time a Congressman,' he commented on the attitude of M.A. Jinnah. 'If today Congress has incurred his wrath, it is because the canker of suspicion has entered his heart.' Speaking in a mood of patriotic fervour, Gandhi declared:

I want freedom immediately, this very night, before dawn, if it could be had. Freedom cannot wait for the realization of communal harmony . . . Congress must win freedom or be wiped out in the effort.

Here is a *mantra*, a short one, that I give you. You may imprint it on your hearts and let every breath of yours give expression to it. The *mantra* is: 'Do or Die'. We shall either free India or die in the attempt; we shall not live to see the perpetuation of our slavery.

Take a pledge with God and your own conscience as witness, that you will no longer rest till freedom is achieved . . . Everyone of you should feel free this very moment, consider yourself a free man or woman and even act as if you are free and no longer under the heel of this imperialism. You have to cultivate the spirit of freedom before it comes physically. The chains of a slave are broken the moment he considers himself a free man . . .

Gandhi proposed to make a last overture to the government before giving the signal. Mirabehn had earlier been sent to Delhi as his spokesperson to the Viceroy. The Viceroy refused to meet her, but she was received by his private secretary, Mr Laithwaite. 'You do not know the latent power lying buried in this coming move,' she informed Laithwaite after a long conversation. 'Even we do not know the force of Gandhiji's spirit, but I sense it, and I tell you that if the rebellion has to burst, this Viceroy will have to face a more terrible situation than any Indian Viceroy has ever had to face before.'

Gandhi's call for freedom 'before dawn, if it could be had', was answered promptly by the authorities. In fact the government of India had their own plans for dealing with the threatening situation. 'After my last night's speech,' Gandhi told his secretary, 'they will never arrest me.' He had intended to wait upon the Viceroy and plead with him for the acceptance of the Congress demands. He was therefore surprised when before dawn on 9 August, moments after he had spoken to his secretary and disciple Mahadev Desai, a police commissioner arrived at Birla House in Bombay to arrest him, together with Mahadev and Mirabehn. The entire Working Committee and other Congress leaders were also arrested, and the All-India Congress Committee and provincial Congress committees declared unlawful associations.

Gandhi, Desai, Sarojini Naidu and Mirabehn were taken to the dilapidated palace of the Aga Khan at Poona. The palace was ringed with barbed wire, and armed police stood at all approaches. Soon after, Kasturbai joined her husband by insisting on addressing a meeting in Bombay.

He had hardly been under detention for a week when profound grief overtook Gandhi. Mahadev Desai, his faithful and able secretary, chronicler and adviser, who had served him for twenty-five years, had a massive heart attack and lost consciousness. The Mahatma stood by his bedside. 'Mahadev, Mahadev,' he called in deep anguish. 'If only he would open his eyes and look at me he would not die.' But he was no more. Mahadev had been more than a son to Gandhi. With trembling hands he helped to wash the body and anointed it with flowers, whispering: 'Mahadev, I thought you would do this for me. Now I have to do it for you.' In the afternoon a small funeral procession followed Mahadev's bier to the improvised cremation site in a corner of the palace grounds. Gandhi followed the body with a staff in one hand and a pot of fire in the other. After a brief religious ceremony he lit the fire. He went daily to the spot where the ashes were buried.

The news of Mahadev Desai's death led people to believe that the arrested leaders were being cruelly treated. The muzzling of the press added to the wild rumours and suspicion of the official communiqués. Clandestine radio stations were set up which announced to the public the news of many happenings concealed by the government. Congress radio stations and the Congress bulletins gave information about a labour strike in Ahmedabad and the closing of the Jamshedpur steel works, the military occupation of the Benares Hindu University, the aerial bombing of Ballia and innumerable incidents of police firing and *lathi* charges.

The arrests of national leaders resulted in mass demonstrations which the government attempted to suppress rigorously. Soon a Quit India revolt flared up that the imprisoned leaders were powerless to control. The programme of nonviolent noncooperation was never carried out. Before it could be implemented, Gandhi and the Working Committee had been arrested, and a campaign of an entirely different character took shape. Their leaders imprisoned, the rank and file of Congress were left to act on their own initiative and resources. Mobs gathered in cities and rural areas and attacked what seemed to them the symbols of British rule and power. They set fire to railroad stations, signal boxes and post offices. Police stations and other government buildings were also attacked. Soon a powerful underground movement sprang into existence and its leaders and workers moved secretly across the land, fomenting rebellion. The rebels cut telephone and telegraph wires, blew up bridges and tore up railroads. The campaign was short but sharp – it lasted a few weeks. The gravest and most extensive disorders occurred in Bihar and the eastern part of the United Provinces, where for some time there was virtual anarchy, and communications were so badly disrupted that the eastern provinces of Bengal and Assam and the armies guarding the eastern frontier against the Japanese were completely cut off from northern India. The government forces, police and military, struck hard. The civilian casualties during August to November numbered about nine hundred killed and many more injured. Some thirty members of the police force and a few other officials and soldiers were also killed in the disturbances. Then, with the arrest of over sixty thousand persons, the uprising gradually flickered out.

'The disturbances', said Churchill, 'have been crushed with all the weight of the government.' Reacting to the Quit India demand, he declared publicly: 'We intend to remain the effective rulers of India for a long and indefinite period . . . We mean to hold our own. I have not become the King's First Minister in order to preside over the liquidation of the British Empire.'

During the Quit India movement and the changes in Delhi, Gandhi was in regular correspondence with the Viceroy. He criticized British propaganda, disclaimed responsibility for the violence, and asked that the Congress leadership be absolved of guilt. In his first letter from jail to the Viceroy, on 14 August, Gandhi accused the government of 'precipitating the crisis' and of 'gross distortions and misrepresentations'. The letter ran to several pages. The Viceroy curtly replied that 'it would not be possible for me either to accept your criticism or your request that the whole policy of the government should be reconsidered'.

# THIRTY-EIGHT

# Detention in the Aga Khan Palace

Some months passed before Gandhi wrote to the Viceroy again. In a 'very personal letter' dated 31 December 1942, he said that he 'must not allow the old year to expire without disburdening myself of what is rankling in my breast against you. I have thought we were friends . . . However, what has happened since 9 August makes me wonder whether you still regard me as a friend. I have not perhaps come in such close touch with any occupant of your throne as with you.' He criticized the manner in which the government had handled the crisis. 'If I have not ceased to be your friend,' he asked, 'why did you not, before taking drastic action, send for me, tell me your suspicions and make yourself sure of your facts?' The government had held him responsible for the violence throughout the country. He was expected to condemn the so-called violence of some people reported to be Congressmen, although he had no accurate information available except the heavily censored reports of the newspapers. 'I thoroughly distrust those reports.'

He went on to complain that the statements made about him in government quarters contained 'palpable departure from truth'. The government had unjustly condemned him and his colleagues and 'wronged innocent men'. In such moments of trial, he wrote, he, as a Satyagrahi, had decided to 'crucify the flesh by fasting'. That was a last resort and there was a way to avoid it. 'Convince me of my errors, and I shall make ample amends,' he concluded. 'You can send for me . . . There are many other ways if you have the will . . . May the New Year bring peace to all!'

In response to Gandhi's letter the Viceroy tried to be 'as frank and as entirely personal as your letter itself'. After the early period of Gandhi's imprisonment newspapers were made available to him and the Working Committee. He should have been aware of the arson and murders that had resulted from 'Congress policy', but 'no word of condemnation for the violence and crime came from you or from the Working Committee . . . It has been a real disappointment to me, all the more when I think of these murders, the burning alive of police officials, the wrecking of trains . . . You may take it from me that the newspaper accounts that you mention are

386

well-founded – I only wish they were not, for the story is a bad one.' Lord Linlithgow wanted to know from Gandhi if he wished to retrace his steps and disassociate himself from the policy of the previous summer. Gandhi replied that if his letter was a growl against the Viceroy, the latter's was a countergrowl, and added: 'Of course I deplore the happenings which have taken place since 9 August last. But have I not laid the whole blame for them at the door of the Government of India?' He felt certain that nothing but good would have resulted if the Viceroy had granted him the interview which he had announced on the night of 8 August. He might still be able to make a positive suggestion if he was put among the Working Committee, and if he was convinced of his errors he would not hesitate to make a full and open confession.

In London the Secretary of State for India, L.S. Amery, had his own difficulties. In a telegram to Lord Linlithgow he referred to a recent cabinet meeting:

> The Gandhi discussion was, as most Indian discussions are, hopelessly confused, because Winston [Churchill], without giving one time ever to explain the situation, or ever really reading the papers himself, sails in with a monologue, and nobody else gets a chance of really setting out their point of view . . . I am afraid we shall go through the usual process of time wasted over confused and unreal discussion to humour Winston, ending in your getting your own way if you are firm enough.

In his letter of 25 January 1943, the Viceroy sought to make it clear to Gandhi that 'the course of events and my familiarity with what has been taking place, has left me no choice but to regard the Congress movement and you as its authorized and fully empowered spokesman at the time of the decision of last August, as responsible for the sad campaign of violence and crime . . . The position remains that it is not the Government of India, but Congress and yourself that are on their justification in this matter.'

Finding that he could get from the Viceroy 'no soothing balm for my pain', Gandhi informed him on 29 January that he would commence after the early morning breakfast of 9 February a fast for twenty-one days. This time he would add citrus fruit juice to make his water drinkable, for his wish was 'not to fast unto death, but to survive the ordeal, if God so wills. The fast can be ended sooner by the government giving the needed relief.'

The Viceroy informed Gandhi that he had sufficient information to indicate that the campaign of sabotage had been conducted under secret instructions, circulated in the name of the All-India Congress Committee. He added rather harshly that he regarded 'the use of a fast for political purposes as a form of political blackmail *(himsa)* for which there can be no moral justification . . . and if you, by any action such as you now appear to be contemplating, find an easy way out, the judgement will go against you by default'.

In his reply of 7 February Gandhi pointed out that the Viceroy's letter, from a Satyagrahi's standpoint, was an invitation to fast. 'No doubt the responsibility for the step and its consequences will be solely mine.' The Viceroy had described the step as an attempt 'to find an easy way out'. The Mahatma was deeply hurt. 'That you, as a friend, can impute such a base and cowardly motive to me passes comprehension.' His fast was not designed to blackmail or coerce anybody, but to express and convince the Viceroy of his innocence. He had no wish to die, he told the Viceroy, but 'if I do not survive the ordeal, I shall go to the Judgement Seat with the fullest faith in my innocence. Posterity will judge between you as a representative of an all-powerful government and me a humble man who tried to serve his country and humanity through it.'

Secret documents reveal that the Viceroy had throughout been consistently in favour of 'letting the Mahatma starve himself to death if he wants to', but under strong pressure from his Executive Council and some governors and top civil servants, Lord Linlithgow decided to release him for the duration of his fast. This prompted Churchill to work himself into one of his states of indignation over India: 'This our hour of triumph everywhere in the world is not the time to crawl before a miserable little old man who had always been our enemy.' Amery wrote to Linlithgow that in the face of that mood the cabinet generally, instead of facing the issue, would begin looking round for minor points of criticism or uncertainty. 'I confess I get very fed up at times with a Cabinet which has no mind of its own and whose members are all terrified of saying anything which would draw Winston's displeasure upon their heads.'

Linlithgow was urged not to release Gandhi, but the Viceroy chose to defy Churchill, cabling in his defence the justification for his action, and stressing that it was not the time to precipitate action against Gandhi. On the eve of the fast, accordingly, the government of India offered to release Gandhi for its duration, thus pointing out clearly that the responsibility for any fast and its consequences rested exclusively with him. In case he decided not to take advantage of this offer of temporary freedom and undertook the fast under detention, he would be at liberty to have his own medical attendants, and also receive visits from friends with the permission of the government during its period. Pyarelal, Gandhi's other secretary, had been transferred to the palace after the death of Mahadev Desai. Pyarelal's sister, Dr Sushila Nayyar, was already there as medical attendant to Kasturbai.

Gandhi was content to take his fast while under detention. 'The impending fast has not been conceived to be taken as a free man,' he wrote in reply to Sir Richard Tottenham, Secretary to the Government of India, Home Department. If he was set at liberty, he would immediately end his fast and would resume it if he was arrested later. Thereupon the government got itself organized to meet all eventualities, including the possibility of his death in captivity.

If death did occur, the Bombay government would send all provincial governments an immediate telegram containing the code word 'RUBICON'. At the same time Bombay would arrange to stop all long-distance telephone calls and telegrams, except official ones from Poona and its neighbourhood, for two hours after the dispatch of the 'RUBICON' telegram. A bare announcement of the death would then be given to the press by Bombay, and the Indian government would issue a brief statement, the format of which had already been prepared.

No official message of condolence would be sent to Gandhi's widow and there would be no half-masting of flags. Full discretionary powers were granted to governors to deal with their local situation. The government of India at first considered closing offices for a day or half a day, as a means of satisfying public sentiment. The idea was later dropped, 'though the Governors will naturally use a wise discretion as to casual leave on or immediately after Gandhi's death, and will probably be disposed to turn a blind eye to unimportant absentees without leave'.

The Bombay government would allow a public cremation 'subject to such regulation in the matter of route, place of cremation, etc., as may be necessary to preserve order'. Gandhi's ashes would be kept in Poona for some time and later secretly conveyed by air to a place selected by his relatives. In no event would these be sent by train as 'there would be great danger from crowds en route, both at stations and on the lines, with serious risk of disorder'. The Bombay governor had already made plans for the deployment of troops in strategic areas. The adviser to the governor, Charles Holditch Bristow, was sent to Poona to make the arrangements for Gandhi's funeral.

The fast commenced on 10 February 1943, a day later than scheduled. For the first two days Gandhi was quite cheerful, but on the third day he discontinued his morning and evening half-hour walks. Dr Manchershah Gilder, who was detained in the Yeravda jail, was brought to the Aga Khan Palace on the second day of the fast. Dr B.C. Roy also arrived, from Calcutta, to attend the Mahatma. As his condition changed for the worse, three Indian members of the Viceroy's Legislative Council resigned from the council in protest against the government accusations which had caused

Gandhi to undertake the fast. Appeals from across India were made for his release, but both Lord Linlithgow and Churchill remained adamant.

On 20 February, the eleventh day of the fast, it appeared that Gandhi would not survive. The following day his condition reached crisis point. A bulletin was issued, signed by six doctors, government as well as non-official physicians: 'After a restless day on 21 February Mr Gandhi entered a crisis at 4 p.m. He was seized with severe nausea and almost fainted and his pulse became nearly imperceptible.' Kasturbai knelt before a sacred *(tulasi)* plant and prayed; she thought he was on the verge of breathing his last.

Finally, on the advice of the doctors, he agreed to add small quantities of fresh *musambi* (sweet lime) juice to his drinking water. Thereafter his condition improved somewhat – the nausea disappeared and he became more cheerful. The fast was successfully completed on the morning of 3 March with the usual ceremonies. Hymns were sung, and passages recited from the *Bhagavad Gita* and the Koran. Then Kasturbai handed her husband a glass containing six ounces of orange juice diluted with water. He sipped it for twenty minutes, then thanked the doctors, weeping while doing so.

Horace Alexander of the Friends' Ambulance Unit wrote to the Governor of Bombay that Gandhi had playfully mentioned to him 'my fraudulent fast', indicating that he had come to know of the insinuation made by the other camp's newspaper reporters that there was an element of fraud in the whole thing and that it was not a real fast.

It was beyond Prime Minister Winston Churchill's comprehension how the old man could survive a fast lasting twenty-one days. From the very beginning he was somewhat baffled by this and was inclined to be suspicious about the genuineness of the fast. In his communication to the Viceroy on 13 February 1943, Churchill observed: 'I have heard that Gandhi usually has glucose in his water when doing his various fasting antics.' Linlithgow, however, informed him that though his medical attendants were trying to persuade Gandhi to take glucose, he had certainly refused. Churchill would not accept this point of view and was anxious that some fraud should be exposed. 'Surely with all these Congress Hindu doctors round him it is quite easy to slip glucose or other nourishment into his food,' he wrote to the Viceroy on 25 February.

Linlithgow now felt happy and encouraged. In a telegram marked 'Most Secret' he informed Churchill that he had known Gandhi as 'the world's most successful humbug'. He had not the least doubt that his physical condition and the bulletins reporting it were distorted 'so as to produce the maximum effect upon public opinion'. The bulletin describing his crisis on 21 February was questionable. The government doctors thought it wise to compromise because the public in India would in those circumstances heed nothing but the bulletins issued by Congress doctors. 'The degree of nervous tension and hysteria engendered by all this Hindu hocus pocus is beyond belief,' the Viceroy said. 'I am suggesting slyly to certain American correspondents here that it has not been so much a matter of having their heart-strings plucked as of their legs being pulled.' The Viceroy however ended the telegram on a rather discouraging note: 'If I can discover any firm evidence of fraud I will let you hear but I am not hopeful of this.'

Churchill praised Linlithgow for his handling of the matter. In his telegram of 28 February to the Viceroy, he said:

> It now seems almost certain that the old rascal will emerge all the better from his so-called fast. I highly approve of the spirit of your [strategy] . . . and the weapon of ridicule, so far as is compatible with the dignity of the Government of India, should certainly be employed . . . How foolish those cowardly Ministers now look who ran away from a bluff and sob-stuff crisis. Your own strong cool sagacious handling of the matter has given me the greatest confidence and satisfaction.

Lord Linlithgow now tried to amuse the Secretary of State. 'We have exposed the Light of Asia – Wardha version – for the fraud it undoubtedly is: blue glass with a tallow candle behind it!'

Looking back at the whole episode, it seems possible that not all Gandhi's personal attendants were dependable, but the Mahatma himself, not unexpectedly, acted throughout in a manner which was beyond reproach. In an attempt to put things in perspective, the secret report of Major-General R.H. Candy, Surgeon General, Bombay Presidency, is quoted at length:

> Mr Gandhi is a man of 74 who is known to have been suffering from high blood pressure for many years. Some of the features noted during his fast may therefore be attributed to these facts either wholly or in part.
>
> He was throughout in charge of his private attendants, and all records and measurements were made by them, except for the presence of the Jail Superintendent at some, but not all, of the occasions when his weight was taken. These records do not appear to be as accurate as might be expected.
>
> Mr Gandhi started his fast in a very good condition. At the time of his arrest he weighed 103 lbs., whilst when he commenced his fast he weighed 109 lbs . . . Nothing noteworthy occurred until the fifth day when he was in difficulties with nausea . . . He lost weight at an average of 2 lbs. a day for the first five days, 1½ lbs. on the sixth day, and weighed 97½ lbs. on the morning of February 16th. Thereafter he was too weak to weigh until February 24th, when we were

informed that he weighed 90 lbs.

In the meantime his general condition rapidly worsened . . . On the 20th, or 11th day of the fast, it appeared that a fatal result was at hand. I had a private conversation with him as a patient and informed him that he had reached 'capacity'. I urged him to consider various points. He made no reply, but I think appreciated the position.

On the following day the 'crisis' appeared . . . the crisis was not witnessed by any Government doctor, but was not unexpected and I see no reason to doubt that it actually occurred. It was an attack of a syncopal nature and would be fully explained by a small coronary thrombosis.

On March 2nd, the last day of the fast, we were told that his weight was 91 lbs., that is he had gained one pound since February 24th. This weighing was done in the presence of the Jail Superintendent, whom I had warned of the importance of being present. At the penultimate weighing, he had been sent on some small errand, and was told of the weight when he returned. It would not have been advisable to have insisted on a reweightment in his presence. He had therefore taken possession of the weights, so that he had to be informed on the next occasion, and in fact this last weightment was done as a routine affair. It is hardly conceivable that one pound could have been added on a diet of water and about 9 oz. of lime juice daily. Either therefore the figure of the penultimate weightment is inaccurate, or the diet was not as stated. As however the general condition was improving it is possible that both conditions were present.

Up to the day of the crisis, Mr Gandhi took nothing but water, salt and alkalies, and small quantities of sour lime juice . . . At the crisis, he took sweet lime juice in his water . . . It does not seem possible that a man could maintain his weight much less increase it on such a diet.

During the course of the fast Dr Roy and Dr Gilder preserved an irreproachable attitude. They are both professionally men of the highest standing . . . I formed the opinion that they were puzzled by the upward course of events.

I am however convinced that if anything was added to his diet, he was ignorant of the fact. If anybody added anything, e.g. glucose, I think the culprit was Dr Sushila Nayyar . . . She is a young woman, and an ardent admirer of Mr Gandhi. She always emphasized the bad points of his decline in health, and even when he was clearly improving laid stress on his weakness, low voice, etc. She had enough sense however not to press her views against the majority . . . I strongly suspect that Dr Nayyar took fright, and sacrificed her principles. This will never be known.

The denigration of Gandhi and Congress was not confined to the British Prime Minister and the Viceroy. Some of the provincial governors were equally enthusiastic. The success of the Muslim League in a by-election in Mardan district in the North-West Frontier Province, hitherto a stronghold of Congress and their allies the Red Shirts, delighted the governor Sir

G. Cunningham. Writing to the Viceroy, he reported:

> It would not, I think, have been possible had not the ground been prepared by the propaganda which we have been doing almost since the war started, most of it on Islamic lines ... I am told that the Muslim League organization for the polling was not really good, and this makes the victory all the more significant.

Cunningham then went on to narrate a story which he was certain would amuse the Viceroy:

> They delighted the people of Peshawar city by dressing up a rather aged stork in a *dhoti*, with big spectacles on its beak, and leading it through the city in a procession with a ticket marked 'Mahatma Gandhi'. I am told it was a cruelly true caricature. The stork died the following day of exhaustion!

Linlithgow was pleased to get the news of the by-election, and was much amused with the governor's story of the aged stork. 'I wonder who the genius was who thought of it as an electioneering device.'

On the conclusion of the fast a number of non-Congress leaders, including Sapru, Jayakar and Bhulabhai Desai, and the ex-Congressman Rajagopalachari (he had resigned from Congress over the Quit India resolution), met in Bombay and issued a statement calling for Gandhi's release and a reconciliation between Congress and the government. It was their conviction that Gandhi, if set at liberty, would do his best to resolve the internal deadlock, and that his release would have no adverse effect on the successful prosecution of the war. The government, the leaders declared, could expect the loyal cooperation of the Indian people during the war only 'if we are permitted to talk with Gandhiji, consult him and obtain his support'.

The Viceroy, in a curt reply, turned down the leaders' appeal, insisting that the matter could be considered only if there were clearer signs of repentance and of 'a change of heart and mind' than Gandhi was willing to offer.

The political breach between the government and Congress was now complete, but Gandhi continued to conduct by letter a sterile controversy with the British authorities over the disturbances of 1942. And when the Viceroy, whose usual five-year term had been extended owing to the war emergency, was finally preparing to quit India, the letters exchanged between the two men, despite the surface politeness, reflected the tautness of their relationship. On 27 September 1943, Gandhi wrote to the Viceroy from the Aga Khan Palace:

Dear Lord Linlithgow,

On the eve of your departure from India I would like to send you a word.

Of all the high functionaries I have had the honour of knowing none has been the cause of such deep sorrow to me as you have been. It has cut me to the quick to have to think of you as having countenanced untruth, and that regarding one whom you at one time considered your friend. I hope and pray that God will some day put it into your heart to realize that you, a representative of a great nation, have been led into a grievous error.

With good wishes,

I still remain,

Your friend,

M.K.Gandhi

Linlithgow replied about a week later:

Dear Mr Gandhi,

I have received your letter of 27th September. I am indeed sorry that your feelings about any deeds or words of mine should be as you describe. But I must be allowed, as gently as I may, to make plain to you that I am quite unable to accept your interpretation of the events in question.

As for the corrective virtues of time and reflection, evidently they are ubiquitous in their operation, and wisely to be rejected by no man.

Yours sincerely,

LINLITHGOW

There appears to be an element of doubt in Gandhi's surmise that the disturbances following the Quit India resolution had arisen spontaneously on the arrest of the Congress leaders. But if the campaign of sabotage was carefully planned, it was not, as the government claimed, the work of the All-India Congress Committee, but of revolutionary groups and the left-wing elements in the lower strata of Congress.

In any event the passing of the Quit India resolution proved to be a fiasco, for it immobilized the entire Congress Committee in jail for three years, leaving the field open to Jinnah and the Muslim League. Jinnah made ample use of this opportunity and increased the forces of the Muslim League throughout the country.

On the war front, meanwhile, British commander Colonel Hunt surrendered his forces of sixty thousand Indian troops to the Japanese. These Indian POWs were handed over to Subhas Bose's command in the borderlands, and in October 1943 he announced the creation of a provisional government of 'Free India'. Three months later he set up his provisional headquarters at Rangoon and started his Indian National Army (INA), promising, 'You give me your blood and I will give you freedom.' In March 1944 Bose and advancing units of the INA crossed the Indian border into Manipur, and a few weeks later had advanced to the periphery of that state's capital, Imphal. The British garrison at Imphal needed to strengthen their eastern wing, and were hoping that the impending monsoon rains that would cause the cessation of all warfare in that jungle region for some months would give them enough time to reinforce themselves.

After the 1944 rains, the tide of battle turned against the INA, and in May 1945 they surrendered in Rangoon. Bose escaped in the last Japanese plane to leave Saigon, but he died in a mysterious plane crash on the island of Formosa in August. Bose's legend survived his own accidental death, which many Indians refused to believe in.

During his detention in the Aga Khan Palace Gandhi disciplined himself to a precise schedule of reading, letter-writing, prayers, half-hour walks and communion with his fellow prisoners. He also spared some time to revert to one of the first serious pursuits of his life, and gave Kasturbai lessons in Indian geography and other subjects. They smiled together over her struggles with Gujarati script and grammar, her failure to memorize the names of the Indian provinces and the larger cities, and her statement under oral examination that Lahore, which is the capital of the Punjab, was the capital of Calcutta, itself a city which is the capital of Bengal. With an orange he would seek to explain the meaning of latitude and longitude, and would point out the equator, but she could not appreciate the significance of these things. It was not that she was simple-minded or devoid of intelligence, she just could not get herself interested about matters that were so remote from her. She was seventy-four.

Unlike Gandhi, who thrived on prison life, Ba, or Mother, as everybody called Mrs Gandhi, felt a sense of inertia in the palace prison, for the restrictions there had deprived her of any real life as she had known it. Once the pious lady asked her husband a pertinent question: 'Why do you ask the British to quit India? Our country is vast. We can all live there. Let them stay if they like.' Gandhi replied quietly that they were welcome if they stayed as brothers and not as rulers.

During the long, hot summer Kasturbai had been ailing, but she improved considerably during the autumn. Then in December 1943 she became seriously ill with chronic bronchitis. Her circulation was bad and she suffered from heart palpitations. Dr Sushila Nayyar and Dr Manchershah Gilder tended her. It was common knowledge that Kasturbai had not long to live. She asked for Dr Dinshah Mehta, a nature-cure therapist who had treated her husband. The government was slow to grant permission. The therapist tried his art for a number of days, but the treatment proved ineffective. Then the modern-medicine physicians, Dr Gilder and Dr Nayyar, resumed their efforts, until they too confessed defeat. Devadas Gandhi sent for penicillin, then virtually unknown in India, but his father advised against it. 'You cannot cure your mother now, no matter what wonder drugs you may muster,' said Gandhi. 'She is in God's hands now.'

One of Kasturbai's last wishes was to see her eldest son, Harilal. Neither Devadas nor Ramdas was able to find him (Manilal was in South Africa). Harilal had vanished into the slums of Poona. On 20 February someone succeeded in tracing his whereabouts. Finally, he lurched into the sickroom in the palace, drunk. Kasturbai wept and beat her forehead. He was promptly removed from her presence, and she never saw him again. Next day Devadas came with Harilal's daughter. Kasturbai was deeply moved to see them and wept. She implored Devadas to look after Harilal's family. 'The burden remains with you.' He promised to take care of his brother's children and stood beside her cot through the night and ministered to her.

By the afternoon of 22 February it appeared unlikely that she had much more time left. As Gandhi sat on her cot with her attendants and visitors around her, she looked at her husband and said: 'There must be no unnecessary mourning for me. My death should be an occasion for rejoicing.' A short while later she closed her eyes, folded her hands and began to pray: 'O Lord, I have filled my belly like an animal. Forgive me. I pray for your grace. All I desire is to be devoted to Thee, nothing more.'

A few hours later she became increasingly restless. 'I am going now,' she said in a lisping voice. 'I am at peace.' She died in her husband's arms while they all sang 'Ramadhun' around her.

The following morning a hundred and fifty relatives and friends were permitted to enter the Aga Khan Palace to attend the funeral rites. Gandhi's request for a public funeral had been refused by the government. Kasturbai was wrapped in a white *sari* made of yarn spun by her husband, and was cremated on the same site as Mahadev Desai. For several hours Gandhi stayed near the pyre, and showed signs of extreme exhaustion. Attempts were made to lead him back to his room, but he refused to leave. For some time he stood leaning on a staff. Later he went and sat under a tree, gazing at the slowly burning body. Finally, he returned and sat on his cot. 'I cannot imagine life without Ba,' he said. 'Her passing has left a vacuum which never will be filled.'

The new Viceroy, Lord Wavell, wrote to Gandhi and expressed to him 'deep sympathy from my wife and myself at the death of Mrs Gandhi. We understand what this loss must mean to you after so many years of companionship.'

Gandhi in reply said: 'Though for her sake I have welcomed her death as bringing freedom from living agony, I feel the loss more than I had thought I should.' They were a couple 'outside the ordinary,' he told the Viceroy, whom he had never met. He spoke of their continence after the age of thirty-seven. 'To my great joy this knit us together as never before. We ceased to be two different entities. Without my wishing it, she chose to lose herself in me. The result was that she became truly my *better* half.'

Some weeks after Kasturbai's death Gandhi had a severe attack of malaria, with a temperature of 105°. At first he tried his own treatment – a fruit juice diet and fasting – but there was no relief. The doctors prescribed quinine, but it was some days before he relented and let the sovereign remedy against malaria work. He took thirty-two grains of quinine in two days and the fever subsided. Soon there was no more trace of malaria in his blood; however, other problems followed. On 3 May 1944, the doctors issued a bulletin saying that he was anaemic and his blood pressure had reached an alarmingly low level. 'His general condition is again giving rise to some anxiety.' The government feared that his death would soon follow the deaths in detention of Mahadev Desai and Kasturbai. Agitation for Gandhi's release swept across India. The government, no doubt, had to consider the fact that he had refused to accept a conditional release at the time of his fast in the Aga Khan Palace. But times had changed now. The war situation was less threatening and the Quit India movement seemed to be losing strength. The Indian Army had grown from its pre-war strength of 175,000 to almost two million men. And Linlithgow had been replaced as viceroy by Lord Wavell, an unpretentious soldier, who accepted as inevitable a role for Congress in the future governance of India.

On the evening of 5 May the superintendent of the jail camp, Colonel Bhandari, entered Gandhi's room to announce quietly that he and his companions would be released unconditionally the next morning. 'Are you joking?' Gandhi asked. 'No, I am serious,' Colonel Bhandari replied. On 6 May the morning prayers were offered as usual at five o'clock, and there was a last visit to the *samadhis* of Mahadev Desai and Kasturbai. 'Yes, Ba and Mahadev laid down their lives on the altar of freedom, and have become immortal,' he murmured. 'Would they have attained that glory if they had died outside of prison?' He then drove away from the Aga Khan Palace, the last of his many prisons. Altogether he had spent 2,089 days in Indian prisons and 249 days in African ones.

Gandhi went to stay at Juhu, the Bombay seaside resort with his old host Shantikumar Morarji. Mrs Naidu and Mrs Vijaya Lakshami Pandit, Nehru's sister, were there at the same time. As a means of ensuring rest Gandhi observed complete silence for two weeks. The sea air and long walks were gradually bringing him back to health.

On learning that he had never seen either a silent movie or a talkie, the Morarjis decided to amuse him with a private showing of a film which was being exhibited in a nearby suburb. The projector was set up in the living room and a hundred guests were invited to view *Mission to Moscow*. It was not a good choice, for the film, depicting the adventures of an American ambassador in the wartime Kremlin, grossly exaggerated the strength of the alliance between the United States and the Soviet Union. Not even the antics of the ambassador could arouse Gandhi's interest in the film.

'How did you like it?' Mrs Morarji asked Gandhi. He did not like it, he replied, chiefly because of the scenes showing provocatively dressed women and couples dancing closely; he considered it improper. They tried an Indian film – *Ram Rajya*, relating to an ancient legend – with happier results, but the Mahatma's dislike of films and cameramen remained to the end of his life.

# THIRTY-NINE

# India in Suspense

Gandhi was still convalescing, this time at a nature clinic at Poona, when on 17 June he wrote to the Viceroy asking for an interview and for permission to consult members of the Working Committee who were all in jail. Lord Wavell declined Gandhi's request to see the Working Committee. He referred to Gandhi's adherence to the Quit India resolution and said:

> I feel that a meeting between us at present could have no value and could only raise hopes which would be disappointed. If after your convalescence and on further reflection, you have a definite and constructive policy to propose for the furtherance of India's welfare, I shall be glad to consider.

But Gandhi was not easily to be put off, and he decided to employ other means to make his views known. During his stay at Panchgani, a hill resort near Poona, he gave a long interview to Stewart Gelder, the correspondent of the English newspaper, the *News Chronicle*, in which he indicated that he had retreated somewhat from the extreme position of the Quit India resolution. Although he had no authority, he said, to withdraw that resolution, he was still in a position to start civil disobedience on the strength of his influence with the masses. But he would be doing so merely to embarrass the British government, and this certainly could not be his object. It was his purpose, he told Gelder, not to hinder but to help the war effort. Much water had flowed under the bridge since 1942. He would now be content with a national government controlling only the civil administration, with the army under Allied control and the Viceroy assuming the role of a constitutional monarch guided by ministers, and he wanted popular government restored to all the provinces.

Report of the interview drew complaints that by his changed attitude he was lending moral weight to the Allied cause, thereby betraying the cause of the country. 'But they forget', Gandhi declared at a press conference, 'that my offer, such as it is, is subject to the condition that the Allies, in this case the British Government, should recognize full independence, qualified during the pendency of the war.' He therefore saw no conflict between the principles defined in the August resolution and what he had suggested in the recent interview. He also spoke of the efficacy of the 1942 rising, which had been independent of him, and stressed that no real Satyagraha had occurred. 'Heroism, suffering and self-sacrifice of those who took part in the struggle', he said, 'are beyond praise; but weighed in the scale of truth and non-violence there are glaring defects in the popular demonstration.' He, however, would continue to believe that the government had magnified popular violence out of proportion, whereas the considerable violence displayed by the authorities had been generally defined as something necessary for the occasion. 'I must, therefore, refuse to judge popular action by the foot-rule of truth and non-violence unless I can apply the same measure for government action.'

A few days after the interview with Stewart Gelder, Gandhi wrote to the Viceroy, offering full cooperation in the war effort if a declaration of immediate Indian independence were made. The Viceroy replied that independence would be possible only after the war, and there must be an agreement by the main elements of India's national life on the framing of a constitution. He was prepared to consider the establishment of a transitional government if the leaders of the Hindus, the Muslims and the important minorities were willing to work within the present constitution. But such a transitional government could succeed only if there was an agreement in principle between the parties concerned as to the method by which the new constitution should be framed. 'Until the Indian leaders have come closer together than they are now, I doubt if I myself can do anything to help,' he reminded Gandhi. Since it was a known fact that the Hindus and Muslims were unlikely to resolve their serious differences, at least within the time that would elapse before the end of the war, Gandhi considered the British to be deliberately stalling. He felt that once India was granted independence, the Hindus and Muslims could fight out the constitutional problems themselves. The British, in his opinion, were engaged in a 'diabolical conspiracy to stifle India's aspirations'.

Lord Wavell, the Viceroy, was a general and a poet, a very well-read man with a wide knowledge of history and literature. He knew long passages of poetry by heart. He liked rhymes and jingles and enjoyed writing parodies and doggerel. A heavily built man, blind in his left eye, which was partly open, he had a rather grim manner, but in congenial company could be talkative and amusing.

A man of great courage and dignity, he was straightforward to the point of exhibiting, at times, a blunt, soldierly manner. Cripps is said to have remarked: 'The trouble about Wavell is that he is no politician' – a remark that Wavell regarded as rather a good testimonial to his honesty. His soldier's mind, however, understood little and cared less about legal and constitutional proprieties, and this caused him to start his viceroyalty on the wrong foot, for he raised with the cabinet at the very beginning, before he had even got out to India, the question of a political move with a view to breaking the deadlock. Apparently he did not appreciate the fact that it was Churchill's intention to appoint a stopgap viceroy who would not precipitate the constitutional issue. Churchill intended him simply to maintain the status quo in the political field for the present and looked forward to a postwar British presence in India. The Prime Minister inevitably ensured that Wavell's proposal was demolished at the cabinet meeting. Wavell wrote in his meticulously maintained journal:

> Prime Minister was menacing and unpleasant when I saw him at 3 p.m.; accused me practically of playing to the gallery . . . and indicated that only on his dead body would any approach to Gandhi take place. I resented this and I am afraid rather replied in kind.

Wavell was of the view that Churchill 'hates India and everything to do with it' and agreed with Amery that he knew 'as much of the Indian problem as George III did of the American colonies'. Wavell discovered that 'the Cabinet is not honest in its expressed desire to make progress in India; and that very few of them have any foresight or political courage'.

Wavell's literary pursuit led him to read *The Man Born to be King* by Dorothy Sayers, and he found the work 'very well done and very interesting'. The result was that for a while he could not help visualizing immortality for himself by sitting on Gandhi's tail, so to speak:

> Curious to think that if Gandhi were a saint, instead of a very shrewd and rather malignant politician (which is possibly how the Sanhedrin thought of Jesus at the time), or became transformed into a saint by history; and if he died on my hands, as he might well do, if he fasts again, I might go down to the readers of 2,000 years hence with the same reputation as Pontius Pilate; my Council would play the part of the Sanhedrin; and perhaps one of the Princes could be cast for Herod.

Meanwhile, Gandhi, rebuffed by the government, turned to 'Brother Jinnah' to discover whether Congress and the Muslim League could come to an agreement which would lead the British authorities to revise their attitude. He offered to talk to Jinnah on the basis of a formula for a Congress-Muslim League understanding evolved by Rajagopalachari, the famous Madras lawyer. The 'Rajaji formula' provided that if the Muslim League endorsed the demand for national independence and cooperated with Congress in forming a provisional interim government during the war, Congress would agree to a future plan of demarcation of contiguous Muslim-majority parts in the north-west and north-east of India, the inhabitants of which should be allowed to decide by plebiscite whether they would remain in a free United India or form a separate state or states of their own. The 'Rajaji formula' brought about hope among Muslims, who rightly believed that it now amounted to Gandhi's acceptance of Pakistan in principle. Gandhi's acceptance of the formula appeared to imply a marked change in his attitude, for he had previously rejected it and had described the partition of the country as 'an untruth, a denial of God, a vivisection on the living flesh of India, and therefore a sin'.

Jinnah had realized that he would be manoeuvring from a position of strength in his future talks with Gandhi. He no doubt had the blessing of the British in his game of poker, not because they saw any merit in his claims – it was just that he was fast becoming, as Linlithgow wrote to Amery, 'a useful counterblast to Congress'. However, Congress seemed unable to appreciate the idea involved in the government's lionization of Jinnah. 'The Hindus', Linlithgow complained on one occasion, 'have made the mistake of taking Jinnah seriously about Pakistan, and as a result they have given substance to a shadow.' Gandhi's preparedness to discuss the position of India with Jinnah aroused bitter criticism. Youths belonging to the Hindu Mahasabha party shouted anti-Congress and anti-Pakistan slogans at Gandhi's prayer meetings. Even some of the Working Committee members detained in Ahmednagar Fort were resentful of the Mahatma's new move, for they saw in it Jinnah further consolidating his position.

Gandhi arrived at Jinnah's palatial residence on Malabar Hill in Bombay at 3.55 p.m. on 9 September 1944, and stayed for two hours. He emphasized at the outset that he had come merely as an individual, representing no one except himself. Jinnah hastened to point out that in his view Gandhi represented the Hindus, or else there was no purpose in continuing the discussion. Their talks continued for eighteen days, and after each meeting their conversations were confirmed in an exchange of letters. There appeared no possibility of Jinnah accepting the 'Rajaji formula'. The Pakistan of his conception was not 'a bundle of contiguous areas' but comprised the whole of six provinces. Moreover he insisted that the division must precede the British departure, whereas Gandhi stressed that any division of India must take place by mutual agreement after the British had left India and not before. Jinnah was convinced that once the British had left, the Hindus would never agree to the partition of the country. In that situation the Muslims, if they wanted a separate homeland, would have to fight for it, and in the civil war that was bound to ensue, the numerically superior Hindus would put them at a great disadvantage. By 15 September it was clear that they were already at variance with each other, with the wall between them the two-nation theory. That evening Gandhi wrote to Jinnah:

In the course of our discussions you have passionately pleaded that India contains two nations, i.e., Hindus and Muslims, and that the latter have their homelands in India as the former have theirs. The more your argument progresses, the more alarming your picture appears to me. It would be alluring if it were true. But my fear is that it is wholly unreal. I find no parallel in history for a body of converts and their descendants claiming to be a nation apart from the parent stock. If India was one nation before the advent of Islam, it must remain one inspite of the change of faith of a very large body of their children.

You do not claim to be a separate nation by right of conquest, but by reason of acceptance of Islam. Will the two nations become one if the whole of India accepted Islam?

In his reply two days later Jinnah said:

We maintain that Muslims and Hindus are two major nations by any definition or test as a nation. We are a nation of a hundred million, and what is more, we are a nation with our own distinctive culture and civilization, language and literature, art and architecture, names and nomenclature, sense of values and proportion, legal laws and moral codes, customs and calendar, history and traditions, aptitudes and ambitions: in short, we have our own distinctive outlook on life and of life. By all the canons of international law, we are a nation.

Jinnah took Gandhi's insistence on the postponement of division as a crafty way of evading it altogether. 'The question of the division of India as Pakistan and Hindustan', he told Gandhi, 'is only on your lips and does not come from your heart.' To Gandhi's final proposal to resolve the issue, 'Brother Jinnah' said no three times. The talks broke down. This was not surprising, for the two men were temperamentally different to such an extent that even in the most favourable circumstances agreement between them would have been very difficult. But the fact that these talks took place at Gandhi's initiative and at Jinnah's house indicated the advantage which the Muslim League had acquired while the Congress was in the wilderness.

In a letter to Gandhi, Dr M.R. Jayakar, the eminent jurist and Liberal leader, sought to sum up the outcome of the talks:

The Muslim League leader has gained more from you than he has lost to you. Though you have resisted the ridiculous two-nation theory, yet you have given him a formula which practically concedes the substance of the Lahore Resolution, viz., vivisection of India into two sovereign communal states without a controlling Centre . . . to a practical politician it makes no difference whether this division takes place as between two 'loving brothers' or between two 'sworn enemies'.

Gandhi's attempts at reconciliation with the British and with the Muslims having both proved unsuccessful, he took no further political initiative. He now devoted more time to his constructive activities, propagating village industries and the cause of the Harijans.

For the British government, wartime unity at home took precedence over an initiative for unity in India. Lord Wavell, the Viceroy, had all along been aware of the way the Indian problems were being treated by London, but it was not until October 1944, after a full year in office, that he took up the constitutional problem again.

During the war years Britain owed India for goods and services 'borrowed' to help win the war, and by 1945 the balance of payments between India and Britain was reversed for the first time. The combination of economic debt and terrorist activity had put Englishmen in India in an awkward position. As the war was drawing to a close, British public opinion, even Conservative opinion, was moving away from Churchill's colonial stand on India. And in the last week of May 1945, when the Prime Minister announced his intention of holding a general election, India was again projected into the political picture. 'If we are returned,' declared Ernest Bevin, 'we shall close the India Office and transfer this business to the Dominions.' The British Labour Party thus pledged itself to grant India dominion status. Lord Wavell, meanwhile, had been summoned to London for consultations.

At about this time, on the eve of the San Francisco Conference to draft the charter of the United Nations, Indian and foreign correspondents approached Gandhi for a statement. The Mahatma declared:

I very much fear that behind the structure of world security sought to be raised lurk mistrust and fear which breed war . . . There will be no peace for the Allies or the world, unless they shed their belief in the efficacy of war and its accompanying terrible deception and fraud, and are determined to hammer out a real peace based on freedom and equality of all races and nations . . . Peace must be just. In order to be that it must neither be punitive nor vindictive. Germany and Japan should not be humiliated . . . the fruits of peace must be shared equally . . . The Allies can prove their democracy by no other means.

On 5 June Lord Wavell returned to India after a stay of two months in

London. He was armed with the so-called Wavell Plan, which incorporated a constitutional offer on behalf of the British government. Churchill at the time still headed the National Government, which included Labour representatives. Soon after Wavell's return, members of the Working Committee were released and India's outstanding politicians were invited by the Viceroy to a conference at Simla, the summer capital, to discuss proposals for the formation of an interim government representative of the principal political parties. Wavell proposed a reconstitution of the Viceroy's Executive Council, which would be an entirely Indian council except for the Viceroy and the Commander-in-Chief, who would retain his position as War Member. The new council would represent the main communities and would provide for equal proportions of Muslims and caste Hindus, i.e., Hindus other than the Harijans. This was a concession to Jinnah and the Muslims, for it inflated the League's political position, but so eager was Congress for a settlement that it accepted the proposed composition.

The Simla Conference which began on 25 June 1945, found the Congress leaders in chastened mood and ready to cooperate. Jinnah attended as president of the Muslim League and Liaquat Ali Khan as its secretary. Master Tara Singh represented the Sikhs and N. Shiva Raj the Harijans. Gandhi did not attend the conference, but was present in Simla throughout the discussions, and although he objected to the projection of the Harijans as separate from caste Hindus, he did not make this grounds for withholding cooperation. The conference, however, soon ran into difficulties. Maulana Azad, a Muslim, was the Congress representative in his capacity as president of the party, but Jinnah insisted that no Muslim should be given a place on the council unless he was a member of the League. Wavell could not persuade Jinnah and would not proceed without his cooperation. Consequently the Simla Conference broke down. The Viceroy was initially determined to go ahead and form the new Executive Council, notwithstanding the possible difficulties. He had assured Azad previously that 'no party to the conference would be allowed to obstruct a settlement out of wilfulness'. But faced with Jinnah's determination, his advisers in both India and Britain counselled him to terminate the conference. The British government thus in effect conceded to the League a power of veto on the country's constitutional advancement. The Congress leaders, though critical of the government, did not for long consider the failure of the conference a great loss, for a few days after its conclusion Labour had come into power in Britain and it was becoming increasingly apparent that India's freedom was not far off. Clement R. Attlee replaced Winston Churchill as prime minister, Lord Pethick-Lawrence, a vegetarian and friend of Gandhi, was the new Secretary of State for India. The surrender of Japan after the atomic bombs were dropped on Hiroshima and Nagasaki in early August also brought a radical change in Britain's policy towards India, while the post-war reconstruction work back home would keep their hands full there for quite some time. The new Labour government promptly announced that it sought 'an early realization of self-government in India', and summoned Lord Wavell to Whitehall. On 19 September Attlee speaking from London and Wavell from New Delhi announced that as a first step fresh elections were to be held to central and provincial legislatures; the Viceroy had been authorized, as soon as the election results were known, to take steps to form an Executive Council. Thereafter a constitution-making body would be convened.

The election results were quite revealing. Congress won the overwhelming majority of the non-Muslim seats in the legislatures. (There were separate Muslim and non-Muslim seats.) Thanks to Abdul Ghaffar Khan, they won most of the Muslim seats as well in the North-West Frontier Province. More significant, however, was the success of the Muslim League. In the Central Assembly it won all the Muslim seats, and in the provincial assemblies 446 out of 495 Muslim seats. Although the League had no clear majority in any provincial assembly, Jinnah managed to form League-led coalition ministries in Bengal and Sind, but not in the Punjab, which remained under the control of the local Unionist party. Congress formed ministries in the remaining eight provinces, including Assam and North-West Frontier, both of which were claimed by the League for Pakistan. Nevertheless the capturing of Muslim seats by the League brought to light this bipolar political picture and gave credence to Jinnah's claim that the League was the sole representative of the Muslims.

Meanwhile discontent swept through the country as a result of shortages of food and cloth. During his visit to Calcutta, Gandhi had spent many hours with Richard Casey, the Australian who served as British governor of Bengal. Casey explained to the Mahatma his irrigation and development projects. These long-term plans were of value, Gandhi agreed, but the millions of unemployed must in the meantime be taught to utilize their idle time. He put forward his scheme of handspinning and handweaving as a means for immediate utilization of human effort. 'The acid question is one of utilizing waste labour . . . under your scheme it is one of utilizing waste water,' he told Casey. The Bengal governor later commented that he found it a 'waste of time . . . trying to argue against his views' on this point. The two men also reviewed the political situation. Summing up his impressions of the Mahatma, Casey recorded:

Mr Gandhi's greatest asset is his warm humanity . . . He can make his point publicly with an opponent and yet leave his opponent without any feeling of bitterness . . . He seldom, if ever, speaks ill of any man. I discussed with him several men who had been harsh to him but he managed to find some good to say of them and no ill . . . He trusts those who trust him . . .

He is credited by many of his followers with being a saint and a statesman. Whilst I have a considerable regard for him, I do not believe that he is either. What claim has Mr Gandhi to statesmanship? There is a simple criterion for determining whether a man is a statesman; the passage of time should show that he was right in his major political decisions three times out of four. I do not think Mr Gandhi can claim this record . . . Perhaps one might say that amongst saints he is a statesman, and amongst statesmen a saint.

# FORTY

# The Cabinet Mission

In the months following the war, certain events helped weaken India's last ties of loyalty to the Raj. Three captured officers of Subhas Bose's Indian National Army – a Hindu, a Muslim and a Sikh – went on trial by court martial in Delhi's Red Fort on charges of treason. From the British standpoint it proved to be an ill-judged trial, for soon it became a dramatic symbol of national unity. Bose's death in a plane crash on the island of Formosa had removed his challenge to the Congress leadership, and for this reason as well as out of national pride Congress lawyers, including Jawaharlal Nehru, defended the officers, and transformed the trial into a eulogy for Bose. Gandhi was watching the progress of the trial. 'Though I have nothing in common with any defence by force of arms,' he wrote to the Viceroy, 'I am never blind to the valour and patriotism often displayed by persons in arms . . . India adores these men who are on trial. No doubt the government have overwhelming might on their side. But it will be a misuse of that power if it is used in the teeth of universal Indian opposition.' The three officers were sentenced to transportation for life, but the Commander-in-Chief, Sir Claude Auchinleck remitted the sentences.

In February 1946 the Royal Indian Navy mutinied in Bombay, where some three thousand naval ratings rose in violent protest against their treatment and living conditions, which contrasted strongly with those of their British counterparts in the Indian Navy. Naval establishments in Karachi, Calcutta and Madras were also affected. Soon the mutineers seized control of several naval vessels in Bombay harbour. Vallabhbhai Patel, the strong man of the Congress high command, personally negotiated with the disgruntled sailors and, on his assurance of the party's assistance to sailors who had 'legitimate grievances', secured the 'surrender' of the ships. The mutiny inflamed the public mood and brought huge crowds into the streets, sparking off serious riots, arson and looting in several of the big cities. Appeals to the public to remain calm went unheeded. Both the military and the police opened fire on several occasions. In six days of disturbances about two hundred people were killed and over one thousand injured.

Gandhi had followed the disturbances with 'painful interest'. In a statement issued on 22 February, he declared:

If the Indian members of the navy know and appreciate non-violence, the way of non-violent resistance can be dignified, manly and wholly effective, if it is corporate. For the individual, it always is. Why should they continue to serve if service is humiliating for them or for India? Action like this, I have called non-violent non-cooperation. As it is, they are setting a bad and unbecoming example for India.

While the naval mutiny was still in progress, the British government announced its decision to send three cabinet ministers to India to seek to resolve India's constitutional problems. The Cabinet Mission, consisting of Lord Pethick-Lawrence, Secretary of State for India, Sir Stafford Cripps, President of the Board of Trade, and A.V. Alexander, the First Lord of the Admiralty, arrived in New Delhi on 24 March, and at once began discussions with Indian leaders. Gandhi travelled to Delhi at the Mission's request and stayed in Bhangi Colony, the municipal sweepers' quarter, on the outskirts of the city, claiming, as usual, to speak only for himself. Members of the Working Committee met at his new abode regularly. Here came British cabinet ministers, statesmen and diplomats of various nations, senior members of the Indian Civil Service and journalists from all over the world, to hold conference with the Mahatma behind his spinning wheel.

The Cabinet Mission remained in India for three months. Gandhi at first took a leading part in the discussions. Rising early in the morning as usual he was sometimes conferring with Lord Pethick-Lawrence by 6.30. The Mission talked to a large number of representative Indians, but the Congress-League deadlock remained and there could be no agreed basis for forming a constitution. The Cabinet Mission then invited Congress and the League to send four delegates each to a conference in Simla, to discuss a tentative scheme put forward by the Mission. Gandhi was not a delegate, but he made himself available in the summer capital for consultation. The Mission proposed a three-tier federal structure with a Union Government at the centre (embracing British India and the princely states), confined to the control of foreign affairs, defence and communications. There would be two groups of provinces, one consisting of the predominantly Hindu provinces, and the other of the predominantly Muslim provinces, dealing with such common subjects as the units within the groups might decide. The third tier related to other subjects and individual provinces in which all residuary powers would be vested. At some later stage the princely states would enter into this three-tier structure on terms to be negotiated with them. The Mission also indicated that in the All-India Union the Hindu-majority and the Muslim-majority groups of provinces might have equal representation, and that there might be provision for a province to have the right to secede from the Union after a period of years.

The Second Simla Conference proved hardly more successful than the first had been. It ended on 12 May, and the venue was thence shifted to Delhi. The Cabinet Mission and the Viceroy said that their object was not to lay out the details of a constitution, but to set in motion the machinery 'whereby a constitution can be settled by Indians for Indians'.

Despite its somewhat confusing details, the Cabinet Mission's plan published on 16 May 1946, was widely accepted as a genuine proposal for ending British rule in India. Gandhi commented: 'My conviction abides that it is the best document the British government could have produced under the circumstances.'

The Mission recommended that an interim government be set up at once to carry on the administration of British India until such time as a new constitution could be brought into being. It was impressed by the acute anxiety of the Muslims and conceded that 'if there is to be internal peace in India, it must be secured by measures that will assure to the Muslims a control in all matters vital to their culture, religion, and economic and other interests'. The Mission, however, rejected the League's demand for a Pakistan consisting of the six provinces of the Punjab, North-West Frontier, Sind, Baluchistan, Bengal and Assam – with their present boundaries – since the size of the non-Muslim minorities in those provinces was very considerable.

The Cabinet Mission then considered whether a smaller sovereign Pakistan confined to the Muslim-majority areas alone might be a possible basis for compromise. 'Such a Pakistan', the statement noted, 'is regarded by the Muslim League as quite impracticable.' The Mission also rejected the alternative of partitioning Bengal and the Punjab, for any such 'radical partition' would be 'contrary to the wishes and interests' of a very large percentage of the people living in both provinces. Moreover, the division of the Punjab would particularly affect the position of the Sikhs, 'leaving substantial bodies of Sikhs on both sides of the boundary'.

There were also weighty administrative, economic and military considerations. The division of India, the Mission said, would weaken the country's defences and gravely upset the communication and transport systems. A further consideration of importance was the question of how then to deal with the princely states. Finally they argued that the League's demand would create a geographically divided and highly vulnerable

Pakistan whose two halves, separated by some seven hundred miles, would render communications between them in both war and peace highly dependent on the goodwill of Hindustan. 'We are therefore unable to advise the British Government that the power which at present resides in British hands should be handed over to two entirely separate sovereign States.' The Cabinet Mission's solution, therefore, was an all-India Union on the old three-tier basis. It was hoped that the provision that any province should have the power to opt out of a group would satisfy the Muslim League's demand for separate Muslim zones in the north-west and north-east, while at the same time preserving intact the conception of a united India with a common centre though limited functions. The Mission conceded that their proposals might not satisfy all parties, but expressed the hope that the leaders and people of India 'will recognize with us that at this supreme moment in Indian history statesmanship demands mutual accommodation'. The acceptance of the plan should enable Indians to attain their independence 'in the shortest time and with the least danger of internal disturbance and conflict'. The only alternative, the Mission feared, would be 'a grave danger of violence, chaos, and even civil war'.

Jinnah criticized the Cabinet Mission's plan, insisting that Pakistan was the only solution. On 4 June, nevertheless, the Muslim League accepted it, affirming that 'the basis of Pakistan' was inherent in the plan. Everything now seemed to depend on what the Congress party would do.

Meanwhile the Viceroy had been striving to bring the two parties to agreement over the formation of a new Executive Council or interim government. He had opened negotiations with Nehru and Jinnah while still in Simla and continued them on his return to Delhi. The League insisted on 'parity' with Congress and the right to nominate all Muslim members. The Congress rejected both claims. In the absence of an agreement between the two parties, Wavell and the Mission at last decided to put forward compromise proposals and hoped that they would be accepted. On 16 June, accordingly, it was announced that the Viceroy had sent invitations to fourteen persons (whose names were given) to serve as members of the interim government. Wavell and the Mission avoided the inclusion of a nationalist Muslim, for they felt sure it would be unacceptable to Jinnah. However, they hoped that the Congress would reconcile itself to this.

Gandhi's oft-repeated advice had been to grant the Muslims the concessions that they wanted. But acceptance of the League's claim to the sole right to nominate Muslim members would have meant abandonment of Congress's own claims to be a truly national party, and not merely a Hindu organization. Gandhi had lately been using one Sudhir Ghosh, a youthful Cambridge University graduate, as his emissary in his communications with the Mission, to which Wavell took strong exception. 'Sudhir Ghosh is I believe a snake in the grass,' the Viceroy noted in his journal, 'and I would certainly never have trusted him.' Ghosh reported that Cripps had told him that the Congress stand in regard to the inclusion of a nationalist Muslim was absolutely logical and legitimate, but had asked whether the Working Committee could not waive it. It was highly improbable that Gandhi would agree to this. A principle was involved which Congress could not give up.

Although Gandhi's moral leadership continued unscathed, a decline in his political leadership now began to become apparent. Congress while conveying on 24 June its rejection of the proposals for an interim government, intimated at last its acceptance of the long-term constitutional proposals contained in the statement of 16 May. In a note to Cripps, Gandhi had observed: 'I propose to advise the Working Committee not to accept the long-term proposition without its being connected with the Interim Government. I must not act against my instinct . . .' But when the Working Committee was preparing to take its decision, Gandhi's was a lone voice. The Mahatma's secretary and biographer, Pyarelal, recorded the event:

> At 8:00 a.m Bapu [Gandhi] went to attend the Working Committee meeting. He asked me to read out the note which he had written to Cripps last night. He then addressed them very briefly: 'I admit defeat. You are not bound to act upon my unsupported suspicion. You should follow my intuition only if it appeals to your reason . . . I shall now leave with your permission. You should follow the dictates of your reason.'
>
> A hush fell over the gathering. Nobody spoke for some time. Azad with his unfailing alertness at once took control of the situation. 'What do you desire? Is there any need to detain Bapu any further?' he asked. Everybody was silent. Everybody understood. In that hour of decision they had no use for Bapu. They decided to drop the pilot. Bapu returned to his residence.
>
> The Working Committee again met at noon and addressed a letter to the Cabinet Mission, rejecting the proposal for the formation of the Interim Government at the Centre and accepting the long term plan with its own interpretation of the disputed clauses. Inspite of it they made Bapu to attend the afternoon session of the Working Committee. At noon the Cabinet Mission invited the members of the Working Committee to meet them. Bapu not being a member was not sent for and did not go. On their return nobody told Bapu about what had happened at the meeting.

A paragraph in the Mission statement of 16 June implied that the Viceroy would go ahead with the formation of an interim government even if only one party accepted the proposed arrangement. Soon after Congress's decision not to enter the interim government, Jinnah said he would. Wavell was in a dilemma, exposing his limitations as a political mediator, and declined to work with one party alone. Jinnah was furious and accused Wavell of having 'chosen to go back on your pledged word'.

On 26 June the Cabinet Mission announced that the plan for an interim government had been shelved, and three days later they left India. Wavell had told the Secretary of State for India at the outset that he did not intend to be a peripheral figure in these negotiations, and played a leading role in them throughout. While the three members of the Mission were able to devote all their time and thought to the negotiations, Wavell had to sustain in addition the whole burden of the viceroy's day-to-day work. He felt depressed at the future prospect, but maintained his sense of humour, giving vent to his feelings in a parody which he wrote shortly before the end of the Mission:

> JABBER-WEEKS
> (from Phlawrence through the Indian Ink)
> Twas grillig; and the Congreelites
> Did harge and shobble in the swope;
> All Jinsy were the Pakstanites,
> And the spruft Sikhs outstrope.
>
> Beware the Gandhiji, my son,
> The satyagraha, the bogy fast,
> Beware the Djinnarit, and shun
> The frustrious scheduled caste.
>
> He took his crippsian pen in hand,
> Long time in draftish mood he wrote,
> And fashioned as his lethal brand
> A cabimissionary note.
>
> And as he mused with pointed phrase,
> The Gandhiji, on wrecking bent,
> Came trippling down the bhangi ways,
> And woffled as he went.
>
> Ek do, Ek do, and blow on blow
> The pointed phrase went slicker snack;
> And, with the dhoti, Ghosh and goat, he
> Came chubilating back.
>
> And hast thou swoozled Gandhiji!
> Come to my arms, my blimpish boy!

Hoo-ruddy-ray! O Labour Day,
He shahbashed in his joy.

Twas grillig; and the Congreelites
Did harge and shobble in the swope,
All jinsy were the Pakstanites
And the spruft Sikhs outstrope.

'It's very interesting,' said Phlawrence a little wearily, 'but it's rather hard to understand.'

'So is nearly everything in this country,' answered Hobson-Jobson. 'Shall I explain some of the difficult words for you?'

'Yes, please,' said Phlawrence.

'Well, grillig is in the hot-weather at Delhi, when everyone's brains are grilled before 2 p.m. and don't get ungrilled till 2 a.m. Congreelites are animals rather like conger eels, very slippery, they can wriggle out of anything they don't like. Harge is a portmanteau word, it means to haggle and argue; to shobble is to shift and wobble; a swope is a place open to sweepers. Pakstanites are rather fierce noisy animals, all green, they live round mosques and can't bear Congreelites. Spruft means spruce and puffed up; outstrope means that they went round shouting out that they weren't being fairly treated and would take direct action about it.'

'That seems a lot for one word to mean,' said Phlawrence.

'The Sikhs don't quite know what it does mean yet,' said Hobson-Jobson.

'Well, anyway, the Gandhiji seems to have been swoozled, whatever that means,' said Phlawrence, 'and I expect that was a good thing.'

'But he wasn't,' said Hobson-Jobson, 'they found out afterwards that he had swoozled everyone else.'

'Thank you very much for your explanation.' said Phlawrence after a pause, 'but I am afraid it is all still very difficult.'

Wavell's relations with most of the leading Congress and League politicians were friendly. He somewhat disliked Jinnah, but got on reasonably well with him, completely disregarding his deliberate discourtesy. He also disliked Gandhi, but there was no trace of any unpleasantness between them till the interview on 27 August 1946 when Gandhi is alleged to have thumped the table and afterward accused Wavell of being minatory. In judging Gandhi, Wavell was strongly influenced by his recollection of the Quit India movement which for some time hampered the British war effort, and held Gandhi responsible for the disturbances. In dealing with Gandhi and Congress the events of 1942 coloured his judgement. Four years after the event, in a letter to the King giving an account of the Cabinet Mission's negotiations, Wavell admitted:

I can never entirely rid my mind of the recollection that in 1942, at almost the most critical period of the war for India, when I was endeavouring as Commander-in-Chief to secure India with very inadequate resources against Japanese invasion, the supporters of Congress made a deliberate effort to paralyse my communications to the Eastern Front by widespread sabotage and rioting.

Although he later acknowledged that it was unlikely that Gandhi had deliberately intended this as a stab in the back, this was, he felt, in effect what it was. 'We must try to leave India united,' the Viceroy wrote to the King, 'and we must secure the cooperation of the Congress which represents the great majority of Indian public opinion, whatever our views on the past record of that party.' Giving his estimate of the performance of the principal Indian personalities concerned, Wavell informed the King:

Gandhi ran entirely true to form: his influence is still great; his line of thought and action at any given moment and on any particular issue is as unpredictable as ever; he never makes a pronouncement that is not so qualified and so vaguely worded that it cannot be interpreted in whatever sense best suits him at a later stage; but however double-tongued he may be, he is quite single-minded on the one objective from which he has never swerved in the last 40 years, the elimination of the hated British influence from India. My distrust of this shrewd, malevolent, old politician was deep before the Conference started; it is deeper than ever now . . . Incidentally, he looks much tougher and in better health than since I first knew him. And I was persuaded that he was at death's door when I released him over two years ago.

I have much sympathy with Jinnah, who is straighter, more positive and more sincere than most of the Congress leaders; but he overcalled his hand in the end, and thereby, I think, missed the opportunity of having a more favourable share in an Interim Government than he is likely to get again . . . He is a curious character, a lonely, unhappy, arbitrary, self-centred man fighting with such resolution what I fear is a losing battle.

Azad, the Congress president, did well. He is a gentleman and stood for good sense and moderation as far as he was able, in spite of poor health and a naturally weak character. But up against Gandhi he was a rabbit faced by a stoat.

I have seen much of Nehru and cannot help liking him. He is sincere, intelligent, and personally courageous . . . but lacks the political courage to stand up to Gandhi when he knows he is wrong.

Vallabhbhai Patel is the recognized 'tough' of the Congress Working Committee, and by far the most forcible character amongst them. I have a good deal more respect for him than for most of the Congress leaders, and he is probably the only one of them capable of standing up to Gandhi. If he takes the line of constitutional progress, he may be valuable; if he goes to the Left, he will be formidable.

The rest of the Congress Working Committee are poor stuff, except that possibly one of the younger ones, Mahatab, Premier of Orissa, who is earnest and likeable, may in time become a capable administrator.

Soon after the departure of the Cabinet Mission, relations between Congress and the League deteriorated further. Nehru, who had replaced Azad as Congress president, flatly declared at a press conference in Bombay that Congress, in accepting the Mission's long-term plan, 'have agreed to go into the Constituent Assembly and have agreed to nothing else'. In regard to grouping of provinces, which the Mission had said was an essential feature of the plan, he went on to say that there would probably be no grouping at all. This virtually repudiated the basis laid down by the Cabinet Mission for accommodation of the minorities. Jinnah and the League retaliated by withdrawing their acceptance of the constitutional plan, and declaring that they would launch 'direct action' to achieve Pakistan. 'Today,' said Jinnah, 'we bid good-bye to constitutional methods . . . why should I sit with folded hands?' Asked if the proposed 'direct action' would be violent or nonviolent, Jinnah replied: 'I am not going to discuss ethics.'

At this critical juncture, Wavell invited Nehru to form an interim government, while keeping the door open for the League, but, in deference to Congress, he stressed that no side could bar the nominees of the other. Jinnah was furious: 'We have forged a pistol and are in a position to use it.' The League proclaimed 16 August 1946 as 'Direct Action Day'. The government of Bengal, headed by H.S. Suharwardy, a Muslim, declared the day a public holiday, and their cavalier attitude ensured that even the police were nowhere in sight. On that day, and for three more days, the streets of Calcutta ran with blood, leaving more than five thousand dead, at least twenty thousand seriously injured, and a hundred thousand residents homeless. After the first shock of 'Direct Action' the Hindu population of Calcutta organized itself and hit back with a parallel fury, thus contributing to turning the city into a charnel house. Despite the fury generated by Direct Action, Nehru took office as Prime Minister on 2 September. 'Our representatives and leaders have broken into the citadel of power,' declared J.B. Kripalani, the new president of Congress. Muslim League leader Ghazanfar Ali Khan reiterated at a public meeting in Delhi: 'The aim of our Direct Action is to paralyse Nehru's Government.'

Gandhi was living in the shanty Untouchables' quarter (inhabited by municipal sweepers) on the day Nehru took charge of the interim government. Early in the morning Nehru and his ministers called on him, and it being a Monday – the Mahatma's day of silence – a written message was read out to them: 'You have been in my thoughts since the prayer. Abolish the salt tax. Remember the Dandi March. Unite Hindus and Muslims. Remove Untouchability. Take to *Khadi*.' There was a short prayer and then each of the ministers received Gandhi's resounding benedictory slap on the back as he bowed to the Mahatma for blessing.

This was a red-letter day in India's history, Gandhi told his evening prayer meeting in a message. Whatever the British might have done in the past, this was no time for 'cavilling at old wrongs or reviving bitter memories'. The British were still in control of the army, but, he assured his audience: 'Sooner, rather than later, complete power will be in your hands if Jawaharlal Nehru, your uncrowned king and Prime Minister, and his colleagues did their part.' The Muslims were the brothers of the Hindus even if they were not in the government as yet, Gandhi continued, and 'a brother does not return anger with anger'. It was an occasion to 'turn the searchlight inward' to find out if any injustice was really done to the Muslim brothers. If there was any, it should be openly admitted and remedied. At the same time, he would respectfully tell the Muslim League that it was 'neither logical nor right' to resort to Direct Action.

But Jinnah declared 2 September a day of mourning, and the inauguration of the new Congress government was greeted by millions of Indian Muslims with black flags. A few weeks later, however, the Muslim League agreed to join the interim government, though their entrance was more tactical than a gesture of consolidation. Jinnah himself did not participate, but permitted Liaquat Ali Khan and three of his colleagues to join. In addition an Untouchable, a staunch opponent of Gandhi, was persuaded to join the cabinet on the League's side. The appointment of an Untouchable, a Hindu, to represent the proclaimed religious Muslim League was ostensibly done to annoy Congress and the caste Hindus. Liaquat Ali Khan, as Finance Minister, made certain that he was able to obstruct the effective functioning of every department by arresting funds. Khan's noncooperative tactics, dictated by Jinnah, were intended to prove that a unified Indian government was not practicable, and it was not long before Wavell and Nehru were made to realize that a Congress-League coalition was simply impossible.

Meanwhile the orgy of communal violence, terror and slaughter spread to eastern Bengal, first to Dacca and then to the remote districts of Noakhali and Tipperah, resulting in mass killings of Hindus. Muslim gangs set fire to Hindu houses, defiled their temples, forced them to profess Islam and raped their women. Deeply distressed, Gandhi decided to proceed in person to Noakhali and to 'bury' himself in East Bengal until such time as 'the Hindus and Muslims learnt to live together in peace and harmony'. Friends tried to dissuade him from setting out on a long journey just then, but he had made up his mind. 'I do not know what I shall be able to do there,' he said. 'All that I know is that I won't be at peace unless I go.'

# FORTY-ONE

# The Ordeal of Noakhali

Gandhi left Delhi for Calcutta, where he planned to spend a few days prior to his departure for Noakhali. Refugees from eastern Bengal had already started pouring into Calcutta and the neighbouring predominantly Hindu province of Bihar. On 25 October, which was proclaimed 'Noakhali Day', the Bihari Hindus began retaliating against the Muslim reign of terror inflicted on the Hindus in Noakhali, and during the following week piled up a verified total of 4,580 corpses. Gandhi was still in Calcutta when the news came of the atrocities inflicted on the Muslims of Bihar. Addressing a manifesto to the Biharis he said:

> Bihar of my dreams seems to have falsified them . . . It is easy enough to retort that things under the Muslim League Government in Bengal were no better, if not worse . . . But a bad act of one party is no justification for a similar act by the opposing party . . . Is it nationalism to seek barbarously to crush the fourteen per cent of the Muslims in Bihar? The misdeeds of the Bihari Hindus may justify Quad-e-Azam [great leader] Jinnah's taunt that Congress is a Hindu organization in spite of its boast that it has in its ranks a few Sikhs, Muslims, Christians, Parsis and others . . . Let not Bihar, which has done so much to raise the prestige of Congress, be the first to dig its grave.

Anticipating retribution in Bengal for the mass murders in Bihar, Nehru and Patel and two Muslim members of the interim government, Liaquat Ali Khan and Abdur Rab Nishtar, rushed by air from Delhi to Calcutta. They had consultations with Gandhi and senior government officials and appealed to the people to remain calm. Soldiers patrolled the city and countryside. From Calcutta Nehru, along with his cabinet colleagues, flew to Patna, the capital of Bihar, and threatened to resort to aerial bombing to quell the disturbances. 'But that was the British way,' Gandhi commented. 'By suppressing the riots with the aid of the military they would be suppressing India's freedom. And what was Pandit Nehru to do if Congress had lost control over the people?' Gandhi now announced that he would keep himself on the 'lowest diet possible' which would become 'a fast unto death if the erring Biharis have not turned over a new leaf'. Fasting seemed to be the only form of Satyagraha that was still possible. But 'the cry of out-raged womanhood' made him feel that his place was in East Bengal. Noakhali, he reckoned, was a plague that might destroy all India unless it was stopped. He gave up the idea of a fast for Bihar.

Gandhi left Calcutta on the morning of 6 November. Noakhali is a densely populated region, forty miles square, situated in the waterlogged delta where the Ganges and Brahmaputra rivers converge. Because of the watercourses transportation is tortuous and access to many villages is pos-sible only by boat. The roads of the district are such that the plying of even the humble bullock cart is beset with difficulties.

The short train journey took Gandhi to the river port of Goalando. He then travelled a distance of about a hundred miles by steamer downriver to Chandpur, reaching there late in the evening. He and his entourage spent the night on the steamer.

One of his first encounters on his peace mission was with a group of twenty Hindu workers, who included some of the prominent Congressmen of the district. They proposed more police or military pro-tection. 'You really confess defeat before the battle has begun,' Gandhi told them characteristically. 'No police or military in the world can pro-tect people who are cowards . . . Your trouble is not numerical inferiority but the feeling of helplessness that has seized you and the habit of depend-ing on others.'

Gandhi's lesson of fearlessness was the main theme of all his talks. The tragedy was not that so many Muslims had gone mad, he remarked to a co-worker. There was nothing courageous in Muslims killing a handful of Hindus in their midst, 'but that the Hindus should have degraded them-selves by such cowardice, being witness to abduction and rape, forcible conversion and forcible marriage of their women folk, is heartrending'. Gandhi, no doubt, considered nonviolence superior to violence, but he did not subscribe to nonviolence of the helpless.

'How can we create a sense of security and self-confidence?' asked a young Hindu man.

'By learning to die bravely. Forget the military and the police. They are broken reeds.'

'But we are burning with indignation.'

'Then turn your wrath against yourself.'

'To whom are we to appeal – the Congress, the League or the British Government?'

'To none of these. Appeal to yourselves; therefore to God.'

'We are men – of flesh and blood. We need some material support.'

'Then appeal to your own flesh and blood. Purify it of all dross,' said Gandhi.

After travelling for some days from one place to another, trying to fulfil his ambition 'to wipe every tear from every eye', he decided to place his own dedicated followers, including the women, one in each affected village chosen for them; they would act as centres of moral force, pledged to protect with their lives, if necessary, the minority Hindu population in their respective villages. 'Those who have ill will against the Muslims or Islam in their hearts or cannot curb their indignation at what has happened should stay away,' he said. 'They will only misrepresent me by working under this plan.' One by one his followers took up residence in the assigned villages, while he set up his own headquarters in the village of Srirampur, from which all but three out of two hundred Hindu families had fled. 'This Noakhali chapter may perhaps be my last,' he wrote to Vallabhbhai Patel. 'If I survive this, it will be a new birth for me. My non-violence is being tested here in a way it has never been tested before.'

Gandhi now devoted himself wholeheartedly to his mission in Noakhali, curtailing his enormous correspondence, and entrusting to others the editing of *Harijan*. He took his lessons in Bengali, did his quota of spinning, received visitors and deputations, and held prayer meetings. He went to the nearby affected areas, some of which could be reached only by boat, visiting the poor in their huts and going round the refugee camps, preaching his message of fearlessness and forgiveness. In that atmosphere charged with fear and suspicion, he wrote to a friend:

> I can sing with cent per cent truth: 'The night is dark and I am far from home, lead Thou me on.'
>
> I have never experienced such darkness in my life before. The night seems to be pretty long. The only consolation is that I feel neither baffled nor disappointed . . . 'Do or Die' has to be put to the test. 'Do' here means Hindus and Muslims should learn to live together in peace and amity. Else, I should die in the attempt . . . God's will be done.

On Christmas Day, a Christian friend brought Gandhi a present from the Friends' Service Unit. It was a soldier's kit containing cigarettes, socks, playing cards, writing paper, towels, soap, etc. The occasion provided Gandhi with a light interlude. He spread all the gifts on a mat and then started distributing them. The packets of cigarettes were kept for Jawaharlal Nehru who was expected to visit him shortly. A heavy mailbag brought among more Christmas presents a handsome edition of the Bible. The Mahatma's face lit up as he received it, and for some time he fondly turned over its pages with reverence. Speaking at his prayer meeting that evening he said that Jesus Christ might be looked upon as belonging to Christians only, but he did not belong to any particular community, inasmuch as the lessons that he gave belonged to the whole world.

On the morning of 2 January 1947, Gandhi, winding up his camp at Srirampur, set out on a more extended village-to-village tour. He was accompanied by Nirmal Kumar Bose, who had taken leave of absence from a teaching post at the University of Calcutta in order to work as Gandhi's Bengali interpreter; Parasuram, his stenographer; and Manubehn Gandhi, the granddaughter of his cousin, who looked after Gandhi's daily requirements.

His present pilgrimage would take him to about fifty villages. He would rise early in the morning, walk a few miles, often barefoot, to a village, stay there for a day or two and then move on. At each village he would hold prayer meetings, which were in effect open forums, and worked intensely to leave an intercommunal peace council functioning. He would also speak on many social and political problems. He would sometimes discourse on such matters while taking a mud bath – part of his celebrated nature cure treatment. A witness reported seeing him in the mild winter weather of Bengal:

> He was lying in the afternoon sun covered with mud from head to foot. I came upon him thus one afternoon in the courtyard of a village house. But he was not alone. He was receiving a deputation that had come to seek his advice on rural reconstruction and uplift. Questions were being asked and answers were coming out of the mud as if from a Delphic oracle.

While Gandhi continued with his pilgrimage of penance, Muslims began to ask him why he did not go to Bihar to provide succour to the Muslim victims of Hindu violence. He replied that he would go there when directed by the 'inner voice'. Even the Premier (chief minister) of Bengal, H.S. Suharwardy, who had welcomed him at first, now felt that Gandhi had overstayed his welcome in the province.

Despite the tense atmosphere, crowds at meetings grew in size, and there were peasants who ran the risk of the resentment of their fellow Muslims by welcoming Gandhi in their midst. In preaching Hindu-Muslim amity he spoke of the virtue of self-sacrifice, but would say that a man whose spirit of sacrifice did not go beyond his own community became selfish himself and also made his community selfish. In fact the spirit of self-sacrifice should be directed towards the welfare of the whole world. 'A drop torn from the ocean perishes without doing any good. But if it remains a part of the ocean, it shares the glory of carrying on its bosom a fleet of mighty ships.'

Opposition to Gandhi's pilgrimage persisted, and in February entered a menacing phase. Muslims began to boycott his prayer meetings as the more politically minded hung threatening placards on his route and advised the peasantry to keep away from him. Hostile elements sometimes strewed broken glass, brambles and filth in the barefoot Mahatma's path. He did not blame them; they had been misled by their politicians.

The pilgrimage to Noakhali brought Gandhi a deep personal crisis. The atrocities on both sides since Direct Action Day made him wonder if non-violence under his leadership had made any headway at all. In his utter state of despondency he blamed himself. As always, he believed that if he had failed to teach *ahimsa*, it was because he had failed to make himself a good enough teacher. He now turned more and more to thoughts of personal salvation. Ever since he could remember, he had yearned for *moksha*. And in his search for God, Brahmacharya, the perfect continence of mind and body, was a central trait of his philosophy. Once again he was striving to perfect Brahmacharya, in the belief that only such sublimation would grant him the spiritual powers to cope with the challenging nightmare of communalism, with its murderous war between Hindus and Muslims, and enable him to overcome Mohamed Ali Jinnah, the father of Pakistan, through nonviolence and repulse Jinnah's plans for partition. It was the Mahatma's aim to divest himself of everything but God's presence; for if he could entirely empty his being, God would possess him. This could be achieved only by intense discipline – perfect Brahmacharya – and at last he would become a fit instrument. However, an argument flared up when Gandhi publicly stated that in his quest to master his sexual drive he had been experimenting by sharing his bed with women disciples. He was seventy-seven.

For some years it had been rumoured that Gandhi occasionally passed the night with a woman in his bed and this, it was explained, was because he suffered from poor circulation, needed warmth, a woman's care and proper nursing. But the exercise was essentially part of his experiment in Brahmacharya. In fact, as the notion took hold of him at Segaon, it also affected the other inmates of the ashram. Ashramites of opposite sexes nursed each other in illness without restraint. At times he received visitors in the bathroom and had his massage administered by young women disciples. 'The sexual sense is the hardest to overcome in my case,' he wrote to Rajkumari Amrit Kaur in May 1938. 'It has been an incessant struggle. It is for me a miracle how I have survived it.' Only a few weeks before, he had discovered that he had not been able to 'subdue passion at all'. Deeply disturbed, he sought Mirabehn's opinion about the matter:

Should I deny myself the service rendered by Sushila? Should I refuse to have *malish* [massage] by Lilavati or Amtul Salaam for instance? Or do you want to say that I should never lean on girls' shoulders? Needless to say you won't pain me at all by telling me frankly whatever you think I should do to get out of the terrible despondency. Just now I am most in need of support from those who surround me with service and affection, undeserved as it seems to me, for the time being.

In a letter of 2 May 1938, addressed to Amritlal T. Nanavati, Gandhi wrote:

I recently discovered that I have not been able to subdue [passion] at all. I don't remember having had an emission while awake at any time during the last fifty years. I am not referring here to the emission in dreams or those brought on by desire. But I was in such a wretched and pitiable condition that in spite of my utmost efforts I could not stop the discharge though I was fully awake. I feel now that the despondency that I had been feeling deep down in me only foreshadowed this occurrence. After the event, restlessness has become acute beyond words. Where am I, where is my place, and how can a person subject to passion represent non-violence and truth? This turmoil goes on in my heart. I keep asking myself: Am I worthy of you all who follow me, am I fit to lead you all? God will answer the question when He pleases.

Writing to Mirabehn on the subject on 3 May, he observed that his Brahmacharya had become steadfast and more enlightened but it had been far from perfection. 'If complete Brahmacharya under the conditions I am trying is like an attempt to climb the craters on the moon, what is the value of the species that requires the nine fortifications?' (The reference is to the nine rules of behaviour known as 'the nine-fold hedge or wall' for the protection of Brahmacharya.) Notwithstanding the progress he had made in this regard, 'that degrading, dirty, torturing experience of April 14 shook me to bits and made me feel as if I was hurled by God from an imaginary paradise where I had no right to be in my uncleanliness'.

But he had now overcome that feeling of misery, he wrote to Amrit Kaur on 15 July 1938. 'My peace cannot be permanently taken away . . . if there is real attempt at purification, it must strengthen me and make me more joyful.' Writing to her two months later he noted:

I stopped on the night of Saturday [17 September 1938] the experiment involving physical contact with women that I had been carrying on . . . I have however been able to discover that the harmless physical contact with women which was habitual with me over many years has not done any harm to my practice of

Brahmacharya. The imperfection of Brahmacharya in me has some other cause. But, as is my nature, when a doubt arose in my mind regarding this it became necessary to make the experiment.

Gandhi's Brahmacharya experiments culminated with the arrival of his cousin's granddaughter, Manu, in Noakhali. The most reliable firsthand account of the episode is to be found in a book entitled *My Days with Gandhi*, written by the Mahatma's Bengali interpreter, Nirmal Kumar Bose. Early on the morning of 20 December, after the usual hour of prayers, Bose entered Gandhi's room and found the Mahatma and Manu in the same bed. They were talking together. Later, Bose says, Gandhi explained that they had been discussing 'a bold and original experiment, whose heat will be great'. He said he had reached the end of one chapter in his life, and a new one was about to begin. He was prepared to part company with anyone who opposed the experiment. On 1 January 1947, his secretary, Parasuram, typed out an enormous letter explaining his own views on the subject and suggesting certain changes to Gandhi's mode of life. Just before leaving Srirampur, Gandhi replied to Parasuram's letter:

I have read your letter with great care . . . It contains half-truths which are dangerous. Since . . . there is a conflict of ideals and you yourself wish to be relieved, you are at liberty to leave me today. That will be honourable and truthful. I like your frankness and boldness . . . You are at liberty to publish whatever wrong you have noticed in me and my surroundings . . .

In Noakhali, according to Nirmal Kumar Bose, Gandhi asked women disciples to share his bed and even the cover which he used, and then tried to ascertain if 'even the least trace of sensual feeling had been evoked in himself or his companions'. In Gandhi's view, such experiments were an integral part of his aspiration to become 'God's eunuch', as he put it, the ultimate in his spiritual quest, but Bose believed that the use of a woman as an instrument in such an experiment was anything but healthy, for it implied her inferiority. He noticed that each woman around Gandhi considered herself to have a special relationship with him, and the resulting feeling of possessiveness led some of them to a kind of emotional unbalance. 'The behaviour of A, B or C [Bose omitted names], for instance, is no proof of healthy psychological relationship,' he wrote to an old associate of the Mahatma. 'Whatever may be the value of the *prayog* [experiment] in Gandhiji's own case, it does leave a mark of injury on the personality of others who are not of the same moral stature as he himself is, and for whom sharing in Gandhiji's experiment is no spiritual necessity.'

When confronted by Bose on the subject, Gandhi said that the women had assured him that holding him or sleeping next to him had no ill effect on them. He knew that his experiment had evoked criticism even among his friends. Most of those whom he took into his confidence about it expressed their dislike, Vallabhbhai Patel describing it as 'irreligious'. But duty could not be shirked even for the sake of the most intimate friends. In a letter to Mirabehn Gandhi wrote: 'The way to truth is paved with skeletons over which we dare to walk.'

In his efforts to seek opinions, he wrote to J.B. Kripalani, then the Congress president:

This [experiment] has cost me dearest associates . . . You as one of the dearest and earliest comrades . . . should reconsider your position in the light of what they have to say . . . I have given the deepest thought to the matter. The whole world may forsake me but I dare not leave what I hold is the truth for me. It may be a delusion and a snare. If so, I must realize it myself . . . I need not argue the point. I have simply conveyed the intensity of my thoughts.

I suggest that you discuss it with X and Y [names omitted in printed text], and then come to a conclusion and let me know. . . . Do not consider my feeling in the matter. I have none. All I want is to *do* the truth at all cost, as I see it.

Kripalani wrote in reply:

These matters are, I find, beyond my depth. Moreover, I have enough to do to keep myself morally straight to sit in judgement on others, and specially those who are morally and spiritually miles ahead of me. I can only say that I have the fullest faith in you. No sinful man can go about his business the way you are doing. Even if I had a lurking suspicion, I would rather distrust my eyes and ears than distrust you, for I believe that my senses are more liable to deceive me than you would. So I remain unperturbed.

Some of Gandhi's dissenting friends, however, persuaded Thakkar Bapa, a man of great moral fibre, to engage with the Mahatma on the subject. The two men met on 25 February 1947.

BAPA: Why this experiment here?
GANDHI: It is not an experiment but an integral part of my *yajna* - a sacred duty. One may forgo an experiment, one cannot forgo one's duty. Now if I regard a thing as a part of my *yajna*, I may not give it up even if public opinion is wholly against me. I am engaged in achieving self-purification . . .
BAPA: But the world does not think of Brahmacharya as you do . . .
GANDHI: If I accept your contention then it would amount to this that I should give up what I hold to be right for me, for fear of displeasing the world. I shud-

der to think where I should have been if I had proceeded like that in my life. I should have found myself at the bottom of the pit. You can have no idea, Bapa, but I can well picture it to myself. I have called my present venture a *yajna* – a sacrifice, a penance. It means utmost self-purification. How can there be that self-purification when in my mind I entertain a thing which I dare not put openly into practice? Does one need anyone's approval or permission to do what one holds with all one's being to be one's duty? . . . My mind is made up. On the lonely way to God on which I have set out, I need no earthly companions. Let those people denounce me if I am the impostor they imagine me to be . . . It might disillusion millions who persist in regarding me as a Mahatma. I must confess, the prospect of being so debunked greatly pleases me. Thousands of Hindu and Muslim women come to me. They are to me like my own mothers, sisters and daughters. But if an occasion should arise requiring me to share the bed with any of them, I must not hesitate if I am the Brahmachari that I claim to be. If I shirk from the test, I write myself down as a coward and a fraud.

BAPA: What if your example is copied?

GANDHI: If there is blind imitation or unscrupulous exploitation of my example, society will not and should not tolerate it. But if there is sincere, bona fide, honest endeavour, society should welcome it and it will be the better for it . . .

BAPA: I for one cannot imagine anything base in you. After all Manu is in place of a granddaughter to you . . . I confess I had my mental reservations in the beginning. I had come in all humility to press upon you my doubts. I did not understand. Only after our talk today have I been able to have a deeper understanding of the meaning of what you are trying to do.

GANDHI: Does that make any real difference? It does not and it should not. You seem to make a distinction between Manu and others like her. My mind makes no such distinction. To me they are all alike – daughters . . .

While the controversy continued, two of Gandhi's colleagues who had temporarily taken up editing *Harijan* during his mission to Noakhali resigned. They refused to publish portions of his prayer addresses bearing on the issue of Brahmacharya. Some weeks later Nirmal Kumar Bose placed before Gandhi a copy of the letter which he had written to two of the Mahatma's co-workers. The document, with a postscript, amounted to a letter of resignation. Gandhi found it 'full of inaccuracies and unwarranted assumptions'. In his reply he wrote:

I go beyond the orthodox view as we know it. My definition does not admit of laxity. I do not call that Brahmacharya that means not to touch a woman. For me Brahmacharya is that thought and practice which puts you in touch with the Infinite and takes you to His presence . . . I am trying to reach that state and, in accordance with my belief, I have made substantial progress in that direction.

I am amazed at your assumption that my experiment implied woman's infer-iority. She would be if I looked upon her with lust with or without her consent . . . My wife was 'inferior' when she was the instrument of my lust. She ceased to be that when she lay with me naked as my sister. Should there be difference if it is not my wife, as she once was, but some other sister? I hope you would acquit me of having any lustful designs upon women or girls who have been naked with me. . .

He amplified his concept of Brahmacharya in a letter to Rajkumari Amrit Kaur:

My meaning of Brahmacharya is this: one who never has any lustful intention, who, by constant attendance upon God, has become capable of lying naked with naked women, however beautiful they may be, without being in any manner whatsoever sexually excited. Such a person should be incapable of being untruthful, incapable of intending doing harm to a single man or woman in the whole world, free from anger and malice and detached in the sense of the *Bhagavad Gita*. Such a person is a full Brahmachari. Brahmachari literally means a person who is making daily and steady progress towards God and whose every act is done in pursuance of that end and no other.

The argument was generally forgotten in the turmoil of India's political storm. As the Muslim League refused to take part in the Constituent Assembly, Nehru and Patel insisted that there was no purpose in the League members remaining in the Cabinet and threatened to resign them-selves if they were retained. All progress towards affecting any sort of peaceful tranfer of power had ceased. Nehru and Patel had, in fact, begun to consider the division of India as a distinct possibility. The British were by now anxious to pull out, finding enough problems at home to occupy all their administrative talents and time. On 20 February 1947, Prime Minister Attlee announced in the House of Commons that it was His Majesty's Government's definite intention to transfer power to responsible Indian hands by a date not later than June 1948. Attlee also announced that Lord Louis Mountbatten would replace Wavell as viceroy.

# FORTY-TWO

# *Vivisection*

The Congress Working Committee met in the first week of March 1947. In view of the deteriorating situation in the Punjab following the campaign of Direct Action launched by the Muslim League, the committee adopted a resolution proposing the division of the Punjab on the basis of the Muslim and non-Muslim majority areas. Gandhi was neither consulted nor forewarned about the resolution, and he rightly saw it as virtual acceptance of the division of the country. He wrote to both Nehru and Patel, asking to be enlightened about its background. In his reply Nehru politely explained that it was necessary to press for division 'so that reality might be brought into the picture', and that this was 'the only answer to partition as demanded by Jinnah'. The resolution, he added, flowed naturally from the previous decisions of the Congress. Patel's reply, however, had a touch of exasperation:

> It is difficult to explain to you the resolution about the Punjab. It was adopted after the deepest deliberation. Nothing has been done in a hurry or without full thought. That you had expressed your views against it, we learnt only from the papers. But you are, of course, entitled to say what you feel right.

In the meantime Muslim opposition to Gandhi's stay in Noakhali had gained momentum, and he was urged to go to Bihar to allay the fears and sufferings of the Muslims there. But he refused to submit to the opposition, for he hoped that he could work with equal effect among the Hindus of Bihar without having to go there. However, an impassioned appeal from Dr Syed Mahmud, a Muslim Congressman in the Bihar government, prompted the Mahatma's 'inner voice' to tell him to interrupt his tour of Noakhali, and by the second week of March he was holding prayer meetings in Patna and collecting money from the Hindus for the relief of Muslim sufferers. At the village of Sipara the villagers stopped his car and presented him with a purse. On opening it he found among the coins a letter signed by them:

> Please forgive us . . . We feel ashamed for the loss of life and property which our

429

Muslim brethren have suffered at our hands. As a token of repentance and to atone for our sin, we present you this purse for the relief of the Muslim victims of the disturbances. We again beg your pardon and assure you that such a thing will never happen again.

It was shortly after his arrival in Bihar that Gandhi had come to know about the Congress resolution proposing the partition of the Punjab. Two weeks later, on 22 March, Lord (Admiral Louis) Mountbatten landed in New Delhi, and at once wrote to the Mahatma to request a meeting. Gandhi was then about to leave for one of the disturbed areas in Bihar, and was therefore unable to say when exactly he would return to Delhi. He wrote to the Viceroy accordingly.

Mountbatten, a great-grandson of Queen Victoria, had been sent to India with a clear brief from the British government – to relinquish one régime and inaugurate a new one. In his first meeting with Gandhi, on the evening of 31 March, in which Lady Mountbatten also participated, the Viceroy was aware of the importance of establishing close rapport with the Mahatma for the hard negotiations ahead. Even when Lady Mountbatten took her leave after an hour of friendly chat, the two men seemed in no hurry to get down to business. The Viceroy found it necessary to 'let him [Gandhi] talk along any lines that entered his mind'. The Mahatma spoke of his life in England, his life in South Africa, his recent tours of Noakhali and Bihar, his discussions with former viceroys and members of cabinet. When they parted after more than two hours, the Viceroy felt satisfied that 'we had progressed along the path of friendship'.

The following day, in a last-minute bid on his part to prevent partition, Gandhi put forward a plan which he had aired from time to time: that Jinnah be invited to form an interim central government. Congress, said Gandhi, should be prepared to accept government by the Muslim League if by so doing they could ensure the unity of the country. He felt that the Muslims' fear must be removed before the present creaky interim government could function better. Once the British had handed over power to a unified India, he reckoned, the Indians themselves would be able to adjust matters and set up some sort of Pakistan, if necessary. Gandhi believed that since the running of the interim government by Congress was wholly unacceptable to Jinnah, the only way was for Jinnah to run it himself and for Gandhi to use his influence to persuade Congress to agree to that. Mountbatten, encountering the idea for the first time, was astonished. He found it 'bold, imaginative and splendidly far-fetched', but had an inkling that the Mahatma's amazing personal influence might induce Congress to accept it. The Viceroy, however, had too clear an idea of where he was going, and notwithstanding the fact that he was fascinated and delighted by Gandhi's personality, he was aware of the importance of eliminating a force which he foresaw would make things difficult in the future. In any event it was becoming more and more apparent that, with the exception of Gandhi, all Congress leaders at least tacitly accepted the fact that a truly united India was inconceivable.

Lord Mountbatten told Gandhi that his plan was 'attractive' and suggested that he should discuss it with Lord Ismay, his Chief of Staff, so that Ismay could cast it into proper shape. In the Viceroy's staff meeting on 5 April, a member described it as 'an old kite flown without disguise'. The consensus of opinion was that 'Mountbatten should not allow himself to be drawn into negotiation with the Mahatma, but should only listen to advice.'

It soon became quite evident to Gandhi that he could not carry the Congress Working Committee with him, and that they no longer shared his basic opposition to any partition under British aegis. Consequently, in a letter to the Viceroy on 11 April, he observed: 'I felt sorry that I could not convince them of the correctness of my plan from every point of view . . . Thus I have to ask you to omit me from your consideration.' The following day he returned to his peace mission in Bihar – the province where thirty years before he had entered the Indian political scene, defending the oppressed indigo peasants in Champaran. The Gandhian era in politics was now drawing to a close, and the Mahatma was painfully aware of it.

The eruption of violence in Bengal and Bihar, and now in the Punjab also, further damaged the concept of a united India. Jinnah made it clear that if he did not achieve his political ends the entire country would be rent by civil war. The riots were a preview. Nehru let it be amply known to Mountbatten that Congress had no objection to partition as such provided it also included the partition of Bengal and the Punjab, where Muslims and non-Muslims existed in more or less equal numbers. The Muslim League would inevitably object to this. In his historic review before the Council of the Royal Empire Society in London some eighteen months after the event, Mountbatten spoke of his crucial meeting with Jinnah:

When I told Jinnah that I had Congress's provisional agreement to partition he was overjoyed. When I said that it logically followed that this would involve partition of the Punjab and Bengal he was horrified. He produced the strongest arguments why these provinces should not be partitioned. He said that they had national characteristics and that partition would be disastrous. I agreed, but I said how much more must I now feel that the same considerations applied to the partitioning of the whole of India. He did not like that, and started explaining why India had to be partitioned, and so we went round and round the mulberry bush until finally he realized that either he could have a United India with an unpartitioned Punjab and Bengal or a divided India with a partitioned Punjab and Bengal, and he finally accepted the latter solution.

During the two weeks prior to his return to Bihar, Gandhi lived in the Untouchables' quarter (Bhangi Colony) in the outer part of Delhi, conducting a prayer meeting there every evening. Hindu refugees from the predominantly Muslim areas of the Punjab and North-West Frontier Province had recently started pouring into the capital, and their tales of woe generated considerable tension. On the first evening, as the customary recitation from the Koran commenced, a Hindu youth stood up and shouted: 'This is a Hindu temple. We won't let you recite from the Muslim holy book at Hindu services.' There were other objectors too. Gandhi immediately broke off the meeting. The episode was repeated in the next two meetings, but by the fourth evening the objectors had withdrawn. After the prayers he addressed the gathering. It had hurt him much to think that they had not been able to hold the prayers, and hundreds had been disappointed because of the objections of a few people. 'We did not pray with the lips but we prayed with our hearts, which is by far the most effective part of prayer,' he added. 'In this those who have opposed have also helped, though unconsciously. Their opposition has helped me to turn the searchlight inward as never before . . . In the end non-violence prevailed . . . In Noakhali, in Bihar, in Punjab, in Delhi, even in this prayer ground the battle of undivided India is being lost and won daily. The experience here today has provided me with the key to success elsewhere.'

While Gandhi spent his time addressing prayer meetings and applying his healing touch to the victims of the communal riots in Bihar, Lord Mountbatten succeeded in evolving a plan for the partition of the country to which all principal parties were willing to agree. The Working Committee was due to meet on 1 May to have a closer look at the 'Mountbatten Plan'. Although Gandhi had no idea of the shaping of the Viceroy's plan, Nehru wrote to him on 23 April requesting his presence in Delhi: 'The first week of May will be of considerable importance and all of us would like you to be near us for advice and guidance.' At the 1 May meeting the Working Committee agreed to accept the principle of partition involving also the partition of Bengal and Punjab. Gandhi was present at this meeting, but the momentous decision was taken against his wishes. 'We are passionately attached to the idea of a united India, but we have accepted the partition of India in order to avoid conflict and compulsion,' Nehru informed the Viceroy. Pleased with his success in persuading the Working Committee to accept his plan, Mountbatten is reported to have remarked to Gandhi: 'The Working Committee is with me and not with you.' In reply Gandhi said: 'Yes, the Working Committee is with you, but the people are still with me.' After a few days in Delhi he resumed his mission in Bihar.

He could see nothing but evil in the partition plan. 'Whatever may be said to the contrary, it would be a blunder of the first magnitude for the British to be a party in any way whatsoever to the division of India,' he wrote to Mountbatten. 'If it has to come, let it come after the British withdraw, as a result of understanding between the parties.' He felt that partition was being accepted for fear of civil war. He personally 'would rather let the whole country be reduced to ashes than yield an inch to violence', but he had been unable to make his views prevail, since Nehru and Patel had finally managed to detach themselves from his leadership strings and were their own masters. It was they who were now guiding the Working Committee. The Mahatma said in anguish:

> My life's work seems to be over. I hope God will spare me further humiliation ... I shall perhaps not be alive to witness it, but should the evil I apprehend overtake India and her independence be imperilled, let posterity know what agony this old soul went through thinking of it. Let it not be said that Gandhi was a party to India's vivisection.

On 25 May, in response to a call from Nehru, Gandhi again returned to New Delhi. Lord Mountbatten had flown to London, where the British cabinet readily approved the plan. The Viceroy praised the role played by the Reform Commissioner, V.P. Menon, in preparing it. He told Alan Campbell-Johnson, his press attaché: 'But for this plan, Dickie Mountbatten would have been sunk, and could have packed his bags.' Before leaving England, Mountbatten saw Churchill, who promised to support the plan in the House of Commons. The former prime minister felt certain that if Jinnah did not accept the plan, it would spell the death-knell of his Pakistan dream. Jinnah was still hesitant about accepting a Pakistan that involved the division of Bengal and Punjab – a 'moth-eaten' Pakistan, as he put it – but the message from Churchill induced him to give the historic nod.

The Congress Working Committee was due to meet on 3 June to formally approve the Mountbatten Plan. Earlier in the morning as Gandhi lay in his bath he observed:

> In all probability, the final seal will be set on the partition plan during the day ... I repeat that the division of India can only do harm to the future of the

country . . . May be that just as God blinded my vision, so that I mistook the non-violence of the weak – which now I see is a misnomer and contradiction in terms – for true non-violence, He has again stricken me with blindness. If it should prove to be so, nobody would be happier than I.

And when Rajkumari Amrit Kaur brought the news that all three parties – the Congress, the Muslim League and the Sikhs – had signed the Mountbatten Plan, the Mahatma heaved a deep sigh. 'May God protect them, and grant them all the wisdom,' he muttered. Henceforth the partition plan would cease to be a live issue with him in the political sense. Mountbatten, in the meantime, had decided that speed in the transfer of power was the essence of the situation, and consequently the earlier deadline of June 1948 was advanced to 15 August 1947.

Some of the Congress leaders were apprehensive that Gandhi in his present emotional and unhappy state would denounce the Viceroy's carefully devised plan, even after the Working Committee had agreed to accept it. However, when the All-India Congress Committee met on 14 June 1947, to consider the Working Committee's stand on the Mountbatten Plan, Gandhi asked its members to honour the commitment made by their leaders. It seems likely that he did contemplate launching another Satyagraha campaign, but at the advanced age of seventy-seven and with no support from his closest associates, Nehru and Patel, he decided against it. It seems that he also felt that a fast unto death would be an exercise in futility. He was deeply hurt by the impending division of the country, he told the Congress Committee, and stressed that the Working Committee's decision should not be accepted out of any false sense of moral compulsion but should come from conviction and a sense of duty. They must also bear in mind that if they rejected or amended the decision it would imply lack of confidence in the Working Committee, who would then be obliged to resign. They should in that case have the strength to carry on the work of Congress and the government without the seasoned leaders who then manned the Working Committee. 'But,' Gandhi added, 'I do not find that strength in us today. If you had it I would also be with you, and if I felt strong enough myself I would, alone, take up the flag of revolt. But today I do not see the conditions for doing so.' This reflected his own failing health and the inadequacy which he had discovered in the practice of nonviolence by Congress and the people at large.

The Congress president, J.B. Kripalani felt that freedom from British rule was the 'prime necessity of our nationhood', even if it was offered at the price of the division of India. Congress had agreed to accept the Mountbatten Plan in the hope that the Muslim League, having got what it wanted, would 'cease its hymn of communal hate'. Concluding his speech at the All-India Congress Committee, Kripalani said:

Even when I have differed from Gandhiji I have considered his political instinct to be more correct than my elaborately reasoned attitudes. Today also I feel that he with his supreme fearlessness is correct and my stand defective. Why then am I not with him now? It is because I feel that he has as yet found no way of tackling the problem on a mass basis. When he taught us non-violent non-co-operation, he showed us a definite method which we had at least mechanically followed. Today he himself is groping in the dark. He was in Noakhali. His efforts eased the situation. Now he is in Bihar and the situation is again eased. But this does not solve in any way the flare-up in the Punjab. He says he is solving the problem of Hindu-Muslim unity for the whole of India in Bihar. May be. But it is difficult to see how that is being done . . . And then unfortunately for us today though he can enunciate policies, they have in the main to be carried out by others and these others are not converted to his way of thinking. It is under these painful circumstances that I have accepted the division of India.

Patel was convinced during interim government that precarious relations between Congress and the Muslim League had reached a point of no return. He agreed to partition as a last resort, 'when we had reached a stage when we would have lost all'. He said that the choice was whether there should be just one division or many divisions. It was better to have one clean fight and then separate than having bickerings every day.

Justifying Congress's acceptance of the Mountbatten Plan, Nehru observed:

A larger India would have constant troubles, constant disintegrating pulls. And also the fact that we saw no other way of getting our freedom – in the near future, I mean. And so we accepted and said, let us build a strong India. And if others do not want to be in it, well, how can we and why should we force them to be in it?

On another occasion, in an interview with Leonard Mosley, the British author, Nehru said:

The truth is that we were tired men, and we were getting on in years too. Few of us could stand the prospect of going to prison again – and if we had stood for a united India as we wished it, prison obviously awaited us. We saw the fires burning in the Punjab and heard every day of the killings. The plan for partition offered a way out and we took it . . . But if Gandhiji had told us not to, we would have gone on fighting, and waiting.

In the summer of 1947 Gandhi's hold over the Congress and the masses had weakened considerably. Most of his mail was abusive and hateful. The letters from Hindus accused him of being partial to Muslims – he was called a 'fifth columnist', a 'slave of Jinnah' and 'Mohamed Gandhi'. The Muslim letters demanded that he stop obstructing the creation of Pakistan. The nation was not responding to the Mahatma's plea for peace and brotherhood. This was the period when he spent long hours in tiring, disappointing, depressing discussions about the goal of his life – independent India's future – and the impending partition. Barbro Alving, a journalist with the Swedish newspaper *Dagens Nyheter*, was then on a journey around the world, on a post-war assignment. She managed a brief meeting with Gandhi. 'Mahatma, India is now at last getting the freedom and independence that you have fought for all your life. How do you react to the fact that India at this point is no longer following your way?' she asked. Gandhi looked at her very sternly and said: 'Madam, you may write in your paper that India has never followed my way.' Years later Barbro Alving summarized her impression of Gandhi thus:

> It was, on the one hand, that he was so very human; that he was impatient, tired, full of a sort of irritated grief and bitterness and also full of that clever sense of humour.
>
> But there was, on the other hand, even in this situation, an atmosphere around him, an aura of spiritual strength, of human greatness and absolute integrity.
>
> I must say that I have never felt anything like that as strongly with any other man or woman during all my long journalistic career.

Gandhi's time and attention were now increasingly claimed by Hindu refugees. Crowds of them could be seen at all hours hovering round the Bhangi Colony. Some of them who had come to him with their heart-rending stories persuaded him to pay a visit to the holy city of Hardwar, where over thirty thousand of them from Rawalpindi and other parts of the Punjab were huddled together in some half a dozen refugee camps. Gandhi, accompanied by Nehru, travelled in blistering heat, and on his arrival was surrounded by perspiring and indignant refugees. The wail of the anguished filled the air. There was a serious lack of sanitation and other amenities in the camps. Gandhi gave the organizers proper advice about arrangements and offered whatever comfort he could to the refugees. In the afternoon, after an exhausting day, he started on his return journey. For a while he dozed off, his feet resting on the lap of Nehru, who gently pressed his limbs. At the usual time in the evening he sat down to prayer in the automobile itself. Nehru sat through the prayer with his eyes closed.

While Gandhi considered the inevitable partition 'a spiritual tragedy', Mountbatten moved ahead with breathtaking speed towards the 15 August deadline, keeping in view the practical consequences of partition. The integration of India's princes and their peoples – hitherto virtually an unconsidered problem – had to be tackled. The Civil Service and armed forces, the railways, the police and the revenue services had to be divided, as did trucks, typewriters, almirahs, carpets, reams of paper, pens and pencils, rupees and pounds. Muslims and Hindus were wrangling over their shares of the inheritance from the British Raj. Fifty committees set up to divide the government's assets proceeded along fifty different lines.

Millions of Muslims, Hindus and Sikhs were convinced that they would be trapped in a nation hostile to their faith. The two-way exodus to and from the India and Pakistan of tomorrow had begun. As the deadline approached, both sectors erupted into intense violence, leading to a holocaust of pain, looting, rape and murder. A boundary force of fifty thousand troops assembled in the Punjab to help keep the transition a peaceful one proved utterly ineffectual, partly because they too were afflicted with communal fever, and for the most part they remained in their barracks, cleaning their weapons and boots. There were both Hindus and Muslims in the boundary force. Soldiers of one community were inclined not to intervene if members of their community were involved in violence; the soldiers of the other community were inclined to remain aloof in order to avoid an open confrontation within the force. Although there were incidences of soldiers belonging to one community firing at peaceful people of the other community, the soldiers mostly remained in a state of inaction. During those few dreadful months an estimated fifteen million people were on the move in the Punjab, most of them on foot, carrying their meagre belongings. Hundreds of thousands of men, women and children were killed in the process. Thus towards the end of the freedom struggle law and order as well as the social fabric of the land had been torn asunder. There was complete anarchy.

The outburst of communal frenzy in the Punjab led Gandhi to make a short tour of the province. He also visited the princely state of Jammu and Kashmir. 'The real test is coming soon,' he told a group of Congress workers at Lahore. The rest of his life, he decided, was going to be spent in Pakistan. 'May be in East Bengal or West Punjab or perhaps the North-West Frontier Province.' For the present time, he would rather be in Noakhali. He hoped to be 'free from Noakhali very soon'.

# FORTY-THREE

# Calcutta

When Gandhi arrived in Calcutta on his way to Noakhali, the situation in the metropolis had changed considerably. Calcutta had never really been peaceful since the Direct Action launched by the Muslim League a year ago, but it was now irrevocably settled that the city was to be included in India and not in Pakistan. H.S. Suharwardy, who still continued to be *de jure* Premier of Bengal, had been previously responsible for the outbreak of violence in Calcutta, using his official position in the Muslims' favour, but he and the Muslim League now found themselves at the receiving end. Keeping in view the possibility of repression by a Hindu government, their instinct was to maintain a low profile. The situation in Noakhali was also tense over the outcome of the imminent partition. The Hindu minority wanted Gandhi's presence there to save them from further atrocities, but Calcutta's Muslims fervently appealed to him to stay on in the city at least until after Independence, as they feared for their own safety. 'We Muslims have as much claim on you as the Hindus,' they implored. 'I am willing,' replied Gandhi to a Muslim deputation, 'but then you will have to guarantee the peace of Noakhali. If I do not go to Noakhali before the 15th [of August] on the strength of your guarantee, and things go wrong there my life will become forfeit; you will have to face a fast unto death on my part.' The leaders of Calcutta's Muslim League immediately prevailed upon their counterparts in Noakhali to restrain their followers so that the Mahatma's presence in Calcutta could assist in saving the large Muslim minority there.

Soon Suharwardy flew in from Karachi and begged Gandhi to stay longer. Suharwardy represented everything that the Hindus detested, but the Mahatma characteristically liked and on the whole trusted him. He said he was prepared to stay on in Calcutta on one condition – that he and Suharwardy should take up abode together, and that they should appear everywhere unprotected by the police or the military, and in 'brotherly fashion' move about among the people, calming their fears and soothing their bitter feelings. They would stay together in one of the deserted houses belonging to Muslims in Beliaghata, an area where there had been looting and murder. A few months earlier Suharwardy had dismissed a similar suggestion as a 'mad offer', but this time after a few hours of thought he accepted it without any reservation. When Gandhi informed Patel of his plans the latter was not too pleased, writing: 'So you have got detained in Calcutta and that too in a quarter which is a veritable shambles and a notorious den of gangsters and hooligans . . . And in what choice company too! It is a terrible risk.'

Crowds of excited young men were waiting when Gandhi drove up to the gate of the abandoned house, Hydari Mansion, on the afternoon of 13 August, two days before Independence Day. The youths shouted: 'Why have you come here? You did not come when we were in trouble. Why don't you go to the places where the Hindus have fled?' A few minutes later Suharwardy arrived. He was surrounded by angry youths who threatened him. It was only after Gandhi had sent some members of his entourage to reason with the demonstrators that Suharwardy was allowed to pass through the gate. The noisy demonstration, however, continued unabated and the crowds began to swell. Hydari Mansion was now under siege. Some of the youths tried to climb in at the windows of the room in which Gandhi was sitting with Suharwardy and an English friend, Horace Alexander. Stones were thrown at the windows as Alexander began to shut them. Finally, when the outcry had somewhat subsided, a deputation was ushered in to meet Gandhi.

The youths asked him why he had come to Calcutta when the Muslims were in danger, but not when the Hindus were in danger. Gandhi replied that he had come to serve 'the Hindus, Muslims and all alike'. Couldn't they see that by taking this step he had put the burden of peace in Noakhali on the shoulders of Suharwardy and his friends? 'But let me tell you,' he told the deputation, 'that if you again go mad, I will not be a living witness to it. I have given the same ultimatum to the Muslims of Noakhali also.' When the youths accused him of being an enemy of the Hindus, he said: 'How can I, who am a Hindu by birth, a Hindu by creed and a Hindu of Hindus in my way of living, be an enemy of the Hindus? Does not that show intolerance on your part?'

His last words seemed to have a pacifying effect, for the youths grew quiet, though still resentful. 'Perhaps we should now go,' one of them said. Gandhi replied: 'Yes, you must go. It is already late. Come again in the morning when you have thought things over.'

The next day they came again and in Suharwardy's presence had a long discussion with Gandhi. The Mahatma stressed that the joint effort on the part of Suharwardy and himself in Beliaghata was only a stepping-stone. Once the Hindus of Beliaghata had invited their Muslim neighbours to return, the two men would move to a predominantly Muslim area where they would stay till the Hindus too were invited to return. The effort would continue till each community had afforded safe return to their neighbours all over Calcutta. That evening over ten thousand people attended his prayer meeting, which was held in the muddy compound of Hydari Mansion. He spoke of the Independence Day, which would begin at the stroke of midnight. The people of India were about to be delivered from the bondage of British rule, but he found no joy in it, for the country would be partitioned too. What concerned him was peace in Calcutta. Gandhi preached his sermon of unity to an attentive audience, but as soon as he returned to the house crowds of youths began screaming for Suharwardy. As the clamour outside became louder, Gandhi went to one of the windows and threw open the shutters. His appearance caused a momentary silence. Suddenly there was a cry: 'Where is Suharwardy?'

Gandhi beckoned Suharwardy and asked him to stand beside him. 'It is Bengal's good fortune that Mahatmaji is in our midst at this hour,' the Muslim leader told the restive gathering. 'Will Bengal realize its high privilege and stop the fratricide?' Someone in the crowd shouted: 'Are you not responsible for the Great Calcutta Killing last year?'

'We are all responsible,' Suharwardy answered.

'Please answer the question.'

'Yes, it was my responsibility.'

This candid admission dramatically changed the atmosphere, and the man who had been so bitterly hated now suddenly found himself cheered by a crowd of Hindu youths. It seemed that the tension of the preceding weeks and months had been released. Hindus and Muslims marched in the streets of Calcutta in their thousands, shouting slogans of unity and harmony. 'Look at the miracle Mahatmaji has wrought in a single day,' exclaimed Suharwardy. Gandhi's residence in Beliaghata became a place of pilgrimage for the citizens of Calcutta.

The Independence celebrations on 15 August presented an unprecedented spectacle of communal fraternization, with people chanting in the street: '*Hindu Muslim bhai-bhai*' (Hindus and Muslims are brothers). Gandhi was, however, absorbed with happenings elsewhere in the dominions of India and Pakistan, and firmly refused to associate himself with the festivities of Independence. Government officials asked him for a statement in honour of 15 August 1947, suggesting that 'if he did not give any message to the nation, it would not be good'. He replied that he 'had run dry . . . There is no message at all. If it is bad let it be so.' When a BBC correspondent came for a message, which would be broadcast all over the world, Gandhi commented tersely: 'I must not yield to the temptation. You must forget that I know English.' He observed the Independence Day by fasting, spinning and praying. Gandhi believed that 'there is no prayer without fasting, and there is no real fast without prayer . . . Abstention from food and even water is [nevertheless] the mere beginning, the least part of the surrender [to God].' His belief in prayer, like his other beliefs, was absolute:

> Prayer is the only means of bringing about orderliness and peace and repose in our daily acts. One has to appear before Him in all one's weakness, empty-handed and in spirit of full surrender, and then He enables you to stand before a whole world and protects you from all harm. Let us pray that He may cleanse our hearts of pettinesses, meannesses and deceit and He will surely answer our prayers.
>
> Worship or prayer is not to be performed with the lips, but with the heart. And that is why it can be performed equally by the dumb and the stammerer, by the ignorant and the stupid. And the prayers of those whose tongues are nectared but whose hearts are full of poison are never heard. He, therefore, who would pray to God, must cleanse his heart.

Gandhi's influence in bringing about peace in Calcutta was largely exercised in persuading the now powerful Hindu majority to refrain from provocation. The appearance of Gandhi and Suharwardy together no doubt helped to create an atmosphere of communal amity, but there was no certainty that it would last. Towards the end of the month tales of atrocities perpetrated by the Sikhs and Hindus on Muslims in East Punjab and by the Muslims on them in West Punjab, caused fresh restiveness in Calcutta.

On the night of 31 August, just after Gandhi had gone to bed, a crowd of young men created a noisy scene in the compounds of Hydari Mansion. They brought with them a man who was heavily bandaged, and alleged that he had been stabbed by Muslims. The shouting youths threw stones at the windows and forced their way into the house. 'Where is Suharwardy?' a youth demanded. Suharwardy was not there, as he had left the previous day to make arrangements for a trip to Noakhali. His absence infuriated the intruders. Before long Gandhi was face to face with enraged rioters. He touched his palms in the traditional Hindu salutation. It was a Monday, his day of silence, but he had always allowed himself to break silence if there was a strong reason to do so. As he appealed to the youths for calm, one of them swung a *lathi*, but it missed him. A brick aimed at him struck a Muslim standing by his side. The Mahatma shook his head sorrowfully. In a barely audible voice, he observed: 'My God asks me, "Where do you stand?" I am deeply pained. Is this the reality of peace that was established on August 15?' The police arrived; the police superintendent appealed to

Gandhi to retire to his room. The rioters were then ejected from the house and the police used tear gas to disperse an unruly mob of Hindus outside.

This incident was followed the next day by violent rioting in which scores of people were killed. 'What was regarded as the "Calcutta Miracle" has proved to be a nine days' wonder,' Gandhi wrote to Patel. 'I am pondering what my duty is in the circumstances.' In a statement to the press on 1 September he said:

> To put an appearance before a yelling crowd does not always work. It certainly did not last night. What my word in person cannot do, my fast may. It may touch the hearts of all the warring factions in the Punjab if it does in Calcutta. I therefore begin from 8:15 tonight to end only if and when sanity returns to Calcutta.

The murders and looting went on, but soon the fast was beginning to have some effect. Representatives of various groups pleaded with the Mahatma to end it. Even leaders of hooligan bands, burly killers, came and sat at Gandhi's bedside and promised to mend their ways. Some of them wept as they confessed their guilt. Hindus and Muslims paraded together through the affected parts of the city to restore communal harmony. Gandhi regarded peace processions as 'empty shows' unless there existed basic honesty of intention on the part of the leaders and the rank-and-file workers. If such volunteer organizations were wedded to nonviolence, ready to make the supreme sacrifice for the achievement of unity and peace, even the state of anarchy would be acceptable. In discussing the subject with an old associate, Gandhi observed:

> I will not mind if the entire police force in the city is withdrawn. And if in the result the whole of Calcutta swims in blood, it will not dismay me. For it will be a willing offering of innocent blood. I know how to tackle such a situation. You and I shall then have to rush barefoot in the midst of the flames and work without respite day and night until either peace is restored or we are all dead.

Finally, on 4 September, municipal officials reported to Gandhi that the city had been absolutely peaceful for twenty-four hours. Interviews and conferences continued, and later in the evening leading members of all three communities, Hindu, Muslim and Sikh, pledged themselves in the form of a document, now that quiet had been restored, never to allow communal strife in the city again and to 'strive unto death to prevent it'. Gandhi agreed to end his fast, which had lasted seventy-three hours. Just before Suharwardy handed him the ceremonial glass of orange juice, there was a short prayer in which all present joined.

There was a vast multitude at the farewell function organized by the citizens of Calcutta to express their gratitude. Gandhi warned the gathering that he had given up his fast as a result of a firm promise by them to keep the peace in the city. 'But do not play with me,' he added. 'If you revert to madness after I leave the place, it will be as silly as dancing on an earthen pot. You will keep me alive if you keep the peace.' The following day he left Calcutta for New Delhi with the intention of proceeding to the Punjab on his mission of peace there.

# FORTY-FOUR

# Anguished Refugees

When Gandhi's train steamed into Delhi station, he found the atmosphere strangely solemn; there were also a strikingly large number of soldiers on the platform. As he drove from the railroad station, a sombre-looking Patel and Rajkumari Amrit Kaur informed the Mahatma that over the past few days the capital had witnessed an orgy of murder, arson and looting, provoked by stories heard from Sikh and Hindu refugees from the Punjab who were flooding the city. They occupied any available place for shelter, and even mosques were being forcibly entered for the purpose. Gandhi's own lodgings in the Bhangi Colony were so packed with these waifs of partition that he had to be accommodated in Birla House, the palatial residence of an industrial magnate friend. There he lived in a spacious ground-floor room. When he arrived he had all the furniture removed. Visitors sat on the floor and he slept on the terrace outside the room. With him at Birla House were his secretary, Pyarelal, Manu and Abha Gandhi, the young wife of another of his cousinly relatives.

Gandhi's intention had been to leave within a few days for the Punjab, but with Delhi ablaze with communal strife, he decided against proceeding further. 'I must do my little bit to calm the heated atmosphere,' he said in a statement to the press. 'I must apply the formula "Do or Die" to the capital of India.' So while the police and the military struggled to quell the riots, he set about the task of 'purging violence from the hearts of the people'. He would visit refugee camps which had been set up in and around Delhi. Some of these camps accommodated Muslims who had been chased out of their homes in the city. Gandhi immediately plunged himself into relief work among the sufferers of all three communities. He wrote articles for *Harijan*, dictated letters, spun, and was in constant touch with the government. His advice to sufferers was to forget and forgive, to bear no malice or hatred and to endure their sufferings with fortitude.

Many Hindus were bitter against him for being 'pro-Muslim', and violent reprisals launched by the Rashtriya Swayam-Sevak Sangh (RSS), a highly disciplined organization of young militant Hindus, continued to send Muslims scurrying towards Pakistan. Nevertheless some Muslim

444

homes remained dumps for bombs, arms and ammunition. During a visit to the city the Deputy Prime Minister, Vallabhbhai Patel, discovered that incessant firing lasting several hours had been going on from a house occupied by Muslims. 'Why has this pocket not been cleared?' he asked a high-ranking military officer accompanying him. The officer replied that this was not possible with the force at their disposal unless they blew up the building. 'Then why did not you do it?' Patel snapped. He had earlier told Gandhi that he had reason to suspect that the vast majority of Muslims in India were not loyal. It was better that such people should move to Pakistan. The Deputy Prime Minister would, however, react indignantly to the suggestion that he was anti-Muslim or that he was bent upon driving them to Pakistan.

In spreading his gospel of love and peace, the Mahatma would confront hostile crowds which, at times, placed his life in danger. Disgruntled, homeless Hindus and Sikhs made menacing gestures, and there could be heard cries of *'Gandhi murdabad'* (Death to Gandhi). At the Purana Qila, an ancient fort, he was surrounded by a wildly shrieking mob of Muslims who were living there in squalor, waiting to be evacuated to Pakistan. His sermon, which he had delivered many times before, was that Hindus and Muslims alike were children of one God, and therefore they should be calm and not angry. Gradually he was able to subdue their frenzy. He urged the Muslims of Delhi to shed all fear and trust God, and appealed to those in possession of unlicensed arms to surrender them to the authorities.

At a prayer meeting two days later he asked to be 'pardoned for putting first blame on the Hindus and Sikhs'. Why couldn't they initiate action so as to 'stem the tide of hatred'? They must take the courageous step of inviting the Muslims who had been driven out of their homes to return. This would undo what migrations had done, and would enable all the refugees to return in safety and honour to their own towns and villages. 'The wrong of Pakistan will be undone by the right of a resolute non-transfer of population.' But the Hindus and Sikhs were afraid to return to their homes, nor were they willing to vacate the homes of Muslims who had fled to Pakistan and whom Gandhi was inviting to return.

He was sad and disillusioned. On 2 October 1947, his seventy-eighth birthday, sheaves of telegrams were delivered from abroad and all parts of India, and all day long visitors streamed into his room at Birla House to congratulate him. He had in the past expressed his wish to live 125 years. But now there was anguish in his heart. 'I have lost all desire to live long, let alone 125 years . . . I cannot live while hatred and killing mar the atmosphere.' The birthday celebrations depressed him. 'Where do congratulations come in?' the Mahatma asked. 'Would it not be more appropriate to

445

send condolences?' He pleaded with the people to purge their hearts of hatred.

As the influx of refugees from Pakistan continued, the authorities became apprehensive about the problem growing unmanageable. The refugee camps were breeding grounds of despair, and their inmates were now beginning to become quite vocal about it. Gandhi visited them as often as he could and listened sympathetically to complaints. But he would not accept the suggestion that Hindus and Sikhs had a perfect right to the houses abandoned by the Muslims; on the contrary, everything belonging to the Muslims who had left Delhi must be kept in custody for them.

At Kurukshetra in East Punjab, about a quarter of a million Hindu and Sikh refugees had arrived to be looked after, and more were pouring in. When Gandhi came to know of this vast assemblage of destitutes he yearned to be with them, but could not leave Delhi at once, as his presence was required at a session of the Congress Working Committee. It was therefore arranged for him to address the camp by radio on 12 November, 1947:

> Yours is not an ordinary camp . . . it is really a city, and your only bond with your co-refugees is your suffering . . . I can serve you best by drawing attention to your shortcomings. That has been my life's motto, for therein lies true friendship and my service is not only to you or to India; it extends to the world, for I know no barriers of race or creed. If you can get rid of your failings, you will not only benefit yourself but the whole of India.
>
> It hurts me to know that so many of you are without shelter. This is a real hardship particularly in the cold weather . . . You must help in the maintenance of discipline . . . You must take the sanitation of the place in your hands . . . I ask you . . . everyone of you, men, women and children, to keep Kurukshetra clean . . . share your rations, be content with what you get . . . You must live for others and not only for yourselves. Idleness is demoralizing . . . All camps should really be self-supporting but, perhaps, that may be too high an ideal to place before you today. All the same, I do ask you not to despise any work but rejoice at doing anything that comes your way in order to serve and thus make Kurukshetra an ideal place.

Meanwhile the relations between the dominions of India and Pakistan had deteriorated over the princely state of Kashmir. This predominantly Muslim state was ruled by a Hindu maharajah who had not yet joined either dominion. Muslim tribesmen, followed by Pakistani troops, soon invaded Kashmir and raised the cry of 'holy war'. An alarmed and helpless maharajah then asked that his state be admitted to the Indian Union. He also informed New Delhi of his intention to appoint Sheikh Abdulla, a

Muslim, whom he had held in prison for long periods, as his prime minister. Sheikh Abdulla's National Conference party now joined in the request to the Indian government to accept the accession and afford all possible help in repelling the invaders. On 29 October India officially announced the accession of Kashmir, and sent in its own troops by air and road. Without the airlift, the entire state would have been overrun and annexed by Pakistan.

Gandhi made it known that he approved of the Indian action. The Pakistan government had been coercing Kashmir to join Pakistan. If the maharajah alone had wanted to accede, said Gandhi, he could not have defended such accession. As it was, both the maharajah and Sheikh Abdulla, who claimed to represent all the people of Kashmir, had urged the Indian government to help repress the attack.

The Mahatma was criticized for condoning the Indian action. But in his view when a situation arose where nobody would practise *ahimsa* as he understood it, violence, as always, was preferable to cowardice. As he had so often explained before, nonviolence could not be taught to a person who feared to die and had no power of resistance:

> Before he can understand non-violence, he has to be taught to stand his ground and even suffer death in the attempt to defend himself against the aggressor who bids fair to overwhelm him. To do otherwise would be to confirm his cowardice and take him further away from non-violence. Whilst I may not actually help him to retaliate, I must not let a coward seek shelter behind non-violence so-called.

Gandhi told his prayer meeting that the Kashmir issue was in the hands of God; he would not shed a tear if all the Indian soldiers were wiped out bravely defending Kashmir, nor would he mind Sheikh Abdulla and his Muslim, Hindu and Sikh comrades dying at their posts in defence of Kashmir. He was critical of Nehru for having submitted, on Mountbatten's persuasion, the Kashmir issue to the United Nations. He felt the parties should resolve it among themselves, perhaps with the help of a British mediator. On the whole he would like to see Kashmir as part of India, for the inclusion of this princely state with a Muslim majority population would be a step in the right direction to making India truly secular.

# FORTY-FIVE

# The Last Fast

Though the riots in Delhi had subsided as a result of Gandhi's presence, he knew that without the police and military the situation could become unmanageable. It was, he felt, 'the peace of the grave, not a peace symbolizing the union of hearts'. He found it intolerable that the Muslims of Delhi could not repossess their homes occupied by the Hindu and Sikh refugees. There were demands that all the Muslim inhabitants of the city be banished. Gandhi wanted to go to Pakistan to help the Hindus and Sikhs there, but how could he when the Muslims of Delhi had not obtained full redress? Vallabhbhai Patel, on the other hand, took it upon himself to give the forty million Indian Muslims, a good proportion of whom, he implied, were either disloyal or half-loyal, some blunt advice. Speaking at a public meeting in Lucknow, the city which had nurtured several advocates of Pakistan, Patel declared:

> To Indian Muslims I have only one question. Why did you not open your mouths on the Kashmir issue? Why did you not condemn the action of Pakistan? . . . It is your duty now to sail in the same boat and sink or swim together. I want to tell you very frankly that you cannot ride two horses. Select one horse. Those who want to go to Pakistan can go there and live in peace.

Gandhi was now becoming increasingly concerned that the feeling of insecurity among Delhi's Muslims had virtually robbed him of the credentials to go to Pakistan. 'I am in a furnace,' he wrote to a friend. 'There is a raging fire all around. We are trampling humanity under foot.' He felt helpless, though 'I have never put up with helplessness in all my life.' The ordeal this time, he remarked, was going to be much more severe. 'I am straining my ear to catch the whispering of the inner voice and waiting for its command.'

At his prayer meeting on 12 January 1948, Gandhi announced his intention once again to fast:

> I have no answer to return to Muslim friends, who see me from day to day, as

to what they should do. My impotence has been gnawing at me. It will go immediately this fast is undertaken. I have been brooding over it for the last three days . . . The fast will end when I am satisfied that there is a reunion of hearts of all communities, brought about not by outside pressure, but from an awakened sense of duty.

The Mahatma commenced his fast at noon on 13 January. During the morning he received a few visitors including Nehru, Patel and Maulana Azad, and then his cot was moved to the adjoining garden, where he took his last meal. There followed his favourite hymns, 'Vaishnava Jana' and 'When I Survey the Wondrous Cross', and finally readings from the Muslim and Sikh holy books and Hindu writings.

At the evening prayer meeting Gandhi conducted the services as usual. Someone asked who was to be blamed for the fast. 'No one,' he replied, 'but if the Hindus and Sikhs insist on turning out the Muslims of Delhi they will betray India and their religions; and it hurts me.' He said that some people had been taunting him by saying that he had undertaken the fast for the sake of the Muslims. They were right. 'All my life I have stood, as everyone should stand, for minorities and those in need . . .' It was essential to have a 'thorough cleansing of hearts'. Hindus and Sikhs ought to protect the lives of Muslims irrespective of what was happening in Pakistan. They should remember Tagore's song: 'If they answer not thy call, walk alone, walk alone.' Gandhi would break his fast only when Delhi became peaceful 'in the real sense of the term'.

His fast inevitably caused widespread concern, but Patel was particularly upset, feeling that the fast was in some sense directed against himself. There were a large number of people who subscribed to this view, for many Muslims had complained to Gandhi that the Home Minister was anti-Muslim. But when a reporter enquired of Gandhi whether 'the fast is more intended to bring about a change of heart in Patel and thereby amounts to a condemnation of the Home Ministry', he repudiated the suggestion in no uncertain terms: 'Vallabhbhai Patel has a bluntness of speech which can sometimes unintentionally hurt, though his heart is expansive enough to accommodate all.'

Patel, in the meantime, sent word to Gandhi that he would do anything he wished. The Mahatma's response, however, was quite startling. A sum of 550 million rupees (£40 million at the prevailing rate of exchange) was due to be paid to Pakistan as its share of united India's cash assets. This had been previously agreed upon, but the cabinet, as a result of the conflict in Kashmir, unanimously decided to withhold the payment. Gandhi called the Indian action 'immoral' and told Patel that the amount must be paid, and that even if Pakistan spent it on armaments to attack Kashmir, the moral obligation remained, and was binding.

On the morning of 14 January Nehru, Patel and S. Chetty, the Finance Minister, met on the lawn of Birla House round Gandhi's fasting bed to consider afresh the issue of Pakistan's share in the cash assets of pre-partition India. The Mahatma was in tears. Patel, as he would admit later, uttered 'extremely bitter words'. A few hours later, however, amid reports of more atrocities against the minority communities in West Punjab, the cabinet decided to pay Pakistan immediately the sum of 550 million rupees. That evening a group of Sikh and Hindu refugees from West Punjab held a demonstration outside Birla House, shouting, 'Blood for blood', 'We want revenge', 'Let Gandhi die'.

By the third day of the fast, Gandhi had become seriously ill. His kidneys were failing; on that day he drank 68 oz. of water and retained a major portion of it, with the result that his body was becoming waterlogged. The medical bulletin issued in the evening added: 'The weakness has increased and his voice is feeble. Acetone bodies have appeared in the urine.' With the presence of these toxins in his bloodstream, the fast had entered the 'danger zone'. Notwithstanding his precarious health, he could still maintain his good humour. In a note to Mirabehn he said:

I am dictating this immediately after the 3:30 a.m. prayer, while I am taking my meal such as a fasting man with prescribed food can take. Don't be shocked. The food consists of 8 oz. of hot water sipped with difficulty. You sip it as poison, well knowing that in result it is nectar. It revives me whenever I take it. Strange to say this time I am able to take about 8 meals of this poison-tasting, but nectar-like meal. Yet I claim to be fasting and credulous people accept it! What a strange world!

That day he was too weak to walk to the prayer ground in Birla House, and arrangements were made for him to speak from his bed into a radio microphone connected with All-India Radio. 'Do not bother about what others are doing,' the Mahatma said in a barely audible voice. 'Each of us should turn the searchlight inward and purify his or her heart as much as possible.' It was his firm belief that if people sufficiently purified themselves, then they would help India and themselves, and also shorten the period of his fast. None should be anxious for him. They should call to mind how best they could improve themselves and work for the good of the country. It was meaningless to worry about the possibility of his dying as a result of the fast. 'No one can escape death. Then why be afraid of it? In fact death is a friend who brings deliverance from suffering.'

While Gandhi was going through the exercise of fasting unto death with a view to bringing about communal harmony, he had an additional burden to bear. There were disagreements between Patel and Nehru; each had his own ideas as to how the government and the party should be run. Patel was angry with Nehru for referring the Kashmir issue to the UN. The Home Minister preferred 'timely action' on the ground. Within days of the attack on Kashmir, Lord Mountbatten (formerly the Viceroy and now Governor-General) had urged Nehru to join him in a visit to Lahore to talk to Jinnah and Liaquat Ali Khan. Patel took strong exception to the suggestion: 'For the Prime Minister to go crawling to Jinnah when we were the stronger side and in the right would never be forgotten by the people of India.' Nehru, however, did not go, though illness was as much a reason as Patel's opposition. Their differences had now become so steep that it appeared that either Patel or Nehru would have to leave the government, and Patel felt certain that it would be him. In fact each offered to resign in favour of the other. Writing to Patel on 23 December 1947, Nehru said:

If I am to continue as Prime Minister, I cannot have my freedom restricted and I must have a certain liberty of direction. Otherwise it is better for me to retire. I do not wish to take any hasty step, nor would you wish to take it . . . If unfortunately either you or I have to leave the Government of India, let this be done with dignity and goodwill. On my part I would gladly resign and hand over the reins to you.

In his reply Patel said:

I have no desire to restrain your liberty of direction in any manner, nor have I ever done so in the past . . . The question of your resignation or your abdicating your functions does not arise at all. I am with you in that the decision may be taken with dignity and goodwill and I will strain every nerve to help you in doing so but you will not, I am sure, want me to continue long as an ineffective colleague.

Patel was further perturbed by Nehru's attitude on the question of the 550 million rupees due to be paid to Pakistan. When Patel told the fasting Mahatma on 14 January that the decision to withhold this amount was a cabinet decision, Gandhi replied that he had just talked to Nehru, who had commented: 'Yes, it was passed but we don't have a case. It is legal quibbling.' Patel's reaction was quite bitter: 'We unanimously agreed, and now the Prime Minister calls it legal quibbling. This is my last meeting.' But he supported the decision to release the money.

The following morning Patel, who was chiefly responsible for successfully negotiating with the princely states to bring them into the Indian Union, flew off to Kathiawar on some urgent business with a number of these states, which were intermittently objecting to joining the Union. Before leaving Delhi he wrote to Gandhi submitting his resignation:

> In the circumstances, it will perhaps be good for me and for the country if you now let me go. I cannot do otherwise than what I am doing. And if thereby I become burdensome to my lifelong colleagues and a source of distress to you and still I stick to office, it could mean – at least that is what I would feel – that I let the lust of power blind my eyes and so was unwilling to quit. You should quickly deliver me from this intolerable situation.

Then Patel requested the Mahatma to give up his fast. Suggesting rather obliquely that the fast was, in fact, directed against him, Patel added that his leaving the government 'may even help remove the causes that have prompted you to fast'.

As Gandhi's condition worsened there began concerted efforts to bring about communal harmony in Delhi. Nehru was addressing public meetings to achieve this goal. Rajendra Prasad, the new Congress president, was interviewing members of numerous organizations, trying to adjust disputes and formulate a joint pledge of communal friendship that would satisfy the Mahatma. Processions began to parade through the streets with everyone shouting slogans in favour of Hindu-Muslim unity. A flood of telegrams arrived from princes, from Muslims in Pakistan, from all over India; however, there was none from Jinnah. On 16 January a group of Hindu and Sikh refugees reported to Gandhi that the situation in the city was fast improving and urged him to end his fast. He told them not to be in too great a hurry. 'I won't pop off suddenly,' he said to them. 'Whatever you do should ring true. I want solid work.' In the evening he spoke to the prayer congregation by microphone from his cot. His doctors had strongly advised him to give up the fast, for even if he survived it, malfunction of his kidneys could lead to permanent, serious injury. 'I did not embark upon the fast after consultation with medical men, be they however able,' he told the prayer meeting. 'My sole guide, even dictator, is God, the Infallible and Omnipotent . . . I am in His hands . . . I dread neither death nor permanent injury even if I survive. But I do feel that this warning of medical friends should, if the country has any use for me, hurry the people up to close their ranks.'

Presently, a telegram was received from Muslim refugees in Karachi who had been driven out of Delhi. They enquired whether they could return to Delhi and reoccupy their houses. 'That is the test,' Gandhi remarked, and dispatched his secretary and disciple, Pyarelal, with the telegram on a round of Hindu and Sikh refugee camps in the city. By nightfall, over a thousand refugees had signed a declaration that they would welcome the Muslims to return and occupy their original homes, even though with their families they might now have themselves to face the biting winter cold of Delhi in refugee camps.

On the fifth day of the fast, the doctors were further perturbed, for the Mahatma's weight over the past three days had remained stationary at 107 lb. The waterlogged system and the failing kidney function meant an added strain on the already enfeebled heart. In his written statement he told the evening prayer meeting about the increasing number of telegrams he had been receiving from people from different walks of life, including the princes, but be warned:

> Nothing is to be done under pressure of the fast . . . If such a thing happens, it would be a tragedy of the high degree. What a spiritual fast does expect is cleansing of the heart . . . Neither the Rajahs and Maharajahs nor the Hindus or Sikhs or any others will serve themselves or India as a whole if at this, what is to me sacred juncture they mislead me with a view to terminating my fast. They should know that I never feel so happy as when I am fasting for the spirit. This fast has brought me higher happiness than hitherto. No one need disturb this happy state unless he can honestly claim that in his journey he had turned deliberately from Satan towards God.

That evening a large procession shouting Hindu-Muslim unity slogans approached Birla House. Nehru spoke movingly to the crowd, which spilled over on to the prayer ground, pleading repeatedly that it was necessary to have peace in Delhi so that the Mahatma should be preserved, and then the crowd dispersed quietly. The Mountbattens came, and Gandhi greeted them with folded hands, saying with a faint smile: 'It takes a fast to bring you to me.' The Governor-General explained that the visit was more than personal; he wanted the world to see that he supported Gandhi in his objective.

On the morning of 18 January the Congress president Rajendra Prasad, who had been feverishly working for an agreement acceptable to Gandhi, led a hundred strong deputation of the Central Peace Committee consisting of representatives from all communities, to Birla House. Nehru and Azad were already there. Prasad was armed with a document signed by the members of the peace committee, pledging communal peace in Delhi and appealing to the Mahatma to end the fast. Soon after the deputation went to Gandhi's room, Prasad read out the document:

We wish to announce that it is our heartfelt desire that the Hindus, Muslims and Sikhs, and the members of other communities should once again live in Delhi like brothers in perfect amity, and we take the pledge that we shall protect the life, property and faith of Muslims, and that the incidents which have taken place in Delhi will not happen again.

We want to assure Gandhiji that the annual fair at Khwaja Qutab-ul-din's mausoleum will be held this year as in previous years.

The Muslims will be able to move about in Subzimandi, Karol Bagh, Paharganj and other localities, just as they did in the past .

The mosques which have been left by Muslims and which are now in the possession of Hindus and Sikhs will be returned. The areas which have been set apart for Muslims will not be forcibly occupied.

We shall not object to the return to Delhi of the Muslims who have migrated from here, if they choose to come back, and Muslims shall be able to carry on their business as before.

We give the assurance that all these things will be done by our personal efforts and not with the help of the police or the military.

We request Mahatmaji to believe us and give up the fast and continue to lead us, as he has done hitherto.

Gandhi was pleased that the signatories included Hindus, Muslims, Sikhs, Christians, Jews and even members of the Hindu Mahasabha and the RSS. He was deeply touched, he said, by their words. Indeed, they had given him all he had asked for. But peace in Delhi was not enough unless it was clearly understood to be the first step towards peace everywhere, a reunion of hearts. 'Delhi', Gandhi added, 'is the heart of the Indian Dominion, and you are the cream of Delhi. If you cannot make the whole of India realize that the Hindus, Sikhs and Muslims are all brothers, it will bode ill for the future of both Dominions. What will happen to India if they both quarrel?' He wept for a moment, and when he resumed, his voice was so faint that Dr Sushila Nayyar, who was in attendance, had to repeat his words to the gathering. He exhorted those present not to ask him to give up his fast unless they found a 'responsive echo' in their hearts. If they fully accepted the implication of their pledge, only then should they release him from Delhi, so that he might be free to go to Pakistan.

He then referred to a book presented to him by a Muslim friend, in which the author expressed the view that according to the Koran, the Hindus were infidels who worshipped idols and were 'worse than poisonous reptiles, fit only to be exterminated'.

Maulana Azad and other Muslim scholars spoke and assured the Mahatma that the observation made in the book did not relate to Islamic tenets. Azad quoted a verse from the holy book to substantiate his assertion.

Ganesh Dutt, speaking for the RSS and the Hindu Mahasabha, made a fervent appeal to Gandhi to break his fast. Zahid Hussain, High Commissioner (Ambassador) of Pakistan in Delhi, also addressed a few friendly words to the Mahatma. 'People of Pakistan enquire about the state of your health. We are ready to render you whatever help we can.' A Sikh representative, Harbhajan Singh, added his pledge. M.S. Randhawa, the Sikh Deputy Commissioner in charge of the Delhi police, who had until this time been distrusted by the Muslims, was pleased to inform Gandhi that the situation in the city was fast approaching normal. Referring to the document read out by Prasad, Randhawa said: 'The administration of Delhi will fulfil all your seven conditions in their entirety.'

When the speeches were over, the assembled deputation waited anxiously. Gandhi sat on his cot, deeply engrossed in thought. Finally he said: 'I will break the fast. God's will be done. All of you may well be a witness to it.'

Then there were prayers, and Buddhist, Japanese, Muslim and Parsi scriptures were read. Members of Gandhi's entourage sang his favourite hymn 'When I Survey the Wondrous Cross', followed by the Hindu *mantra*:

> Lead me from untruth to truth,
> From darkness to light,
> From death to immortality.

Thereupon, Gandhi accepted from Maulana Azad the ceremonial glass of orange juice and slowly drank it. Soon after the gathering dispersed Gandhi learned that Nehru had gone on a sympathy fast since the previous day. Deeply moved, he sent a note to the Prime Minister punning on the meaning of *jawahar* (jewel): 'Now break your fast . . . May you long remain the jewel of India.'

He addressed the evening prayer meeting from his bed. It was a happy day for him, he said. If the solemn pledge was honoured, it would revive his intense desire that he might live for 125 years. He stressed that the main concern ought to be the act itself, not the result of the action. 'If there is darkness in the Indian Union,' he continued, 'it would be folly to expect light in Pakistan. But if the night in the Union is dispelled beyond the shadow of a doubt, it cannot be otherwise in Pakistan.'

## FORTY-SIX

# *Message to Congress*

On the first day after the fast Gandhi was carried in a chair to his prayer meeting, where he proclaimed himself a failure, for a few hours earlier an official of the right-wing Hindu Mahasabha party had repudiated the Delhi peace pledge. But the Mahatma was far from being cast down. He was planning his mission to Pakistan, bearing fully in mind that his fast had resulted in a studied silence on the part of Jinnah. He had expected the beginnings of sympathetic treatment for the Hindus in Pakistan, but there was no sign of it. Soon after the prayer meeting a delegation from Pakistan met Gandhi, leaving him uncharacteristically exasperated. 'No settlement can now be arrived at through Jinnah,' he angrily informed Nehru. 'Nobody need go to Pakistan. I should not go there even in my personal capacity.' But his anger was a passing one, and in the following days he would explain how imperative it was for him to make the journey.

On 20 January he was again carried to the prayer meeting. As he was speaking about the peace pledge – that 'excellent decision taken by us with God as witness, which would take us to rise to a much higher plane' – there was a loud explosion near the garden wall. A part of the wall was demolished. While the noise of the explosion caused many in the audience to run helter-skelter, Gandhi appealed for calm. 'Don't worry about it,' he said. 'Listen to me.'

A few minutes later a young refugee named Madanlal Pahwa was being searched and interrogated in the police box at the entrance to Birla House. A hand grenade was found on him. He was removed to the local police station, and although he did not admit it, the police had no doubt that there were other conspirators in the plot to kill Gandhi.

The next day the Mahatma was able to walk to the prayer meeting. He told the congregation that innumerable telegrams and telephone calls had been received, complimenting him for remaining calm during the previous day's incident. But, he said, he deserved no credit at all. He had really thought it was military target practice.

On 23 January someone reminded Gandhi that it was Subhas Chandra Bose's birthday. He was glad that there was special reason to take note of

Bose's birthday, in spite of the fact that the deceased patriot had believed in violence. Paying him a rich tribute, the Mahatma said:

He gambled away his own life for the sake of his country. What a huge army he raised, making no distinction of caste or creed! His army was also free from provincialism and colour prejudice. Being the commander of this army, he did not seek comforts for himself while denying them to others. Subhas Chandra Bose was tolerant of all religions, and consequently he won the hearts of all men and women of his country. He accomplished what he had set his heart on. We should call to mind his virtues and practise them in our lives.

The congregation at Gandhi's prayer meeting on 25 January was larger than usual. He was pleased about the reports that peace continued in the capital. 'It has gladdened my heart to be informed by Hindu and Muslim friends that Delhi has experienced a reunion of hearts,' he told the meeting. Two days later, addressing a mammoth gathering at the annual Muslim fair of Urs on the outskirts of Delhi, he spoke of people with different religious affiliations as 'leaves of the same tree'. He advised the Muslims to write to their brothers in Pakistan, urging them to purge their hearts of hatred and not to massacre Hindus.

Apart from the problem of Hindu-Muslim disunity, the prevailing state of affairs of Congress distressed Gandhi immensely. Some time earlier he had dwelt on the subject at a large prayer meeting:

The Congress has come to have a tradition of its own. For years – for more than sixty years – it has fought the British Government. As [poet] Tulsidas says, 'The name of Rama has become greater than Rama Himself.' Similarly the name of the Congress has become greater than the Congress.

But what is the condition of the Congress now? Congressmen think that now it is their Government . . . Truly speaking one can only be a servant of the people, not their leader. It would be a misfortune if the spirit of service disappears . . . if devoid of the spirit of service we concern ourselves only with serving our own ends or those of our relatives and friends by seeking the favours of the Chief Minister or by capturing the Congress office to further our own interest. Everywhere Congressmen are thus scrambling for power and favours. If this continues, I am afraid, we shall not be able to hold the reins of the Congress firmly, nor will those who are in the Government be able to run it efficiently.

A government seems to have only military power behind it, but it cannot run on the strength of that power alone. What is the real power of the Government? The real power is in your hands. Their power is only what you delegate to them. Therefore once you have your own government you become your own masters. It is a different matter if you fail to recognize your own strength and remain in darkness. But if we realize that real power is now in the hands of India, i.e., in our own hands, we should use it judiciously . . .

A rot has set in in the Congress. It means that Congressmen are no more honest. If those who are selfish capture the Congress it cannot function well. Now there are various groups in the Congress and all of them have the one thought of capturing the Congress. But in this way none of the groups will be able to hold the organization. The Congress would slip from their hold and pass into the hands of unscrupulous men. And they are white-[clad] *goondas* who appear respectable but are *goondas* at heart. How can our purpose be served if the reins of the Congress pass into their hands? We will all perish if we ourselves disintegrate into groups such as the Forward Bloc, the Socialists, and so on. We all belong to the Congress. The Congress aims at serving the whole nation, not any particular party or group.

For many years he had been of the view that when freedom came the Congress party should eschew the business of government and confine itself to selfless service of the people. He now felt that the need of the hour was to concentrate on constructive work. A group of prominent Congressmen, including Kripalani, suggested to Gandhi that all constructive workers could form themselves into a separate body for the vigorous prosecution of the constructive work. Such a body should not abjure politics, but go into the government, take power and use it for the furtherance of the constructive programme. 'Today politics has become corrupt,' the Mahatma told the Congressmen. 'Anybody who goes into it is contaminated. Let us keep out of politics altogether.'

He was not any less explicit while talking to a group of Socialists who called on him:

Note down these words of an old man past the age of three score and ten: In the times to come the people will not judge us by the creed we profess or the label we wear or the slogans we shout, but by our work, industry, sacrifice, honesty and purity of character. They will want to know what we have actually done for them. But if you do not listen, if taking advantage of the prevailing misery and discontent of the people, you set about to accentuate and exploit it for party ends, it will recoil upon your head and even God will not forgive you for your betrayal of the people.

Gandhi planned to go to Sevagram ashram for a week or two to recover his strength. Meanwhile he resumed writing for *Harijan* and expounded his proposals that Congress should convert itself into a body dedicated to social service, contenting itself with exercising moral pressure on whatever government happened to be in power. He had over the years felt that the desire and opportunity for service could be the only incentive for a Congressman to aspire to become a legislator. 'In an organization which exists for the sake of service and which has boycotted titles and other such paltry things, the sentiment that to be selected as candidates for the legislatures is a mark of honour is harmful,' he said. 'If such a sentiment takes root, it will finally prove to be Congress's ruin . . . who will then put flesh and blood into India's millions of skeletons? On whom will India and the world rely?' He was distressed by the opulent living of the high Congress government officials. He could not reconcile himself to the practice of holding dinner parties in Government House 'when the people are experiencing acute food shortage'. He saw no reason why in a poverty-stricken country the governors and ministers should take up residence in palatial homes. If he had his way he would provide ministers with small, cosy, unostentatious houses, but would give no armed bodyguards either to Congress governors or to ministers, 'who are committed to non-violence as their policy. And if as a result some of them should get killed, I would not mind.'

He had foreseen that once the Congress associated itself with the government of the country it would soon be converted from a party dedicated to service to a party obsessed with power and privilege. What he feared had come to pass. On 27 January the Mahatma wrote:

> The Congress has won political freedom, but it has yet to win economic freedom, social and moral freedom. These freedoms are harder than the political one if only because they are constructive, less exciting and not spectacular . . .
>
> In its difficult ascent to democracy Congress has inevitably created rotten boroughs, leading to corruption and creation of institutions, popular and democratic only in name . . . It must do away with its special register of the members who cannot be easily identified . . . It should ensure that no fictitious name gets in and no legitimate name is left out . . . Let the Congress now proclaim to itself and the world that it is only God's servant – nothing more, nothing less. If it engages in the ungainly skirmish for power, it will find one fine morning that it is no more.

On the morning of 29 January Gandhi sketched a draft constitution for the Congress. Now that its political objective of independence had been achieved, he proposed that Congress in its present form be disbanded and converted into a *lok sewak sangh* (organization for the service of the people) based on the village *panchayat* (council of five persons), abjuring political power and devoting itself only to social, moral and economic reform and the constructive programme.

That afternoon a group of refugees from Bannu, survivors of a massacre on a train in Pakistan, came to see Gandhi. They narrated their experience in mounting excitement and anger, and at last one of them, a powerfully built old man, advised the Mahatma in a vehement tone: 'Why do you not take a rest? You have done enough harm. You have ruined us utterly. You ought to leave us now and retire to the Himalayas.'

'My Himalayas are here,' Gandhi replied in a harsh voice. 'To remove your sufferings and to die in your service is for me like going to the Himalayas.'

The old man said: 'It is God who is speaking to you through us. We are beside ourselves with grief.'

'My grief is no less than yours,' Gandhi replied, and gradually he was able to pacify them.

Among the people received by Gandhi on that day was Margaret Bourke-White of *Life* magazine. She asked him about the atomic bomb: 'If an aircraft actually drops one on a city, what should believers in *ahimsa* do?' Gandhi's reply was his last message to the world. The falling of the atomic bomb, he said, should not scare the soldiers of nonviolence. They should not dive for the shelter, for they must have faith in the indestructibility of *ahimsa*. If those thousands who were done to death in Hiroshima had come out and stood firm, looking up, watching without fear, and praying for the pilot, 'their sacrifice would not have gone in vain'. The previous day the Mahatma had told the American author Vincent Sheean:

> They claim that one atom bomb changed the entire course of the war and brought the end of the war so much nearer. Has it conquered the Japanese spirit? It has not and it cannot. Has it crushed Germany as a nation? It has not and it cannot. To do that would require resorting to Hitler's method, and to what purpose? In the end it will be Hitlerism that will have triumphed.

There was an endless procession of visitors on 29 January, and though at the end of the day Gandhi felt thoroughly exhausted, he devoted some time to the draft of the Congress constitution which he had undertaken to prepare for the Congress Working Committee. He was deeply concerned about the mounting evidence of corruption in the Congress. Congressmen who had worked and sacrificed for the sake of freedom were now succumbing to the lure of office and power. To Manubehn, who was massaging his head with oil, he said: 'How can we look the world in the face? The honour of the whole nation hinges on those who have participated in the freedom struggle. If they too misuse their powers we are sure to lose our footing . . . Where do I stand and what am I doing?'

# FORTY-SEVEN

# The Last Journey

On Friday 30 January 1948, Gandhi woke up at his usual hour, 3.30 a.m. After the morning prayer he put the final touches to the new constitution for Congress which he had been unable to finish the previous night. The rest of the morning was spent answering letters. Someone mentioned the fact that despite poor health he was working incessantly. 'Tomorrow', he explained, 'I may not be here.' He was aware of the strengthening of the police guard on Birla House, but notwithstanding Home Minister Patel's earnest request Gandhi would not permit the police to search those attending the prayer meetings: 'If I have to die I should like to die at the prayer meeting. You are wrong in believing that you can protect me from harm. God is my protector.'

Gandhi had been busy since the early morning. It was now nearly four o'clock in the afternoon, and soon there would be a meeting with Patel. Gandhi had earlier been drawn into the ideological differences and rivalry between Patel and Nehru, and had expressed the view that one of the two should withdraw from the cabinet. He had since come to the conclusion that both were indispensable, pointing out that the government would be seriously weakened if it lost either.

Patel arrived with his daughter, Manibehn, and was promptly ushered into the room where Gandhi sat at his spinning wheel. The conversation with Patel was a long and absorbing one. Gandhi stressed that any breach between the two senior cabinet colleagues would be disastrous. He would seek out Nehru after the evening prayer and discuss the whole matter with him as well. Earlier in the day someone had shown him a clipping from the London *Times*, an article suggesting that the conflict between Nehru and Patel was irreconcilable. He was determined to put an end to the disunity between them, even if it meant delaying his journey to Sevagram. While the conversation continued he took his evening meal consisting of goat's milk, cooked and raw vegetables, oranges and a kind of sauce made with ginger and strained butter. It was now past 5 p.m., but Gandhi did not notice that he was late for the prayer meeting. Abhabehn, the young wife of Kanu Gandhi, grandson of the Mahatma's cousin, held up a watch, but neither Gandhi nor Patel paid any attention. After some minutes Patel's daughter said: 'It is ten minutes past five,' whereupon the two men rose. It had been decided that Gandhi, Patel and Nehru would together discuss the matter the following day.

Patel and his daughter immediately left Birla House while Gandhi, a little vexed at being unpunctual, made his way to the prayer meeting. Leaning lightly on the two girls, Manu and Abha, his 'walking sticks', he took a short cut across the grass, walking briskly to make up for lost time and then mounted the six low steps up to the level of the prayer ground. As he took a few paces in the direction of the wooden platform on which he sat during services, the crowd opened to enable him to pass through, bowing to his feet as he went by. Gandhi took his arms off the girls' shoulders and for a moment stood there smiling, touching his palms together in the traditional *namaskar*. Just then a stocky young man in a khaki bush jacket jostled through the crowd, roughly pushing Manu away, and when he was directly in front of Gandhi he fired three shots at point-blank range. The Mahatma's hands, folded in friendly greeting, descended slowly. 'He Ram [Oh, God],' he murmured, and sighed softly as the frail old body slumped to the ground. The assassin was overpowered after a short and fierce struggle, and the police quickly took custody of him.

Gandhi was carried indoors, but he was already unconscious. Within a few moments a doctor pronounced him dead. Patel, who lived not far from Birla House, had hardly reached home when he rushed back. A few minutes later Nehru arrived. The Prime Minister knelt by the side of his dead master and wept unrestrainedly while Patel managed an outward calm. Soon one of Gandhi's disciples appeared at the door of Birla House to speak to the anxiously waiting crowd: 'Bapuji is finished.' A moan went up from the crowd.

Mountbatten, on hearing the news, came immediately, but had to push his way through the crowd to the door. As he was about to go in, someone shouted in a loud voice: 'It was a Muslim that did it.' Mountbatten turned round and shouted back: 'You fool! Don't you know it was a Hindu?' Some in the crowd wanted it to be a Muslim, for they could then have a pretext to run a riot. Mountbatten's spirited response with his characteristic presence of mind had a calming effect on the excited crowd. A member of the Governor-General's staff remarked to him: 'How can you possibly know it's a Hindu?' Mountbatten replied: 'I don't. But if it is a Muslim we're all finished, so it may as well be a Hindu.'

Mountbatten stood by the Mahatma's body momentarily and then, seeing both Patel and Nehru together in the room, he acted with his instinctive sense of drama and timing. He drew the two leaders aside and told them of his recent meeting with Gandhi, when the Mahatma had said how deeply he wished that they would resolve their differences. Nehru and Patel looked at each other, and then at Gandhi, who now lay before them on the floor, wrapped in his shroud of *khadi*. They moved towards each other and embraced in a gesture of reconciliation.

For a long time Manu and Abha cradled the dead Mahatma's head on their laps, while the other women watched in silence or chanted verses from the *Bhagavad Gita*.

> Freedom from pride and pretentiousness; non-
> violence, forgiveness, uprightness, service of the
> Master, purity, steadfastness, self-restraint.
> Aversion from sense-objects, absence of conceit,
> realization of the painfulness and evil of birth,
> death, age and disease.
> Absence of attachment, refusal to be wrapped up
> in one's children, wife, home and family, even-
> mindedness whether good or evil befall . . .

> Thou mournest for them whom thou
> shouldst not mourn, and utterest vain
> words of wisdom. The wise mourn neither
> for the living nor for the dead. For
> never was I not, nor thou nor these kings,
> nor will any of us cease to be hereafter.

> This [the soul] no weapons wound,
> This no fire burns; This no waters wet,
> This no wind doth dry . . . For certain
> is the death of the born, and certain
> is the birth of the dead; therefore what
> is unavoidable thou shouldst not regret.

> This [the soul] is never born nor ever dies,
> nor having been will ever not be any more;
> unborn, eternal, everlasting, ancient,
> This is not slain when the body is slain . . .
> As a man casts off worn-out garments and
> takes others that are new, even so
> the embodied one casts off worn-out bodies
> and passes on to others new.

Soon the room was crowded with prominent Indians and diplomats, as well as young men and women who had been Gandhi's constant attendants.

The vast crowds outside Birla House, anxious to have a last glimpse of their departed leader, caused such a crush that the body was finally put on a tilted plank on an outside balcony, and bathed in floodlights so that all might see.

That evening Nehru spoke to the nation over All-India Radio. Speaking impromptu, in a choked voice, he said:

The light has gone out of our lives and there is darkness everywhere and I do not quite know what to tell you and how to say it. Our beloved leader, Bapu as we called him, the father of our nation, is no more. Perhaps I am wrong to say that. Nevertheless, we will not see him again as we have seen him these many years. We will not run to him for advice and seek solace from him, and that is a terrible blow not to me only but to millions and millions in this country. And it is difficult to soften the blow by any advice that I or anyone else can give you.

The light has gone out, I said, and yet I was wrong. For the light that shone in this country was no ordinary light. The light that has illumined this country for these many years will illumine this country for many more years, and a thousand years later that light will still be seen in this country, and the world will see it and it will give solace to innumerable hearts. For that light represented the living truth, and the eternal man was with us with his eternal truth reminding us of the right path, drawing us from error, taking this ancient country to freedom.

All this has happened. There is so much more to do. There was so much more for him to do. We could never think that he was unnecessary or that he had done his task. But now, particularly, when we are faced with so many his not being with us is a blow most terrible to bear.

On that fateful Friday, Gandhi's industrialist friend G.D. Birla was at Pilani. When he heard the sad news he immediately felt like rushing to Delhi by car, but his friends advised him to go by plane the following morning. Birla describes the restless night he spent at Pilani:

I know not if and when I slept or whether I was dreaming or my spirit had flown to Gandhiji. As if in a trance all of a sudden I was with Bapu.

I saw his dead body lying exactly at the place where he used to sleep. I saw Pyarelal and Sushila [Nayyar] sitting by his side. Seeing me Gandhiji got up as if from his sleep, and affectionately patting me said: 'I am glad you have also come. Don't worry about me, even though I have fallen victim to a conspiracy. But I am going to dance with joy as my mission is now over.' Then he pulled out his watch and said: 'Oh, it is nearing eleven now and you have to take me to Jumna *Ghat* [the cremation site on the banks of the river Jumna]. So I had better lie down again.'

Suddenly I woke up and wondered whether it was a dream or an occult reality.

At about midnight the body was lowered from the outside balcony into the house. All night mourners kept a vigil in the room and, between sobs, recited from the Hindu scriptures. Gandhi's disciples then washed his body according to the ancient Hindu rites to prepare him for his last journey to cremation grounds. He was covered up to the waist with a rose-strewn blanket. 'I asked for the chest to be left bare,' the Mahatma's youngest son, Devadas, explained. 'No soldier ever had a finer chest than Bapu's.'

During the morning the crowds outside resumed their demand that they should have *darshan*. Accordingly the body was once again placed on the balcony for public view. The funeral was being delayed until the arrival of Ramdas, Gandhi's third son, from Nagpur in the Central Provinces. Manilal, his second son, was still in South Africa.

Ramdas arrived at eleven o'clock in the morning and there was no reason for waiting further. The body was brought down into the house and then lifted on to a weapons carrier in an open coffin. Nehru, Patel, Kripalani, Rajendra Prasad and several others took up their places beside the bier. Those in charge of the arrangements, recalling Gandhi's opposition to machines, ensured that the weapons carrier's motor would not propel it. A non-commissioned officer sat at the steering wheel. Two hundred uniformed servicemen with four stout ropes drew the carrier through the streets, and this concession to Gandhi was indeed symbolic. Six thousand soldiers, sailors, airmen and policemen, and countless citizens marched before and after the bier. In front of the bier walked, among others, Ramdas and Devadas, barefoot.

The vast crowds which had gathered along the roads crowded round the weapons carrier to have *darshan*, and consequently the procession moved at an extremely slow pace. Hymns of all religions went up from the onlookers, mingling with the roars of '*Mahatma Gandhi ki jai*', while low-flying Dakotas dropped rose petals on Gandhi's bier. It took almost five hours for the marchers to cover the six miles to the banks of the sacred river Jumna, where about 700,000 people awaited the cortège.

The weapons carrier reached the cremation ground where the Department of Public Works had built overnight a small, elevated platform made of stone, brick and earth. Gandhi's body was laid tenderly on the funeral pyre – a pile of sandalwood logs, mixed with *ghee*, incense, coconuts and camphor. At 4.15 p.m. Ramdas lit his father's funeral pyre. Most of the members of the Indian government, and Lord and Lady Mountbatten, sat on the grass, watching quietly. As the flames, red and gold, leapt into the air, a groan went up from the vast assemblage and then from nearly a million throats came the chant: '*Mahatma Gandhi amar ho gae*' (Mahatma

Gandhi has become immortal), echoing instinctively the age-old message contained in the *Vedas*:

Holy soul, may sun, air and fire be auspicious unto thee. Thy dear ones on this earth do not lament at thy departure, for they know that thou art gone to the radiant regions of the blessed. May the waters of all rivers and oceans be helpful unto thee, and serve thee ever in thy good deeds for the welfare of all beings; may all space and its four quarters be open unto thee for thy good deeds.

The pyre burned for fourteen hours while priests recited the entire text of the *Bhagavad Gita*. Among the many visitors who came to the cremation ground that night was Harilal Gandhi, the prodigal son. Pale and emaciated, suffering from tuberculosis, he mingled unrecognized with the crowd, and spent the rest of the night in the house of his brother Devadas. A few months later he was found in a coma 'in some locality' of Bombay.

When the last embers had grown cold, the ashes were gently scooped into a homespun cotton bag, while the *asthis* – the bones as distinguished from the ashes – were deposited in a copper urn. The ashes were divided up and given to the governors of each province for immersion in the rivers or, as at Bombay, the sea.

The chief immersion ceremony took place at Allahabad, in the United Provinces, at the Triveni, the place where the sacred Ganges, the Jumna and the Saraswati meet. A special train carrying the flower-decked urn left New Delhi at 4 a.m. on 11 February, stopping at a number of stations *en route* to let the people standing on crowded platforms pay homage. At Allahabad the urn was mounted on a motor truck, which moved slowly through a throng of over a million people. At the river bank the urn was transferred to a small amphibious landing craft, and minutes later the *asthis* and the ashes were emptied into the river. As Dakotas flew overhead, dropping roses, the landing craft with Nehru, Patel, Azad, Ramdas, Devadas, and Mrs Naidu, among those aboard, turned towards the shore. The guns of the fort fired a salute as the *asthis* rode seaward.

The impact of Gandhi's assassination was universal. The Indian authorities received over three thousand unsolicited messages from abroad. The Pope, the Archbishop of Canterbury, the Chief Rabbi of London, King George VI, the political heads of all important countries and most minor ones publicly expressed grief at Gandhi's passing; indeed people from all walks of life paid tribute to the peacemaker.

Léon Blum, the French Socialist, spoke for millions: 'I never saw Gandhi. I do not know his language. I never set foot in his country and yet I feel the same sorrow as if I have lost someone near and dear . . .' The novelist Pearl S. Buck described Gandhi's assassination as 'another crucifixion'. Lord Mountbatten expressed the hope that Gandhi's life might 'inspire our troubled world to save itself by following his noble example'. General George C. Marshall, United States Secretary of State, said: 'Mahatma Gandhi was the spokesman for the conscience of all mankind.' 'A prince among men has passed away,' said General Smuts. Lord Halifax (Irwin) declared: 'There can be few men in all history who, by personal character and example have been able so deeply to influence the thought of their generation.' The British Prime Minister, Clement Attlee, described him as 'their greatest citizen' who 'seemed to belong to a different period of history'.

Professor Albert Einstein observed: 'Gandhi had demonstrated that a powerful human following can be assembled not only through the cunning game of the usual political maneuvers and trickeries but through the cogent example of a morally superior conduct of life.' General Douglas MacArthur, supreme Allied military commander in Japan, asserted: 'In the evolution of civilization, if it is to survive, all men cannot fail eventually to adopt Gandhi's belief that the process of mass application of force to resolve contentious issues is fundamentally not only wrong but contains within itself the germs of self-destruction.'

In the words of the *New York Times*, 'Gandhi strove for perfection as other men strive for power and possessions . . . the power of his benignity grew stronger as his political influence ebbed . . . He tried in the mood of the New Testament, to love his enemies, and to do good to those who despitefully used him. Now he belongs to the ages.'

The *Times* of London said in an editorial: 'No country but India and no religion but Hinduism could have given birth to a Gandhi.'

Lord Wavell was on his travels in South Africa when he came to know of Gandhi's death. Wavell recorded in his journal, which he still maintained:

We got to Johannesburg . . . I was greeted with the news of Gandhi's assassination, an unexpected end for a very remarkable man. I never accepted him as having much of the saint in his composition but he was an extremely astute politician. Whether he did more harm or good for India it would be hard to say, but Indians will have no doubt, and he certainly hastened the departure of the British, which was his life's aim. But he wrecked the plan of the Cabinet Mission which might possibly have secured a united India and saved all the massacres. I do not believe that he really worked for an understanding with the Muslims, when his influence might have secured it. He was always the lawyer and the Bania who would drive a hard bargain and then find some legal quibble to deprive his opponent of what he had seemed to gain. I always thought he had more of malevolence than benevolence in him, but who am I to judge, and how can an Englishman estimate a Hindu? Our standards are poles apart; and by Hindu standards Gandhi may have been a saint; by any standards he was a very remarkable man.

Some twenty-five years later authors Larry Collins and Dominique Lapierre interviewed Lord Mountbatten for their book *Mountbatten and Independent India*. Collins and Lapierre describe the scene when they first touched on the subject of Gandhi's assassination with the former Viceroy:

Neither of us, we are sure, will ever forget the afternoon we first talked to Mountbatten of Gandhi's death. It was a winter evening, with premature shadows darkening the Broadlands living room and the great green lawn running down to his salmon stream. Suddenly we both realized that this man who prided himself on being a professional warrior, a man who'd rolled over with his dying ship rather than leave his captain's bridge, was crying. Openly, unashamedly crying, as he described entering Birla House that January afternoon and seeing Gandhi's body laid out on his straw pallet.

# FORTY-EIGHT

# The Hatching of the Plot

Soon after the Mahatma's announcement at the prayer meeting on 12 January 1948, that he had decided to go on a fast, the news was being transmitted by the media. In Poona two men sitting in a small and shoddy newspaper office read it over their teleprinter. It took them little time to make their profound decision: Gandhi had to be eliminated.

The two men, Nathuram Godse and Narayan Apte, were respectively the editor and manager of a Marathi newspaper, *Hindu Rashtra*. Their cause was the unification and revitalization of the Hindus so that they should be in a position to fight for their political rights instead of 'giving in to the Muslims' as they had done in the past. The supreme goal of their unification movement, however, was to prevent the vivisection of India – a cause already lost, for India had been partitioned and there was nothing they could do to reverse the division.

Nathuram Godse and Narayan Apte were bitter, angry, frustrated. The partition of India perpetrated by the British was a fraud, and the Congress party, by accepting partition, had betrayed the nation. The independence of India to them was a farce and an insult, and they had observed the Independence Day on 15 August as a day of mourning.

In the weeks before the murder of Gandhi it was becoming evident that his life was being threatened by a small band of resolute conspirators. In the beginning the evidence was in the form of reports of speeches made against him, pamphlets denouncing him and accusing him of being pro-Muslim, increasing number of visitors to Birla House who complained openly against him for having 'lost touch with the people', urging him to retire from politics. These developments, coupled with an increased traffic in arms, made it apparent that Gandhi's life was endangered, but still the evidence had no clear outlines of a conspiracy. Some of those who were in close proximity to Gandhi said later that they could perceive the menace taking shape before their eyes.

Gandhi was well aware that he was exposed to a violent attack on his life. The greatest danger was from people who had suffered during the period of anarchy just before and following the partition, when Hindus, Sikhs and

Muslims all lost sight of reason and committed atrocities. Many of the survivors proceeded to retaliate with a vengeance. Incidentally, only one of the conspirators had witnessed such scenes of violence. This was Madanlal Pahwa, the youth who ignited the guncotton slab on 20 January. The rest had been virtually unaffected throughout the communal disturbances, for they lived in relatively safe areas like Bombay and Poona.

Only one of the persons arrested in connection with the murder had a long history of terrorist activity behind him. This was Vinayak Damodar Savarkar, who had been dispatched by the British to the penal colony in the Andamans. He was a former president of the right-wing Hindu Mahasabha, a party dedicated to militant Hinduism in opposition to the nonviolence of Gandhi.

Although the main conspirators, Godse and Apte, had known Savarkar for many years, the minor conspirators appeared late on the scene and were unknown to one another until a few weeks prior to the assassination.

Nathuram Godse was arrested moments after shooting Gandhi, and was taken to the nearby Tughlak Road police station. A reporter who managed to see him briefly in a cell at the police station asked him whether he had anything to say. 'For the present I only want to say that I am not at all sorry for what I have done,' he replied. 'The rest I will explain in court.' The police then cautioned him not to say anything more, and soon he was removed to the Parliament Street police station, where tighter security could be placed around him.

Preliminary investigations revealed that he was the editor of a newspaper and a well-known member of the Hindu Mahasabha. Clean-cut, sober, intelligent, the thirty-seven-year-old bachelor hardly seemed a candidate for the role of assassin. From time to time he had written scathing editorials denouncing Gandhi and the Congress party, though acquaintances could not recall an occasion when he had spoken bitterly against the Mahatma.

He was of medium height, well built and fair-complexioned, with finely carved features. Born into an orthodox Brahmin family in 1910, his father was a minor official in the postal department. The family was large – four sons and two daughters – and poor. The father was frequently transferred to be postmaster in small townships in the Bombay Presidency. After Nathuram had finished primary schooling in his mother-tongue, Marathi, he was sent to Poona to continue his studies there. He read books on history, mythology and scriptures in the Marathi language, but showed no particular interest in school and left without matriculating, having failed to pass the examination in English. He was about sixteen when he opened up a small shop selling cloth, but this proved to be an unsuccessful venture. He then tried his hand at tailoring and made a poor living. Meanwhile he was endeavouring to catch up with his education and improve his English.

When he was about twenty Nathuram became an active member of the Hindu Mahasabha. He participated in the civil disobedience movement in Hyderabad, where Hindus were complaining of being deprived of their rights by the Muslim government of the Nizam. He was arrested and sentenced to a short term of imprisonment. He had, by now, become deeply involved in politics, devoting all his energies to the Hindu cause, and abandoned all thoughts of matrimony. He read widely in history and sociology. He would read the history of India with a kind of intoxication and, glorifying in the spirit of the past, came to believe that Hindustan belonged to the Hindus because 'they have no other place which they can call their own . . . To the Hindus largely this country owes its fame and glory, its culture and art, knowledge, science and philosophy.' He raved at the Muslim conquest of India and rebelled against the British subjugation.

At Poona Godse met Narayan Apte, a schoolteacher, and started a Marathi newspaper, *Agrani*. The name was later changed to *Hindu Rashtra*. Godse was fervently opposed to what he called Mahatma Gandhi's policy of appeasement towards the Muslims, and criticized any move to concede Jinnah's demands. As Godse's writings became more and more virulent, which the authorities deemed dangerous to public peace, his security deposit under the Press Security Act was forfeited. He was asked to make a fresh deposit, and the money was hurriedly collected from the sympathizers with the Hindu Mahasabha cause.

He had a special devotion to the *Bhagavad Gita* and knew most of its verses by heart. He liked to quote them to justify acts of violence in pursuing a righteous aim and, unlike Gandhi, he was convinced that Krishna was talking to Arjuna about real battles and not battles which take place in the soul.

Godse's brother Gopal was arrested while on his way to his ancestral village, Uksan, where his aged parents lived. He was twenty-seven. Gopal had received more formal education, for he had passed his matriculation, but lacked Nathuram's air of refinement. For a short period of time he too joined the tailoring shop where Nathuram worked. Gopal was married and had two daughters. During the war he joined the Army as a storekeeper at the Motor Transport Spares Sub-Depot in Kirkee, near Poona, and saw service in Iraq and Iran. Like his brother, he was greatly influenced by Savarkar's philosophy and his crusade against the proposal to divide India, and now subscribed to revolutionary violence. 'You are a married man with responsibilities and commitments,' Nathuram cautioned him. 'Think twice before embarking on this dangerous course.' Gopal thought over the matter and decided to throw in his lot with his brother.

Narayan Apte came from a middle-class Brahmin family. After taking his Bachelor of Science degree he taught in a school at Ahmednagar where, during his tenure, he started a rifle club. He was quick-witted, lively and intelligent but somewhat vain and considered himself a kind of Casanova. For some time he belonged to the Rashtra Dal, a society of Hindu militant youths which he helped to organize at Poona with Nathuram Godse. The youths set themselves up as defenders of their motherland, and practised military drill with sticks and batons. In 1943 he joined the Royal Indian Air Force and was awarded a King's commission, but four months later he resigned from the service for family reasons, the chief one being that the condition of his two-year-old son (who was born retarded) was getting worse. He could not remain in service in which he was liable to be trans-ferred away from Poona. During the following year he joined Nathuram Godse to help him with the management of his newspaper. He was thirty-four years old.

Madanlal Pahwa, a twenty-year-old Punjabi Hindu, came from the small town of Pakpattan, now deep in Pakistan. He ran away from home to join the Royal Indian Navy, but failed to pass the entrance examination. He then went to Poona and managed to join the Army. After a brief period of training he asked for and obtained his release order and returned to his home town, where he remained until large-scale rioting broke out early in 1947. Pakpattan was predominantly Muslim and the Hindus were driven out of the town. He saw people being massacred by Muslim mobs before he slipped out, making his way to Ahmednagar near Poona, where he lived for some weeks in a refugee camp. Pahwa was a restless, disgruntled youth, with a ferocious temper, and was not averse to using his hands to make a living and his fists to get what he considered his due. In December 1947 he came to blows with a speaker from the Congress party who was propagat-ing Hindu-Muslim amity. About this time he came in contact with Godse and Apte, who felt that he could be a dependable member of the conspir-acy they were already hatching.

Vishnu Karkare, proprietor of a tawdry travellers' lodge in Ahmednagar, had had an unenviable childhood and adolescence. His parents were too poor to support him and gave him to an orphanage. When he was in his teens he ran away and earned his livelihood by taking up odd jobs. Then he joined a troupe of travelling actors and finally settled down to run a cheap restaurant and hotel. He became an active member of the Hindu Mahasabha and, with Apte's assistance, successfully contested the election to the Ahmednagar municipal committee. As an official representative of the municipal committee he accompanied a relief party to Noakhali in 1946 to render assistance to victims of Muslim mob violence. He stayed there for three months and witnessed the kidnapping of Hindu women by Muslims. By the time he returned to Ahmednagar, he was an intensely embittered man, and fell more and more under the influence of Nathuram Godse, who could fearlessly publish his reports of atrocities in Noakhali. At the time of the trial he was thirty-seven.

Dr Dattatraya Parchure was the son of a senior official in the education department in the princely state of Gwalior. For some time he worked in the Gwalior medical service, but was obliged to resign in 1934 and then went into private practice. He got himself keenly involved in the activities of the Hindu Mahasabha and was elected 'dictator' of the local Hindu Rashtra Sena, a militant group. In this capacity he became acquainted with Godse and Apte. Dr Parchure was not endowed with any great force of character and the conspirators, whilst using him for their own purposes, never really trusted him. He was forty-nine and, barring Savarkar, the oldest prisoner in the dock.

Shankar Kistayya, the youngest accused, was the son of a village carpenter, but had no schooling or trade. After a series of temporary jobs he took up employment with Digambar Badge, a bookseller, running errands and looking after the domestic chores. But when his wages fell into arrears, he decamped with a sum of money which he had collected from an old woman on his master's behalf. After the money was spent he returned and Badge assigned him even more important duties. In addition to selling books, Badge dealt in daggers, knives, knuckle-dusters and, surreptitiously, firearms and ammunition. Shankar Kistayya became Badge's trusted agent for carrying contraband weapons to his customers, while his wages still continued to fall overdue. Badge had little education and lived on his wits. He joined the dangerous adventure on an impulse inspired by monetary gain, and at the trial became an 'approver', informing on the other defendants and thus gaining pardon for himself.

The most prominent and controversial among the accused was Vinayak Damodar Savarkar. Now ailing and emaciated, looking much older than his sixty-five years, he was still domineering in manner. He sat alone in the last row in the prisoners' dock, giving the appearance of a Hindu family priest. Forty years earlier he had been in close touch with Gandhi, although their basic views differed on many matters. They had had little occasion or felt any necessity to meet in the ensuing years; however, they are known to have met in March 1927 when Gandhi was visiting Ratnagiri, where Savarkar was living under house arrest after his release from the Andaman Islands. Ratnagiri was the birthplace of Bal Gangadhar Tilak, the renowned nationalist, and in his speech to the welcoming committee Gandhi described his visit as a pilgrimage. He also recalled that Savarkar, whom he had known well in England, and whose sacrifice and patriotism were unquestionable, was now residing in Ratnagiri. 'We had our differences,' Gandhi observed, 'but difference of opinion should never mean hostility.' Savarkar sent a note to Gandhi inviting him to his residence and a brief meeting followed. They spoke about their encounters in London, but neither was convinced of the other's view. The real object of Gandhi's visit to Savarkar was to measure the extent of his revolutionary fervour. Now Savarkar sat in the dock accused of being the mastermind behind the assassination of the Mahatma.

While the prosecution had no difficulty in establishing Nathuram Godse's role as the organizer of the conspiracy, they were quite vague about the direct complicity of Savarkar. He stated that he was keeping indifferent health during the months preceding the assassination and received few visitors. He had associated with Nathuram Godse and Apte in their capacity as workers for the Hindu Mahasabha, but had not been in communication with them for more than a year. In the past he had corresponded with them on a regular basis, for in order to secure wide publicity and influence they were continually pressing him to allow his name to be linked with their paper, *Hindu Rashtra*, either as chief editor or at least as a patron, which he never agreed to do, nor did he write any articles for them. He had, however, permitted them to join his entourage on some of his tours. Godse and Apte were among innumerable other equally enthusiastic volunteers and were therefore neither specially chosen nor exclusively trusted. Savarkar asserted that all this belonged to the past. He had since retired from politics and lived quietly in his house in Bombay, protected from public glare by his secretary and his bodyguard.

Digambar Badge, the informer, had an altogether different story to tell. He claimed that on 17 January, three days before the assassination attempt was made on Gandhi, he accompanied Godse and Apte to Savarkar's house in Bombay at nine o'clock in the morning. While Badge waited downstairs, Godse and Apte went upstairs to Savarkar's study to receive final instructions from their political leader. After about ten minutes they came down with Savarkar, who said to them: 'Be successful and come back.'

Savarkar, in his defence, asserted that he never made such a statement, did not meet Godse and Apte that morning, nor was he aware of their visit if it did take place. He explained that visiting his two-storey house, 'Savarkar Sadan', did not necessarily mean visiting him. The ground floor contained an office which carried on the work of the Hindu Mahasabha. There was a reading room and a telephone on this floor. The ground floor of the house was thus frequented by party workers and sympathizers.

Besides, Savarkar's secretary, G.V. Damle, resided with his family in a second set of rooms. Another party worker, A.S. Bhide, had also taken up residence with his family as tenant on the upper floor. Damle, Bhide and Savarkar's bodyguard, A. Kesar, were usually found on the ground floor, and both Godse and Apte were well acquainted with them. Savarkar denied that he had said: 'Be successful and come back.' Yet he accepted the fact that he was present in the house on the day that Godse and Apte visited it. He defended himself systematically, pointing out several possibilities of error that arose from hearsay evidence, and bringing out various discordant elements in Badge's confession.

The prosecution reiterated that Savarkar bore a heavy responsibility for the murder, but he presented himself as a man who thoroughly deplored the death of Gandhi. And yet, in 1909, he had had no compunction about ordering a young Indian to kill Sir Curzon Wyllie, the government's prosecutor in the cases against some terrorists in Bengal. He had given Madanlal Dhingra a nickel-plated revolver and while bidding him farewell ordered: 'Don't show me your face if you fail this time.' The London police had strongly suspected Savarkar's involvement in the crime, but had failed to provide enough evidence to convict him. However, some eighteen months later, he was convicted of complicity in the murder of Mr A.M.T. Jackson at the Nasik conspiracy trial and sentenced to transportation for life to the Andaman Islands and forfeiture of all his property.

At the Gandhi murder trial, Savarkar's statement in his defence covered fifty-two pages. By way of introduction, he projected himself as a man of learning and dignity, who had graduated from Bombay University in 1905, read law at Gray's Inn in London and qualified himself for the Bar 'in 1909 or thereabout'. He had since been the author of several books of history, literature and drama in Marathi and English, and was the recipient of an honorary doctorate from Nagpur University in recognition of his contribution to literature. He had been elected to preside over innumerable conferences and conventions, political, social, religious and others in various parts of India. These statements were true except that although Savarkar had passed the final examination of the Gray's Inn, the Inn's specially appointed committee had decided not to call him to the Bar unless he gave them a written undertaking that he would never participate in politics. Savarkar had rejected their offer *in toto*.

His knowledge of law and correct behaviour in a courtroom stood him in good stead. He minutely examined all the evidence linking him to Godse, showing that he did not commit any of the offences charged against him, nor had he reason to do so, and that all such links could be interpreted as innocent associations. He had never met the conspirators; if he had, then the meeting had nothing to do with the conspiracy; he never came down the stairs with Godse and Apte; if he did, and spoke the parting words, 'Be successful and come back', then he could have been talking about something which had no connection whatsoever with the conspiracy, such as civil resistance to the government of the Nizam of Hyderabad or the sale of shares of *Hindu Rashtra* or any one of numerous legitimate undertakings. He also took apart Badge's story in the same way. 'So whether Badge has lied or Godse or Apte lied to exploit the moral influence which my name exercised on people to further their alleged criminal conspiracy,' Savarkar argued, 'in either case it cannot incriminate me, in the absence of any independent direct and material proof to connect me with the criminal knowledge of or participation in that conspiracy.'

There was clear-cut evidence that Savarkar had moulded the minds of countless Hindus to militancy and was strongly opposed to the attitudes of Gandhi and the Congress party. But there was only circumstantial evidence available to show that he was a part of the conspiracy to kill the Mahatma.

The evidence revealed that the plan to kill Gandhi had first been considered by Godse and Apte at the time of the partition of India in August 1947. They believed that it was Gandhi's weak-kneed policy of appeasement towards the Muslims that was responsible for the catastrophe. For various reasons their plan to murder Gandhi was delayed, and it was not until November that they began actively searching for weapons and ammunition and for associates who would help them to execute the plan. In the course of the weeks that followed, others joined the two principal conspirators, and details of the plan were worked out. The original plan was to overwhelm Gandhi from all sides; the simultaneous use of pistols and hand grenades should leave no possibility of his survival. Digambar Badge, the arm dealer, was asked to supply a minimum of two revolvers, two guncotton slabs and five hand grenades. A few days later he notified Godse and Apte that the guncotton slabs and hand grenades, together with detonators and primers, had been acquired and would be sent to the Hindu Mahasabha office in Bombay by 14 January. He was, however, unable to find two revolvers. Godse now began to search for them. Meanwhile Karkare, Pahwa and Kistayya had joined the conspirators, acting for the moment mainly as messenger boys.

The final decision to assassinate Gandhi was taken on 12 January when it was learned that the Mahatma was about to undertake a fast unto death. There were several reasons for undertaking the fast, but what disturbed Godse and Apte most was Gandhi's determined pressure on the government of India to compel it to review its former decision to withhold the pay-

ment of 550 million rupees to Pakistan. When after three days the government yielded to Gandhi's demand by declaring that the agreement between
India and Pakistan relating to financial adjustment should be implemented
forthwith, the chief conspirators became restive. They could wait no longer.
Over the next few days their plan was nurtured in Poona, Bombay and New
Delhi, till they had created a multi-limbed monster. The plan to kill Gandhi
became a plan of indiscriminate massacre. They even put a pistol into the
hands of that most inoffensive of men, Badge's henchman Shankar
Kistayya. Poor Shankar, very close to being a half-wit, did not have a clue as
to who Gandhi was, or why he was to fire the pistol at him.

The first thing that Godse did after his final decision to assassinate
Gandhi was to make an assignment of his assets, for he expected to die in
the attempt or to be arrested and sentenced to death. He himself was
unmarried and had no commitments to leave behind, but the two persons
for whom he felt most concern were his brother, Gopal, and his friend and
associate, Apte, who had joined him in this perilous undertaking. On 13
January he nominated Gopal's and Apte's wives as beneficiaries of his life
insurance policies. Godse was a man of modest means, and the policies
amounted to only 5,000 rupees.

The following day Godse and Apte left Poona for Bombay by train, taking up two window seats facing each other. Apte noticed that a very pretty
woman was going up and down looking for a window seat. He offered his
seat to her and moved across to sit next to Godse. Apte asked her if she was
not Bimba, the well-known screen actress. She was Shanta Modak; Bimba
was indeed her screen name. A friendly conversation followed. The three
of them were to get down at Dadar, a suburb of Bombay. Miss Modak's
destination was Shivaji Park, almost next to Savarkar Sadan, the house
where the Hindu Mahasabha leader lived. Apte told her that since he was
going to hire a taxi he would be pleased to give her a ride home. Miss
Modak expected her brother to pick her up at the station and offered to
drop Apte and Godse instead, if they were going close to where she lived.

Apte and Godse were actually on their way to the Hindu Mahasabha
office, about half a mile from where Savarkar lived, but Apte cheerfully
accepted the charming young lady's offer. She dropped them in front of
Savarkar Sadan, but did not see them enter the house. By giving in to his
vanity as a lady's man, Apte was not only creating evidence against himself
but was also dragging in Savarkar who, in all probability, had no idea about
the plot. The film actress clearly remembered the dashing young man and
his serious-looking friend, and where she had dropped them, and her
evidence in court reinforced the prosecution case against Savarkar as the
mastermind behind the conspiracy.

Gopal Godse, in the meantime, had requested seven days' leave of absence from his office, effective from 15 January, to attend to some 'immediate farm affairs in my village'. This was not granted. He repeated his request, asking leave from 17 January instead. Only after this was sanctioned did he proceed with his mission.

While the plan to kill Gandhi was being worked out, Dr Jagdish Chandra Jain, a professor who taught Hindi at Ruia College in Bombay, had a chance meeting with Madanlal Pahwa in the street. The professor had helped Pahwa in the past, giving him some odd jobs so that he could settle down after his nightmarish experiences in West Punjab. Pahwa was under severe strain and asked Dr Jain if he could come and have a chat with him. At the meeting, which was arranged for eight o'clock in the evening, Pahwa spoke about his activities at Ahmednagar with a group of conspirators financed by Vishnu Karkare. Arms and ammunition were being collected with a view to striking at the Muslims. He also spoke of a plot to kill an Indian leader, but declined to name the leader, saying he did not know about it. Finally he admitted that the leader in question was none other than Gandhi, and that he had been assigned the task of hurling a bomb at the Mahatma's prayer meeting. The confusion caused by the explosion would enable the conspirators to 'overpower' Gandhi. Dr Jain did not take Pahwa's story seriously because at this time angry and dispirited refugees from the Punjab often made vague threats against Gandhi and several other Congress leaders. The professor warned Pahwa of the perils of following so dangerous a project and tried to dissuade him from his wild talk and plan. When Pahwa called on him a day or two later, Dr Jain asked if he had paid any heed to the advice he had been given. Pahwa replied that he regarded the professor as a father and if he failed to take this advice he was bound to face dire consequences. Dr Jain was lulled into the belief that all was well.

Madanlal Pahwa was, in fact, a dedicated member of the conspiracy and participated in the meeting held on the evening of 14 January at the Hindu Mahasabha office in Bombay, which was attended by Godse, Apte, Karkare, Badge and Kistayya. Badge brought with him a khaki canvas bag containing two guncotton slabs and five hand grenades, and was promptly paid. Arrangements for travel to Delhi were explained, and each conspirator was given instructions as to the precise nature of his task. The meeting began at around 8.00 p.m. An hour later, according to Badge, he accompanied Godse and Apte to Savarkar's house, a visit that lasted five or ten minutes. Nothing was ever discovered about this alleged visit. Badge said that they took the khaki bag containing the arsenal with them, and they still had it when they returned to the waiting taxicab. Godse was anxious to find a place where it could be deposited for safekeeping, and on Badge's advice they took it to the house of Dixit Maharaj, a prominent nationalist and religious leader, whose elder brother was the chief priest of the local Vaishnava temple. Dixit Maharaj had on several occasions bought knives, daggers and other weapons from Badge, saying that they would be distributed to Hindus living in the Muslim-ruled princely states, for their protection. He could therefore be expected to be tight-lipped, and the bag with its contents would be safe in his custody. By the time the conspirators arrived at his house it was about 10.00 p.m. and Dixit Maharaj had gone to bed. Badge decided to leave the bag with one of the servants, saying that he would pick it up the next morning.

Badge spent the night at the Hindu Mahasabha building, and in the morning Godse and Apte met him there. Pahwa and Karkare had been in Bombay since 10 January and they too joined the deliberations to discuss the details of their plan. After the meeting at the Mahasabha office, all five of them went to Dixit Maharaj's to retrieve the bag containing the explosives. Dixit Maharaj was lying ill in bed, but had a friendly talk with the visitors and volunteered to explain the best manner of working and throwing a hand grenade. But when Apte asked him for the loan of a revolver, he was quite indifferent to the suggestion and gave an evasive reply. At the trial, when he was produced as a witness, he explained that he clearly remembered the visit of these five persons because an astrologer had predicted that he would suffer serious bodily harm on 17 January. In fact on that day he fell and broke a leg, and he remembered subsequently that it was exactly two days before the accident that Badge and his companions had come to visit him. He testified that he was never informed about the conspiracy, and that his advice on the working and throwing of a hand grenade was given solely in the belief that the weapons would be used against Muslims in Hyderabad.

Badge claimed that as they were coming out of Dixit Maharaj's house on 15 January, Apte asked him to go to Delhi with them, but gave no indication as to the purpose of such a visit. It is inconceivable that Badge, who had been sitting through most of the discussions that had so far taken place, did not have any idea what they were all about. Yet he testified that he asked Apte what they were going to do in Delhi and was told that Savarkar had commanded Apte and Nathuram to 'finish' Gandhi and Nehru. He said that it was in response to a casual question thrown at him by Apte that he volunteered to become a member of the conspiracy to murder Gandhi. And where Badge went, so did Kistayya, even though he had absolutely no idea whom they were going to kill.

Pahwa and Karkare left Bombay by train on the evening of 15 January. The khaki bag was given to Pahwa with instructions that it should be wrapped up in his bedding roll. Both conspirators reached Delhi two days later, and after an unsuccessful attempt to find accommodation at the already crowded Hindu Mahasabha building they found a room in an inexpensive hotel in Chandni Chowk in Old Delhi. Karkare gave the hotel clerk an assumed name, but Pahwa made no secret of his identity except that he did not divulge his correct address.

Godse went back to Poona and was relieved to learn that Gopal's leave had been sanctioned. One reason why Gopal Godse was taken into the conspirator's confidence was that he possessed a service revolver which he had had with him since he was posted abroad. Badge and Kistayya were also back in Poona. When Badge came to the *Hindu Rashtra* office, Godse impressed upon him the utmost necessity of obtaining another revolver. Badge dashed off to see an old client of his named Suryadeo Sharma, and was able to buy back a revolver.

Badge and Kistayya left for Bombay on 17 January by the 2.40 a.m. train. At Dadar, Kistayya detrained with Sharma's revolver and proceeded to the Hindu Mahasabha office, while Badge stayed on the train, reaching the Victoria Terminus at the break of dawn. He met Godse and Apte at the ticket barrier. 'I am glad you have come, Badge,' said Apte. 'Before leaving for Delhi we have to collect some funds.' They went round Bombay in a taxi on their money-raising campaign, and by representing that they needed the funds for the Hyderabad movement were able to collect about 2,000 rupees from a number of people. Later they went to the Mahasabha office and picked up Kistayya. Thereafter, according to Badge, they went to Savarkar's house to seek his blessing. Much was made of this visit at the trial, when Badge testified that Savarkar had uttered those parting words: 'Be successful and come back.' Soon after they left Savarkar's house, Badge added, Apte told him that Savarkar had predicted that Gandhi's hope to live for a hundred years would not be fulfilled. 'There is therefore no doubt that our mission will be successfully accomplished.'

The same afternoon Godse and Apte travelled to Delhi by plane. Their tickets were under assumed names – D.N. Karmarkar and S. Marathe, respectively. Dada Maharaj, the priest of the Vaishnava temple, travelled on the same plane as far as Ahmedabad. He had heard about their political activities and plans from his brother Dixit and now had a chance to have a few words with Apte, who was boasting of the great changes his small organization would soon bring about. 'You have been talking a lot,' Dada Maharaj commented, 'but it does not appear that anything has been done.' Apte replied in no uncertain terms: 'When we do the work, then you will know.'

In Delhi the chief conspirators stayed in the Marina Hotel, registering themselves under aliases different from those used for booking the plane tickets. They stayed in this hotel till 20 January.

Badge and Kistayya travelled to Delhi by train, reaching the city on the evening of the 19th. They went to the Hindu Mahasabha Bhavan (the building containing the party's office and accommodation for staff and visitors) and stayed there. Gopal Godse reached Delhi on the evening of the 18th. His train was late, and he was fast asleep when it arrived at New Delhi station. His brother Nathuram, who had come to meet him, was thus unable to find him there. The train proceeded on to Old Delhi, and there Gopal got down, spending the night on the platform crowded with refugees. The following morning he went to the Bhavan and met his associates. By the evening of 19 January all the conspirators had arrived in Delhi.

The Marina Hotel, where Apte and Godse had checked in was one of the better establishments in New Delhi's Connaught Place. They requested a room on the upper floor, and but for their unusual preference for a corner room, the receptionist would not later have been able to identify Nathuram Godse and Narayan Apte as S. and M. Deshpande who had occupied room number 40 for three days. It never became clear which was which; nor did it matter.

After dinner on the 17th, Godse and Apte went to the Hindu Mahasabha Bhavan, where Karkare was waiting for them. They had a brief chat with him and then returned to their hotel. The next morning Karkare joined them for breakfast, then the conspirators travelled in a *tonga* to take a look at Birla House, where Gandhi was staying. Entry to the compound to attend the Mahatma's five o'clock meeting presented no difficulty, but for the rest of the day it was difficult to get past the police guard at the gate. However, to get a general idea of the layout of the garden and the place where Gandhi held his prayers, it was not necessary to go through the main gate, for there were service lanes on both sides of the house and at the back, and a separate entrance to the servants' quarters and garages was situated at the rear.

The three conspirators made another trip to Birla House, this time to attend Gandhi's prayer meeting. The Mahatma was resting and his message was read out over the public address system. This was the day when Gandhi had decided to give up his fast. After wandering all over the garden, they finalized their plan of action. Now that the fast was over they were confident that Gandhi would come out and resume his prayers within a day or two. The morning newspapers of 19 January described how the Muslim citizens of Delhi were moving about freely and how some of them had even formed a procession and been greeted by Hindus and Sikhs with gifts of fruits and sweets. The extremists in the Hindu Mahasabha criticized the party and wanted to know how they had been browbeaten by Congress leaders into subscribing to the peace pledge in the face of the declared policy of the party to the contrary. The Hindu Mahasabha party's secretary, Ashutosh Lahiri, announced that neither he nor anyone authorized by him had signed the seven-point pledge.

That morning Godse and Apte went to see Lahiri at the Hindu Mahasabha office, but it is not clear what time they arrived or what was the duration of their stay. However, the question was to assume importance later since that morning someone booked a long-distance telephone call to Bombay from Lahiri's office number. In India in those days long-distance calls booked at the telephone exchange of the caller required full information to be recorded about telephone numbers, time of call, with whom the caller wished to speak, etc.

This call, an urgent one, was booked at 9.20 a.m. The number requested was that of Savarkar's house. The names of the people the caller wished to speak to were given as G. Damle, Savarkar's secretary, or Appa Kesar, Savarkar's bodyguard. The prosecution later made every effort to capitalize on this episode to connect Savarkar's name with the plot to kill Gandhi. In the wake of Gandhi's murder, no one would confess to having placed the call for fear of falling victim to the witch-hunting on the part of officials and politicians. The identity of the person who had booked this call was thus never established. Lahiri himself could have placed the call to discuss with Savarkar the statement he was going to make – disclaiming that the Hindu Mahasabha party had participated in the peace committee's pledge of 18 January that led Gandhi to break his fast – since Lahiri's statement was bound to generate a storm of protest from the public as well as the government. The urgent call, however, never came through and was cancelled.

According to Karkare, however, at least an hour before that time Gopal arrived, and they hastily took him into a room and anxiously asked him whether he had brought the revolver. He had. Apte, Nathuram and Karkare then left him in the room to have a bath and rest, and themselves once again proceeded to Birla House for another tour of the grounds. On the night of 19 January Madanlal Pahwa and Gopal shared a room in the Hindu Mahasabha Bhavan, and Badge and Kistayya slept in the entrace hall outside. Karkare stayed with Apte and Godse in the Marina Hotel room.

# FORTY-NINE

# A Permissive Assassination

Shortly after 8.00 a.m. on 20 January Apte and Karkare entered the hall at the Hindu Mahasabha Bhavan. Apte then asked Badge and Kistayya to accompany him to Birla House so that he could show them precisely what he wanted them to do. Nathuram Godse did not take part in this reconnaissance, as he was suffering from a migraine. Pahwa and Gopal, who had been assigned equally important roles in the murder plot, had never been to Birla House and failed to go with Apte even this time because they were waiting for water to be heated for their baths. Karkare did not find it necessary to make another trip to Birla House since he had already familiarized himself with the layout.

The three conspirators, Apte, Badge and Kistayya, drove to the main gate of Birla House. After hanging around in front of it they went to the back of the estate, to the small gate which led past about a dozen servants' quarters to the prayer ground. There was a small pavilion at the back of the quarters, and just inside it was a raised wooden platform where Gandhi would hold his prayers. The pavilion itself could seat only about twenty people. The rest of the audience would dispose themselves on the ground. The wall behind Gandhi's divan contained a trellis-work window designed to provide ventilation to the room beyond, which was occupied by a certain Chotu Ram. Apte measured the openings of the trellis-work with a piece of string and came to the conclusion that if they could gain entrance to the servants' quarters behind the trellis, it would be possible to shoot Gandhi in the back, and that the openings were wide enough to allow even the passage of a hand grenade of the size they had brought with them.

It was now imperative that their weapons were in order. When the reconnaissance team returned to the Hindu Mahasabha Bhavan, Apte asked Gopal to join them to try out the two revolvers in the woods some distance behind the building. Badge's revolver, which he had bought back from one of his customers, was an old one and the service revolver belonging to Gopal Godse had remained unused for several years. It was noticed that Badge's weapon was defective, for when Kistayya fired at a tree the shot fell far short of the target. The chamber of Gopal's revolver would not function either. As Gopal proceeded to repair the revolvers, Kistayya was sent back to the building to fetch a bottle of oil and a penknife. Then there was a moment of panic. While Gopal was still at work, three forest guards appeared and asked them what they were doing. Gopal Godse said they were tourists, and that they had come for a quiet walk and were resting for a few minutes. After the guards left, satisfied with the glib explanation, there was no further trial firing, and Apte took his team back to the Mahasabha building. Karkare and Pahwa met them in the hall and Apte asked them both to go to the Marina Hotel without delay. A few moments later the others followed, Gopal carrying the bag containing the 'stuff'.

When they arrived in room number 40, Godse was lying in bed, still suffering from a severe headache, and looking rather gloomy. Gopal deposited his bag in a corner as Badge and Kistayya went downstairs to the restaurant for lunch. When they returned, Badge testified, he found Gopal repairing the revolvers. Soon after, Karkare, Pahwa and Badge himself got busy in the attached bathroom, fixing primers to the guncotton slabs and detonators to the hand grenades. A little while later Nathuram Godse stepped into the bathroom. 'This is our last chance,' he admonished them. 'The work must be accomplished, and make sure that everything is done properly.' Then he withdrew and shut the door.

When they all got back into the room, Apte took over the proceedings of the meeting. He said that the time had come for a final disposition of the weapons. Apte suggested that he and Badge should take the revolvers, Madanlal and Kistayya should each be given one guncotton slab and a hand grenade, while the Godses and Karkare should each be armed with a hand grenade. Apte anticipated no difficulty in shooting Gandhi through the trellis-work, but he had made no effort to get into the room behind the pavilion – and it was easily possible to do so on some pretext – mainly because a one-eyed man was sitting in front of the door to this room. A one-eyed man proverbially brings ill-luck.

For a while no one spoke. Then Badge, who was far more knowledgeable about weapons than anyone else in the group, said that since the general idea was to commence the operation by creating a commotion, one guncotton slab was sufficient for the purpose. He suggested that Pahwa should be given a guncotton slab and a hand grenade, while a revolver and a hand grenade should be taken by himself and his servant Kistayya. Gopal Godse and Karkare should be given a hand grenade each, and Nathuram Godse and Apte would make themselves available to give signals. According to the revised plan, Badge would shoot through the trellis-work the moment Pahwa exploded the guncotton slab, and after he had exhausted all his ammunition he would also throw the hand grenade. By this time Kistayya would have repeated his master's performance at close range. The revolver shots would be the signal for the other grenade throwers. Apte would give the signal to Pahwa and Nathuram Godse would give the signal to Badge behind the trellis-work; Kistayya would have managed to worm his way close to Gandhi. This multiple attack was bound to cause utter confusion, and the conspirators would then simply mingle with the crowd.

Apte decreed that they should all assume aliases, but it occurred to nobody that in the confusion of the moment it would be impossible for all seven of them to remember everyone else's false name. Karkare's suggestion that they should also assume disguises was unanimously accepted too. Godse put on khaki shorts and a half- sleeved shirt, Apte wore a dark-blue suit, Karkare a *dhoti*, a Nehru shirt and a Gandhi cap. As a former actor he followed the tradition of the stage and further disguised himself by thickening his eyebrows and painting on a false moustache. The remaining conspirators also assumed disguises and so attired they set out to murder the Mahatma.

The first to leave for Birla House were Nathuram Godse, Karkare and Pahwa. It was about 4.30 p.m. Some twenty minutes later Apte emerged from the Marina Hotel with Badge, Kistayya and Gopal, and near the Regal cinema on Connaught Place they hired a taxi for a return trip with a thirty-minute stopover at Birla House. On their arrival they were notified by their fellow conspirators, who had preceded them, that things were quite in order. Madanlal Pahwa had placed the guncotton slab in position. Karkare had arranged with Chotu Ram, the occupant of the room behind the trellis-work, for Badge to take 'photographs' of Gandhi during the prayer meeting, which had by now already started. As Badge, along with Apte and Nathuram Godse, approached the entrance to this room, Badge noticed the one-eyed man sitting on a cot in front of the door. The very sight of him now virtually paralysed Badge, who was convinced that if he entered the room for the task assigned to him, it would prove to be a death-trap. He begged the two principal conspirators to let him strike Gandhi from the front. Apte and Godse finally accepted Badge's suggestion. According to the new plan hashed out in a hurry, Pahwa would explode the guncotton slab and in the confusion that was bound to ensue Gandhi would be eliminated by revolver shots and hand grenades.

At this point, Badge claimed at the trial, he signalled to Kistayya and they both went to their waiting taxi. There, in the absence of the taxi driver, he took the two revolvers, his own and Kistayya's, wrapped up in a towel, and threw them into the back of the taxi. He passed on his hand grenade to Kistayya. On their return to the prayer meeting Badge met Apte and assured his leader that he was ready to strike. The remaining weapons comprised five hand grenades, one held by Pahwa, one by Gopal, one by Karkare, and two by Kistayya.

The stage was now fully set. Pahwa was about to ignite the guncotton slab and the others had completely surrounded the unsuspecting Mahatma, who, at this moment, was preaching his gospel of truth and nonviolence.

Suddenly a blast shook the ground. Gandhi's last moments on earth had come. Revolver shots and hand grenades would now rain upon him. But, miraculously enough, nothing happened: no shots were fired, no hand grenades hurled. Barring a minor commotion, there was hardly any confusion. Gandhi asked the audience to remain calm, and the prayer meeting went on almost as if nothing had happened.

Pahwa's igniting of the guncotton slab was witnessed by a young woman, Sulochana Devi, who happened to be there along with her three-year-old son. Because of their being so close to the explosion, Pahwa had asked her to pick up her child and run. Pahwa had never been to Birla House before, and took off in the direction of what he thought was an exit. The police arrested him as Sulochana Devi pointed at him and screamed: 'That is the man.'

When Gopal returned to the waiting taxi, he was surprised to see the bundle containing the two revolvers. The taxi driver had still not come back. It suddenly occurred to Gopal that this was a rare chance to finish the job on his own. He thrust the bundle into the bag containing the grenade he was carrying and dashed in the direction of the servants' quarters, where curious occupants had flocked to the prayer ground to see what all the noise was about. Gopal walked into Chotu Ram's room, shut the door behind him and fastened it with the chain, then took out the .38 revolver.

But he had no chance to shoot. Some years ago Gopal Godse took the present author to that room, and his dilemma on 20 January 1948 appeared quite evident. A glance at the trellis-work made him realize that it was set too high in the wall to afford a view of the prayer ground. The level of the room's floor was in fact much lower than the level of the ground just outside the trellis-work. He tried frantically to grab a ledge with one hand while using the other to grip the revolver. It was an impossible task. He ran back to the door, and for a moment was terrified to realize that he could not release the chain. When he managed to do so, he ran to the waiting taxi, where Nathuram, Apte and Karkare were waiting for him. They excitedly urged the taxi driver to start the automobile and drive them back. The first attempt to assassinate Gandhi was a washout.

On arrival near the Regal cinema, Karkare and Gopal hired a *tonga* to take them to the Hindu Mahasabha Bhavan. Godse and Apte walked the short distance to the Marina Hotel and at once checked out. They took a taxi to the Bhavan and there encountered Badge. They demanded why he had not accomplished the task assigned. This annoyed Badge, who asked them to go away.

It is likely that Badge never wanted to proceed with the plot to the end. He was no doubt deceitful and rascally shrewd, but by no means a fool. A born mercenary, personal safety was always his prime concern, and he exhibited this trait at the trial when cross-examined about his peculiar behaviour at Birla House on the afternoon of 20 January:

COUNSEL: Were you not afraid of keeping the bag containing the revolvers in the taxi?

BADGE: Why should I be afraid? If anybody was arrested it would be the driver of the taxi and not I.

COUNSEL: Why did you transfer the hand grenade to Shankar Kistayya?

BADGE: After a shot is fired the revolver remains in the hand, but after throwing away the hand grenade nothing incriminating remains in the hand.

COUNSEL: Why did not you do anything [after the guncotton slab explosion by Madanlal Pahwa]?

BADGE: If after the explosion Karkare and Gopal [Godse] had thrown their hand grenades at Mahatma Gandhi I would have asked Shankar to hurl the two hand grenades at Gandhiji.

One of the persons who got himself involved over Madanlal Pahwa's arrest was his professor friend in Bombay, Dr J.C. Jain. That he should have originally treated Pahwa's revelation as that of a disgruntled refugee was understandable. Now that Pahwa had been arrested, Dr Jain considered it his clear duty to report the matter to the authorities. But instead of rushing to the nearest police station, he telephoned frantically one government department after another. Deputy Prime Minister Vallabhbhai Patel was in Bombay, but he was unavailable. S.K. Patil, the president of the Bombay Provincial Congress, was out of town. Dr Jain finally managed to arrange an interview with the premier of the Bombay province, B.G. Kher, but it was not till four o'clock in the afternoon on the following day that he was admitted to the Premier's office, where he recounted how he had met Madanlal Pahwa a few months earlier and tried to rehabilitate him by giving him odd jobs. He found Pahwa to be a hardworking, intelligent young man. However, when he met him in January he found him tense and ill at ease, talking about a strange conspiracy to kill Indian leaders, including Mahatma Gandhi. Pahwa had described Vishnu Karkare as the man financing the conspiracy.

Kher saw no reason to disbelieve Jain's story and arranged to put him in touch with Morarji Desai, the Home Minister of the Bombay government.

Some thirty years later Desai would become Prime Minister of India.

Morarji Desai, a former magistrate under the British, was a man of considerable administrative talent. Lean and hawk-faced, Desai's self-righteousness was the hallmark of his personality. He found Jain's story highly improbable, and saw no reason why Pahwa would confide in a professor of languages met by chance on a busy Bombay street. Jain answered Desai's questions as best as he could, but the Home Minister brushed the replies aside. Desai, who also held the police portfolio, failed to arrange for someone in his office to have Dr Jain's statement recorded. One result of this was that both Jain and Desai later relied solely on their memories to recall exactly what had been said at this interview. After Gandhi's murder, what Jain claimed to have told Desai and what Desai believed he heard was to spark angry exchanges between the two men.

Desai was, however, sufficiently impressed by Dr Jain's story to summon to his office J.D. Nagarvala, the deputy commissioner of the Bombay Intelligence Branch. The deputy commissioner was too busy to come, but he did arrange to meet Morarji Desai later in the evening at the railroad station. The Home Minister was taking the train to Ahmedabad, and he had just a few minutes to talk to Nagarvala about the possible threat on Gandhi's life.

At the railroad station Desai told Nagarvala what Jain had reported to him, without revealing Jain's name. The professor had requested that in view of his safety his name should not be divulged. Jain had reported to Desai that Madanlal Pahwa had told him that he had been taken by his friend Karkare to see Savarkar who, after listening to Pahwa's detailed narration of his exploits, had patted him on the back and told him to 'carry on'. While Gandhi was preaching nonviolence, Hindu–Muslim unity and universal brotherhood, and Nehru was advocating secularism and a new world order, Savarkar, an ultra Hindu nationalist, was considered as much a thorn in the flesh of the Congress Raj as he was of the British Raj. Nagarvala initiated the obvious measures to prevent the murder of Gandhi, and at the same time he also decided, perhaps at Desai's suggestion, that a watch should be kept on Savarkar's house.

After the unsuccessful attempt on Gandhi's life on 20 January, Karkare and Gopal spent the night at the Frontier Hindu Hotel in Old Delhi under assumed names, before taking the train back to Poona. Badge and Kistayya took the night train for Poona, while Nathuram Godse and Apte made their way to Cawnpore, where they stayed overnight before taking another train, arriving in Bombay at noon on 23 January. Godse and Apte travelled first class to Cawnpore and were alone in a four-berth sleeping compartment. At about six o'clock in the morning when Apte was still half-asleep, he heard

Nathuram speak: 'Nana, did you sleep well?' Apte mumbled: 'And you?' Nathuram did not answer the question. Instead he said: 'I am going to do it. I don't need any help, not another man. No recruiting of people, no depending on anyone else.' As Apte later recounted: 'My eyes were still closed, and I swear that in that instant I saw Gandhi dead.'

Almost immediately after his arrest, Pahwa was taken to the Marina Hotel's room number 40, where the police found in a drawer of a table a copy of Ashutosh Lahiri's statement made the previous day that his party had not signed the seven-point peace pledge. If instead of jumping to the conclusion that the Hindu Mahasabha had had a hand in the murder plot, they had used it to seek clarification from its author, he would at the very least have told them that the editor mentioned by Madanlal Pahwa was none other than Nathuram Godse of the *Hindu Rashtra*.

During the next ten days the investigation officers of the Delhi police were busy grilling Pahwa, but did not extend their investigation to the Hindu Mahasabha office in New Delhi. India's Home Minister, Vallabhbhai Patel, ordered some extra guards sent to Birla House, though the extent of Patel's intervention proved to be of no consequence. Neither Patel nor Morarji Desai, nor the police felt any urgency in discovering the conspirators, who had anyway returned to Bombay or Poona. Twenty years later, when a commission of inquiry was established under Mr Justice Kapur to investigate some of the more elusive aspects of the assassination, it was revealed that no questions were asked about the Hindu Mahasabha Bhavan in New Delhi, where the majority of the conspirators had stayed, nor of Ashutosh Lahiri, who personally knew both Nathuram Godse and Apte. It brought to the fore the cavalier attitude of the police and high government officials. A permissive assassination was destined to take place.

The absence of any systematic and determined line of action hampered the police investigation. The lack of cooperation between the Delhi and Bombay police departments created further difficulties in proper and efficient investigation. Within twenty-four hours of Pahwa's arrest two officers of the Delhi police were flown to Bombay with instructions to later proceed to Poona to apprise the authorities concerned of the facts. J.D. Nagarvala, the deputy commissioner of the Bombay Intelligence Branch, who outranked the two Delhi police officers, treated them with contempt and thought they were interfering with his department's investigative work. They were asked to get out of their uniforms and leave. The officers returned to Delhi with nothing to show to their superiors. The senior officers in Delhi did not consider it necessary even to try to reach their counterparts in Bombay on the telephone.

With Pahwa under arrest, and a disillusioned Badge refusing to take any further part in the conspiracy, there remained only Nathuram and Gopal Godse, Apte and Karkare. They had to strike at once, for they feared that Pahwa would find it extremely difficult to maintain his silence when subjected to police interrogation, and it would only be a matter of time before they would be traced and arrested.

The police pressure to which Madanlal Pahwa was subjected included third-degree tactics. According to Pahwa, he was made to lie on the floor with two legs of a string bed resting on his hands while a policeman jumped up and down on the bed. They also treated him to 'the ordeal by ants' – releasing wet red ants on his naked body. Pahwa screamed and howled like an animal, but he talked too, purporting to be telling the truth, revealing too many irrelevant details, and his utterances went down in police records as a confession made voluntarily because his companions 'had deserted him and run away and he considered it his duty to get them arrested'. The net result was that he was able to throw the police off the right trail for just long enough to prevent them from arresting the determined conspirators, who were yet to launch their mortal attack.

Nathuram Godse had decided not to involve his brother in the assassination, and there were now only three members left in the conspiracy, Apte, Karkare and Godse himself, although Gopal arrived in Bombay from Poona on 24 January and was there till the 26th. Once more they sought the help of Dixit Maharaj, who possessed an excellent revolver, but again they were unable to acquire it. On the night of 26 January Nathuram Godse, Apte and Karkare had a secret meeting in the freight yard of Thana railroad station in suburban Bombay. It was a moonlit night, and they discussed their plans in whispers and with the utmost caution. Godse was calm but concerned that Pahwa's arrest would lead the police to the other conspirators, and the plan to assassinate Gandhi would fail. He reckoned that the original plan involving nine or ten people was unwieldy. Just one person could accomplish the task ahead, and he kept insisting that he would take up the responsibility single-handed. Apte and Karkare chose to stand by him to afford companionship and support.

Godse anticipated no difficulty in procuring a good revolver, for he and Apte had managed to secure a loan of ten thousand rupees from a wealthy sympathizer with the Hindu cause, on the pretext that they required the money urgently for their newspaper.

Apte and Godse were at that time staying under assumed names at the Elphinstone Annex Hotel, but when they arrived at the Air India office on 25 January to book their flights to Delhi two days later, they gave their address as the Sea Green Hotel, Bombay. They booked two seats under assumed names, Godse giving his name as N.Vinayak Rao – his full name was Nathuram Vinayak Godse – while the seat for Apte was reserved in the name of D. Narayan Rao, Apte's full name being Narayan Dattatray Apte. If the police in Bombay and Poona had shown any semblance of efficiency and cooperation, an intelligent detective should by this time have been able to identify them and pull them off the plane.

Neither of the conspirators encountered any trouble during their travels. They arrived in Delhi at 12.40 p.m. on 27 January, drove to the Old Delhi railroad station, and took the express train to Gwalior, two hundred miles to the south. They arrived late in the evening, and immediately hired a *tonga* to take them to the residence of Dr Dattatraya Parchure. Parchure and Godse had met several times before in the course of their work for the Hindu Mahasabha, and Godse and Apte felt confident that Dr Parchure would help in getting a revolver in good repair. The following morning Dr Parchure sent his son and his bodyguard to fetch one G.S. Dandvate, then, after assuring his house guests that they could trust him completely, went off to his dispensary. Dandvate showed the visitors a 'country-made' pistol which they found unsatisfactory. It was not till the evening that Dandvate again came to Dr Parchure's house, this time with a revolver, a 9mm Beretta in excellent working order. Dandvate, who sold the revolver to Godse for five hundred rupees, said in his statement that he had bought it from a man called Jagdish Prasad Goel, which the latter did not deny, but Goel did not explain how he himself had come by it. In any event, since Godse had admitted his guilt, the court did not deem it necessary to examine the chain of ownership of the revolver before it reached Godse.

Godse and Apte left Gwalior soon after procuring the weapon, reaching Delhi on the morning of 29 January. They checked into a retiring room at the Old Delhi railroad station in the name of N. Vinayak Rao. A few hours later they walked to the nearby park, some two hundred yards across the road, where they had arranged to meet Karkare. The three conspirators walked back towards the railroad station, Karkare following his companions into the retiring room, and as Apte shut and bolted the door Godse reached for the blue-black weapon. Like a trophy won by a team, the shiny Beretta passed from hand to hand before Godse put it away again.

Although Gandhi held a prayer meeting that afternoon, Godse had decided to defer the assassination till the following day. The last three days had been quite hectic and he was tired. The weapon had not yet been tested. They dined at a vegetarian restaurant in Chandni Chowk, then Godse returned to his retiring room while Apte and Karkare, needing some diversion to take their minds off the business of the following day, went to see a movie.

Godse did not need any such diversion, and was content to read a book.

He was in a mood of calm elation, savouring his approaching triumph. He had earlier explained to Karkare his motives for taking the entire burden upon himself.

Apte has responsibilities. He has a wife and child. I have no family. Moreover, I am an orator and a writer, and I shall be able to justify my act and impress the Government and the court of my good faith in killing Gandhi. Now Apte, on the other hand, is a man of the world. He can contact people and carry on the *Hindu Rashtra*. You, Karkare, must help in the conduct of the newspaper and carry on the work of the Hindu Mahasabha.

On the morning of 30 January Godse appeared calm despite strange mixed feelings of elation and inner turmoil. He awoke earlier than usual and was already bathed and dressed while Apte and Karkare were still asleep. They had a light breakfast, and then drove to the Birla Temple and walked a few hundred yards into the wooded area at the back, almost to the same spot where, ten days before, some of them had had their first target practice. Godse fired three or four shots at a tree and was pleased with the performance of the Beretta. He put on the safety catch and slipped the automatic into his pocket. He continued to wear a determined expression and became increasingly silent as the day wore on.

By the time they had finished lunch and returned to the retiring room, it was nearing 1.00 p.m. The retiring room was available for only twenty-four hours, and despite Godse's request, their stay there could not be extended for another day. They carried their baggage to the common waiting room for second-class passengers, but it was too crowded to discuss anything secret.

They found an empty cane-bottomed bench for Godse to rest on. For a while the other two sat near him, feeling like relatives sitting near a man's deathbed. Apte then beckoned Karkare and told Godse that they would be back in about an hour. The would-be assassin just smiled and did not ask them where they were going.

Apte and Karkare took a taxi to Birla House. On their return Apte told Godse in whispers that though there were a lot more policemen at the gate, they were all from the northern parts of the country and none of them appeared to hail from their region. At 4.30 p.m. Nathuram Godse hired a *tonga* and, waving a final goodbye, drove to Birla House. A few minutes later Apte and Karkare followed him in another *tonga*. Godse mingled with the crowd of about five hundred people on the prayer ground. Apte and Karkare had pushed their way forward and stood on either side of him, but if he saw them he gave no sign of recognition. Suddenly there was some restlessness in the gathering, and everyone stood up to form a passage for Gandhi, who was seen coming up slowly with his hands resting on the shoulders of his two great-nieces. As Gandhi reciprocated the people's greeting with folded hands, Nathuram Godse slid forward the safety catch on the Beretta while it was still in his pocket, then darted out of the crowd, brushed past Manubehn with such swiftness that she almost fell, and fired three shots in quick succession at point-blank range. The Mahatma collapsed and fell.

Godse made no effort to escape. For a few moments, while he held the smoking revolver, the dazed crowd stood still, then things moved fast. A uniformed man from the Royal Indian Air Force sprang at Godse, gripped him by the wrist, rained blows on his face with his other hand, and retrieved the weapon. Other people, perhaps a dozen, joined in the attack. Momentarily there was a hush, until people on the prayer ground realized fully what had happened, when there arose a wild screaming, loud sobbing, hysterical weeping, and cries of 'Kill him! Kill him!' In the utter confusion hardly anyone noticed the bruised and bleeding assassin being led away by the police. Apte and Karkare blended well with the people rushing from Birla House. They made their way to the Old Delhi railroad station and took the train to Bombay.

With Gandhi's murder it became evident that Madanlal Pahwa's revelation to Dr Jain had not been just a figment of the imagination of a discontented and misguided young refugee. There was clearly a wider and deeply laid plan involving several people. The police now broadened the field of their investigation, covering the entire country.

Within a few days most of the conspirators were rounded up. Badge was taken into custody on 31 January, Gopal Godse on 5 February, when he had almost reached his village, and Dr Parchure was arrested at his house in Gwalior the same day. Shankar Kistayya was apprehended the following day. Apte and Karkare were on the run for a while before they were arrested on 14 February in the lobby of Pyrke's Apollo Hotel in Bombay, where a police party was awaiting the return of the occupants of room number 29.

All the conspirators were interrogated intensively and long statements were made by each of them. Hundreds of other persons were questioned, and consequently the complete picture of the conspiracy and the manner of its execution was pieced together. It also became evident that while the conspirators were merrily leaving a blazing trail of clues, the police in Delhi and Bombay had spared no effort in being complacent.

# FIFTY

# The Judicial Verdict

The trial of Nathuram Godse and other conspirators implicated in the murder of Mohandas Karamchand Gandhi opened in the searing heat of summer on 27 May 1948, in the historic Red Fort at Delhi. Eight men were charged with murder, conspiracy to commit murder, and other charges connected with violations of the Explosive Substances Act.

The Red Fort had been the venue of only the most important political trials. Here, nine decades earlier, the last of the Mughal emperors, Bahadur Shah Zaffar, was put on trial by the British and sentenced to banishment for life. It was also at the Red Fort that the trial of officers of the Indian National Army was held in 1945 which generated so much fervour throughout the country that the accused were acquitted.

The judge at the trial known as Rex *versus* Nathuram Godse and others, was Mr Justice Atma Charan, a member of the Indian Civil Service. There was no jury. It was decided that since the evidence was complex and the issues involved intricate questions of law, a jury of laymen would have been far from competent. A vindictive jury would have frustrated the very purpose of the trial. Men with legal training, on the other hand, though suitable, would have made dangerous jurymen. In the circumstances, the destiny of the accused was safe in the hands of a single judge of national repute.

Atma Charan was both astute and detached, and neither the accused nor their lawyers had any cause for dissatisfaction with regard to the conduct of the protracted trial. There were altogether 149 prosecution witnesses. The examination of the witnesses and the recording of the evidence lasted about six months. The whole exercise was especially time-consuming because each question and answer had to be translated by Hindustani, Marathi and Telugu interpreters. But the salient features of the conspiracy were soon identified by the prosecution.

At the trial the defence of the conspirators was a simple one. Godse maintained that his killing of Gandhi was an individual act, and nobody had any knowledge of what he had planned to do. He had to admit, however, that he and Apte travelled from Bombay to Delhi by air on 17

January, and again on 27 January, each time under false names. He further admitted that he and Apte had stayed at the Marina Hotel in New Delhi from 17 to 20 January and registered their arrival under assumed names. He admitted having paid a visit to Dr Parchure at Gwalior and the fact that on his return he booked a retiring room at the Old Delhi railroad station under an assumed name.

Apte admitted travelling from Bombay to Delhi with Nathuram Godse on 17 and 27 January. He said that he had stayed with him at the Marina Hotel during their first visit to Delhi. He also admitted travelling to Gwalior and meeting Dr Parchure, but insisted he did not travel back to Delhi with Godse. He stated that he had returned to Bombay directly from Gwalior.

Karkare admitted coming to Delhi along with Pahwa on 17 January, and staying at the Sharif Hotel in Old Delhi under the false name of B.N. Bias. But he denied having visited Delhi again and being present there on the day the Mahatma was assassinated. He claimed that he had no knowledge of the plot.

Shankar Kistayya, when examined by the trial judge after the conclusion of the evidence for the prosecution, made a statement along similar lines to the deposition of his employer, Badge, pleading that he had merely carried out his employer's orders. But once the case was placed before the court, and no police influence could be exercised upon him, the simple-minded Kistayya did not hesitate to let the cat out of the bag. He made his statement in his native Telugu:

> In the beginning, when Badge and I were kept in one room, Nagarvala and Khan Sahib [another police officer] came to see us and took us to the jailer's office. Nagarvala and Khan Sahib asked Badge to instruct me as to what to say. Khan Sahib said to me: 'Don't be frightened. Be with Badge and do as he tells you to do.' At that time there used to be another jailer, the senior one. The senior jailer used to supply liquor and cigarettes to Badge and myself. I was not used to taking liquor, but Badge introduced me to it. The senior jailer had said that I could ask for whatever I wanted. He used to supply Badge and me with eggs, meat, omelette and sweets. The senior jailer is not here any more. For the last one and a half months the supply of liquor has been stopped, and the quantity of other items has been greatly reduced.
>
> Nagarvala had come to the jail about twenty times. He used to meet Badge and ask: 'Have you instructed Shankar?' And to the jailer he had said: 'If he instructs Shankar, give Badge liquor.' Badge was instructing me as to what to say. I had said to Badge: 'When I do not know anything, why should I say all this?' Then Badge would say: 'What should you know? If you want to be acquitted, do as I tell you to do . . .' I used to repeat all that he instructed me.

About eight or nine days before my statement was recorded, Nagarvala had come to me with some papers. He asked Badge: 'Have you given Shankar enough practice?' Nagarvala asked me in Hindustani what I had to say. I made five or six mistakes. He again read out what I was required to say. Nagarvala then said to me: 'Don't be worried. Don't associate with these Brahmins. Even if you are given ten years' imprisonment, we shall see to it that you are acquitted. Whatever you need, take it from the jailer.'

Badge had told me that Nagarvala was sending to his home one hundred rupees every month. Badge asked me to give him my address, which I gave to him. He told me that he would arrange to send some money to my home, but I am not certain if he has done so.

Just two days before my statement was recorded, Khan Sahib came to the jail at night. He said to me: 'There are two days left. Let me see what you are going to say.' I told him all that I could. Khan Sahib had brought me a bottle of liquor and some eatables. Badge was also called there. When I repeated everything, Khan Sahib told me that what I had said was alright. 'Don't be afraid,' he said. I said: 'When I know nothing, is there any use my saying all this.' Khan Sahib told me not to worry.

Recently I had a meeting with my counsel [the court-appointed counsel who was to defend him] and told him about the whole affair. Somehow the news reached the jailer. He got angry with me and said: 'Is this a legal case or some kind of fun?' Badge slapped me before the jailer and said: 'You want to be acquitted, and you want us to supply you with various things, and you behave like this.'

The jailer does not allow me to talk to the other accused except Badge. I know nothing and I have no connection with this case. Whatever Badge had instructed me to say, I have repeated it.

Of the other accused, Gopal Godse denied that he had participated in the conspiracy. He totally rejected the allegation that he had gone to Delhi on 17 January and was present there on the 20th. And yet forty years later, in January 1988, as Gopal Godse and the present author, on their way to Birla House, approached 30 January Marg (formerly Albuquerque Road and renamed to signify the day of the Mahatma's assassination), Gopal observed: 'If we had managed to finish our job on the 20th this road would have been called 20 January Marg.'

Madanlal Pahwa claimed that his sole purpose in going to Delhi was to demonstrate his indignation against the shabby treatment meted out to refugees like himself. He had ensured that the slab of guncotton was exploded at a safe distance so that no harm should be caused to any person.

Dr Parchure's defence was that Nathuram Godse and Apte, during their visit to Gwalior, had asked him to send some volunteers for the purpose of staging a peaceful demonstration in Delhi, but he had declined to comply with their request. He denied that he had assisted them in any manner to procure the revolver.

The defence plea thus simply amounted to this: There was no conspiracy to kill Gandhi. The explosion of 20 January and the assassination of the Mahatma on 30 January were individual and unrelated acts of Pahwa and Godse respectively. The prisoners, however, offered no evidence in support of their pleas.

Quite early in the trial it became clear that Nathuram Godse wanted to assume the entire responsibility for the murder. Night after night he had devoted to the preparation of his ponderous statement. 'After firing the shots at Mahatma Gandhi,' he had declared, 'it was not my intention to run away . . . I did not try to shoot myself. It was never my intention to do so, for it was my ardent desire to give vent to my thoughts in an open court.' Finally, on 8 November 1948, he was allowed his day in the sun when he rose to make his statement. Reading quietly in English from a typed manuscript, he sought to explain why he had killed Gandhi. His thesis covered ninety-three pages, and he was on his feet for five hours. Godse's statement should be quoted extensively, for it provides an insight into his personality.

Born in a devotional Brahmin family, I instinctively came to revere Hindu religion, Hindu history and Hindu culture. I had, therefore, been intensely proud of Hinduism as a whole. As I grew up I developed a tendency to free thinking unfettered by any superstitious allegiance to any isms, political or religious. That is why I worked actively for the eradication of untouchability and the caste system based on birth alone. I openly joined anti-caste movements and maintained that all Hindus were of equal status as to rights, social and religious, and should be considered high or low on merit alone and not through the accident of birth in a particular caste or profession. I used publicly to take part in organized anti-caste dinners in which thousands of Hindus, Brahmins, Kshatriyas, Vaisyas, Chamars and Bhangis participated. We broke the caste rules and dined in the company of each other.

I have read the speeches and writings of Dadabhai Naoroji, Vivekanand, Gokhale, Tilak, along with the books of ancient and modern history of India and some prominent countries like England, France, America and Russia. Moreover I studied the tenets of Socialism and Marxism. But above all I studied very closely whatever Veer [brave] Savarkar and Gandhiji had written and spoken, as to my mind these two ideologies have contributed more to the moulding of the thought and action of the Indian people during the last thirty years or so, than any other single factor has done.

All this reading and thinking led me to believe it was my first duty to serve Hindudom and Hindus both as a patriot and as a world citizen. To secure the freedom and to safeguard the just interests of some thirty *crores* of Hindus would automatically constitute the freedom and the well-being of all India, one fifth of the human race. This conviction led me naturally to devote myself to the Hindu Sanghatanist ideology and programme, which alone, I came to believe, could win and preserve the national independence of Hindustan, my Motherland, and enable her to render true service to humanity as well.

Since the year 1920, that is, after the demise of Lokamanya Tilak, Gandhi's influence in the Congress first increased and then became supreme. His activities for public awakening were phenomenal in their intensity and were reinforced by the slogan of truth and non-violence which he paraded ostentatiously before the country. No sensible or enlightened person could object to these slogans. In fact there is nothing new or original in them. They are implicit in every constitutional public movement. But it is nothing but a mere dream if you imagine that the bulk of mankind is, or can ever become, capable of scrupulous adherence to these lofty principles in its normal life from day to day. In fact, honour, duty, and love of one's own kith and kin and country might often compel us to disregard non-violence and to use force. I could never conceive that an armed resistance to an aggression is unjust. I would consider it a religious and moral duty to resist and, if possible, to overpower such an enemy by use of force. [In the *Ramayana*] Rama killed Ravana in a tumultuous fight and relieved Sita. [In the *Mahabharata*], Krishna killed Kansa to end his wickedness; and Arjuna had to fight and slay quite a number of his friends and relations including the revered Bhishma because the latter was on the side of the aggressor. It is my firm belief that in dubbing Rama, Krishna and Arjuna as guilty of violence, the Mahatma betrayed a total ignorance of the springs of human action.

In more recent history, it was the heroic fight put up by Chhatrapati Shivaji that first checked and eventually destroyed the Muslim tyranny in India. It was absolutely essential for Shivaji to overpower and kill an aggressive Afzal Khan, failing which he would have lost his own life. In condemning history's towering warriors like Shivaji, Rana Pratap and Guru Gobind Singh as misguided patriots, Gandhi has merely exposed his self-conceit. He was, paradoxical as it may appear, a violent pacifist who brought untold calamities on the country in the name of truth and non-violence, while Rana Pratap, Shivaji and the Guru will remain enshrined in the hearts of their countrymen for ever for the freedom they brought to them.

The accumulating provocation of thirty-two years, culminating in his last pro-Muslim fast, at last goaded me to the conclusion that the existence of Gandhi should be brought to an end immediately. Gandhi had done very good work in South Africa to uphold the rights and well-being of the Indian community there. But when he finally returned to India he developed a subjective mentality under which he alone was to be the final judge of what was right or wrong. If the country wanted his leadership, it had to accept his infallibility; if it did not, he would stand aloof from the Congress and carry on in his own way. Against such an attitude there can be no halfway house. Either Congress had to surrender its will to his and had to be content with playing second fiddle to all his eccentricity, whimsicality, metaphysics and primitive vision, or it had to carry on without him. He alone was the judge of everyone and every thing; he was the master brain guiding the civil disobedience movement; no other could know the technique of that movement. He alone knew when to begin it and when to withdraw it. The movement might succeed or fail, it might bring untold disaster and political reverses but that could make no difference to the Mahatma's infallibility. 'A Satyagrahi can never fail' was his formula for declaring his own infallibility and nobody except himself knew what a Satyagrahi is.

Thus the Mahatma became the judge and jury in his own cause. These childish insanities and obstinacies, coupled with a most severe austerity of life, ceaseless work and lofty character made Gandhi formidable and irresistible. Many people thought that his politics were irrational but they had either to withdraw from the Congress or place their intelligence at his feet to do with as he liked. In a position of such absolute irresponsibility Gandhi was guilty of blunder after blunder, failure after failure, disaster after disaster.

Gandhi's pro-Muslim policy is blatantly illustrated in his perverse attitude on the question of the national language of India. It is quite obvious that Hindi has the most prior claim to be accepted as the premier language. In the beginning of his career in India, Gandhi gave a great impetus to Hindi but as he found that the Muslims did not like it, he became a champion of what is called Hindustani. Everybody in India knows that there is no language called Hindustani; it has no grammar, it has no vocabulary. It is a mere dialect, it is spoken, but not written. It is a bastard tongue and cross-breed between Hindi and Urdu, and not even the Mahatma's sophistry could make it popular. But in his desire to please the Muslims he insisted that Hindustani alone should be the national language of India. His blind followers, of course, supported him and the so-called hybrid language began to be used. The charm and the purity of the Hindi language was to be prostituted to please the Muslims. All his experiments were at the expense of the Hindus.

From August 1946 onwards the private armies of the Muslim League began a massacre of the Hindus. The then Viceroy, Lord Wavell, though distressed at what was happening, would not use his powers under the Government of India Act of 1935 to prevent the rape, murder and arson. The Hindu blood began to flow from Bengal to Karachi with some retaliation by the Hindus. The Interim Government formed in September was sabotaged by its Muslim League members right from its inception, but the more they became disloyal and treasonable to the government of which they were a part, the greater was Gandhi's infatuation for them. Lord Wavell had to resign as he could not bring about a settlement and he was succeeded by Lord Mountbatten. King Log was followed by King Stork.

The Congress which had boasted of its nationalism and secularism secretly accepted Pakistan literally at the point of the bayonet and abjectly surrendered to Jinnah. India was vivisected and one-third of the Indian territory became foreign land to us from August 15, 1947. Lord Mountbatten came to be described in Congress circles as the greatest Viceroy and Governor-General this country ever had. The official date for handing over power was fixed for June 30, 1948, but Mountbatten with his ruthless surgery gave us a gift of vivisected India ten months in advance. This is what Gandhi had achieved after thirty years of undisputed dictatorship and this is what the Congress party calls 'freedom' and 'peaceful transfer of power'. The Hindu-Muslim unity bubble was finally burst and a theocratic state was established with the consent of Nehru and his crowd and they have called it 'freedom won by them with sacrifice' – whose sacrifice? When top leaders of Congress, with the consent of Gandhi, divided and tore the country – which we consider a deity of worship – my mind was filled with direful anger.

One of the conditions imposed by Gandhi for his breaking of the fast unto death related to the mosques in Delhi occupied by the Hindu refugees. But when Hindus in Pakistan were subjected to violent attacks he did not so much as utter a single word to protest and censure the Pakistan Government or the Muslims concerned. Gandhi was shrewd enough to know that while undertaking a fast unto death, had he imposed for its break some condition on the Muslims in Pakistan, there would have been found hardly any Muslims who could have shown some grief if the fast had ended in his death. It was for this reason that he purposely avoided imposing any condition on the Muslims. He was fully aware from past experience that Jinnah was not at all perturbed or influenced by his fast and the Muslim League hardly attached any value to the inner voice of Gandhi.

Gandhi is being referred to as the Father of the Nation. But if that is so, he has failed in his paternal duty inasmuch as he has acted very treacherously to the nation by his consenting to the partitioning of it. I stoutly maintain that Gandhi has failed in his duty. He has proved to be the Father of Pakistan. His inner voice, his spiritual power and his doctrine of non-violence of which so much is made of, all crumbled before Jinnah's iron will and proved to be powerless.

Briefly speaking, I thought to myself and foresaw that I shall be totally ruined, and the only thing I could expect from the people would be nothing but hatred and that I shall have lost all my honour, even more valuable than my life, if I were to kill Gandhiji. But at the same time I felt that the Indian politics in the absence of Gandhiji would surely be practical, able to retaliate, and would be powerful with armed forces. No doubt, my own future would be totally ruined, but the nation would be saved from the inroads of Pakistan. People may even call me and dub me as devoid of any sense or foolish, but the nation would be free to follow the course founded on reason which I consider to be necessary for sound nation-building. After having fully considered the question, I took the final decision in the matter, but I did not speak about it to anyone whatsoever. I took courage in both my hands and I did fire the shots at Gandhiji on 30th January 1948, on the prayer-grounds in Birla House.

I do say that my shots were fired at the person whose policy and action had brought rack and ruin and destruction to millions of Hindus. There was no legal machinery by which such an offender could be brought to book and for this reason I fired those fatal shots.

I bear no ill will towards anyone individually but I do say that I had no respect for the present government owing to their policy which was unfairly favourable towards the Muslims. But at the same time I could clearly see that that policy was entirely due to the presence of Gandhi. I have to say with great regret that Prime Minister Nehru quite forgets that his preachings and deeds are at times at variance with each other when he talks about India as a secular state in season and out of season, because it is significant to note that Nehru has played a leading role in the establishment of the theocratic state of Pakistan, and his job was made easier by Gandhi's persistent policy of appeasement towards the Muslims.

I now stand before the court to accept the full share of my responsibility for what I have done and the judge would, of course, pass against me such orders of sentence as may be considered proper. But I would like to add that I do not desire any mercy to be shown to me, nor do I wish that anyone else should beg for mercy on my behalf. My confidence about the moral side of my action has not been shaken even by the criticism levelled against it on all sides. I have no doubt that honest writers of history will weigh my act and find the true value thereof some day in future.

Nathuram Godse sought to present himself as a duty-bound righteous man. As he spoke he was quite aware that he was not making an ordinary speech in defence of an ordinary crime. He made an impassioned appeal to the Hindus to hold and preserve their motherland, and to fight for it. The great sermon spoken by Krishna to Arjuna in the *Bhagavad Gita* was implicit throughout the argument. As Godse finished his statement, there was a disturbing silence. Justice G.D Khosla, one of the three judges appointed to hear the appeal by Godse and his accomplices, recalled the scene:

The audience was visibly and audibly moved. There was a deep silence when he ceased speaking. Many women were in tears and men were coughing and searching for their handkerchiefs. The silence was accentuated and made deeper by the sound of an occasional subdued sniff or a muffled cough. It seemed to me that I was taking part in some kind of melodrama or in a scene out of a Hollywood feature film. Once or twice I had interrupted Godse and pointed out the irrelevance of what he was saying, but my colleagues seemed inclined to hear him and the audience most certainly thought that Godse's performance was the only worthwhile part of the lengthy proceedings . . . I have, however, no doubt that had the audience of that day been constituted into a jury and entrusted with the task of deciding Godse's appeal, they would have brought in a verdict of 'not guilty' by an overwhelming majority.

After Godse's speech, which sounded more like a cry of triumph, the trial seemed strangely irrelevant. For the whole month of December the counsels continued their arguments, although there was hardly anything left to argue about. Savarkar was able to demonstrate meticulously that he had had nothing whatsoever to do with the conspiracy and, unlike Godse, he spared no effort in defending himself by continual appeals to the law of evidence, showing in clear terms that there was no reason to believe that he was part of the conspiracy to assassinate the Mahatma.

The final judgement of the Red Fort Trial was handed down on 10 February 1949. Nathuram Godse and Narayan Apte were sentenced to death while the other prisoners, with the exception of Savarkar, were sentenced to transportation for life. Savarkar was found not guilty on all charges and acquitted.

Long after Savarkar had been cleared of any complicity in the plot and some years after he retired as the Inspector General of Police, Nagarvala insisted that 'to my dying day I shall believe that Savarkar was the man who organized Gandhi's murder'. Perhaps by saying so Nagarvala was attempting to find a way to diminish to some extent the gross inefficiency of his police force.

The convicted men were sent to the Central Jail in Ambala, about 120 miles north of Delhi. From there, all of them, including Nathuram Godse, appealed against the verdict. Godse's appeal was not against his own sentence, but against the charge of conspiracy for which the others had been convicted. The appeal was heard in the Punjab High Court, then located at Simla. The court, with three judges sitting on the bench, finally gave Dr Parchure and Shankar Kistayya the benefit of the doubt and they were both acquitted, but the sentences on the others were confirmed.

Early in the morning of 15 November, 1949, Nathuram Godse and Narayan Apte came out of their cells and walked towards the hanging shed. They shouted at brief intervals the slogan *'Akhand Bharat Amar Rahe'* (India united, may it be for ever). A single gallows had been prepared for the execution of both. Two ropes, each with a noose, hung from a high crossbar in parallel lines. They went towards it singing in unison a Sanskrit verse with the refrain: 'Even as we die, we salute you, our land of birth.' They were made to stand side by side, their hands were tied behind their backs, and black cloth bags were drawn over their heads and tied at the necks. The nooses were adjusted, the executioner pulled the lever, and the bodies hurtled down.

Godse and Apte were cremated inside the prison. The ground where the pyres had been erected was ploughed over lest someone should try to make relics from the ashes, and the earth and ashes were ritually immersed in the nearby Ghaggar river under a cloak of secrecy.


Nathuram Godse was hanged in accordance with the law of the land. His justification in murdering Gandhi notwithstanding, the Mahatma would have been distressed by the execution of his assassin, for 'to die by the hand of a brother rather than by disease or in some other way cannot be for me a matter of sorrow . . . I would deserve praise only if I fell as a result of such an [attack] and yet retained a smile on my face and no malice against the doer . . . All perpetrators should be won over through love.'

# Glossary

| | |
|---|---|
| *ahimsa* | nonviolence (opposite of *himsa*) |
| anna | one-sixteenth of a rupee |
| ashram | religiously oriented community, often clustered round a holy man |
| *asthis* | burned bones collected from a funeral pyre |
| Babu | mister |
| Bania | person of commercial caste (Modh Bania was Gandhi's own sub-caste). *Bania* is a synonym in India for a shrewd, grasping businessman |
| Bapu | Father; term of affection used for Gandhi |
| *bhai-bhai* | *bhai* means brother; the term *bhai-bhai* is used for brothers or sisters |
| *bhangi* | sweeper, Untouchable |
| Brahmachari | person observing celibacy |
| Brahmacharya | celibacy |
| Brahmin | the highest Hindu caste |
| *charkha* | spinning wheel |
| *crore* | ten million |
| *dal* | lentils |
| *darshan* | the vision of sanctity |
| *dewan* | a princely state prime minister |
| *dharma* | religion or religious duty |
| *dhoti* | the long cloth worn by Indians from the waist |
| *ghee* | clarified butter used in cooking and in Hindu devotional practice |
| *goonda* | hooligan |
| *guru* | spiritual teacher |
| *hakim* | a Muslim physician practising the Unani system of medicine that originated in ancient Greece |
| Harijans | name given by Gandhi to people formerly considered untouchable; literally: 'children of God' |
| *hartal* | strike, traditionally used to indicate mourning or protest |
| *himsa* | violence (opposite of *ahimsa*) |
| *inquilab zindabad* | long live revolution |

| | |
|---|---|
| *-ji* | suffix suggesting affection and respect |
| *khadi* | handspun cloth |
| *khaddar* | handspun cloth |
| Khilafat | movement in support of the Sultan of Turkey, the spiritual head of Islam |
| *ki jai* | to him victory |
| *kurta* | long, collarless shirt |
| *lathi* | long cane, usually iron-tipped, used as weapon by Indian police |
| Mahatma | 'Great Soul'; honorific title used of Gandhi |
| *mantra* | sacred verse |
| Maulana | title of respect given to learned Muslims |
| *moksha* | salvation, spiritual realization in Hindu thought |
| *murdabad* | death to |
| Musalman | Moslem |
| Muslim | Moslem |
| *namaskar* | the Hindu salute with folded hands |
| Pandit | title given to a learned man or teacher, especially a Brahmin |
| Parsi | member of the Zoroastrian religious community |
| *purna swaraj* | complete self-rule |
| Raj | rule; hence the British Raj |
| Ram(a) | a name for God in Hindu mythology |
| *Ramadhun* | song made up of repetitions of Rama's name |
| *Ramanama* | the repetition of Rama's name |
| *sadhu* | Hindu wandering holy man, ascetic |
| *samadhi* | a monument erected over the ashes of the deceased or on the site of cremation |
| *sanyasi* | Hindu religious recluse |
| Satyagraha | truth force, soul force; name given by Gandhi to nonviolent resistance |
| Satyagrahi | one who practises Satyagraha |
| *swami* | Hindu ascetic or religious teacher |
| *swaraj* | self-rule |
| *tonga* | two-wheeled horse-driven vehicle |
| Urdu | language based on Hindi, with a Persian and Arabic vocabulary |
| *vaidya* | A physician practising Ayurvedic (ancient Hindu) system of medicine |
| Vaishnava | Hindu giving special reverence to god Vishnu |
| *vakil* | lawyer |
| *zindabad* | long live |

# Bibliography

There are six necessary sources for a biography of Gandhi: his two biographical writings, *The Story of My Experiments with Truth* and *Satyagraha in South Africa;* his *Collected Works* (90 volumes); D.G. Tendulkar's *Mahatma* (8 volumes); Pyarelal's unfinished biography, *The Early Phase* and *The Last Phase;* and Mansergh and Moon's *The Transfer of Power* documents 1942–7 (12 volumes).
The following is the list of books which I found useful in clarifying further the life and thought of Mahatma Gandhi:

Andrews, C.F. *Mahatma Gandhi's Ideas.* London, George Allen & Unwin, 1949.
Ashe, Geoffrey. *Gandhi: A Study in Revolution.* Bombay, Asia Publishing House, 1968.

Bhattacharya, Bhabani. *Mahatma Gandhi.* New Delhi, Arnold-Heinemann, 1977.
Bhuyan, A.C. *The Quit India Movement.* New Delhi, Manas Publications, 1975.
Birkenhead, Earl of. *Halifax.* London, Hamish Hamilton, 1965.
Birla, G.D. *In the Shadow of the Mahatma.* Bombay, Orient Longmans, 1953.
Bolitho, Hector. *Jinnah: Creator of Pakistan.* London, John Murray, 1954.
Bolton, Glorney. *The Tragedy of Gandhi.* London, George Allen & Unwin, 1934.
Bondurant, Joan V. *Conquest of Violence: The Gandhian Philosophy of Conflict.* Princeton, Princeton University Press, 1958.
Bose, Nirmal Kumar. *My Days with Gandhi.* Bombay, Orient Longmans, 1974.
Bose, Subhas Chandra. *The Indian Struggle.* Bombay, Asia Publishing House, 1964.
——*Crossroads: Being the Work of Subhas Chandra Bose.* Bombay, Asia Publishing House, 1962.

Brecher, Michael. *Nehru: A Political Biography*. London, Oxford University Press, 1959.

Broad, Lewis. *Winston Churchill*. London, Sidgwick & Jackson, 1963.

Brock, Peter. *The Mahatma and Mother India*. Ahmedabad, Navajivan Publishing House, 1983.

Brown, D. Mackenzie. *The White Umbrella*. Westport, Greenwood Press, 1981.

Brown, Judith M. *Gandhi: Prisoner of Hope*. Delhi, Oxford University Press, 1990.

——*Gandhi's Rise to Power*. Cambridge, Cambridge University Press, 1972.

——*Modern India: The Origins of an Asian Democracy*. Oxford, Oxford University Press, 1986.

Campbell-Johnson, Alan. *Mission with Mountbatten*. Bombay, Jaico Publishing House, 1951.

Casey, R.G. *An Australian in India*. London, Hollis & Carter, 1947.

Catlin, George. *In the Path of Mahatma Gandhi*. London, Macdonald and Company, 1948.

Chaplin, Charles. *My Autobiography*. New York, Simon & Schuster, 1964.

Chaturvedi, Benarsidas, and Sykes, Marjorie. *Charles Freer Andrews*. London, George Allen & Unwin, 1949.

Chaudhri, Sandhya. *Gandhi and the Partition of India*. New Delhi, Sterling Publishers, 1984.

Collins, Larry, and Lapierre, Dominique. *Mountbatten and Independent India*. New Delhi, Vikas Publishing House, 1984.

Connell, John. *Wavell: Scholar and Soldier*. London, Collins, 1964.

Copley, Antony. *Gandhi: Against the Tide*. Oxford, Basil Blackwell, 1987.

Cousins, Norman (ed.). *Profiles of Gandhi*. Delhi, Indian Book Company, 1969.

Das, Hari Hara. *Subhas Chandra Bose and the Indian National Movement*. New Delhi, Sterling Publishers, 1983.

Das, Manmath Nath. *Partition and Independence of India*. New Delhi, Vision Books, 1982.

Desai, Valji Govindji (ed.). *The Diary of Mahadev Desai*. Ahmedabad, Navajivan Publishing House, 1953.

Doke, Joseph J. *M.K. Gandhi: An Indian Patriot in South Africa*. London, The London Indian Chronicle, 1909.

Draper, Alfred. *The Amritsar Massacre*. London, Buchan & Enright, 1985.

Durant, Will. *The Case for India*. New York, Simon & Schuster, 1930.

Durgadas (ed.). *Sardar Patel's Correspondence* 1945–50 (Vol. VI). Ahmedabad, Navajivan Publishing House, 1973.

Edwardes, Michael. *A History of India*. London, Thames & Hudson, 1961.
Erikson, Erik H. *Gandhi's Truth: On the Origins of Militant Nonviolence*. London, Faber and Faber, 1970.

Fischer, Louis. *The Life of Mahatma Gandhi*. New York, Harper & Row, 1983.

Gandhi, Manubehn. *Last Glimpses of Bapu*. Delhi, Shiva Lal Agarwala, 1962.
——*The Miracle of Calcutta*. Ahmedabad, Navajivan Publishing House, 1959.
Gandhi, M.K. *An Autobiography or The Story of My Experiments with Truth*. Ahmedabad, Navajivan Publishing House, 1990.
——*Bapu's Letters to Mira*. Ahmedabad, Navajivan Publishing House, 1949.
——*The Collected Works*. New Delhi, Publication Division of the Government of India, 1958–84.
——*Delhi Diary*. Ahmedabad, Navajivan Publishing House, 1948.
——*Freedom's Battle*. Madras, Ganesh & Co., 1921.
——*Gandhiji's Correspondence with the Government, 1944–47*. Ahmedabad, Navajivan Publishing House, 1959.
——*Hind Swaraj*. Ahmedabad, Navajivan Publishing House, 1984.
——*Satyagraha in South Africa*. Ahmedabad, Navajivan Publishing House, 1972.
Gandhi, Rajmohan. *Patel: A Life*. Ahmedabad, Navajivan Publishing House, 1990.
Ghosh, P.C. *Mahatma Gandhi as I Saw Him*. Delhi, S. Chand & Co., 1968.
Ghosh, Tapan. *Gandhi Murder Trial*. Bombay, Asia Publishing House, 1974.
Glendevon, John. *The Viceroy at Bay: Lord Linlithgow in India*. London, Collins, 1971.

Halifax, Earl of (Lord Irwin). *Fulness of Days*. London, Collins, 1957.
Hancock, W.K. *Smuts: The Sanguine Years*. Cambridge, Cambridge University Press, 1962.
Hodson, H.V. *The Great Divide*. London, Hutchinson, 1969.
Holmes, John Haynes. *My Gandhi*. London, George Allen & Unwin, 1954.
Hunt, James D. *Gandhi in London*. New Delhi, Promilla & Co. Publishers, 1978.

Hutchins, Francis G. *India's Revolution: Gandhi and the Quit India Movement.* Cambridge, Harvard University Press, 1973.
——*Spontaneous Revolution: The Quit India Movement.* Delhi, Manohar Book Service, 1971.
Huttenback, Robert A. *Gandhi in South Africa.* Ithaca, Cornell University Press, 1971.
Hyde, H. Montgomery. *Lord Reading.* London, Heinemann, 1967.

Inamdar, P.L. *The Story of the Red Fort Trial.* Bombay, Popular Prakashan, 1979.

James, Robert Rhodes (ed.). *Winston S. Churchill: His Complete Speeches* (Vol. V). New York, Chelsea House Publishers, 1974.
Jamil-Ud-Din (ed.). *Some Recent Speeches and Writings of Mr Jinnah.* Lahore, Muhammad Ashraf, 1946.
Jha, Manoranjan. *Civil Disobedience and After.* Delhi, Meenakshi Prakashan, 1973.
Jog, N.G. *In Freedom's Quest.* New Delhi, Orient Longmans, 1969.

Kalarthi, Mukulbhai. *Ba and Bapu.* Ahmedabad, Navajivan Publishing House, 1962.
Keer, Dhananjay. *Mahatma Gandhi.* Bombay, Popular Prakashan, 1973.
——*Veer Savarkar.* Bombay, Popular Prakashan, 1966.
Khosla, G.D. *The Murder of the Mahatma.* London, Chatto & Windus, 1963.
Krishnadas. *Seven Months with Mahatma Gandhi.* Madras, S. Ganesan, 1928.
Kytle, Calvin. *Gandhi: Soldier of Nonviolence.* New York, Grosset & Dunlap, 1969.

Lester, Muriel. *Entertaining Gandhi.* London, Ivor Nicholson & Watson, 1932.

Mahadevan, T.K. *The Year of the Phoenix.* New Delhi, Arnold-Heinemann, 1982.
Malgonkar, Manohar. *Men who Killed Gandhi.* Madras, Macmillan, 1978.
Manchester, William. *The Last Lion: Winston Spencer Churchill.* London, Michael Joseph, 1983.
Mansergh, Nicholas, and Moon, Penderel (eds). *The Transfer of Power 1942–47* (12 vols). London, Her Majesty's Stationery Office, 1972–83.
Mayo, Katherine. *Mother India.* London, Jonathan Cape, 1935.

Mehta, Ved. *Mahatma Gandhi and His Apostles.* London, André Deutsch, 1977.

Menon, K.P. Kesava (ed.). *The Great Trial.* Madras, Ganesh & Co., 1922.

Moon, Penderel. *Divide and Quit.* London, Chatto & Windus, 1961.

——*Gandhi and Modern India.* London, English Universities Press, 1968.

——(ed.). *Wavell: The Viceroy's Journal.* London, Oxford University Press, 1973.

Moore, R.J. *Churchill, Cripps and India.* Oxford, Clarendon Press, 1979.

Moraes, Frank. *Jawaharlal Nehru.* New York, Macmillan, 1956.

——*Sunlight and Shadow.* Bombay, Jaico Publishing House, 1964.

——*Witness to an Era.* Delhi, Vikas Publishing House, 1973.

Moran, Lord. *Winston Churchill: Taken from the Diaries of Lord Moran.* London, Constable, 1966.

Mosley, Leonard. *The Last Days of the British Raj.* London, Weidenfeld & Nicolson, 1961.

Muzumdar, Haridas T. *Gandhi Versus the Empire.* New York, Universal Publishing Company, 1932.


Nanda, B.R. *Mahatma Gandhi.* London, George Allen & Unwin, 1958.

Nayyar, Sushila. *Kasturba: A Personal Reminiscence.* Ahmedabad, Navajivan Publishing House, 1960.

Nehru, Jawaharlal. *An Autobiography.* London, The Bodley Head, 1953.

——*The Discovery of India.* London, Meridian Books, 1956.

——*Jawaharlal Nehru's Speeches* (Vol. I). New Delhi, Publication Division, Government of India, 1967.


Pandit, H.N. *Fragments of History.* New Delhi, Sterling Publishers, 1982.

Panjabi, K.L. *The Indomitable Sardar.* Bombay, Bhartiya Vidya Bhavan, 1962.

Payne, Robert. *The Life and Death of Mahatma Gandhi.* London, The Bodley Head, 1969.

Philips, C.H., and Wainwright, Mary Doreen (eds). *The Partition of India.* London, George Allen & Unwin, 1970.

Polak, Millie Graham. *Mr Gandhi: The Man.* Bombay, Vora and Company, 1950.

Prasad, Bimal. *Gandhi, Nehru and J.P: Studies in Leadership.* Delhi, Chanakya Publications, 1985.

Prasad, Rajendra. *Mahatma Gandhi and Bihar.* Bombay, Hind Kitabs, 1949.

Pyarelal. *Mahatma Gandhi: The Birth of Satyagraha.* Ahmedabad, Navajivan Publishing House, 1986.

———*Mahatma Gandhi: The Discovery of Satyagraha.* Bombay, Sevak Prakashan, 1980.
———*Mahatma Gandhi: The Early Phase.* Ahmedabad, Navajivan Publishing House, 1965.
———*Mahatma Gandhi: The Last Phase* (2 vols). Ahmedabad, Navajivan Publishing House, 1956, 1958.

Radhakrishnan, S. (ed.). *Mahatma Gandhi: Essays and Reflections.* Allahabad, Kitabistan, 1944.
Rose, Kenneth. *King George V.* London, Weidenfeld & Nicolson, 1983.

Saggi, P.D. (ed.). *Life and Work of Netaji Subhas Chandra Bose.* Bombay, Overseas Publishing House, 1949.
Sanger, Margaret. *An Autobiography.* New York, W. W. Norton, 1938.
Sharp, Gene. *The Politics of Nonviolent Action.* Boston, Porter Sargent Publisher, 1973.
Shimoni, Gideon. *Gandhi, Satyagraha and the Jews.* Jerusalem, The Hebrew University of Jerusalem, 1977.
Shridharani, K.J. *War Without Violence.* New York, Harcourt Brace and Company, 1939.
Shukla, Chandrashanker (ed.). *Incidents of Gandhiji's Life.* Bombay, Vora and Company, 1949.
Slade, Madeleine. *The Spirit's Pilgrimage.* London, Longmans, 1960.
Stokes, S.E. *To Awaking India.* Madras, Ganesh and Company, 1922.
Sunderland, Jabez T. *India in Bondage: Her Right to Freedom.* Calcutta, R. Chatterjee, 1929.
Swan, Maureen. *Gandhi: The South African Experience.* Johannesburg, Ravan Press, 1985.
Swinson, Arthur. *Six Minutes to Sunset.* London, Peter Davies, 1964.

Templewood, Viscount (Sir Samuel Hoare). *Nine Troubled Years.* London, Collins, 1954.
Tendulkar, D.G. (ed.). *Gandhiji: His Life and Work.* Bombay, Karnatak Publishing House, 1945.
———*Mahatma* (8 vols). New Delhi, Publication Division of the Government of India, 1969.
Tinker, Hugh. *The Ordeal of Love: C.F. Andrews and India.* Delhi, Oxford University Press, 1979.
Tolstoy, Leo. *Letter to a Hindu.* London, Peace News, 1963.

Walker, Roy. *Sword of God.* New Delhi, Orient Longmans, 1969.

Wallbank, T. Walter (ed.). *The Partition of India.* Boston, D.C. Heath and Company, 1966.

Watson, Blanche. *Gandhi: Voice of the New Revolution.* Calcutta, Saraswaty Library, 1921.

Watson, Francis. *Talking of Gandhi.* Bombay, Orient Longmans, 1957.

Winsten, Stephen. *Salt and His Circle.* London, Hutchinson, 1951.

Wolpert, Stanley. *A New History of India.* New York, Oxford University Press, 1982.

——*Jinnah of Pakistan.* New York, Oxford University Press, 1982.


Yajnik, Indulal K. *Gandhi as I Knew Him.* Delhi, Danish Mahal, 1943.


Ziegler, Philip. *Mountbatten.* London, Collins, 1985.

Zinkin, Taya. *Reporting India.* London, Chatto & Windus, 1962.

# Chapter Notes

References to major sources are indicated in abbreviated form: *The Story of My Experiments in Truth* appears as *Story; Satyagraha in South Africa* is given as *Satyagraha; The Collected Works* as *Works;* D.G. Tendulkar's *Mahatma* is shown as Tendulkar; and *The Transfer of Power* is given as *TOP*.

Whilst volume numbers are in Roman, page numbers appear as Arabic numerals. In the case of *The Transfer of Power*, the references relate to the document numbers.

**Biographer's Note**

| | | |
|---|---|---|
| vii | There is no hope | *Harijan*, 29 June 1947 |
| viii | A disciple cannot | *Works*, XIV, 199 |

**Chapter 1**

| | | |
|---|---|---|
| 1 | Generations to come | Tendulkar, *Gandhiji: His Life and Work*, xi |
| 4 | My father was | *Story*, 3–4 |
| 5 | The outstanding | *Story*, 4 |
| 5 | These many things | *Story*, 28 |
| 6 | He is the true | Krishnadas, *Seven Months with Mahatma Gandhi*, 293 |
| 6 | But one thing | *Story*, 29 |
| 6 | Moniya could be | Pyarelal, *Mahatma Gandhi: The Early Phase*, 194 |
| 9 | I could never be | *Story*, 6 |
| 11 | Take one step | *Works*, XXX, 88–9 |
| 12 | And oh! that first | *Story*, 9 |
| 12 | It is my painful | *Story*, 7 |
| 13 | I was a coward | *Story*, 17–18 |
| 13 | Behold the mighty | *Story*, 18 |
| 14 | I could see | *Story*, 23–4 |
| 15 | I broke her bangles | *Works*, LXXII, 127 |
| 15 | The dreadful night | *Story*, 25–6 |

**Chapter 2**

| | | |
|---|---|---|
| 18 | You will have to | *Works*, I (1979 edition), 4 |
| 20 | I hope that | *Works*, I, 1 |
| 20 | My mother was | *Works*, I, 45 |
| 21 | In the opinion of | *Story*, 34–5; *Works*, I, 46 |
| 22 | One dark night | *Works*, I, 10 |
| 23 | When you land | *Works*, I, 13 |

**Chapter 3**

| 25 | The doors were | *Works*, I, 16 |
| 25 | When I first saw | *Works*, I, 83 |
| 25 | Do not touch | *Story*, 38 |
| 28 | I read Salt's | *Story*, 41 |
| 28 | You are too clumsy | *Story*, 42 |
| 29 | My landlady's | *Story*, 54–5 |
| 30 | I am glad God has | *Story*, 56–7 |
| 30 | Gandhi was wearing | Fischer, *The Life of Mahatma Gandhi*, 24 |
| 32 | My life was | *Story*, 47 |
| 33 | And in the very | Winsten, *Salt and His Circle*, 118 |
| 35 | If one ponders | *Story*, 57 |
| 38 | Well, sir, you | *Story*, 59 |
| 39 | Hindus as a rule | *The Vegetarian*, 28 February 1891 |
| 40 | when the great | *The Vegetarian Messenger*, 1 June 1891 |
| 40 | Whence this devil | *Story*, 60-1 |
| 41 | In conclusion | *The Vegetarian*, 20 June 1891 |
| 41 | In a word | *The Vegetarian*, 13 June 1891 |
| 41 | So much attached | *The Vegetarian*, 9 April 1892 |
| 42 | The breakfast menu | *The Vegetarian*, 9 April 1892 |
| 43 | The second night | *The Vegetarian*, 16 April 1892 |
| 43 | My grief was | *Story*, 73 |
| 43 | Austerity implies | Desai, *The Diary of Mahadev Desai*, I, 51–2 |

**Chapter 4**

| 45 | My head was | *Story*, 79 |
| 46 | I exhausted | *Story*, 74 |
| 46 | But I have passed | *Story*, 80 |
| 47 | You do not know | *Story*, 82 |
| 47 | Your brother is | *Story*, 82–3 |
| 47 | Tell Gandhi | *Story*, 83 |
| 48 | those were my | *Story*, 86 |

**Chapter 5**

| 50 | I simply stood | *Story*, 87 |
| 54 | Sami, you sit | *Story*, 95–6 |
| 55 | That does not matter | *Story*, 98 |

**Chapter 6**

| 56 | I am a Hindu | *Story*, 100 |
| 56 | Lord, show the | *Story*, 101–2 |
| 57 | This superstition | *Story*, 103 |
| 58 | I had great | Pyarelal, *Mahatma Gandhi: The Early Phase*, 315 |
| 58 | My difficulties | *Story*, 113 |
| 59 | What is God? | *Works*, I, 127–8 |
| 59 | If you have | Pyarelal, *Mahatma Gandhi: The Early Phase*, 329 |

**Chapter 7**

| | | |
|---|---|---|
| 63 | My joy was | *Story*, 112 |
| 64 | During 1893 | Mahadevan, *The Year of the Phoenix*, 71 |
| 64 | It is the first | *Story*, 116 |
| 65 | I am inexperienced | *Works*, I, 140 |
| 66 | I wanted to | *Story*, 123 |
| 67 | There are many | *Natal Witness*, 4 January 1895 |
| 68 | What we want | *Natal Mercury*, 6 June 1896 |
| 68 | Mr Gandhi writes | *Works*, II, 36 |

**Chapter 8**

| | | |
|---|---|---|
| 69 | A pamphlet published | *Works*, II, 187–8 |
| 70 | Mr Gandhi, on his | *Works*, II, 188 |
| 70 | The man in the | *Works*, II, 4 |
| 71 | In Dundee | *Works*, II, 5 |
| 71 | An Indian | *Works*, II, 36 |
| 71 | Such feeling of | *Works*, II, 8–10 |
| 72 | We would often | *Works*, II, 43 |
| 72 | Is your speech | *Story*, 145 |
| 73 | Don't you see | *Story*, 150 |
| 76 | Our forefathers | *Works*, II, 221–2 |
| 77 | Mr Bale, MLA | *Natal Witness*, 11 January 1897 |
| 79 | What essential | Pyarelal, *Mahatma Gandhi: The Discovery of Satyagraha*, 101 |
| 79 | You will injure | *Satyagraha*, 52 |
| 81 | What do you want? | *Satyagraha*, 56 |
| 81 | The leaders and | *Story*, 163 |
| 82 | Ours is one | *Works*, II, 74 |

**Chapter 9**

| | | |
|---|---|---|
| 84 | I will not tolerate | *Story*, 232 |
| 85 | The barber was | *Story*, 178–9 |
| 86 | If any class | *Satyagraha*, 67 |
| 87 | After a night's | Andrews, *Mahatma Gandhi's Ideas*, 364 |
| 87 | British Indians Natal | *Works*, III, 173–4 |
| 88 | It was hard to | *Works*, III, 193 |
| 88 | KASTURBAI: You may | *Story*, 184–5 |

**Chapter 10**

| | | |
|---|---|---|
| 90 | Gandhi, it seems | *Story*, 186 |
| 91 | There was no limit | *Story*, 187 |
| 91 | Well, then, here is | *Story*, 188–9 |
| 95 | I searched here | *Story*, 202 |
| 96 | In getting my | *Story*, 219 |
| 97 | Barrister Gandhi | *Works*, III, 263 |

| 139 | I will not | *Story*, 270 |
| 140 | Although I think | *Works*, IX, 205–9 |

**Chapter 15**

| 141 | My aspirations | *Works*, IX, 218 |
| 142 | I am sure | *Works*, IX, 269 |
| 143 | Everyone seems | Tendulkar, I, 101–2 |
| 143 | We cannot recognize | Hunt, *Gandhi in London*, 119 |
| 143 | We cannot have | *Satyagraha*, 209–10 |
| 146 | I must say | *Works*, IX, 303 |
| 146 | Don't show me | Keer, *Veer Savarkar*, 53 |
| 147 | Those who believe | Tendulkar, I, 103 |
| 147 | Hindus are the | Keer, *Veer Savarkar*, 64 |

**Chapter 16**

| 150 | It is wrong | *Works*, VIII, 373–4 |
| 158 | I do not know | *Works*, IX, 446 |
| 159 | I have just | Tendulkar, I, 327 |
| 159 | Looking at this | *Works*, IX, 389 |
| 161 | EDITOR: . . . Why do you | Gandhi, *Hind Swaraj*, 29–72 |

**Chapter 17**

| 166 | But this or | *Satyagraha*, 212 |
| 169 | I have often | *Satyagraha*, 222 |
| 170 | The longer I live | Tendulkar, I, 122–3 |

**Chapter 18**

| 173 | SMUTS: . . . You as a | *Works*, XI, 32–4 |
| 176 | You do not know my | *Satyagraha*, 228 |
| 177 | You do not know the | *Satyagraha*, 244–5 |
| 177 | Your future is largely | Tendulkar, I, 130 |
| 177 | Will you forgive | *Works*, XI, 351 |
| 178 | You will always have | *Satyagraha*, 243 |

**Chapter 19**

| 179 | We in India have | *Satyagraha*, 250 |
| 181 | Going Transvaal | *Works*, XII, 117–18 |
| 181 | A settlement without | *Indian Opinion*, 13 September 1913 |
| 183 | The pilgrims which | Tendulkar, I, 141 |
| 183 | General Smuts will | *Satyagraha*, 273 |
| 184 | You are my prisoner | *Satyagraha*, 277 |
| 185 | Gandhi had no business | Nanda, *Mahatma Gandhi*, 118 |
| 187 | 'Yes,' Gandhi responded | Chaturvedi and Sykes, *Charles Freer Andrews*, 95 |
| 187 | I do not like | *Satyagraha*, 295 |
| 188 | Christianity in its | Tinker, *The Ordeal of Love*, 88 |
| 189 | The greatest grief | Tendulkar, I, 150 |
| 190 | Never before have I | *Works*, XII, 410–11 |

| 191 | For me there can be | *Works*, XII, 455 |
| 191 | The saint has left | Hancock, *Smuts: The Sanguine Years*, 345 |
| 191 | It was my fate | Radhakrishnan, *Mahatma Gandhi: Essays and Reflections*, 296–8 |
| 192 | There is a law | *Satyagraha*, 306–7 |
| 192 | Persons in power | Tendulkar, I, 151 |
| 194 | Those who confine | *Story*, 291–3 |
| 195 | I had before me | *Story*, 297 |
| 195 | Just now my own | *Works*, XII, 556–7 |
| 196 | You cannot possibly | *Story*, 300 |
| 196 | I have been so often | *Works*, XII, 566 |

**Chapter 21**

| 204 | I caught a glimpse | Mehta, *Mahatma Gandhi and His Apostles*, 210 |
| 205 | I would like you | *Story*, 312–13 |
| 205 | Are you prepared | *Story*, 315 |
| 205 | Is not this a | *Story*, 316–17 |
| 207 | Launching on the | *Story*, 321 |
| 209 | It was they | *Works*, XIII, 52–3 |
| 209 | I know that a | *Works*, XIII, 59-60 |

**Chapter 22**

| 212 | It is a matter of | *Works*, XIII, 210–16 |

**Chapter 23**

| 220 | I have come to the | *Story*, 341 |
| 220 | We quite agree with you | Brown, *Gandhi's Rise to Power*, 65 |
| 221 | My desire is purely | Tendulkar, I, 202 |
| 221 | I have entered | *Works*, XIII, 375 |
| 222 | I do not wish | Tendulkar, I, 204 |
| 222 | You want Mr Andrews | Prasad, *Mahatma Gandhi and Bihar*, 15 |
| 224 | I can only say | Tendulkar, I, 209 |
| 224 | We may look on | Nanda, *Mahatma Gandhi*, 159 |

**Chapter 24**

| 227 | If you succeed | *Works*, XIV, 229–30 |
| 227 | One morning | *Story*, 359 |
| 228 | I am at present | *Works*, XIV, 262–3 |
| 230 | If you agree | *Story*, 369 |
| 230 | I have an idea | *Works*, XIV, 382 |
| 230 | There are 600 | Tendulkar, I, 230 |
| 230 | There can be no | *Works*, XIV, 440 |
| 231 | There was a danger | *Works*, XIV, 511 |
| 231 | recruiting mad | *Works*, XV, 17 |
| 232 | The will to live | *Story*, 379 |
| 232 | When friends told | *Works*, XIV, 475 |
| 234 | When we have | *Works*, XV, 186–7 |

| 276 | Cows we cannot protect | *Works*, XXXI, 524–5 |
| 276 | It is better for you | *Works*, XXXII, 42 |
| 276 | I do not think that | *Young India*, 11 November 1926; 18 November 1926 |
| 277 | Gandhi, you killed | Watson, *Talking of Gandhi*, 48 |
| 279 | We have lost hold | *Works*, XXXIII, 365 |
| 280 | What you say | Jha, *Civil Disobedience and After*, 32 |
| 280 | The book is cleverly | *Works*, XXXIV, 539-47 |
| 282 | Challenge the government | Tendulkar, II, 329 |
| 282 | He closely studied | *Works*, XXXVI, 261–3; 280 |
| 283 | Not that I distrust | *Works*, XXXVI, 266–7 |
| 283 | My love to you | *Works*, XXXVIII, 150 |
| 284 | Independence is a thing | Tendulkar, II, 335 |

**Chapter 29**

| 288 | We believe it is | *Works*, XLII, 427 |
| 289 | Dear Friend | *Works*, XLIII, 2–8 |
| 291 | I repudiate the law | *Works*, XLIII, 52 |
| 291 | 'This will be,' he said | *Works*, XLIII, 46 |
| 292 | Today we are defying | *Works*, XLIII, 100 |
| 293 | For me there is no | *Works*, XLIII, 149 |
| 293 | I shall return | Tendulkar, III, 30 |
| 293 | The will-power | Birkenhead, *Halifax*, 281–2 |
| 294 | Our path has been | *Works*, XLIII, 215 |
| 294 | If we are to | Tendulkar, III, 34 |
| 295 | You may condemn | *Works*, XLIII, 392 |
| 296 | Suddenly, at a word of | Tendulkar, III, 40–1 |
| 297 | Your Majesty | Birkenhead, *Halifax*, 284 |
| 298 | In a few seconds | *Time*, 7 July 1930; Shridharani, *War Without Violence*, 38–9 |

**Chapter 30**

| 300 | It is alarming | James, *Winston S.Churchill: His Complete Speeches*, 4985 |
| 300 | I think that | Birkenhead, *Halifax*, 298–9 |
| 301 | This did not | Halifax, *Fulness of Days*, 149 |
| 302 | I exhorted him | Halifax, *Fulness of Days*, 151 |
| 302 | I am against | Broad, *Winston Churchill*, 325–6 |
| 302 | There was a | Halifax, *Fulness of Days*, 147 |
| 302 | I could not conceive | Halifax, *Fulness of Days*, 149 |
| 303 | Mr Gandhi thought | Halifax, *Fulness of Days*, 150 |
| 303 | You must know | *Works*, XLV, 349 |
| 303 | The deed itself | *Young India*, 30 July 1931 |
| 304 | I go to London | *Works*, XLVII, 368–9 |

**Chapter 31**

| 306 | You are strange | Holmes, *My Gandhi*, 42–3 |

| 307 | We have adopted | *Works*, XLVIII, 8–10 |
| 308 | This street | Lester, *Entertaining Gandhi*, 68–9 |
| 308 | The first feeling | *Works*, XLVIII, 27 |
| 309 | I am absolutely | Shukla, *Incidents of Gandhiji's Life*, 24 |
| 309 | If we are intent | *Works*, XLVIII, 18 |
| 310 | 'The Congress,' he declared | Tendulkar, III, 128 |
| 311 | October 16, 1931 | Muzumdar, *Gandhi Versus the Empire*, 153–4 |
| 312 | Well, Mr Slocombe | Tendulkar, III, 113–14 |
| 312 | If you went to | *Works*, XLVIII, 69 |
| 313 | One of the most | Slade, *The Spirit's Pilgrimage*, 140–1 |
| 314 | It requires | *Works*, XLVIII, 272–3 |
| 314 | What! Have the rebel | Templewood, *Nine Troubled Years*, 59–60 |
| 315 | He is a perfect master | *The Parliamentary Debates, The House of Commons*, 2 December 1931, vol. 260, p. 1195 |
| 315 | Mr Gandhi has left | *The Parliamentary Debates, The House of Lords*, 8 December 1931, vol. 83, p. 355 |
| 316 | Speaker after speaker | *Works*, XLVIII, 358–68 |
| 318 | The little man | Slade, *The Spirit's Pilgrimage*, 147 |
| 318 | I am against | Tendulkar, III, 146–7 |
| 318 | I have a feeling | Tendulkar, III, 146 |
| 319 | His mind proceeds | Tendulkar, III, 149 |
| 319 | He does not understand | Slade, *The Spirit's Pilgrimage*, 149 |

**Chapter 32**

| 321 | I do not know | *Works*, XLVIII, 459 |
| 323 | If the India of | Tendulkar, III, 158 |
| 324 | Birth control has no | Desai, *The Diary of Mahadev Desai*, I, 173 |
| 324 | It may be that | *Works*, L, 384 |
| 325 | In the establishment | *Works*, LI, 31 |
| 325 | I felt angry | Nehru, *An Autobiography*, 370 |
| 326 | It is worth | Tendulkar, III, 167 |
| 326 | What I want | *Works*, LI, 118–19 |
| 327 | There will be | *Works*, LIII, 260 |
| 328 | You have a perfect | Tendulkar, III, 173 |
| 330 | A tempest | *Works*, LV, 74 |
| 331 | If I resort to | *Works*, LV, 271 |
| 332 | The strain of | *Works*, LV, 353 |
| 332 | Mere money | Tendulkar, III, 223 |
| 333 | Physical catastrophes | Tendulkar, III, 249–50 |
| 333 | I confess my utter | *Harijan*, 16 February 1934 |
| 334 | This is the least | *Works*, LVIII, 159–60 |
| 334 | I must advise | Tendulkar, III, 260–1 |
| 335 | For me, this is a | *Works*, LIX, 6 |
| 336 | Mechanization is good | *Young India*, 13 November 1924; 5 November 1925; 17 June 1926; *Harijan*, 16 November 1934; 14 September 1935; 27 January 1940 |

| 370 | For the Congress | *Works*, LXXII, 195 |
| 371 | The Viceregal | *Works*, LXXII, 384 |
| 371 | I do not want | *Works*, LXXIII, 16–20 |

**Chapter 37**

| 375 | Why did you come | Tendulkar, VI, 72 |
| 376 | I see Gandhi | *TOP*, II, # 241 |
| 377 | The wrong sort | Tendulkar, VI, 78 |
| 378 | Leave India to | Tendulkar, VI, 81 |
| 378 | And what is | *Harijan*, 19 July 1942 |
| 379 | The British statesmen | *Works*, LXXVI, 98–100 |
| 379 | Did the French | *Harijan*, 19 July 1942 |
| 380 | You will be | *Works*, LXXVI, 311–12 |
| 381 | 'That question' | Tendulkar, VI, 125 |
| 381 | India is not | *Works*, LXXVI, 331 |
| 382 | PM: As I get | Moran, *Winston Churchill*, 52 |
| 382 | The Qaid-e-Azam | *Works*, LXXVI, 386 |
| 382 | I want freedom | *Works*, LXXVI, 389–92 |
| 383 | You do not know | Slade, *The Spirit's Pilgrimage*, 237 |

**Chapter 38**

| 387 | The Gandhi discussion | *TOP*, III, # 337 |
| 388 | This our hour | *TOP*, III, # 437 |
| 388 | I confess | *TOP*, III, # 437 |
| 390 | I have heard | *TOP*, III, # 463 |
| 390 | Surely with all | *TOP*, III, # 538 |
| 391 | The degree of | *TOP*, III, # 546 |
| 391 | It now seems | *TOP*, III, # 553 |
| 391 | We have exposed | *TOP*, III, # 555 |
| 391 | Mr Gandhi is | *TOP*, III, # 568 |
| 393 | It would not | *TOP*, IV, # 89 |
| 393 | I wonder who | *TOP*, IV, # 96 |
| 394 | Dear Lord Linlithgow | *TOP*, IV, # 145 |
| 394 | Dear Mr Gandhi | *TOP*, IV, # 167 |
| 396 | O Lord | Nayyar, *Kasturba: A Personal Reminiscence*, 95 |
| 396 | Though for her sake | Tendulkar, VI, 240 |
| 397 | Are you joking? | Tendulkar, VI, 249 |

**Chapter 39**

| 399 | I feel that | *TOP*, IV, # 544 |
| 399 | But they forget | Tendulkar, VI, 261–2 |
| 401 | Prime Minister was | Moon, *Wavell: The Viceroy's Journal*, 23 |
| 401 | Curious to think | Moon, *Wavell: The Viceroy's Journal*, 88 |
| 403 | In the course of | *Works*, LXXVIII, 101 |
| 403 | We maintain | *Works*, LXXVIII, 407 |
| 404 | I very much fear | Tendulkar, VII, 2–3 |
| 407 | Mr. Gandhi's | Casey, *An Australian in India*, 59–62 |

## Chapter 40

| | | |
|---|---|---|
| 408 | Though I have | Tendulkar, VII, 18 |
| 409 | If the Indian | Tendulkar, VII, 69 |
| 411 | Sudhir Ghosh is | Moon, *Wavell: The Viceroy's Journal*, 314 |
| 412 | At 8:00 a.m. | Pyarelal, *Mahatma Gandhi: The Last Phase*, I, 239 |
| 413 | JABBER-WEEKS | Moon, *Wavell: The Viceroy's Journal*, 315–17 |
| 415 | I can never entirely | Pyarelal, *Mahatma Gandhi: The Last Phase*, I, 494–5 |

## Chapter 41

| | | |
|---|---|---|
| 419 | Bihar of my | *Works*, LXXXVI, 81 |
| 420 | How can we | Tendulkar, VII, 263 |
| 421 | Those who have | *Works*, LXXXVI, 114 |
| 421 | This Noakhali | *Works*, LXXXVI, 119 |
| 421 | I can sing | Tendulkar, VII, 280 |
| 422 | He was lying | Moon, *Gandhi and Modern India*, 253 |
| 422 | A drop torn | Tendulkar, VII, 343 |
| 423 | The sexual sense | *Works*, LXVII, 69 |
| 424 | Should I deny | *Works*, LXVII, 60–1 |
| 424 | I recently discovered | *Works*, LXVII, 58 |
| 424 | If complete | *Works*, LXVII, 60–1 |
| 424 | My peace cannot | *Works*, LXVII, 171 |
| 424 | I stopped on | *Works*, LXVII, 362–3 |
| 425 | I have read | *Works*, LXXXVI, 299-300 |
| 425 | The behaviour of | Bose, *My Days with Gandhi*, 151 |
| 426 | This [experiment] has | Pyarelal, *Mahatma Gandhi: The Last Phase*, I, 581–2 |
| 426 | These matters | Pyarelal, *Mahatma Gandhi: The Last Phase*, I, 582 |
| 426 | BAPA: Why this | Pyarelal, *Mahatma Gandhi: The Last Phase*, I, 585–7 |
| 427 | I go beyond | *Works*, LXXXVII, 103–4 |
| 428 | My meaning of | *Works*, LXXXVII, 108 |

## Chapter 42

| | | |
|---|---|---|
| 429 | It is difficult | Pyarelal, *Mahatma Gandhi: The Last Phase*, II, 35 |
| 429 | Please forgive us | Pyarelal, *Mahatma Gandhi: The Last Phase*, I, 653 |
| 431 | I felt sorry | Pyarelal, *Mahatma Gandhi: The Last Phase*, II, 85 |
| 431 | When I told | *United Empire*, November–December 1948 |
| 432 | We did not | Pyarelal, *Mahatma Gandhi: The Last Phase*, II, 96 |
| 432 | The first week | Pyarelal, *Mahatma Gandhi: The Last Phase*, II, 149 |
| 432 | We are passionately | *TOP*, X, # 267 |
| 433 | Whatever may be | *Works*, LXXXVII, 435 |
| 433 | My life's work | Pyarelal, *Mahatma Gandhi: The Last Phase*, II, 210-11 |
| 433 | But for this | Mosley, *The Last Days of the British Raj*, 127 |
| 433 | In all probability | Pyarelal, *Mahatma Gandhi: The Last Phase*, II, 215 |
| 434 | 'But,' Gandhi | *Works*, LXXXVIII, 154 |
| 435 | Even when I | Tendulkar, VIII, 19 |

| 435 | A larger India | Brecher, *Nehru: A Political Biography*, 377 |
| 435 | The truth is | Mosley, *The Last Days of the British Raj*, 248 |
| 436 | It was, on the | *Gandhi Marg*, April 1974 |

**Chapter 43**

| 438 | We Muslims | Pyarelal, *Mahatma Gandhi: The Last Phase*, II, 363 |
| 439 | So you have | Pyarelal, *Mahatma Gandhi: The Last Phase*, II, 365 |
| 439 | Why have you | Pyarelal, *Mahatma Gandhi: The Last Phase*, II, 365 |
| 439 | But let me | Pyarelal, *Mahatma Gandhi: The Last Phase*, II, 366–7 |
| 440 | It is Bengal's | Pyarelal, *Mahatma Gandhi: The Last Phase*, II, 369 |
| 441 | My God asks | Pyarelal, *Mahatma Gandhi: The Last Phase*, II, 404 |
| 442 | What was regarded | *Works*, LXXXIX, 133 |
| 442 | To put an | *Works*, LXXXIX, 132 |
| 442 | I will not mind | Pyarelal, *Mahatma Gandhi: The Last Phase*, II, 413 |
| 443 | If you revert | Manubehn Gandhi, *The Miracle of Calcutta*, 100 |

**Chapter 44**

| 445 | Why has this | Pyarelal, *Mahatma Gandhi: The Last Phase*, II, 438 |
| 446 | Yours is not | *Works*, XC, 15–17 |
| 447 | Before he can | *Works*, LXI, 265 |

**Chapter 45**

| 448 | To Indian Muslims | Rajmohan Gandhi, *Patel: A Life*, 461 |
| 448 | I am in a | Pyarelal, *Mahatma Gandhi: The Last Phase*, II, 698 |
| 448 | I have no answer | *Works*, XC, 408–9 |
| 449 | Vallabhbhai Patel | *Works*, XC, 427 |
| 450 | I am dictating | Gandhi, *Bapu's Letters to Mira*, 383 |
| 451 | For the Prime Minister | Hodson, *The Great Divide*, 458 |
| 451 | If I am to | Durgadas, *Sardar Patel's Correspondence*, 11–12 |
| 451 | I have no | Durgadas, *Sardar Patel's Correspondence*, 12–13 |
| 452 | In the circumstances , | Durgadas, *Sardar Patel's Correspondence*, 25 |
| 452 | I won't pop off | Pyarelal, *Mahatma Gandhi: The Last Phase*, II, 722 |
| 452 | I did not embark | Tendulkar, VIII, 261–2 |
| 453 | Nothing is to be | *Works*, XC, 439–40 |
| 454 | We wish to | *Harijan*, 1 February 1948 |
| 454 | worse than poisonous | Tendulkar, VIII, 266 |
| 455 | I will break | Manubehn Gandhi, *Last Glimpses of Bapu*, 198 |
| 455 | Lead me from | Tendulkar, VIII, 268 |
| 455 | If there is | Gandhi, *Delhi Diary*, 357 |

**Chapter 46**

| 456 | No settlement | Manubehn Gandhi, *Last Glimpses of Bapu*, 216 |
| 457 | He gambled away | Manubehn Gandhi, *Last Glimpses of Bapu*, 247 |
| 457 | The Congress has come | *Works*, LXXXVII, 513–14 |
| 458 | Today politics has | Tendulkar, VIII, 230 |
| 459 | who are committed | Pyarelal, *Mahatma Gandhi: The Last Phase*, II, 642 |

# Acknowledgements

During the course of my work on this book, which spanned several years, I inevitably consulted innumerable books, documents, newspapers and journals. In this connection, I wish to place on record my appreciation and indebtedness for assistance afforded to me by the staff of the following: Newspaper Library, Colindale, London; National Archives of India, New Delhi; Gandhi Memorial Museum and Library, New Delhi; Nehru Memorial Museum and Library, New Delhi; Central Secretariat Library, New Delhi; Indian Council of World Affairs Library, Sapru House, New Delhi; British Council Library, New Delhi; American Center Library, New Delhi; State Library, Simla; Metropolitan Toronto Reference Library, Toronto.

Most of the photographs in this book were made available to me by the Gandhi Memorial Museum and Library, New Delhi.

# Index

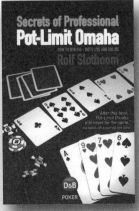